Using Turbo Pascal

Michael Yester

CORPORATION

LEADING COMPUTER KNOWLEDGE

Using Turbo Pascal®

Library of Congress Catalog No.: 88-62185
ISBN No.: 0-88022-396-0

93 92 91 90 89   8 7 6 5 4 3 2 1

Interpretation of the printing code: the rightmost double-digit number is the year of the book's printing; the rightmost single-digit number, the number of the book's printing. For example, a printing code of 89-4 shows that the fourth printing of the book occurred in 1989.

Using Turbo Pascal is based on Version 5.0 of Turbo Pascal.

ABOUT THE AUTHOR ▽

Michael Yester

For the last ten years, Michael Yester has been involved in the design, development, and management of financial systems. He holds an M.B.A. in finance and an M.S. in computer science and has taught courses in both systems design and accounting. Currently, he is an independent consultant residing in Los Angeles, California.

Publishing Manager

Allen L. Wyatt, Sr.

Product Development Specialist

Bill Nolan

Acquisitions Editor

Pegg Kennedy

Senior Editor

Gregory Croy

Editing and Indexing

Brown Editorial Service

Editorial Assistant

Ann K. Taylor

Technical Editor

Chris Land

Illustrator

Susan Moore

Book Design and Production

Dan Armstrong	Cindy L. Phipps
Cheryl English	Dennis Sheehan
Lori A. Lyons	Carolyn A. Spitler
Jennifer Matthews	

Composed in Garamond and American Typewriter
by Que Corporation

CONTENT OVERVIEW

TABLE OF CONTENTS

I   Learning Turbo Pascal

II   Programming

III   Advanced Programming

IV   Reference

ACKNOWLEDGMENTS

I would like to thank my friends (assuming any of them are still speaking to me) who somehow managed to tolerate me while I was working on this book.

I'd also like to thank the editors and staff at Que Corporation for the support and guidance they provided during this project. Special thanks go to Pegg Kennedy and Allen Wyatt, who were willing to risk commissioning a first-time author; Greg Croy and Chris Land, who had to wade through impenetrable material; and especially Bill Nolan, who (miraculously) never lost faith.

TRADEMARK
ACKNOWLEDGMENTS

Que Corporation has made every attempt to supply trademark information about company names, products, and services mentioned in this book. Trademarks indicated below were derived from various sources. Que Corporation cannot attest to the accuracy of this information.

Introduction

What Is Turbo Pascal 5.0?

Turbo Pascal 5.0 from Borland International is the latest stage in the evolution of the Pascal language. Turbo Pascal 5.0 is a powerful, integrated applications development package that includes a compiler, an editor, a debugger, and a library manager. With Turbo Pascal 5.0, programmers can create highly readable, modular programs that generate fast, efficient executable code.

Almost any high-level programming problem that can be expressed in English can also be expressed in Turbo Pascal. In addition, because of the ease with which it can access both PC hardware and the operating system itself, Turbo Pascal is well suited for many low-level systems programming tasks.

Who Should Use This Book?

Using Turbo Pascal is written for everyone with an interest in Turbo Pascal programming—from the novice to the seasoned veteran.

Although it would be helpful if you've already had some prior exposure to Pascal and DOS, this book makes no assumptions about your background. First and foremost, it is the goal of this book to explain *how* Turbo Pascal programs operate—not just to present a cookbook of rules and recipes. *Using Turbo Pascal* treats Turbo Pascal programming as a natural extension of DOS. In the process, it improves the reader's knowledge of and skill with both Turbo Pascal and DOS itself.

Using Turbo Pascal takes a simple, linear approach. It begins with basic system installation instructions, proceeds through a course in Turbo Pascal programming, demonstrates how to use the unique features of the Turbo Pascal language, and closes with an explanation of how to develop sophisticated systems-level applications such as memory-resident programs. This book is not intense, but it *is* thorough. No matter what your level of expertise, this book will be of interest to you.

1

What Is in This Book?

Using Turbo Pascal is divided into three parts. Essentially, they form an introduction to Pascal programming, an introduction to Turbo Pascal programming in particular, and an introduction to advanced Turbo Pascal programming applications. Practical software tools are presented throughout.

Part I, "Learning Turbo Pascal," introduces the fundamentals of the Pascal language and introduces the major features specific to the Turbo dialect. The design and operation of a typical Turbo Pascal program are examined, including how data are represented and controlled, how memory is organized, and how units are used.

❑ Chapter 1, "Getting Started with Turbo Pascal," leads the novice Turbo Pascal user through the stages of taking the compiler out of the box, installing it on the PC, and performing an actual step-by-step programming session.

❑ Chapter 2, "The Structure of a Turbo Pascal Program," introduces the individual components of the Pascal language—including reserved words, symbols, identifiers, numbers, and strings—and shows how they combine to form the basic structure of a Turbo Pascal program.

❑ Chapter 3, "Data and Data Types," discusses the nature of data and identifies the various groupings, called *types*, used to categorize data and shows how data types are used in a program.

❑ Chapter 4, "Expressions, Operands, and Operators," presents the instructions that control the flow of programming operations and that manipulate and manage program data.

❑ Chapter 5, "Procedures and Functions," covers how to combine related data and code statements.

❑ Chapter 6, "Dynamic Data Structures," explains how the PC manages memory and how memory can be used to store data objects.

❑ Chapter 7, "Units," discusses the standard units of Turbo Pascal and describes Turbo's separate compilation feature.

❑ Chapter 8, "Debugging Your Programs," presents Turbo's integrated debugger and shows how you can use it to solve complex programming puzzles.

Part II, "Programming," reveals how Turbo Pascal programming is a logical extension of DOS and demonstrates how you can write programs that use both Turbo Pascal and DOS to their full potential.

❑ Chapter 9, "Keyboard Input," explains the design, operation, and management of the keyboard and demonstrates how to read and interpret any key combination.

❑ Chapter 10, "Text Display," discusses the design, operation, and management of the text screen and how to develop programs that exploit such features as windows, colors, and intensity.

❑ Chapter 11, "Graphics Display," presents and demonstrates the extensive Turbo Pascal graphics subroutine library.

❑ Chapter 12, "Accessing DOS," describes how to access and control the operating system of your PC, including date, time, and sound commands. In addition, the chapter discusses the DOS environment and the Program Segment Prefix (PSP) and demonstrates how to execute child processes and control program termination.

❑ Chapter 13, "File Handling," discusses the characteristics and management of text, typed, and untyped files.

❑ Chapter 14, "Directory Handling," discusses the management of collections of files in the form of directories and disk drives.

Part III, "Advanced Programming," provides an introduction to some of the advanced systems-level applications available with Turbo Pascal.

❑ Chapter 15, "Overlays," demonstrates how to allow different parts of a single Turbo Pascal program to occupy the same internal memory locations.

❑ Chapter 16, "BIOS, DOS, and Assembly Language," describes how your program can access the major software services available in your PC and explains how to incorporate low-level assembly language instructions.

❑ Chapter 17, "The 8087 and External Devices," demonstrates the various ways Turbo Pascal allows you to access all of the equipment connected to your PC, including special floating-point data types, hardware ports, and both predefined and custom device drivers.

❑ Chapter 18, "Interrupt Service Routines," explains how DOS uses both the BIOS routines and its own subroutine library to maintain control of the PC. Further, the chapter explains how you can directly access those routines and even add to them for your own special purposes.

❑ Chapter 19, "Memory-Resident Programs," reveals the procedures and techniques to develop memory-resident programs that either run continuously or are user-activated with "hot" keys.

Part IV, "Reference," provides a library of all of the procedures and functions available in Turbo Pascal 5.0. The reference also includes a summary of the Turbo Pascal compiler directives, including conditional compilation instructions.

Part I

Learning Turbo Pascal

Getting Started with Turbo Pascal

One reason Turbo Pascal enjoys such immense popularity is its ease of use. Like most Pascal developers, Borland offers a command-line compiler, TPC.EXE, that you can use to create executable files from stand-alone programs written with an independent editor. TPC.EXE is run from the DOS prompt; it will either compile your program into an executable .EXE file or provide you with error messages to explain why your program failed. TPC.EXE will most often be used during those phases of project management in which all you need to do is make a few changes to otherwise functional code. TPC.EXE can be used in batch files, for example, to expedite compilation in large programming projects.

In addition, Borland provides a second version of the compiler, TURBO.EXE, known as the integrated environment. TURBO.EXE is a highly sophisticated interactive system that provides you with almost every tool you need for program development through its built-in, pull-down menus and multiple windows. TURBO.EXE is ideal for developing new programs and for modifying existing ones. It is, undoubtedly, the version you will use most often. Consequently, TURBO.EXE is the version used throughout this book.

This chapter discusses the essential information you need to take Turbo Pascal out of the package and be up and running in as short a time as possible. In addition, this chapter takes you on a brief tour of the integrated environment, discussing every command and function you need to know to begin using Turbo Pascal. This chapter is written for those of you who aren't current users of an earlier Turbo Pascal version. If you're already familiar with the process of installing the compiler, then you should probably just skim through the next few pages.

The Turbo Pascal Package

The Turbo Pascal compiler package contains three diskettes and two manuals. The diskettes are labeled Install/Compiler, Help/Utilities, and BGI/Demos/Doc/Turbo3. Following are the major files contained on the distribution diskettes:

1. Contents of the Install/Compiler Disk (Volume PASCAL1):

INSTALL.EXE	The Turbo Pascal installation program
TURBO.EXE	The main compiler—the Turbo Pascal Integrated Development Environment
TURBO.TPL	Library files of Turbo Pascal "units"
TPC.EXE	The Turbo Pascal command-line compiler
README.COM	Program to display or list the README file
README	Text file containing information not included in the Turbo Pascal manuals.
THELP.COM	Memory-resident help utility

2. Contents of the Help/Utilities Disk (Volume PASCAL2):

TURBO.HLP	The Turbo Pascal on-line help file
TINST.EXE	TURBO.EXE customizing program
TPUMOVER.EXE	Unit manager
MAKE.EXE	Project management utility
GREP.COM	Text file search utility
TOUCH.COM	Utility to change file date and time stamps
BINOBJ.EXE	Conversion program: binary to .OBJ
TPCONFIG.EXE	Conversion program: .TP to .CFG
TINSTXFR.EXE	Conversion program: 4.0 options to 5.0

3. Contents of the BGI/Demos/Doc/Turbo3 Disk (Volume PASCAL3):

UNPACK.COM	Archive file "unpacker"
BGI.ARC	Archive file containing graphics documentation (*.DOC), drivers (*.BGI), fonts (*.CHR), and examples (*.PAS). BGI.ARC also contains

	the file GRAPH.TPU, which is required for any graphics programming
DEMOS.ARC	Archive file containing sample programs (*.PAS)
DOC.ARC	Archive file containing listings of the interface sections of the SYSTEM, DOS, CRT, PRINTER, and OVERLAY units, plus documentation for the THELP.EXE help utility
MCALC.ARC	Archive file containing the source code to the MicroCalc spreadsheet program
TURBO3.ARC	Turbo 3.0 compatibility files, including the UP-GRADE.EXE conversion program, documentation, and the TURBO3 and GRAPH3 unit files
HELPME!.DOC	Answers to the questions most often received by Borland's Technical Support department

The first manual, the *User's Guide*, only briefly describes the language of Pascal but exhaustively describes the functions and options of the compilers and utilities. The second manual, the *Reference Guide*, describes in detail the syntactic and semantic intricacies of the Turbo Pascal language, including a description of every individual procedure and function.

Preparing Your Diskettes

After you open the package, the first thing you should do is read, sign, and mail Borland's No-Nonsense License Statement. Among other things, it explains that you have the right to make as many backup copies as you need for your own personal use. You should take advantage of this to safeguard your original diskettes; use them as seldom as possible. You prepare backups in three simple steps:

1. To prevent any possibility of accidental erasure, attach write-protect tabs to the three distribution diskettes.

2. Use the DISKCOPY command to make working copies of each of the original diskettes. (Consult your DOS manual if you're not familiar with this command.) Be sure to label each of the copies correctly.

3. Store the original diskettes in a safe place. From now on, you need to use only the copies.

Next, insert your working copy of the Install/Compiler disk in drive A:, and enter the following command.

A:README

The README.COM program displays the contents of the README file, which contains supplementary information not found in either of your manuals. Because one of the topics README usually covers involves installation procedures, now is the time to review its contents. It's generally a good idea to use the README.COM program to print a copy of the file so that you have a hard copy for future reference. Press P to begin. You can see a complete list of program options by pressing the F1 function key.

Installing Turbo Pascal 5.0

Turbo Pascal Version 5.0 comes complete with an installation utility, IN-STALL.EXE, which considerably simplifies the process of configuring your system. One of the following sections explains how to use INSTALL.EXE on floppy-based systems. Another section explains its use on hard disk systems. Read through the appropriate section before you begin. If you're comfortable with the way the INSTALL.EXE program operates, go ahead and use it. However, if you're not satisfied with its options—and particularly if you want to minimize the disk space it consumes—then follow the steps in one of the other two sections that describe how Turbo Pascal can be installed without the INSTALL.EXE program. Remember that unlike some copy-protected software, you can install Turbo Pascal as often as you wish. If you dislike the configuration you've chosen, you can always rearrange files among the disks and directories.

Throughout this discussion, I'm assuming that your floppy disk is drive A:, your second floppy disk (if you have one) is drive B:, and your hard disk (if you have one) is drive C:.

Hard Disk Installation with INSTALL.EXE

When you use INSTALL.EXE to place the compiler on your hard disk system, three directories are created:

C:\TP   Stores the compiler files themselves, the help file, the various support utilities, print drivers, and sample programs

C:\TP\DOC   Contains documentation, consisting principally of listings of the constant, variable, procedure, and function declarations of the Turbo units

C:\TP\TURBO3   Contains the files necessary for programs written with Turbo Pascal Version 3.0 (and earlier) to be successfully compiled and executed under Version 5.0

All tallied, you are expected to provide about 1.2 megabytes of storage. However, many of these files are discretionary:

1. The C:\TP directory contains the README file, which contains the "latest word" from Borland on added features, typographical errors in the documentation, helpful hints, and so forth. It can be read and printed with the README.COM program. After you've done that, you can remove both files from your hard disk.

2. The C:\TP\DOC directory contains listings of unit headers. While extremely informative, the headers don't need to be physically present in order for the compiler to run. (You should, however, print them and keep the hard copies as reference.) This directory also holds the HELPME!.DOC file that contains answers to the questions the Borland Technical Support department receives most frequently. You should most definitely print and read this file, but again, it isn't necessary for it to remain resident on your hard disk.

3. If you're using Turbo Pascal for the first time with Version 5.0, or if you're upgrading from Version 4.0, then you probably won't need the contents of C:\TP\TURBO3. This directory contains the program UPGRADE.EXE and the files necessary to convert the BCD, graphics, and older Turbo routines from versions prior to 4.0.

As you can see, using INSTALL.EXE is convenient but costly. If you have the space, or if it's simply more convenient to transfer the files to your hard disk before you print them, use the INSTALL.EXE program.

To install Turbo Pascal Version 5.0 on your hard disk with the INSTALL.EXE utility, follow these steps, which assume that your hard disk is drive C:.

1. Insert your working copy of the Install/Compiler diskette in drive A:, then enter

   A:INSTALL

   to begin. The first thing you see is the Turbo 5.0 Installation Utility sign-on screen, as shown in figure 1.1.

Fig. 1.1. The main screen of the INSTALL.EXE installation utility.

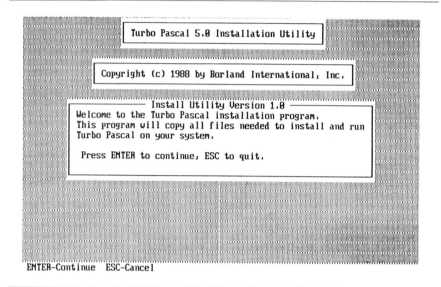

2. Press the Enter key to proceed. INSTALL.EXE then asks you for the drive that you're using for diskettes. Press Enter to accept the default of drive A: and proceed.

3. INSTALL.EXE then inquires about the desired configuration, as shown in figure 1.2. You're asked to select from installing on a hard disk, upgrading Version 4.0 on a hard disk, and installing on a floppy system. Choose Install Turbo Pascal on a Hard Drive.

4. Figure 1.3 shows the installation menu for the hard disk. Essentially, you're being asked to confirm that the default directory names are acceptable. In addition, you should agree to "unarchive" files, which means only that you want the files on the diskettes converted to a usable format. Use the down-arrow key to select the Start Installation option.

INSTALL.EXE creates the named directories, then copies and unarchives files. The installation proceeds automatically. You will be prompted to insert the Help/Utilities and BGI/Demos/DOC/Turbo3 diskettes.

Fig. 1.2. The installation options of the INSTALL.EXE program.

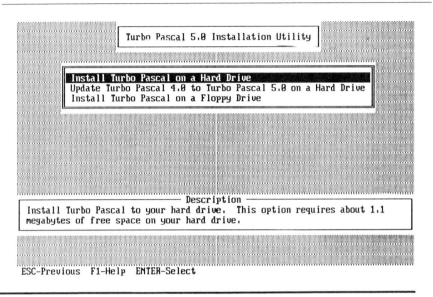

Fig. 1.3. Configuration options for installing Turbo Pascal 5.0 on a hard disk drive.

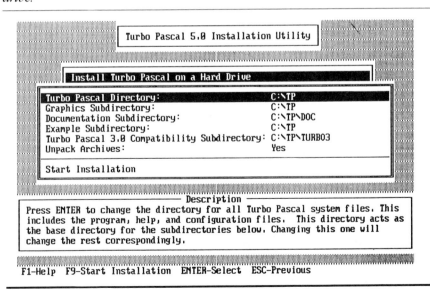

When INSTALL.EXE finishes, you can run the TINST.EXE program to customize the compiler if you want. You will probably find the defaults acceptable, however.

Hard Disk Installation without INSTALL.EXE

You can install the compiler yourself without using the INSTALL.EXE program. Follow these steps:

1. Create a separate subdirectory for the compiler. You can use any name you want; in these instructions TP is used. Assuming that your hard disk is drive C:, use the following commands:

   C:
   CD C:
   MD TP

   Enter the TP directory with the following command:

   CD TP

2. Choose the files you want to copy, based on the earlier discussion for INSTALL.EXE. At a minimum, you need the TURBO.TPL file and either the TURBO.EXE or TPC.EXE compiler. All three files can be found on the Install/Compiler diskette. So, for example, if you want to load only the smallest number of files for running the Interactive Development Environment, insert the Install/Compiler diskette in drive A: and issue the following commands:

   COPY A:TURBO.TPL C:\TP
   COPY A:TURBO.EXE C:\TP

3. Alternatively, you can copy every file from every diskette and then erase any files you don't want to keep. For each of the three working disks, place the disk in drive A: and issue the following command:

   COPY A:*.* C:\TP

4. If your system executes an AUTOEXEC.BAT file when it's booted, you should initialize a PATH to the TP subdirectory by including the following line:

   PATH =C:\TP

   If you already have a PATH statement, add the TP subdirectory as follows:

   PATH =C:\DOS;C:\SPRINT;C:\TP

Floppy Diskette Installation with INSTALL.EXE

Almost incredibly, everything you need to run Turbo Pascal Version 5.0 can fit comfortably on just one double-density diskette. To install Turbo Pascal Version 5.0 on your floppy disk with the INSTALL.EXE utility, follow these steps, which assume that your floppy disk drives are A: and B:.

1. If you have a dual floppy system, insert the blank diskette you want to use for your Turbo work in drive B: and your regular system diskette in drive A:. Use the FORMAT command to create a bootable system disk by entering the following command at the DOS prompt:

   FORMAT B:

2. If you have a single drive system, use the same FORMAT command shown in the preceding step. Your computer will prompt you through the process by expecting the blank diskette when it calls for drive B: and your system diskette when it calls for drive A:.

3. Place your working copy of the Install/Compiler diskette in drive A:, then enter

   A:INSTALL

   to begin. The first display is the Turbo 5.0 Installation Utility sign-on screen, as shown in figure 1.1.

4. Press the Enter key to proceed. INSTALL.EXE then asks you for the drive that you will use for the working diskettes. Press Enter to accept the default of drive A:.

5. INSTALL.EXE then prompts you to select your configuration, as shown in figure 1.2. You're asked to select among installing on a hard disk, upgrading Version 4.0 on a hard disk, and installing on a floppy system. Choose the third option to install Turbo Pascal on your floppy drive.

6. Figure 1.4 shows the installation menu for the floppy disk. You can choose between the integrated environment compiler, TURBO.EXE, and the command-line version, TPC.EXE, by pressing the Enter key. The assumption here is that you prefer the integrated environment compiler, TURBO.EXE. The help utility is optional for both compilers, but you should allow it to be copied as well. Use the down-arrow key to select the Start Installation option.

Fig. 1.4. Configuration options for installing Turbo Pascal 5.0 on a floppy drive.

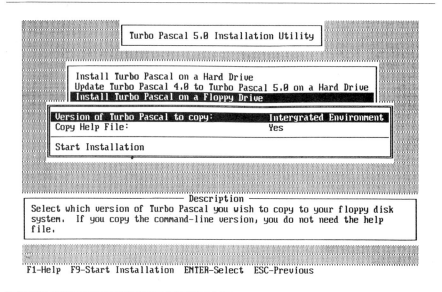

INSTALL.EXE prompts you alternately to insert your working copy of the Install/Compiler disk and your newly formatted diskette. If you opted to copy the help utility, you will also be prompted to insert the Help/Utilities diskette.

When the process is complete, label the formatted diskette as your "Turbo Pascal System Diskette."

Floppy Diskette Installation without INSTALL.EXE

If you would prefer not to use the INSTALL.EXE utility, you should still begin by following steps 1 and 2 of the preceding list to create a formatted disk. Then continue with the following steps:

1. Insert your working copy of the Turbo Pascal Install/Compiler diskette in drive A: and your newly formatted diskette in drive B:. Enter the command

   COPY A:TURBO.TPL B:

   to copy the Turbo system files.

2. To use the integrated environment version of the compiler, enter the command

   COPY A:TURBO.EXE B:

   If, instead of the TURBO.EXE integrated environment compiler, you want to use the command-line version, which isn't too likely for now, enter the command

   COPY A:TPC.EXE B:

3. To copy the on-line help file, place the Help/Utilities diskette in drive A:, and enter the command

   COPY A:TURBO.HLP B:

If you have a single drive system, the same commands are used, but your system will prompt you to insert the appropriate diskette. For example, you will use the working copy of the Turbo Pascal Install/Compiler disk when the prompt asks for drive A:, and you will use your newly formatted diskette when it asks for drive B:.

Reading Archive Files

If you just installed Turbo Pascal on a floppy system or just installed the compiler manually on a hard disk, the next step is learning how to use the files on the third distribution disk. (If you just installed on a hard disk and answered Yes to the Unpack Archives option, you can skip this section.)

Several of these files have the extension .ARC. They're called *archive* files because they actually contain other files stored in a compressed format. This process reduces the number of disks required to ship the final product, but the files need a "dearchiving" step with the UNPACK.COM program before they can be used. One of these files, BGI.ARC, must be dearchived in order to run graphics routines.

You can obtain further instructions on how to use UNPACK.COM from the program itself. Insert your working copy of the BGI/Demos/Doc/Turbo3 disk in drive A:, and enter the following command:

A:UNPACK

Because no additional parameters were provided on the command line, the program displays operating instructions. The command to dearchive the BGI.ARC file is

A:UNPACK BGI.ARC C:

or

A:UNPACK BGI.ARC B:

depending on whether you're installing on a hard disk (C:) or a floppy system (on B:).

Configuring Your System for Turbo Pascal Version 5.0

Before you begin, ensure that your system has a CONFIG.SYS file in the root directory. CONFIG.SYS contains special DOS instructions concerning device drivers and system parameters that must be known by the operating system when you boot the computer.

For example, as a default, DOS allows only 8 files to be open at any one time. The Turbo Pascal compilers require more; Borland recommends that you increase the allowance to 20 files.

In addition, DOS offers a device driver file, ANSI.SYS, which provides enhanced keyboard and screen support. ANSI.SYS is an industry standard, so programs that rely on ANSI support can run successfully on PCs from a variety of manufacturers. The Turbo Pascal compilers themselves don't require the ANSI.SYS driver, but some of the applications discussed in this book assume that it's available.

The ANSI.SYS driver file was supplied with your PC. If the driver file is not already installed, locate it on your master system disk and copy it to the root directory of your hard disk. If you're using a floppy diskette system, copy it to your system diskette.

Generally, CONFIG.SYS is a user-created file. If you already have a CONFIG.SYS file and you have a word processor, ensure that the file includes the following lines:

DEVICE =ANSI.SYS
FILES =20

Note that you can have more than one DEVICE = statement. If you don't have a word processor, but you do have a CONFIG.SYS file, enter the following command:

TYPE CONFIG.SYS

This enables you to see the current contents of the file. You need to add the DEVICE and FILES statements using the COPY command. Enter the following lines as shown, pressing the Enter key at the end of each line.

COPY CON CONFIG.SYS
DEVICE =ANSI.SYS
FILES =20

If a CONFIG.SYS file already existed, add its contents line by line at this point. When you've finished, press the F6 function key and then the Enter key. The screen will display:

    1 File(s) copied

to show that you've been successful.

You need to reboot the computer so that the operating system can reconfigure for the new CONFIG.SYS parameters. Now you're ready to run the compiler.

Running Turbo Pascal Version 5.0

Once the Turbo Pascal compiler is installed, you can use it by following a few simple steps. (Remember that in the following discussion, I'm assuming that you've selected the TURBO.EXE integrated environment.)

Starting Turbo Pascal on Hard Disk Systems

To bring up Turbo Pascal on a hard disk system, change to the Turbo Pascal subdirectory by entering the following command:

CD \TP

You may want to use the directory command, DIR, to verify that you're in the correct subdirectory. Next invoke the compiler by entering the command

TURBO

The computer then loads the compiler.

Starting Turbo Pascal on Floppy Diskette Systems

To bring up Turbo Pascal on a floppy diskette system, insert your Turbo Pascal System disk in drive A: and enter the command

TURBO

The computer then loads the compiler.

When the compiler is loaded—from either the hard disk or from a floppy drive—the monitor displays the Turbo Pascal Version 5.0 logon screen, as shown in figure 1.5.

Fig. 1.5. *The main screen of Turbo Pascal 5.0.*

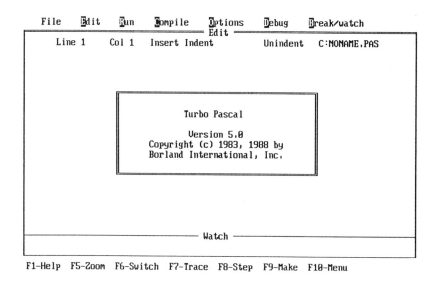

Press the Enter key to begin operation.

Turbo Pascal Menu Displays

Welcome to the integrated environment! The screen may appear somewhat empty, but every tool you need for developing a Turbo Pascal program can be found in the main menu across the top. You will also notice two windows: an Edit window used to enter and modify programs, and a Watch window at the bottom used for debugging. The Watch window is covered in Chapter 8. Because you don't need it yet, you can eliminate it by pressing the F5 function key.

When you first run the compiler, the File option is highlighted; press the Enter key to select it. Immediately, you see the options shown in figure 1.6.

***Fig. 1.6.** The File menu.*

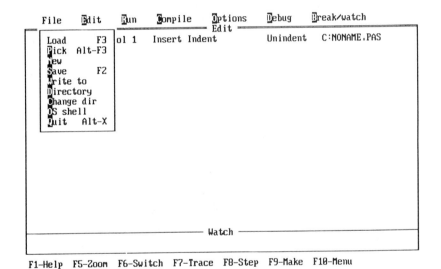

You can use the left- and right-arrow keys to see all of the other menu options.

In the File menu and also across the bottom of the screen, you will notice that several commands are shown with a corresponding "hot key." For example, the Quit selection is shown as being Alt-X. There are three ways to select a menu offering:

1. Use the arrow keys on your numeric pad to position the cursor over the desired option; then press the Enter key.

2. When you're within a menu, type the first letter of the instruction. When you're in the File menu, you can quit the Turbo Pascal program by typing Q.

3. Use the hot key. For example, you can also quit the compiler by pressing Alt-X.

No method is best; you will develop your own preferences shortly. By the way, you now know three ways to terminate the compiler.

Let's briefly review the main menu options:

File — This is your connection to the outside world. The File menu enables you to load, save, and create program files; to select directories; and—with the OS shell option—to suspend temporarily the execution of the compiler by returning to the operating system (you just type the command EXIT to return to Turbo).

Edit — When you select Edit, the cursor is positioned in the main part of the screen, where you can use the built-in word processing program to enter and edit your programs. You can return to the main menu by pressing the F10 function key or by holding down the Alt key and entering the first letter of your menu selection. For example, Alt-F takes you directly to the File menu.

Run — As the name implies, this is the option that actually runs your code. If your program hasn't been compiled, the Run option will do that first.

Compile — Most of the time, you will want to run your programs immediately. Occasionally, though, you will prefer to compile and store them on disk in order to run them later outside of the integrated environment. The Compile option handles this for you.

Options — The default settings of the compiler are adequate for almost every programming task. For now, simply accept them as given.

Debug — The integrated environment comes complete with a sophisticated debugger that helps you "look under the hood" of your PC while a program is running. Debugging is discussed in Chapter 8.

Break/Watch — The Break/Watch option enables you to run your program in sections, which you can then analyze individually. As with debugging, this feature is discussed in Chapter 8.

Even in this quick tour, you can begin to appreciate the power of the integrated environment. Some of these features you will use later; others you may never use.

Steps in Creating a Turbo Pascal Program

The remainder of this chapter concentrates on the features you use in every session: entering, saving, loading, editing, and running a program.

Entering and Editing the Program

One of the attractions of the integrated environment is the built-in editor. To try it, choose the Edit option from the main menu and enter the following program. (Except for the message within the quotation marks, capitalization and spacing don't matter.)

```
program First;
begin
    writeln( 'Hello, world!' )
end.
```

The writeln (pronounced "write line") statement instructs the compiler to display whatever it finds between the parentheses.

If you're familiar with the WordStar word processing package, then you're already familiar with the basic Turbo Pascal editing functions. If you don't know WordStar—in fact, if you've never touched a word processor before —there are only a few things you really need to remember.

1. The cursor (the flashing underline character that marks your current position) can be moved around the screen with the arrow keys on your numeric pad. Whatever you type will be inserted where the cursor is located when the key is pressed. Notice that the editor keeps track of your current line and column.

2. End each line by pressing the Enter key.

3. If you make a mistake, move the cursor over the mistake and type any new material. If you need to erase a character, position the cursor over the unwanted character and press the Del (delete) key. You can remove several unwanted characters by holding down the Del key a bit longer.

Your screen should now look like the one in figure 1.7.

Fig. 1.7. The "Hello, world!" program.

```
  File    Edit    Run    Compile    Options    Debug    Break/watch
                                    Edit
      Line 4    Col 5    Insert Indent           Unindent * C:NONAME.PAS
  program First;
  begin
    writeln( 'Hello, world!' )
  end.












                                    Watch
```

```
F1-Help  F5-Zoom  F6-Switch  F7-Trace  F8-Step  F9-Make  F10-Menu
```

Although several additional editing features are available, these are the only ones you really need to know for now. Editing is that simple. In fact, many experienced programmers use Turbo as their word processing system.

Running the Program

Now it's time to run your first program. Press the F10 function key to leave the editor and return to the main menu. Then select the Run option, as shown in figure 1.8. This instructs the integrated environment to compile and execute your program. (Alternatively, you could have gone directly from the editor to the Run menu by pressing Alt-R.)

Notice that the hot key for the Run option is Ctrl-F9. Even from within the editor, if you press Ctrl-F9, your program will compile and execute.

If you made a typing error, Turbo stops the compilation, returns you to the editor, positions the cursor over the offending section of code, and tells

Fig. 1.8. The Run menu.

```
  File   Edit   Run   Compile   Options   Debug   Break/watch
┌──────────────┬──────────────────────┬─────────────────────────────┐
│      Line 4  C│ Run           Ctrl-F9│  Unindent * C:NONAME.PAS     │
│program First:│ Program reset Ctrl-F2 │                              │
│begin         │ Go to cursor      F4  │                              │
│   writeln( 'Hello│ Trace into     F7 │                              │
│end.          │ Step over         F8  │                              │
│              │ User screen    Alt-F5 │                              │
│              └───────────────────────┘                             │
│                                                                    │
│                                                                    │
│                                                                    │
│                                                                    │
│                                                                    │
│                                                                    │
├─────────────────────────── Watch ──────────────────────────────── │
│                                                                    │
└────────────────────────────────────────────────────────────────────┘
  F1-Help  F5-Zoom  F6-Switch  F7-Trace  F8-Step  F9-Make  F10-Menu
```

you—in English—the problem it found. If this happens, correct the problem and rerun the program. If this doesn't happen, you may want to commit an error deliberately (omit a quotation mark, for example) and see how the compiler helps you locate the error.

If you didn't make any typing mistakes, you will probably notice that the screen flashes for a second, then returns you to the editor. You've probably figured out that the program is supposed to display a message, but where?

Take another look at figure 1.8. The bottom option is User screen or Alt-F5. Run this option now; you can either call up the menu or press the hot key—the choice is yours. A "user screen" similar to figure 1.9 appears. You can see your first message at the end of whatever was on the screen before you ran the compiler. Press any key to return to the integrated environment.

Saving the Program

Notice in figure 1.8 the characters C:NONAME.PAS (or A:NONAME.PAS if you're using floppies) on the second line in the upper right corner. This is the

Fig. 1.9. Output from the "Hello, world!" program.

```
C>turbo
Hello, world!
```

name of the file in which your program is saved; but in this case, of course, you haven't yet saved the program. Let's remedy that right now.

If you've been following the chapter closely, the current directory is the one you were in when you invoked TURBO—C:\TP on a hard disk system or A:\ for a floppy system. Select the File option. Notice that one of the options enables you to change the current directory. As you write and acquire more programs, you will probably want to segregate some of your files. For now, just remember that the opportunity exists.

Now select the Write to option. You are prompted for a file name. Use FIRST since it's also the name of the program. After you type in the name but before you press the Enter key, your screen should look like figure 1.10. After you press Enter, you will notice that the NONAME characters in the upper right corner have changed to FIRST.

Fig. 1.10. Choosing a file name for the "Hello, world!" program.

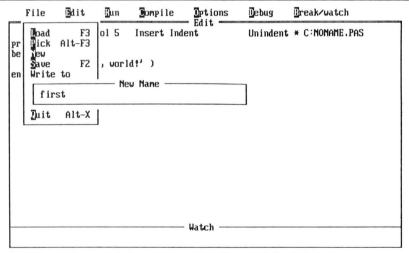

Note that you don't need to specify an extension; Turbo Pascal assumes that all program files use .PAS.

The Write to option is only used to create a file on the disk. From now on, if you edit the program and wish to save its current version, you can simply select Save to store the file. Remember to save frequently. Most programs are considerably longer than the four-line demonstration you just created, and they're extremely painful to lose. Note that the hot key to Save is F2; you can use this key to save your program at frequent intervals while you're editing.

Now select Quit to exit the compiler; you are about to find out how to retrieve the program from disk.

Loading the Program

Once again, invoke the compiler by entering TURBO at the DOS prompt. After the program loads, select the File option, as shown in figure 1.6. You're probably in the same subdirectory you were in when you invoked TURBO for the first time (C:\TP or A:\ in these examples). If not, now would be the time to select the Change dir option and specify the directory you're using to store your programs.

Now choose the Load option. The integrated environment responds, as shown in figure 1.11, with a small window containing a template you can use to narrow the search for your program. For now, you can simply press Enter and accept the default; the integrated environment responds by scanning the current directory for all Pascal program files. It then alphabetizes them and displays them in a larger window. Use the arrow keys on your numeric pad to select FIRST.PAS; position the cursor over the name, as shown in figure 1.12, then press the Enter key.

The FIRST.PAS program now displays in the Edit window. Edit the program by changing the word "world" to the word "again." Remember that you position the cursor over the spot where you want to type new material or over the spot where you want to use Del to remove something. After you make the change, your program should look like the following:

```
program First;
begin
   writeln( 'Hello, again!' )
end.
```

Next, rerun the program. You can use F10 to return to the main menu where you can select Run, or you can simply use the Ctrl-F9 hot key; the choice is yours. The result can be examined with the User screen option (Alt-F5).

Fig. 1.11. Choosing the name of the next file you want to load.

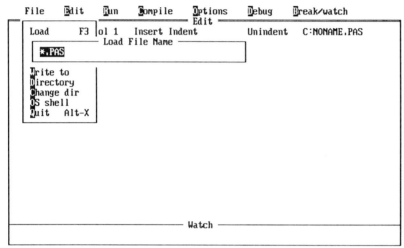

*Fig. 1.12. All files in the C:\TP directory that match *.PAS.*

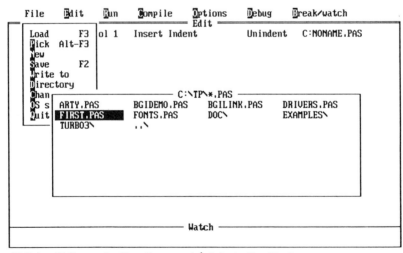

Instead of the original Hello, world! message, you now see Hello, again!

Now, quit the compiler by selecting that option in the File menu or by using Alt-X. The compiler reacts with a warning, as shown in figure 1.13. Because you've changed the program, the integrated environment displays a Verify box and forces you to choose consciously either to save the file or lose your work. You should save it.

Fig. 1.13. *Verifying whether to save or lose your changes.*

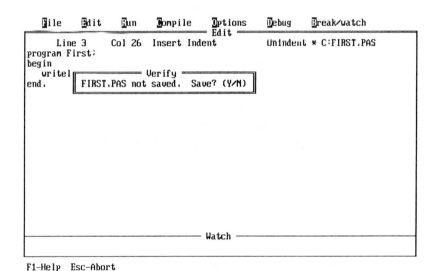

Consider what you just did. By telling the compiler to save the latest version of your program, you've implicitly told it to overwrite the previous contents of the FIRST.PAS file. The integrated environment will do that, but not before it copies FIRST.PAS to a new file, FIRST.BAK, in the same directory. Only one "generation" of your program is saved as backup (as .BAK files are called). If you want more, you can save your files under different names. More than one professional programmer (and author) has used backup files to salvage work that otherwise would have been lost forever.

Running the Program
Directly from DOS

So far, you've seen how to run a Turbo Pascal program from within the integrated environment, but you may have written a utility program that's only useful when it's run directly from DOS. Or you may have written a game program that you want to share with a friend who doesn't have a copy of the compiler. You might even have developed a business application that will run on several PCs in your office.

Invoke the compiler by entering TURBO at the DOS prompt. After the program loads, select the File option, and load the FIRST.PAS program.

To run the program directly from DOS, select the Compile menu. The fourth option, Destination, enables you to choose between compiling to memory and compiling to disk. Press the Enter key to toggle between the two choices. As shown in figure 1.14, you want to choose to compile to disk. Select the first option, Compile (Alt-F9). The integrated environment responds with a status window similar to the one shown in figure 1.15. After you see the Success message, press the Enter key to return to the editor, then Quit the compiler.

Fig. 1.14. *The Compile menu.*

```
   File    Edit    Run    Compile    Options    Debug    Break/watch
 ┌─────────────────────────┬───────────────────────────┐ ┌──────────
 │    Line 3      Col 26    │Compile  Alt-F9            │ │:FIRST.PAS
 │program First;            │Make        F9            │ └──────────
 │begin                     │Build                     │
 │   writeln( 'Hello, again │Destination        Disk   │
 │end,                      │Find error                │
 │                          │Primary file:             │
 │                          │Get info                  │
 │                          └───────────────────────────┘
 │
 │
 │
 │
 │
 │
 │
 │
 │
 │                          ── Watch ──
 └──────────────────────────────────────────────────────────────────
   F1-Help  F5-Zoom  F6-Switch  F7-Trace  F8-Step  F9-Make  F10-Menu
```

Fig. 1.15. Progress messages when compiling to disk.

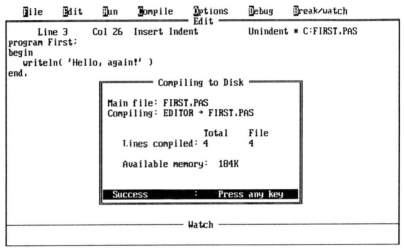

Refer to figure 1.16. If you enter the command DIR FIRST, you will find three files:

Fig. 1.16. The files created during the current session.

```
C>dir first

    Volume in drive C has no label
    Directory of  C:\tp

FIRST    PAS      59    9-08-88    4:26p
FIRST    BAK      59    9-08-88    4:26p
FIRST    EXE    1040    9-08-88    8:18p
        3 File(s)    696320 bytes free

C>first
Hello, again!

C>
```

FIRST.PAS   Your current "Hello, again!" program

FIRST.BAK   Your original "Hello, world!" program

FIRST.EXE   The executable file

The FIRST.EXE program can be run by entering the following command:

FIRST

This loads the program and displays the Hello, again! message.

Summary

In this short chapter, you learned everything you needed to know to take the Turbo Pascal compiler out of the package and:

❏ Install Turbo Pascal on your PC.

❏ Enter a program.

❏ Edit a program.

❏ Save a program.

❏ Load a program.

❏ Compile a program.

❏ Execute a program within the integrated environment.

❏ Execute a stand-alone program directly from DOS.

This chapter also described the menu system of the Turbo Pascal integrated environment and familiarized you with the commands and options that you will begin to use routinely as you progress through the remainder of the book.

The Structure of a Turbo Pascal Program

This chapter introduces Pascal by presenting a fundamental overview that explains both the essential components and the overall structure of a program. At the end of the chapter, we will look at a typical Turbo Pascal program.

If you are already familiar with Pascal, and especially if you are already familiar with the Turbo dialect, feel free to bypass the next few pages or else just skim through them. But if you have never written a Pascal program, this chapter is for you.

A word of advice before you continue; unless you try very, very hard, nothing you do in a Turbo Pascal program is likely to break your PC or damage any software. So feel free to try the examples, and don't worry about making errors. Soon you will be impressed with how protective and helpful Turbo can be. The most horrible situation you are likely to encounter is the one where your program "hangs" (in an infinite loop, for example). When this happens, just press the Alt, Ctrl, and Del keys simultaneously to reboot your PC. Just remember that whatever you haven't saved to disk will be lost. In other words, save your work frequently!

For now, we begin at the beginning.

What Is a Computer Language?

Think of a computer as a purely mechanical device—a pocket calculator with a program pushing the keys. (In many ways, in fact, a four-function pocket calculator is more sophisticated than the CPU of a personal computer.) A calculator is able to load, add, display, and store data by relying completely on its built-in circuitry. Even though it's invisible to the user, pressing the plus key (+) triggers a sequence of events (adding the contents of the input buffer to main memory, displaying main memory, clearing the input buffer, and so on) comparable to what would be done by a computer performing a similar job.

While the PC is capable of the same internal sequence of events as the calculator, its built-in functions, called *machine code*, are—individually, at least—far more primitive. Numbers can be input, added, stored, and displayed in several ways, and each method requires a complicated sequence of machine-code instructions to carry it out.

Rather than "reinvent the wheel" with each new program, computer languages such as Pascal collect these machine-code instruction sequences into standard routines. In Pascal, each one of these routines is called a *procedure* or a *function*, and each one has a name. If you look in the index of the *Reference Guide*, you will see that Turbo Pascal has over 200 of them, with names like ClrScr, Write, and Sound. These names are *standard*, meaning that whenever one of the names appears in a program, the compiler automatically assumes that your intent was to execute the machine code in the underlying procedure or function.

A procedure is called by stating the name of the procedure followed by its parameters, if any, enclosed in parentheses. A function is called just as if the function name (along with its parameters, if any) were a variable.

A Note on Procedures and Functions

Procedures and functions are essentially identical; in fact, most functions can be rewritten in the more general form of a procedure. So for now, just think of them as collections of machine code.

What Is a Compiler?

A *compiler* is a program that takes program statements written in a computer language and rephrases them into instructions that the PC's microprocessor understands. The Borland Turbo Pascal compiler translates the lines of a Pascal program into the machine-readable code of the 8086-family microprocessor. It does this primarily by recognizing the presence of predefined procedure and function names and executing the packets of machine code they represent. A program—through a compiler—causes a computer to perform actions.

By using these standard machine-language building blocks and enforcing some simple rules of grammar, a compiler can effectively and efficiently convert a human-oriented, high-level language such as Pascal to machine-readable, executable code.

Language Components

Before you can begin the formal study of any language—whether it's a language you already know, such as English; a foreign language like French, German, or Farsi; or a computer language like Pascal—you must begin by defining the components.

In a spoken language, the components consist of the ordinary parts of speech such as nouns, verbs, prepositions, and the like. A computer language's "parts of speech" are reserved words, identifiers, tokens, separators, comments, numbers, symbols, characters, and strings.

Reserved Words

In Chapter 1, the program named FIRST illustrated how Turbo Pascal's integrated environment can be used. You saw how the words program, begin, and end have special meaning in Pascal. These words belong to a family of *reserved words*, that provide structure and context in a Pascal program.

The complete list of reserved words is as follows:

absolute	file	mod	shr
and	for	nil	string
array	forward	not	then
begin	function	of	to
case	goto	or	type
const	if	packed	unit
div	implementation	procedure	until
do	in	program	uses
downto	inline	record	var
else	interface	repeat	while
end	interrupt	set	with
external	label	shl	xor

Each reserved word has a special meaning and can't be used for any other purpose. Some, like begin and end, you will use frequently. Others, unless you run the examples in this book, you will probably never see again.

Always remember that although *you* might be able to see the entire program on your screen, the compiler is "blind." *You* can probably determine the intent of a section of code just by looking at it, but the compiler must process your program one word at a time. Some of the most interesting error conditions (and error messages) appear when a reserved word is used incorrectly on one line, but the effect of the error isn't seen until several lines later.

Identifiers

An *identifier* is any name you assign in your program. An identifier denotes the program name as well as any units, labels, constants, variables, procedures, or functions the program defines. Each identifier can have only one meaning in a program.

An identifier can consist of any number of continuous letters, digits, and underscores, but the first character must be a letter. Upper- and lowercase letters are considered identical; therefore, all of the following names are considered the same word.

```
PrintMessage, priNTmessaGE, printMessage, PRINTMESSAGE
```

Turbo Pascal uses only the first 63 characters. If, for example, you use an identifier with 100 characters, the last 37 will be ignored. Alternatively, if the first 63 characters of one identifier match the first 63 characters of another, you get a duplicate identifier error.

Reserved words can't be used as identifiers. If a reserved word is used inappropriately, strange error messages are likely to result.

Valid identifiers include the following:

```
X                        FlightNumber
Passenger_Name           Gate17
Seat4_Aisle8             Seven
```

Invalid identifiers include the following:

```
2x4BoardFeet            (Can't begin with a digit)
Type-3A_Conduit         (Hyphen is an illegal character)
Unit                    (Can't use a reserved word)
```

Through your choice of identifiers you can develop highly readable, self-documenting programs. The following programs (listing 2.1) are functionally equivalent, but you can see for yourself which one is easier to understand:

Listing 2.1

```
program Q;                          program TestForRightTriangle;
var                                 var
   x,                                  SideA,
   y,                                  SideB,
   z  : real;                          Hypotenuse : real;
begin                               begin
   x := 12.0;                          SideA := 12.0;
   y := 5.0;                           SideB := 5.0;
   z := 13.0;                          Hypotenuse := 13.0;
   if z =                              if Hypotenuse =
      Sqrt(x*x +y*y) then                 Sqrt(SideA*SideA +SideB*SideB) then
         writeln( 'Right' );                 writeln( 'Right' );
end.                                end.
```

Characters

A *character* is any one of the 256 standard or extended ASCII characters. You can enter a character in any of three ways:

1. You can simply type its "normal" symbol; for example, the letter A.

2. You can hold down the Alt key and enter the ASCII value of the character from the numeric keypad on the right of the keyboard. (A complete list of ASCII characters can be found in table 3.4.) If you have never done this before, give it a try. The letter A is ASCII 65; hold down the Alt key, enter 65 on the numeric keypad, and release the Alt key. The letter A will appear. This is the usual means for entering graphics and accent marks (sometimes called *extended* characters) that don't appear anywhere on your keyboard.

3. You can precede the ASCII value (an integer in the range 0 through 255) with the # symbol. Therefore, the letter A can be written as #65. This has limited appeal when you enter the normal symbols on a keyboard, but it greatly eases the difficulty of entering special (sometimes called *unprintable*) characters. For example, the character pair #7 represents the single character corresponding to the bell sound. Similarly, #10 is a line feed, #12 is a form feed, and #13 is a carriage return; all are treated by the compiler as single ASCII characters.

Strings

A *string* is a sequence of zero or more ASCII characters contained in a single program line and enclosed in apostrophes (single quotation marks). A string with no characters between the apostrophes is called a *null string*. If an apostrophe is desired *within* a string, it must be written twice.

Examples of valid strings are

```
'Enter your selection: '
'File wasn''t found. Program terminated.'
'Didn''t receive valid response;  can''t continue!'
'The formula used was y = 4x + 7.'
```

Most of the time, strings consist of letters and numbers, but any ASCII character may be included. If you want to include one of the unprintable or extended characters, place it outside any apostrophes; if the control character is in the middle of a string, the string must be temporarily closed and then reopened.

Some character string examples follow:

```
'Hello, world.'
'This part of the string is above'#13#10'this part of the string'
'This is on the page before'#12'this page'
```

Remember that #13#10 is the ASCII code for a carriage return and line feed and that #12 is the ASCII code for a form feed.

Numbers

Numbers, as you might expect, consist of any valid combination of digits, plus and minus signs, and decimal points. Commas may not be used.

Numbers can be broadly grouped as real or integer. Quite simply, a real number is one that contains a decimal point; an integer doesn't.

Any decimal point used in a real number must be preceded by a digit. If, for example, the number 0.6 was written as .6, the compiler may interpret the decimal point as a period and assume (prematurely) that you want the program to terminate. At best, Turbo will display an error message.

Real numbers may be written in scientific notation using the letter *E* (or *e*) to designate "times 10 to the power of." Table 2.1 shows the relationships.

Table 2.1. Real Number Formats in Turbo Pascal

In Turbo Pascal	In Scientific Notation	In Normal Usage
3.4E7	3.4×10^7	34,000,000
3.4E–7	3.4×10^{-7}	.00000034
–7.1E2	-7.1×10^2	–710

Hexadecimal numbers are written with a leading dollar sign. Therefore, $10 equals 16 decimal, but 10 equals ten. The letters *A, B, C, D, E,* and *F* (or *a, b, c, d, e,* and *f*) designate decimal 10, 11, 12, 13, 14, and 15, respectively. For example, $C equals 12, $FF equals 255, and $a0 equals 160. Turbo Pascal limits the use of hexadecimal numbers to integers.

Symbols

Pascal uses special symbols in addition to letters and digits. The following symbols have special meanings:

=	Used in type and constant declarations
( )	Grouping symbols for complex expressions; also used for subroutine headings and calls and for declaring enumeration types
$	Used before a number to indicate that the number is hexadecimal
#	Used before a number to indicate that the number is to be interpreted as the ASCII value of the number
;	Used to separate statements and terminate declarations
: =	Assignment symbol
:	Used in variable declarations, labels, case statements, function headings, and in formatting output
'	(single quotation mark) Used with quoted and constant strings
.	(period) Used as a decimal point to terminate programs and units and to access the fields of a record
,	(comma) Used to separate identifiers and parameters
..	(double period) Subrange. Also used in array subscript declaration
^	Used to denote a pointer
(. .) or [ ]	Brackets for arrays or sets
(* *) or { }	Comment delimiters

The following symbols are used as arithmetic operators. Their operation will be discussed in greater detail in Chapter 4.

*	Multiplication/set intersection
+	Addition/concatenation/set union

–	Subtraction/set difference/unary negate
/	Real division
<	Less than
<=	Less than or equal to/set inclusion
<>	Not equal to
=	Equal to
>	Greater than
>=	Greater than or equal to/set inclusion
@	Address

All other symbols, including foreign and graphics characters, are *undefined* and can only appear in a Turbo Pascal program within a string.

Tokens and Separators

Each sequence of characters having a common meaning is called a *token*. For example, reserved words, numbers, strings, and symbols are all considered tokens. An individual token can be clearly identified because two adjacent tokens must be divided by at least one separator, which consists of a space or a comment. Note that as far as Pascal is concerned, not only is the standard space character (ASCII 32 or #32) considered a space, but so are all of the following:

Space	(#32)
Carriage return	(#13)
Line feed	(#10)
Form feed	(#12)
Tab	(#09)

These are often referred to as white space characters.

Separators are required between tokens but may not occur within them. (Of course, within a string, a space is treated as the space character itself and not as a separator.) There must be at least one separator between two tokens, but any number of separators may be used. In other words, any number of spaces is regarded by the compiler as a single separator.

With such a broad definition, the format of a Pascal program is quite flexible. For example, a carriage return is regarded as a separator, so statements and declarations may extend over several lines, and the spacing on a single line (indentations, for example) is left to the programmer. The FIRST program from the previous chapter could have been written as:

```
program First; begin writeln( 'Hello, again!' ) end.
```

Viewed in this way, you can see how the program corresponds to the imperative sentence, "Write 'Hello, Again!' on the screen!!!" But you can also see how line spacing and indentation can play important roles in adding clarity to your work. You will be surprised at how quickly you adopt a legible style.

Comments

The characters

```
{ This is a comment }
```

constitute a comment—a special form of a separator that defines an area of text that's completely ignored by the compiler. Comments are principally used for program documentation. To separate each comment from the rest of the program, enclose the comment within braces, as shown in the preceding comment line, or within asterisk-parentheses pairs as follows:

```
(* This is a comment *)
```

The compiler treats the entire comment exactly like a single space. A comment can appear anywhere in the program or not at all. Everything inside a comment is ignored unless a dollar sign ($) is placed in its first position. This special form of a comment is called a directive and is discussed in the Compiler Directive reference section of this book.

One comment can appear within another comment (a process called *nesting*) only if each of the comments uses a different set of end symbols. For example, the following lines are considered to be a single comment:

```
(* Temporarily commenting out the next two lines
PageNumber := PageNumber + 1;   { Turn the page }
LineNumber := 0;                { Start at first line }
*)
```

The (* opening symbol alerted the compiler to search for the *) closing symbol; the curly braces were ignored.

The Organization of a Pascal Program

A computer program consists fundamentally of action-oriented instructions, commonly called *code*, and the data manipulated by these instructions. Taken together, program data and code (declarations and statements) are commonly called the *program block*. Everything you need to express an idea in a computer language can be found in a block.

In fact every action-oriented Pascal component (that is, every program, unit, procedure, and function) contains its own block. To keep them separate, you begin each block with a separate header.

Units, procedures, and functions are described in later chapters. For now, concentrate on the program itself.

Pascal's Parts of Speech

If you give someone the English language commands "Walk!" or "Lift!" the responses are likely to be "Where?" and "What?" More complicated commands like "Travel!" are likely to be answered with "Where, when, and how?"

Even though a computer language is action-oriented, action-oriented statements are not sufficient for communicating with a computer any more than verbs are sufficient for communicating in a spoken language. In English, people rely on nouns to serve as the subjects of sentences and the objects upon which the action of a verb is performed. In Pascal, you use data.

The analogy between English and Pascal isn't as forced as you might think. Pascal was originally intended as a language that would be used primarily for teaching students how to program. Consequently, the original vision of Pascal was an elegantly simple set of English-like programming building blocks from which progressively more complicated programs could be constructed. The Pascal programming language is, in essence, a set of rules for writing imperative sentences.

The Parts of a Pascal Program

For a Pascal program, the *header* is the program declaration and the *block* is the program itself. Therefore, every Pascal program consists of the same three major components:

1. The *header*, consisting of the reserved word program, followed by the program name.

2. The *data* to be manipulated by the instructions in the program, as defined in label, constant, type, and variable declarations. You place data immediately after the header but before the first program code statement.

3. Program *code* statements describing the actions to be performed. Any procedures or functions defined by the program are placed at the start of the code area. Code statements follow and are enclosed by the reserved words begin and end.

Every program is terminated with a period.

General Format

The general format of a Pascal program is as follows:

```
program name;
    { Data declarations }
begin
    { Code statements }
end.
```

The header, the data declarations, and the code statements are all optional. However, since it's considered good programming style to include a header in your programs, all programs in this book will follow that convention. The following three lines:

```
program Trivial;
begin
end.
```

form a legitimate (although incredibly boring) program. You can enter it into the compiler, and actually (yawn) run it. Nevertheless, it does demonstrate how three reserved words (program, begin, and end) separate the regions where data and code belong.

A Program Example

The following program, LAYOUT (listing 2.2), demonstrates the three-part structure of a program in greater detail.

Listing 2.2

```
{*** Header ***}   program Layout;
{**************}   label   Start;
{     Data     }   const  Secret = 'aardvark';
{ Declarations }   type   Format = string[ 8 ];
{**************}   var    Response : Format;
{**************}   begin
{              }       Start:  write( 'Make a guess: ' );
{     Code     }               readln( Response );
{  Statements  }               if Response  <> Secret then goto Start;
{              }               writeln( 'Correct!!' );
{**************}   end.
```

Here the program asks the user to guess the name of an animal. (The correct answer is "aardvark." Don't tell anyone.) The program continues until the user is successful. The program can be terminated early by pressing Ctrl-Break.

The header consists of the reserved word program followed by Layout, the program's name.

The data section consists of four declarations:

1. A label, Start, that, although it's used within the code section, just marks a location rather than performs an action or stores some information.

2. A constant, Secret, that keeps the same value throughout the operation of the program.

3. A type, Format, that defines the structure of variables. Here, the program defines an eight-character string.

4. A variable, Response, that stores each guess and changes its contents every time a guess is entered. Response is defined to have the properties identified as Format. In other words, Response is defined to consist of an eight-character string.

The code section consists of four lines:

1. A write statement that tells the user to make a guess. The label can be used to reference this line throughout the remainder of the program; other than that, Start has no effect on program execution.

2. A readln (pronounced "read line") statement that accepts data input from the keyboard. Press the Enter key after each guess.

3. An if...then statement that tests a condition and performs an action based on the result of that test. Here, the program tests whether the user answer Response is equal to the correct answer, Secret. If the two don't match (the <> symbol stands for an inequality) then the goto Start instruction redirects the flow of the program back to the line following the label Start.

4. A writeln (pronounced "write line") statement that congratulates the user when the correct animal name is entered. Notice that because of the preceding if...then statement, the writeln statement is reached only if the user answer, Response, matches the correct answer, Secret.

When a program runs, the computer reserves storage (memory space) according to the contents of the data declaration section. Then the program proceeds to execute the first instruction following the begin statement. After that statement is finished executing, the statement on the next line is executed. After that statement is finished executing, the statement on the next line is executed, and so on. The program continues executing statements line-by-line until the final period is reached.

In the LAYOUT program, storage space is reserved for only two data items: Secret and Response. The label Start doesn't reside in memory; it simply marks a location in memory. This location is only needed by the compiler to generate the machine code to perform the goto statement; because the location is incorporated within the machine code itself, Start can be discarded when the program executes. Similarly, the Format type simply told the compiler how to reserve space for the Response variable (as an eight-character string); once the compiler knew the style to use, Format was no longer needed.

After the program arranges storage for Secret and Response, control is passed to the statement following the begin. The Make a guess message is displayed, the user response is read in, and the comparison is performed. Here, the flow of the program can be changed. If an incorrect guess is entered, the if...then test allows the goto statement to transfer program flow to the Start line. The flow of the program continues sequentially only when the correct response is entered.

Program Data Declarations

Although program declarations can occur in any sequence, they usually appear in the following order:

❑ Labels

❑ Constants

❑ Types

❑ Variables

The only restriction is that all identifiers must be defined before being used.

The following sections discuss each of these declarations in more detail.

Label Declarations

In the BASIC language that came with your PC, every line in every program begins with a number. When you want to transfer control to another line (or when you want to bypass several lines), you jump to the new line using a goto statement.

Instead of a line number, Pascal uses a *label* to mark a location within a block of program code.

Labels are declared with the reserved word label followed by the desired identifiers. In standard Pascal, each identifier may consist of a whole number in the range 0 through 9999.

Because the only practical application of labels is as the target of goto statements and because integers are less user friendly than ordinary alphanumeric identifiers, this restriction was supposed to be a deterrent to the use of goto. It didn't work. The goto statement has remained (perhaps unfortunately) extremely popular. In fact, Turbo Pascal allows labels to be normal alphanumeric identifier names. If several labels are declared, each pair must be separated with a comma. The final label must be followed by a semicolon.

When a label is used in the program, it must be the first identifier on the line. Each label must be immediately followed by a colon (:).

In the LABELER program (listing 2.3), the label Start is used to mark the beginning of a loop.

Listing 2.3

```
program Labeler;
label
   Start;
var
   Counter : byte;
begin
           Counter := Ø;
           Writeln( 'The loop is now beginning.' );
   Start:  Counter := Counter + 1;
           Writeln( 'This is line ', Counter );
           if Counter  < 1Ø then Goto Start;
           Writeln( 'Done' );
end.
```

Labels may also be inserted in your program in order to provide additional comments.

Constant Definitions

A *constant* is an identifier that—once defined—has a single, unchangeable meaning.

The constant declaration section begins with the reserved word const. Each individual constant is declared as an identifier, followed by an equal sign (=), followed by the value to be assigned to the identifier, and finally followed by a semicolon.

Within a program statement, constants and variables are treated equivalently—except, of course, that constants cannot be redefined. Wherever the compiler detects a constant identifier, however, it treats the line exactly as if it were written with the value itself. For example, in the following:

```
const
   MinSize = 1;
   MaxSize = 20;
var
   Students : array [ MinSize..MaxSize ] of word;
   i : byto;
begin
   .
   .

   .
   for i := MinSize to MaxSize do
      Writeln( Students[ i ] );
```

the size of the array is interpreted by the compiler as [1..20] just as if the digits had appeared in place of the constant identifiers. In a similar way, the identifiers used in the for...do loop allow it to range from 1 through 20.

Constant Expressions

Turbo Pascal further allows *constant expressions* to be used in the place of a single constant. In the following lines:

```
const
   Radius        = 12;
   Diameter      = 2 * Radius;
   Circumference = 3.14159 * Diameter;
```

Turbo treats both the Diameter and Circumference identifiers as constants even though their values were completely derived from the value of Radius.

Remember that Turbo is a one-pass compiler. Anything appearing in a constant expression must be completely defined by the time the expression is encountered. Consequently, expressions can't contain references to variables, typed constants, function calls, or the address operator (@). The following standard functions, however, may be used:

Abs	Lo	Ptr	Swap
Chr	Odd	Round	Trunc
Hi	Ord	SizeOf	
Length	Pred	Succ	

(These functions will be defined in later chapters.) With the exception of these few restrictions, constant expressions operate just like the normal expressions described in Chapter 4.

Several uses of constant expressions can be seen in the following extract of a report writing program:

```
const
    Title             = 'Turbo Programming Notes';
    TopLineOfPrint    = 6;
    BottomLineOfPrint = 60;
    LeftMargin        = 10;
    RightMargin       = 75;
    PageLength        = BottomLineOfPrint - TopLineOfPrint + 1;
    PageWidth         = RightMargin - LeftMargin + 1;
    CharactersPerPage = PageLength * PageWidth;
    FormFeed          = Chr(12);
    TopLine           = FormFeed + Title;
    PositionOfTopLine = ((PageWidth - Length(Title)) div 2) + LeftMargin;
```

Constant expressions are only evaluated once, when the program is first compiled. They don't detract from either the execution speed or the size of the final program. Yet, as you can see in the example, they can considerably simplify the process of program development.

Typed Constants

Turbo Pascal supports the use of *typed constants*, which enable you to assign not only an initial value to a variable, but a type as well.

Typed constants are declared within the constant section. Despite this fact (and despite their unfortunate name), typed constants are really variables.

Each typed constant is written in the form: identifier, colon (:), type, equal sign (=), and initial value.

The following examples demonstrate their use:

```
const
    NumberOfFlights : integer = 4;
    MatrixRows      : byte    = 6;
```

Both NumberOfFlights and MatrixRows can be redefined whenever you wish.

Type Definitions

Type is the property of a Pascal variable that defines the size of the storage it requires, the range of values it can be assigned, and the operators that can act on it. Once a type has been declared for a variable, the compiler will ensure that the variable is used appropriately; for example, you won't be allowed to assign a string to a variable defined as an integer.

A type declaration section begins with the reserved word type. Each individual type is written in the form of an identifier, followed by an equal sign (=), followed by a description of the type, followed finally by a semicolon.

Table 2.2 lists Turbo Pascal's broad range of predefined data types that can be used on individual variables. The basic Pascal data types are numbers, which may be either real or integer; logical Boolean values, which may be either True or False; and ASCII characters, called *char* when used singly and *string* when multiple characters are used. More complicated data types, such as the array, record, and set, are also available. Integer and real types are further divided into categories depending on the size and allowable range of the data.

Table 2.2. *Turbo Pascal Standard Data Types*

Type	Description
Boolean	True or False
	Whole Numbers:
byte	$0 \ldots +255$
integer	$-32,768 \ldots +32,767$
longint	$-2,147,483,648 \ldots +2,147,483,647$
shortint	$-128 \ldots +127$
word	$0 \ldots +65,535$
	Real Numbers:
real	$2.9 \times 10^{-39} \ldots 1.7 \times 10^{38}$
single	$1.5 \times 10^{-45} \ldots 3.4 \times 10^{38}$
double	$5.0 \times 10^{-324} \ldots 1.7 \times 10^{308}$
extended	$3.4 \times 10^{-4932} \ldots 1.1 \times 10^{4932}$
comp	$-2^{63} + 1 \ldots 2^{63} - 1$
char	Any one of the ASCII characters
string	A sequence of up to 255 ASCII characters. If a size isn't specified, a default of 255 will be used.
pointer	A location in memory rather a value itself

The Boolean, the char, and the five whole number types are together referred to as *ordinal* types.

These predefined types are most often used within the variable declaration section when a simple variable is first defined. The type declaration section is used to define more complicated data structures based on the specific needs of the program. These user-defined types always use the standard types as building blocks.

Through the use of user-defined data types, shown in table 2.3, your Turbo Pascal programs can comfortably manipulate extremely sophisticated data structures. For example, in the following section of code, the Student Array type defines an array of records, one field of which consists of a user-defined set.

```
type
    Specialties  = ( Math, Physics, English, History );
    StudentData  = record
                       StudentName : string[ 20 ];
                       Major       : Specialties;
                       Graduation  : word;
                   end;
    StudentArray = array [ 1..25 ] of StudentData;
```

Table 2.3. *Turbo Pascal User-Defined Data Types*

Type	Description
enumerated	A set of values
subrange	A subset of another type
array	A repeating data structure
set	A collection of values
file	A data type that stores data on an auxiliary storage device
record	A combination of variables of other types

Data types are discussed in greater detail in Chapter 3.

Variable Declarations

A variable declaration section begins with the reserved word var. Each individual variable is written in the form of an identifier, followed by a colon (:), followed by the type of the variable, followed finally by a semicolon. A variable may be of any standard or user-defined type.

Examples of variable declarations include the following:

```
var
    i            : byte;
    ProductKey   : string[ 12 ];
    SalesHistory : array [ 1..12 ] of real;
```

Further illustrations of variable declarations can be found in the other examples in this book.

Program Code Statements

Program code is defined by executable statements that specify the actions to be taken by the program. Statements are the active data movement and manipulation commands. From their content, the compiler determines the machine instructions to be generated.

The following sections discuss Pascal statements in more detail.

Simple and Compound Statements

Wherever Pascal allows a statement to be used, it may be either simple or compound. A simple statement is a single command such as an assignment, case, for...do, or repeat...until statement. A compound statement consists of the reserved words begin and end, between which any number of other valid statements may be located. As far as the compiler is concerned, the begin and end pair define a single statement.

For example, the standard form of an if...then...else statement is as follows:

```
if <condition> then
    statement
else
    statement;
```

Through the use of the reserved words begin and end, you can actually perform several statements in the place of one, as shown in the following example:

```
if QuantitySold > 1000 then
    begin
        writeln( 'Great job!  You are getting a bonus!' );
        Commission := QuantitySold * 5.00;
    end
else
    begin
        writeln( 'You didn''t hit your quota. Try harder!' );
        Commission := 0;
    end;
```

The Assignment Statement

The most fundamental statement in Pascal, the assignment statement replaces the contents of a variable. The identifier of the variable to be changed is stated first, followed by the assignment operator (:=), then followed by the new value. The new value can either be explicitly defined, as in

```
Quantity := 45;              { Assignment of a number }
Warning  := 'File not found';  { Assignment of a string }
SaveData := Y;               { Assignment of a variable }
```

or it can be stated as an expression (which may contain functions) from which the value can be derived, as in

```
X := 45 div 9;              { Assignment of an expression }
Y := 3 * X = 6;            { Assignment of a Boolean }
Z := Sqrt( Sqr(X)+Sqr(Y) ); { Assignment of a function }
```

The *Case* Statement

A case statement selects one action out of several depending on the result of a single test. The expression to be tested is called the *selector* and each option is called a *case constant*. If the selector doesn't match any of the case constants, the statement identified with the word else will be executed. Each case statement must be terminated with an end. The else statement is optional; if it isn't present and no case constant matches the selector, the compiler simply moves along to the first statement that follows the end.

The selector expression should evaluate to an ordinal value within the range –32,768 through +32,767. Therefore, strings, real numbers, and the integer types longint and word can't be used as selectors. This still leaves a variety of options, including char, Boolean, and set types, as well as integer types such as byte and shortint.

The case statements are among the most useful in Pascal. Their operation can be demonstrated with the following examples:

```
case Answer of
   'Y' : DoTheTask;
   'N' : CancelFutureWork;
   else  ShowHelpMessage;
end;
case Month of
   Jan..Mar : writeln( 'Winter' );
   Apr..Jun : writeln( 'Spring' );
   Jul..Sep : writeln( 'Summer' );
   Oct..Dec : writeln( 'Fall' );
end;
case MenuOption1 of
   1 : DoTask1;
   2 : DoTask2;
   3 : case MenuOption2 of
          1 : DoTask3A;
          2 : DoTask3B;
       end;
   4 : DoTask4;
 else  DemandRetype;
end;
```

The case statement is functionally equivalent to a long series of potentially confusing if...then...else statements.

The *For...To/DownTo...Do* Statement

The for statement executes a statement a predetermined number of times. A control variable assumes a different sequential value during each pass.

A for statement is extremely efficient, because—unlike a while or repeat loop—you don't need to perform a condition test on each pass, and the code that changes the control variable is highly optimized.

There are two forms of for statements. In the first, the control variable increases in its sequence. In the second, the control variable decreases with each pass. The reserved word to indicates an increase, and downto indicates a decrease, as follows:

```
for i := 'a' to 'z' do write( i );       { Outputs the alphabet }
for i := 'z' downto 'a' do write( i );   { Reverses the alphabet }
```

The control variable must be ordinal and must have been defined within the block in which the for statement is used.

The for statement is frequently the most convenient means of manipulating arrays. For example, the following code calculates the result of multiplying an $m \times n$ matrix A and an $n \times p$ matrix B. The product, C, is an $m \times p$ matrix.

```
for i := 1 to m do
   for j := 1 to p do begin
      C[i,j] := 0;
      for k := 1 to n do
         C[i,j] := C[i,j] + A[i,k]*B[k,j];
   end;
```

The initial and final values of the loop are determined as soon as the for statement begins. They cannot be affected by any actions *within* the statement being executed. Therefore, in the code:

```
j := 5;
for i := 1 to j do
   begin
      j := j + 8;
      writeln( i );
   end;
```

the writeln statement is executed only five times, even though the variable j changes with each pass.

The *Goto* Statement

A goto statement, written in the form

```
goto LabeledLine;
```

changes the flow of program execution by jumping to the statement immediately following the referenced label, which must be located within the same
block as the goto itself.

The goto statement is deceptively simple to use. Nevertheless, you should
avoid it. Other statements—most notably the while...do and repeat...until
loops—can always be used instead and with greater reliability, readability, and
control. The goto statement does not appear in any other programs in this
book.

The LABEL2 program (listing 2.4) shows how a label can actually be
defined within an if...then statement. When executed, LABEL2 displays a
single Hello message.

Listing 2.4

```
program Label2;
label
    Intrude;
var
   i : integer;
begin
          i := 23;
          if i = Ø then
   Intrude:    begin
                  write( 'Hello' );
                  i := 1ØØ;
               end;
          if i <> 1ØØ then
             goto Intrude;
end.
```

The *If...Then...Else* Statement

The if...then statement tests a condition; if the condition is True, then a
statement is executed. For example:

```
if RecordCount > 1ØØ then
   Write( 'It''s time to save your file!' );
```

If you want an action to occur when the condition is True and some other
action to occur when the condition is False, you can use the option else to
specify the alternate action, as in:

```
if FileExists then
   OpenTheFile
else
   CreateTheFile;
```

Some extremely useful (although extremely complicated) structures arise when the statement is itself another if...then...else. For example:

```
if Salary < 20000 then
    HourlyRate := HourlyRate + 0.75    { Flat rate }
else
    if Salary < 40000 then
        HourlyRate := HourlyRate * 1.08
    else
        HourlyRate := HourlyRate * 1.05;
```

The compiler assumes that each else is associated with the last unmatched if. You should indent your code to reflect the pairing.

The *Repeat...Until* Statement

A repeat statement defines the beginning of a series of statements that is executed at least once and that continues to be executed until a certain condition is met.

For example, in the following code:

```
Counter := 10;
repeat
writeln( 'Hello' );
    Counter := Counter - 1;
until Counter < 5;
```

the message Hello is displayed six times.

Because the statements between repeat and until must execute before the test is made, repeat loops are most useful to ensure that a certain sequence of code will continue to repeat until some condition is True.

```
repeat
    write( 'Enter the time: ' );
    readln( Hour );
until Hour in [ 0..24 ];
```

The *While...Do* Statement

The while statement executes another statement, identified by the prefix do, as long as a specified condition is True. Unlike the repeat...until loop, the while statement tests the condition *before* the loop is executed. Examples of the while...do loop include the following:

```
while not Eof( DataFile ) do begin  { Test for end of file }
   Statement1;
   Statement2;
   Statement3;
end;
while index > 0 do
   begin
      TargetString[ index ] := SourceString[ index ];
      index := index - 1;
   end;
```

The *With* Statement

A with statement can reference the fields of a record without specifying the record name every time. For example, given the following declarations:

```
type
   TravelData = record
                   Name       : string;
                   Flight     : word;
                   TicketPrice : real;
                end;
var
   Passenger : TravelData;
```

the following sets of code are identical:

```
begin                                with Passenger do
   Passenger.Name       := 'Smith';  begin
   Passenger.Flight     := 703;         Name       := 'Smith';
   Passenger.TicketPrice := 324.65;     Flight     := 703;
end;                                    TicketPrice := 324.65;
                                     end;
```

Procedures and Functions

A procedure is a subroutine that results in a series of actions directed toward a single purpose. A function is a subroutine specifically designed to return a single value; accordingly, functions are only called within expressions. Certain procedures and functions are of such widespread importance that they are provided as standard services in Pascal. As such, they need not be defined before they are invoked. For example, writeln and readln are standard procedures; Sqr and Sqrt are standard functions. The complete list of over 200 standard procedures and functions can be found in the *Reference Guide*.

When these standard procedures and functions are not adequate for the task at hand, you can define a customized subroutine using a procedure declaration or a function declaration. The new subroutine can then be invoked in the same way that the standard routines are invoked.

These user-defined procedures and functions have the same basic structure as the program itself—a header followed by a block. Each procedure and function can have its own label, constant, type, and variable declarations.

These are said to be *local* to the procedure. They remain active and can be accessed only within the procedure; they disappear when the procedure is finished executing.

Within a procedure or function, a block will appear just as if it were a main program. It begins with the reserved word begin, contains a number of statements to be executed, and closes with the reserved word end. Procedures and functions, however, end with a semicolon rather than a period.

Program PFDEMO (listing 2.5) illustrates how a procedure and function can be used. The program itself is designed to produce a simple 5 × 5 addition table. The procedure DoHeadings prepares the table headings. The function Total performs the individual additions. Total and DoHeadings must be positioned after all program data has been declared but before the first begin statement in the main body of the program.

Listing 2.5

```
program PFdemo;
var
   Value1, Value2 : byte;

function Total : byte;
begin
   Total := Value1 + Value2;
end;

procedure DoHeadings;
begin
   writeln( 'Addition Table' );
   writeln( '==============' );
   writeln;
   writeln( '        1    2    3    4    5' );
   writeln( '----------------------------' );
end;

begin
   DoHeadings;
   for Value1 := 1 to 5 do begin
      write( '   ', Value1, '|' );
      for Value2 := 1 to 5 do
         write( '   ', Total );
      writeln;
   end;
end.
```

When PFDEMO executes, it produces the addition table shown in figure 2.1.

Fig. 2.1. Addition Table Created by PFDEMO

```
          1      2      3      4      5
-------------------------------------------
   1|     2      3      4      5      6
   2|     3      4      5      6      7
   3|     4      5      6      7      8
   4|     5      6      7      8      9
   5|     6      7      8      9     10
```

Within the main body of the program, the DoHeadings procedure was treated just like a standard procedure, and the Total function was treated just like a standard function.

A complete discussion of procedures and functions can be found in Chapter 5. For now, you only need to be comfortable with their basic structure.

Summary

In this chapter, you have learned about the individual components of the Turbo Pascal language, and you have seen how they combine to form a complete program. A *reserved word* has a unique and special meaning related to program structure and control. An *identifier* is any user-defined name. A *character* is any one of the ASCII characters. A string is a sequence of zero or more ASCII characters. A *number* consists of any valid combination of digits, plus and minus signs, and decimal points. A *comment* is an area of text that's completely ignored by the compiler. You have learned the meanings of the special symbols used by Turbo Pascal.

You have learned that a Turbo Pascal program is structured in three major sections. The header consists of the reserved word program followed by the program name. Program data consists of the items of information that are to be manipulated by the instructions in the program. Program code statements describe the actions to be performed.

You have learned about the major categories of data. A *label* is used to mark a location within a program. A *constant* is an identifier that has a single, unchangeable meaning. *Typed constants* enable you to assign an initial value to a variable. A *variable* is information that can change during the course of the program.

You have learned how to use the statements available in a Turbo Pascal program. The *assignment* statement replaces the value of a variable. *Case* selects one statement to be executed out of a list of many. *For* executes a statement repeatedly, and a sequence of values is assigned to a control variable. *Goto* transfers the flow of the program. *If* tests a condition and performs actions based on the result. *Repeat* repeats a series of statements one or more times. *While* repeats a series of statements zero or more times. *With* allows the fields of a record to be referenced without having to identify the record name with each use. You have learned that all statements appearing between the reserved words begin and end are treated as a single statement.

You have learned that statements can be combined into units called procedures and functions. A *procedure* is a subroutine that results in series of actions directed toward a single purpose. A *function* is a subroutine specifically designed to return a single value.

Data and Data Types

I n everyday life, people tend (for better or worse) to assign categories for everything they see and every action they perform. These categories are what give the subject—be it an object or an event—its identity and character. The journalist's technique of "Who, What, Where, When, Why, and How" is an example of categories that can be used to gather, structure, and present information quickly, efficiently, and eloquently. People say that they have the facts about something when the most important categories have been objectively identified and accurately evaluated.

Data are the facts that you use to solve a specific problem. Data are usually expressed as numbers, characters, or conditions (true or false, for example). The different categories of data are called data *types*. Data items might include *red*, *42*, and *Ralph*; the corresponding data types might be *color, hours worked*, and *first name*.

Knowing the data type helps you determine the validity of an individual data item. For example, hours worked is probably not a negative number, and a first name is probably something containing letters.

Similarly, the data type defines the set of actions that can be performed with the data. It makes no sense to take the square root of a first name, and it makes no sense to capitalize hours worked.

Perhaps not too surprisingly, this programming definition of a type—a valid range of data, plus a meaningful set of operations—is the same as the dictionary definition of the word *algebra*. Just as the use of algebra helps to solve mathematical problems with pencil and paper, the use of data types allows programming problems to be solved with the PC.

The previous chapter briefly discussed the types supported by Turbo Pascal. This chapter describes those types in greater detail and shows how you can define entirely new data types to better handle specific programming problems.

Integers

Turbo Pascal provides five data types for storing integer formats: Byte, ShortInt, Integer, Word, and LongInt. Table 3.1 summarizes these types.

Table 3.1. *Data Types for Integer Formats*

Type	Size	Ranges of allowed values
Byte	1 byte	0..255
ShortInt	1 byte	–128..+127
Integer	2 bytes	–32,768..+32,767
Word	2 bytes	0..65,535
LongInt	4 bytes	–2,147,483,648..+2,147,483,647

Note that ShortInt is the signed version of Byte, and Integer is the signed version of Word. LongInt is a data type you can use when you need to manipulate relatively large numbers accurately.

Notice that both Byte and ShortInt occupy a single byte, and both Word and Integer both occupy a single word. Each member of the pair interprets the bit patterns of a variable differently. If you're using *only* Bytes or *only* ShortInts, for example, these differences won't matter. But if you mix the types (and this happens all the time), you might get some unexpected results. To understand this process better, you need to know something about how integer arithmetic works.

Clarification of Integer

Pascal groups the five data types Byte, ShortInt, Integer, Word, and LongInt in the category called *integers*. Unfortunately, the word *integer* describes both the category and an individual type. A similar problem arises when Pascal users discuss *reals*. This situation came about because over the years, Borland has increasingly offered more features (the ShortInt and LongInt data types, for example) than most other compilers, so the single word *integer* used in most books and articles has come to be applied to a much broader range of types when used for Turbo Pascal. The meaning I intend should always be clear from the context in which the word is used.

Integer Arithmetic

Human beings use addition and subtraction. Computers use two's complement arithmetic.

There's nothing more confusing than base 2 arithmetic, so forget about it for now. Consider instead the ordinary decimal (base 10) system. If a computer operated entirely on base 10 instead of just 0 and 1, you could use these digits:

0, 1, 2, 3, 4, 5, 6, 7, 8, and 9.

Every number would be stored in a series of one or more bytes. Assume that you are using a decimal-system computer with each byte capable of holding the digits from 0 through 9. Further assume that you want to work with a "decimal-word" sized number of two bytes. Each decimal-word, therefore, can hold the following numbers:

00, 01, 02, 03,...,96, 97, 98, and 99.

Because your decimal word is only two "decimal bytes" long, any three-digit number (100 and above) is truncated back to two digits.

Given such a structure, most arithmetic operations are quite normal. After all,

04 + 76 = 80
54 – 32 = 22
16 × 03 = 48
72 ÷ 09 = 08

Your decimal-system computer can handle results greater than 99 (that is, greater than can fit in a "decimal-word") by simply truncating all of the extra columns.

53 + 82 = 35   (135, truncated)
43 × 65 = 95   (2795, truncated)

But how does it answer questions such as

53 – 82 = ??
43 – 65 = ??

when negative numbers weren't part of the definition? The answer is that you use numbers that "act like" negatives. The formal definition of a negative number is: Given a number X, its negative (–X) is the value that satisfies the equation:

X + (–X) = 0

You want to find the negatives of 82 and 65, so what numbers in your decimal computer could be added to 82 and 65 to produce zero (00)? The answer is 18 and 35. Remember that any total greater than 99 is simply truncated. As a result, any multiple of 100 is equal to 0, including 0, 00, 100, 500, 1000400, and 87623945300.

Of course, common sense tells you that 18 isn't equal to (–82), and 35 isn't equal to (–65), but when you use them in formulas where only the two right-hand columns of the result are significant, you quickly find that there's no other explanation for the answers you get.

Because 100 is the same as zero, you find that

(–82) = 0 – 82 = 100 –82 = 28   so   (–82) = 28
(–65) = 0 – 65 = 100 – 65 = 35   so   (–65) = 35

Alternatively, you can do the math normally, then convert the answers.

53 – 82 = – 29   and   100 – 29 = 71   so   53 – 82 = 71
43 – 65 = – 22   and   100 – 22 = 78   so   43 – 65 = 78

When you also consider that

53 – 82 = 71   and   53 + 28 = 71
43 – 65 = 78   and   43 + 35 = 78

you see that (–82) does equal (+28) and (–65) does equal (+35).

Still not convinced? In an ordinary decimal system, the negative sign in a multiplication can float freely. Compare $-(43 \times 68)$ with $(-43) \times 68$ and $43 \times (-68)$.

$-(43 \times 68)$	$(-43) \times 68$	$43 \times (-68)$
$-(2924)$	$(+57) \times 68$	$43 \times (+32)$
$-(24)$	3876	1376
76	76	76

So (–24) equals 76. Negative numbers in your decimal-word don't need the traditional format in order to act the same. You can find a positive number that's equivalent to any negative number within range. Therefore, your decimal-system computer has the following equalities:

$$-01 = +99$$
$$-02 = +98$$
$$-03 = +97$$
$$\vdots \quad \vdots \quad \vdots$$
$$-47 = +53$$
$$-48 = +52$$
$$-49 = +51$$
$$-50 = +50$$

As a practical matter, *50* should not denote both a negative and positive amount, so you can arbitrarily say that *50* means (–50) and further say that (+50) is *out of range*.

Now slip back to binary, because the PC operates on base 2, not base 10. Instead of recycling to zero at decimal 100, each byte returns to zero with each multiple of 256. Hence, for a byte:

$$
\begin{array}{rcl}
-1 & = & +255 \\
-2 & = & +254 \\
-3 & = & +253 \\
\vdots\ \vdots & & \vdots \\
-125 & = & +131 \\
-126 & = & +130 \\
-127 & = & +129 \\
-128 & = & +128
\end{array}
$$

Again, you don't want *128* to mean both a negative and positive amount, so you can say that *128* means (–128) and further say that (+128) is *out of range*. Notice however, that as a result of this definition, all binary negative numbers are in the range 128 through 255; in other words, all binary negative numbers have a 1 in their highest bit, and all binary positive numbers have a 0 in their highest bit.

Similarly, each word recycles to zero with each multiple of 65,536. Therefore, for a word:

$$
\begin{array}{rcl}
-1 & = & +65,535 \\
-2 & = & +65,534 \\
-3 & = & +65,533 \\
\vdots\ \vdots & & \vdots \\
-32,765 & = & +32,771 \\
-32,766 & = & +32,770 \\
-32,767 & = & +32,769 \\
-32,768 & = & +32,768
\end{array}
$$

Once more, *32,768* should not denote both a negative and positive amount, so you can say that *32,768* means (–32,768) and further say that (+32,768) is *out of range*. Notice that here again all negative numbers have a 1 in their highest bit, and all positive numbers have a 0 in their highest bit.

This discussion repeatedly states that (+65,534) "acts like" (–2). Obviously, however, it must also act like (+65,534). In other words, when you need a negative number, you now know how to obtain its functional equivalent. But when you need only a positive number, you can use the positive number itself. So in the eight bits of a byte, you can have the values

   –128, –127,...,–2, –1, 0, +1, +2..+126, +127

or

   0, 1, 2, 3,...,253, 254, 255

depending upon whether or not you want negative numbers. You could, of course, have both +254 and –2 in the same byte, but to avoid confusion, don't let this happen. The N numbers that can be stored in a set of bytes are either

0, 1, 2,...,N–2, N–1

or

$-(N/2)$, $-(N/2)+1$,...,–2, –1, 0, 1, 2,...,$(N/2)-2$, $(N/2)-1$

Therefore, you represent positive and negative numbers in the same bytes just by shifting the range of values the bit patterns represent. When you use negatives, the numbers are *signed*, because the numbers have an implied positive or negative sign in the form of the highest bit; when the bit is 1, the number is negative, and when the bit is 0, the number is positive. When you use the full set of positives, the numbers are *unsigned*, and the highest bit has no special meaning.

Using Integer Types

The processor itself makes no distinction between signed and unsigned numbers. The choice is entirely dependent upon the programmer's intent; ensure that your program's instructions are used appropriately. An error is generated if you try to assign a value too large for the type of the specified variable.

To avoid undesirable results (truncation or rounding, for example) when you use integers of different types in the same expression, Turbo converts all of its terms into a *common type* before performing any operations. A common type is simply the smallest type that can hold all of the values. If the right side of the equation contains a Byte and a ShortInt, the equation will be evaluated as if all terms are Integers. Similarly, a Byte and a Word will both be evaluated as Words. A Word and an Integer will be evaluated as LongInts.

If the common type of an evaluated expression is larger than the assigned type of the variable on the left side of the equation, its contents may be truncated or converted, as necessary. For example:

```
{ Ø..255 }    { Ø..255 }   { –128.. +127 }
ValueByte1 := ValueByte2  + ValueShortInt;
```

If ValueByte2 = (+99) and ValueShortInt = (–100), Turbo will evaluate the sum as (–1), just as if both variables were Integer types. When the result is assigned to ValueByte1, it will be converted to (+255).

The format you select to represent an integer-type variable depends on its minimum and maximum bounds. In order to avoid unwanted surprises in your programs, always use integer types large enough to contain the full expected range comfortably.

Real Numbers

Unfortunately, only a narrow subset of all integer numbers can be handled by the PC. For example, integer types are too small to track the dollar value of a Fortune 500 company. They're also too inexact to contain the changes in thrust required by the space shuttle to attain orbit. Very large and very small numbers are handled by a different family of data types—the reals.

At the risk of oversimplifying the entire subject of number theory, mathematicians say that a number is *real* if it is either rational or irrational. A *rational* number is one that can be expressed as a fraction of whole numbers, such as 3/1, 13/19, and 1/2. A number is *irrational* if no whole number fraction can be found and it can only be expressed approximately, such as pi and the square root of 2. Real numbers are typically written as decimal values, such as 2.0, 3.14159, 1.414, and 0.5.

In Turbo Pascal, this definition is greatly simplified: a real number is any number that contains a decimal point. Table 3.2 lists Turbo's real-number data types, together with the size in bytes that they occupy, the range of values they can assume, and the number of significant digits they hold.

***Table 3.2.** Real Number Data Types*

Type	Size	Ranges of allowed values	Significant Digits
Real	6 bytes	2.9×10^{-39} to 1.7×10^{38}	11–12
Single	4 bytes	1.5×10^{-45} to 3.4×10^{38}	7–8
Double	8 bytes	5.0×10^{-324} to 1.7×10^{308}	15–16
Extended	10 bytes	1.9×10^{-4951} to 1.1×10^{4932}	19–20
Comp	8 bytes	$-2^{63}+1$ to $2^{63}-1$	19–20

Single, Double, Extended, and Comp data types can be used on an 8087 math coprocessor chip. This capacity is discussed more fully in Chapter 17, and in the reference section on compiler directives.

Real numbers, which are also called *floating-point* numbers, compress large values into a small number of bytes by using a format similar to that of scientific notation. Whereas scientific notation uses base 10, floating-point types store the binary representations of a sign (+ or –), an exponent, and a significand:

(+/–) significand $\times 2^{\text{exponent}}$

The actual bit layout doesn't really matter. Notice, though, that both the significand and the exponent are stored as binary numbers; this is why the table of reals shows ranges that seem so unusual.

When you define a real number as a constant, Turbo Pascal stores the value in the smallest possible type. All of the numbers in the following example are stored as reals:

```
const
    NormalTemp     = 98.6;
    ExchangeRate   = 1.65;
    LifeSavings    = 43935.21;
    DiscountFactor = 0.76;
    NormalFactor   = 1.0;
```

Notice that the value of DiscountFactor, which is less than 1, is preceded by a zero, whereas the value of NormalFactor, which is an integer, is written in decimal form. These concessions to style are required if Turbo Pascal is to understand the intended type; remember that a period not preceded by a number is treated as the final period of the program, and a number not written in decimal form is interpreted as an integer.

Boolean Types

Boolean logic is named for George Boole, the English mathematician who studied the algebra of two elements. In Turbo Pascal, the two elements are True and False.

Actually, Boolean values are stored as numbers in a single byte. False is stored as zero. True is nonzero, but is typically stored as +1.

Boolean values are the most common method of controlling the flow of a program through their use in conditional and looping statements. When you assign a Boolean value to a variable, you effectively turn the variable into a condition. For example, given the following declaration:

```
var
    FirstParagraph : Boolean;
    DoneYet        : Boolean;
```

the Boolean variables can be assigned values of either True or False, as follows:

```
begin
    :
    FirstParagraph := True;
    DoneYet        := False;
```

and can be used in Pascal statements just like conditions, as in the following:

```
if FirstParagraph then
    DoPageEjectAndTitle;

while not DoneYet do
    ProcessTheNextRecord;
```

Char Types

All information in the PC is managed in the fundamental unit, the *byte*, which may assume any one of 256 states. Turbo Pascal provides three data types for handling individual bytes: Char, Byte, and ShortInt. When a byte is used to represent the eight-bit number itself, the Byte or ShortInt type is used. When a byte is used to represent one of the 256 extended ASCII characters, the Char type is used. Even though all three data types are internally identical, a variable of type Char cannot be used in an arithmetic expression.

The best way to understand the Char type is to view every possible ASCII value. The values are listed in table 3.3.

As you can see, the digits from 0 through 9 are stored as ASCII 48 through ASCII 57; uppercase letters are stored as ASCII 65 through ASCII 90; and lowercase letters are stored as ASCII 97 through ASCII 122.

As strange as these patterns might seem, they have (or at least *had*) their uses. ASCII originated in the old teletype days. Originally, only the low 128 characters—called the *standard* ASCII character set—were used. Because each character could be represented with seven bits, the eighth bit was available to test the accuracy of the transmission. By setting or clearing the eighth bit, every byte could be transmitted with an odd number of bits (odd parity) or an even number of bits (even parity).

The low ASCII values—0 through 31—were used as control characters; the abbreviations shown have meanings like "enquiry" and "acknowledgment." (In other words, if the sixth and seventh bits were zero, the byte contained a control character.)

Because uppercase letters begin at ASCII 65, if the seventh bit was set, the byte probably contained an alpha character. Also, uppercase and lowercase letters differ by 32 positions, so the setting of the sixth bit determined whether a letter was capitalized.

When it developed the PC, IBM decided the machine should perform parity testing with special circuits. Consequently, the eighth bit became available; as a result, an *additional* 128 characters could be introduced to handle foreign and graphics characters. The full 256 characters are commonly called the *extended ASCII character set*.

Except for special characters like the form feed (number 12) and carriage return (13), you'll almost always refer to a standard character by the symbol itself (that is, a letter A instead of 65). The extended character set shown in figure 3.1 is most frequently used for drawing boxes.

Table 3.3. *ASCII Values*

Hex	Dec	Screen	Hex	Dec	Screen	Hex	Dec	Screen
00h	0		2Ch	44	,	58h	88	X
01h	1	☺	2Dh	45	–	59h	89	Y
02h	2	●	2Eh	46	.	5Ah	90	Z
03h	3	♥	2Fh	47	/	5Bh	91	[
04h	4	♦	30h	48	0	5Ch	92	\
05h	5	♣	31h	49	1	5Dh	93	]
06h	6	♠	32h	50	2	5Eh	94	^
07h	7	•	33h	51	3	5Fh	95	_
08h	8	◘	34h	52	4	60h	96	`
09h	9	○	35h	53	5	61h	97	a
0Ah	10	◙	36h	54	6	62h	98	b
0Bh	11	♂	37h	55	7	63h	99	c
0Ch	12	♀	38h	56	8	64h	100	d
0Dh	13	♪	39h	57	9	65h	101	e
0Eh	14	♫	3Ah	58	:	66h	102	f
0Fh	15	☼	3Bh	59	;	67h	103	g
10h	16	►	3Ch	60	<	68h	104	h
11h	17	◄	3Dh	61	=	69h	105	i
12h	18	↕	3Eh	62	>	6Ah	106	j
13h	19	‼	3Fh	63	?	6Bh	107	k
14h	20	¶	40h	64	@	6Ch	108	l
15h	21	§	41h	65	A	6Dh	109	m
16h	22	▬	42h	66	B	6Eh	110	n
17h	23	↨	43h	67	C	6Fh	111	o
18h	24	↑	44h	68	D	70h	112	p
19h	25	↓	45h	69	E	71h	113	q
1Ah	26	→	46h	70	F	72h	114	r
1Bh	27	←	47h	71	G	73h	115	s
1Ch	28	∟	48h	72	H	74h	116	t
1Dh	29	↔	49h	73	I	75h	117	u
1Eh	30	▲	4Ah	74	J	76h	118	v
1Fh	31	▼	4Bh	75	K	77h	119	w
20h	32		4Ch	76	L	78h	120	x
21h	33	!	4Dh	77	M	79h	121	y
22h	34	"	4Eh	78	N	7Ah	122	z
23h	35	#	4Fh	79	O	7Bh	123	{
24h	36	$	50h	80	P	7Ch	124		
25h	37	%	51h	81	Q	7Dh	125	}
26h	38	&	52h	82	R	7Eh	126	~
27h	39	'	53h	83	S	7Fh	127	∆
28h	40	(	54h	84	T	80h	128	ç
29h	41	)	55h	85	U	81h	129	ü
2Ah	42	*	56h	86	V	82h	130	é
2Bh	43	+	57h	87	W	83h	131	â

Table 3.3. *continued*

Hex	Dec	Screen	Hex	Dec	Screen	Hex	Dec	Screen
84h	132	ä	ADh	173	¡	D6h	214	╓
85h	133	à	AEh	174	«	D7h	215	╫
86h	134	å	AFh	175	»	D8h	216	╪
87h	135	ç	B0h	176	░	D9h	217	┘
88h	136	ê	B1h	177	▒	DAh	218	┌
89h	137	ë	B2h	178	▓	DBh	219	█
8Ah	138	è	B3h	179	│	DCh	220	▄
8Bh	139	ï	B4h	180	┤	DDh	221	▌
8Ch	140	î	B5h	181	╡	DEh	222	▐
8Dh	141	ì	B6h	182	╢	DFh	223	▀
8Eh	142	Ä	B7h	183	╖	E0h	224	α
8Fh	143	Å	B8h	184	╕	E1h	225	β
90h	144	É	B9h	185	╣	E2h	226	Γ
91h	145	æ	BAh	186	║	E3h	227	π
92h	146	Æ	BBh	187	╗	E4h	228	Σ
93h	147	ô	BCh	188	╝	E5h	229	σ
94h	148	ö	BDh	189	╜	E6h	230	µ
95h	149	ò	BEh	190	╛	E7h	231	τ
96h	150	û	BFh	191	┐	E8h	232	Φ
97h	151	ù	C0h	192	└	E9h	233	θ
98h	152	ÿ	C1h	193	┴	EAh	234	Ω
99h	153	Ö	C2h	194	┬	EBh	235	δ
9Ah	154	Ü	C3h	195	├	ECh	236	∞
9Bh	155	¢	C4h	196	─	EDh	237	φ
9Ch	156	£	C5h	197	┼	EEh	238	∈
9Dh	157	¥	C6h	198	╞	EFh	239	∩
9Eh	158	₧	C7h	199	╟	F0h	240	≡
9Fh	159	ƒ	C8h	200	╚	F1h	241	±
A0h	160	á	C9h	201	╔	F2h	242	≥
A1h	161	í	CAh	202	╩	F3h	243	≤
A2h	162	ó	CBh	203	╦	F4h	244	⌠
A3h	163	ú	CCh	204	╠	F5h	245	⌡
A4h	164	ñ	CDh	205	═	F6h	246	÷
A5h	165	Ñ	CEh	206	╬	F7h	247	≈
A6h	166	ª	CFh	207	╧	F8h	248	°
A7h	167	º	D0h	208	╨	F9h	249	∙
A8h	168	¿	D1h	209	╤	FAh	250	·
A9h	169	⌐	D2h	210	╥	FBh	251	√
AAh	170	¬	D3h	211	╙	FCh	252	ⁿ
ABh	171	½	D4h	212	╘	FDh	253	²
ACh	172	¼	D5h	213	╒	FEh	254	■
						FFh	255	

Fig. 3.1. ASCII values of characters used to draw boxes.

String Types

A string type consists of a series of ASCII characters. A string is declared with the following format:

```
var
    StrVar : string[ StringSize ];
```

The maximum StringSize is 255 characters. If the reserved word string appears *without* a size indicator, 255 is used as the default.

When stored in memory, each string occupies as many bytes as its maximum length plus one. The zero byte contains the working length of the string, and the following bytes contain the individual characters of the string. For example, if the string Name is defined as follows:

```
var
    Name : string[ 30 ];
```

then Name requires 31 bytes of storage. The zero byte keeps track of the length of the most recently assigned string. The individual characters in a string can be accessed with subscripts; for example, Name[5] references the fifth character. If the following assignment is made:

```
Name := 'SHEILA';
```

then byte zero contains 6 (the length of the string), byte one contains *S*, byte two contains *H*, and so on. *Name* will be treated exactly as if it physically contains only six characters. For example, the statement:

```
writeln( 'Start of string +', Name, ' + End of string' );
```

will produce

```
Start of string  +SHEILA + End of string
```

If Name is reassigned:

```
Name := 'ILANA';
```

then byte zero contains 5, byte one contains *I*, byte two contains *L*, and so on. *Name* will be treated exactly as if it physically contains only five characters.

The STRING1 program (Listing 3.1) demonstrates how the effective length of a string can vary.

Listing 3.1

```
program String1;
var
    TestString : string[ 15 ];
procedure ShowString;
var
    i : byte;
begin
    writeln( '   ***', TestString, '***' );
    for i := Ø to 15 do
        write( ord( TestString[i] ):4 );    {Allow 4 spaces}
    writeln;
    write( '     ' );    { 4 spaces, to bypass the size byte }
    for i := 1 to 15 do
        write( TestString[ i ]:4 );    {Allow 4 spaces}
    writeln;
    writeln;
end;
begin
    TestString := 'abcdefghijklmnopqrstuvwxyz';
    ShowString;
    TestString := 'ZYXWVUT';
    ShowString;
    TestString := '';
    ShowString;
    TestString := 'a1b2c3d4e5';
    ShowString;
end.
```

The *string* TestString is defined as being 15 characters long. Actually, the *variable* TestString is 16 bytes long; the first byte contains the length of the string. When you first initiate the string, its contents are undefined (in other words, the contents are meaningless), so begin by assigning it the alphabet.

```
TestString := 'abcdefghijklmnopqrstuvwxyz';
```

TestString was defined to be 15 characters long, so only the first 15 characters are captured. When the ShowString procedure is called, TestString turns out to contain the contents of figure 3.2

Fig. 3.2. The contents of TestString *with a 15-character assignment.*

abcdefghijklmno														
Size Byte	String Contents													
15	97	98	99	100	101	102	103	104	105	106	107	108	109	110	111
	a	b	c	d	e	f	g	h	i	j	k	l	m	n	o

Next, TestString is assigned ZYXWVUT, which is only seven characters long. After ShowString is called, TestString contains the contents of figure 3.3.

Fig. 3.3. The contents of TestString *with a seven-character assignment.*

*** ZYXWVUT ***															
Size Byte	String Contents														
7	90	89	88	87	86	85	84	104	105	106	107	108	109	110	111
	Z	Y	X	W	V	U	T	h	i	j	k	l	m	n	o

As indicated by the size byte, only the first seven characters are significant, even though the eighth through fifteenth characters (here, *h* through *o*) are still in the string.

Next, TestString is assigned the null string (that is, a string of length zero). ShowString reveals the contents of figure 3.4.

Fig. 3.4. The contents of TestString *with a null string.*

******															
Size Byte	String Contents														
0	90	89	88	87	86	85	84	104	105	106	107	108	109	110	111
	Z	Y	X	W	V	U	T	h	i	j	k	l	m	n	o

Here, the size byte of zero clearly indicates that the string is to be considered empty, even though no other changes have been made to the contents of the individual characters in TestString.

Finally, the string a1b2c3d4e5 is assigned to TestString. As the ShowString procedure demonstrates, the size byte now contains 10, and only the first 10 characters in TestString have been overwritten (see fig. 3.5)

Fig. 3.5. The contents of TestString *with the string a1b2c3d435.*

a1b2c3d4e5														
Size Byte	String Contents													
10	97	49	98	50	99	51	100	52	101	53	107	108	109	110	111
	a	1	b	2	c	3	d	4	e	5	k	l	m	n	o

Using the default type string without a size indicator allocates 256 bytes of storage. You may be tempted to use such a type so that you don't have to worry about whether a string will fit, but you can quickly see how a great deal of storage can be consumed unnecessarily. For example, in the following definition:

```
var
    StrArray : array [ 1..1ØØ ] of string;
```

the StrArray array consumes 100 × (255 + 1) or 25,600 bytes of storage.

At first, the dynamic nature of strings may seem wasteful, but fixed-length strings are relatively awkward to use. Collections of names, addresses, labels, and titles rarely have the same size. Conversely, "true" strings—strings that physically vary in length depending on the number of characters required—are extremely difficult to implement in a compiler.

Turbo Pascal provides a good compromise; it supports physically fixed-length strings, but the contents of the strings allow different sizes.

Enumerated Types

Suppose that your company is divided into four regions—North, South, East, and West—and that your program needs a variable, Region, to identify which geographic area it's currently processing. In many languages, you'd be forced to use an integer to identify the choices, as follows:

```
var
    Region : byte;
    :
begin
    :
    for Region := 1 to 4 do
        case Region of
            1 : writeln( 'Northern Region' );
            2 : writeln( 'Southern Region' );
            3 : writeln( 'Eastern Region' );
            4 : writeln( 'Western Region' );
        end;
```

Using numbers to represent nonnumeric data is awkward at best, however, and can lead to confusion when reading a longer (or more complicated) program. Turbo Pascal provides the *enumerated* type for just such a purpose. The enumerated type is simply a list of *identifiers* enclosed in parentheses. The intention is to enable you to manipulate variables with understandable English descriptions instead of being forced to use arbitrarily assigned integer values.

For example, with enumerated types the preceding program can be rewritten as shown in Listing 3.2.

Listing 3.2

```
program Enum;
type
    RegionType = ( North, South, East, West );
var
    Region : RegionType;
begin
    for Region := North to West do
        case Region of
            North : writeln( 'Northern Region' );
            South : writeln( 'Southern Region' );
            East  : writeln( 'Eastern Region' );
            West  : writeln( 'Western Region' );
        end;
end.
```

When the ENUM program executes, it produces the following output:

```
Northern Region
Southern Region
Eastern Region
Western Region
```

Notice that the for loop cycles through the entire sequence: North, South, East, and West. Internally, Turbo Pascal stores each value in the enumeration as an integer—beginning with zero and based on its sequence in the list—and automatically converts each identifier to its numeric equivalent. Enumeration provides a natural ordering that can be used by comparison operators. In the ENUM program, North is stored as zero, South is stored as one, East is stored as two, and West is stored as three. The Ord function must be used to access the numeric value of the identifier; Ord(North) is zero, Ord(South) is one, and so on.

Obviously, every identifier in the list must be individually enumerated. This might seem, at first, to be something of a pain, but depending on the application, enumerated types can add immeasurably to the legibility of your programs. For example, if your program deals with the colors of the rainbow, you can define the enumerated type Spectrum and variables that use it as follows:

```
type
    Spectrum = ( Red, Orange, Yellow, Green, Blue, Indigo, Violet );
var
    Color : Spectrum;
    Tint  : array [ Red..Violet ] of integer;
```

The variables Color and Tint can take on any of the identifiers defined by Spectrum, such as

```
Color := Green;
Tint[ Orange ] := 7*4;
```

The compiler doesn't allow enumerated types to be input or output; your program can only use them internally. The statement

```
writeln( 'The color is ', Color );
```

will produce a compilation error.

Subrange Types

Frequently, you will want to limit the use of a variable to a range of values. Turbo Pascal provides the *subrange* type for such a purpose.

The subrange must be a subset of a previously defined type, called the *host* type. The range itself must be continuous. You define it by declaring the upper and lower bounds with two periods (..) separating them.

The compiler ensures that any variable of a subrange type remains within the specified range. An error results if you attempt an assignment outside that range. Subranges are particularly useful for guaranteeing that subscripts of arrays remain within predetermined bounds. For example, given the following subrange definitions:

```
const
    LowTeen  = 13;
    HighTeen = 19;
```

```
var
    Grade      : Ø..1ØØ;
    Floor      : 1..5;
    UpperCase  : 'A'..'Z';
    WorkingAge : 18..65;
    TeenYear   : LowTeen..HighTeen;
```

the following assignments are legal:

```
Grade := 96;
Floor := 3;
UpperCase := 'M';
WorkingAge := 43;
TeenYear := 17;
```

but each of the following assignments generates a range error:

```
Grade := 1Ø4;
Floor := 7;
UpperCase := 'm',
WorkingAge := 12;
TeenYear := 6;
```

For obvious reasons, a subrange of real numbers isn't allowed, because there are an infinite number of floating point numbers between any two reals.

Set Types

A *set* is a finite collection of elements that share the same previously defined type, called the *base* type. A set variable is declared as:

```
var
    Bunch : set of BaseType;
```

The maximum number of elements in a set is 256. Further, the upper and lower bounds of the base type must have ordinal values that are themselves within the range 0 through 255. Consequently, the base type of a set can't be a ShortInt, Integer, LongInt, or Word. This isn't a serious restriction. For example, sets can be defined as follows:

```
type
    Days      = ( Sun, Mon, Tue, Wed, Thu, Fri, Sat );
    LowerCase = 'a'..'z';
    Healthy   = ( Tofu, Sprouts, WheatGerm, PureWater );
    Parts     = ( Nuts, Bolts, Metal, Plastic, Cardboard );
var
    OneDay    : Days;
    WorkDays  : set of Days;
    Vowels    : set of LowerCase;
    Spelling  : set of char;
    InStock   : set of Parts;
    Menu      : set of Healthy;
```

When you assign a value to an enumerated type, such as OneDay, you do it directly, as follows:

```
OneDay := Wed;
```

But sets can contain several values. When you assign values to a set type, such as WorkDays, you place the identifiers within brackets, as follows:

```
WorkDays := [ Mon, Fri ];
```

Set operations are discussed in detail in Chapter 4.

Pointers

Pointer variables contain the memory *address* of a data structure rather than the data structure itself. A pointer type is stored as a double word, with the offset part in the low word and the segment part in the high word.

A pointer variable can be defined in either of the following ways:

```
var
    Var1 : ^BaseType;
    Var2 : pointer;
```

Var1 is a pointer to a variable of type BaseType. BaseType may be either a standard type—like Byte or String—or it may be a user-defined type that appeared in a previous type declaration statement. Var1 can only be used to point to BaseType variables. Var2 is a general pointer and can be used to point to a variable of any type.

Pointers are discussed in detail in Chapter 6.

Arrays

An *array* is a fixed number of variables that all have the same type. Each element of the array can be accessed by specifying its *index*.

An array type is declared with an array declaration, as follows:

```
var
    ArrayName : array [ IndexType ] of ArrayType;
```

IndexType is a subrange that specifies the array's dimensions. ArrayType may be any standard or user-defined data type. ArrayType may even be another array, in which case the declaration would appear as follows:

```
var
    Array1 : array [ 1..5 ] of array [ 1..10 ] of integer;
```

There's no restriction to the number of dimensions of an array. Multidimensional arrays can also be defined in the following manner:

```
var
    Array2 = array [ 1..5, 1..10 ] of integer;
```

Arrays are usually associated with mathematical and list processing, but any ordinal subrange is allowed with the exception of LongInt and subranges of LongInt.

```
type
    Months = ( Jan, Feb, Nov, Dec );
    Days   = ( Sun, Mon, Fri, Sat );
var
    Calendar : array [ Jan..Dec, Sun..Sat ] of byte;
```

Records

A *record* is a data type that consists of any combination of *fields*, each of which is a variable of any data type. In other words, the record type enables you to reference any predetermined number of variables through a single identifier. Records are usually used with files and dynamic data structures.

An example of a record definition is as follows:

```
Passenger1 = record
            Name         : string;
            FlightNumber : word;
            Date         : array [ 1..3 ] of byte;
        end;
```

Each record can be composed of even smaller records, such as:

```
Passenger2 = record
            Name         : record
                            First,
                            Last    : string;
                        end;
            FlightNumber : word;
            Date         : record
                            Month,
                            Day,
                            Year    : byte;
                        end;
        end;
```

Each field can be individually accessed in the form

```
RecordIdentifier.FieldName
```

For example, if a variable Ticket is defined as type Passenger1, then Ticket.Name references the passenger's name. If, instead, Ticket is defined as type Passenger2, then Ticket.Name still references the entire Name record, but Ticket.Name.First and Ticket.Name.Last are used to subdivide it. In both cases, Ticket references the entire record.

Occasionally, when you're considering what should be included in a record, you realize that some fields are never used at the same time, such as

MaidenName and WifesName. At other times, you realize that entire sets of fields may be mutually exclusive. Rather than force you to list every field in every record, which rapidly consumes large blocks of memory that will never be accessed, Turbo Pascal enables you to use a variant record.

A *variant record* is, simply, a single record identifier that references physically different collections of fields. Some fields may be common to all records; the fields that differ form the *variant* part of the record.

A variant record is defined by first listing all common fields, then by using a case statement to identify the individual groups or variants. Each variant may be a different length but must be referenced with an ordinal constant. For example:

```
type
   Registers = record
                  case integer of
                    1 : ( AX, BX, CX, DX : word );
                    2 : ( AL, AH, BL, BH, CL, CH, DL, DH : byte );
                  end;
var
   Settings : Registers;
```

The Registers record consists of either a record of four words or a record of eight bytes. If you make the following assignment:

<pre>
                              { ---Hi----   ---Low---   }
Settings.CX := 256;   { 0000 0001   0000 0000 in binary }
</pre>

then the following equalities are true:

Settings.CL = 0   and   Settings.CH = 1

because the CL and CH variables reside in the *same physical memory* as the CX variable. Therefore, a variant record helps you to access the same physical memory in several ways.

Frequently, you will need to keep track of which variant is in use. This can be accomplished by introducing an extra field, called a *tag field*, to identify the active variant.

```
type
   FlightType = ( Domestic, Overseas );
   PassRec    = record
                  Name         : string;
                  FlightNumber : word;
                  Date         : array [ 1..3 ] of byte;
                  case Destination : FlightType of
                     Domestic  : ( DestCity,
                                   DestState   : string[ 30 ] );
                     Overseas  : ( OverseasTax : real;
                                   DestCountry : string[ 20 ] );
                  end;
var
   Traveler : PassRec;
```

In the PassRec record, Destination is the tag field. Destination is actually stored as a separate field within the PassRec record. Its value can either be Domestic or Overseas, depending on the assignment you make, as follows:

```
Traveler.Destination := Domestic;
```

The presence of a tag field is a convenience for the programmer; no restrictions are placed on accessing variant fields. The tag field is used primarily when you retrieve an unknown record from an array or from a file; the tag field tells you which variant is being used and enables you to avoid inappropriate access of any data, which could cause a run-time error. For example, in the PassRec record, DestCity (a string) and OverseasTax (a real) reference some of the same memory locations; the Destination field can be tested to determine how the current record is being used.

File Types

A *file* is a *sequence* of components of the same type. A component may be a standard type, such as Byte or Word, or it may be a user-defined type, such as a record. There may be any number of components, but they may only be accessed one at a time.

A file can be declared in one of three ways:

```
var
    First   : File of PassRec;
    Second  : Text;
    Third   : File;
```

The First file consists of records of the type PassRec. The Second file contains text characters organized into lines of (possibly) varying lengths. Notice that the format File of *FileType* is ideal for data files, and the Text file type, as the name implies, is ideal for storing text. Both of these formats are called *typed* files. The Third file is *untyped*. An untyped file may contain data of many different types; when you use an untyped file, you must ensure that the individual data elements are handled correctly.

Files are discussed in greater detail in Chapter 13.

Procedure Types

With Turbo Pascal you assign a procedure or function to a variable declared as a procedure type. The procedure types are discussed in greater detail in Chapter 5.

Summary

In this chapter, you have learned that a data type specifies a range of values and the set of operations that can be performed on those values.

You have learned about the standard Turbo Pascal data types. The integer types integer, shortint, longint, byte, and word handle whole numbers. Five real data types are available for handling decimal numbers: real, single, double, extended, and comp. Boolean data types can either be true or false. The char data type defines single ASCII characters, while a string is a series of ASCII characters. A pointer data type specifies the memory address of a data structure rather than the data structure itself.

You have learned how to define your own, customized data types to solve a variety of specialized programming problems. An enumerated data type consists of a user-defined list of identifiers. A subrange is a continuous subset of a previously defined type. A set is a finite collection of elements that share the same previously defined type. An array is a fixed number of variables that all have the same type. A record allows you to reference any predetermined number of fields through a single identifier. A file is a sequence of components—all of the same type—that may only be accessed one at a time. A procedure data type is an advanced feature of Turbo Pascal that allows your program to handle a procedure or function as an ordinary data object.

CHAPTER 4

Expressions, Operands, and Operators

Most people associate computers with "number crunching"—processing extremely complex (or exceedingly tedious) mathematical problems accurately and rapidly.

It's easy to understand how this impression arises. Looking back over the history of computing, it was the detail-oriented and number-intensive applications, like payroll processing, which were first able to economically justify commercial computer installations. Even today, most cost justifications begin by identifying which number-intensive applications can be performed better by the computer than by human hands. There are, after all, few ways to use a computer that don't demand some degree of numerical power.

Fortunately, almost every problem with a numeric origin can be reduced to one or more equations, which in turn can be expressed as the evaluation of a formula. In Turbo Pascal, expressions are the principal means of both defining and solving problems; everything from simple arithmetic through condition testing to trigonometry is phrased as a expression.

This chapter discusses how expressions are used in Turbo Pascal programs.

Overview of Operators and Operands

To put it simply, an expression consists of a operation on one or more operands. To calculate the area of a rectangle, you use the expression (height * width), where height and width are operands, and the multiplication symbol (*) is an operator.

Analyzing Operands

Each operator has two basic properties: operand count and precedence.

Operand count refers to the number of operands used by the operator. In Turbo Pascal, an operator is either *unary*, meaning that it has only one operand, or *binary*, meaning that two operands are required. The multiplication operator * is binary; it's used to obtain the product of two numbers. The minus sign can be used as either a unary operator (as, for example, in -4) or as a binary operator (as in $5 - 2$) depending upon context.

Precedence refers to the priority Turbo Pascal assigns to the operation. For example, multiplication is generally regarded as having a higher priority than addition. When you see the equation

X = 2 + 4 * 3

your math classes taught you to evaluate the multiplication operator first, obtaining $2 + (4 * 3) = 14$ rather than $(2 + 4) * 3 = 18$.

Parentheses can be used to force the processing sequence. If you had written the previous formula as

X = (2 + 4) * 3

you would have forced the addition to occur first and obtained 18 as the value for X. Parentheses are always evaluated outward from the innermost pair. Although precedence enables you to avoid excessive parentheses, you should still insert parentheses as often as necessary to clarify processing order.

The order of operator precedence is given in table 4.1. Unless otherwise grouped by parentheses, all operators on the same line have equal precedence and are evaluated in the order they are written. When an operand is between two operators, it is assumed to belong to the operator with the higher precedence.

Table 4.1. *Operator Precedence*

Priority	Operators
1 (high)	@ NOT unary + −
2	* / DIV MOD AND SHL SHR
3	binary + − OR XOR
4 (low)	= <> < > <= >= IN

The fact that there are only four operator precedence levels considerably increases the readability of a Pascal program. In contrast, the C language has more than 15!

Arithmetic Operators

Of all the operators supported by Turbo Pascal, the addition, subtraction, multiplication, and division operators are the easiest to understand, performing just as their names imply (see table 4.2). There are, however, different rules to observe depending on whether the operators are applied to integer or real values.

Table 4.2. *Arithmetic Operators*

Operator	Syntax	Meaning
+	+expression	Positive (unary)
+	expression1 + expression2	Addition (binary)
−	-expression	Negative (unary)
−	expression1 - expression2	Subtraction (binary)
*	expression1 * expression2	Multiplication
/	expression1 / expression2	Real division
DIV	expression1 DIV expression2	Integer division
MOD	expression1 MOD expression2	Remainder (modulus)

If an expression is being assigned to an integer variable, every individual term must also be an integer type. Further, if division is being performed, the integer division operator, DIV, must be used rather than the slash (/) operator, which denotes real division. Real terms can (and must) be converted to integers with the Round and Trunc functions.

Conversely, a real value is returned if *any* individual term is real. Further, a real value is returned whenever the slash real division operator is used, even if the dividend and divisor are both integers.

The DIV integer division operator cannot be used with real operands. It returns the integer portion of the quotient. The MOD operator (referring to *modular arithmetic*) returns the remainder. For example, the number 6 can be divided into 45 seven times, with a remainder of three; hence:

45 DIV 6 = 7   and   45 MOD 6 = 3

The MATH1 program (listing 4.1) is a simple four-function calculator that creates an output similar to an adding machine tape.

Listing 4.1

```
program Math1;
uses Crt;
var
   LastOperator,
   LastEntry,
   Entry          : char;
   Operand1,
   Operand2       : LongInt;
begin
   Operand1 := Ø;
   Operand2 := Ø;
   Entry := ' +';
   LastOperator := ' +';
   repeat
      LastEntry := Entry;
      Entry := ReadKey;
      if (Entry = ' +') and (Entry = LastEntry) then
         Operand1 := Ø;    { Two ' +' entries cause a zero }
      case Entry of
         'Ø'..'9' : begin
                       write( Entry );
                       Operand2 := Operand2*1Ø + (ord( Entry ) - 48);
                    end;
         ' +',
         '-',
         '*',
         '/' : begin
                  case LastOperator of
                     ' +' : Operand1 := Operand1 + Operand2;
                     '-' : Operand1 := Operand1 - Operand2;
                     '*' : Operand1 := Operand1 * Operand2;
                     '/' : Operand1 := Operand1 div Operand2;
                  end;
                  Operand2 := Ø;
                  writeln;
                  writeln( Operand1:1Ø );
                  writeln( Entry );
                  LastOperator := Entry;
               end;
      end;
   until not (Entry in [ 'Ø'..'9', ' +', '-', '*', '/' ]);
end.
```

Each integer is entered, followed by one of the keys +, –, *, or /. By storing and testing the LastEntry variable, two successive + keys will clear the total. The LastOperator variable is stored because the sequence

12345 + 23 –

adds and displays the total of 12345 and 23 only after the – key is pressed. The entry of an operator triggers the execution of the previous operator. The program terminates with the entry of any key other than a digit or an operator. (If you use the number keypad, be sure to set the NumLock key!)

Shift Operators

Figure 4.1 shows how the SHL (shift bits left) and SHR (shift bits right) operators are used to slide the bits in an integer left and right, respectively. Bits shifted off either end of the expression are lost. Bits on the right for SHL and on the left for SHR are zero-filled as their original contents are moved over.

Fig. 4.1. *The SHL and SHR operators.*

Shifting by one bit to the left is equivalent to multiplying the expression by two. Shifting by one bit to the right is equivalent to dividing the expression by two. You can take advantage of this to do fast multiplication and division by the powers of two. Shifting left twice multiplies by four, shifting left three times multiplies by eight, and so on.

When Turbo Pascal compiles a SHR or SHL operator, it produces a machine code shift instruction that is considerably faster than a functionally equivalent multiply or divide instruction. Multiplying and dividing are among the slowest instructions on the 8086-family processors, so using shifts can often speed operations by a factor of 10 or more.

The program SHIFT2 in listing 4.2 demonstrates the result of using the SHR and SHL operators. Each time the ShowShifts procedure is called it displays the results of different shift instructions. The RevealBits procedures illustrate the effect of the instructions on the bits themselves.

Listing 4.2

```
program Shift2;
var
   i : ShortInt;
procedure RevealBits( Subject : integer );
var
   j : byte;
   Compare : word;
begin
   Compare := 32768;   { In binary:  1000 0000 0000 0000 }
   write( '     ' );   { 5 spaces }
   for j := 15 downto 0 do begin
      if Compare and Subject  <> 0 then write( '1' )
                                   else write( '0' );
      Compare := Compare div 2;
   end;
end;
procedure ShowShifts( Orig : ShortInt );
begin
   writeln( 'Shift Left   Right           Left            Right' );
   writeln( '----- ----   -----           ----            -----' );
   for i := 0 to 8 do begin
      write( i:3, (Orig shl i):8, (Orig shr i):8 );
      RevealBits( Orig shl i );
      RevealBits( Orig shr i );
      writeln;
   end;
   writeln;
end;
begin
   ShowShifts(  +53 );
   ShowShifts(  -53 );
end.
```

The numbers +53 and –53 were chosen arbitrarily. When SHIFT2 executes, it produces the results shown in figure 4.2.

Fig. 4.2. The output produced by the SHIFT2 program.

Shift	Left	Right	Left	Right
0	53	53	0000000000110101	0000000000110101
1	106	26	0000000001101010	0000000000011010
2	212	13	0000000011010100	0000000000001101
3	424	6	0000000110101000	0000000000000110
4	848	3	0000001101010000	0000000000000011
5	1696	1	0000011010100000	0000000000000001
6	3392	0	0000110101000000	0000000000000000
7	6784	0	0001101010000000	0000000000000000
8	13568	0	0011010100000000	0000000000000000

Shift	Left	Right	Left	Right
0	-53	-53	1111111111001011	1111111111001011
1	-106	32741	1111111110010110	0111111111100101
2	-212	16370	1111111100101100	0011111111110010
3	-424	8185	1111111001011000	0001111111111001
4	-848	4092	1111110010110000	0000111111111100
5	-1696	2046	1111100101100000	0000011111111110
6	-3392	1023	1111001011000000	0000001111111111
7	-6784	511	1110010110000000	0000000111111111
8	-13568	255	1100101100000000	0000000011111111

Note that SHR can divide only positive numbers. Shifting –53 by one bit to the right produced +32741, not –26 as you might expect.

The SHL and SHR operators return zero if the expression is shifted right or left by a number greater than or equal to the number of bits in the integer; for example, if X is a word-type variable, then

    X shl 16

will always return zero, regardless of the current value of X.

Boolean Operators

The Boolean operators AND, NOT, OR, and XOR do double duty. They serve either as *logical* or *bitwise* operators. Table 4.3 summarizes what they do.

Table 4.3. *Boolean Operators*

Operator	Syntax	Meaning
NOT	NOT expression	Complement
AND	expression1 AND expression2	AND
OR	expression1 OR expression2	Inclusive OR
XOR	expression1 XOR expression2	Exclusive OR

The bitwise operators perform Boolean operations on each bit of an expression. The logical operators perform Boolean operations on the operands, each of which is itself considered either Boolean True or False. Turbo Pascal can tell the difference between the operator categories from context.

The logical and bitwise operators are shown in table 4.4, together with their meanings.

Table 4.4. *Logical and Bitwise Operators*

Values Returned by Bitwise Operations for Each Bit Pair						Values Returned by Logical Operations Where X and Y are Operands					
X	Y	NOT X	X AND Y	X OR Y	XOR Y	X	Y	NOT X	X AND Y	X OR Y	XOR Y
1	1	0	1	1	0	T	T	F	T	T	F
1	0	0	0	1	1	T	F	F	F	T	T
0	1	1	0	1	1	F	T	T	F	T	T
0	0	1	0	0	0	F	F	T	F	F	F

Logical Operators

Logical operators perform Boolean manipulations that use entire operands. AND compares two operands and returns True only if both operands are True. OR compares two operands and returns True if either operand is True. XOR compares two operands and returns True only if the operands are different. NOT returns the opposite state of an operand.

By default, Turbo Pascal evaluates Boolean expressions only as far as necessary to determine the result of the entire expression. This feature, called *short-circuit evaluation*, results in extremely efficient program execution. For example, in the expression

```
if (A=4) OR (B>16) OR ((B*B-4*A*C)>0) then  <statement>
```

if A is equal to 4, Turbo executes <statement> without bothering to test the second or third conditions. Similarly, if A doesn't equal 4, but B is greater than 16, Turbo executes <statement> without testing the third condition.

A similar process results when conditions are connected by AND operators. In the expression

```
if (A=4) AND (B>16) AND ((B*B-4*A*C)>Ø) then  <statement>
```

if A doesn't equal 4, then Turbo won't execute <statement>; the second and third conditions are never checked.

You can disable short-circuit evaluation by turning off the B compiler directive with {$B-}, which then forces every condition to be evaluated. This is only desirable when the conditions include function calls that also contain side-effects. This topic is discussed in detail in the "Compiler Directives" reference section.

Bitwise Operators

The bitwise operators do Boolean manipulations on individual bits. Each bit of the result is determined by individually testing the corresponding bits in the operands. AND compares two bits and sets the result if both bits are set. OR compares two bits and sets the result if either bit is set. XOR compares two bits and sets the result if the bits are different. NOT reverses a single bit.

The AND instruction can clear the value of specific bits regardless of their current settings. To do this, AND the original value with a *mask* containing 0 for any bit positions you want to clear and 1 for any bit positions you want to remain unchanged. For example, to clear bits 4 through 6 of the byte variable X, you would use the following instruction:

```
X := X AND $8F;   { 1ØØØ 1111 to clear bits 4, 5, and 6 }
```

The OR instruction can set the value of specific bits regardless of their current settings. To do this, OR the original value with a mask containing 1 for any bit positions you want to set and 0 for any bit positions you want to remain unchanged. If you want to set bits 4 through 6 of the byte variable X, no matter what those bits contained previously, you could use the instruction:

```
X := X OR $7Ø;   { Ø111 ØØØØ to set bits 4, 5, and 6 }
```

The XOR instruction can be used to toggle the value of specific bits (reverse them from their current settings) regardless of their current settings. To do this, XOR the original value with a mask containing 1 for any bit positions you want to toggle and 0 for any bit positions you want to remain unchanged. To change the setting of bit 4 in the byte variable X, the instruction would be:

```
X := X XOR $1Ø;   { ØØØ1 ØØØØ to toggle bit 4 }
```

The unary NOT instruction is used to completely change the state of every bit in an integer. By itself, NOT isn't a particularly useful arithmetic operator; you don't often need to know, for example, that for the byte values 70 and 213, NOT 70 equals 185, and NOT 213 equals 42. NOT is most commonly used in combination with the AND and OR operators. To set every bit *except* bits 4 through 6 of the byte variable X (that is, to set bits 0 through 3 and bit 7), no matter what those bits contained previously, you could use the instruction:

```
X := X OR NOT $70;    { 0111 0000 becomes 1000 1111 }
```

Relational Operators

The relational operators compare two expressions and return True if the condition specified by the operator is satisfied, or False if it is not. Relational operators are typically used with conditional directives. The operators and their return values are listed in table 4.5.

Table 4.5. *Relational Operators*

Operator	Syntax	Returns True if:
=	expression1 = expression2	Expressions are equal
<>	expression1 <> expression2	Expressions are not equal
<	expression1 < expression2	expression1 is less than expression2
<=	expression1 <= expression2	expression1 is less than or equal to expression2
>	expression1 > expression2	expression1 is greater than expression2
>=	expression1 >= expression2	expression1 is greater than or equal to expression2

Relational tests can be used wherever Boolean expressions are allowed. This includes if..then, repeat..until, while...do, and case statements, as the BOOL1 program (listing 4.3) shows.

Listing 4.3

```
program Bool1;
var
   i, j : integer;
begin
   writeln( 'Enter two integers: ' );
   write( 'First number:   ' );
   readln( i );
   write( 'Second number: ' );
   readln( j );
   case (i <j) of
      True  : writeln( i, ' is less than ', j );
      False : writeln( i, ' is not less than ', j );
   end;
end.
```

A typical session with BOOL1 is as follows:

```
Enter two integers:
First number:   2
Second number: 6
2 is less than 6
Enter two integers:
First number:   -5
Second number: -9
-5 is not less than -9
```

Each Boolean clause in a compound expression must be enclosed in parentheses, as in:

```
if (DinerCount >= RoomMax) OR (Expense > Profit) then
```

The NOT operator negates (that is, reverses) the state of a Boolean value. For example, if the expression (X >= 3) is False, then (NOT (X >= 3)) is True. Notice, though, that for each relational operator, you can use its functional opposite; for example, > for NOT =, < for NOT >=, and > for NOT =.

Notice in table 4.1 that NOT has a higher precedence than any relational operator. In the program NEG1 (listing 4.4), the first writeln procedure produces True, but the second writeln procedure produces False.

Listing 4.4

```
program Neg1;
var
   i, j : byte;
begin
   i := 100;
   j := 1;
   writeln( NOT i > j );
   writeln( NOT (i > j) );
end.
```

In the first writeln statement, the instruction NOT i is treated as NOT 100 and results in 155 (the number 100 in binary is 01100100; its negation is 10011011, or 155), and when 155 is found to be greater than 1, the result is True. In the second writeln statement, 100 is found to be greater than 1, so its negation returns False. You can avoid such problems through the liberal use of parentheses.

Two strings are compared lexicographically. This is a fancy way of saying that the same rules that sequence dictionary entries are used when strings are being compared. Strings are sorted according to the ASCII value of each character. Therefore, "CATS"< "DOG" is True, even though "CATS" contains more characters. The defined size of a string is ignored; only the current contents matter.

For purposes of comparison, an operand of type char is treated as a string of length one.

Unfortunately, Boolean values can be compared other than for equality and inequality. In the program BOOL2 in listing 4.5, two Boolean variables are compared to test a "greater than" condition. True is stored as +1 and False is stored as 0, so True *is greater than* False and the message

```
VarI is greater than VarJ
```

is displayed. You should avoid such constructions whenever possible.

Listing 4.5

```
program Bool2;
var
   VarI, VarJ : Boolean;
begin
   VarI := True;
   VarJ := False;
   if VarI > VarJ then
      writeln( 'VarI is greater than VarJ' )
   else
      writeln( 'VarI is not greater than VarJ' );
end.
```

Set Operators

Sets are intended to bridge the gap between the esoteric, artificial world of the computer program and the hard, cold, concrete world of everyday existence. Because sets define collections of objects that represent the real world, it seems only fitting that the common logic of everyday life can be applied to their manipulation.

The relational set operators test either for equality or *inclusion*. The only consideration is the presence or absence of elements; neither the ordering of elements in a set operand nor the relative magnitude of individual elements has any bearing on the result of the test. Table 4.6 summarizes these operators.

Table 4.6. *Set Operators*

Operator	Syntax	Returns True if:
=	Set1 = Set2	Set1 and Set2 are identical. Every element in Set1 is contained in Set2, and every element in Set2 is contained in Set1.
<>	Set1 <> Set2	One of the sets contains at least one element that isn't in the other set.
<=	Set1 <= Set2	Every element in Set1 is also in Set2.
<	Set1 < Set2	Every element in Set1 is also in Set2. In addition, Set2 contains at least one other element not found in Set1.
>=	Set1 >= Set2	Every element in Set2 is also in Set1.
>	Set1 > Set2	Every element in Set2 is also in Set1. In addition, Set1 contains at least one other element not found in Set2.
IN	elem IN Set1	The element elem is found in Set1.

Just as it does with arithmetic relation operators, the NOT operator negates (reverses) the state of a Boolean value. Therefore, if Set1 = Set2 is True, then NOT (Set1 = Set2) is False.

Three main operations can be performed on the elements of sets: union, difference, and intersection. The results of these operations conform to the ordinary rules of logic.

The union operator + produces a set that contains one of every element found in either operand. For example, the union

    [1, 2, 3, 4, 5] + [3, 4, 5, 6, 7]

produces the set

    [1, 2, 3, 4, 5, 6, 7]

which can also be written

    [1..7]

The difference operator – (sometimes called the *complement* operator) produces a set that contains all elements of the first set that are not found in the second set. For example, the difference

[1, 2, 3, 4, 5] - [3, 4, 5, 6, 7]

produces the set

[1, 2]

The intersection operator * returns a set containing elements common to both set operands. For example, the intersection

[1, 2, 3, 4, 5] * [3, 4, 5, 6, 7]

produces the set

[3, 4, 5]

The union, difference, and intersection operators have their greatest value in defining new sets rather than in direct problem solving situations. For example, the program SET2 in listing 4.6 uses these operators to define sets.

Listing 4.6

```
program set2;
type
    Rainbow       = ( Red, Yellow, Orange, Blue, Green, Violet );
    DaysOfTheWeek = ( Sunday, Monday, Tuesday, Wednesday,
                      Thursday, Friday, Saturday );
    Months        = ( Jan, Feb, Mar, Apr, May, Jun,
                      Jul, Aug, Sep, Oct, Nov, Dec );
var
    Primaries, Composites, Crayons : set of Rainbow;
    FullWeek, WeekDays, WeekEnd     : set of DaysOfTheWeek;
    NoSchool, WarmEnough, Vacation : set of Months;
begin
    Primaries   := [ Red, Blue, Green ];
    Composites  := [ Orange, Green, Violet ];
    Crayons     := Primaries + Composites;   { All colors in Rainbow }
    FullWeek    := [ Sunday..Saturday ];
    WeekEnd     := [ Saturday, Sunday ];
    WeekDays    := FullWeek - WeekEnd;        { Contains Monday..Friday }
    NoSchool    := [ May..Sep ];
    WarmEnough  := [ Apr..Aug ];
    Vacation    := NoSchool * WarmEnough;   { Contains May..Aug }
    { Remainder of code follows }
end.
```

The Address Operator

The address operator @ returns the address of any variable, procedure, or function. It produces the same result as the Addr function, although much more efficiently. The @ operator returns a value that is compatible with all pointer types.

Listing 4.7

```
program PtrFunct;
var
    P1 : byte;          { Defines a normal byte variable }
    P2 : ^byte;         { Defines a pointer to a byte }
begin
    P1 := 14;           { Assigns "14" to the byte variable }
    P2 := @P1;          { Finds the address of P1 }
    writeln( P2^ );     { Outputs "14".  Notice the pointer symbol! }
end.
```

The PTRFUNCT program defines the pointer variable P2, then uses the @ operator to make it functionally equivalent to the byte variable P1.

The Concatenation Operator

Most string and character operations are handled by functions or procedures. The one exception is the + operator, which is equivalent to the Concat function.

Using + on operands of string or char types returns a single string that is the concatenation of the two operands. The resulting string cannot exceed 255 characters; any excess characters are truncated on the right.

The new string consists of only the active portions of the operands. For example, in the code

```
var
    S1, S2, S3 : string[ 25 ];
begin
    S1 := 'abc';
    S2 := '12345678';
    S3 := S1 + S2;
```

the string S3 has become 'abc12345678' even though all three strings were defined to be 25 characters long.

Summary

In this chapter, you have learned how to use expressions in Turbo Pascal.

You have learned the behavior of individual Turbo Pascal operators and that each operator is processed in order of precedence. The results of arithmetic operators depend on whether the operands are integer or real values. Shift operators "slide" the bits in an operand left or right. Logical operators perform Boolean operations on entire operands; bitwise operators perform Boolean operations on the individual bits of an operand. Relational operators compare the magnitude of operands. Set operators test for equality or inclusion. The address operator returns the memory location of a data object. The concatenation operator combines two strings.

Procedures and Functions

There is no one *right* way for a program to solve a given problem. In fact, the more complicated the programming task, the harder it is to ensure that *any* approach is correct. A variety of methods can help you simplify program design, however. Almost all involve breaking a problem down into smaller, more manageable tasks called subroutines. In Turbo Pascal, subroutines consist of procedures and functions.

Because of its extensive use of procedures and functions (actually, because of its almost total *reliance* on them), Turbo Pascal is considered a *structured* language. A *structured program* consists of subroutines that, when combined, create a working program. Most programs of any interest are broken up into subroutines.

This chapter discusses how you can use procedures and functions to write structured programs and offers guidance on how you can exploit the more advanced features of procedures and functions.

The Need for Structure

Many famous stories about software errors have been circulated. The original avionics software for the F-16 jet fighter contained a small bug that caused the plane to flip upside down whenever it crossed the equator. One of the early NASA space probes to Venus went off-course and was lost because of a software glitch. The Bank of New York lost millions of dollars in interest payments because a two-day computer "crash" prevented the bank from determining how much money it needed to repay the Federal Reserve Bank. In the PC world, almost every major software house has experienced some sort of delay in releasing a new product; many others have simply gone out of business because design errors made their products unmarketable.

These systems are a bit more complicated than the ones you are likely to develop with Turbo Pascal. Nevertheless, the same quality guidelines that now apply to the design of cruise missile guidance software can also be applied to the smallest programming chore.

Exhaustive Testing

Most introductory programming classes explain that one way to test your program is to trace its flow, keeping track of the contents of its variables as you go. Unfortunately, that technique has its limitations. For example, suppose that your program contains a loop with five sections that transfer control according to the diagram in figure 5.1.

Fig. 5.1. A flowchart of a small program with only five sections.

If every path is equally likely to be taken, there are four possible routes through the program. After 10 loops, there are 4^{10} or 1,048,576 possible routes. Even if you only needed 1 second for each pass, your test would still take over 12 days. (After 20 passes, over 1 *trillion* combinations are possible. Your test would take about 35,000 years.)

Obviously, exhaustive testing isn't the answer. But how else can you be sure that your program will work?

The solution is to test each of the components individually. If each component is itself formed from several other components, then each of those must be tested as well. In other words, if a problem is too difficult or too complex, then break it down into something more manageable.

In programming, this particular technique is commonly called *divide and conquer*. If the term sounds militaristic, it's because it was first used by Julius Caesar. It's been a successful tool ever since. You divide a difficult problem into a set of smaller, independent problems that are easier to understand and solve.

In Turbo Pascal, each "subproblem" is solved with a procedure or function.

The Use of Procedures and Functions

There are several advantages to using subroutines and structured design, including:

❏ Programs are more readable because subroutines identify the single purpose behind several lines of code.

❏ Programs are more efficient because every common action is defined (and stored) only once.

❏ Programs are more reliable because the underlying problem has been simplified as a result of being broken down into subroutines.

❏ Programs are easier to maintain because changing a single subroutine doesn't require modification of the entire program.

❏ Programs can be developed in less time because you don't need to develop new techniques for each new application.

In addition, structured programming imposes a discipline on the overall programming effort. That's not something you can quantify, but it's a very real advantage because it results in a final product of generally higher quality.

Procedure and Function Structure

Procedures and functions have the same basic structure as the program itself—a header followed by a block. They can be thought of as sub*programs* that will always be referenced—and executed—as a single unit.

A *procedure* is a subroutine that—like a statement—results in a series of actions directed toward a single purpose. A function is a subroutine specifically designed to return a value; accordingly, functions are only called within expressions. Certain procedures and functions are of such widespread importance, they're already defined by the compiler. These subroutines—such as write, writeln, and readln—are called *standard*. The complete list of over 200 standard procedures and functions can be found in the *Reference Guide*.

When the standard subroutines aren't adequate for the task at hand, the programmer may define a new subroutine through a procedure declaration or a function declaration. Once defined, the new subroutine can then be invoked by simply stating its name—the same way that the standard routines are invoked.

Procedures

A *procedure* consists of a collection of instructions that you want to execute as a single unit. A *parameter* is information (usually a variable) that's transferred between a procedure and a calling program. A procedure is executed simply by listing its name, together with any required parameters.

Components of a Procedure

Like a program, a procedure consists of three components:

❏ The *header*, consisting of the reserved word procedure, followed by the procedure name and any required parameters.

❏ The *data* that are to be manipulated by the instructions in the procedure, as defined in label, constant, type, and variable declarations. Data are located immediately after the header but before the first procedure code statement.

❏ Program *code* statements describing the actions to be performed. Any procedures or functions defined by the procedure are placed at the start of the code area. Code statements follow, enclosed by the reserved words begin and end.

Every procedure is terminated with a semicolon.

The general format of a Pascal procedure is as follows:

```
procedure name( optional parameters );
   { Data declarations }
begin
   { Code statements }
end;
```

The header is always required, but both data and code are optional. For example, the following:

```
procedure Trivial;
begin
end;
```

defines a procedure that does absolutely nothing. If the Trivial procedure is called later in a program, its only effect would be to slow down the execution of the program.

The rule in Pascal that says that a variable must be declared before it can be used applies to procedures and functions as well. However, once defined, the procedure or function name may be used just like other predefined procedure and function names. Through the act of creating your own subroutine, you temporarily extend the language.

A Procedure Example

The following procedure, SayHello, clears the screen and then displays the Hello message.

```
procedure SayHello( Col, Row : byte );
begin;
   ClrScr;              { Clears the screen and positions the }
                        { cursor in the upper left-hand corner }
   GotoXY( Col, Row );  { Moves the cursor to column Col of row Row }
   Write( "Hello" );    { Displays "Hello" on the screen }
end;
```

The SayHello procedure itself relies on three other procedures:

❏ ClrScr clears the screen and positions the cursor in the upper left corner of the screen

❏ GotoXY positions the cursor at the X and Y coordinates specified as its parameters

❏ Write displays a message, provided as a parameter, on the screen

After the SayHello procedure is defined, it can be executed with a statement such as:

```
SayHello( 1Ø, 5 );   { Places "Hello" in column 1Ø of row 5 }
```

There are only two differences between the SayHello procedure and an equivalent program:

1. The procedure terminates with a semicolon, whereas a program terminates with a period.

2. In the procedure, the variables Col and Row are undefined. Their values must come from an external source.

These aren't big distinctions. A *program*, consisting of a header and a block, can invoke a *procedure*, which itself consists of a header and a block. Further, any given procedure can invoke other procedures and functions.

Functions

A *function* is similar to a procedure. It consists of a collection of instructions that you want to execute as a single unit. However, its specific purpose is to return a value.

Components of a Function

Like a procedure, a function consists of three components:

❑ The *header*, consisting of the reserved word function, followed by the function name and any required parameters. In addition, the function must itself be defined as a certain *type*.

❑ The *data* that are to be manipulated by the instructions in the function, as defined in label, constant, type, and variable declarations. Data are located immediately after the header but before the first function code statement.

❑ Program *code* statements describing the actions to be performed. Any procedures or functions defined by the function are placed at the start of the code area. Code statements follow, enclosed by the reserved words begin and end.

Every function is terminated with a semicolon.

The general format of a Pascal function is as follows:

```
function name( optional parameters ) : functiontype;
    { Data declarations }
begin
    { Code statements }
end;
```

The header is always required, but both data and code are optional. However, a function generally contains at least one line of code that determines the value returned by the function. For example, the following:

```
function Trivial : integer;
begin
    Trivial := Ø;
end;
```

defines a function called Trivial that is *functionally equivalent* to using zero. Once Trivial is defined, the following codes are identical:

```
    X := Ø;    and    X := Trivial;
```

A Function Example

Two of the simplest standard functions are Sqrt(x), which returns the square root of its parameter, and Sqr(x), which returns the square of its parameter. By *return*, I mean that the entire function is equivalent to the variable it defines; hence it can be used wherever a single variable is allowed.

For example, the function LongSide, which returns the hypotenuse of a right triangle, is defined as follows:

```
function LongSide( A, B : real ) : real;
begin
    LongSide := Sqrt( Sqr(A) + Sqr(B) )
end;
```

A function is executed simply by listing its name, together with any required parameters. LongSide can be used wherever an ordinary variable can be used, such as in the following code:

```
if LongSide( 3.Ø, 4.Ø ) = 5.Ø then
    writeln( '3, 4, and 5 are Pythagorean triples!' );
```

Structured Programs and the Limits of Scope

In Turbo Pascal, subroutines may be *nested*. That is, each subroutine may contain another subroutine, which in turn may contain yet another subroutine, and so on.

Each nested subroutine can access the label, constant, type, and variable declarations of any of the parent subroutines that "surround" it. However, no parent subroutine can access any of the label, constant, type, and variable declarations of a subroutine that nests within it. This limitation is called the *scope of an identifier.*

Similarly, a nested subroutine can only be used by the parent that defined it. This limitation is called the *scope of a subroutine.*

The following sections explain the effect of scope on program design and operation.

Global and Local Variables

All identifiers defined in any of the parent subroutines are called *global,* and all identifiers defined within a nested procedure or function are said to be *local* to the procedure or function.

In the program SCOPE1 (listing 5.1), the variables First, Second, and Average are *global* to the CalculateAverage procedure; therefore, they may be freely used within it. The variable Total is *local* to CalculateAverage; it cannot be used outside of the procedure itself. Local variables are created by saving stack space for the variable at the start of the subroutine; this space is returned to the stack when the subroutine terminates.

Listing 5.1

```
program Scope1;
var
   First, Second, Average : integer;
procedure CalculateAverage;
var
   Total : integer;
begin
   Total := First + Second;
   Average := Total div 2;
end;
begin
   First  := 12;
   Second := 38;
   CalculateAverage;
   Writeln( 'The average of ', First, ' and ', Second, ' is ', Average );
end.
```

Variable Definition

Clearly, the compiler is able to segregate identifiers according to the block in which they are defined. Whenever an identifier is used, the compiler looks to the declarations of the current block; if the identifier isn't found, the compiler then checks the next higher block, then the next, and so on, until a declaration is found.

Once the declaration is located, no further searches are made. Consequently, each procedure and function can declare a local identifier that has the same name as a global identifier. In the SCOPE2 program (listing 5.2), the variable i is defined both globally within the program itself and locally within the ShowI procedure.

Listing 5.2

```
program Scope2;
var
   i : byte;
procedure ShowI;
var
   i : byte;
begin
   i := 48;
   writeln( 'Within the procedure, the value of "i" is ', i );
end;
begin
   i := 35;
   ShowI;
   writeln( 'Within the main program, the value of "i" is ', i );
end.
```

When SCOPE2 executes, it produces the following result:

```
Within the procedure, the value of "i" is 48
Within the main program, the value of "i" is 35
```

Notice that the global variable i is unaffected by either the declaration or assignment of the local variable with the same name.

Side Effects

Because of the rules of scope, variables can be created, stored, and used for as long as they're needed. Their life expectancy might be the duration of the entire program or the duration of a single subroutine. Although the tendency is to define every variable globally, a better approach is to reduce the life of a variable to as short a time as possible.

For example, if one subroutine needs to pass information to another subroutine, the information can be passed as a parameter. If the data are only used by the two routines, there is no need to define the data globally.

This is more than just good housekeeping. One of the most common programming errors is for procedures and functions to redefine (often unintentionally) the values of global variables. This process is known as the *side effect* of the subroutine, because it's rarely something that the programmer deliberately sets out to do.

Parameter Passing

The parameters specified in a procedure or function heading are called *formal parameters*. These parameters, like the variables defined within the subroutine itself, are *local* to the subroutine; no permanent space is reserved for them anywhere in memory. When the subroutine is called, the *actual parameters* to be sent to the subroutine are temporarily placed—in order—in a special area of memory called the *stack*. The subroutine reads this data—in order—from the stack. In other words, formal and actual parameters are transferred and matched by their order in the declaration, which becomes their order in the stack, not by name. The return value of a function is placed in one of the registers of the PC.

In the ACTFORM program (listing 5.3), *Factor1* and *Factor2* are formal parameters; *A* and *B* are actual parameters.

Listing 5.3

```
program ActForm;
var
   A, B : integer;

procedure Product( Factor1, Factor2 : integer );
begin
   writeln( Factor1, ' x ', Factor2, ' = ', Factor1*Factor2 );
end;

begin
   A := 12;
   B := 17;
   Product( A, B );
end.
```

By using the stack to transfer data, Turbo Pascal effectively isolates each procedure and function from the part of the program that calls it. Conceivably, each subroutine can process in total independence, without ever affecting the contents of any other program variable. For this reason, procedures and functions are commonly called *subprograms*.

Now, obviously, there are times when you *want* a subroutine to access the variables in the main body of the program. When you want to replace the value of a single variable, you can use a function. But at other times, you need a subprogram to compute a number of results rather than just one (for example, to compute an array), or you need to both use and modify the same variable (as when you increment a page number). For these situations, a function is not appropriate, and a procedure is needed instead.

Finally, a third situation arises where you want a subroutine to *ignore the type* of a variable passed to it.

Turbo Pascal supports all of these situations by providing three ways to specify a parameter.

❏ A parameter *not* preceded by the reserved word var, but followed by a specific type, is called a *value parameter*.

❏ A parameter preceded by the reserved word var and followed by a specific type is called a *variable parameter*.

❏ A parameter preceded by the reserved word var and *not* followed by a specific type is called an *untyped variable parameter*.

Each of these methods is described fully in this section.

Value Parameters

When a parameter is passed by *value*, it's copied into the stack. Value parameters are completely local to the subroutine. Whenever the variable is used within the subroutine, it's the *copy* of the variable on the stack that is read or modified; the *original* variable (the actual parameter) is never touched.

The types of the actual and formal parameters must be compatible; for example, you can't send a string to a procedure that expects a number. But beyond that, the only restriction is that the actual parameter must represent data whose value *can* be copied to the stack. In other words, within the limits of the type constraint, any format of actual parameter is allowed: expression, function, variable name, constant name, number, or string.

Note that a file type doesn't directly contain data (you have to read the data from the file itself) and consequently can't be placed on the stack.

Therefore, neither a `file` type variable nor a structured type variable that contains a `file` type can be used as a value parameter.

In the VALUE1 program (listing 5.4), the variables i and j are passed as value parameters to the `AddUp` function. When the function is called, the program copies the contents of i and j to the stack. While the function executes, only the stack copies of the variables can be accessed. Although the function changes both the `Val1` and `Val2` parameters, only the stack is affected; the variables i and j were never touched and consequently retain their original values.

Listing 5.4

```
program Value1;
var
   i, j : word;
function AddUp( Val1, Val2 : word ) : word;
begin
   Val1 := Val1 + Val2;    { Deliberate use of Val1 }
   Val2 := Ø;              { Deliberate use of Val2 }
   AddUp := Val1;
end;
begin
   i := 1Ø;
   j := 5;
   writeln( AddUp( i, j ), ' is the total of ', i, ' and ', j );
end.
```

When VALUE1 executes, it produces the following result:

```
15 is the total of 1Ø and 5
```

Variable Parameters

A *variable parameter* is used when you want to directly access—and, presumably, modify—a variable defined outside the scope of the subroutine itself. A variable parameter is passed by *reference*. This means that instead of using the stack to store a copy of the variable, the compiler uses the stack to store a *pointer* to the memory location where the actual variable can be found.

While the subroutine executes, every reference to the variable parameter is passed—via the pointer—to the actual variable. Therefore, when you change a variable parameter, you are really changing the original variable.

The VAR1 program (listing 5.5) is designed to perform simple screen animation. A block character (ASCII 219) is moved across the screen, from left to right, on line 10. The horizontal position is determined by the action of the MoveRight procedure. When the block reaches column 80 (the right-hand side of the screen), MoveRight returns to column 1. To do this, MoveRight needs to be able to both read and modify the current column number; Consequently, MoveRight is passed a variable parameter containing the current column. It moves the block character one position to the right until it hits column 80, when it resets the block to the far left side.

VAR1 uses the Delay procedure to pause long enough for each position to be observable. The format of the procedure is Delay(Msec), where Msec is the number of milliseconds you want to wait before the program proceeds to the next statement. Delay bases its actions on the system clock; this is superior to using a loop or other counting device, which varies in duration depending on the type of computer you are using.

Listing 5.5

```
program Var1;
uses Crt;
const
   Column : word = 1;    {Initialize Column to 1}
var
   i : word;
procedure MoveRight( var Xposition : word );
begin
   if Xposition = 80 then
      Xposition := 1
   else
      Inc( Xposition );
end;
procedure Horizontal;
begin
   GotoXY( Column, 10 );   writeln( ' ' );  {Erases the previous block}
   MoveRight( Column );
   GotoXY( Column, 10 );   write( #219 );
   Delay( 50 );
end;
begin
   ClrScr;
   for i := 1 to 160 do Horizontal
end.
```

One of the most common programming errors you will experience is forgetting the reserved word var in the subroutine header. In that case, the subroutine can only access a copy of the variable on the stack, leaving the original variable untouched. You can see the result of such an error in the VAR1 program. Delete the reserved word var, and rerun the program. With a variable parameter, the MoveRight procedure causes the block character to make two horizontal passes across the screen. With a value parameter,

MoveRight has no effect on the Column variable; 160 lines are written with the block remaining in the far left column.

> A variable parameter puts only a pointer on the stack instead of the data object itself, so large data objects such as arrays can be more efficiently handled as variable parameters even if you don't intend to modify them.

Untyped Variable Parameters

When you define a subroutine with a value or variable parameter, you are implicitly telling the compiler that you want it to test for—and ensure—type compatibility between the formal and actual parameters.

Type compatibility is highly desirable while you are developing your program. If you transpose, omit, or otherwise bungle a subroutine call, it's a relief to know that Turbo Pascal will tell you about it immediately. However, you may want to allow a single subroutine to use parameters of different types.

Turbo Pascal enables you to bypass type-checking through the use of *untyped variable parameters*. This is an advanced feature of the compiler, so use it carefully; debugging programs without type-checking can be extremely painful. However, one useful result of untyped variables is that you can use the same subroutine to process *similar* structures. For example, with type-checking in place, formal and actual array parameters must be both the same type and the same size. Untyped parameters aren't so restrictive.

The UNTYPED program (listing 5.6) contains a procedure called Write-Array, which is defined with the untyped variable parameter ArrType. Write-Array is designed to display the contents of any integer array up to 100 elements long. WriteArray is called by providing it with the name of an array, together with the array's lower and upper bounds.

Listing 5.6

```
program Untyped;
var
   i      : word;
   Array1 : array [ 1..10 ] of integer;      { 10 elements }
   Array2 : array [ 5..9 ] of integer;       {  5 elements }
```

Listing 5.6 continues

Listing 5.6 continued

```
procedure WriteArray( var ArrType; Min, Max : word );
type
   GeneralArray = array [ 1..1Ø0 ] of integer;
var
   i : word;
   WorkArray : GeneralArray absolute ArrType;
begin
   writeln( '             Index    Value' );
   for i := 1 to ( Max - Min + 1 ) do
      writeln( i:8, ( Min + i - 1 ):8, WorkArray[ i ]:8 );
end;

begin
   for i := 1 to 1Ø do Array1[ i ] := i*i;
   for i := 5 to 9 do Array2[ i ] := i*i*i;
   writeln( 'Array1' );
   WriteArray( Array1, 1, 1Ø );
   writeln;
   writeln( 'Array2' );
   WriteArray( Array2, 5, 9 );
end.
```

When UNTYPED executes, it produces the following results:

```
Array1
            Index    Value
     1        1        1
     2        2        4
     3        3        9
     4        4       16
     5        5       25
     6        6       36
     7        7       49
     8        8       64
     9        9       81
    1Ø       1Ø      10Ø
Array2
            Index    Value
     1        5      125
     2        6      216
     3        7      343
     4        8      512
     5        9      729
```

Exiting a Subroutine

The Exit procedure can be used to terminate gracefully the current procedure or function. Before you use Exit, be sure that any values returned by your procedure or function have already been assigned.

Suppose that you need to evaluate the roots of a quadratic equation:

$$Ax^2 + Bx + C = 0$$

You remember that the *roots* are those values of x for which the equation is *true*. For example, the equation:

$$x^2 - 5x + 6 = 0$$

has A equal to 1, B equal to –5, and C equal to 6. The equation only holds when x is equal to either 2 or 3. Sometimes no numbers can be found to solve the equation; in that case, the roots are called *imaginary*.

The roots can be found with the *quadratic formula*:

$$x = \frac{-B \pm \sqrt{(B^2 - 4AC)}}{2A}$$

Roots only exist if $(B^2 - 4AC)$ is nonnegative. The RealQuadraticRoots procedure uses the quadratic formula to test whether the roots exist. If they do exist, the roots are returned; if they don't, the procedure terminates early with a call to the Exit routine.

```
procedure RealQuadraticRoots( A, B, C : real; var Root1, Root2 : real );
var
    Hold : real;
begin
    Root1 := Ø;
    Root2 := Ø;
    Hold := Sqr(B)-4*A*C;
    if Hold < Ø then Exit;           { Imaginary roots! }
    Root1 := (-B - Sqrt(Hold))/(2*A);
    Root2 := (-B + Sqrt(Hold))/(2*A);
end;
```

The SquareRoot function returns the square root of a number to any desired degree of precision. It operates by making a series of guesses; each new guess is halfway between the two prior "best" guesses. Each guess is tested; if it's accurate to within a specified (user-defined) range, the function terminates with the Exit procedure. (In fact, if it weren't for the EXIT procedure, the repeat loop would never terminate!)

```
function SquareRoot( X : real ) : real;
var
    Top, Bottom, Guess : real;
begin
    Top := Abs(X);    { Note absolute value }
    Bottom := Ø.Ø;
    repeat
        Guess := (Top + Bottom) / 2;
        SquareRoot := Guess;
        if abs(Sqr(Guess)-X) < Ø.ØØØØ1 then Exit;
        if Guess*Guess > X then Top    := Guess
                           else Bottom := Guess;
    until False;
end;
```

Although it might seem as if SquareRoot is nothing but trial and error, it actually converges quickly. The technique can be used to solve a variety of other numerical problems.

You can also call the Exit procedure within the main body of your program; if you do, it will cause your program to terminate immediately. Note, though, that the preferred way to end your program early is with a call to the Halt procedure discussed in Chapter 12.

Recursion

A *recursive* subroutine is one that calls itself directly (that is, it uses its own name) or calls another subroutine that, in turn, calls the original. At first, this might seem either unwise or downright illegal, but consider that in Turbo Pascal, every time a subroutine is called, storage space is allocated for a completely new set of local variables.

In most traditional languages—including BASIC, Cobol, and Fortran—if a subroutine calls itself, then every one of its local variables is overwritten. If a Turbo Pascal subroutine calls itself, each use of the routine is completely independent of every other.

The BACK program (listing 5.7) will ask you to keep entering animal names until it detects a null string. Notice that the writeln statement can only be executed *after* the null string is entered; after that, the Backwards procedure terminates, and control is returned to the line following the most recent procedure call. If the procedure was called by another copy of itself, control returns to that copy, and the writeln statement for the parent copy of the procedure is executed. This chain continues until the original procedure call in the main body of the program is reached.

Listing 5.7

```
program Back;
procedure Backwards;
var
   Animal : string[ 15 ];
begin
   write( 'Select an animal: ' );
   readln( Animal );
   if Animal  <> " then Backwards;
   writeln( Animal );
end;
begin
   Backwards
end.
```

The following is typical of the program's operation:

```
Select an animal: Antelope
Select an animal: Bear
Select an animal: Cat
Select an animal: Dog
Select an animal: Elephant
Select an animal: Fox
Select an animal: Giraffe
Select an animal: Hyena
Select an animal:
Hyena
Giraffe
Fox
Elephant
Dog
Cat
Bear
Antelope
```

Each Select an animal message was produced from a separate copy of the Backwards procedure. Each writeln was executed by those same copies as they terminated in reverse order.

This opens up some interesting possibilities. Clearly, Turbo Pascal can support the use of subroutines that are defined in terms of themselves (so-called *recursive subroutines*). Uses of recursive subroutines abound in mathematics, language theory, and artificial intelligence.

Factorials

If you have two objects, you can arrange them in only two ways (AB and BA). Three objects can be arranged in six ways (ABC, ACB, BAC, BCA, CAB, and CBA). In general, N objects can be arranged in N! ways. The exclamation mark is called a *factorial* sign. If N is a positive integer, then the number N! (pronounced "N factorial") is defined to be equal to:

$$N \times (N - 1) \times (N - 2) \times (N - 3) \times ... \times 4 \times 3 \times 2 \times 1$$

Therefore

$1! = 1$
$2! = 2 \times 1 = 2$
$3! = 3 \times 2 \times 1 = 6$
$4! = 4 \times 3 \times 2 \times 1 = 24$ and
$8! = 8 \times 7 \times 6 \times 5 \times 4 \times 3 \times 2 \times 1 = 40,320$

Because of the availability of recursion in Turbo Pascal, *factorial* can be defined as follows:

if N = 1 then N! = 1 else N! = N × (N – 1)!

Such a definition is said to be *recursive*. You can apply it in the FACT1 program (listing 5.8), as follows:

Listing 5.8

```
program Fact1;
var
   number : longint;
function Fact( n : longint ) : longint;
begin
   if n = 1 then
      Fact := 1
   else
      Fact := n * Fact( n-1 );
end,
begin
   for number := 1 to 10 do
      writeln( number:2, '! = ', Fact( number ) );
end.
```

When FACT1 executes, it produces the following:

```
 1! = 1
 2! = 2
 3! = 6
 4! = 24
 5! = 120
 6! = 720
 7! = 5040
 8! = 40320
 9! = 362880
10! = 3628800
```

FACT1 operates by calling the Fact function N times; each time the Fact function calls itself, it uses the next lower integer as the parameter.

For something as simple as a factorial calculation, a nonrecursive solution is also possible, as shown in the FACT2 program (listing 5.9).

Listing 5.9

```
program Fact2;
var
   number : longint;
function fact( n : longint ) : longint;
var
   Index, Hold : longint;
begin
   Hold := 1;
   for Index := 1 to n do
      Hold := Hold * Index;
   fact := Hold;
end;
begin
   for number := 1 to 10 do
      writeln( number:2, '! = ', fact( number ) );
end.
```

At this level, it's difficult to determine which program is easier to define, understand, and use. Now it's time to add some complexity.

The Greatest Common Divisor

The *greatest common divisor (GCD)* of two integers is the largest whole number that can be evenly divided into both of them. The GCD of 12 and 18 is 6. The GCD of 18 and 36 is 18. The GCD of 17 and 53 is 1.

Program GCD1 (listing 5.10) uses a technique called *Euclid's method* to compute the GCD of two numbers. Essentially, Euclid's method states that the GCD of two numbers must equal the GCD of the smaller number of the original pair and the difference between the pair. By applying that observation repetitively, you can quickly arrive at the GCD of the original set.

Listing 5.10

```
program GCD1;
var
   First, Second, Answer : longint;
function GCD( a, b : longint ) : longint;
begin
   writeln( a:1Ø, b:1Ø );
   if b = Ø then
      GCD := a
   else
      GCD := GCD( b, a mod b );
end;
begin
   write( 'Enter the first integer:  ' );
   readln( First );
   write( 'Enter the second integer: ' );
   readln( Second );
   Answer := GCD( First, Second );
   writeln( 'The greatest common denominator is: ', Answer );
end.
```

A sample execution of GCD1 is as follows:

```
Enter the first integer:   48
Enter the second integer: 36
         48         36
         36         12
         12          Ø
The greatest common denominator is: 12
Enter the first integer:   747346
Enter the second integer: 543469
```

```
          747346      543469
          543469      203877
          203877      135715
          135715       68162
           68162       67553
           67553         609
             609         563
             563          46
              46          11
              11           2
               2           1
               1           0
   The greatest common denominator is: 1
```

Again, a nonrecursive approach can be taken, as demonstrated in the GCD2 program (listing 5.11). GCD2 uses an iterative technique to apply the same method.

Listing 5.11

```pascal
program GCD2;
var
    First, Second, Answer : longint;
function GCD( a, b : longint ) : longint;
var
   c : longint;
begin
   writeln( a:10, b:10 );
   while b  <> 0 do begin
      c := a mod b;
      a := b;
      b := c;
      writeln( a:10, b:10 );
   end;
   GCD := a;
end;
begin
   write( 'Enter the first integer:  ' );
   readln( First );
   write( 'Enter the second integer: ' );
   readln( Second );
   Answer := GCD( First, Second );
   writeln( 'The greatest common denominator is ', Answer );
end.
```

The Fibonacci Sequence

The Fibonacci sequence is the basis of most spiral designs. The sequence is defined by specifying the first two elements; every subsequent element is the sum of the previous pair. The FIB1 program (listing 5.12) includes a Fibonacci function that solves for the Nth element of the sequence by looping through every lower-order element. This approach is called *iteration*.

Listing 5.12

```
program Fib1;
var
  i : word;
function Fibonacci( Element : longint ) : longint;
var
  Index, Current, First, Second : longint;
begin
  First   := 1;
  Second  := 1;
  Current := 1;
  if Element > 2 then
    for Index := 1 to Element - 2 do begin
      Current := First  + Second;
      Second  := First;
      First   := Current;
    end;
  Fibonacci := Current;
end;
begin
  for i := 1 to 1Ø do
    writeln( i:3, Fibonacci( i ):8 );
end.
```

The FIB2 program (listing 5.13) defines a Fibonacci function using a recursive approach. Intuitively, you can see that FIB2 is a bit simpler than FIB1.

Listing 5.13

```
program Fib2;
var
  i : word;
function Fibonacci( Element : longint ) : longint;
begin
  if Element  <= 2 then
    Fibonacci := 1
  else
    Fibonacci := Fibonacci( Element - 1 ) + Fibonacci( Element - 2 );
end;
begin
  for i := 1 to 1Ø do
    writeln( i:3, Fibonacci( i ):8 );
end.
```

When either of these programs is run, it produces the following output:

```
1      1
2      1
3      2
4      3
5      5
6      8
7      13
8      21
9      34
1Ø     55
```

When To Use Recursion

Three major rules apply to the use of recursion.

Rule 1: In general, for every recursive technique you can devise, an iterative approach can also be found.

Rule 2: Each recursive call must apply to a simpler case than the previous one.

Rule 3: A means of easy escape must exist, so the recursion is not infinite. It is called the *basis* of the recursive definition.

Unfortunately, no such hard and fast rules can be found to help determine *when* recursion *should be* used.

One of the most famous uses of recursion is to solve the puzzle of the *Towers of Hanoi*. This is a game consisting of three poles and a set of rings of different diameters. As the game opens, all of the rings are on the left pole, arranged in order of their size; the smallest ring is on the top and the largest is on the bottom.

The object of the game is to move all of the rings from the pole on the left to the pole on the right. There are, however, just a few restrictions to make things interesting. First, you can only move one disk at a time. Each move consists of removing the topmost ring from one pole and placing it immediately on another pole. Second, you can't place a larger ring on top of a smaller ring.

For two rings, you make three moves: move the small ring from the left to center, move the large ring from the left to the right, and finally move the small ring from the center to the right.

For three rings, you need seven moves, as shown in figure 5.2.

Fig. 5.2. *Solving the Towers of Hanoi puzzle with three rings.*

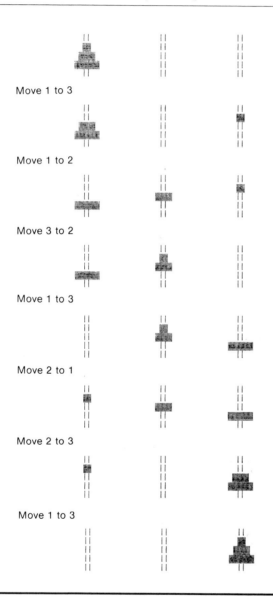

Move 1 to 3

Move 1 to 2

Move 3 to 2

Move 1 to 3

Move 2 to 1

Move 2 to 3

Move 1 to 3

With just a little thought, you can see that in order to move N disks from the left pole to the right pole, you do the following:

1. Move N −1 disks from the left pole to the center pole.

2. Move the largest disk from the left pole to the right pole.

3. Move the N −1 disks from the center pole to the right pole.

The HANOI1 program (listing 5.14) automates this strategy for any number of rings.

Listing 5.14

```
program Hanoi1;
var
   NumberOfDisks : integer;
procedure transfer( Disk, StartFrom, Target, StopOver : integer );
begin
   if Disk > Ø then begin
      transfer( Disk-1, StartFrom, StopOver, Target );
      writeln( 'Move ', StartFrom, ' to ', Target );
      transfer( Disk-1, StopOver, Target, StartFrom );
   end;
end;
begin
   write( 'Enter the number of disks: ' );
   readln( NumberOfDisks );
   transfer( NumberOfDisks, 1, 3, 2 );
end.
```

For three rings, HANOI1 provides the following advice:

```
Move 1 to 3
Move 1 to 2
Move 3 to 2
Move 1 to 3
Move 2 to 1
Move 2 to 3
Move 1 to 3
```

Of course, for anything larger, results presented in this manner could become boring quickly. Eight rings require 255 moves. Ten rings require 1,023 moves. The HANOI2 program (listing 5.15) animates the process by displaying the disks and the moves on the screen.

Listing 5.15

```
program Hanoi2;
uses Crt;
var
    i, j, NumberOfDisks : byte;
    GameBoard          : array[ 1..3, 1..10 ] of boolean;
procedure SetUp;
begin
    ClrScr;
    for i := 1 to 3 do                      { Clear the board }
        for j := 1 to 10 do
            GameBoard[ i, j ] := False;
    for i := 1 to NumberOfDisks do begin
        GameBoard[ 1, i ] := True;          { Put rings on left pole }
        GotoXY( 20-i, i );                  { Position for display }
        for j := 1 to 2*i do write( #219 ); { Write the block symbol }
    end;
end;
procedure transfer( Disk, StartFrom, Target, StopOver : integer );
procedure DisplayTheMove;
var
    k, k1 : byte;
begin
    k := 0;                                 { Find level of peg }
    repeat Inc(k) until GameBoard[ StartFrom, k ] = True;
    for k1 := 1 to abs(Target-StartFrom)*20 do begin
        if Target > StartFrom then begin    { Move disk left to right }
            GotoXY( StartFrom*20 +k +k1-1, k );        write( #219 );
            GotoXY( StartFrom*20 +k +k1-1-2*k, k );  write( ' ' );
        end else begin                      { Move disk right to left }
            GotoXY( StartFrom*20-k1-k, k );      write( #219 );
            GotoXY( StartFrom*20-k1-k +2*k, k);  write( ' ' );
        end;
        delay( 50 );                        { So movement is visible }
    end;
    GameBoard[ StartFrom, k ]  := False; { Remove from the old peg }
    GameBoard[ Target, k ] := True;         { Drop it on the new peg }
    delay( 500 );                           { Wait between moves }
end;
begin
    if Disk > 0 then begin
        transfer( Disk-1, StartFrom, StopOver, Target );
        DisplayTheMove;
        transfer( Disk-1, StopOver, Target, StartFrom );
    end;
end;
begin
    write( 'Enter the number of Disks: ' );
    readln( NumberOfDisks );
    SetUp;
    transfer( NumberOfDisks, 1, 3, 2 );
end.
```

In order for the animation feature to work best, no more than 10 disks should be specified when Hanoi2 is executed.

As an exercise, try to rewrite either of these programs *without* using recursion. It *can* be done (hint: use arrays to store intermediate results), but the resulting code quickly becomes complicated.

Recursion should be used whenever and wherever it is easier to use than iteration. In general, the more difficult the problem, the more likely that recursion will be the technique you prefer!

Forward Declarations

In the preceding section, I defined a *recursive subroutine* as one that calls itself either directly or indirectly. An example of an *indirect* call is when subroutine A calls subroutine B, and subroutine B calls subroutine A. When two or more subroutines call each other in such an indirect manner, they are said to exhibit *mutual recursion*.

But if A calls B, and B calls A, which one is defined first? After all, we said that every procedure and function has to be declared before it can be used. Take it one step further; how can *ordinary* recursion be allowed, because the subroutine obviously hasn't been totally defined before a call instruction is encountered?

The answer is that only the procedure or function *header* must be defined before the first call is made. Turbo Pascal needs to know the *name* of the subroutine (it must be able to recognize a call when it sees one), and it needs to know the parameter and function types, if any, in order to check the syntax of the call.

For two subroutines, each of which calls the other, one must obviously be listed second—*after* the first subroutine that needs to use it. But if you include a special *forward declaration* of its header *prior* to the first subroutine, the problem is solved.

The forward declaration is written exactly as the ordinary subroutine header, except that it's followed by the reserved word forward. Later, when the actual subroutine is defined, you don't need to repeat any of the parameters.

Actually, you can use forward declarations for any subroutine, even those that aren't used recursively. You will sometimes find programs where, for purposes of documentation, *every* procedure or function is listed as a forward at the beginning of a program.

An *expression parser* is a program that can evaluate legal algebraic expressions. *Precedence* refers to the order in which each operation is evaluated. In Turbo Pascal, multiplication has a higher precedence than addition; hence,

```
2 + 3 * 4
```

will evaluate as $2 + (3*4)$, or *14*, rather than as $(2+3)*4$, or *20*. Parentheses are used to specify the parts of the expression that must be evaluated first. Hence, the statement

```
(2 + 3) * 4
```

does evaluate to 20.

The EXPRESS program (listing 5.16) is a simple expression parser with the functions and levels of precedence shown in table 5.1.

Table 5.1. *Precedence in the EXPRESS Program*

	Precedence	Operators	Name
Highest	1	( )	Parentheses
	2	- +	Unary plus and minus
	3	* /	Multiplication and division
Lowest	4	- +	Binary plus and minus

Within the EXPRESS program, the DoParentheses, DoUnaries, DoMultDiv, and DoBinaries procedures process each level of precedence separately. Each procedure is called in sequence in order to ensure that statement operators are evaluated in the proper order. Before any procedure can process operands at its own level, it must ensure that all higher-precedence operations have completed. Hence, DoBinaries calls DoMultDiv, DoMultDiv calls DoUnaries, and DoUnaries calls DoParentheses.

Consider, however, that if parentheses are detected, the expression *within* the parentheses must be evaluated independently; hence, the processing sequence must begin again at the lowest precedence level. Since DoParentheses must be able to call DoBinaries "out of order," the DoBinaries procedure must be declared forward.

Listing 5.16

```
program Express;
type
    TokenType = ( Number, Space, LParen, RParen,
                  Plus, Minus, Star, Slash, EndLine );
var
    Value,
    Result  : LongInt;
    Token   : TokenType;
    LinePos : byte;
    Line    : string[ 80 ];
procedure DoBinaries( var Result : LongInt ); forward;
procedure Error( Message : string );
begin
    writeln( Message );
    Halt;
end;
procedure ScanLine;
begin
    if LinePos > Length( Line ) then
        Token := EndLine
    else begin
        case Line[ LinePos ] of
            '0'..'9' : begin
                           Token := Number;
                           Value := 0;
                           repeat
                               Value := 10*Value +Ord( Line[ LinePos ] )-48;
                               Inc( LinePos );
                           until ( LinePos > Length(Line) ) or
                                 ( Line[ LinePos ]  < '0' ) or
                                 ( Line[ LinePos ]  > '9' );
                       end;
            '(' : Token := LParen;
            ')' : Token := RParen;
            '+' : Token := Plus;
            '-' : Token := Minus;
            '*' : Token := Star;
            '/' : Token := Slash;
            ' ' : Token := Space;
        else    Error( 'Illegal characters on line' );
        end;
        if Token  <> Number then Inc( LinePos );
    end;
    while Token = Space do ScanLine;
end;
procedure GetNextNumber( var Result : LongInt );
begin
    if Token = Number then begin
        Result := Result + Value;
        ScanLine;
    end else
        Error( 'Syntax error' );
end;
```

Listing 5.16 continues

Listing 5.16 *continued*

```
procedure DoParentheses( var Result : LongInt );    { Zero Level }
begin
   if Token = LParen then
      begin
         ScanLine;
         DoBinaries( Result );
         if Token = Rparen then ScanLine
                        else Error( 'Unbalanced parentheses' );
      end
   else
      GetNextNumber( Result );
end;
procedure DoUnaries( var Result : LongInt );   { First Level }
var
   Operation : TokenType;
begin
   Operation := Token;
   if (Token = Plus) or (Token = Minus) then
      ScanLine;
   DoParentheses( Result );
   if Operation = Minus then
      Result := -Result;
end;
procedure DoMultDiv( var Result : LongInt );   { Second Level }
var
   Next : LongInt;
   Operation : TokenType;
begin
   DoUnaries( Result );
   while (Token = Star) or (Token = Slash) do
      begin
         Operation := Token;
         ScanLine;
         Next := Ø;
         DoUnaries( Next );
         case Operation of
            Star  : Result := Result * Next;
            Slash : if Next = Ø then Error( 'Division by Ø' )
                              else Result := Result div Next;
         end;
      end;
end;
procedure DoBinaries{( var Result : LongInt )};   { Third Level }
var
   Next : LongInt;
   Operation : TokenType;
begin
   DoMultDiv( Result );
   while (Token = Plus) or (Token = Minus) do
      begin
```

Listing 5.16 *continues*

Listing 5.16 continued

```
               Operation := Token;
               ScanLine;
               Next := Ø;
               DoMultDiv( Next );
               case Operation of
                  Plus  : Result := Result + Next;
                  Minus : Result := Result - Next;
               end;
         end;
end;
procedure Evaluate;    { Only process if something was entered }
begin
   if Length( Line )  <> Ø then begin
      LinePos := 1;
      ScanLine;
      Result := Ø;
      DoBinaries( Result );
   end;
end;
begin
   repeat
      writeln;
      writeln( 'Enter your expression:' );
      readln( Line );
      Evaluate;
      if Length( Line ) > Ø then
         writeln( Result );
   until Length( Line ) = Ø;
end.
```

When EXPRESS executes, it asks you to enter an equation.

```
Enter your expression:
12-4
8

Enter your expression:
 (  (12- 4) * (12  /4))
24

Enter your expression:
-4Ø/ +1Ø
-4

Enter your expression:
(1 +2)*(4*5)/(1Ø* +1)
6

Enter your expression:
1Ø + (3*4
Unbalanced parentheses
```

The program terminates with a null line or after any of these error conditions are detected:

- ❏ Illegal characters on line
- ❏ Syntax error
- ❏ Unbalanced parentheses
- ❏ Division by 0

Procedure Types

In Turbo Pascal, you can define a *procedure type* to enable a procedure or function to be treated just like an ordinary data object. This is an extremely clever method of allowing subroutines to be assigned to variables and passed as parameters, but it's also a technically complicated technique that you should use carefully.

A procedure-type declaration is designed to capture the type of the subroutine parameters and the type returned by a function. Therefore, it's declared just like an ordinary procedure or function header but without the subroutine name, which is immaterial.

Sample procedure type declarations are as follows:

```
type
    Binary   = function ( First, Second : word ) : word;
    ProcHold = procedure;
    SumProc  = procedure ( var X, Y; ActionProc : ProcHold );
    Rooter   = function ( RealPart, ImaginaryPart : real ):real;
```

Identifiers used in the declarations are similar to the formal parameters in an actual subroutine. The sequence is what's important, not the actual names you use. Any procedure or function having a *similar combination* of types defined in its header may be assigned to any variable defined as a compatible type.

Normally, when Turbo Pascal compiles a procedure or function call, it generates the most efficient machine code possible based on where the subroutine physically resides. In order to use a procedure-type variables anywhere in your program, any subroutine you want to assign a procedure-type variable must be compiled with the {$F +} Force Far Calls option in force. This directive is discussed in greater detail in the Compiler Directives reference section.

A Procedure-Type Example with Procedures

The PROC1 program (listing 5.17) is a password validation routine that uses procedure-type variables to determine the action to take when an unauthorized user tries to access the system.

Three sign-on attempts are allowed; the first two result in warning messages, and the third causes the program to terminate completely. Depending on the try, the TestPassword procedure is given the name of either the Warning or Fatal response procedure.

Listing 5.17

```
program Proc1;
const
   Attempt : byte = Ø;
   GoodGuy : Boolean = False;
type
   String8    = string[ 8 ];
   ErrorLevel = procedure ( Try : byte );
var
   Response : String8;
{$F +}
procedure TestPassword( Answer : String8;  Severity : ErrorLevel );
const
   Secret  = 'Borland';
begin
   if Answer = Secret then
      GoodGuy := True
   else
      Severity( Attempt );
end;
procedure Warning( Try : byte );
begin
   writeln( #7'Incorrect response number ', Try );
   writeln( 'Please try again!' );
end;
procedure Fatal( Try : byte );
begin
   writeln( #7'After ', Try, ' tries, access is denied!' );
   Halt;
end;
```

Listing 5.17 continues

Listing 5.17 *continued*

```
{$F-}
procedure UserSignOn;
begin
   repeat
      Inc( Attempt );
      write( 'Enter your password: ' );
      readln( Response );
      if Attempt  < 3 then
         TestPassword( Response, Warning )
      else
         TestPassword( Response, Fatal );
   until GoodGuy;
   writeln( 'Welcome to the program' );
end;
begin
   UserSignOn;
{  program code goes here    }
end.
```

If the correct password is provided, the program executes normally.

```
Enter your password: Borland
Welcome to the program
```

If the correct password hasn't been entered after three attempts, an error message is generated and the program halts.

```
Enter your password: Fred
Incorrect response number 1
Please try again!
Enter your password: Bob
Incorrect response number 2
Please try again!
Enter your password: Rosebud
After 3 tries, access is denied!
```

A Procedure-Type Example with Functions

Procedure-type parameters can also be applied to functions. The FUNC1 program (listing 5.18) is a simple set of routines used to determine the maximum and minimum values of a function. A variation of FUNC1 could be used as part of a routine to determine the scale to be used in displaying a graph.

Listing 5.18

```
program Func1;
type
   Func = function ( Param : real ) : real;
var
   Minimum, Maximum : real;
{$F +}
function Sine( X : real ) : real;
begin
   Sine := Sin( X );
end;
function Cosine( X : real ) : real;
begin
   Cosine := Cos( X );
end;
procedure FindMaxAndMin( CurrFunction : Func );
var
   i      : word;
   Param,
   Result : real;
begin
   Maximum := -10000.0;
   Minimum := +10000.0;
   for i := 1 to 100 do begin
      Param := i / 10;
      Result := CurrFunction( Param );
      if Result > Maximum then
         Maximum := Result;
      if Result < Minimum then
         Minimum := Result;
   end;
   writeln( 'Minimum= ', Minimum:0:6, ' Maximum= ', Maximum:0:6 );
end;
{$F-}
begin
   write( 'For the Sine function:   ' );
   FindMaxAndMin( Sine );
   write( 'For the Cosine function:  ' );
   FindMaxAndMin( Cosine );
end.
```

When FUNC1 executes, it produces the following output:

```
For the Sine function:  Minimum= -0.999923 Maximum= 0.999574
For the Cosine function:  Minimum= -0.999693 Maximum= 0.999859
```

Summary

In this chapter, you have learned how a complex programming problem can be broken down into subroutines. Within Turbo Pascal, subroutines consist of procedures and functions.

You have learned the differences between a procedure and a function, including how each is structured and called. A procedure consists of a collection of statements, possibly including other procedures, that operate as a group. A procedure is invoked by simply writing its name, just like an ordinary Pascal statement. A function is similar to a procedure except that a function is designed to return a value of a specified type. A function can be used in any expression in which a variable of the same type would be permitted. You have seen how the Exit procedure can terminate the processing within a subroutine.

You have learned how a series of subroutines can be nested, and you have learned the scope limits associated with the nesting process.

You have learned how subroutines access information through parameters. Value parameters allow access to a copy of the original data. Variable parameters allow access to the original data itself. Untyped variable parameters allow subroutines to access data of different types.

You have learned how subroutines can be called recursively, and thus mimic common recursive problem-solving techniques. You have seen how forward declarations allow subroutines to be called before they are formally defined.

You have learned that a special data object called a procedure type allows Turbo Pascal programs to pass procedures and functions as parameters to other procedures and functions.

CHAPTER 6

Dynamic Data Structures

L ike most microprocessors, those in the 8086-family (the 8086, 80286, and 80386) have internal word-sized areas called *registers*. Some registers are specifically designed to hold memory addresses, whereas others are intended primarily for data storage and manipulation.

One common misconception is that for data to be used by a processor, it must first be placed in one of the registers. Although it's true that data in registers can be accessed much more quickly than data in memory, most microprocessor instructions (including arithmetic ones like add and subtract) have options that allow for one or more operands to *remain* in memory. For example, the instruction that compares two 100-byte strings for equality requires only that the registers contain the strings' starting addresses and length—a considerable time savings over the brute force method of moving each pair of bytes to separate registers and comparing them individually.

A memory address is usually referenced by combining two words: a 16-bit segment and a 16-bit offset within the segment—the common syntax of the segment:offset format. Because any memory location can be completely specified by a four-byte address and most 8086 instructions allow memory addresses to be used in place of the actual data, program performance can be considerably enhanced using memory references wherever possible. Turbo Pascal provides a special data type called the pointer for just such a purpose.

This chapter discusses how PC memory is structured and accessed and then proceeds to explain dynamic memory management in Turbo Pascal.

137

Referencing Memory

Most people believe that if their PC has 640K of memory, it must have 10 distinct physical segments of 64K each. In reality, segment boundaries and memory addressing are much more flexible.

The 8086-family processor has 20 address lines that control which byte of memory is accessed. There are 20 lines, so 220 bytes (1,048,576 bytes or 1 megabyte) are accessible, even though DOS or hardware constraints limit *actual* memory to 640K on most machines.

Because a register is only 16 bits long, identifying a specific memory location requires the use of two registers, as follows:

❏ The first register (the *segment*) selects a paragraph that begins on—or just less than—the desired byte. All segments begin on paragraph boundaries. A *paragraph* is a 16-byte memory area; hence, a *paragraph boundary* is a memory location that is evenly divisible by 16. There are 64K paragraphs throughout the 1 megabyte of memory space. When DOS loads a program into the lowest available memory location, DOS is really selecting the next paragraph boundary above the last memory byte in current use.

❏ The second register (the *offset*) specifies the distance, or *displacement*, between the desired byte and the starting byte of the referencing paragraph. This is why the size of a segment is generally considered to be 64K; once a segment is selected by having the index number of a paragraph loaded into a segment register, no 16-bit offset can access a memory location outside of a 64K range.

Most programmers already know this, but in a slightly different form. Programming texts usually explain that the *true* address (called the *absolute* address) is found by shifting the segment word over one column to the left and adding the offset word. In hexadecimal, shifting one place to the left means multiplying by $10, which is 16 decimal. This is illustrated as follows:

Segment:	B800	(The paragraph index)
Offset:	+ 0000	(Distance from start of paragraph)
Absolute address:	B8000	(The 20-bit physical address)

The absolute address represents the actual memory location physically accessed by the 20-bit data bus.

Addresses within the current segment are termed *near*; those outside the current segment are termed *far*. Accessing a near address requires that only the offset register be changed. Accessing a far address requires changing both the segment and offset registers.

As a consequence of specifying addresses with two registers, any specific byte may be written and accessed in thousands of different ways. Consider the addresses B800:0000, B700:1000, and A8FF:F010.

Table 6.1. *Absolute Addresses of Three Memory Locations*

	B800:0000	B700:1000	A8FF:F010
Segment Register:	B800	B700	A8FF
Offset Register:	+ 0000	+ 1000	+ F010
Absolute Address:	B8000	B8000	B8000

As shown in table 6.1, all three addresses point to the same physical byte in the PC's memory, despite the fact that they have unique segment and offset register values.

So you can see that a 640K PC doesn't have 10 distinct *physical* 64K segments. Instead, the PC's memory consists of—potentially—40,960 overlapping *logical* segments. (640K equals 655,360 bytes, divided by 16 bytes per paragraph to give 40,960 paragraphs.) A logical segment takes up only as many 16-byte paragraphs as it needs. If one logical segment doesn't require the maximum 64K available space, DOS feels free to take the next free paragraph and use it as the start of the next logical segment.

Segment Usage

Data declaration (or data allocation) statements reserve and optionally initialize memory space for program variables and data. Instruction statements specify the machine instructions to be generated; they are the active, data movement, and manipulation commands (add, move, compare, and so on).

All program data and instructions are stored in memory. The 8086 has been physically designed in such a way that it expects the memory location of the instructions of its currently executing program to be specified with one unique combination of register pairs, the memory location of that program's data to be defined with a second register pair, and the memory area to be used as a stack to be defined with a third register pair. These areas are the code segment of memory, the data segment of memory, and the stack segment of memory, respectively. The locations of these memory areas are determined by the contents of the segment and offset register pairs shown in table 6.2.

Table 6.2. *Segment and Offset Register Pairs*

	Segment Name	Segment Register	Offset Register	Seg:Ofs
Program code	Code	CS	IP	CS:IP
Program data	Data	DS	SI	DS:SI
Stack	Stack	SS	SP	SS:SP

The Code Segment

The code segment (CS) register identifies the start of the program's instructions. The actual memory address of the next byte to be executed is found by locating the paragraph specified in the CS register, then adding the value in the instruction pointer (IP) register. To the 8086, running a program consists of starting at the first byte in a block of executable code and processing the instructions it finds there, one at a time.

The IP register always contains the address of the *next* instruction to be executed. Because alteration of this register will probably "crash" the program, the instruction pointer cannot be directly accessed or changed.

Although no direct way of learning the value of the IP register is available, the current value of the CS register can be found with the Turbo Pascal function CSeg.

The Data Segment

The data segment (DS) register identifies the start of the program's data.

When the compiler encounters a data declaration, it reserves space in the data segment based on the size of the data item. If the data item is a typed constant, its initial value is inserted into memory; otherwise, the value of a data item consists of whatever was residing in the location prior to the start of the program.

The source index (SI) register is used for pointing to (indexing) a data item within the data segment. When an instruction requires data movement, the SI register points to the source data while another register, the destination index (DI) register, points to (indexes) the destination data.

The Turbo Pascal function DSeg returns the current value of the DS register. The SI and DI registers may be accessed indirectly, through an interrupt call, as explained in Chapter 16.

The Stack Segment

The stack segment (SS) register identifies the start of the program's stack. The stack pointer (SP) register always points to the current offset within the stack segment.

The *stack* is the area of memory used by your program as a scratch pad. Any data that must be temporarily stored is placed "on the stack" until it's needed. Although most programming texts explain a stack with the "first in, first out" analogy of a stack of cafeteria trays, in truth, every byte in the stack is directly accessible. The only reason that data is stored in the stack segment from, for example, left-to-right and read back right-to-left is to minimize memory use. Any other technique would create "holes" in the stack and result in an inefficient need for more memory than would be necessary.

The Turbo Pascal function SSeg returns the current value of the SS register. Similarly, the SPtr function returns the current value of the SP register.

Reading Segment and Offset Values

Turbo Pascal provides two functions, Seg and Ofs, to return the segment and offset, respectively, of any data object.

The MEMORY1 program in listing 6.1 demonstrates how you access the various memory addresses with Turbo Pascal.

Listing 6.1

```
program Memory1;
uses Crt;
var
    StackLoc,
    SegWork,
    OfsWork  : word;
function HexByte( BinaryForm : byte ) : char;
const
    HexSymbols : array [ 0..15 ] of char = '0123456789ABCDEF';
begin
    HexByte := HexSymbols[ BinaryForm ];
end;
function HexWord( WordForm : word ) : string;
begin
    HexWord := '$' + HexByte( Hi( WordForm ) div 16 ) +
                     HexByte( Hi( WordForm ) mod 16 ) +
                     HexByte( Lo( WordForm ) div 16 ) +
                     HexByte( Lo( WordForm ) mod 16 );
end;
function SizeOfHexWord : longint;
```

Listing 6.1 continues

Listing 6.1 continued

```
begin
   SizeOfHexWord := Ofs( SizeOfHexWord ) - Ofs( HexWord );
end;
procedure ShowStackActivity( StartLoc : word );
begin
   writeln( (StartLoc - SPtr):3,
            ' bytes were used by the stack during this call ');
end;
begin
   ClrScr;
   writeln( 'Program segments begin as follows: ' );
   writeln;
   writeln( '        Code        ', CSeg:6, ' or ', HexWord( CSeg ) );
   writeln( '        Data        ', DSeg:6, ' or ', HexWord( DSeg ) );
   writeln( '        Stack       ', SSeg:6, ' or ', HexWord( SSeg ) );
   writeln( '-----------------------------------------------------------' );
   writeln( 'Segment:Offset of program code can be found at: ' );
   writeln;
   writeln( 'HexByte             ', Seg( HexByte ):6, Ofs( HexByte ):6 );
   writeln( 'HexWord             ', Seg( HexWord ):6, Ofs( HexWord ):6 );
   writeln( 'SizeOfHexWord       ', Seg( SizeOfHexWord ):6,
                                    Ofs( SizeOfHexWord ):6 );
   writeln( 'ShowStackActivity   ', Seg( ShowStackActivity ):6,
                                    Ofs( ShowStackActivity ):6 );
   writeln;
   writeln( 'The size of the HexWord function itself is ',
            SizeOfHexWord, ' or ',
            HexWord( SizeOfHexWord ), ' bytes' );
   writeln( '-----------------------------------------------------------' );
   writeln( 'Segment:Offset of program data can be found at: ' );
   writeln;
   writeln( 'StackLoc            ', Seg( StackLoc ):6, Ofs( StackLoc ):6 );
   writeln( 'SegWork             ', Seg( SegWork ):6, Ofs( SegWork ):6 );
   writeln( 'OfsWork             ', Seg( OfsWork ):6, Ofs( OfsWork ):6 );
   writeln( '-----------------------------------------------------------' );
   writeln( 'A use of the stack is demonstrated by: ' );
   writeln;
   StackLoc := SPtr;
   ShowStackActivity( StackLoc );
end.
```

When MEMORY1 executes, the program produces an output similar to that of figure 6.1.

***Fig. 6.1.** The output produced by the MEMORY1 program.*

```
Program segments begin as follows:

        Code        28673  or  $7001
        Data        28890  or  $70DA
        Stack       28935  or  $7107
```

```
Segment:Offset of program code can be found at:

HexByte             28673      0
HexWord             28673      39
SizeOfHexWord       28673      220
ShowStackActivity   28673      310
```

```
The size of the HexWord function itself is 181 or $00B5 bytes
```

```
Segment:Offset of program data can be found at:

StackLoc            28890      76
SegWork             28890      78
OfsWork             28890      80
```

```
A use of the stack is demonstrated by:

 10 bytes were used by the stack during this call
```

The program will probably report different memory locations when it is executed on your PC. The actual values depend, among other things, on which memory-resident programs are currently running on your machine.

Notice that all global variables have a segment value equal to the contents of the DS register, and all functions and procedures have a segment value equal to the contents of the CS register. The offsets grow depending on the size required for each entry.

Ten bytes were used by the stack to execute the ShowStackActivity procedure. Two bytes were taken up by the StartLoc parameter. Eight other bytes were required to save the word-sized BP, SP, SS, and DS registers—an action performed whenever a procedure or function is called. By preserving these registers, the compiler can regain control of the program no matter what happens inside the subroutine itself.

A Note on .COM and .EXE Formats

In .COM programs, such as those generated by Turbo Pascal Version 3.0 and prior versions, all segment registers contain the same value. Hence, the entire program must fit within a single 64K segment.

This format offers several advantages. Such a program compiles quickly, because no code needs to be generated to allow for switching segment registers. A .COM program also executes quickly, because segment registers don't need to be saved and restored while the program runs. The result is a highly efficient program—as long as the 64K limit isn't a problem.

Sometimes, however, the 64K limit is simply too tight for developing programs. In these cases, programs need more than one 64K segment in which to store code or data. This is the advantage of the .EXE file. Pascal programs resulting in .EXE files can call subroutines and access data in any memory location (that is, both the segment and the offset registers are free to change).

If your code or data requires more than one *physical* 64K segment, it follows that you also need more than one *logical* segment to define it. In Pascal, this means that more than one program module—called a *unit*—is needed. Units are discussed further in Chapter 7.

Dynamic Memory Allocation

Each of the code, data, and stack segments can only have a maximum size of 64K, so there must be a considerable amount of memory remaining in the PC just waiting to be used. Turbo Pascal allows this memory area, called the *heap*, to be accessed and manipulated by pointer variables.

By default, the heap can be as large as the unused portion of memory in the PC. However, its actual size grows and shrinks dynamically, depending on the size required to hold the desired variables. No single variable, however, can exceed 64K.

An ordinary variable represents a value, and the space to hold this value is allocated in the data segment when the variable is declared. A fixed amount of memory is allocated by the compiler depending on the declared type and size of the particular variable, and that much memory is consumed regardless of the actual size of the variable at run-time. A 100-element array of char consumes 100 bytes even if only the first five elements are used. Similarly, a 100-element array of records, each 20 bytes in length, consumes 2000 bytes even if only the first two records are used.

Pointers, on the other hand, are *dynamic* because the amount of allocated storage is controlled by the program during run-time. A *pointer variable* contains the address of the first byte in memory where a data object is stored rather than containing the data object itself.

The allocation of storage to the object being referenced occurs when the program is executed rather than when it's compiled. The data item being referenced can be any legal type, including a number, string, record, or even a procedure, function, or another pointer. Pointer variables can be used anywhere ordinary variable names would be used.

A pointer is stored as a double word, with the offset part in the low word and the segment part in the high word.

Declaring Pointer Variables

To declare a pointer data type, simply insert a caret (the ^ symbol) followed by the name of the type being referenced. A few examples should serve to illustrate this method.

```
type
    Structure1 = array [ 1..100 ] of longint;
var
    Var1 : ^byte;
    Var2 : ^real;
    Var3 : ^Structure1;
```

Here, Var1 is declared as a pointer to a byte, Var2 is declared as a pointer to a real, and Var3 is declared as a pointer to a 100-element array of longint.

The pointer is the only declaration that can define itself as something declared *later* in the same section. Technically, this is called a *forward pointer declaration*. The following set of declarations is completely legal and quite typical of those that appear in programs that use lists:

```
type
DataArrow = ^DataStuff;
DataStuff = record
                Info1    : real;
                Info2    : integer;
                DataPtr  : DataArrow;
            end;
```

Although at first it looks like a dog chasing its tail, this declaration is nothing more than a very clever device to enable you to create an entire series of DataStuff records, each of which contains a pointer to the *next* record in the chain.

Allocating Memory
with the *New* Procedure

Because a pointer variable contains a memory address, four bytes of storage must be allocated for it in the data segment when the program is compiled. Storage for the referenced memory area itself won't be created until the program actually runs and the New procedure is called, as follows:

```
New( VarName );
```

If VarName is declared as a pointer to the type PointerType, then the New procedure sets aside (allocates) an area of memory large enough to contain a single variable of the size of PointerType and sets the VarName variable equal to the memory address where PointerType begins.

The area of memory now pointed to by VarName doesn't have its own name; it can only be referred to—a process sometimes called *indirection*—as VarName^. Notice the caret appearing after the variable name; the *address* of the PointerType data is VarName, but the *value* of the PointerType data is VarName^.

This distinction is further demonstrated in the POINTER1 program in listing 6.2.

Listing 6.2

```
program Pointer1;
Type
   Message   = String[ 255 ];
   MsgPtr    = ^Message;
   IntPointer = ^Integer;
var
   Message1 : Message;
   Message2 : MsgPtr;
   VarX     : IntPointer;
   VarY     : Integer;
begin
   New( Message2 );
   Message1  := 'Message1 is stored in a string';
   Message2^ := 'Message2 is stored where Message2 points';
   writeln( Message1 );
   writeln( Message2^ );
   New( VarX );
   VarX^ := 12;
   VarY  := 3;
   writeln( 'The product of VarX and VarY is ', VarX^ * VarY );
   writeln( 'The size of Message1 is ', SizeOf( Message1 ) );
   writeln( 'The size of Message2 is ', SizeOf( Message2 ) );
   writeln( 'The size of Message2^ is ', SizeOf( Message2^ ) );
   writeln( 'The size of VarX is ',     SizeOf( VarX ) );
   writeln( 'The size of VarX^ is ',    SizeOf( VarX^ ) );
   writeln( 'The size of VarY is ',     SizeOf( VarY ) );
end.
```

When executed, POINTER1 generates the output shown in figure 6.2.

Fig. 6.2. Output produced by the POINTER1 program.

```
Message1 is stored in a string
Message2 is stored where Message2 points
The product of VarX and VarY is 36
The size of Message1 is 256
The size of Message2 is 4
The size of Message2^ is 256
The size of VarX is 4
The size of VarX^ is 2
The size of VarY is 2
```

Notice the difference between the Message1 and Message2 variables, and between the VarX and VarY variables. Both Message2 and VarX are 4-byte pointers, although Message2^ and VarX^ are treated as a 255-byte string and an integer, respectively, just like Message1 and VarY. The contents of Message1 and Message2 differ considerably, but Message1 and Message2^ (with the caret) are *absolutely equivalent* from a functional standpoint.

Even though this memory-referencing technique seems to have tremendous flexibility, it's still necessary to obey some fundamental programming rules. Every pointer references a specific type; when a pointer is used, it must conform to the syntax of this type. For example, it's legal to multiply a constant by the pointer to an integer, but it's illegal to multiply a constant by the pointer to a string.

Reusing Memory
with the *Dispose* Procedure

The advantage of using dynamic variables is that not only is memory allocated only when needed, but it can also be *de*allocated once it's no longer required.

Memory can be returned to the heap for reuse through the Dispose procedure. The POINTER2 program in listing 6.3 demonstrates how this is done.

Listing 6.3

```
program Pointer2;
type
   RealPntr = ^real;
var
   index : byte;
   NumberList : array[ 1..20 ] of RealPntr;
begin
   for index := 1 to 20 do begin
      New( NumberList[ index ] );
      NumberList[ index ]^ := sqrt( index );
      writeln( index:3, NumberList[ index ]^:10:5 );
      Dispose( NumberList[ index ] );
   end;
end.
```

When POINTER2 executes, it allocates, uses, and deallocates 20 pointers in the NumberList array.

Dispose isn't quite the inverse of New. With New, the pointer was automatically assigned the memory address of the allocated area of the heap. Dispose simply tells the compiler that the area is *available* for reuse; neither the contents of the heap nor the address in the pointer variable is changed.

Identifying an Unused Pointer

The predefined pointer constant Nil doesn't point to anything. (Actually, the value of Nil is equal to a double-word zero.) Nil may be assigned to a pointer variable of any type to indicate that the pointer no longer references an active memory location.

```
Dispose( Message2 );
Message2 := Nil;
Dispose( VarX );
VarX := Nil;
```

Note that you assign Nil to Message2 and VarX, *not* to Message2^ and VarX^.

Once you get into the habit of using Nil as the default value for all of your program's pointers, you can be sure that a pointer is active before you try to use it, as follows:

```
if VarX = Nil then
   New( VarX );
VarX^ := 17;
```

Allocating Memory with the *Mark* and *Release* Procedures

Dispose deallocates space for one pointer-type variable at a time. If many pointer variables have been created, Dispose can be highly inefficient, because an individual procedure call must be done for each item to be deallocated. For this reason, Turbo Pascal provides the Mark and Release procedures.

The compiler always allocates space in the heap sequentially. If a long series of data is to be defined by a succession of New procedure calls, Mark can be used to flag the position in the heap *prior* to the start of the allocations. When space for the pointer variables is no longer needed, Release can deallocate all the space allocated *since* the Mark procedure was executed. In this way, large amounts of memory can be freed with a single procedure call.

Mark is called with one pointer argument. In effect, it sets the pointer equal to the memory location at the current top of the heap.

Release is called with the same pointer argument used in the Mark procedure. Release resets the top of the heap to the memory location referenced by the pointer.

Just as with Dispose, use of the Release procedure frees the heap of unwanted variables but doesn't affect either the contents of the heap or the contents of the individual pointers.

The POINTER3 program in listing 6.4 demonstrates how Mark and Release can be used.

Listing 6.4

```
program Pointer3;
type
   RealPntr = ^real;
var
   index : byte;
   HeapMarker : ^pointer;
   NumberList : array[ 1..20 ] of RealPntr;
begin
   Mark( HeapMarker );
   for index := 1 to 20 do begin
      New( NumberList[ index ] );
      NumberList[ index ]^ := sqrt( index );
      writeln( index:3, NumberList[ index ]^:10:5 );
   end;
   Release( HeapMarker );
end.
```

When POINTER3 executes, the Mark procedure saves a pointer to the current top of the heap in HeapMarker. The program then allocates and uses heap memory equal in size to 20 real numbers. After the program finishes with this space, the Release procedure resets the top of the heap to the position stored in HeapMarker.

The choice of whether to use Dispose or Mark and Release depends principally on two issues:

❏ No memory deallocation is really necessary unless a memory constraint is reached. For short programs such as POINTER5 and POINTER6 (listings 6.6 and 6.7), there's really no need to bother; for a spreadsheet or database program, frequent deallocation may be required.

❏ Mark and Release free entire *blocks* of heap memory. If your program creates even a single pointer reference between the two procedure calls you might need to use later, you will have to use the Dispose procedure to return heap memory selectively.

Allocating Memory with the *GetMem* and *FreeMem* Procedures

When you allocate variables with the New procedure, one byte of heap space is used for each byte of the data structure being referenced.

One method of dynamic memory allocation that is unique to Turbo Pascal is the combination of the GetMem and FreeMem procedures. They are similar to New and Dispose in that they allocate and deallocate memory one variable at a time, but they differ in that with GetMem and FreeMem you can actually specify how much memory in the heap you want to control, regardless of the size implied by the pointer type.

The POINTER4 program in listing 6.5 demonstrates how GetMem and FreeMem procedures are used.

Listing 6.5

```
program Pointer4;
type
   SqrPntr = ^Squares;
   Squares = array[ 1..100 ] of integer;
var
   index   : byte;
   Array1,
   Array2  : SqrPntr;
   Message : ^string;
```

Listing 6.5 continues

Listing 6.5 continued

```
begin
    GetMem( Array1, 10 );
    GetMem( Array2, 20 );
    New( Message );
    Message^ := 'This is the start of the program.';
    writeln( Message^ );
    Message^ := 'This is the terminating message line.  Good-bye.';
    writeln( 'The size of Array1 is ', SizeOf( Array1^ ) );
    writeln( 'The size of Array2 is ', SizeOf( Array2^ ) );
    for index := 1 to 20 do Array1^[ index ] := index * index;
    for index := 1 to 20 do Array2^[ index ] := index * index;
    for index := 1 to 15 do
        writeln( index:6, Array1^[ index ]:8 );
    writeln( Message^ );
    Dispose( Message );
    FreeMem( Array1, 10 );
    FreeMem( Array2, 20 );
end.
```

When POINTER4 executes, it generates the output shown in figure 6.3.

Fig. 6.3. Output produced by the POINTER4 program.

```
This is the start of the program.
The size of Array1 is 200
The size of Array2 is 200
     1       1
     2       4
     3       9
     4      16
     5      25
     6       1
     7       4
     8       9
     9      16
    10      25
    11      36
    12      49
    13      64
    14      81
    15     100
    É ┌ ─ ρ  ⊟!⊡D⊟¡⊡É⊟ting message line.  Good-bye.
    ⊟ ñµ?⊟???????PAS⊟ ↓A≤ é⊟ ↵►!!◄W⊟ ODD2.P
```

The garbage appears in the final message because memory sizes weren't properly tested. The GetMem allocation procedures

```
GetMem( Array1, 10 );
GetMem( Array2, 20 );
```

reserved 10 bytes and 20 bytes, respectively, for Array1 and Array2. Because both of these variables consist of arrays of integers, and integers are each two bytes in length, Array1 was effectively set to a size large enough to hold 5 integers, whereas Array2 was slightly larger with a 10-integer capacity.

When the first 20 integers in Array1 were initialized to the squares of the index, the first five elements fit comfortably inside the memory area allocated for Array1 in the heap, while the last 15 overflowed this area and began to fill up the heap memory area set aside for Array2. Then, when the first 20 integers in Array2 were initialized to the squares of the index, the first 10 elements fit inside the memory area allocated in the heap for Array2, while the last 10 overflowed this area and began to fill up the heap memory area set aside for the message.

The compiler never generated an error, because its syntax checking logic believed that the arrays were each 100 integers (200 bytes) long. Obviously, there's some danger in using GetMem and FreeMem, but there's also one major advantage. So long as you are willing to assume responsibility for range checking within the body of your program, you have complete control over the size of your data objects.

When memory is deallocated with the FreeMem procedure, the number of bytes specified must exactly match the number of bytes originally allocated with the GetMem call. If it doesn't, the wrong amount of memory will be returned to the heap for reuse, and the other pointers declared in your program will become fair game.

Pointer Operations

The only operations directly allowed on pointer variables are assignments and comparisons.

Assignments can only take place between pointers of compatible type. This can be accomplished by executing another New procedure, assigning the Nil value to the pointer, or setting the pointer equal to the address of another pointer of the same type.

Similarly, the equality and inequality operators (= and <>) can only be used on compatible pointer-type operands. When Turbo Pascal compares two pointers, it actually compares the segment and offset parts individually. (It's much more efficient for the compiler to test two word-sized pairs than to first compute and then compare two four-byte numbers.)

Because two logically different pointers can point to the same physical memory location, pointers returned by the New and GetMem procedures are always normalized. *Normalized* means that the compiler returns a segment value that's as large as possible to make the offset value 15 bytes or less, regardless of the actual content of the segment register that controls the address.

Linked Lists

Pointers offer several unique advantages over other data types. For example, the array structure has several limitations when used for list processing:

- ❏ The array has a fixed size regardless of the actual number of elements used and regardless of whether your program even needs the full size at any given time.
- ❏ The full size of the array consumes space in the data section of the program, regardless of how many elements are actually used and whether your program needs to use it at any given time.
- ❏ When an item is inserted into the middle of an array, every entry after the insertion point must be moved down toward the end of the array to make room for the new entry.
- ❏ When an entry is removed, every element after the removal point must be moved over toward the beginning of the array to fill the open space.

The linked list, one of the most common uses of pointers, sidesteps these limitations. If one of the fields of a record is a pointer to another record of the same type, several records can be linked together into a list, the size of which can be changed as records are added and deleted. You start with a pointer to the first record in the list; the pointer in the last record is set to Nil.

Setting the final pointer to Nil allows each record to be tested before it's processed. For example, given the following definitions:

```
type
    PtrType    = ^DataRecord;
    DataRecord = record
                    DataStuff : integer; { or real, or whatever }
                    NextPtr   : PtrType;
                 end;
```

the list can be written when the pointer to the first record is passed to the following procedure:

```
procedure WriteList( FirstPtr : PtrType );
var
   Scooter : PtrType;
begin
   Scooter := FirstPtr;
   while Scooter  <> Nil do begin
      writeln( Scooter^.DataStuff );
      Scooter := Scooter^.NextPtr;
   end;
end;
```

A linked list is actually an advanced data type and, as such, is not used during the remainder of this book. However, the following example introduces you to a simple but typical linked-list application.

The POINTER5 program in listing 6.6 clears the screen and lists the names of the files in the current subdirectory that have the extension .PAS. Essentially, POINTER5 produces an unsorted directory listing, similar to the sequence of the DOS DIR command.

Listing 6.6

```
program Pointer5;
uses Dos, Crt;
var
   FileInfo : SearchRec;
begin
   ClrScr;
   FindFirst( '*.PAS', AnyFile, FileInfo );
   while DosError = Ø do
      begin
         writeln( FileInfo.Name );
         FindNext( FileInfo );
      end;
end.
```

The FindFirst and FindNext procedures are discussed in more detail in Chapter 14.

The POINTER6 program in listing 6.7 begins with this same file-retrieval mechanism. However, as each file is read, the program maintains a linked list where each new record is inserted into the list based on the alphabetical sequence of the file names.

Listing 6.7

```
program Pointer6;
uses Dos, Crt;
type
   HeapRecordPtr = ^HeapRecord;
   HeapRecord = record
                   NextOne   : HeapRecordPtr;
                   DirRecord : SearchRec;
                end;
var
   FileInfo : SearchRec;
   Trace,
   First,
   Fresh,
   Prior    : HeapRecordPtr;
begin
   ClrScr;
   FindFirst( '*.pas', AnyFile, FileInfo );
   New( Fresh );                  { Create the last record              }
   Fresh^.NextOne := Nil;         { There's no record after the last one }
   First := Fresh;                { "First" points to the first record in }
                                  {    the list--namely, the last record }

   while DosError = Ø do
      begin
         Trace := First;          { Start search in first record in chain }
         Prior := Trace;          { Next record will be inserted        }
                                  {    between Prior and Trace           }
         while (Trace^.NextOne <> Nil) and
               (Trace^.DirRecord.Name < FileInfo.Name) do
            begin
               Prior := Trace;                { Move Prior over one      }
               Trace := Trace^.NextOne;       { Now move Trace over one }
            end;
         New( Fresh );                  { Reserve memory for the new record }
         if First = Trace then          { First record in list           }
            First := Fresh
         else                           { Insert between Prior and Trace  }
            Prior^.NextOne := Fresh;
         Fresh^.NextOne := Trace;            { Set new pointer field      }
         Fresh^.DirRecord := FileInfo;       { Set new data field         }
         writeln( FileInfo.Name );      { Write each record as it's read }
         FindNext( FileInfo );          { Retrieve the next record       }
      end;
   writeln( '----------------------------' );
   Trace := First;
   while Trace^.NextOne <> Nil do            { Write out the linked list }
      begin                                  {    in alphabetical order  }
         writeln( trace^.DirRecord.Name );
         First := Trace;
         Trace := Trace^.NextOne;
      end;
end.
```

When POINTER6 executes, it displays the names of all Turbo Pascal source files (actually, all files with the .PAS extension). The names are displayed twice. The first time, the names are in random order, in the same sequence as a DIR command. The second time, the names appear in alphabetical order.

The *Addr* Function and the @ Operator

Both the Addr function and the @ operator return the memory address of any data object, including variables, procedures, and functions. Like Nil, both Addr and @ are compatible with all pointer-type variables.

Preference of the @ Operator

The @ operator is functionally equivalent to the Addr function, but because of its greater economy, the @ form is preferred. The only real advantage of the Addr function is in maintaining compatibility with other Pascal compilers. If you plan to transfer your programs to another compiler—a process called *porting*—and that compiler doesn't recognize the @ operator, you can continue to use the Addr function. For the remainder of this book, however, only the @ operator will be shown.

When the @ operator is applied to a procedure, function, or global variable (or when it's applied to a local variable inside a procedure or function), the results are straightforward: @ returns a pointer to the memory address where the data item is stored.

The @ operator can also be applied to a parameter passed to a procedure or function. The mechanics are slightly different depending on whether the parameter is passed as a value parameter, as in:

```
procedure SampleProc1( Param1 : Anytype v );
```

or as a variable parameter, as in:

```
procedure SampleProc2( var Param2 : Anytype );
```

Value parameters are copied onto the stack. Variable parameters only have their addresses placed on the stack. The application of the @ operator to a parameter follows similar rules. Applying @ to a value parameter results in a pointer to the stack location containing the copy of the value. Applying @ to a variable parameter results in a pointer to the actual variable.

The PARMPASS program in listing 6.8 uses the TypicalProc procedure to demonstrate this difference. TypicalProc is declared with one variable parameter and one value parameter; the memory locations of these parameters are displayed when the procedure is invoked.

Listing 6.8

```
program ParmPass;
uses Crt;
var
    Var1,
    Var2  : byte;
procedure TypicalProc( var Param1 : byte;  Param2 : byte );
begin
    writeln( 'Param1 is at        ', Seg( Param1 ):8, Ofs( Param1 ):8 );
    writeln( 'Param2 is at        ', Seg( Param2 ):8, Ofs( Param2 ):8 );
end;
begin
    ClrScr;
    Var1 := 100;
    Var2 := 100;
    writeln( 'Code segment is at   ', CSeg:8 );
    writeln( 'Data segment is at   ', DSeg:8 );
    writeln( 'Stack segment is at ', SSeg:8 );
    writeln;
    writeln( 'Var1 is at           ', Seg( Var1 ):8, Ofs( Var1 ):8 );
    writeln( 'Var2 is at           ', Seg( Var2 ):8, Ofs( Var2 ):8 );
    TypicalProc( Var1, Var2 );
end.
```

When PARMPASS is executed, it produces the results shown in figure 6.4. Both global variables reside in the data segment. Notice how the memory location of the variable parameter is identical to the original global variable itself; the memory address of the value parameter, however, is somewhere in the stack segment.

Fig. 6.4. Output produced by the PARMPASS program.

```
Code segment is at      28648
Data segment is at      28717
Stack segment is at     28760

Var1 is at              28717       60
Var2 is at              28717       61
Param1 is at            28717       60
Param2 is at            28760    16376
```

Selecting Addresses

So far, whenever you have used a pointer, you haven't needed to worry about the area of memory it referenced. It's enough to know that the Turbo Pascal compiler always selects a safe place for the pointer in the heap. Every time you request another area of memory with New or GetMem, you can be sure that the new region won't overlap any other areas of memory that were allocated previously.

Sometimes, however, situations arise when you need to be able to read from (or write to) a *specific* area of memory. In this section, you will learn how Turbo Pascal enables you to select and use specific memory regions.

Creating Absolute Pointers

The Ptr function can be used to *create* a pointer to any desired memory location. Ptr accepts two parameters: The first specifies the segment, and the second specifies the offset within the segment. No specific data type is associated with the Ptr function, so you can use it with any pointer variable.

Every IBM-compatible PC uses certain memory regions for system control purposes. This is one of the reasons that DOS is able to run successfully on computers from different manufacturers. For example, the word beginning at $0040:$0013 contains the size of the PC's internal memory, in 1K blocks. This value, which is reset whenever the PC boots up, is freely available to any program that needs to know how much memory is installed in the machine.

You can read this value using the Ptr function, as demonstrated in the ABS0 program in listing 6.9.

Listing 6.9

```
program Abs0;
var
   MemorySize : ^word;
begin
   MemorySize := Ptr( $0040, $0013 );
   writeln( 'This PC has ', MemorySize^, 'K bytes of internal memory.' );
end.
```

Here, MemorySize is a variable, defined as a pointer to a word. Of course, the memory *location* of the variable should never change. MemorySize was intended to reference only one memory address, even though in using the compiler you could freely reassign it.

Overlaying Absolute Variables

You can restrict a variable to a specific memory address by declaring it with the reserved word absolute. Program ABS1 in listing 6.10 "freezes" the first byte of MemorySize at the absolute location $0040:$0013.

Listing 6.10

```
program Abs1;
var
   MemorySize : word absolute $0040:$0013;
begin
   writeln( 'This PC has ', MemorySize, 'K bytes of internal memory.' );
end.
```

In the ABS1 program, MemorySize is *not* a pointer. Rather, it's an ordinary word-sized variable that happens to be located at $0040:$0013 instead of somewhere in the data segment. There are no restrictions placed on its use. Consequently, if you change its contents with an ordinary assignment statement, such as:

```
MemorySize := 64;
```

then the next program that needs to know how much memory is in your PC will assume that 64K bytes are installed—regardless of the actual size. Obviously, the absolute clause and the Ptr function should only be used with extreme care.

Both the absolute clause and the Ptr function require you to know the exact segment and offset of the memory you want to reference. Absolute demands that you explicitly identify the location at compile time, whereas Ptr allows the location to be derived during execution. Absolute is used most often when you want to access those specific memory addresses used by the PC or DOS itself, as you did in the ABS1 program. Ptr is used most often when you want a single variable to access several different memory locations while a program is executing.

A third (and more common) situation arises when you want to reference the same program data item by two different names. The simplest solution is often to use a variant record, as demonstrated in the ABS2A program (listing 6.11).

Listing 6.11

```
program Abs2A;
type
   Combined = record
                 case integer of
                    1 : ( ByteForm : byte );
                    2 : ( CharForm : char )
              end;
var
   BC : Combined;
begin
   BC.ByteForm := $41;
   writeln( BC.ByteForm:5, BC.CharForm:5 );
end.
```

ABS2A defines its single variable, BC, as a variant record of the type Combined. The two components of Combined—ByteForm and CharForm—are both one byte long, and both refer to the same memory location. When the ByteForm field is used, the data item is treated as a simple number, from 0 through 255. When the CharForm field is used, the data item is treated as one of the 256 ASCII characters.

ABS2A begins by assigning the hexadecimal value $41 to the BC.ByteForm field. When the writeln procedure executes, ByteForm interprets $41 as the decimal value 65, whereas CharForm interprets $41 as the capital letter A.

In a similar way, Turbo allows a modified version of the absolute statement that accepts the name of a previously declared variable rather than a specific address. Program ABS2B in listing 6.12 shows how this form of the absolute directive can be used.

Listing 6.12

```
program Abs2B;
var
   ByteForm : byte;
   CharForm : char  absolute ByteForm;
begin
   for ByteForm := 65 to 77 do
      write( ByteForm:5 );
   writeln;
   for ByteForm := 65 to 77 do
      write( CharForm:5 );
   writeln;
   writeln;
   writeln;
   for ByteForm := 78 to 90 do
      write( ByteForm:5 );
   writeln;
   for ByteForm := 78 to 90 do
      write( CharForm:5 );
   writeln;
end.
```

Because `CharForm` is declared as being `absolute` to `ByteForm`, both variables begin at the same memory location, but both regard the data as having different types. When ABS2B executes, it produces the table of ASCII values shown in figure 6.5.

Fig. 6.5. Output produced by the ABS2B program.

65	66	67	68	69	70	71	72	73	74	75	76	77
A	B	C	D	E	F	G	H	I	J	K	L	M

78	79	80	81	82	83	84	85	86	87	88	89	90
N	O	P	Q	R	S	T	U	V	W	X	Y	Z

Variable Names As Memory References

Remember that to the Turbo Pascal compiler, every variable name is, itself, a memory reference. For example, when you write a statement such as:

```
A := B + C;
```

the compiler adds the value stored at memory location B to the value stored at memory location C, and moves the sum to the memory location of A.

Accessing Memory as an Array

All of the memory referencing techniques you have seen here so far allow access to only a single segment and offset address. As useful as they are, many applications require free access to large blocks of memory.

Turbo Pascal provides an extremely powerful method of memory management in the form of the predefined arrays `Mem`, `MemW`, and `MemL`. Each of these arrays treats the entire one megabyte internal memory of the PC as a single array. `Mem` is an array of bytes, `MemW` is an array of words, and `MemL` is an array of `longInts`.

All three arrays are one-dimensional, but each takes an index in segment:offset form—that is, a word-sized value representing a segment, followed by a colon (`:`), followed by another word-sized value representing the offset within the segment.

The ABS3 program in listing 6.13 uses the Mem array to access the byte at $0040:$0049, which contains information on the type of display adapter installed in your PC. If the byte contains the number 7, the display is monochrome. Every other value represents one of the possible color adapters.

Listing 6.13

```
program Abs3;
function ScreenIsInColorMode : Boolean;
begin
   if Mem[ $0040 : $0049 ] = 7 then
      ScreenIsInColorMode := False
   else
      ScreenIsInColorMode := True;
end;
begin
   case ScreenIsInColorMode of
      True  : writeln( 'Color Adapter Card Installed' );
      False : writeln( 'Monochrome Display Adapter Installed' );
   end;
end.
```

The ABS3 program might detect a color adapter card even if you have only a monochrome screen. Most COMPAQ® portables, for example, are equipped with screens that display individual colors as different shades of green.

Throughout this book, I use the Mem array extensively to develop powerful system-level applications. A short example can be found in the ABS4 program in listing 6.14.

Listing 6.14

```
program Abs4;
uses Printer;
var
   Row, Column,
   SegmentNumber : word;
function VideoSegment : word;
begin
   if Mem[ $0040 : $0049 ] = 7 then
      VideoSegment := $B000
   else
      VideoSegment := $B800;
end;
begin
   SegmentNumber := VideoSegment;
   for Row := 0 to 24 do begin
      for Column := 0 to 79 do
         write( Lst, chr( Mem[ SegmentNumber : 2*Column + 160*Row ] ) );
      writeln( Lst );
   end;
   write( Lst, #12 );
end.
```

The operation of ABS4 is similar to the hardware "Print Screen" function on your PC. When you press Shift-PrtSc, the current screen image is listed on your system printer. When you execute ABS4, the program itself causes the screen image to print. The program first tests the memory location at $0040:$0049 to determine whether a monochrome or color graphics display adapter is installed. Monochrome adapters store data in segment $B000, whereas color adapters use segment $B800. Once the video memory segment is known, ABS4 outputs its contents to the system printer.

A complete discussion of video memory can be found in Chapter 10. For now, it's enough to accept many of the features of the ABS4 program on faith.

Memory Use

The memory map of a Turbo Pascal program is shown in figure 6.6.

The major components of memory are discussed here. The final two sections, "Determining the Size of the Heap" and "The Heap Error Function," are *advanced* topics presented as reference material only. Feel free to skip these sections if you wish.

The Program Segment Prefix

The Program Segment Prefix (PSP) is a 256-byte area established by MS-DOS when the .EXE file is loaded. It contains information needed by the operating system to transfer control of the computer to the program in order for it to run, and it contains information needed to return control to the operating system once the program finishes. The segment address of the PSP is stored in the predeclared word PrefixSeg. The Program Segment Prefix is discussed in greater detail in Chapter 12.

The Code Region

The instructions in each Turbo Pascal unit are placed in separate code segments. In other words, the CS register is changed depending on whether the currently executing code is from the main program or from one of the separate units. (Units are discussed in greater detail in Chapter 7.)

The individual code segments are placed in sequence: the main program occupies the first segment, whereas the code segments that follow it are occupied by the individual unit code in reverse order from how they are listed in the uses clause of the main program. The last code segment is occupied by the run-time library—that is, the System unit.

Fig. 6.6. *The memory map of a Turbo Pascal program.*

Any number of code segments may exist (up to the available memory of the system) but the size of an individual code segment cannot exceed 64K. Notice that even when separate modules aren't used (that is, when no uses clause exists), the program incorporates at least two code segments.

The Data Region

Although program code may occupy as many segments as necessary, program data (consisting of all typed constants followed by all global variables) must reside completely within a single segment; the DS register is never changed during program execution. Hence, programs that require more than the maximum 64K data area must rely on dynamically allocated memory in the heap.

The Stack Region

Like the data area, the stack segment also cannot exceed 64K; the SS register is never changed during program execution. When the program begins, the stack segment register (SS) and the stack pointer (SP) are loaded so that SS:SP points to the first byte past the stack segment. The stack grows downward, meaning that as a new variable is placed on the stack, the SP register points to lower and lower memory locations depending on the variable's size.

The Heap Region

The heap is the area of memory set aside for dynamic variable allocation. It can conceivably use all of the memory remaining in a PC after the program is loaded.

The heap is also the region of memory where the overlay buffer, discussed in Chapter 15, and the graphics buffer, discussed in Chapter 11, reside.

Although the size requirements for the code and data segments are known during compilation, the size of the stack and heap can only be determined approximately, because they depend upon the exact use of the program. Consequently, *ranges* of memory can be specified with the {$M} compiler directive. The default stack size is 16K. By default, the heap will occupy all remaining memory.

The pointer to the bottom of the heap is stored in the variable HeapOrg, which stays unchanged during program execution. The pointer to the top of the heap is stored in the variable HeapPtr, which moves upward by the size of each dynamic variable allocated by the New or GetMem procedures.

The Free List

When the Dispose or FreeMem procedure is used to free up a dynamic variable other than the last one allocated, gaps of free memory are created within the heap, causing *memory fragmentation*. The addresses and sizes of these free blocks are kept on a *free list*, an area within the heap that grows downward from high memory. The free list begins at the memory location pointed to by FreePtr. The variable FreeMin can be set to control the minimum allowable distance between HeapPtr and FreePtr.

If any deallocation frees up an area bordering on another unassigned region, the free list entry for the unassigned region is modified to encompass the complete free zone. Each block of free heap space is defined by a single free list entry.

Whenever a dynamic variable is allocated, the free list is checked before the heap is expanded. If the compiler finds a large enough block of free memory, it gets used before any new space is apportioned.

The Release procedure clears all memory between the address of its pointer argument and the address pointed to by HeapPtr. Because this process destroys the free list, it is never a good idea to mix calls to Mark and Release with calls to Dispose and FreeMem.

Determining the Size of the Heap

To find out the true memory availability of the heap, Turbo provides the MaxAvail and MemAvail functions. MaxAvail returns a value equal to the largest *single* free block of space in the heap. MemAvail returns a value equal to the *sum* of all free blocks in the heap.

Of course, if you never deallocated any heap space, or if you only deallocated memory at the top of the heap, MaxAvail and MemAvail return the same value. Conversely, after you Dispose of memory in the middle of the heap, MemAvail may not represent a meaningful value, especially if you're using pointers to data objects of different sizes.

This can be demonstrated by the POINTER7 program (listing 6.15).

Listing 6.15

```
program Pointer7;
type
   WastedArray = array[ 1..100 ] of real;
var
   index : byte;
   NumberList : array[ 1..100 ] of ^WastedArray;
   OriginalMemAvail : longint;
   OriginalMaxAvail : longint;
begin
   OriginalMemAvail := MemAvail;
   OriginalMaxAvail := MaxAvail;
   writeln( 'Allocating...' );
   for index := 1 to 10 do begin
      New( NumberList[ index ] );
      writeln( index:3,
               MemAvail:10, MaxAvail:10,
               (OriginalMemAvail - MemAvail):10,
               (OriginalMaxAvail - MaxAvail):10 );
   end;
```

Listing 6.15 *continues*

Listing 6.15 *continued*

```
    writeln( 'Deallocating...' );
    for index := 2 to 9 do begin
{
        if index mod 3 = Ø then
}
            Dispose( NumberList[ index ] );
        writeln( index:3,
                 MemAvail:1Ø, MaxAvail:1Ø,
                 (OriginalMemAvail - MemAvail):1Ø,
                 (OriginalMaxAvail - MaxAvail):1Ø );
    end;
    writeln( 'Final results:' );
    writeln( '   MemAvail is ', MemAvail );
    writeln( '   MaxAvail is ', MaxAvail );
end.
```

The results of the execution of POINTER7 are shown in figure 6.7.

Fig. 6.7. *Output produced by the POINTER7 program, with only one memory "hole."*

```
Allocating...
    1    177544    177544     600     600
    2    176944    176944    1200    1200
    3    176344    176344    1800    1800
    4    175744    175744    2400    2400
    5    175144    175144    3000    3000
    6    174544    174544    3600    3600
    7    173944    173944    4200    4200
    8    173344    173344    4800    4800
    9    172744    172744    5400    5400
   10    172144    172144    6000    6000
Deallocating...
    2    172736    172136    5400    6000
    3    173336    172136    4800    6000
    4    173936    172136    4200    6000
    5    174536    172136    3600    6000
    6    175136    172136    3000    6000
    7    175736    172136    2400    6000
    8    176336    172136    1800    6000
    9    176936    172136    1200    6000
Final results:
    MemAvail is 176936
    MaxAvail is 172136
```

First, the available heap space decreases as 10 new arrays are allocated. Next, the middle eight arrays are returned to the heap, leaving a "hole" of increasing size as more memory frees up. There are, in effect, two blocks of memory available, separated by a single array.

The eight-byte discrepancy between the two sets of numbers is caused by the free-list record defining the boundaries of the available gap. The eight bytes consist of two four-byte pointers: one for the top of the block, and one for the bottom. To illustrate, if the commenting braces around the statement

```
if index mod 3 = Ø then
```

are removed, the program produces the results shown in figure 6.8.

Fig. 6.8. Output produced by the POINTER7 program, with three memory "holes."

```
Allocating...
    1    177528      177528       600        600
    2    176928      176928      1200       1200
    3    176328      176328      1800       1800
    4    175728      175728      2400       2400
    5    175128      175128      3000       3000
    6    174528      174528      3600       3600
    7    173928      173928      4200       4200
    8    173328      173328      4800       4800
    9    172728      172728      5400       5400
   10    172128      172128      6000       6000
Deallocating...
    2    172128      172128      6000       6000
    3    172720      172120      5408       6008
    4    172720      172120      5408       6008
    5    172720      172120      5408       6008
    6    173312      172112      4816       6016
    7    173312      172112      4816       6016
    8    173312      172112      4816       6016
    9    173904      172104      4224       6024
Final results:
   MemAvail is 173904
   MaxAvail is 172104
```

Notice that every time a free block is created, Turbo adds another eight-byte free record to the heap.

The Heap Error Function

It's far better to retain control of a program than for it to terminate with a run-time error. For example, within a spreadsheet program where the value of each cell is dynamically allocated, the typical user would prefer to see an Insufficient Memory message and have the opportunity to save the current file rather than to watch helplessly while the program ends with a Turbo system message and the consequent loss of several hours of work.

When New or GetMem encounters any memory allocation problem, the procedure immediately calls the Turbo Pascal heap error function. If the heap error function itself is unable to resolve the problem, New or GetMem simply terminates the program with a run-time error.

You can install your own customized version of the heap error function by assigning its address to the predefined HeapError pointer variable, as follows:

```
HeapError := @HeapFunc;
```

The syntax of the default heap error function is as follows:

```
{$F +}   function HeapFunc( Size : word ) : integer;   {$F-}
```

Your HeapError function must obey the same structure. Remember that the default heap error function resides in the Turbo Pascal System unit—a different code segment than the one that contains your program. Consequently, the {$F +} compiler directive forces HeapError to use the far call model, which creates the proper pointer format.

The Size parameter contains the size of the allocation request that generated the error. The default Turbo Pascal heap error function would try to find Size bytes of free memory. Your function should be less ambitious and settle for providing a means to terminate the program gracefully without causing it to abort uncontrollably.

Both New and GetMem expect one of the following return values from the heap error function:

0   Failure. A run-time error occurs immediately.

1   Failure. No run-time error is generated; rather, the New or GetMem procedure is forced to return a Nil pointer.

2   Success. The originating New or GetMem procedure is tried once again. Note, however, that another call to the heap error function could result, so some code must be provided to prevent the program from locking up.

The standard heap error function always returns 0, which triggers a run-time error. If, instead, your customized heap error function always returns a value of 1, your program can test the results of every call to New and GetMem to see if Nil is returned. If so, you know that the allocation was unsuccessful and you can provide a harmless way for the program to end.

The MEMORY2 program (listing 6.16) demonstrates how this works.

Listing 6.16

```
program Memory2;
uses Crt;
type
    BigArray = array[ 1..10000 ] of integer;
var
    Pntr : ^BigArray;
    Counter : word;
{$F + }
function HeapFunc( Size : word ) : Integer;
begin
    writeln( 'Error in attempt to allocate ', Size, ' bytes on the heap' );
    HeapFunc := 1;
end;
{$F- }
begin
    ClrScr;
    HeapError := @HeapFunc;
    Counter := 0;
    repeat
        New( Pntr );
        Counter := Counter + 1;
        writeln( 'Allocation number ', Counter );
    until Pntr = Nil;
    writeln( 'Ending program' );
end.
```

When MEMORY2 executes, it generates the results shown in figure 6.9.

Fig. 6.9. *Output produced by the MEMORY2 program.*

```
Allocation number 1
Allocation number 2
Allocation number 3
Allocation number 4
Allocation number 5
Allocation number 6
Allocation number 7
Allocation number 8
Error in attempt to allocate 20000 bytes on the heap
Allocation number 9
Ending program
```

Note that the failure of the New procedure triggered the call to HeapError, but once it executed, the program returned control to the statement following New.

Summary

In this chapter, you have learned the general structure and operation of PC memory, and you have seen the specific memory-management tools available in Turbo Pascal.

You have learned how the segment registers allow the CPU to simultaneously access different memory regions. You have seen how to identify the segment and offset of any Turbo Pascal data object, and you have learned how to position variables in any desired memory location.

You have learned how the unused portion of PC memory, called the heap, is available for you program to use for data storage. You have learned how Turbo Pascal manages heap memory, and you have seen how to recover from heap errors. You have learned how heap memory can be allocated and deallocated and how it can be accessed with pointers.

7

Units

A *program* is the main module of Turbo Pascal source code that you write and execute. A *unit* is simply a collection of subroutines that the program can invoke; but the unit is physically compiled, stored, loaded into memory, and accessed independently of the program itself.

Prior to the release of Version 4.0, Turbo Pascal required all program code to fit within a single 64K segment. Programs consisting of many small, relatively independent components could circumvent this restriction by being developed as chain files or overlays. However, many other programs—generally, the more sophisticated applications—simply couldn't be conveniently designed in such a format.

Units broke the 64K barrier. Because there's no limit to the number of units your program uses, and each unit is loaded into its own memory segment, your applications are limited only by the size of memory in your machine.

And as if this isn't enough, units offer several other administrative advantages:

- ❏ Units allow each program component to be developed, tested, and debugged independently.

- ❏ Programs incorporating units don't always need to be completely recompiled every time they're used or modified.

- ❏ Units enable you to build a library of precompiled, tested code that you can easily incorporate in any program.

This chapter explains what a unit is and how units are used. It also discusses the standard units available in Turbo Pascal. Finally, it discusses how you can develop and manage your own units.

Standard Units

Turbo Pascal supports over 200 procedures and functions, together with dozens of lower-level instructions, such as addition and set membership. Instead of including the machine code for every one of these operations in every program you compile, Turbo stores the subroutines in eight *standard units*.

The eight standard units are as follows:

Crt	Display and keyboard support
Dos	Use general DOS functions
Graph	Use graphics support
Graph3	Implement Turbo Pascal 3.0 Turtlegraphics
Overlay	Implement the overlay manager
Printer	Access the printer
System	Use Turbo Pascal's run-time library
Turbo3	Maintain compatibility with Turbo Pascal 3.0

The Graph unit resides in the GRAPH.TPU file. The Turbo3 and Graph3 units reside in the TURBO3.TPU and GRAPH3.TPU files, respectively. All other standard units reside in the TURBO.TPL library file. Each unit in a library can be extracted selectively by the compiler and merged, or *linked*, with your program as needed. Whenever you compile a program, Turbo automatically accesses the TURBO.TPL file and pulls out the routines it requires. This is why the installation procedures in Chapter 1 told you to place the TURBO.TPL file in the same directory as the compiler itself.

Crt and Dos versus CRT and DOS

Crt and Dos (with only the first letter capitalized) refer to the Crt and Dos standard units. CRT and DOS (with all capital letters) refer to cathode-ray tube and disk operating system, respectively.

Using a Standard Unit

Even though five of the standard units (System, Crt, Dos, Printer, and Overlay) physically reside in the same library file (TURBO.TPL), Turbo Pascal treats each unit as a unique entity and, except for the System unit, accesses each unit only when you specifically direct the program to do so. For example, if your program uses a routine in the Crt unit, then you *must* include a uses clause immediately after the program header, as follows:

```
uses Crt;
```

If you want to access data objects in more than one unit, name each one in the uses clause. Separate each name with a comma, and terminate the final name with a semicolon. For example, if you need both the Crt and the Dos units, the clause should appear as follows:

```
uses Crt, Dos;
```

The System unit is the only exception. The compiler *always* accesses the System unit because it contains the most frequently used data objects required by literally every program you write.

As you can see, the standard units may be an efficient way to store Turbo Pascal code and data, but standard units are not automatically accessed. Remember that it's *your* responsibility to tell the compiler which units to use. Turbo's first assumption is that every data object used in your program is defined within the System unit or within the program itself. Failure to include the proper uses clause usually results in an Unknown identifier error.

To help you avoid such problems, your Turbo Pascal distribution disks contain a documentation (.DOC) file for each one of the standard units. Every procedure and function header, and every global type, constant, and variable are listed. You may wish to print these files out and keep them nearby for ready reference. In addition, each procedure and function description in the Turbo Pascal *Reference Guide* (and in the reference section at the end of this book) indicates the unit that contains it.

The System Unit

The *System unit* contains Turbo Pascal's run-time library, which includes every one of Turbo's standard built-in procedures and functions. Essentially, the System unit contains everything needed to support every *standard* procedure, function, or operation. In other words, whatever the compiler needs to produce a basic, no-frills program can be found there.

Because the System unit is required by every application you write, it need not be directly declared in your program. The System unit is automatically linked with your code during compilation.

The Dos Unit

The *Dos unit* provides excellent system-level support for all of the most commonly used DOS functions. These include routines for the system date and time, directory search, and file handling. The Dos unit contains the majority of the Turbo Pascal product enhancements; in fact, none of its procedures or functions is considered part of standard Pascal.

The VERSION program (listing 7.1) demonstrates how the Dos unit can be used. DosVersion is a function contained in the Dos unit that returns a word containing the version number of the operating system currently running on your machine. The major number (the 2 in 2.10) is returned in the low byte, and the minor number (the 10 in 2.10) is in the high byte.

Listing 7.1

```
program Version;
uses Dos;                  { Accesses the Dos unit }
var
   Level : word;           { Defines a word-sized work variable }
begin
   Level := DosVersion;    { Gets the current version number }
   writeln( 'Your machine is currently running DOS Version ',
            Lo( Level ),    { Low byte contains the major number }
            '.',
            Hi( Level ) )   { High byte contains the minor number }
end.
```

The following is typical of the output of the VERSION program:

```
Your machine is currently running DOS Version 2.10
```

The Crt Unit

The *Crt unit* includes sophisticated screen and keyboard management functions. Normally, Turbo Pascal programs use standard DOS routines for all input and output operations. Although this ensures that your programs can run successfully on PCs from almost every manufacturer, the reliance on DOS adds considerable system overhead. Use of the Crt unit enables your program to bypass DOS and directly access the low-level BIOS routines and video memory in your machine. Use of the Crt unit must be restricted to programs that run on IBM PCs, ATs, PS/2s, and true compatibles.

The CRTOUT program (listing 7.2) demonstrates the use of the Crt unit. It clears the screen, positions the cursor in the center of the display, then writes the Hello, world! message.

Listing 7.2

```
program CrtOut;
uses Crt;                         { Accesses the Crt unit }
begin
    ClrScr;                       { Clears the screen }
    GotoXY( 34, 12 );             { Positions the cursor }
    write( 'Hello, world!' )      { Displays the Hello message }
end.
```

The Printer Unit

The *Printer unit* has only one purpose: it defines the file Lst and assigns it to your system printer. Well, technically, it assigns the file to your LPT1 device, which is *most likely* your system printer. Therefore, a program that uses this unit allows write and writeln statements specifying the Lst file to output directly to the printer.

The PRINTOUT program (listing 7.3) demonstrates the use of the Printer unit. It prints the Hello, world! message followed by a form feed.

Listing 7.3

```
program PrintOut;
uses Printer;                          { Accesses the Printer unit }
begin
    write( Lst, 'Hello, world!'#12 )   { Prints out the message and }
                                       { triggers a form feed (#12) }
end.
```

The Overlay Unit

The *Overlay unit* contains the code to support the use of Turbo Pascal's overlay management system. Overlays are sections of a single program that execute at different times and consequently can occupy—or *overlay*—the same physical memory area when they run. With overlays, a large program can utilize the smallest possible internal memory.

The ADDUP2 and USEADD2 programs (listings 7.4 and 7.5) demonstrate the use of the overlay unit. ADDUP2 is the component being overlaid. ADDUP2 is stored in a separate file and is compiled independently to the disk. USEADD2 is the calling program.

Listing 7.4

```
unit AddUp2;
{$O +,F +}
interface
   function WastefulAdd( Var1, Var2 : word ) : word;
implementation
   function WastefulAdd;
   begin
      WastefulAdd := Var1 + Var2
   end;
end.
```

Listing 7.5

```
program UseAdd2;
{$F +}
uses Overlay, AddUp2;
{$O AddUp2}
begin
   OvrInit( 'UseAdd2.OVR' );
   writeln( WastefulAdd( 5, 6 ) )
end.
```

Overlays are discussed in greater detail in Chapter 15.

The Graph Unit

The *Graph unit* is a sophisticated library of over 50 separate graphics routines that can be run on a wide variety of machines. Because of the size and complexity of its procedures and functions, the Graph unit is contained in its own file, GRAPH.TPU, separate from the other standard units. When Turbo compiles a graphics program, it accesses both TURBO.TPL and GRAPH.TPU, as well as one of the graphics driver files—that is, one of the files with the extension .BGI. In addition, if special display fonts are required, one or more of the .CHR files must also be accessible.

The BALLOON program (listing 7.6) demonstrates how you can use the Graph unit. The program draws circles of increasing diameter, giving the illusion of an inflating balloon. When you run it within the integrated environment, you even experience a "pop" when the program terminates. (Note that the InitGraph procedure assumes that your graphics files are in the C:\TP directory; you may need to modify this parameter based on your own configuration.)

Listing 7.6

```
program Balloon;
uses Graph;                            { Accesses the Graph unit }
var
   Driver,                             { Graphics driver type }
   Mode   : integer;                   { Graphics mode type }
   i      : word;
begin
   Driver := Detect;                   { Identify the graphics driver }
   InitGraph( Driver, Mode, 'C:\TP' ); { Initiate graphics }
   for i := 1 to 100 do
      Circle( 250, 100, i );           { Blow up the balloon }
   CloseGraph;
end.
```

Graphics routines are discussed in greater detail in Chapter 11.

Compatibility with Earlier Versions of Turbo Pascal

Borland has substantially enhanced Turbo Pascal since Version 3.0 was first introduced. Version 5.0, for example, is an order of magnitude more sophisticated than its grandfather product. As a result of these improvements, a program written with an earlier version of the compiler may not be completely compatible with the latest release.

The Turbo3 unit and Graph3 unit are included to improve the *downward compatibility* with the earlier code. If you have any problems compiling a program written with an earlier version of Turbo Pascal, you *might* be able to use the Turbo3 and Graph3 units to avoid rewriting major portions of the code.

The Turbo3 Unit

The *Turbo3 unit* includes variables and procedures that have ceased to be supported or have been substantially modified since Version 3.0 was introduced. The procedures included in the Turbo3 unit principally involve keyboard handling, screen display, and some minor I/O routines.

If you have trouble compiling a program written in an earlier version of Turbo Pascal, add the following line after the program header:

```
uses Turbo3;
```

Note that some program modifications may still be necessary. Consult the Turbo Pascal *User's Guide* and *Reference Guide* for further details.

The Graph3 Unit

The *Graph3 unit* implements the full set of Turbo Pascal Version 3.0 graphics, including Turtlegraphics.

If you have trouble compiling a graphics program written in an earlier version of Turbo Pascal, follow these steps:

1. Remove the {$I GRAPH.P} compiler directive in the older code.

2. If only the graphics routines are causing the compile-time or run-time errors, add the following line after the program header:

   uses Graph3;

3. If other procedures have also changed, use the following line instead:

   uses Turbo3, Graph3;

Remember: Use only the Graph unit—not the Graph3 unit—in future programs.

The Structure of a Unit

Each unit has four components—header, interface, implementation, and initialization—arranged as shown here:

```
unit identifier;

interface
uses list-of-units;    { Optional }
    { Public declarations of constants, types, and variables }
    { intended to be accessible to the user of the unit, plus }
    { the headings of all public subroutines.                }

implementation
uses list-of-units;    { Optional }

    { Private declarations of constants, types, and variables }
    { intended to be inaccessible to the user of the unit,     }
    { including all private procedures and functions in their }
    { entirety, and the bodies of all subroutines declared in  }
    { the interface section.                                   }
begin
    { Optional initialization statements                       }
end.
```

Let's consider each section individually.

The Heading

Every unit begins with a *unit header* similar in format to a program header. As an example, the first line of a unit named Trig would appear as follows:

```
unit Trig;
```

The presence of the reserved word unit tells the compiler two things:

1. The file *is* a unit, so it contains interface and implementation sections.

2. When the unit is compiled, its output file should have the extension .TPU rather than .EXE.

The Interface

The interface section declares every data object—that is, every constant, type, variable, procedure, and function—that you want the unit to share with any program or unit that calls it. Labels can't be declared because the target label of a goto statement must be in the same block as the goto statement itself.

Only the headers of the procedures and functions need to be declared. Other programs need to know the types of the parameters and functions but not their innermost details. The bodies of the subroutines are defined later in the implementation section.

If the unit needs to use another unit and you wish the other unit to also be available to the calling program, then that other unit is declared in a uses clause at the beginning of the interface section.

The Implementation

The implementation section is the meat of the unit. It contains all of the procedures and functions that make the unit useful, including the bodies of the subroutines whose headings were previously declared in the interface section.

Any constant, type, or variable declared in the interface is automatically available to the code in the implementation section. Additional private declarations can be made in the implementation section, but they will be local to the unit itself.

If the unit needs to use another unit and you don't wish the other unit to automatically be available to the calling program, then that other unit is declared in a uses clause at the beginning of the implementation section.

The Initialization

Most units are passive; they store procedures and functions and wait to be called by the host program. Some units, however, require variables to be initialized or require some code to be executed (such as opening a file) before the unit can be used.

Turbo Pascal provides a means for a unit to execute an opening set of instructions, called *initialization code*, before the first statement in the main program is executed. Simply place all initialization code at the end of the implementation section and preface the statements with the reserved word begin.

Initialization code is optional. The presence of the word begin tells the compiler to perform an initialization; if no begin statement is present, no initialization occurs.

If the main program uses several units, each unit is initialized in the order in which it is declared in the uses clause.

Developing Your Own Units

Now that you have seen the components of an individual unit, it's time to see how units and programs work together.

A program uses the subroutines in a unit in the same manner as it uses a forward procedure or function. The program doesn't care where the subroutine resides or when it's defined as long as the header is declared.

Suppose that you create a simple addition function called Adder, as follows:

```
function Adder( Var1, Var2 : word ) : word;
begin
   Adder := Var1 + Var2
end;
```

Suppose further that because of its general usefulness, you decide to turn it into a unit called ADDUP (listing 7.7).

Listing 7.7.

```
unit AddUp;
interface
    function Adder( Var1, Var2 : word ) : word;
implementation
    function Adder;
    begin
        Adder := Var1 + Var2
    end;
end.
```

Once the ADDUP unit is compiled to disk, the Adder function becomes available to any program that calls for it. One such program is USEADDER (listing 7.8).

Listing 7.8.

```
program UseAdder;
uses AddUp;
begin
    writeln( Adder( 5, 6 ) )
end.
```

Because USEADDER includes the uses AddUp directive, the Adder function is available just as if it had been declared within the USEADDER program itself.

Conceptually, a unit and its calling program fit together like a lock and key. Figure 7.1 shows the combination of the USEADDER program and the ADDUP unit.

The following sections discuss the rules of creating and using your own units.

Using a Unit

You can use a custom unit in the same way you use the predefined ones—by declaring it in a uses clause in the main program. If several units are to be accessed, each name in the uses clause is separated by a comma. The final unit is terminated with a semicolon.

When the main program is compiled, Turbo looks for every unit named in the uses clause. It assumes that the name of the unit file is the same as the name of the specified unit but with the .TPU extension. Suppose that the compiler sees the following declaration in the main program:

```
uses FileA, FileB;
```

Turbo Pascal assumes that the code for the units is contained in the files FileA.TPU and FileB.TPU, respectively.

Fig. 7.1. The combination of the USEADDER program and the ADDUP unit.

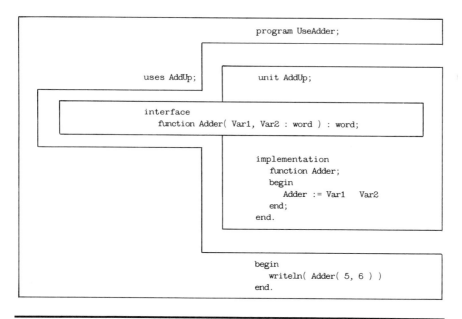

```
                                    program UseAdder;


       uses AddUp;              unit AddUp;

              interface
                 function Adder( Var1, Var2 : word ) : word;


                              implementation
                                 function Adder;
                                 begin
                                    Adder := Var1    Var2
                                 end;
                              end.



                              begin
                                 writeln( Adder( 5, 6 ) )
                              end.
```

Writing Units

Although capable of doing almost anything a regular program can do, a unit is primarily used to hold general-purpose procedures and functions that you want to access from several different programs. Alternatively, a large program may use units to collect related code segments that—as units—operate independently of each other.

Believe it or not, because of the similarities that a unit shares with a program, creating a unit is a simple, almost mechanical process. To prove this point, the following is a set of rules for you to follow.

1. Begin with the unit skeleton presented earlier. The unit header (the reserved word *unit* followed by an identifier) is placed in the first line.

2. Identify all *public* data objects—all *global* constants, types, variables, procedures, and functions—contained in the unit and declare them within the interface section. If any global data objects require the use of another unit, then that other unit must be named in a uses statement at the beginning of the interface section.

3. Identify all *private* data objects—all *local* constants, types, variables, procedures, and functions—and include them within the implementation section. In addition, include the code for the global procedures and functions you declared in the interface section. If any local data objects require the use of a unit not already identified in the interface section, then that other unit must be named in a uses statement at the beginning of the implementation section.

4. If the unit contains any initialization code (most units won't have any), place the initialization code just before the final end statement in the file, then segregate the code from the rest of the implementation section by placing a begin statement before its first line.

5. Save the unit to disk.

6. Compile the unit to disk. Even though a unit is entered, debugged, and compiled just like a program, it cannot be directly *run*. Instead, the unit must be made available to other programs by being compiled to disk with the Compile/Destination disk option discussed in Chapter 1. Turbo Pascal automatically assigns the .TPU extension to the file name of a compiled unit.

Unfortunately, describing how to create a unit is a bit like describing a spiral staircase without using your hands; it's much easier to point to an example.

Example 1: Trigonometric Functions

The only trigonometric functions defined by Turbo Pascal are Sin, Cos, and ArcTan. Fortunately, these functions can be combined to derive any other trigonometric value.

For example, the Trigs unit contains derived tangent, secant, cosecant, and cotangent functions. As you read the following steps to create the unit, refer to its final form in listing 7.9.

1. Begin the unit with the header:

    unit Trigs;

2. Because the tan, sec, csc, and cot functions are public, insert their headers into the interface section, as shown. No other data objects are global, and no other units are required, so you do not need to make additional entries.

3. Insert the bodies of the four functions into the implementation section. Because their complete headers appeared in the interface section, you don't need to declare their parameters and return types. However,

you can include the information here as comments to improve overall program documentation.

4. No initialization code is required, so the unit is complete.

5. Save the unit as TRIGS.PAS.

6. Compile the unit to disk, as shown in figure 7.2.

Fig. 7.2. Compile the TRIGS.PAS unit to disk.

```
   File    Edit    Run    Compile    Options    Debug    Break/watch

      Line 1      Col 1   Compile   Alt-F9              :TRIGS.PAS
unit Trigs;                Make           F9
                          Build
interface                 Destination        Disk
                          Find error
function tan( Radians : r  Primary file:
function sec( Radians : r  Get info
function csc( Radians : r
function cot( Radians : real ) : real;    { cotangent }

implementation

function tan { ( Radians : real ) : real };    { tangent }
var
   cosine : real;
begin
   cosine := cos( Radians );
   if abs( cosine ) <= 0.001 then
      tan := 99999.999999
                          ─────── Watch ───────

F1-Help  F5-Zoom  F6-Switch  F7-Trace  F8-Step  F9-Make  F10-Menu
```

Listing 7.9

```
unit Trigs;

interface
   function tan( Radians : real ) : real;    { tangent }
   function sec( Radians : real ) : real;    { secant }
   function csc( Radians : real ) : real;    { cosecant }
   function cot( Radians : real ) : real;    { cotangent }

implementation
   function tan { ( Radians : real ) : real };    { tangent }
   var
      cosine : real;
```

Listing 7.9 continues

Listing 7.9 continued

```
begin
   cosine := cos( Radians );
   if abs( cosine )  <= 0.001 then
      tan := 99999.999999
   else
      tan := sin( Radians ) / cosine;
end;

function sec { ( Radians : real ) : real };    { secant }
var
   cosine : real;
begin
   cosine := cos( Radians );
   if abs( cosine )  <= 0.001 then
      sec := 99999.999999
   else
      sec := 1.0 / cosine;
end;

function csc { ( Radians : real ) : real };    { cosecant }
var
   sine : real;
begin
   sine := sin( Radians );
   if abs( sine ) <= 0.001 then
      csc := 99999.999999
   else
      csc := 1.0 / sine;
end;

function cot { ( Radians : real ) : real };    { cotangent }
var
   sine : real;
begin
   sine := sin( Radians );
   if abs( sine )  <= 0.001 then
      cot := 99999.999999
   else
      cot := cos( Radians ) / sine;
end;

end.
```

The USETRIGS program (listing 7.10) demonstrates how simple it is to use the Trigs unit. USETRIGS contains a uses clause similar in format to one you would use to access a standard unit. No other special conditions apply. The output of USETRIGS is shown in figure 7.3. Notice how the number 99999.999999 is used to avoid division by zero.

Listing 7.10

```
program UseTrigs;
uses Trigs;
var
   Degrees : word;
   Radians : real;
begin
   writeln( 'Degs         Sin         Cos         Tan',
            '             Sec         Csc         Cot' );
   writeln;
   for Degrees := 0 to 20 do begin
      Radians := (5*Degrees) * Pi / 180.0;
      writeln( (5*Degrees):4, '  ',
               sin( Radians ):12:6,
               cos( Radians ):12:6,
               tan( Radians ):12:6,
               sec( Radians ):12:6,
               csc( Radians ):12:6,
               cot( Radians ):12:6 );
   end;
end.
```

Fig. 7.3. Output produced by the USETRIGS program.

Degs	Sin	Cos	Tan	Sec	Csc	Cot
0	0.000000	1.000000	0.000000	1.000000	99999.999999	99999.999999
5	0.087156	0.996195	0.087489	1.003820	11.473713	11.430052
10	0.173648	0.984808	0.176327	1.015427	5.758770	5.671282
15	0.258819	0.965926	0.267949	1.035276	3.863703	3.732051
20	0.342020	0.939693	0.363970	1.064178	2.923804	2.747477
25	0.422618	0.906308	0.466308	1.103378	2.366202	2.144507
30	0.500000	0.866025	0.577350	1.154701	2.000000	1.732051
35	0.573576	0.819152	0.700208	1.220775	1.743447	1.428148
40	0.642788	0.766044	0.839100	1.305407	1.555724	1.191754
45	0.707107	0.707107	1.000000	1.414214	1.414214	1.000000
50	0.766044	0.642788	1.191754	1.555724	1.305407	0.839100
55	0.819152	0.573576	1.428148	1.743447	1.220775	0.700208
60	0.866025	0.500000	1.732051	2.000000	1.154701	0.577350
65	0.906308	0.422618	2.144507	2.366202	1.103378	0.466308
70	0.939693	0.342020	2.747477	2.923804	1.064178	0.363970
75	0.965926	0.258819	3.732051	3.863703	1.035276	0.267949
80	0.984808	0.173648	5.671282	5.758770	1.015427	0.176327
85	0.996195	0.087156	11.430052	11.473713	1.003820	0.087489
90	1.000000	0.000000	99999.999999	99999.999999	1.000000	0.000000
95	0.996195	-0.087156	-11.430052	-11.473713	1.003820	-0.087489
100	0.984808	-0.173648	-5.671282	-5.758770	1.015427	-0.176327

Example 2: Hexadecimal Conversion

The Hexes unit contains useful hexadecimal conversion functions. As you read the following steps to create the unit, refer to its final form in listing 7.11.

1. Begin the unit with the header:

   unit Hexes;

2. The HexNybble, HexByte, and HexWord functions are public, so you insert their headers into the interface section as shown. Notice that the return type for HexByte is a two-character string type named String2, and the return type for HexWord is a four-character string type named String4. Neither of these types is standard, so both must be declared within the interface section prior to the function headers. No other data objects are global, and no other units are required, so no other entries need to be made.

3. Insert the bodies of the three functions into the implementation section. Because their complete headers appeared in the interface section, their parameters and return types don't need to be redeclared. However, you can include information as comments to improve overall program documentation.

4. No initialization code is required, so the unit is complete.

5. Save the unit as HEXES.PAS.

6. Compile the unit to disk, as shown in figure 7.4.

Listing 7.11

```
unit Hexes;

interface
   type
       String2 = string[ 2 ];
       String4 = string[ 4 ];

   function HexNybble( Number : byte ) : char;
   function HexByte( Number : byte ) : String2;
   function HexWord( Number : word ) : String4;

implementation
   function HexNybble { ( Number : byte ) : char };
   begin
       if Number < 10 then HexNybble := Chr( 48 + Number )
                   else HexNybble := Chr( 55 + Number );
```

Listing 7.11 continues

Listing 7.11 *continued*

```
   end;
   function HexByte { ( Number : byte ) : String2 };
   begin
      HexByte := HexNybble( Number div 16 )  + HexNybble( Number mod 16 );
   end;
   function HexWord { ( Number : word ) : String4 };
   begin
      HexWord := HexByte( Hi(Number) )  + HexByte( Lo(Number) );
   end;
end.
```

The USEHEX program (listing 7.12) demonstrates how simple it is to use the Hexes unit. USEHEX contains a uses clause similar in format to one you would use to access a standard unit. No other special conditions apply.

Fig. 7.4. *Compile the HEXES.PAS unit to disk.*

```
    File    Edit    Run    Compile    Options    Debug    Break/watch

         Line 1      Col 1   Compile  Alt-F9          :HEXES.PAS
unit Hexes;                   Make        F9
                              Build
interface                     Destination       Disk
                              Find error
type                          Primary file:
   String2 = string[ 2 ];     Set info
   String4 = string[ 4 ];

function HexNybble( Number : byte ) : char;
function HexByte( Number : byte ) : String2;
function HexWord( Number : word ) : String4;

implementation

function HexNybble { ( Number : byte ) : char };
begin
   if Number < 10 then HexNybble := Chr( 48+Number )
                  else HexNybble := Chr( 55+Number );
                                  Watch

 F1-Help  F5-Zoom  F6-Switch  F7-Trace  F8-Step  F9-Make  F10-Menu
```

Listing 7.12

```
program UseHex;

uses Hexes;
var
   i : byte;
   j : word;
begin
   for i := 14 to 18 do writeln( i:8, HexByte( i ):6 );
   writeln;
   for j := 32765 to 32770 do writeln( j:8, HexWord( j ):6 )
end.
```

When executed, USEHEX produces the output shown in figure 7.5.

Fig. 7.5. Output produced by the USEHEX program.

```
   14    0E
   15    0F
   16    10
   17    11
   18    12

32765  7FFD
32766  7FFE
32767  7FFF
32768  8000
32769  8001
32770  8002
```

Using the TPUMOVER
Unit Mover Program

Every program that uses a unit must be able to access that unit's .TPU file. If, as frequently happens, the .TPU file is in a different directory than the program you're developing, you need to help the compiler find it. There are two ways to do this.

1. Copy the .TPU file into the current directory. This is the simplest technique, but you can end up with multiple versions of your unit program scattered throughout your disks.

2. Tell the integrated environment where the .TPU file resides. You do this by appending the unit's path to the current Unit directories entry, located in the Options/Directories menu, as shown in figure 7.6.

Fig. 7.6. *The Directories menu.*

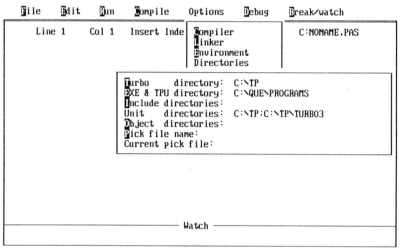

```
 File    Edit    Run    Compile    Options    Debug    Break/watch
┌─────────────────────────────────────┬─────────────────────────┐
│      Line 1     Col 1    Insert Inde│ Compiler    C:NONAME.PAS │
│                                      │ Linker                   │
│                                      │ Environment              │
│                                      │ Directories              │
│                                      └──────────────┐           │
│             ┌─────────────────────────────────────┐│           │
│             │ Turbo      directory:  C:\TP         ││           │
│             │ EXE & TPU directory:   C:\QUE\PROGRAMS│          │
│             │ Include directories:                 ││           │
│             │ Unit     directories:  C:\TP;C:\TP\TURBO3│       │
│             │ Object  directories:                 ││           │
│             │ Pick file name:                      ││           │
│             │ Current pick file:                   ││           │
│             └─────────────────────────────────────┘│           │
│                                                      │           │
│                              Watch                   │           │
├──────────────────────────────────────────────────────────────┤
└──────────────────────────────────────────────────────────────┘
 F1-Help  F5-Zoom  F6-Switch  F7-Trace  F8-Step  F9-Make  F10-Menu
```

Of course, both of these methods can become tiresome or impractical when several units in other directories must be accessed by the same program. In fact, as the number of units proliferate, before long the mundane house-keeping chores (listing directories, copying units, keeping track of current unit versions, and so on) will make you wonder why you started using units in the first place.

Fortunately, Turbo Pascal provides an answer. Although an individual unit is stored in its own .TPU file, several units can be combined into a single .TPL library file similar to the way the TURBO.TPL library stores the standard units. To the compiler, reading a unit from a library is functionally equivalent to reading it from the disk and also provides several practical advantages.

1. Because one library can store several units, you don't need the individual .TPU files cluttering up your directories.

2. Program reliability is increased, because having one "official" unit library ensures that you always use the latest version of a unit.

3. Libraries simplify code sharing. It's much easier to copy or erase one .TPL library file than a dozen .TPU files.

4. It takes less disk space to store one .TPL library than to store its component .TPU units individually.

5. Libraries reduce compile times by minimizing disk access.

TPUMOVER.EXE is the library management program for Turbo Pascal units. You run it to create and maintain your own library files and even to manage the standard TURBO.TPL library. TPUMOVER.EXE is frequently called the *mover* utility because it is used principally to move units into and out of libraries. Specifically, its most common application is to ensure ease of access to your custom units by adding them to the TURBO.TPL library itself.

Protect Your Library File

Modifying the TURBO.TPL library is serious, but not hazardous. Nevertheless, you should make a backup copy of the file before you begin.

Let's assume that you want to add the Hexes and Trigs units to the TURBO.TPL library. You can do this with the TPUMOVER.EXE program interactively or directly from the command line. I will briefly demonstrate each method.

The following discussion assumes that the TPUMOVER.EXE program is either in the current directory or a directory specified in your current search path. It also assumes that both the HEXES.TPU and TRIGS.TPU files are in the current directory and that the TURBO.TPL library is in the \TP directory. Be sure you specify the complete path names wherever necessary.

Running TPUMOVER from the Command Line

Like all Turbo products, TPUMOVER.EXE is extremely user friendly. To see for yourself, enter the following command:

TPUMOVER ?

The question mark parameter tells the program that you want it to display help messages. TPUMOVER.EXE responds by listing the complete command-line syntax, as shown in figure 7.7.

Fig. 7.7. *The help screen for the TPUMOVER.EXE utility.*

```
C>tpumover ?
TPUMOVER  Version 5.0  Copyright (c) 1987,1988 Borland International


Command Line Usage:

    TPUMOVER [libfile] /[option]unit1 /[option]unit2 ...

    [options]: +  Adds a unit
               -  Deletes a unit
               *  Extracts a unit
               ?  Lists syntax

Examples:

    tpumover turbo.tpl /+myunit.tpu
    tpumover turbo.tpl /+myunit.tpu /+myunit2.tpu
    tpumover turbo.tpl /-turbo3
    tpumover turbo.tpl /*graph3

C>
```

Now let's cheat a little. To see the current contents of the TURBO.TPL library, use this command:

TPUMOVER \TP\TURBO.TPL

TPUMOVER.EXE responds by displaying two windows, side by side, as shown in figure 7.8. The units in the TURBO.TPL library are listed individually on the left. Press Esc to return to DOS.

Refer to the command-line syntax in figure 7.7 as you add the Hexes and Trigs units to the TURBO.TPL library with the command:

TPUMOVER \TP\TURBO.TPL / +HEXES / +TRIGS

If the process is successful, the *only* message will be the program header:

TPUMOVER Version 5.0 Copyright © 1987,1988 Borland International

The default file extension is .TPU, so you must specify .TPL as part of the library name. If you don't, TPUMOVER.EXE will assume that you want to

---

Fig. 7.8. The contents of the TURBO.TPL library.

```
                      Turbo Pascal Unit Librarian
                              Version 5.0

        C:\TP\TURBO.TPL                        C:\TP\NONAME.TPU
   Unit     Code  Data  Syms Uses        Unit     Code  Data  Syms Uses

   SYSTEM  21332   664  4036
   OVERLAY  1586    10   696
   CRT      1555    20  1651
   DOS      1589     6  4143
   PRINTER    37   256   276




        File size:    42 K
        Drive C:    1000 K free

   F1-Help F2-Save F3-New F4-Info F6-Switch +-Mark Ins-Copy Del-Delete Esc-Quit
```

---

create a *new* library named TURBO.TPU instead of adding the units to TURBO.TPL, as you intended. No status or error message is produced in either case.

Cheat once again by entering the command:

TPUMOVER \TP\TURBO.TPL

TPUMOVER.EXE now displays the screen shown in figure 7.9. Both Hexes and Trigs are included in the modified TURBO.TPL library. Press Esc to return to DOS.

Running TPUMOVER Interactively

The TPUMOVER.EXE program can also be run interactively. The following instructions assume that you're using the original TURBO.TPL library in the \TP directory and that the HEXES.TPU and TRIGS.TPU units are in the current directory.

1. Enter the following command at the DOS prompt:

TPUMOVER \TP\TURBO.TPL

Fig. 7.9. The units in the modified TURBO.TPL library.

```
                      Turbo Pascal Unit Librarian
                            Version 5.0

   ══════ C:\TP\TURBO.TPL ══════        ────── C:\TP\NONAME.TPU ──────
   Unit      Code  Data  Syms Uses      Unit      Code  Data  Syms Uses

   SYSTEM   21332   664  4036
   OVERLAY   1586    10   696
   CRT       1555    20  1651
   DOS       1589     6  4143
   PRINTER     37   256   276
   HEXES      218     0   763
   TRIGS      533     0   882




        File size:   45 K
        Drive C:     992 K free

   F1-Help F2-Save F3-New F4-Info F6-Switch +-Mark Ins-Copy Del-Delete Esc-Quit
```

This loads TPUMOVER.EXE and displays the side-by-side window format you have already seen in figure 7.8. (If you have any self-doubts about proceeding, note that the F1 function key displays a help screen whenever you want.)

2. As you can see, the left window is framed with double lines, and the first unit in the list, SYSTEM, is highlighted. These features indicate the *active window*. Press the F6 function key to change the active window to the empty window on the right side.

3. Press F3 to load a file. A template appears, enabling you to narrow your search. If HEXES.TPU and TRIGS.TPU are in the current directory, press the Enter key. Position your cursor on HEXES.TPU, as shown in figure 7.10. Press Enter to select the file.

4. The HEXES.TPU unit now appears in the window on the right. Press the plus sign (+) to mark HEXES as the active unit. A small triangle appears in front of the name as shown in figure 7.11.

5. Press the Ins key to copy the unit to the TURBO.TPL library on the left. The HEXES name now appears in the left window.

6. Repeat steps 3, 4, and 5 for the TRIGS.TPU unit. The screen appears as figure 7.12.

Fig. 7.10. Select the HEXES.TPU unit.

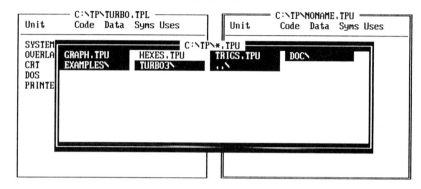

```
                    Turbo Pascal Unit Librarian
                           Version 5.0

      ┌─ C:\TP\TURBO.TPL ──┐              ┌─ C:\TP\NONAME.TPU ──┐
      │ Unit    Code Data Syms Uses │     │ Unit    Code Data Syms Uses │
      │                             │     │                             │
      │ SYSTEM ┌──────────────── C:\TP\*.TPU ────────────────┐
      │ OVERLA │ GRAPH.TPU      HEXES.TPU    TRIGS.TPU   DOC\ │
      │ CRT    │ EXAMPLES\      TURBO3\      ..\              │
      │ DOS    │                                             │
      │ PRINTE │                                             │
      │        │                                             │
```

```
              File size:    42 K
              Drive C:      960 K free
```

```
    F1-Help F2-Save F3-New F4-Info F6-Switch +-Mark Ins-Copy Del-Delete Esc-Quit
```

Fig. 7.11. Mark the HEXES.TPU unit.

```
                    Turbo Pascal Unit Librarian
                           Version 5.0

      ┌─ C:\TP\TURBO.TPL ──┐              ┌─ C:\TP\HEXES.TPU ──┐
      │ Unit    Code Data Syms Uses │     │ Unit    Code Data Syms Uses │
      │                             │     │                             │
      │ SYSTEM  21332  664 4036     │     │►HEXES    218    0  763      │
      │ OVERLAY  1586   10  696     │     │                             │
      │ CRT      1555   20 1651     │     │                             │
      │ DOS      1589    6 4143     │     │                             │
      │ PRINTER    37  256  276     │     │                             │
```

```
              File size:    42 K              File size:     1 K
              Drive C:      960 K free        Drive C:      960 K free
```

```
    F1-Help F2-Save F3-New F4-Info F6-Switch +-Mark Ins-Copy Del-Delete Esc-Quit
```

Fig. 7.12. The contents of the modified TURBO.TPL library.

```
                        Turbo Pascal Unit Librarian
                               Version 5.0

   ┌───── C:\TP\TURBO.TPL ─────┐      ┌═════ C:\TP\TRIGS.TPU ═════┐
   │ Unit    Code  Data  Syms Uses│   │ Unit    Code  Data  Syms Uses│
   │                              │   │                              │
   │ SYSTEM  21332  664  4036     │   │ TRIGS    533    0   882      │
   │ OVERLAY  1586   10   696     │   │                              │
   │ CRT      1555   20  1651     │   │                              │
   │ DOS      1589    6  4143     │   │                              │
   │ PRINTER    37  256   276     │   │                              │
   │►HEXES     218    0   763     │   │                              │
   │►TRIGS     533    0   882     │   │                              │
   │                              │   │                              │
   │                              │   │                              │
   │                              │   │                              │
   │                              │   │                              │
   └──────────────────────────────┘   └──────────────────────────────┘

      File size:    42 K              File size:     2 K
      Drive C:    952 K free          Drive C:     952 K free

   F1-Help F2-Save F3-New F4-Info F6-Switch +-Mark Ins-Copy Del-Delete Esc-Quit
```

7. Press Esc to end the program. TPUMOVER.EXE responds with a verification prompt, shown in figure 7.13, which asks if you want to accept the changes. Answer Y for Yes. TPUMOVER.EXE terminates with the two new units included in the TURBO.TPL library.

Summary

This chapter began by introducing you to the standard Turbo Pascal units.

❏ The System unit contains the code that supports Turbo's built-in subroutines.

❏ The Dos unit supports the most commonly used DOS functions.

❏ The Crt unit provides screen and keyboard services.

❏ The Printer unit helps you use your system printer.

❏ The Overlay unit supports Turbo's overlay management system.

❏ The Graph unit is a library of graphics routines.

❏ The Turbo3 and Graph3 units provide compatibility with earlier Turbo Pascal versions.

Fig. 7.13. *Save the modified TURBO.TPL library.*

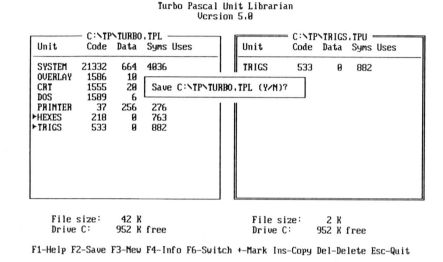

```
                        Turbo Pascal Unit Librarian
                              Version 5.0
        ┌──────── C:\TP\TURBO.TPL ────────┐  ┌════════ C:\TP\TRIGS.TPU ════════┐
        │ Unit    Code  Data  Syms Uses   │  ║ Unit    Code  Data  Syms Uses   ║
        │                                 │  ║                                 ║
        │ SYSTEM  21332   664 4036        │  ║ TRIGS    533     0   882        ║
        │ OVERLAY  1586    10             │  ║                                 ║
        │ CRT      1555    20  ┌Save C:\TP\TURBO.TPL (Y/N)?─────────┐
        │ DOS      1589     6  └───────────────────────────────────┘
        │ PRINTER    37   256  276        │  ║                                 ║
        │►HEXES     218     0  763        │  ║                                 ║
        │►TRIGS     533     0  882        │  ║                                 ║
        │                                 │  ║                                 ║
        └─────────────────────────────────┘  └─────────────────────────────────┘

            File size:    42 K               File size:     2 K
            Drive C:     952 K free          Drive C:     952 K free

        F1-Help F2-Save F3-New F4-Info F6-Switch +-Mark Ins-Copy Del-Delete Esc-Quit
```

You also saw how several individual units can be combined to form a single library.

Next, the major components of a unit—heading, interface, implementation, and initialization—were explained. You then learned how to develop units of your own design. Rules were presented for writing and using custom units. Two examples were presented; the first contained common trigonometric functions, and the second provided hex conversion routines.

Finally, you saw how to use the TPUMOVER library management program.

Debugging Your
Programs

Almost all programs contain errors sometime during their lives. In fact, as soon as you think your program is perfect, give it to someone else to run. Suddenly, the strangest things start to happen! Printers jam, disks fill up, and power fails. The smallest task exhausts every byte of internal memory. Impatient users "type ahead" in the program, only to find that they have made a mistake and can't undo the effect of their responses. All at once, your "perfect" program is riddled with holes.

Errors—both large and small—are a fact of programming life. Strangely enough, the big errors are usually the easiest to fix. Sometimes, it's difficult even to be sure that a small error is present—until the program crashes, of course. When you ask programmers how they learned the process of debugging, you are likely to get a single word in response: *experience*.

Fortunately, programming in Turbo Pascal is different. Turbo provides a powerful, built-in debugger that helps you *look inside* a program while it's running. With the debugger, you can trace the complete flow of the program, and you can see how each variable changes every step of the way. In this chapter, you will learn how to use the debugger to solve even the most troublesome programming challenges.

Categories of Errors

There are three major categories of errors: compile-time, run-time, and logic.

Compile-Time Errors

A compile-time error is generally the result of lexical or syntactic mistakes. A lexical error occurs when an individual word, number, or program symbol is illegal, such as writing the hexadecimal value *$23* as *23h*. A syntactic error happens when your program breaks one of the formal rules of Turbo Pascal, such as specifying the wrong number of parameters in a subroutine or forgetting a semicolon. Turbo won't let your program run until all compile-time errors are repaired.

Most compile-time errors are obvious and easy to fix. When Turbo detects one, it halts compilation, moves the cursor (and scrolls the screen, if necessary) to the offending line of code, and displays both an error number and a brief English-language error message.

Run-Time Errors

A run-time, or semantic, error arises when perfectly valid Turbo Pascal statements are combined illegally. Examples include trying to write to files not opened for output, range errors, memory overflows, and division by zero—in short, any of the numerous things that Turbo Pascal can detect while the program is running.

Run-time errors terminate the program and cause an error number and message to be displayed. If the program was running within the integrated environment, Turbo will return to the editor and move the cursor to the line of code that triggered the problem. Run-time errors can be a nuisance, but because you know which line of code was running when the error occurred, it's usually a simple matter to analyze and repair the problem.

Logic Errors

A logic error is generated when the program does something you don't want or doesn't do something you expect. A logic error is a design fault in the program. Logic errors are the most difficult to isolate. After all, Turbo believes that it's running a good program.

Sometimes, of course, a logic error is obvious. If the first page number on a report is 38, then you probably forgot to initialize your page-counter variable. At other times, depending on the complexity of your program's design, you might not even know which part of the program contains the error. The most complicated and time-consuming problems are usually caused by the combination of two or more individually trivial mistakes.

The debugger is designed to detect logic errors.

A Debugging Example

Now run the TURBO.EXE editor and enter the BAD1 program in listing 8.1. After you have proofread your typing, press F2 and save the program to disk.

Do *not*—repeat, do *not*—run the program. BAD1 contains an example of the most difficult species of bug to find, the kind that completely hangs up the machine.

Listing 8.1

```
program Bad1;
var
    i : integer;
    X : array [ 1..3 ] of integer;
begin
    i := 0;
    while i  <> 3 do begin
        X[i] := i*i  + 5;
        Inc( i );
    end;
    for i := 1 to 3 do
        writeln( X[i] );
end.
```

From a quick glance, BAD1 appears to be designed to calculate, store, and display values using the formula

```
X[i]  := i*i  + 5;
```

Even without a computer, you can determine that the contents of the first three elements of the X array will be 6, 9, and 14.

However, BAD1 contains a fatal flaw. Because the variable i is initially set to zero, the first formula computed by the program is the one for array element zero, as follows:

```
X[0]  := 0*0  + 5;
```

Even though the X array is only declared for elements 1 through 3, the compiler dutifully calculates the position of element 0 to be the two bytes *immediately in front of* the X array. In other words, the compiler believes that X[0] occupies the same memory location as the index variable i itself. Consequently, the assignment

```
X[Ø] := 5;
```

is the same as

```
i := 5;
```

In the next program statement, the Inc procedure increases i to 6; therefore, the second pass through the while loop assigns X[6]. Similarly, the third pass assigns X[7], the fourth pass assigns X[8], and so on. Just as the compiler used the location of the X array to calculate where X[0] must reside, it also derives the locations for X[6], X[7], and X[8].

Because the value of i will never be 3, the while loop will never terminate. The program will continue until the value of i is large enough that array element X[i] overwrites a critical memory location. If you actually run the BAD1 program, you will probably find that you have to reboot your PC. (In fact, if you disregarded the warning and actually ran the program, you should probably reboot even if you *don't* find any problems with your PC).

If the {$R +} range-checking option had been enabled, this error would have been discovered fairly quickly. This discussion assumes that range checking remains at its default setting of {$R-}.

Traditional Debugging Techniques

If you didn't already know what was wrong with BAD1, you would probably begin your debugging effort by inserting writeln statements at key points throughout the program, as follows:

```
       begin
          i := Ø;
          while i <> 3 do begin
{* 1 *}     WRITELN( 'Now at statement 1:', I:5, X[I]:5 );
             X[i] := i*i + 5;
{* 2 *}     WRITELN( 'Now at statement 2:', I:5, X[I]:5 );
             Inc( i );
{* 3 *}     WRITELN( 'Now at statement 3:', I:5, X[I]:5 );
          end;
{* 4 *}     WRITELN( 'Now at statement 4:', I:5, X[I]:5 );
          for i := 1 to 3 do
             writeln( X[i] );
       end.
```

Next, you would save the program to disk under a different name, then compile and run it. Using this technique, the results of the first seven passes through the while loop are shown in figure 8.1.

Fig. 8.1. The initial output produced by the modified BAD1 program.

```
Now at statement 1:     0    0
Now at statement 2:     5  359
Now at statement 3:     6  105
Now at statement 1:     6  105
Now at statement 2:     6   41
Now at statement 3:     7   54
Now at statement 1:     7   54
Now at statement 2:     7   54
Now at statement 3:     8   69
Now at statement 1:     8   69
Now at statement 2:     8   69
Now at statement 3:     9 1538
Now at statement 1:     9 1538
Now at statement 2:     9   86
Now at statement 3:    10    0
Now at statement 1:    10    0
Now at statement 2:    10  105
Now at statement 3:    11    0
Now at statement 1:    11    0
Now at statement 2:    11  126
Now at statement 3:    12 3785
```

The value of i changes immediately from 0 to 5 between the first and second lines, so it's obvious that the execution of the assignment statement

```
X[i] := i*i + 5;
```

is what changed the value of i. It's also clear that the PC "hangs up" and needs to be rebooted because assignments are being made to nonexistent elements of the X array—a process that is likely to adversely affect control of the operating system itself.

Using the Integrated Debugger

Now try to perform the same analysis using the Turbo Pascal integrated debugger.

To use the debugger, both the {$D} and the {$L} options must be enabled. The default settings are {$D +} and {$L +}. The {$D} option can be controlled by the Options/Compiler/Debug menu selection. The {$L} option can be controlled by the Options/Compiler/Local Symbols menu selection. Make sure you haven't changed the defaults; otherwise, simply include the following as the first line of your program:

{$D +,L +}

To the debugger, keeping track of a variable throughout the execution of a program is called *watching*. Specifying which variable to track is called *adding a watch*. The following steps explain how to watch the i and X variables:

1. Load the original BAD1 program.

2. Choose the Add watch option from the Break/watch menu. (Notice that pressing Ctrl-F7 selects the option directly.) An Add Watch window appears in the center left of the display, as shown in figure 8.2.

Fig. 8.2. The Add Watch window.

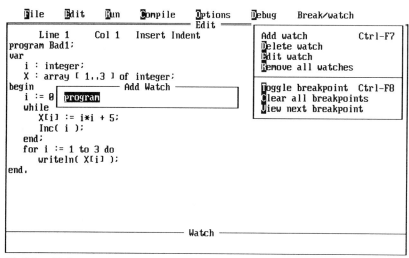

The word *program* has no significance here; by default, the window contains the word currently being referenced by the cursor. After you become comfortable with the debugger and its features, you will be in the habit of positioning the cursor and pressing Ctrl-F7. For now, add your first watch expression by entering **i** and then pressing the Enter key. The i variable appears in the Watch window at the bottom of the screen, together with the phrase Unknown identifier.

3. Repeat step 2 for the X variable. You can either press Ctrl-F7 or, again, select the Add watch option from the Break/watch menu. Either way, another Add Watch window appears. Type **X**, and press the Enter key. Both the i and X variables appear at the bottom of the screen, as shown in figure 8.3.

Fig. 8.3. *The BAD1 program, with* i *and* X *selected as watch variables.*

```
  File    Edit    Run    Compile    Options    Debug    Break/watch
                                     Edit
      Line 1    Col 1    Insert Indent         Unindent    C:BAD1.PAS
  program Bad1;
  var
     i : integer;
     X : array [ 1,,3 ] of integer;
  begin
     i := 0;
     while i <> 3 do begin
        X[i] := i*i + 5;
        Inc( i );
     end;
     for i := 1 to 3 do
        writeln( X[i] );
  end,




                              Watch
  •X: Unknown identifier
   i: Unknown identifier

  F1-Help  F5-Zoom  F6-Switch  F7-Trace  F8-Step  F9-Make  F10-Menu
```

Now start running the program. Notice the bottom line of the display; the F7 function key is marked Trace. *Tracing* is the process of stepping through a program one executable statement at a time.

1. Press the F7 key to begin the trace. Three things immediately happen. First, Turbo compiles the program. Second, because of the compilation, i and X are no longer "unknown identifiers" but known numeric variables; hence, the Watch window now shows that i and X contain numbers. Third, the first executable line in the program—the begin statement in front of the main body—is highlighted. The resulting screen is shown in figure 8.4.

Fig. 8.4. The initial contents of the i *and* X *variables.*

```
   File     Edit     Run     Compile     Options     Debug     Break/watch
                                  Edit
      Line 5      Col 1     Insert Indent          Unindent    C:BAD1.PAS
program Bad1;
var
   i : integer;
   X : array [ 1..3 ] of integer;
begin
   i := 0;
   while i <> 3 do begin
      X[i] := i*i + 5;
      Inc( i );
   end;
   for i := 1 to 3 do
      writeln( X[i] );
end.



                                  Watch
·X: (12544,-17966,100)
 i: 15521

F1-Help  F5-Zoom  F6-Switch  F7-Trace  F8-Step  F9-Make  F10-Menu
```

Throughout the tracing process, Turbo highlights the line containing the *next* instruction to be executed.

2. Continue to press the F7 key to advance the trace. With each keystroke, another executable statement is processed.

   Check the Watch window as you go. When the highlighted line passes the assignment statement—that is, immediately after the assignment statement is processed—the variable i changes its value to 5, as shown in figure 8.5.

3. Press the F7 key again. The Inc statement changes the value of i to 6. Keep pressing F7 until you have cycled through the while loop a second time. The value of i changes to 7, as shown in figure 8.6, but the values in the X array remain unchanged.

Fig. 8.5. The value of the variable i *is set to 5.*

```
     File     Edit     Run     Compile     Options     Debug     Break/watch
┌──────────────────────────────────── Edit ──────────────────────────────────┐
│     Line 9      Col 1     Insert Indent          Unindent    C:BAD1.PAS      │
│program Bad1;                                                                 │
│var                                                                          │
│  i : integer;                                                               │
│  X : array [ 1..3 ] of integer;                                             │
│begin                                                                        │
│  i := 0;                                                                    │
│  while i <> 3 do begin                                                      │
│     X[i] := i*i + 5;                                                        │
│     Inc( i );                                                               │
│  end;                                                                       │
│  for i := 1 to 3 do                                                         │
│     writeln( X[i] );                                                        │
│end.                                                                         │
│                                                                             │
│                                                                             │
│                                                                             │
│─────────────────────────────────── Watch ──────────────────────────────────│
│•X: (12544,-17966,100)                                                       │
│ i: 5                                                                        │
└─────────────────────────────────────────────────────────────────────────────┘
  F1-Help  F5-Zoom  F6-Switch  F7-Trace  F8-Step  F9-Make  F10-Menu
```

Fig. 8.6. The value of i *has changed; the contents of* X *remain the same.*

```
     File     Edit     Run     Compile     Options     Debug     Break/watch
┌──────────────────────────────────── Edit ──────────────────────────────────┐
│     Line 10     Col 1     Insert Indent          Unindent    C:BAD1.PAS      │
│program Bad1;                                                                 │
│var                                                                          │
│  i : integer;                                                               │
│  X : array [ 1..3 ] of integer;                                             │
│begin                                                                        │
│  i := 0;                                                                    │
│  while i <> 3 do begin                                                      │
│     X[i] := i*i + 5;                                                        │
│     Inc( i );                                                               │
│  end;                                                                       │
│  for i := 1 to 3 do                                                         │
│     writeln( X[i] );                                                        │
│end.                                                                         │
│                                                                             │
│                                                                             │
│                                                                             │
│─────────────────────────────────── Watch ──────────────────────────────────│
│•X: (12544,-17966,100)                                                       │
│ i: 7                                                                        │
└─────────────────────────────────────────────────────────────────────────────┘
  F1-Help  F5-Zoom  F6-Switch  F7-Trace  F8-Step  F9-Make  F10-Menu
```

Just as with the earlier writeln method, the integrated debugger enables you to conclude that the assignment statement is what changed the value of i.

The Debug Menu

Now that you have gotten a taste of what the built-in debugger can do, it's time to examine each of its features more fully. The Debug menu, shown in figure 8.7, contains many of the commands that control the use of the debugger.

Fig. 8.7. *The Debug menu.*

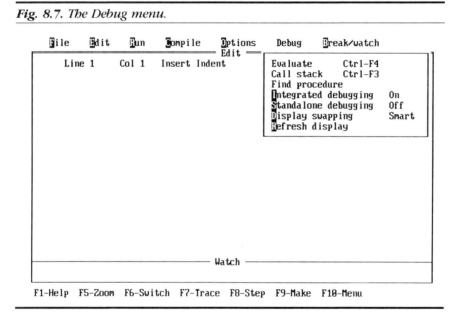

In this section, you will learn about each command in greater detail.

Evaluate (Ctrl-F4)

During a debugging session, the Evaluate command enables you to test the value of any expression or variable. In addition, it helps you to actually *change* the value of any variable.

To see how the Evaluate command helps debug your program, pick up the debugging session from where you left off (fig. 8.6). Recall that by cycling through the while loop, you determined that the value of i was out of bounds and that the X array wasn't receiving any assignments.

Now, within the debugging session itself, modify the value of i by choosing the Evaluate option from the Debug menu. (The equivalent hot key is Ctrl-F4.) The compiler displays a window containing three long horizontal boxes, labeled Evaluate, Result, and New value. Enter **i** in the Evaluate box, then press the Enter key. The current value of i, the number 7, appears immediately in the Result box. Now use the Tab key to move the cursor to the New value box. Enter the number 1, then press the Enter key. The Result box changes to reflect the new value. Note that the value of i shown in the Watch window is still equal to 7. The screen appears as shown in figure 8.8.

Fig. 8.8. The Evaluate *option from the Debug menu.*

```
    File     Edit     Run     Compile    Options    Debug     Break/watch
 ══════════════════════════════════════ Edit ═══════════════════════════════
    Line 10     Col 1    Insert Indent              Unindent    C:DAD1.PAS
 program Bad1;
 var                        ┌────────────────── Evaluate ──────────────────┐
    i : integer;            │ i                                            │
    X : array [ 1..3 ] o    └──────────────────────────────────────────────┘
 begin                      ┌────────────────── Result ────────────────────┐
    i := 0;                 │ 1                                            │
    while i <> 3 do begi    └──────────────────────────────────────────────┘
       X[i] := i*i + 5;     ┌───────────────── New value ──────────────────┐
       Inc( i );            │ 1                                            │
    end;                    └──────────────────────────────────────────────┘
    for i := 1 to 3 do
       writeln( X[i] );
 end.



                          ┌────────────────── Watch ─────────────────────┐
 *X: (12544,-17966,100)
  i: 7
 ────────────────────────────────────────────────────────────────────────────
   F1-Help   F7-Trace   F8-Step   F10-Menu   TAB-Cycle   <─┘-Modify
```

Now press the Esc key to return to the debugging session. The value of i showing in the Watch box changes to 1, indicating that your new value has been accepted.

Press F7 several times to cycle through the while loop. Notice that the debugger uses your new value of i just as if it had been assigned within the program itself. As you cycle through the while loop, you will also notice the values in the X array changing. After the second loop, when i is equal to 3, the highlighted line drops down to the for loop. The screen now appears as shown in figure 8.9.

Fig. 8.9. *The values of the* i *and* X *variables immediately after completion of the* while *loop.*

```
  File    Edit    Run    Compile   Options   Debug    Break/watch
──────────────────────────────── Edit ─────────────────────────────
      Line 11    Col 1    Insert Indent        Unindent   C:BAD1.PAS
program Bad1;
var
   i : integer;
   X : array [ 1..3 ] of integer;
begin
   i := 0;
   while i <> 3 do begin
      X[i] := i*i + 5;
      Inc( i );
   end;
   for i := 1 to 3 do
      writeln( X[i] );
end.



──────────────────────────────── Watch ────────────────────────────
 •X: (6,9,100)
  i: 3
────────────────────────────────────────────────────────────────────
 F1-Help  F5-Zoom  F6-Switch  F7-Trace  F8-Step  F9-Make  F10-Menu
```

Clearly, the condition in the while statement prevented the value of X[3] from being modified by the assignment statement.

Now it's time to fix the program. Move the cursor and change the line

    i := 0;

to

    i := 1;

and also change the line

    while i <> 3 do begin

to

    while i < 4 do begin

Press F7 to continue the debugging session. As figure 8.10 shows, a verification window appears, asking if you want these changes to be reflected in the compiled code. Respond with Y for yes. Turbo recompiles the program. The new version of the program can be saved by pressing F2.

Fig. 8.10. *The Verify box.*

```
 File    Edit    Run    Compile    Options    Debug    Break/watch
───────────────────────────────────── Edit ──────────────────────────
   Line 7     Col 15  Insert Indent          Unindent * C:BAD1.PAS
program Bad1;
var
   i : in┌───────── Verify ──────────┐
   X : ar│ Source modified, rebuild? (Y/N) │
begin    └──────────────────────────┘
   i := 1;
   while i < 4 do begin
      X[i] := i*i + 5;
      Inc( i );
   end;
█for i := 1 to 3 do██████████████████████████████████████
      writeln( X[i] );
end.



──────────────────────────── Watch ──────────────────────
•X: (6,9,100)
 i: 3
─────────────────────────────────────────────────────────
F1-Help  Esc-Abort
```

Using the Evaluate Box As a Calculator

Whenever you wish, you can use the *Evaluate* box as a calculator —whether or not a debugging session is in progress. Just enter any arithmetic expression, press Enter, and the result appears in the Result box.

Call Stack (Ctrl-F3)

During a debugging session, you can use the Call stack command to display the list—in sequence—of the currently executing procedure and function calls together with their parameters. By examining this list, you can quickly learn your program's flow of control.

To see how the Call stack command works, follow these steps:

1. Enter the Turbo Pascal editor, and load the HANOI1 program (listing 5.15 in Chapter 5).

2. Place the cursor on the end statement that terminates the transfer procedure.

3. Execute the Go to cursor option of the Run menu. (This is equivalent to pressing the F4 function key.) Turbo will compile the program and run it until it reaches the marked line. One of the program's first actions is to ask you for the desired number of disks; enter 4 at the prompt. At this point, the screen looks like figure 8.11.

Fig. 8.11. *The HANOI1 program after the first completion of the transfer procedure.*

```
    File   Edit   Run   Compile   Options   Debug   Break/watch
      Line 11    Col 1    Insert Indent       Unindent   C:HANOI1.PAS
program Hanoi1;
var
   NumberOfDisks : integer;
procedure transfer( Disk, StartFrom, Target, StopOver : integer );
begin
   if Disk > 0 then begin
      transfer( Disk-1, StartFrom, StopOver, Target );
      writeln( 'Move ', StartFrom, ' to ', Target );
      transfer( Disk-1, StopOver, Target, StartFrom );
   end;
end;
begin
   write( 'Enter the number of disks: ' );
   readln( NumberOfDisks );
   transfer( NumberOfDisks, 1, 3, 2 );
end.
```

```
 F1-Help  F5-Zoom  F6-Switch  F7-Trace  F8-Step  F9-Make  F10-Menu
```

4. Now perform the Call stack option (Ctrl-F3 is its equivalent hot key). The Call Stack window appears in the upper right corner, as shown in figure 8.12.

The *call stack* is a LIFO (last-in, first-out) list showing which procedures and functions are currently open. The HANOI1 program itself called the transfer procedure with the parameters (4,1,3,2). The transfer procedure then called itself recursively, using the parameters (3,1,2,3). transfer was called three more times, the final time with the parameters (0,1,3,2).

Use the cursor keys to select any one of the entries in the list, then press the Enter key. The cursor immediately moves to the line that invoked the procedure or function call.

Fig. 8.12. The contents of the Call Stack window.

```
    File    Edit   Run    Compile   Options   Debug   Break/watch
      Line 11    Col 1   Insert Indent           Unindent  C:HANOI1.PAS
program Hanoi1;
var                                              ┌─── Call Stack ───┐
   NumberOfDisks : integer;                      │TRANSFER(0,1,3,2)│
procedure transfer( Disk, StartFrom, Target, StopOver : in│ TRANSFER(1,1,2,3)│
begin                                            │ TRANSFER(2,1,3,2)│
   if Disk > 0 then begin                        │ TRANSFER(3,1,2,3)│
      transfer( Disk-1, StartFrom, StopOver, Target );│ TRANSFER(4,1,3,2)│
      writeln( 'Move ', StartFrom, ' to ', Target );│ HANOI1          │
      transfer( Disk-1, StopOver, Target, StartFrom );└──────────────────┘
   end;
end;
begin
   write( 'Enter the number of disks: ' );
   readln( NumberOfDisks );
   transfer( NumberOfDisks, 1, 3, 2 );
end.




   F1-Help   ↑↓→←-Scroll   <─┘-View call
```

Find Procedure

As Turbo performs a compilation, it stores the location of each procedure and function in your program, including those in any include files your program might have used.

The Find command prompts you for the name of any of these routines, locates it, and moves the cursor to its first line.

Integrated Debugging (On)

The Integrated debugging switch controls whether Turbo maintains the tables and performs the extra routines required to support interactive debugging.

By default, Turbo's debugging features are ready for use. If you plan to compile a program to disk, interactive debugging isn't needed; in these cases, you can save internal memory space by turning the option off.

Standalone Debugging (Off)

The Standalone debugging switch should be turned on when you want to use Borland's Turbo Debugger product on a program that you compile to disk.

When the option is turned on, the compiler stores all of its debugging tables within a separate section of the .EXE file. Although the .EXE file is larger because of it, program execution speed isn't affected.

The stand-alone Turbo Debugger product is available as a separate software package. Although it's an excellent tool for developing large programming applications, you will probably find that Turbo Pascal's built-in debugger offers more than enough power and performance for most purposes.

Display Swapping (Smart)

The Display swapping switch enables you to select the way Turbo handles screen displays during debugging sessions. There are three available options.

❑ Smart. Temporarily displays the output screen whenever your program performs an output operation. The swapping is fast, but noticeable; you can press the Alt-F5 key to examine your output more leisurely.

❑ Always. Temporarily displays the output screen after *every* program statement.

❑ None. *Superimposes* the output and editor screens. Use this setting only for programs that don't do any screen output. Otherwise, the display can become hopelessly muddled. The Refresh display command can be used to restore the screen's appearance.

The default setting is Smart.

Refresh Display

The Refresh display command provides a convenient way to restore the screen after your program—debugged when the Display swapping switch was set to None—overwrites the display.

The Break/Watch Menu

Earlier in the chapter, you saw how Turbo's integrated debugger helps you to watch as variables are changed during the execution of a program. You also saw how the Go to cursor option of the Run menu enables you to temporarily set a program breakpoint—that is, a location in a program where the debugger temporarily interrupts its processing and waits for new instructions from the user.

The Break/watch menu contains all of the options that control these processes. The menu is displayed in figure 8.13.

Fig. 8.13. The Break/watch menu.

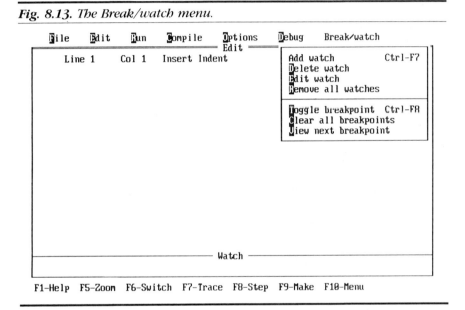

In this section, you learn about these options in greater detail.

Add Watch (Ctrl-F7)

With the Add watch command you can add a variable or an expression to the top of the Watch window. The debugger displays the value of each of the selected items throughout the remainder of the debugging session or until the Watch window is cleared with the Remove all watches command.

The value of each watched variable and expression is displayed beside its name. The Watch window expands in size with the addition of each item, up to the limit you selected when you installed the compiler with the TINST.EXE program. If you add more items, the contents of the window can be scrolled with the cursor keys.

You can switch between the Turbo Editor and the Watch window by pressing the F6 key. When the Watch window is active, you can use the Ins key to add more items.

Delete Watch

The Delete watch command deletes the current watch item. The current item can be identified by the presence of a small bullet to the left of its name.

To change the current item, switch to the Watch window by pressing the F6 key. When the Watch window is active, the current item is the one that's highlighted. You can change the selection using the cursor control keys. Press F6 once more to return to the editor.

Within the Watch window itself, you can delete an item using the Del key.

Edit Watch

The Edit watch command copies the current watch expression to a special *Edit Watch* window. You can then use the standard Turbo Pascal editing keys to modify the expression any way you want. Press Enter to install the change or press Esc to cancel it.

When the Watch window is active, you can select the current item for editing more easily by simply pressing the Enter key.

Remove All Watches

The Remove all watches command clears all items from the Watch window and returns it to its original size.

Toggle Breakpoint (Ctrl-F8)

The Toggle breakpoint command selects the line containing the cursor as a breakpoint. Every selected line is highlighted. If the line is already a break-point, the Toggle breakpoint command cancels the selection.

Clear All Breakpoints

The Clear all breakpoints command cancels all current breakpoint selections.

View Next Breakpoint

The View next breakpoint command moves the cursor to the next break-point selection, scrolling the screen or even loading another file if necessary. No code is executed as a result of using the command. If no more breakpoints remain in the program, then the View next breakpoint command selects the first breakpoint at the beginning of the program.

The Run Menu

You have already been using the Run menu extensively. It contains the Run command itself—the instruction you have issued every time you have wanted to execute a program. The Run menu also contains special commands that allow programs to execute within the debugger.

This section explains each of these commands in more detail.

Run (Ctrl-F9)

The Run command initiates program execution. If necessary, Turbo automatically compiles the program before the execution occurs. If you have changed the program since its last compilation, Turbo will ask you if it should recompile the code before it proceeds.

If you are in the middle of a debugging session, you can use the Run command to resume program execution from the point at which it was last interrupted.

Program Reset (Ctrl-F2)

The Program reset command tells the compiler to terminate the current debugging run. Any dynamic memory allocated by the program is released. Any open files are closed. Typed constants are reset, but any variables are left untouched. The next line to be executed will be the first executable line of the program.

Breakpoints and watch expressions are unaffected by this command. If you want to terminate the debugging session completely and run the program normally, you may also need to execute the Remove all watches and Clear all breakpoints commands.

Go to Cursor (F4)

The Go to cursor command executes all program statements until it reaches the line containing the cursor. Using the command enables you to bypass large blocks of program code without forcing you to first establish a breakpoint.

If you are already in the middle of a debugging session, then the Go to cursor command starts its run with the line immediately following the last line executed. If the program hasn't yet run or you have just issued a Program reset command, the program starts running with its first executable line. If necessary, Turbo will first compile the program.

Trace into (F7)

The Trace into command executes the next program statement. By repeatedly using the Trace into command, you can run your program one line at a time. If the next line is a procedure or function call, then the procedure or function itself is also executed a line at a time. If the next executable line happens to reside in another unit or in an include file, the debugger automatically loads that file before proceeding.

Step over (F8)

The Step over command is similar to the Trace into command, except that if the next line is a procedure or function call, the procedure or function is executed in a *single* step. The debugger then moves the highlighted line to the first statement following the subroutine call.

User Screen (Alt-F5)

The User screen command enables you to view the output screen.

Summary

In this chapter, you have learned how to use Turbo Pascal's built-in debugger to identify and fix logic errors in your programs. Through a simple case study, you have seen that the process of debugging consists primarily of observing and controlling the contents of selected variables during the execution of small sections of a program or even through the program as a whole.

This process of observing is called *tracing*. The specific variables to be traced are called watch variables. The lines that border the statements to be executed during the trace are called breakpoints.

Within the Turbo Pascal integrated environment, a debugging session is controlled with the Debug, Break/watch, and Run menus.

You have learned that the options of the Debug menu activate the debugger and control its use.

❏ Evaluate tests the value of any expression or variable.

❏ Call stack displays the list of the currently executing procedure and function calls together with their parameters.

❏ Find procedure moves the cursor to the first line of any specified procedure or function.

❏ Integrated debugging controls whether or not to support interactive debugging.

❏ Standalone debugging prepares a program for later processing by Borland's Turbo Debugger product.

❏ Display swapping selects screen display options.

❏ Refresh display restores the screen.

You have learned that the options of the Break/watch menu establish the program's breakpoints and determine which variables to watch.

❏ Add watch adds a variable or an expression to the Watch window.

❏ Delete watch deletes the current watch item.

❏ Edit watch allows you to edit the current watch expression.

❏ Remove all watches clears all items from the Watch window.

❏ Toggle breakpoint either creates or cancels a breakpoint.

❏ Clear all breakpoints cancels all breakpoints.

❏ View next breakpoint moves the cursor to the next breakpoint.

You have learned that the options of the Run menu initiate and control the execution of the program during the debugging session.

❏ Run initiates program execution.

❏ Program reset terminates the current debugging run.

❏ Go to cursor executes all statements before the line containing the cursor.

❏ Trace into executes the next statement.

❏ Step over is similar to Trace into but executes procedures and functions in a single step.

❏ User screen displays the output screen.

Part II

Programming

9

Keyboard Input

Buried somewhere in the documentation of almost every software product —from word processors to Turbo Pascal itself—is the inevitable phrase that assures the reader that the keyboard acts "just like a typewriter."

And—for the most part—it's true. The keyboard and screen are electronically connected; when you press a key on the keyboard, you know from experience that the character appears immediately on the screen. The cursor can be positioned, mistakes can be removed with the Backspace or Del keys, and uppercase letters can be entered when the Shift key is pressed. To borrow the slogan of desktop publishing packages: "What you see is what you get."

But what appears at first to be a single event is actually the combination of three distinct activities: keyboard entry, screen display, and editing. Most of the time they occur together so quickly that you don't notice (or appreciate) the complexity of each component. Turbo Pascal, however, *does* make the distinction, and in the process offers the programmer the means to develop some powerful data entry tools.

This chapter introduces the techniques your programs can use to acquire information from the keyboard. It does this by discussing how the keyboard actually operates, how (and where) the information is stored, and how you can use the tools provided by Turbo Pascal to access and manipulate keyboard data. By understanding the data flows, you will be better able to understand how to exploit the full power of Turbo Pascal.

Command-Line Parameters

There are two distinct times when a Turbo Pascal program can get data from the keyboard: within the program itself (that is, while the program is running, as with the read and readln routines) and as part of the command line. Perhaps not surprisingly, two distinct methods are involved.

Programs frequently allow or expect command-line parameters, for example:

COPY infile,outfile

DUMP details.obj

PAYABLES july

Within a program, you can work interactively with the user. Prompting messages can appear (File name:), input editing code can be used (That number was out of range. Please retype.), and validations can be obtained (Are you sure?). In short, you develop a dialog. When you enter information as part of the command line, this flexibility doesn't usually exist. The prime objective is simply to capture the data.

Turbo Pascal provides two functions for just that purpose. ParamCount returns the number of parameters on the command line. ParamStr is an array of strings, each element of which contains a single parameter. For example, ParamStr(3) returns the third parameter from the command line. (Beginning with DOS 3.0, ParamStr (Ø) returns the path and file name of the executing program.)

These functions can be demonstrated with the CLINE program (listing 9.1), which simply returns each command-line parameter on a separate line.

Listing 9.1

```
program CLINE;
var
   i : byte;
begin
   if ParamCount < 1 then
      writeln( 'Please try again with some command-line parameters.' )
   else
      for i := 1 to ParamCount do
         writeln( 'Parameter', i:2, ': ', ParamStr( i ) );
end.
```

To run CLINE from the DOS prompt, you would enter the following:

C>CLINE infile.pas outfile.lst

Parameter 1: infile.pas
Parameter 2: outfile.lst

C>CLINE opt1 opt2 opt3

Parameter 1: opt1
Parameter 2: opt2
Parameter 3: opt3

Parameters are assumed to be separated by spaces or tabs. Commas, slashes, and semicolons are all treated as ordinary characters—*not* as separators. This can create some problems, especially if you (or your users) expect to employ traditional separators, as demonstrated by the following examples. Try the following entries:

C>CLINE opt1,opt2,opt3

Parameter 1: opt1,opt2,opt3

C>CLINE file1/opt3;suboption2

Parameter 1: file1/opt3;suboption2

C>CLINE city ='Los Angeles'

Parameter 1: city='Los
Parameter 2: Angeles'

It may be easier to access the entire command line as a single string and process it on a character-by-character basis. As you will see in Chapter 12, the contents of the command line can be found at a memory location stored 128 bytes into the Program Segment Prefix. The CLINE2 program in listing 9.2 demonstrates how the command line can be accessed.

Listing 9.2

```
program CLINE2;
type
    CmdLineArray = string[ 127 ];
var
    CmdLine : ^CmdLineArray;
begin
    CmdLine := Ptr( PrefixSeg, $80 );
    if Length( CmdLine^ ) < 1 then
        writeln( 'Please try again with some command-line parameters.' )
    else
        write( Length( CmdLine^ ), ' characters: ', CmdLine^ );
end.
```

The command-line string—no matter how complicated—is captured and returned in its entirety.

C>CLINE2 opt1,opt2,opt3/sub4; a,b..c

28 characters: opt1,opt2,opt3/sub4; a,b..c

The Program Segment Prefix is described in greater detail in Chapter 12.

Keyboard Operation

The keyboard is more than a collection of simple switches and wires. It contains (and is controlled by) its own microprocessor, an Intel 8048 (or an Intel 8042 for the AT), which is also called the *keyboard controller*.

Each one of the 83 keys on the keyboard is numbered—arbitrarily—from 1 through 83. This number, called a *scan code*, was assigned by the PC's designers based on the key's physical location; it has no relationship either to the meaning of the key or to the ASCII value of the character being typed. (A table of scan codes can be found in the Turbo Pascal handbook.) Each time you press one of the keys, you send its scan code to the 8048. When you release the key, another scan code gets sent to the 8048, but this time with a value 128 higher than the first. In other words, the eighth bit of the scan code is zero when the key is pressed and one when it's released. The AT is slightly different; it sends the same scan code each time, but precedes the release signal with an $F0 byte.

Chapter 3 discussed how each ASCII character can be defined by a single eight-bit byte. The standard ASCII character set consists of 128 values (the eighth bit is zero) and includes upper- and lowercase letters, numbers, and punctuation. IBM introduced an "extended" version of ASCII that defines an additional 128 values (the eighth bit is set) and includes line drawing symbols, foreign character sets, and technical symbols. Yet nowhere is a key such as "Function Key 1" or "Alt-A" defined. Such keys are called "specials" and further increase the number of usable characters.

Obviously, there are fewer keys on the keyboard than potential symbols; by separately recognizing the press and release (or "make" and "break") scan codes, special key combinations (such as shift, alternate, and control-key prefixes) can be captured. For example, the four actions:

1. Pressing the Shift key
2. Pressing the Q key
3. Releasing the Q key
4. Releasing the Shift key

must together be identifiable as the single character known as a "capital Q."

The keyboard controller makes no attempt to evaluate the meaning of any scan code signals. Instead, it simply alerts the 8086 to the availability of keyboard input. The CPU itself converts the scan code sequences into useful data. Every recognized character is stored in one word of data. The high byte is called the *ASCII byte*, and the low byte is called the *extended byte*.

If the character is one of the 256 standard ASCII characters, its ASCII code is stored in the high byte of the word and the extended byte is undefined (but generally it's the scan code of the chosen key). For the capital Q example, the ASCII byte will contain 81 (the ASCII code for *Q*).

If the character is a special key, the ASCII byte contains a zero, and the extended byte contains an "extended" key code. Pressing the PgUp key, for example, results in a zero in the ASCII byte and 73 in the extended byte.

To summarize, *every single* character entered on the keyboard produces *two* bytes. Either the first byte is the ASCII value of the character, and the second byte can be ignored; or the first byte is zero, and the second byte has a special (non-ASCII) meaning called an "extended" code.

Reading Data from the Keyboard

In most of your programs, you will want to input ASCII characters with either `read` or `readln`, just as all of the examples have done up to now. Remember that neither procedure is directly connected to the keyboard; both get their data *indirectly*, by accessing the buffer.

Information from the keyboard is input one line at a time and stored—in its entirety—in the internal buffer. When variables are read, this buffer is used as the input source.

The Read and Readln Procedures

Both the `read` and the `readln` procedures read data items into variables. The difference between them is that wherever a `read` procedure is positioned when it terminates, the next `read` or `readln` procedure begins; but when a `readln` procedure terminates, the remainder of the line (including the carriage return and line feed) is ignored.

This difference is best illustrated with an example. The READER1 and READER2 programs (listing 9.3) are identical except that the variable YorN is input with a `read` procedure in READER1 and a `readln` procedure in READER2.

Listing 9.3

```
program Reader1;
var
    YorN : char;
    Name : string;
begin
    write( 'Should we continue? (Y)es or (N)o: ' );
    read( YorN );
    writeln( 'Your answer was ', UpCase( YorN ) );
    write( 'What is your name? ' );
    readln( Name );
    writeln( 'Hello, ', Name );
end.
```

Listing 9.4

```
program Reader2;
var
    YorN : char;
    Name : string;
begin
    write( 'Should we continue? (Y)es or (N)o: ' );
    readln( YorN );
    writeln( 'Your answer was ', UpCase( YorN ) );
    write( 'What is your name? ' );
    readln( Name );
    writeln( 'Hello, ', Name );
end.
```

Both programs accept one char variable followed by one string variable. Run the READER1 program, but don't cooperate—instead of a single character, enter five: abcde, followed by a carriage return. The read procedure assigns the letter *a* to YorN but won't advance the position in the buffer. Consequently, the remaining characters, *bcde, plus the carriage return*, will be read without a pause by the readln procedure.

```
Should we continue? (Y)es or (N)o: abcde
Your answer was A
What is your name? Hello, bcde
```

In READER2, the readln procedure assigns the letter *a* to the variable YorN, and then advances the buffer position. The remaining characters, *bcde, plus the carriage return*, will be completely ignored.

```
Should we continue? (Y)es or (N)o: abcde
Your answer was A
What is your name? Fred
Hello, Fred
```

The read procedure is used primarily for file input. You should always use the readln procedure for keyboard entry, and, further, you should try to use a single readln procedure for each variable.

Line Input

By temporarily storing data in the buffer, read and readln help you to edit your work as you go along. The following editing commands are available:

Backspace	Deletes the last character entered
Escape	Deletes the entire input line
Enter	Terminates the input line and stores the end-of-line marker (the carriage return/line feed combination of #13#10) in the buffer

You have probably already used these keys by now, but if you haven't, enter the LINEIN0 program (listing 9.5) and try them. Note that the program must be terminated with a Ctrl-C.

Listing 9.5

```
program LineIn∅;
var
   Str : string;
begin
   writeln( 'Please enter some lines.' );
   repeat
      readln( Str );
      writeln( Str );
   until False;
end.
```

If you include the Crt unit in your program with the statement

uses Crt;

several additional editing features become available:

Ctrl-A	Same as Escape
Ctrl-D	Recalls one character from the last input line
Ctrl-F	Recalls the remainder of the last input line
Ctrl-S	Same as Backspace

The LINEIN1 program (listing 9.6) illustrates the inclusion of the Crt unit. Execute the program, and try out the new editing commands. Except for the uses clause, no other change to the program has been made.

Listing 9.6

```
program LineIn1;
uses Crt;
var
   Str : string;
begin
   writeln( 'Please enter some lines.' );
   repeat
      readln( Str );
      writeln( Str );
   until False;
end.
```

Ctrl-Z and the End of the File

When you include the Crt unit in your program, you transform the keyboard from a simple input device into the functional equivalent of a text file. As a consequence, you have the option of actually testing for an "end-of-file" condition.

The predefined Boolean variable CheckEof is used by the Crt unit to determine whether end-of-file testing is allowed. Normally, CheckEof is False and the test is disallowed. However, if you set CheckEof to True, entering Ctrl-Z during the execution of a read or readln statement sets Eof (the end-of-file flag) to True. Once this happens, no further input will be allowed unless the procedure

```
Reset( input );
```

is executed, which resets Eof to False. In essence, the Reset procedure reopens the keyboard for input.

The LINEIN2 program in listing 9.7 demonstrates the end-of-file test. The program continues to ask for lines to display until either a Ctrl-C or a Ctrl-Z is entered. Ctrl-C terminates the program. Ctrl-Z is interpreted as an end of file; Eof is set to True, and the No more data can be entered message is displayed.

Listing 9.7

```
program LineIn2;
uses Crt;
var
   Str : string;
begin
   CheckEof := True;
   writeln( 'Please enter some lines.' );
```

Listing 9.7 continues

Listing 9.7 continued

```
    repeat
        readln( Str );
        writeln( Str );
    until Eof;
    writeln( 'No more data can be entered' );
end.
```

Note that entering Ctrl-Z during the execution of the `readln` procedure causes a null string to be assigned to the variable `Str`. If `readln` had a numeric variable as its parameter, the variable would have been assigned a zero.

Text files are discussed in greater detail in Chapter 13.

Reading a Single Character

The Turbo Pascal function `ReadKey` can be used to identify a single keystroke. If the entry is one of the ASCII characters, `ReadKey` returns its ASCII value. If the entry is a special character, `ReadKey` returns a null value (that is, an ASCII zero). In the latter case, `ReadKey` must be executed a second time to pick up the extended code of the entry.

The KEY1 program in listing 9.8 displays the values returned by `ReadKey`. The program can be terminated by entering a lowercase z.

Listing 9.8

```
program Key1;
uses Crt;
var
    Selection : char;
begin
    repeat
        Selection := ReadKey;
        if Selection = chr( Ø ) then
            writeln( '    Ø and ', ord( ReadKey ) )
        else
            writeln( Selection, '  ', ord( Selection ) );
    until Selection = 'z';
end.
```

When KEY1 is executing, entering the characters a, b, c, Q, R, S, Function 1, Function 2, Home, and Alt-H results in the following:

```
a  97
b  98
c  99
Q  81
R  82
S  83
```

Ø and 59
Ø and 6Ø
Ø and 71
Ø and 35

The numbers 97, 98, 99, 81, 82, and 83 correspond to the ASCII values of the letters that were entered. The numbers 59, 60, 71, and 35 correspond to the extended key codes for the special characters.

Reading without Echoing

Sometimes it's desirable to prevent keyboard input from being displayed on the screen. The best example of this situation is when you ask for a password.

The PASS1 program (listing 9.9) reads each keystroke and, instead of displaying the character itself, displays an asterisk. PASS1 allows two attempts at guessing the password before terminating.

Listing 9.9

```
program Pass1;
uses Crt;
const
    Secret = 'BLAISE';
type
    String8 = string[ 8 ];
function Password : String8;
var
    Count : byte;
    WorkString : String8;
    Entry : char;
begin
    Count := Ø;
    WorkString := '';
    Entry := ' ';
    repeat
        if KeyPressed then begin
            Entry := UpCase( ReadKey );
            write( '*' );
            if ord(Entry)  <> 13 then
                WorkString := WorkString + Entry;
            Inc( Count );
        end;
    until (Count = 8) or (ord(Entry) = 13);
    Password := WorkString;
end;
begin
    ClrScr;
```

Listing 9.9 continues

Listing 9.9 *continued*

```
    gotoXY( 1, 5 );
    write( 'Please enter your password: ' );
    if Password  <> Secret then begin
       writeln;
       write( 'One more try: ' );
       if Password  <> Secret then begin
          writeln;
          writeln( 'Sorry.  Please obtain authorization.' );
          Exit;
       end;
    end;
    writeln;
    writeln( 'Welcome to the program!' );
end.
```

One interesting consideration of this program is that the password variable Secret may have contained *any* eight characters. Most people think of a password as being alphanumeric; the PASS1 program allows it to contain, for example, function keys and backspaces. Some of the most secure passwords consist of unprintable characters. For example, to change the password to include a backspace after the A, change the definition of Secret to 'BLA'#8'ISE' (#8 is the code for backspace). Similarly, you can define Secret as 'BLA'#0#68'ISE' to use the F10 function key.

Esc, Ctrl-Break, and Ctrl-C

If you have been entering and running the examples in this book, you have probably had more than one occasion to use Ctrl-Break to terminate a contrary program. Further, if you have had any experience with PCs whatsoever, you have probably pressed the Escape key fairly often.

These keystrokes have advantageous results during program development, but they aren't often desirable during the execution of a real-world application. Imagine the user of one of your programs who finishes an hour or more of boring but important data entry, then—for whatever reason—presses Ctrl-Break. The following worst-case events transpire immediately:

1. The program terminates.

2. No files will have been closed, so all the data is lost.

3. The diskette requires repair with the CHKDSK utility.

4. You get a phone call.

Fortunately, Turbo Pascal provides a way to disable early termination. The Crt unit uses the Boolean variable CheckBreak to enable and disable the action of Ctrl-Break. When CheckBreak is True—the default state—pressing Ctrl-Break will cause the program to abort when it next writes to the display. But when CheckBreak is False, pressing Ctrl-Break has no effect.

The CHECKCB program (listing 9.10) disables the Ctrl-Break key, then displays English equivalents for several of the "special" keys. Compile it to disk and run it outside of the integrated environment. To end the program, press Escape, Ctrl-Break, or Ctrl-C.

Listing 9.10

```
program CheckCB;
uses Crt;
const
   EndLoop : Boolean = False;
var
   ch, Answer : char;

procedure TerminateRoutines;
begin
   EndLoop := True;
   { Any other file closings, screen displays, etc. }
   { required for smooth program termination }
end;

begin
   CheckBreak := False;
   ClrScr;
   writeln( 'Enter special keys.' );
   writeln( 'Terminate with Escape, Ctrl-C, or Ctrl-Break.' );
   repeat
      if KeyPressed then begin
         ch := ReadKey;
         if (ord( ch ) = 3) or               { Ctrl-C or Ctrl-Break? }
            (ord( ch ) = 27) then begin      { Escape key?            }
            repeat
               write( 'Are you sure you want to stop? (Y/N) ' );
               readln( Answer );
            until UpCase( Answer ) in [ 'Y', 'N' ];
            if UpCase( Answer ) = 'Y' then
               TerminateRoutines;
         end;
         if ch = chr(Ø) then begin
            ch := ReadKey;
            case ord(ch) of
                    71 : writeln( 'Home' );
                    72 : writeln( 'Up arrow' );
                    73 : writeln( 'PgUp' );
                    75 : writeln( 'Left arrow' );
                    77 : writeln( 'Right arrow' );
                    79 : writeln( 'End' );
                    8Ø : writeln( 'Down arrow' );
                    81 : writeln( 'PgDn' );
                    82 : writeln( 'Ins' );
                    83 : writeln( 'Del' );
                   114 : writeln( 'Ctrl-PrtSc' );
                   115 : writeln( 'Ctrl-Left Arrow' );
                   116 : writeln( 'Ctrl-Right Arrow' );
```

Listing 9.10 continues

Listing 9.10 continued

```
              117 : writeln( 'Ctrl-End' );
              118 : writeln( 'Ctrl-PgDn' );
              119 : writeln( 'Ctrl-Home' );
         120..128 : writeln( 'Alt-', ord(ch)-119 );
                                { Alt + digits 1..9 }
              129 : writeln( 'Alt-Ø' );
              130 : writeln( 'Alt-Minus' );
              131 : writeln( 'Alt-Equal' );
              132 : writeln( 'Ctrl-PgUp' );
          59..68 : writeln( 'F', ord(ch)-58 );
                                { Function keys 1..10 }
          84..93 : writeln( 'Shift-F', ord(ch)- 83 );
                                { Shift + Function keys 1..10 }
          94..103 : writeln( 'Ctrl-F', ord(ch)- 93 );
                                { Ctrl + Function keys 1..10 }
         104..113 : writeln( 'Alt-F', ord(ch)-103 );
                                { Alt + Function keys 1..10 }
            end;
          end;
        end;
     until EndLoop;
  end.
```

Disabling Ctrl-Break only works for a program compiled to your diskette. Ctrl-Break always terminates a program run within the integrated environment, because it is the integrated environment itself—not your program—that senses the key.

Changing the State of Ctrl-Break Checking

If, when `CheckBreak` is True, you want Ctrl-Break to terminate the program immediately rather than wait for the next screen output, use the `SetCBreak` procedure to change the current state of Ctrl-Break checking. The syntax is as follows:

```
SetCBreak( BreakTest : Boolean );
Executing the statement
SetCBreak( True );
```

and causes DOS to test for Ctrl-Break during *every* system call, not just during I/O routines. You can return to the default setting by executing

```
SetCBreak( False );
```

The `GetCBreak` procedure returns a variable that tells you the current state of Ctrl-Break checking.

```
GetCBreak( var BreakTest : Boolean );
```

The Keyboard Buffer

The ASCII and extended byte pairs generated by each keystroke are placed in a 16-word (32 byte) circular buffer in the main memory of the PC. Any program requesting keyboard input reads data from this buffer one word (two bytes) at a time.

A circular buffer is like a queue. Characters are stored on a first-come, first-served basis. The only difference is that there's no clearly defined "beginning" or "end" in a circular buffer. Characters from the keyboard simply fill up the spaces in sequence. The start of the queue is called the *head* of the buffer. The *tail* of the buffer points to the next open slot. When a character fills the highest memory location in the buffer, the tail "wraps around" and is reset to the lowest memory location, where it awaits the next character to be entered.

When the head and tail both point to the same location, the buffer is empty. After 15 characters have been entered, the tail can't advance further, because no open slots remain. Hence, the buffer can only hold 15 characters; trying to enter another one generates the familiar beep sound that indicates the buffer is full.

Figure 9.1 shows how the command

DIR *.*

(which is executed when you press the Enter key) can be inserted into a circular buffer. Note that the starting point is completely arbitrary.

Data entered in the keyboard buffer aren't really erased; new keystrokes simply overwrite the old. The actual starting location of the buffer can be found in the main memory of the PC at $0040:$001E. The head is located at $0040:$001A, and the tail is located at $0040:$001C. The bytes in the head and tail positions contain values from $1E through $3C, indicating the offsets of the locations they reference.

The memory locations for the head and tail aren't part of the buffer itself. The head and tail could have been placed anywhere in memory, but for the sake of convenience, DOS puts them just before the start of the buffer. After the entry of the DIR *.* command, the buffer and pointers might look like the diagram in figure 9.2.

Again, the head location is completely arbitrary.

The best way to understand how the buffer works is to actually see it in action. The SHOWBUFF program in listing 9.11 continuously displays the contents of the buffer on the screen, together with the head and tail locations. The program terminates after 500 displays or after Ctrl-C is pressed.

Fig. 9.1. Processing the DIR *.* command in the keyboard buffer.

Tail ⟶   ⟵ Head

Here, the circular buffer is empty. The head and tail both point to the same word.

⟵ Tail

D   ⟵ Head

The buffer begins to be filled. The first entry, an uppercase D, is placed in the word referenced by the head pointer. The tail pointer advances to the next open word.

R   *   .   *

I   C/R

D   ⟵ Head   Tail ⟶

The complete command:
    DIR *.*
is now in the buffer and will wait for a program to read it. Reading will begin with the word pointed to by head and will proceed until the head and tail once again point to the same word.

R   *   *

I   C/R

D   Tail ⟶   ⟵ Head

The command has been read. The head and tail again point to the same word.

The buffer is now awaiting a new entry, which will begin where the head now points. The original command remains in the buffer and will be overwritten with the next set of keystrokes.

Fig. 9.2. *An example of how the DIR *.* command might be entered in the keyboard buffer.*

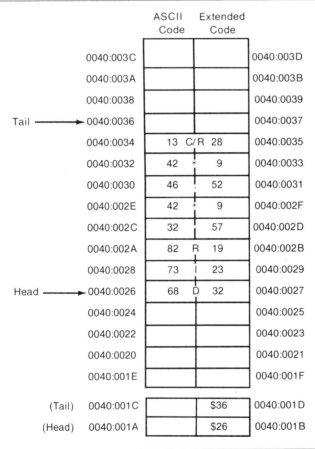

	ASCII Code		Extended Code	
0040:003C				0040:003D
0040:003A				0040:003B
0040:0038				0040:0039
Tail ⟶ 0040:0036				0040:0037
0040:0034	13	C/R	28	0040:0035
0040:0032	42	*	9	0040:0033
0040:0030	46	.	52	0040:0031
0040:002E	42	*	9	0040:002F
0040:002C	32		57	0040:002D
0040:002A	82	R	19	0040:002B
0040:0028	73	I	23	0040:0029
Head ⟶ 0040:0026	68	D	32	0040:0027
0040:0024				0040:0025
0040:0022				0040:0023
0040:0020				0040:0021
0040:001E				0040:001F
(Tail) 0040:001C			$36	0040:001D
(Head) 0040:001A			$26	0040:001B

Listing 9.11

```
program ShowBuff;
uses Crt;
var
   i, Pass, Row : byte;
   BlankRow,
   HeadRow,
   TailRow      : byte;
   KeyBuffer    : array[ 1..32 ] of byte absolute $0040:$001E;
   HeadPointer  : byte                   absolute $0040:$001A;
   TailPointer  : byte                   absolute $0040:$001C;
```

Listing 9.11 continues

Listing 9.11 continued

```
begin
    Pass := Ø;              { Track how many times the buffer is displayed }
    BlankRow := 1Ø;
    ClrScr;
    GotoXY( 31, 1 ); write( 'The Keyboard Buffer' );
    GotoXY( 33, 3 ); write( 'ASCII  Extended' );
    repeat
        Pass := Pass  + 1;
        Row := 5;
        for i := 16 downto 1 do begin
            GotoXY( 32, Row );
            write( KeyBuffer[i*2-1]:4, chr( KeyBuffer[i*2-1] ):3 );
            GotoXY( 41, Row );
            writeln( KeyBuffer[i*2]:4 );
            Row := Row  + 1;
        end;
        TailRow := 35 - ( TailPointer div 2 );
        HeadRow := 35 - ( HeadPointer div 2 );
        GotoXY( 2Ø, TailRow );
        write( '(', TailPointer:2, ') Tail->' );
        if BlankRow  <> TailRow then begin
            GotoXY( 2Ø, BlankRow );
            write( '           ' );  { 11 spaces }
            BlankRow := TailRow;
        end;
        GotoXY( 47, HeadRow );
        write( ' <-Head (', HeadPointer:2, ')' );
    until Pass > 5ØØ;    { Stop after 5ØØ passes }
end.
```

For example, the program might begin as shown in figure 9.3.

The head and tail point to the same word, so the buffer is empty. The characters currently in the buffer will be overwritten. The first character in the command (the D) is entered where the tail was pointing. After entry, the tail advances to the next slot to be filled, as shown in figure 9.4.

The next character (the I) is placed where the tail had been pointing. This position is the highest location in the buffer, so the tail must now wrap around and point to the lowest location, as shown in figure 9.5.

Fig. 9.3. *An empty keyboard buffer.*

```
                    The Keyboard Buffer

                    ASCII  Extended

                    32     32
        (58) Tail->  32     32     <-Head (58)
                    32     32
                    32     32
                    32     32
                    32     32
                    32     32
                    32     32
                    32     32
                    32     32
                    32     32
                    32     32
                    32     32
                    32     32
                    32     32
                    32     32
```

Fig. 9.4. *The keyboard buffer after a capital* D *is entered.*

```
                    The Keyboard Buffer

                    ASCII  Extended

        (60) Tail->  32     32
                    68  D  32     <-Head (58)
                    32     32
                    32     32
                    32     32
                    32     32
                    32     32
                    32     32
                    32     32
                    32     32
                    32     32
                    32     32
                    32     32
                    32     32
                    32     32
```

Fig. 9.5. *The keyboard buffer after a capital I is entered.*

```
The Keyboard Buffer

ASCII   Extended

          73  I    23
          68  D    32    <-Head (58)
          32       32
          32       32
          32       32
          32       32
          32       32
          32       32
          32       32
          32       32
          32       32
          32       32
          32       32
          32       32
          32       32
(30) Tail->  32    32
```

The third character (the R) is entered in the normal manner. The buffer now appears as shown in figure 9.6.

Fig. 9.6. *The keyboard buffer after a capital R is entered.*

```
The Keyboard Buffer

ASCII   Extended

          73  I    23
          68  D    32    <-Head (58)
          32       32
          32       32
          32       32
          32       32
          32       32
          32       32
          32       32
          32       32
          32       32
          32       32
          32       32
          32       32
(32) Tail->  32    32
          82  R    19
```

After the rest of the characters are entered, including the Enter key (an ASCII 13), the buffer appears as shown in figure 9.7.

Fig. 9.7. *The keyboard buffer after the* DIR *.* *command has been entered.*

```
                 The Keyboard Buffer

                 ASCII  Extended

                 73  I   23
                 68  D   32   <-Head (58)
                 32      32
                 32      32
                 32      32
                 32      32
                 32      32
                 32      32
                 32      32
   (42) Tail->   32      32
                 13      28
                 42  *    9
                 46  .   52
                 42  *    9
                 32      57
                 82  R   19
```

After the DIR *.* command is processed, the buffer appears as shown in figure 9.8.

The head advanced as characters were read from the buffer. Because the head and tail now point to the same byte, the buffer is "empty." The current contents of the buffer will be overwritten when more keys are pressed.

Note that when you run the SHOWBUFF program, you will probably find that it contains characters. Even so, since the head and tail begin by pointing to the same byte, DOS treats the buffer as being completely empty.

Remapping Scan Codes

All of this may seem unnecessarily complicated at first. For example, why even bother using scan codes when the ASCII characters themselves are available?

The answer is that scan codes give you the flexibility to redefine the keyboard. Different countries, for example, have different standard keyboard

---

***Fig. 9.8.** The keyboard buffer after the DIR *.* command has been processed.*

The Keyboard Buffer

ASCII Extended

		ASCII		Extended	
		73	I	23	
		68	D	32	
		32		32	
		32		32	
		32		32	
		32		32	
		32		32	
		32		32	
		32		32	
(42) Tail->		32		32	<-Head (42)
		13		28	
		42	*	9	
		46	.	52	
		42	*	9	
		32		57	
		82	R	19	

---

layouts. (These are described in greater detail in your operating system manual.) Similarly, the ECHO command in DOS can be used to redefine keys to any desired string. Your CONFIG.SYS file must include the statement DEVICE =ANSI.SYS in order for key reconfiguration to work on your machine.

The REDEF1 program in listing 9.12, for example, redefines all lowercase letters to their uppercase equivalents. Run the program, then exit Turbo and type a command at the DOS prompt. No matter what you do (short of another redefinition) you won't be able to make lowercase letters appear.

Listing 9.12

```
program Redef1;
var
   letter : char;
begin
   for letter := 'a' to 'z' do    { Redefine lowercase to uppercase }
      writeln( 'echo ', chr(27), '[', ord(letter), ';', ord(letter)-32, 'p' );
end.
```

To solve this slight annoyance, you can either reboot your machine or run the REDEF2 program (listing 9.13) to map lowercase scan codes to their default lowercase letters.

Listing 9.13

```
program Redef2;
var
   letter : char;
begin
   for letter := 'a' to 'z' do    { Redefine lowercase back to lowercase }
      writeln( 'echo ', chr(27), '[', ord(letter), ';', ord(letter), 'p' );
end.
```

On a more practical level, the REDEF3 program (listing 9.14) redefines the F10 function key to the instruction pair:

CD\TP

TURBO

Run the REDEF3 program, then exit the compiler. You can now begin Turbo Pascal from any directory simply by pressing F10.

Listing 9.14

```
program Redef3;
begin
   writeln( 'echo ', chr(27),'[Ø;68;"CD\TP";13;"TURBO";13p' );
end.
```

Entering Data into the Buffer

You can actually insert characters into the buffer and have your program chain to another program upon completion. The ADDBUFF program (listing 9.15) introduces the NextCommand procedure, which places any desired string in the buffer, just as if the characters were entered through the keyboard. When ADDBUFF finishes its run, the DIR *.* command is executed.

Listing 9.15

```
program AddBuff;
procedure NextCommand( Command : string );
type
   KeyArray = array[ $1E..$3D ] of byte;
var
   i : byte;
   CmdSize : byte;
   HeadPointer : byte absolute $ØØ4Ø:$ØØ1A;
   TailPointer : byte absolute $ØØ4Ø:$ØØ1C;
   KeyBuffer : ^KeyArray;
begin
   KeyBuffer := Ptr( $ØØ4Ø, $ØØ1E );
   TailPointer := $1E;
```

Listing 9.15 continues

Listing 9.15 continued

```
      HeadPointer := TailPointer;
      CmdSize := Length( Command );
      for i :- 1 to CmdSize do begin
         KeyBuffer^[ TailPointer ] := ord( Command[ i ] );
         write( command[ i ] );
         TailPointer := TailPointer + 2;
      end;
      KeyBuffer^[ TailPointer ] := 13;
      KeyBuffer^[ TailPointer + 1 ] := 28;
      TailPointer := TailPointer + 2;
   end;
begin
   NextCommand( 'DIR *.*' );
end.
```

Testing the Buffer

The Turbo Pascal KeyPressed function returns True if an entry is available to be read from the keyboard. KeyPressed is handy when you want to provide for input, but you don't want to stop processing if no input is available. In a game program, for example, animation should continue, although the keyboard should be periodically tested for new commands.

In the KEY1A program (listing 9.16), all letters of the alphabet are displayed continuously at the same cursor position. To move the cursor (and create a chain of random letters), the Up Arrow, Down Arrow, Right Arrow, and Left Arrow keys can be used. The program terminates when the End key is pressed.

Listing 9.16

```
program Key1A;
uses Crt;
const
   Row      : byte = 12;
   Column   : byte = 40;
   GameOver : Boolean = False;
   OutSpot  : word = 0;
begin
   ClrScr;
   repeat
      if KeyPressed then
         if ReadKey = chr(0) then    { Special character }
            case ord(ReadKey) of
                72 : Row     := Row - 1;       { Up Arrow }
                75 : Column  := Column - 1;    { Left Arrow }
                77 : Column  := Column + 1;    { Right Arrow }
                80 : Row     := Row + 1;       { Down Arrow }
                79 : GameOver := True;         { "End" key }
```

Listing 9.16 continues

Listing 9.16 *continued*

```
            end;
        if not (Row in [ 1..25 ]) then Row := 1;
        if not (Column in [ 1..80 ]) then Column := 1;
        gotoXY( Column, Row );
        OutSpot := (OutSpot mod 26) + 1;
        write( chr(OutSpot + 64) );
    until GameOver;
end.
```

Note that the Pascal code

```
if KeyPressed then ...
```

is equivalent to

```
if Mem[$0040:$001A] <> Mem[$0040:$001C] then ...
```

Frequently, the opposite situation arises. You want to read characters from the keyboard, but you don't want to pick up any characters that may have been typed ahead and are idly sitting in the buffer. The most familiar example is the DOS ERASE command. If you enter the command ERASE *.*, you must *wait* for the Are you sure? message before you can answer Y or N.

Two versions of a FlushBuffer procedure follow.

Version 1 reads the contents of the buffer, if any, into the dummy variable Empty. A uses Crt; statement is required at the beginning of the module.

```
procedure FlushBuffer;   { Version 1 }
var
    Empty : char;
begin
    while KeyPressed do Empty := ReadKey;   { Requires "uses Crt;" }
end;
```

Version 2 simply sets the location referenced by the head pointer equal to the location referenced by the tail pointer. The two pointers are now equal, so the buffer is considered to be empty.

```
procedure FlushBuffer;   { Version 2 }
begin
    Mem[$0040:$001A] := Mem[$0040:$001C];   { HeadPointer := TailPointer }
end;
```

Shift and Toggle Keys

Some keys are never (or rarely, at least) used alone, and consequently they leave no trace in the keyboard buffer. For example, knowing that the Shift key has been pressed is of little value by itself. Turbo programs operate quite comfortably by directly processing the upper- or lowercase form of a letter; they would bog down quickly if each letter had to be tested for the presence of a preceding Shift or CapsLock.

When you press one of the *shift* keys (that is, a Shift, Ctrl, or Alt), the keyboard interrupt routines modify the next character to be entered before placing it in the keyboard buffer. Similarly, the interrupt routines examine the current state of each of the *toggle* keys (CapsLock, NumLock, ScrollLock, and Ins).

Each shift and toggle key is mapped to at least one bit in the pair of bytes at memory locations $0040:$0017 and $0040:$0018.

In the byte at $0040:$0017, the upper four bits indicate the status of the four toggle keys. If CapsLock is on, for example, bit 6 is set and continues to be set until CapsLock is pressed again. The lower four bits indicate whether the Alt, Ctrl, or Shift keys are down. (Notice in figure 9.9 that the left and right shift keys are treated as having separate meanings.) These bits are set only while the key is pressed.

Fig. 9.9. The keyboard status byte at $0040: $0017.

$0040:$0017

7	6	5	4	3	2	1	0
Insert	CapsLock	NumLock	Scroll Lock	Alt Down	Ctrl Down	Left Shift Down	Right Down
Toggle Status: On =1 Off =0							

In the byte at $0040:$0018, the upper four bits indicate whether the four toggle keys are pressed. If CapsLock is pressed, for example, bit 6 will be set only until CapsLock is released. Bit 3 indicates that the Ctrl-NumLock combination (which temporarily suspends program execution) is currently in force. As figure 9.10 shows, the lowest three bits are undefined. (On the PCjr, bit 2 controls whether the keyboard click is on or off.)

These bits are updated automatically whenever one of the toggle or shift keys is pressed or released. The Ins key is the only one of these keys that also creates an entry in the keyboard buffer; specifically, it produces 0 for the ASCII byte and 82 for the extended byte.

Because the keyboard interrupt routine checks the contents of the keyboard status bytes before determining the final entry to make to the keyboard buffer, changing these bytes has the same effect as the key action indicated by the values of the bits.

Fig. 9.10. The keyboard status byte at $0040: $0018.

$0040:$0018

7	6	5	4	3	2	1	0
Insert Down	CapsLock Down	NumLock Down	Scroll Lock Down	Ctrl-Num Lock On			
Key Status: Down = 1 Up = 0							

The SHOWKEY program (listing 9.17) reveals how these bits change with various character entries. The program terminates when you enter a lower-case z.

Listing 9.17

```
program SHOWKEY;
uses Crt;
var
   Selection : char;
   KeyFlag1  : byte absolute $0040:$0017;
   KeyFlag2  : byte absolute $0040:$0018;
procedure ShowBits( Specimen : byte );
var
   i,
   Compare : byte;
begin
   Compare := 128;
   for i := 7 downto 0 do begin
      if Specimen and Compare = 0 then write( '0' )
                                  else write( '1' );
      Compare := Compare shr 1;
   end;
end;
begin
   repeat
      Selection := ReadKey;
      write( Selection, ' ', ord( Selection ):4, ' ' );
      ShowBits( KeyFlag1 );
      write( ' ' );
      ShowBits( KeyFlag2 );
      writeln;
   until Selection = 'z';
end.
```

Fig. 9.11. Sample output produced by the SHOWKEY program.

SHOWKEY Program Output				Key Entered
a	97	00000000 00000000	Lowercase *a*	
A.	65	00000010 00000000	Left-Shift *a*	
A	65	00000001 00000000	Right-Shift *a*	
☺	1	00000100 00000000	Control-*a*	
	0	00001000 00000000	Alternate-*a*	
▲	30	00001000 00000000	Alternate-*a*	CapsLock key pressed
A	65	01000000 00000000	Lowercase *a*	
a	97	01000010 00000000	Left-Shift *a*	

Notice in figure 9.11, for example, that the combination of CapsLock and Shift cancel out and produces a lowercase *a*.

The KEYSET program (listing 9.18) alternately clears and sets the CapsLock toggle bit to force a change in the default of the case of any letters being entered. Notice how the constants are defined.

Listing 9.18

```
program KEYSET;
uses Crt;
const
    InsertOn      = $80;   { Key Flag at 0040:0017 }
    CapsLockOn    = $40;
    NumLockOn     = $20;
    ScrollLockOn  = $10;
    AltKeyDown    = $08;
    CtrlKeyDown   = $04;
    LeftShiftDown = $02;
    RightShiftDown = $01;
    InsertKeyDown = $80;   { Key Flag at 0040:0018 }
    CapsLockDown  = $40;
    NumLockDown   = $20;
    ScrollLockDown = $10;
    CtrlNumLockOn = $08;
var
    TypedItem : char;
    KeyFlag1 : byte absolute $0040:$0017;
    KeyFlag2 : byte absolute $0040:$0018;
begin
    ClrScr;
    KeyFlag1 := KeyFlag1 and (not CapsLockOn);    { Turns caps off }
```

Listing 9.18 continues

Listing 9.18 continued

```
   writeln( 'CapsLock isn''t on' );
   repeat
      TypedItem := ReadKey;
      write( TypedItem );
   until TypedItem = 'z';
   writeln; writeln;
   KeyFlag1 := KeyFlag1 or CapsLockOn;    { Turns caps on }
   writeln( 'CapsLock is on' );
   repeat
      TypedItem := ReadKey;
      write( TypedItem );
   until TypedItem = 'Z';
end.
```

The KEYSET program first clears the CapsLock setting so all characters can be entered normally. When a lowercase z is typed, KEYSET turns the CapsLock bit on, just as if the key had been physically pressed on the keyboard itself. The program terminates when an uppercase Z is typed. The output from the program looks like the following:

```
CapsLock isn't on
iuwrye fdgvvkjhgoeiwrty eryowytw dkjhgfkz
CapsLock is on
REWOIUYTOIEYKDFHGKLSHACDJHFO YEWRQ 2396Z
```

After the program is finished, the CapsLock setting remains enabled until it is reset from the keyboard.

It's common to run programs that affect—or are affected by—the settings of the toggle keys. The KEYSTAT program (listing 9.19) can be executed from the DOS prompt or included in a batch file to establish specific toggle key states.

Listing 9.19

```
program KEYSTAT;
const
   InsertOn      = $80;    { Key Flag at 0040:0017 }
   CapsLockOn    = $40;
   NumLockOn     = $20;
   ScrollLockOn  = $10;
var
   i, j        : byte;
   UpperString : string[ 10 ];
   KeyFlag1    : byte absolute $0040:$0017;
procedure DisplayHelp;
begin
   writeln;
   writeln( 'Syntax:' );
   writeln( 'keys condition(s)' );
```

Listing 9.19 continues

Listing 9.19 continued

```
       writeln;
       writeln( 'where "condition" is one or more of the following, in any' );
       writeln( 'order, separated by spaces:' );
       writeln;
       writeln( '   ion = Insert mode on    ioff = Insert mode off' );
       writeln( '   con = CapsLock on       coff = CapsLock off' );
       writeln( '   non = NumLock on        noff = NumLock off' );
       writeln( '   son = ScrollLock on     soff = ScrollLock off' );
       writeln;
       writeln( 'Letters may be either upper- or lowercase.' );
    end;
begin
    if ParamCount < 1 then
       DisplayHelp
    else
       for i := 1 to ParamCount do begin
          UpperString := ParamStr( i );
          for j := 1 to length( UpperString ) do
             UpperString[ j ] := UpCase( UpperString[ j ] );
          if UpperString = 'ION' then
             KeyFlag1 := KeyFlag1 or InsertOn
          else if UpperString = 'IOFF' then
             KeyFlag1 := KeyFlag1 and (not InsertOn)
          else if UpperString = 'CON' then
             KeyFlag1 := KeyFlag1 or CapsLockOn
          else if UpperString = 'COFF' then
             KeyFlag1 := KeyFlag1 and (not CapsLockOn)
          else if UpperString = 'NON' then
             KeyFlag1 := KeyFlag1 or NumLockOn
          else if UpperString = 'NOFF' then
             KeyFlag1 := KeyFlag1 and (not NumLockOn)
          else if UpperString = 'SON' then
             KeyFlag1 := KeyFlag1 or ScrollLockOn
          else if UpperString = 'SOFF' then
             KeyFlag1 := KeyFlag1 and (not ScrollLockOn)
          else begin
             DisplayHelp;
             Halt;
          end;
       end;
end.
```

The program accepts parameters that specify desired toggle key states. For example, to ensure that all toggle keys are disabled, enter:

KEYSTAT ioff coff noff soff

Similarly, to enable the CapsLock state, enter

KEYSTAT con

Summary

In this chapter, you have learned how your programs can read and process information entered through the keyboard. You have learned how to read data from the command line, and you have learned several techniques for editing data entered with the Read and Readln procedures.

You have learned that every keystroke produces two bytes of information. Either the first byte is the ASCII value of the character, and the second byte can be ignored; or the first byte is zero, and the second byte has a special (non-ASCII) meaning called an "extended" code.

You have learned that these bytes are placed in a special keyboard buffer that your program uses as its source of input. The ReadKey function can be used to identify a single keystroke and process extended keystrokes. You have learned how the KeyPressed function can be used to test if a character is available to be read from the keyboard buffer. You have seen that you can insert characters into the buffer and have your program execute a DOS command upon completion.

You have learned how to prevent input from appearing on the screen, and you have learned how to handle the Esc, Ctrl-Break, and Ctrl-C keys.

You have learned how you can use the ECHO command to redefine the meaning of keystrokes entered from DOS.

You have learned how to control the settings of the shift keys (Shift, Ctrl, and Alt) and the toggle keys (CapsLock, NumLock, ScrollLock, and Ins) by accessing the keyboard status bytes at memory locations $0040:$0017 and $0040:$0018.

CHAPTER 10

Text Display

Suppose that you have sweated endless hours developing the world's most sophisticated spreadsheet program. It manipulates n-dimensional data structures, performs marvelously fast data retrieval, and achieves miraculously faster internal processing. It also displays all of its data in the lower left corner of the screen and scrolls up one line per cell, just like an adding machine tape. Your program is brilliant, but no one wants to use it.

This happens more often than you might think.

Together with keyboard entry routines, screen layouts constitute the *user interface*. Through the user interface a program communicates with the outside world; consequently, it's the user interface that establishes the program's character and identity. If a program has a personality, it can be read on the screen. In less fanciful terms, the images on the screen help determine how "user-friendly" your program is. In order to improve the quality of your program, you need to improve the quality of the screens that your program displays.

This chapter discusses screen management techniques using the Monochrome Display Adapter (MDA) and the text display modes of the various color and graphics adapter boards. Graphics routines are discussed in Chapter 11.

Screen Memory

Even though only 640K of memory is available to your program, the 8086-family processor can—and does—physically access the full 1 megabyte of address space. For example, if your PC has color capability, the memory beginning at $B800:0000 (which is B80000h or 753,664 decimal) is where

255

the PC places its screen images. This area is referred to as *screen memory* or *video memory*. If your PC has a monochrome display, screen memory begins at $B000:0000.

The 8086 never writes "to the screen"; instead, it writes to this particular memory area. Manufacturers of monitors and color adapter boards design their products to read these memory locations continuously and move their contents to specific cursor positions on the screen. In other words, the chore of writing "to the screen" is actually the responsibility of specially designed hardware circuits over which the CPU has no control.

Contents of Video Memory

A 25-line by 80-column screen has 2,000 possible cursor positions. The 2,000 words that begin at the memory location $B800:0000 (or $B000:0000 if your machine is monochrome) define the current screen image. The first byte of each word is the ASCII character to be displayed, and the second byte is the *attribute* of the display, which controls such characteristics as color and whether the character should blink.

Therefore, beginning at memory location $B800:0000 (or $B000:0000 in a monochrome system), the PC stores an image of whatever it wants to display on the screen. The first word in this memory region represents the upper left corner of the screen. Each successive word in memory defines cursor positions to the right of the previous character. The 81st word in memory defines the first character on the second line of the screen. The 2,000th word defines what appears on the lower right corner of the screen.

Writing to Video Memory

Because anything in this memory area is automatically displayed, it follows that you can directly control the contents of the screen by writing directly to this area of memory, as demonstrated by the program SCR1 (listing 10.1).

Listing 10.1

```
program Scr1;
var
    i, Slider, Disp : word;
    Attrib          : byte;
begin
    Attrib := Ø;
    for Slider := Ø to 255 do begin
        Disp := Ø;
        for i := Ø to ( (23 * 8Ø) - 1 ) do begin
```

Listing 10.1 continues

Listing 10.1 *continued*

```
        Mem[ $B8ØØ : 2*i ]      := Lo( Disp );
        Inc( Disp );
        Mem[ $B8ØØ : 2*i  + 1 ] := Attrib;
        if Attrib = 255 then Attrib := Slider else Inc( Attrib );
      end;
    end;
  end.
```

Remember that the segment address $B800 must be changed to $B000 in a monochrome system.

By simply changing the contents of the memory array, the SCR1 program cycles through and displays every combination of ASCII character and attribute byte. Running the program results in an explosion of colors and styles, only one phase of which is illustrated in figure 10.1.

Fig. 10.1. *Output produced by the SCR1 program.*

Screen Coordinates

If you use the standard (X, Y) coordinate system to define a cursor position on the screen, with the upper left corner at (1,1) and the lower right corner at (80,25), then with a little algebra you can see that the offset value for a cursor position can be found at:

Words: 80*(Row–1) + (Column–1)

or

Bytes: 160*(Row–1) + 2*(Column–1)

Therefore, if you want to display a box of asterisks in the center of your screen (for example, rows 10 through 15 and columns 20 through 60), you can simply determine the appropriate offsets, as shown in the program SCR1A (listing 10.2).

***

Listing 10.2

```
program Scr1A;
var
   Row,
   Column : byte;
begin
   for Row := 10 to 15 do
      for Column := 20 to 60 do begin
         Mem[ $B800 : 160*(Row-1) +2*(Column-1) ]     := ord( '*' );
         Mem[ $B800 : 160*(Row-1) +2*(Column-1)  + 1 ] := 4;   { Red }
      end;
end.
```

***

Figure 10.2 shows the output from the program displayed against the image generated by the SCR1 program. SCR1A uses the byte form of the displacement. By setting each attribute to 4, the program ensures that the asterisks are all red. (Colors are covered in more detail shortly.)

***

Fig. 10.2. *Output produced by the SCR1A program.*

A more practical application is found in the rapid display of messages. The WriteString procedure in the SCR1B program (listing 10.3) outputs a string directly to video memory.

Listing 10.3

```
program Scr1B;
var
   Message : string;
procedure WriteString( OutString : string; Column, Row : byte );
var
   X : byte;
begin
   X := 1,
   while ( X  <= Length( OutString ) ) do begin
      Mem[ $B8ØØ : 2*(8Ø*(Row-1) +Column +X-2)    ] := ord( OutString[ X ] );
      Mem[ $B8ØØ : 2*(8Ø*(Row-1) +Column +X-2) +1 ] := 4;    { Red }
      X := X  + 1;
   end;
end;
begin
   Message := 'Hello.  Special program now beginning...';
   WriteString( Message, 2Ø, 1Ø );
end.
```

Screen Output

Normally, programs that write "to the screen" don't go to all this trouble. DOS itself offers a complete line of screen management services. One DOS call displays a character, another erases the screen, still another scrolls the screen, and so on. (Consider the code you would otherwise have to develop to scroll the screen by one line!) Nevertheless, for simply displaying blocks of characters, direct screen addressing (that is, direct screen *memory* addressing) is the fastest technique available.

Using the Crt Unit

Like most programs, Turbo Pascal normally relies on the DOS and BIOS functions when it generates screen output. However, when the Crt unit is included with a program, Turbo automatically performs its screen output with the faster direct memory method. Each use of a write or writeln bypasses the slower DOS routines in favor of directly positioning the output strings in the appropriate memory locations, which are then directly transferred to the screen. Therefore, the Crt unit allows screen displays to be as fast as memory access times. If your program performs screen writing extensively, it should include a uses Crt; line even if no other procedures or functions from the Crt unit are needed.

Because the standard output file (the screen) is bypassing the normal DOS control code, one side-effect of using the Crt unit is that output from write and writeln statements can't be redirected or piped with the | or > characters on the command line. For example, in the program CRTR1 (listing 10.4), two writeln statements use the standard output device, whereas two others use a defined file. (Files are discussed in more detail in Chapter 13.)

Listing 10.4

```
program Crtr1;
uses Crt;
var
    AnyFile : Text;
begin
    writeln( 'Line 1:  This text is sent to the standard output device.' );
    writeln( 'Line 2:  It bypasses DOS and can''t be redirected.' );
    Assign( AnyFile, '' );
    Rewrite( AnyFile );
    writeln( AnyFile, 'Line 3:  This text is sent to a different file. It' );
    writeln( AnyFile, 'Line 4:  uses DOS services, so it can be redirected.' );
end.
```

All four lines are displayed when CRTR1 executes from the command line.

```
Line 1:    This text is sent to the standard output device.
Line 2:    It bypasses DOS and can't be redirected.
Line 3:    This text is sent to a different file. It
Line 4:    uses DOS services, so it can be redirected.
```

However, if you try to redirect its output to the printer, only the lines that use DOS procedures are captured. Lines 1 and 2 bypass DOS, so they continue to be displayed on the screen.

```
Line 1:    This text is sent to the standard output device.
Line 2:    It bypasses DOS and can't be redirected.
```

This isn't a problem for most applications. A program that optionally allows CRT or printer output usually offers the user a choice at the beginning of its run, when the file parameter is assigned either to the printer or to a null file. This technique allows the program to use only a single set of write and writeln procedures. For example, in Lines 3 and 4 of the CRTR1 program, the AnyFile parameter could have been assigned to either *PRN* or *null* depending upon the user's selection. Unfortunately, this means that the direct memory output routines would be sacrificed.

Using the *AssignCrt* Procedure

To assign the file parameter to the CRT while not abandoning the direct memory optimizations, Turbo Pascal offers the AssignCrt procedure. It operates just like an ordinary Assign, except that no file name needs to be specified. Program CRTR2 in listing 10.5 demonstrates how the output mechanism can be selected. Again, because AssignCrt uses direct memory output and bypasses DOS, write and writeln procedures directed to the CRT can't be redirected.

Listing 10.5

```
program Crtr2;
uses Crt;
var
   AnyFile : Text;
   Choice  : char;
begin
   repeat
      write( '(P)rinter or (C)rt : ' );
      Choice := ReadKey;
   until UpCase(Choice) in [ 'P', 'C' ];
   writeln( Choice );
   case UpCase(Choice) of
      'P' : Assign( AnyFile, 'PRN' );
      'C' : AssignCRT( AnyFile );
   end;
   Rewrite( AnyFile );
   writeln( AnyFile, 'Line 1:   This text is sent to the CRT or to' );
   writeln( AnyFile, 'Line 2:   the printer.  It cannot be redirected.' );
end.
```

Disabling Direct Video Output

Inevitably, the situation arises in which you need a procedure or function in the Crt unit, but you don't want Turbo Pascal to use the direct memory writes. In this case, you can either assign the output to a null file, as listing 10.4 did for Lines 3 and 4 of the CRTR1 program, or you can simply switch off the optimized routines by setting the predefined Boolean variable DirectVideo to False.

You should note that the TextMode procedure, discussed later in this chapter, resets DirectVideo to True whenever it's called.

Contending with Snow

The monochrome screen uses 720 horizontal and 350 vertical dots or *pixels* for its display. Therefore, each of its 80 × 25 characters takes a 9 × 14 image. Color Graphics Adapters (CGAs) use 640 horizontal and 200 vertical pixels. Therefore, each CGA character takes up an 8 × 8 pattern.

There are two differences between a monochrome display and a CGA display. First, a monochrome display always displays crisper and cleaner text images than a CGA display. Second, the CGA is *slower* than a monochrome.

Because it's slower, an *older* CGA sometimes has trouble with interference—lines or spots commonly called *snow*—when the adapter writes directly to video memory. Snow is produced when the CGA board is trying to display *both* the regular screen image *and* your new video memory input. The distortion is caused when the CGA board tries to jump back and forth between them.

To compensate for this, the Crt unit includes special code that ensures that CGA video memory writes occur only during the nondisplaying horizontal retrace intervals. This code is enabled or disabled by the value of the predefined Boolean variable CheckSnow, which is set to True when the program first runs and after each execution of the TextMode procedure.

If your PC has a newer CGA, you can disable this "snow-checking" logic by setting CheckSnow to False. This should result in significantly faster displays.

Snow generally isn't a problem when you are working with monochromes, Extended Graphics Adapters (EGAs), Video Graphics Adapter (VGAs), or the newer CGAs. And, of course, snow isn't a problem at all if you disable direct video by setting DirectVideo to False. (More advanced snow-handling techniques are discussed in Chapter 17.)

The Attribute Byte

Each character on the screen consists of a rectangular cursor block of a certain color over which an ASCII character (also of a certain color) is superimposed. Associated with each screen position is a word-size memory value. The first byte in the word defines the ASCII character, and the second byte (the *attribute* byte) defines the color pattern to use in the display.

Attribute Bit Settings

The eight bits in the attribute byte are used in the manner shown in figure 10.3.

Fig. 10.3. *The structure of the attribute byte.*

```
Background/Foreground Combinations with Blinking
0 0 1 0 2 0 3 0 4 0 5 0 6 0 7 0 8 0      0 0 1 0 2 0 3 0 4 0 5 0 6 0 7 0 8 0
0 1 1 1 2 1 3 1 4 1 5 1 6 1 7 1 8 1      0 1 1 1 2 1 3 1 4 1 5 1 6 1 7 1 8 1
0 2 1 2 2 2 3 2 4 2 5 2 6 2 7 2 8 2      0 2 1 2 2 2 3 2 4 2 5 2 6 2 7 2 8 2
0 3 1 3 2 3 3 3 4 3 5 3 6 3 7 3 8 3      0 3 1 3 2 3 3 3 4 3 5 3 6 3 7 3 8 3
0 4 1 4 2 4 3 4 4 4 5 4 6 4 7 4 8 4      0 4 1 4 2 4 3 4 4 4 5 4 6 4 7 4 8 4
0 5 1 5 2 5 3 5 4 5 5 5 6 5 7 5 8 5      0 5 1 5 2 5 3 5 4 5 5 5 6 5 7 5 8 5
0 6 1 6 2 6 3 6 4 6 5 6 6 6 7 6 8 6      0 6 1 6 2 6 3 6 4 6 5 6 6 6 7 6 8 6
0 7 1 7 2 7 3 7 4 7 5 7 6 7 7 7 8 7      0 7 1 7 2 7 3 7 4 7 5 7 6 7 7 7 8 7
0 8 1 8 2 8 3 8 4 8 5 8 6 8 7 8 8 8      0 8 1 8 2 8 3 8 4 8 5 8 6 8 7 8 8 8
0 9 1 9 2 9 3 9 4 9 5 9 6 9 7 9 8 9      0 9 1 9 2 9 3 9 4 9 5 9 6 9 7 9 8 9
0 A 1 A 2 A 3 A 4 A 5 A 6 A 7 A 8 A      0 A 1 A 2 A 3 A 4 A 5 A 6 A 7 A 8 A
0 B 1 B 2 B 3 B 4 B 5 B 6 B 7 B 8 B      0 B 1 B 2 B 3 B 4 B 5 B 6 B 7 B 8 B
0 C 1 C 2 C 3 C 4 C 5 C 6 C 7 C 8 C      0 C 1 C 2 C 3 C 4 C 5 C 6 C 7 C 8 C
0 D 1 D 2 D 3 D 4 D 5 D 6 D 7 D 8 D      0 D 1 D 2 D 3 D 4 D 5 D 6 D 7 D 8 D
0 E 1 E 2 E 3 E 4 E 5 E 6 E 7 E 8 E      0 E 1 E 2 E 3 E 4 E 5 E 6 E 7 E 8 E
0 F 1 F 2 F 3 F 4 F 5 F 6 F 7 F 8 F      0 F 1 F 2 F 3 F 4 F 5 F 6 F 7 F 8 F
```

The color of the background rectangle is determined by the setting of the *Background* bits.

The color of the character itself is controlled by the *Foreground* bits. The Foreground field is generally considered as being four bits long, but functionally it consists of a three-bit color selector and a one-bit *intensifier*. If the character is to be displayed in high-intensity form, the Intense bit is set.

Finally, if you want the character to blink, the Blink bit is set.

The Blink and Intense bits affect only the character and not the background.

Choosing Colors

In order to help select color combinations, Turbo Pascal predefines several color constants. The values 0 through 7 correspond to the colors black through light gray. Both the background rectangle and the character itself (in the foreground) can have any combination of these colors.

Foreground and Background	Value
Black	0
Blue	1
Green	2
Cyan	3

Red	4
Magenta	5
Brown	6
LightGray	7

When the intensity bit is set, the Foreground field can assume eight new values. Don't be confused by the "Light" prefixes. Light colors are simply less dark and therefore significantly brighter.

Foreground	*Value*
DarkGray	8
LightBlue	9
LightGreen	10
LightCyan	11
LightRed	12
LightMagenta	13
Yellow	14
White	15

Finally, to enable blinking, just add the Blink constant.

Blinking	*Value*
Blink	128

Using Colors

To display a blinking red asterisk on a blue background at a general cursor position (column, row), you could use the following lines of code:

```
Mem[ $B800 : 160*(Row-1) +2*(Column-1) ] := ord( '*' );
Mem[ $B800 : 160*(Row-1) +2*(Column-1) + 1 ] :=
    Blink + (Blue Shl 4) + Red;
```

Fortunately, Turbo Pascal offers a simpler technique. The procedure TextColor selects the color of the foreground character, and the procedure TextBackground selects the background color. Adding the Blink constant to the parameter of either function enables the blinking process. Therefore, to display the asterisk, all you need do is:

```
GotoXY( Column, Row );
TextColor( Red + Blink );
TextBackground( Blue );
write( '*' );
```

Turbo Pascal uses a default attribute byte called TextAttr. Once its value is adjusted with the TextColor and TextBackground procedures, the colors (and the blinking) become the new defaults for all subsequent write and writeln procedures. Of course, you can adjust the TextAttr variable directly, but executing the TextColor and TextBackground procedures is easier and provides better program documentation. Although Turbo provides no procedures to directly identify the current color scheme, you can obtain this information by testing the bits of the TextAttr variable.

To display the complete set of color combinations for your hardware, execute the ATTR2 program (listing 10.6). Each background and foreground pair is presented, with and without blinking enabled. The background number is shown first, followed by the foreground value (in hexadecimal, in order to comfortably fit it on the screen). Sample output is shown in figure 10.4. (Remember, however, that in the actual program, the right-hand side of the screen will be blinking.)

Listing 10.6

```
program Attr2;
uses Crt;
var
   Blinker,
   Color,
   Background : byte;
begin
   ClrScr;
   writeln( 'Background/Foreground Combinations with Blinking' );
   for Color := 0 to 15 do begin
      for Blinker := 0 to 1 do begin
         TextColor( Color + 128*Blinker );
         for Background := 0 to 7 do begin
            TextBackground( Background );
            write( Background:2 );
            if Color > 9 then write( chr(55 +Color):2 )
                         else write( Color:2 );
         end;
         TextBackground( Black );                  { Reset }
         if Blinker = 0 then write( '       ' );  { 7 spaces }
      end;
      writeln;
   end;
end.
```

Not too surprisingly, characters disappear when the foreground and background colors are the same.

Obviously, colors will be displayed only if your PC is equipped with color capability. On a monochrome system, the attribute byte can display only five formats: hidden, normal, highlighted, underlined, and reverse video. Hidden text corresponds to black characters on a black background. Reverse video is a

Fig. 10.4. Output produced by the ATTR2 program.

```
Background/Foreground Combinations with Blinking
00 10 20 30 40 50 60 70         00 10 20 30 40 50 60 70
01 11 21 31 41 51 61 71         01 11 21 31 41 51 61 71
02 12 22 32 42 52 62 72         02 12 22 32 42 52 62 72
03 13 23 33 43 53 63 73         03 13 23 33 43 53 63 73
04 14 24 34 44 54 64 74         04 14 24 34 44 54 64 74
05 15 25 35 45 55 65 75         05 15 25 35 45 55 65 75
06 16 26 36 46 56 66 76         06 16 26 36 46 56 66 76
07 17 27 37 47 57 67 77         07 17 27 37 47 57 67 77
08 18 28 38 48 58 68 78         08 18 28 38 48 58 68 78
09 19 29 39 49 59 69 79         09 19 29 39 49 59 69 79
0A 1A 2A 3A 4A 5A 6A 7A         0A 1A 2A 3A 4A 5A 6A 7A
0B 1B 2B 3B 4B 5B 6B 7B         0B 1B 2B 3B 4B 5B 6B 7B
0C 1C 2C 3C 4C 5C 6C 7C         0C 1C 2C 3C 4C 5C 6C 7C
0D 1D 2D 3D 4D 5D 6D 7D         0D 1D 2D 3D 4D 5D 6D 7D
0E 1E 2E 3E 4E 5E 6E 7E         0E 1E 2E 3E 4E 5E 6E 7E
0F 1F 2F 3F 4F 5F 6F 7F         0F 1F 2F 3F 4F 5F 6F 7F
```

black foreground on a LightGray (white) background. Underlined characters appear when the foreground color is set to Blue. Normal and highlighted states are the same as those in a color system.

Modifying Intensity

Although listed as two distinct colors, pairs such as Red and LightRed appear to the eye as two different intensities of the same color.

Turbo Pascal provides three procedures to change the Intense bit of the TextAttr default attribute. LowVideo clears the Intense bit, whereas HighVideo sets it. The NormVideo procedure sets the entire TextAttr byte to the value it had when the program started.

As the INTENSE1 program in listing 10.7 executes, the color of the display changes from Red (for low intensity) to LightRed (for high intensity) back to the default color contained in TextAttr when the program began. Again, the only action taken by the LowVideo and HighVideo procedures is to clear and set the default Intense bit. Executing TextColor(Red) followed by HighVideo has the same effect as executing TextColor(LightRed). Consequently, both lines display the same color characteristics.

Although the intensity procedures don't add any more colors to the set you already have, they can be used quite effectively for highlighting screen messages. A partial set of choices can be displayed by executing the INTENSE2 program (listing 10.8).

Listing 10.7

```
program Intense1;
uses Crt;
begin
   TextColor( Red );    { As an example }
   LowVideo;   write( 'Low Low Low...' );
   HighVideo;  write( 'High High High...' );
   NormVideo;  write( 'Norm Norm Norm' );
   writeln;
   TextColor( LightRed );
   LowVideo;   write( 'Low Low Low...' );
   HighVideo;  write( 'High High High...' );
   NormVideo;  write( 'Norm Norm Norm' );
   writeln;
end.
```

Listing 10.8

```
program Intense2;
uses Crt;
var
   Cycle : byte;
begin
   ClrScr;
   for Cycle := 1 to 24 do begin
      TextColor( Random( 15 ) + 1 );
      TextBackground( Random( 8 ) + 1 );  write( 'Color Color Color....' );
      LowVideo;                           write( 'Low Low Low....' );
      HighVideo;                          write( 'High High High....' );
      NormVideo;                          write( 'Normal Normal Normal' );
      writeln;
   end;
end.
```

Each level of intensity is displayed, together with the color number, as shown in figure 10.5.

Text Mode

A text screen can be either 40 or 80 columns wide and 25, 43, or 50 lines long. It can display either color characters or a single color (usually green or amber) with shading to simulate colors. Taken together, size and color define the *mode* of a screen.

Programs that use 80-columns don't work well on 40-column screens. Similarly, some programs deliberately display only 40 columns on a screen capable of 80 in order to show larger character sizes. If you develop a program

Fig. 10.5. Output produced by INTENSE2 program.

```
Color Color Color....Low Low Low....High High High....Normal Normal Normal
Color Color Color....Low Low Low....High High High....Normal Normal Normal
Color Color Color....Low Low Low....High High High....Normal Normal Normal
Color Color Color....Low Low Low....High High High....Normal Normal Normal
Color Color Color....Low Low Low....High High High....Normal Normal Normal
Color Color Color....Low Low Low....High High High....Normal Normal Normal
Color Color Color....Low Low Low....High High High....Normal Normal Normal
Color Color Color....Low Low Low....High High High....Normal Normal Normal
Color Color Color....Low Low Low....High High High....Normal Normal Normal
Color Color Color....Low Low Low....High High High....Normal Normal Normal
Color Color Color....Low Low Low....High High High....Normal Normal Normal
Color Color Color....Low Low Low....High High High....Normal Normal Normal
Color Color Color....Low Low Low....High High High....Normal Normal Normal
Color Color Color....Low Low Low....High High High....Normal Normal Normal
Color Color Color....Low Low Low....High High High....Normal Normal Normal
Color Color Color....Low Low Low....High High High....Normal Normal Normal
Color Color Color....Low Low Low....High High High....Normal Normal Normal
Color Color Color....Low Low Low....High High High....Normal Normal Normal
Color Color Color....Low Low Low....High High High....Normal Normal Normal
Color Color Color....Low Low Low....High High High....Normal Normal Normal
Color Color Color....Low Low Low....High High High....Normal Normal Normal
Color Color Color....Low Low Low....High High High....Normal Normal Normal
```

with a color monitor, you may wish to switch to a black and white mode to see how it looks when executing on a monochrome display. If you have EGA or VGA capability, you may wish to display 43 or 50 lines on your screen instead of the default of 25.

Turbo Pascal predefines several constants that can be used to identify the mode of the screen, as shown in table 10.1.

Table 10.1. Screen Mode Constants

Mode	Value	Meaning
BW4Ø	0	40 × 25 B/W on Color Adapter
CO4Ø	1	40 × 25 Color on Color Adapter
BW8Ø	2	80 × 25 B/W on Color Adapter
CO8Ø	3	80 × 25 Color on Color Adapter
Mono	7	80 × 25 on Monochrome Adapter
Font8×8	256	Add-on for ROM font

To set a specific mode, call the TextMode procedure with one of the predefined constants as a parameter. Note that TextMode always clears the screen before resetting it. TextMode is demonstrated in the MODE2 program (listing 10.9), which switches through all available screen options.

Listing 10.9

```
program Mode2;
uses Crt;
begin
   TextMode( BW4Ø );
   writeln( '4Øx25 Black & White on a Color Adapter' );
   readln;
   TextMode( CO4Ø );
   writeln( '4Øx25 Color on a Color Adapter' );
   readln;
   TextMode( BW8Ø );
   writeln( '8Øx25 Black & White on a Color Adapter' );
   readln;
   TextMode( CO8Ø );
   writeln( '8Øx25 Color on a Color Adaptor' );
   readln;
   TextMode( Mono );
   writeln( '8Øx25 on a Monochrome Adapter' );
   readln;
   { ================================================ }
   TextMode( CO8Ø + Font8x8 );
   writeln( '8Øx25 Color on a Color Adapter' );
   writeln( 'with Add-in ROM Font' );
   readln;
end.
```

The Font8x8 constant is added to CO8Ø to activate the compressed EGA or VGA modes. EGA compressed text is 80 columns by 43 lines. VGA compressed text is 80 columns by 50 lines. If these special adapters aren't available, the use of the Font8x8 constant has no effect.

When you run MODE2, you will probably notice that several of the messages appear identical. That's to be expected. After all, changing the mode of your screen doesn't change its capabilities. You may, for example, disable color generation on a color system, but the color video adapter card is still present in your PC and video memory remains in the $B800 segment. On a color system, the call

```
TextMode( Mono );
```

is equivalent to

```
TextMode( BW8Ø );
```

Similarly, on a monochrome system, the mode can't be changed to color.

To keep track of the mode, Turbo Pascal provides the predefined word-sized variable LastMode. In spite of its confusing name, LastMode actually contains the *current* video mode. To learn how your PC is configured, your program can examine this variable, as demonstrated by the MODE1 program in listing 10.10.

Listing 10.10

```
program Mode1;
uses Crt;
begin
   case Lo( LastMode ) of
      BW4Ø : writeln( 'Mode is 4Ø x 25 B/W on Color Adapter' );
      CO4Ø : writeln( 'Mode is 4Ø x 25 Color on Color Adapter' );
      BW8Ø : writeln( 'Mode is 8Ø x 25 B/W on Color Adapter' );
      CO8Ø : writeln( 'Mode is 8Ø x 25 Color on Color Adapter' )
      Mono : writeln( 'Mode is 8Ø x 25 on Monochrome Adapter' );
      else   writeln( 'Non-standard mode' );
   end;
   if Lastmode and 256  <> Ø then
      writeln( 'Extended display enabled' );
end.
```

LastMode can be tested to determine which segment ($B800 or $B000) contains the video memory for your PC. The MODE1A program (listing 10.11) performs such a test.

Listing 10.11

```
program Mode1A;
uses Crt;
var
   VideoSegment : word;
procedure SetVideoSegment;
begin
   if LastMode = 7 { Mono } then
      VideoSegment := $BØØØ
   else
      VideoSegment := $B8ØØ;
end;
begin
   SetVideoSegment;
   :
   :  { Continue }
   :
end.
```

The variable VideoSegment can now be used as the segment value when you are using video memory.

Generally, one mode is selected and used throughout the entire program. Occasionally, however, a program operates in more than one mode, in which case LastMode should be saved prior to the mode change.

```
var
  StoredMode : word;
   :
begin
   :
```

```
        StoredMode := LastMode;
        TextMode( BW4Ø );                { Switch to 4Ø-column Black & White mode }
          :
        TextMode( StoredMode );          { Return to original mode }
          :
    end;
```

Cursor Positioning and Screen Control

Turbo Pascal provides several screen positioning and line control routines. Many of them, such as GotoXY, you have already used. This section will increase your familiarity with those tools, and introduce a few new ones.

Setting Cursor Position

The GotoXY routine enables you to place the cursor at any desired position on the screen. Through the repeated use of GotoXY and write, you can "paint the screen."

The program GOTO3 (listing 10.12) displays a screen, shown in figure 10.6, designed to capture the entries for a mailing list. Each individual field (Name, Address, City, State, and Zip) is read as a string, and edited to remove leading blanks. All letters are capitalized, and within each field, multiple blanks are transformed to single blanks. For example, the field:

"   LoS   aNgeLeS" becomes "LOS ANGELES"

Each field is redisplayed after each entry and edit.

Listing 10.12

```
program Goto3;
uses Crt;
var
    Name    : string[ 2Ø ];
    Address : string[ 3Ø ];
    City    : string[ 25 ];
    State   : string[ 2 ];
    Zip     : string[ 5 ];
function EditedStr( Column, Row, StrLength : byte ) : string;
var
    BlankTest, i : byte;
    StrEntry,
    StrExit : string;
    InChar : char;
```

Listing 10.12 continues

Listing 10.12 *continued*

```
begin
   repeat
      GotoXY( Column, Row );
      for i := 1 to StrLength do write( '_' );
      GotoXY( Column, Row );
      StrEntry[ Ø ] := chr( Ø );    { Length of "StrEntry" now equals zero }
      repeat
         InChar := ReadKey;
         if InChar <> chr( 13 ) then
            StrEntry := StrEntry + InChar;
         write( InChar );
      until (InChar = chr( 13 )) or (Length( StrEntry ) = StrLength);
      StrExit[ Ø ] := chr( Ø );    { Length of "StrExit" now equals zero }
      if Length( StrEntry ) > Ø then begin
         { Strip leading blanks }
         BlankTest := 1;
         while (StrEntry[ BlankTest ] = ' ') and
               (BlankTest <= Length( StrEntry )) do
            Inc( BlankTest );
         { Convert to upper case and disallow multiple blanks }
         if Length( StrEntry ) >= BlankTest then
            for i := BlankTest to Length( StrEntry ) do
               if not ((StrEntry[ i ] = ' ') and (StrEntry[ i-1 ] = ' ')) then
                  StrExit := StrExit + UpCase( StrEntry[ i ] );
      end;
   until Length( StrExit ) > Ø;
   GotoXY( Column, Row ); for i := 1 to StrLength do write( ' ' );
   GotoXY( Column, Row ); write( StrExit );
   EditedStr := StrExit;
end;
begin
   ClrScr;
   GotoXY( 1Ø,  8 );    write( 'Name: _____' );
   GotoXY(  7, 1Ø );    write( 'Address: _____' );
   GotoXY( 1Ø, 12 );    write( 'City: _____' );
   GotoXY(  9, 14 );    write( 'State: __' );
   GotoXY( 11, 16 );    write( 'Zip: _____' );
   Name    := EditedStr( 16,  8, 2Ø );
   Address := EditedStr( 16, 1Ø, 3Ø );
   City    := EditedStr( 16, 12, 25 );
   State   := EditedStr( 16, 14,  2 );
   Zip     := EditedStr( 16, 16,  5 );
end.
```

Line Control

The ClrScr procedure was called at the beginning of the GOTO3 program. ClrScr, one of several screen-management procedures offered by Turbo Pascal, erases the screen and positions the cursor in the upper left corner.

Fig. 10.6. Output produced by the GOTO3 program.

```
           Name: _____  _____
        Address: _____
           City: _____
          State: __
            Zip: _____
```

The ClrEol procedure erases all characters on the current line to the right of the cursor. The position of the cursor remains unchanged.

The DelLine procedure deletes the line containing the cursor. All lines below the current line scroll up. The relative position of the cursor remains unchanged.

The InsLine procedure inserts an empty line in the same line as the cursor. All lines below the current line scroll down. The relative position of the cursor remains unchanged.

The actions of the ClrScr, ClrEol, DelLine, and InsLine procedures can be explored in the WHERE1 program (listing 10.13). It fills the screen with characters, positions the cursor in a random location, and enables you to call one of the four procedures. It begins with the screen shown in figure 10.7.

Listing 10.13

```pascal
program Where1;
uses Crt;
const
   Width  : byte = 80;
   Bottom : byte = 24;
var
   Row, Column,
   RowCode     : byte;
   Choice      : char;
begin
   ClrScr;
   Randomize;
   for Column := 1 to 80 do
      for Row := 1 to 23 do begin
         RowCode := Row mod 10;
         GotoXY( Column, Row );
         TextColor( Random( 6 ) + 1 );
         write( RowCode );
      end;
```

Listing 10.13 continues

Listing 10.13 continued

```
repeat
   NormVideo;
   GotoXY( 1, 25 );
   write( '(1)ClrEol  (2)DelLine  (3)InsLine  (4)ClrScr  (5)End' );
   Row    := Random( Bottom ) + 1;
   Column := Random( Width ) + 1;
   GotoXY( Column, Row );
   TextColor( Red  + Blink );
   write( ' +' );
   repeat
      Choice := ReadKey;
   until Choice in [ '1'..'5' ];
   GotoXY( 1, 25 );  ClrEol;
   GotoXY( Column, Row );  TextColor( White );   write( ' +' );
   case Choice of
      '1' : ClrEol;
      '2' : begin
               DelLine;
               Dec( Bottom );
            end;
      '3' : begin
               InsLine;
               Inc( Bottom );
            end;
      else  ClrScr;
   end;
   until Choice = '5';
end.
```

Fig. 10.7. Output produced by the WHERE1 program.

```
11111111111111111111111111111111111111111111111111111111111111111111111111111111
22222222222222222222222222222222222222222222222222222222222222222222222222222222
33333333333333333333333333333333333333333333333333333333333333333333333333333333
44444444444444444444444444444444444444444444444444444444444444444444444444444444
55555555555555555555555555555555555555555555555555555555555555555555555555555555
66666666666666666666666666666666666666666666666666666666666666666666666666666666
77777777777777777777777777777777777777777777777777777777777777777777777777777777
88888888888888888888888888888888888888888888888888888888888888888888888888888888
99999999999999999999999999999999999999999999999999999999999999999999999999999999
00000000000000000000000000000000000000000000000000000000000000000000000000000000
11111111111111111111111111111111111111111111111111111111111111111111111111111111
22222222222222222222222222222222222222222222222222222222222222222222222222222222
33333333333333333333333333333333333333333333333+33333333333333333333333333333333
44444444444444444444444444444444444444444444444444444444444444444444444444444444
55555555555555555555555555555555555555555555555555555555555555555555555555555555
66666666666666666666666666666666666666666666666666666666666666666666666666666666
77777777777777777777777777777777777777777777777777777777777777777777777777777777
8888888888888888888888888888888888888888888888888888888888888888888888888888888
99999999999999999999999999999999999999999999999999999999999999999999999999999999
00000000000000000000000000000000000000000000000000000000000000000000000000000000
11111111111111111111111111111111111111111111111111111111111111111111111111111111
22222222222222222222222222222222222222222222222222222222222222222222222222222222
33333333333333333333333333333333333333333333333333333333333333333333333333333333
```

(1)ClrEol (2)DelLine (3)InsLine (4)ClrScr (5)End

Locating the Cursor Position

Of course, the WHERE1 program had one major advantage: Even though the target cursor location was assigned randomly, you always knew where the cursor was located. Most programs that allow the cursor to roam freely still keep track of its location in special variables. The variables are passed as parameters to any procedure dependent upon cursor location. For example, in the Turbo Editor itself, the cursor row and column positions are always displayed; if auto-indent is turned off, pressing the Enter key repositions the cursor to the first column of the next row.

Sometimes it's simply not convenient to keep track of cursor position. In an operational version of the GOTO3 program, cursor location would be precisely controlled. Yet the user might be in the process of entering data in a field before he or she presses a Help key. That action would trigger the display of a help message, then reposition the cursor on the same spot where the help feature was invoked. Without using much imagination, you can see that maintaining fields with cursor position in a form-entry program is more trouble than it might be worth.

A simple alternative is provided by Turbo Pascal. The WhereX and WhereY functions return the X and Y coordinates, respectively, of the cursor at any time. A procedure that needs to know the current cursor location can simply call these functions, as demonstrated in the WHERE2 program (listing 10.14).

Listing 10.14

```pascal
program Where2;
uses Crt;
var
    Row, Column, RowCode : byte;

procedure ClearEndScreen;
var
    CurrentX, CurrentY, RowWork, MaxRows : byte;
begin
    CurrentX := WhereX;                        { Locate current X-coordinate }
    CurrentY := WhereY;                        { Locate current Y-coordinate }
    ClrEol;                                    { First, clear the current line }
    MaxRows := Hi( WindMax ) + 1;    { Number of rows in current window }
    if MaxRows > CurrentY then
        for RowWork := CurrentY + 1 to MaxRows do begin
            GotoXY( 1, RowWork );              { Go to start of each successive line }
            ClrEol;                            { Clear each successive line }
        end;
    GotoXY( CurrentX, CurrentY );     { Return to the original spot }
end;
```

Listing 10.14 continues

Listing 10.14 *continued*

```
begin
   ClrScr;
   Randomize;
   for Column := 1 to 80 do
      for Row := 1 to 23 do begin
         RowCode := Row mod 10;
         GotoXY( Column, Row );
         TextColor( Random( 6 ) + 1 );
         write( RowCode );
      end;
   GotoXY( Random( 80 ) + 1, Random( 24 ) + 1 );
   TextColor( Red + Blink );
   write( '+' );
   Delay( 2000 );
   ClearEndScreen;
   GotoXY( 1, 25 );
   NormVideo;
   write( 'Hit enter to end...' );
   readln;
end.
```

The WHERE2 program fills the screen with characters, then randomly positions the cursor. After a short delay, it calls the ClearEndScreen procedure, which clears all characters to the right of the cursor and all characters on all lines below the cursor.

Using the WhereX and WhereY functions, ClearEndScreen can determine its starting point without having been passed separate position parameters. Notice, in fact, that the main body of the program doesn't even bother storing the cursor's coordinates.

The predefined variable WindMax was used by ClearEndScreen to determine the number of rows to erase. WindMax is discussed in greater detail in the next section.

Managing Windows

The SCR1A program presented in listing 10.1 at the beginning of the chapter displayed characters to a small rectangular area of the screen. Such a region, commonly called a *window*, can be managed easily in Turbo Pascal.

Windows are used most frequently to display information or interact with the user without destroying or obscuring most of the original screen. In the Turbo Pascal interactive environment, for example, pull-down menus appear and disappear in windows as needed, leaving the bulk of the screen intact.

The Turbo Pascal Window procedure is called with four byte-sized location parameters as follows:

```
Window( left, top, right, bottom );
```

Window changes the default screen into a rectangle with an upper left position of (left, top) and a lower right position of (right, bottom).

After `Window` executes, all standard screen display instructions (such as `GotoXY`, `ClrScr`, and `writeln`) will be processed relative to the new window, not to the original screen. One exception is another `Window` instruction, which always uses absolute references. The original screen size is restored by the call:

```
Window( 1, 1, 80, 25 );
```

The minimum window size is 1 column by 1 row. The maximum window size is the original system default of 25 rows by 80 columns.

Identifying the Current Window

The coordinates of the upper left corner of the current window can be found in the predefined variable `WindMin`, Similarly, `WindMax` contains the coordinates of the lower right corner. `WindMin` and `WindMax` are word-sized variables, with the upper byte holding the Y coordinate and the lower byte holding the X coordinate. Unlike every other screen procedure, `WindMin` and `WindMax` assume that screen coordinates range from (0,0) to (79,24). These variables can be used as follows:

```
Left   := Lo( WindMin ) + 1;   { Upper-left hand X-coordinate  }
Top    := Hi( WindMin ) + 1;   { Upper-left hand Y-coordinate  }
Right  := Lo( WindMax ) + 1;   { Lower-right hand X-coordinate }
Down   := Hi( WindMax ) + 1;   { Lower-right hand Y-coordinate }
Width  := Right - Left  + 1;
Height := Bottom - Top  + 1;
Area   := Width * Height;
```

Using a Single Window

The SCR3 program (listing 10.15) fills the screen with asterisks, opens a window in the center of the screen, then displays the attention-getting message ERROR in blinking red letters, as shown in figure 10.8.

Listing 10.15

```
program Scr3;
uses Crt;
var
   Row, Column : byte;
begin
   ClrScr;
   for Column := 1 to 80 do
      for Row := 1 to 23 do begin
```

Listing 10.15 continues

Listing 10.15 continued

```
        GotoXY( Column, Row );
        TextColor( Random( 6 ) + 1 );
        write( '*' );
      end;
    Window( 25, 8, 55, 16 );
    ClrScr;
    GotoXY( 13, 5 );
    TextColor( Red + Blink );
    write( 'ERROR' );
  end.
```

Fig. 10.8. Output produced by the SCR3 program.

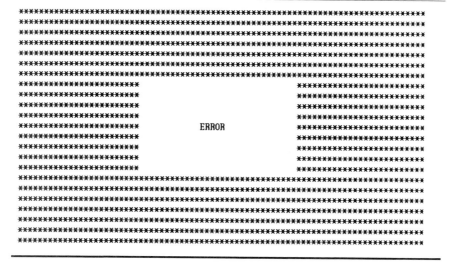

Notice that the second `ClrScr` and `GotoXY` calls affect only the current window, not the entire screen. The window itself effectively becomes the new screen.

Saving and Restoring Multiple Windows

In most windowing applications, a window appears, characters are displayed, input is received, and the window closes, leaving no trace of its presence. Turbo Pascal makes generating and using a window easy. It does not, however, provide a direct way to save the contents of a screen before a window is called, nor does it offer an easy way to restore the screen to its original image after the window is no longer needed.

The WIND2 program in listing 10.16 introduces the OpenWindow and CloseWindow procedures. OpenWindow saves the original screen image before it executes the call to the Window procedure. CloseWindow closes the most recently opened window and restores the prior screen image. OpenWindow and CloseWindow allow up to 10 windows to be opened at once.

Listing 10.16

```
program Wind2;
uses Crt;
type
    ScreenImage  = array [ Ø..1999 ] of word;
    FrameRec     = record
                        UpperLeft,
                        LowerRight   : word;
                        ScreenMemory : ScreenImage;
                    end;
var
    SnapShot     : ^ScreenImage;
    FrameStore   : array [ 1..1Ø ] of ^FrameRec;
    WindowNumber : byte;

procedure OpenWindow( UpLeftX, UpLeftY, LoRightX, LoRightY : byte );
begin
    WindowNumber := WindowNumber + 1;
    New( FrameStore[ WindowNumber ] );
    with FrameStore[ WindowNumber ]^ do begin
        ScreenMemory := SnapShot^;
        UpperLeft    := WindMin;
        LowerRight   := WindMax;
    end;
    Window( UpLeftX, UpLeftY, LoRightX, LoRightY );
end;

procedure CloseWindow;
begin
    with FrameStore[ WindowNumber ]^ do begin
        SnapShot^ := ScreenMemory;
        Window( (Lo(UpperLeft) +1),   (Hi(UpperLeft) +1),
                (Lo(LowerRight) +1),  (Hi(LowerRight) +1) );
    end;
    Dispose( FrameStore[ WindowNumber ] );
    WindowNumber := WindowNumber - 1;
end;

procedure FillScreen( Filler : byte );
var
    Row, Column : byte;
begin
    ClrScr;
    TextBackground( Filler + 1 );    { Not black }
```

Listing 10.16 continues

Listing 10.16 *continued*

```
    for Column := 1 to 80 do
       for Row := 1 to 23 do begin
          TextColor( Random( 6 ) + 1 );
          write( Filler );
       end;
    NormVideo;
 end;

 begin
    SnapShot := Ptr( $B800, $0000 );    { Set to $B000 if monochrome }
    WindowNumber := 0;
    OpenWindow( 10, 5, 40, 15 );
    FillScreen( 2 );
    OpenWindow( 20, 10, 65, 13 );
    FillScreen( 3 );
    OpenWindow( 5, 2, 25, 20 );
    FillScreen( 4 );
    GotoXY( 1, 1 ); write( 'Hit enter... ' ); Readln;
    CloseWindow;
    GotoXY( 1, 1 ); write( 'Hit enter... ' ); Readln;
    CloseWindow;
    GotoXY( 1, 1 ); write( 'Hit enter... ' ); Readln;
    CloseWindow;
 end.
```

The FillScreen procedure shows the location and shape of each window by filling it with a number, as shown in figure 10.9.

Fig. 10.9. *Output produced by the WIND2 program.*

The `OpenWindow` procedure dynamically stores a record containing the current screen image and the current `WindMin` and `WindMax` variables. `Close-Window` retrieves that record, restores the screen, then uses `WindMin` and `WindMax` to call `Window` and reset the screen size. More efficiently written procedures might only save and restore the area of the window itself.

Notice that the first line in the main body of the program identifies the start of video memory. Incorporating a procedure such as `SetVideoSegment` (shown in the MODE1A program in listing 10.11) would enable WIND2 to work on all PC types. Instead of the command

```
SnapShot := Ptr( $B800, $0000 );    { Set to $B000 if monochrome }
```

you could use

```
SnapShot := Ptr( VideoSegment, $0000 );
```

Summary

In this chapter, you have learned how Turbo Pascal programs can manage the Monochrome Display Adapter (MDA) and the text display modes of the various color and graphics adapter boards.

You have learned about the screen memory of your PC, and you have seen how any data moved to this region is automatically displayed on the screen. You have learned that each cursor position is defined by a word of memory. The first byte of this word is the ASCII character to be displayed, and the second byte is the `attribute` of the display. Individual bits in the attribute byte determine the foreground and background colors, the intensity, and whether the character is to blink. You have learned about the Turbo Pascal procedures that control color and intensity.

You have learned that when the Crt standard unit is included with a program, Turbo automatically performs its screen output with the faster direct memory method. You have learned how to disable direct output to video memory, and you have learned how "snow" can be controlled.

You have learned how to use screen positioning and line control routines, and you have learned how to locate the X and Y coordinates of the cursor.

You have learned how to use windows, and you have seen how multiple windows can be managed in Turbo Pascal.

Graphics Display

No matter how many rows and columns of numbers your programs produce, numeric amounts always tend to be regarded as *data*. It isn't until patterns emerge and relationships are perceived that data becomes *information*.

Probably the most powerful visual method of projecting information is graphics. A single graphic image can provide more information in one glance than entire libraries of data. Scientists and engineers use graphics to understand the meaning of their experiments. Business people use graphics to gain quick insight into financial trends. Magazine publishers and network news programs use graphics to compress long stories into succinct facts. A well-designed graph has impact, and the message it conveys is remembered because of it.

This chapter will provide you with a solid foundation in the use of Turbo Pascal graphics routines.

The Graphics Screen

The default text screen consists of a rectangle of 25 rows of 80 characters. If you stare closely at one of the characters, you will notice that it consists of its own rectangular pattern of dots. Each of these dots is called a *pixel*, short for picture element. The monochrome screen contains 252,000 of them, densely packed in 350 lines of 720 columns.

In text mode, these pixels can only be used in 2,000 discrete blocks, 9 pixels wide by 14 pixels high. Each block contains one of the 256 ASCII characters. The actual pattern is controlled by PC hardware that automatically turns each pixel on or off depending on the ASCII value in the corresponding screen memory address. Other characteristics, such as color and intensity, are also determined for the entire block.

In graphics mode, each pixel can be individually traced, or *bit-mapped*, to its own unique memory location and consequently can be directly controlled by your program.

The Borland Graphics Interface

In text mode, you can write ASCII characters directly to screen memory. If you try that in graphics mode, you are likely to get bizarre (but interesting) results. Special software is required to convert the images you wish to display into the appropriate dots on the screen. This software is the Borland Graphics Interface, or BGI. Different graphics board manufacturers use various mapping techniques, so a different interface—provided in a file with the extension .BGI—is used for your specific configuration.

Graphics Adapters

The .BGI files available in Turbo Pascal are listed in table 11.1.

Table 11.1. *Graphics Adapter Driver Files*

Name	Driver
Color Graphics Adapter	CGA.BGI
Multicolor Graphics Array	CGA.BGI
Enhanced Graphics Adapter	EGAVGA.BGI
Video Graphics Adapter	EGAVGA.BGI
Hercules Monochrome Graphics	HERC.BGI
AT&T 400 Line Graphics	ATT.BGI
IBM PC 3270 Graphics	PC3270.BGI
IBM 8514 Graphics	IBM8514.BGI

Before you try to run any of the graphics routines in this book, make sure that the correct interface file for your graphics adapter is available to the Turbo Pascal compiler.

A .BGI file is commonly called a *driver*, because it is, technically, a device driver for the graphics display. Each vendor's product is driven by a different set of software signals. A device driver converts Turbo Pascal commands into instructions that can be understood by the graphics hardware.

Graphics Resolution and Modes

The *resolution* of a screen is determined by the number of pixels it contains. The greater the resolution, the cleaner and crisper the display. You see a consequence of poor resolution every day: newspaper photographs are notoriously "grainy" compared to the pictures you take with your own camera. It's natural, then, that computer users demand new, higher resolution graphics adapters.

The PC needs only 4,000 bytes to define the contents of a text screen completely—one character byte and one attribute byte for each of the 2,000 possible cursor positions. Graphics screens, because of their greater need for detail, are allocated 16K bytes of memory. Even this fourfold increase only provides about 130,000 bits, considerably fewer than the 252,000 pixels available in text mode.

Your PC sidesteps this problem in three ways.

1. Most graphics adapters use fewer pixels than a monochrome screen. For example, one of the most popular graphics adapters (and the only one supported by the earlier versions of Turbo Pascal) is the Color Graphics Adapter (CGA). Normally, CGA offers 200 rows of pixels, with each row consisting of only 320 columns of pixels. A quick calculation reveals that such a screen contains 64,000 pixels—only a quarter of those in text mode. Even in "high resolution mode," a CGA screen is arranged in a 640×200 pattern—still only half the number of a text display.

2. The graphics adapters themselves contain memory. This reduces the burden on the PC but makes it impossible to write directly to video memory. That's one of the functions of the Borland Graphics Interface.

3. Most graphics adapters offer fewer colors than the 16 found in text mode. For example, the high-resolution CGA screen can only draw in two colors.

The resolution of a screen, together with the number of available colors and memory pages (defined later), are described by the *mode* of the graphics adapter. Graphics modes for each driver are compared in table 11.2.

Table 11.2. *Turbo Pascal Graphics Drivers and Modes*

Graphics Adapter	Graphics Driver	Mode Name	Value	Resolution (Col × Row)	Palette	Pages
CGA	CGA.BGI	CGAC0	0	320 × 200	C0	1
		CGAC1	1	320 × 200	C1	1
		CGAC2	2	320 × 200	C2	1
		CGAC3	3	320 × 200	C3	1
		CGAHi	4	640 × 200	2 colors	1
MCGA	CGA.BGI	MCGAC0	0	320 × 200	C0	1
		MCGAC1	1	320 × 200	C1	1
		MCGAC2	2	320 × 200	C2	1
		MCGAC3	3	320 × 200	C3	1
		MCGAMed	4	640 × 200	2 colors	1
		MCGAHi	5	640 × 480	2 colors	1
EGA	EGAVGA.BGI	EGALo	0	640 × 200	16 colors	4
		EGAHi	1	640 × 350	16 colors	2
		EGA64Lo	0	640 × 200	16 colors	1
		EGA64Hi	1	640 × 350	4 colors	1
		EGAMonoHi	3	640 × 350	2 colors	1*
		EGAMonoHi	3	640 × 350	2 colors	2†
Hercules	HERC.BGI	HercMonoHi	0	720 × 348	2 colors	2
AT&T	ATT.BGI	ATT400C0	0	320 × 200	C0	1
		ATT400C1	1	320 × 200	C1	1
		ATT400C2	2	320 × 200	C2	1
		ATT400C3	3	320 × 200	C3	1
		ATT400Med	4	640 × 200	2 colors	1
		ATT400Hi	5	640 × 400	2 colors	1
VGA	EGAVGA.BGI	VGALo	0	640 × 200	16 colors	4
		VGAMed	1	640 × 350	16 colors	2
		VGAHi	2	640 × 480	16 colors	1
3270 PC	PC3270.BGI	PC3270Hi	0	720 × 350	2 colors	1
IBM 8514	IBM8514.BGI	IBM8514LO	0	640 × 480	256 colors	1
		IBM8514HI	1	1024 × 768	256 colors	1

    *1 page if the graphics board contains 64K of memory.

    †2 pages if the graphics board contains 256K of memory.

The Palette column identifies the colors available in each mode. Each entry in the column is either a specified number of colors or a C followed by an integer in the range 0 through 3. These integers identify a palette—a set of three colors, plus the "background" color. The colors in each palette are listed in table 11.3.

Table 11.3. *Turbo Pascal CGA, MCGA, and AT&T Graphics Palettes*

Palette	Color 0	Color 1	Color 2	Color 3
C0	Background	LightGreen	LightRed	Yellow
C1	Background	LightCyan	LightMagenta	White
C2	Background	Green	Red	Brown
C3	Background	Cyan	Magenta	LightGray

Using the background color is like writing with an empty pen; whatever you draw is invisible. Note that the background color is always included in every total. As a result, each entry described as "2 colors" is really monochrome.

A Note on *Mode*

Unfortunately, the word *mode* is a bit overused. For the remainder of this chapter, unless I specifically refer to text mode or graphics mode, the word *mode* will be used solely to indicate a resolution, color, and page count option of a graphics adapter. For example, the CGA adapter offers five modes. Each mode can be referenced by an integer in the range 0 through 4 or by one of the predefined constants CGAC0, CGAC1, CGAC2, CGAC3, or CGAHi.

The Coordinate System

Just as in text mode, every pixel on the graphics screen is referenced with an (X, Y) coordinate system. The upper left corner's coordinates are (0, 0), and the lower right corner's coordinates can be obtained from the screen resolution. For example, a CGA adapter in mode CGAC0 has (319, 199) for its lower right corner. The center of the same screen would be addressed as (160, 100).

The Current Pointer

In text mode, the cursor is always visible. Unless changed with a GotoXY statement, the cursor always comes to rest one space to the right of the last position written. If the last write was in column 80, the cursor would advance to the first position of the following line. If the last referenced position was the 80th column of the 25th line, the entire screen would scroll up one line, and the cursor would appear in the first column of the 25th line.

Both the cursor's appearance and its tendency to "wrap around" characters from the end of a line to the next line are directly controlled by DOS or, alternatively, by the software routines that emulate DOS in the Crt unit. Graphics mode is different. Because the screen image is under control of the circuitry on the graphics board itself, DOS rules don't apply.

The cursor on the text screen referenced the entire 9×14 pixel block. In graphics mode, only a single pixel is referenced at any one time. The location of this pixel is called the *current pointer*, or *CP*. Its position is directly over the last referenced character itself, not one space beyond as it is in text mode. Because a blinking CP would distort the graphics image, the CP isn't visible on the screen.

Entering and Exiting Graphics

When you include the Crt unit in your program, all `Write` and `Writeln` statements automatically bypass DOS and use the faster direct video memory routines. The Graph unit operates differently. Even if you include the Graph unit in your program, Turbo Pascal still assumes that the default mode is text rather than graphics.

There's good reason for this. Although you can, of course, write programs specifically to display graphics images, most applications use graphics as a supplement rather than as an end in itself. Spreadsheets and database managers, for example, may switch to graphics mode temporarily, but the majority of their efforts rely on text displays. In general, most interactive user interfaces are programmed in text mode.

In addition, graphics displays tend to be considerably slower than text displays. On some systems, the delay is hardly noticeable, but on others, the delay can irritate even the most patient user. You can avoid this problem by switching back to text mode when you do not use graphics.

Initializing Graphics Mode

You enter graphics mode by calling the `InitGraph` procedure.

```
procedure InitGraph( var GraphDriver  : integer;
                     var GraphMode    : integer;
                         PathToDriver : String );
```

The `GraphDriver` and `GraphMode` parameters identify the graphics driver and mode, respectively. `PathToDriver` holds the name of the subdirectory that contains the graphics drivers; simply use a null string if the files are in the current directory.

There are two ways to use InitGraph.

1. If you set GraphDriver to zero before calling InitGraph, Turbo Pascal will initialize graphics using the defaults for your machine.

```
GraphDriver :- Detect;
InitGraph( GraphDriver, GraphMode, 'C:\TP' );
```

The predefined constant Detect (which is equal to zero) is used as the starting value for GraphDriver when InitGraph is first called. Because GraphDriver is a variable parameter, it can't directly accept a constant parameter.

After InitGraph ends, GraphDriver contains a value corresponding to the graphics adapter Turbo detected, and GraphMode will contain a value corresponding to what Turbo believes to be the adapter's optimal mode. The values returned in the GraphDriver parameter can be compared to the predefined constants given in table 11.4. The values for GraphMode are the same as those in table 11.2. For example, if your PC is equipped with the Color Graphics Adapter, GraphDriver will be equal to CGA, and GraphMode may equal CGAHi.

Table 11.4. Graphics Drivers

Driver	Value
Detect	0
CGA	1
MCG	2
EGA	3
EGA64	4
EGAMono	5
IBM8514	6
HercMono	7
ATT400	8
VGA	9
PC3270	10

2. Of course, it's highly unlikely that your PC contains more than one graphics adapter, but some PCs and some adapters may not be properly detected. To initialize graphics using a specific driver and mode, choose a valid combination of values for the GraphDriver and Graph-Mode parameters before you call InitGraph.

```
GraphDriver := CGA;
GraphMode := CGAHi;
InitGraph( GraphDriver, GraphMode, 'C:\TP' );
```

If InitGraph is successful, it loads the .BGI driver file into heap memory, enters graphics mode, initializes all graphics settings to their defaults, and clears the screen.

> These examples, as well as all other examples in this book, assume that the graphics files reside in the C:\TP directory.

Detecting Graphics Hardware

If you are curious about the configuration of your PC, you can, of course, call InitGraph to learn which graphics adapter is installed and which mode Turbo Pascal believes is optimal. Unfortunately, one of the effects of InitGraph is to convert the PC to graphics mode. A more direct approach is to use the DetectGraph procedure:

```
procedure DetectGraph( var GraphDriver, GraphMode : integer );
```

DetectGraph is the procedure InitGraph itself uses when you call it with a GraphDriver parameter of zero. By calling DetectGraph directly, you are assured of obtaining the same values. The DetectGraph procedure is demonstrated in the GRAFINFO program in listing 11.1.

Listing 11.1

```
program GrafInfo;
uses Graph;
var
   GraphDriver, GraphMode : integer;
begin
   DetectGraph( GraphDriver, GraphMode );
   writeln( GraphDriver:8, GraphMode:8 )
end.
```

If you run the GRAFINFO program on a COMPAQ PLUS®, it reveals a driver of 1 and a mode of 4. Table 11.4 shows that the graphics adapter is a CGA. Table 11.2 reveals that CGA mode 4 (CGAHi) is high-resolution, with a 640 × 200 pixel screen.

If DetectGraph doesn't find a graphics adapter, GraphDriver returns a value of –2.

Detecting Graphics Modes

As you have seen, graphics adapters usually offer more than one mode. Although the DetectGraph procedure recommends an optimal mode, several other Turbo Pascal subroutines help you learn other modes that are available for your adapter.

```
function GetDriverName : string;
function GetGraphMode : integer;
function GetMaxMode : integer;
function GetModeName( GraphMode : integer ) : string;
procedure GetModeRange( 1GraphDriver : integer;
var LoMode, HiMode : integer);
```

The `GetDriverName` function returns the name of the current driver. This function wasn't used in the GRAFINFO program, because `GetDriverName` operates by accessing the currently loaded .BGI file; therefore, it can only run when the graphics system is active.

`GetGraphMode` returns the number of the current mode, as given in table 11.2. It can be used as the parameter for `GetModeName`, which returns the name of a given mode.

Except for EGAMono, the currently loaded graphics driver has mode numbers ranging from 0 through `GetMaxMode`. The `GetModeRange` procedure returns the lowest and highest graphics modes for any given driver.

The GRFINFO2 program in listing 11.2 combines all of these routines into a display that could be used as a help screen or as part of a menu.

Listing 11.2

```
program GrfInfo2;
uses Graph;
var
   GraphDriver, GraphMode, Low, High, Driver : integer;
begin
   GraphDriver := Detect;
   InitGraph( GraphDriver, GraphMode, 'C:\TP' );
   GetModeRange( GraphDriver, Low, High );
   writeln( 'Currently using the ', GetDriverName, ' driver ',
            'in mode ', GetModeName( GetGraphMode ) );
   writeln;
   writeln( '   Lowest mode is  ', Low );
   writeln( '   Highest mode is ', High );
   writeln;
   writeln;
   writeln( 'Other modes supported by the ', GetDriverName,
            ' driver are:' );
   writeln;
   for Driver := Ø to GetMaxMode do
      writeln( '   ', GetModeName( Driver ) );
   readln;          { Press Enter to continue }
   CloseGraph;
end.
```

When GRFINFO2 executes on a COMPAQ PLUS, it produces the output shown in figure 11.1.

Fig. 11.1. *Output produced by the GRFINFO2 program.*

```
Currently using the CGA driver in mode 640 x 200 CGA

Lowest mode is  0
Highest mode is 4

Other modes supported by the CGA driver are:

320 x 200 CGA C0
320 x 200 CGA C1
320 x 200 CGA C2
320 x 200 CGA C3
640 x 200 CGA
```

The Run/User Command (Alt-F5)

The Run/User screen menu command (the Alt-F5 hot key) can be used to examine output in text mode only. Graphics images are cleared by the CloseGraph procedure when graphics mode terminates and text mode is restored. Consequently, most of the programs in this chapter use the readln procedure to retain the graphics display while waiting for the Enter key to be pressed.

Detecting the Size of the Screen

Unless you can guarantee that your programs will always run in a specific mode on a specific graphics adapter, you should avoid writing code that assumes a constant resolution. Of course, you could maintain a table of graphics drivers, modes, and screen sizes—and continue to update it as new products are developed—but Turbo Pascal provides a simpler method:

```
function  GetMaxX : integer;
function  GetMaxY : integer;
```

The GetMaxX and GetMaxY functions return the number of the pixel in the extreme right column and bottom row, respectively. For example, on a COMPAQ PLUS, which has a high-resolution CGA 640 × 200 graphics adapter, GetMaxX returns 639 and GetMaxY returns 199.

Since the upper left corner of the display is (0, 0) and the bottom right corner is (GetMaxX, GetMaxY), the code that locates the center of any screen is given by the coordinates:

```
Xmidpoint := GetMaxX div 2;
Ymidpoint := GetMaxY div 2;
```

Using this technique, the BALLOON program from Chapter 7 can be rewritten as shown in listing 11.3.

Listing 11.3

```
program Balloon2;
uses Graph;
var
   Driver, Mode : integer;
   Xmidpoint, Ymidpoint, Radius : word;
begin
   Driver := Detect;
   InitGraph( Driver, Mode, 'C:\TP' );
   Xmidpoint := GetMaxX div 2;
   Ymidpoint := GetMaxY div 2,
   for Radius := 1 to GetMaxY div 4 do
      Circle( 250, 100, Radius );
   CloseGraph
end.
```

Note that even the maximum radius of the circle can be expressed in terms of GetMaxY.

Locating the Pointer Position on the Graphics Screen

Any time during a graphics session, you can locate the current pointer (CP) by using the GetX and GetY functions:

```
function  GetX : integer;
function  GetY : integer;
```

GetX and GetY return the X and Y coordinates, respectively. These functions are particularly useful because, unlike the cursor in text mode, the CP in graphics mode is invisible.

Ending the Graphics Session

The CloseGraph procedure ends the graphics session. It frees the heap of the graphics driver and any buffers used by the graphics routines, and restores the screen to its original mode. If the screen was in text mode when Init-Graph was called, the screen returns to text mode after CloseGraph is through.

If you don't call CloseGraph, your program will still end quite normally, but your screen will remain in graphics mode. You will have to restore the text mode yourself, either by executing a DOS MODE command or by rebooting the PC.

Switching between Text and Graphics Modes

You will often develop programs that switch between text and graphics modes. Turbo Pascal provides the following routines to help you do this smoothly:

```
procedure RestoreCrtMode;
procedure SetGraphMode( Mode : integer );
```

RestoreCrtMode exits the graphics mode and restores the screen to its mode when InitGraph was invoked. The SetGraphMode procedure returns the system to graphics mode, resets all graphics settings to their defaults, and clears the screen. SetGraphMode can also be used while you are within a graphics session to change to a new mode.

Using RestoreCrtMode and SetGraphMode is preferable to using a combination of CloseGraph and InitGraph. RestoreCrtMode doesn't clear the .BGI driver from memory; therefore, you can avoid the disk file loading process performed by InitGraph.

The SWITCH program in listing 11.4 demonstrates how RestoreCrtMode and SetGraphMode can be used.

Listing 11.4

```pascal
program Switch;
uses Crt, Graph;
var
   Driver, Mode : integer;
   Radius, CenterX, CenterY : word;
begin
   ClrScr;
   write( 'Press ENTER to see a hole' );
   readln;
   Driver := Detect;
   InitGraph( Driver, Mode, 'C:\TP' );
   CenterX := GetMaxX div 2;
   CenterY := GetMaxY div 2;
   Circle( CenterX, CenterY, CenterY );
   OutText( 'Press ENTER' );
   readln;
   RestoreCrtMode;
   write( 'Press ENTER to see it close' );
   readln;
   SetGraphMode( Mode );
   for Radius := CenterY downto 1 do
      Circle( CenterX, CenterY, Radius );
   OutText( 'Press ENTER to end the program' );
   readln;
   CloseGraph;
end.
```

SWITCH alternates modes—from text to graphics, from graphics to text, and finally from text to graphics. You might want to experiment by replacing RestoreCrtMode and SetGraphMode with CloseGraph and InitGraph; if you do, you may notice a reduction in performance.

Handling Graphics Errors

Graphics are usually a supporting portion of an application, so Turbo Pascal doesn't allow run-time graphics errors to terminate a program. Instead, a subroutine simply fails to perform; it sets an internal variable to a value that indicates the nature of the error, but otherwise the program proceeds normally.

This internal value can be examined with the GraphResult function:

```
function  GraphResult : integer;
```

You can interpret the error codes returned by GraphResult according to the values in table 11.5. Note that the error code is reset to zero after the call.

Table 11.5. GraphResult Error Codes

Constant Name	Error Code	Error
grOk	0	No error
grNoInitGraph	–1	(BGI) graphics not installed
grNotDetected	–2	Graphics hardware not detected
grFileNotFound	–3	Device driver file not found ( )
grInvalidDriver	–4	Invalid device driver file ( )
grNoLoadMem	–5	Not enough memory to load driver
grNoScanMem	–6	Out of memory in scan fill
grNoFloodMem	–7	Out of memory in flood fill
grFontNotFound	–8	Font file not found ( )
grNoFontMem	–9	Not enough memory to load font
grInvalidMode	–10	Invalid graphics mode for selected driver
grError	–11	Graphics error
grIOerror	–12	Graphics I/O error
grInvalidFont	–13	Invalid font file ( )
grInvalidFontNum	–14	Invalid font number

The Name column in the table contains the names of predefined constants provided by Turbo Pascal. A typical use of GraphResult is as follows:

```
InitGraph( GraphDriver, GraphMode, 'C:\TP' );
if GraphResult <> grOK then
    Halt( 1 );
```

For each valid ErrorCode, the GraphErrorMsg function

```
function GraphErrorMsg( ErrorCode : integer ) : String;
```

returns an English error message corresponding to that in table 11.5. (In a real error message, the parentheses shown in the table would hold the name of the file that provoked the error.) With GraphErrorMsg, you can include more informative error messages.

```
InitGraph( GraphDriver, GraphMode, 'C:\TP' );
GraphError := GraphResult; { Save the value, because }
                           { GraphResult resets to zero }
                           { after each call }
if GraphError <> grOK then begin
    writeln ( GraphErrorMsg( GraphError ));
    Halt( 1 );
end;
```

You can list all graphics error descriptions by using the GRAPHERR program in listing 11.5.

Listing 11.5

```
program GraphErr;
uses Graph;
var
    ErrorNumber : integer;
begin
    for ErrorNumber := 0 downto -14 do
        writeln( ErrorNumber:8, '    ', GraphErrorMsg( ErrorNumber ) );
end.
```

Calling GraphResult

You can call GraphResult after using any of the following routines: Bar, Bar3D, ClearViewPort, CloseGraph, DetectGraph, DrawPoly, Fill-Poly, FloodFill, GetGraphMode, ImageSize, InitGraph, Install-UserDriver, InstallUserFont, PieSlice, RegisterBGIdriver, RegisterBGIfont, SetAllPalette, SetFillPattern, SetFillStyle, SetGraphBufSize, SetGraphMode, SetLineStyle, SetPalette, SetText-Justify, and SetTextStyle. The examples in this book don't test for errors in order to present cleaner code, but your programs should check GraphResult after every critical command.

Plotting Individual Points

The most direct way of drawing graphics characters on the screen is to access individual pixels. Turbo Pascal provides the PutPixel and GetPixel subroutines for that purpose.

```
procedure PutPixel( X, Y : integer; Pixel : word );
function  GetPixel( X, Y : integer ) : word;
```

The PutPixel procedure paints the single pixel located at (X, Y) with the color specified by the Pixel parameter. The GetPixel function gets the color of the pixel located at (X, Y).

Colors are discussed in more detail later. For now, think of the colors as the same set of predefined constants and values discussed in the last chapter, repeated here in table 11.6.

Table 11.6. *Predefined Color Constants*

Name	Value
Black	0
Blue	1
Green	2
Cyan	3
Red	4
Magenta	5
Brown	6
LightGray	7
DarkGray	8
LightBlue	9
LightGreen	10
LightCyan	11
LightRed	12
LightMagenta	13
Yellow	14
White	15

PutPixel and GetPixel are demonstrated in the DNAHELIX program in listing 11.6.

Listing 11.6

```
program DNAhelix;
uses Graph;
var
   grDriver, grMode, Swing : integer;
   Width, Crest, Ypos, i : word;
begin
   grDriver := Detect;
   InitGraph( grDriver, grMode, 'C:\TP' );
   Ypos := GetMaxY div 2;
   Crest := GetMaxY div 8;
   Width := GetMaxX;
   for i := 0 to Width do begin
      Swing := Round( Crest * Sin( 10*Pi*i / Width ) );
      PutPixel( i, Ypos + Swing, i mod 15 );
      PutPixel( i, Ypos - Swing, (GetPixel( i, Ypos + Swing ) + 8 ) mod 15 );
   end;
   readln;
   CloseGraph;
end.
```

When DNAHELIX executes, it uses PutPixel to produce a string of multi-colored pixels in the shape of a sine wave. As it moves across the screen, a second PutPixel call accesses the color of the pixel in the first wave by a call to GetPixel, then produces a mirror image shape in a different color, as shown in figure 11.2.

Fig. 11.2. *Output produced by the DNAHELIX program.*

Line Routines

You *could* draw every graphics image by using a (rather large) number of PutPixel instructions. Fortunately, Turbo Pascal includes most fundamental shapes as standard features. The following sections discuss the various ways you can generate lines.

Drawing a Straight Line

Next to turning on a single pixel, drawing a line is the most intuitive process in graphics.

```
procedure Line( X1, Y1, X2, Y2 : integer );
```

The Line procedure draws a straight line from (X1, Y1) to (X2, Y2).

The TANLINES program in listing 11.7 uses a combination of Line instructions to draw four sets of tangents within a box.

Listing 11.7

```
program TanLines;
uses Graph;
var
    grDriver, grMode : integer;
    y, Ymax, Ymid : word;
begin
    grDriver := Detect;
    InitGraph( grDriver, grMode, 'C:\TP' );
    Ymax := GetMaxY;
    Ymid := Ymax div 2;
    for y := 1 to Ymid do begin
        Line( Ymid - Y, 0, 0, Y );              { Upper left }
        Line( Ymid + Y, 0, Ymax, Y );           { Upper right }
        Line( 0, Ymid + Y, Y, Ymax );           { Lower left }
        Line( Ymid + Y, Ymax, Ymax, Ymax - Y ); { Lower right }
    end;
    readln;
    CloseGraph;
end.2
```

When TANLINES executes, it creates the illusion of an oval in silhouette, as shown in figure 11.3.

Fig. 11.3. *Output produced by the TANLINES program.*

Keeping Track of the Current Pointer

After you execute the procedure

```
Line( X1, Y1, X2, Y2 );
```

the current pointer is repositioned to the pixel at (X2, Y2). Now suppose that you want to draw a second line, as follows:

```
Line( X2, Y2, X3, Y3 );
```

Instead of having to specify the current pointer explicitly as the start of the line, you could use the simpler procedure

```
procedure LineTo( X, Y : integer );
```

LineTo draws a straight line from the current pointer to the pixel at (X, Y) and resets the current pointer to (X, Y). Therefore, the pairs of instructions

```
Line( X1, Y1, X2, Y2 );
Line( X2, Y2, X3, Y3 );
```

and

```
Line( X1, Y1, X2,  Y2 );
LineTo( X3, Y3 );
```

are equivalent, but the second pair operates slightly faster.

You can move the current pointer to any desired pixel with the following:

```
procedure MoveTo( X, Y : integer );
```

MoveTo moves the CP to (X, Y), but it has no visible impact on the screen. Consequently, the instructions:

```
Line( X1, Y1, X2, Y2 );
```

and

```
MoveTo( X1, Y1 );
LineTo( X2, Y2 );
```

are equivalent. This is demonstrated in the TANLINE2 program in listing 11.8, which is functionally identical to TANLINES.

Listing 11.8

```
program TanLine2;
uses Graph;
var
    grDriver, grMode : integer;
    Y, Ymax, Ymid : word;
begin
    grDriver := Detect;
    InitGraph( grDriver, grMode, 'C:\TP' );
```

Listing 11.8 continues

Listing 11.8 continued

```
Ymax := GetMaxY;
Ymid := Ymax div 2;
for y := 1 to Ymid do begin
    MoveTo( Ymid - Y, Ø );      LineTo( Ø, Y );             { Upper left  }
    MoveTo( Ymid + Y, Ø );      LineTo( Ymax, Y );          { Upper right }
    MoveTo( Ø, Ymid + Y );      LineTo( Y, Ymax );          { Lower left  }
    MoveTo( Ymid + Y, Ymax );   LineTo( Ymax, Ymax - Y );   { Lower right }
end;
readln;
CloseGraph;
end.
```

Drawing Relative Lines

The MoveTo, Line, and LineTo procedures are useful only when you know specific coordinates in advance. Frequently, it's easier to move or draw a line a *relative distance* from the current pointer.

```
procedure MoveRel( DX, DY : integer );
procedure LineRel( DX, DY : integer );
```

Remember that GetX and GetY return the X and Y coordinates of the current pointer, respectively. MoveRel(DX, DY) is equivalent to

```
MoveTo( GetX + DX, GetY + DY );
```

and

```
LineRel( DX, DY )
```

is equivalent to

```
LineTo( GetX + DX, GetY + DY );
```

The LineRel procedure is particularly useful for drawing shapes. For example, given a specific coordinate for one of the corners of a square, a hexagon, and an octagon, what are the coordinates of the remaining corners? The square is easy, but the other figures take some thought. Consider, though, that instead of identifying the *specific* coordinate of each corner, it might be easier to determine their *relative* coordinates. The SHAPES program in listing 11.9 uses relative movements to display a rectangle, a hexagon, and an octagon.

Listing 11.9

```
program Shapes;
uses Graph;
const
   S2 = 1.414;   { Square root of 2 }
   S3 = 1.732;   { Square root of 3 }
   DeltaXØ : array[ 1..4 ] of real = ( 2, Ø, -2, Ø );
   DeltaYØ : array[ 1..4 ] of real = ( Ø, 1, Ø, -1 );
   DeltaX1 : array[ 1..6 ] of real = ( 2, 1, -1, -2, -1, 1 );
   DeltaY1 : array[ 1..6 ] of real = ( Ø, S3/2, S3/2, Ø, -S3/2, -S3/2 );
   DeltaX2 : array[ 1..8 ] of real = ( 2, S2, Ø, -S2, -2, -S2, Ø, S2 );
   DeltaY2 : array[ 1..8 ] of real = ( Ø, S2/2, 1, S2/2, Ø, -S2/2, -1, -S2/2 );
   Factor : integer = 3Ø;   { Scaling factor }
var
   Height, Width : word;
   grDriver, grMode : integer;
   i : byte;
begin
   grDriver := Detect;
   InitGraph( grDriver, grMode, 'C:\TP' );
   Height := GetMaxY div 5;
   Width := GetMaxX div 7;
     {Display a rectangle}
   MoveTo( Width, Height );
   for i := 1 to 4 do
     LineRel( Round( Factor*DeltaXØ[ i ] ), Round( Factor*DeltaYØ[ i ] ) );
     {Display a hexagon}
   MoveTo( 3*Width, Height );
   for i := 1 to 6 do
     LineRel( Round( Factor*DeltaX1[ i ] ), Round( Factor*DeltaY1[ i ] ) );
     {Display an octagon}
   MoveTo( 5*Width, Height );
   for i := 1 to 8 do
     LineRel( Round( Factor*DeltaX2[ i ] ), Round( Factor*DeltaY2[ i ] ) );
   readln;
   CloseGraph;
end.
```

When SHAPES executes, it uses the values in the typed constant arrays to draw relative lines. Three figures are produced: a rectangle, a hexagon, and an octagon, as shown in figure 11.4.

Fig. 11.4. *Output produced by the SHAPES program.*

> The figures (see fig. 11.4) might not appear symmetrical on your screen. Unfortunately, the pixels on the typical graphics screen aren't distributed in a perfect square. You will learn how to compensate for this deficiency later when the aspect ratio is discussed.

Line Styles

Having a choice of line style and thickness is especially useful when you want to identify or even emphasize one small feature of a larger image. This is the same technique employed in architectural drawings, in which a thick line indicates an outer wall, a thin line indicates an inner wall, and a dotted line shows the location of hidden pipes or wiring.

So far, all of our drawings have used solid lines. We can change that with the following routine:

```
procedure SetLineStyle( LineStyle : word;
                        Pattern   : word;
                        Thickness : word );
```

SetLineStyle enables you to modify both the width and style of your lines. The LineStyle parameter can have any one of the following values:

```
SolidLn   = 0;
DottedLn  = 1;
CenterLn  = 2;
DashedLn  = 3;
```

As the names of the constants imply, you can choose from among solid, dotted, center-dotted, and dashed lines. The Thickness parameter enables you to draw each line with normal or thick width.

```
NormWidth  = 1;
ThickWidth = 3;
```

If you are using one of the four standard LineStyle options, set Pattern equal to zero.

The GRID program in listing 11.10 shows every combination of style and width.

Listing 11.10

```
program Grid;
uses Graph;
var
   GraphDriver, GraphMode : integer;
   Swath, Xjump, Yjump, Thickness : word;
begin
   GraphDriver := Detect;
   InitGraph( GraphDriver, GraphMode, 'C:\TP' );
   Xjump := GetMaxX div 11;
   Yjump := GetMaxY div 11;
   for Swath := 0 to 10 do begin
      if Odd( Swath ) then Thickness := 1
                      else Thickness := 3;
      SetLineStyle( Swath mod 4, 0, Thickness );
      Line( Swath*Xjump, 0, Swath*Xjump, 10*Yjump );
      Line( 0, Swath*Yjump, 10*Xjump, Swath*Yjump );
   end;
   readln;
   CloseGraph;
end.
```

When GRID executes, it produces the display shown in figure 11.5.

Fig. 11.5. *Output produced by the GRID program.*

To increase your available options even more, you can define your own customized line styles. Just set the LineStyle parameter equal to the predefined constant UserBitLn, which equals 4, and select the pattern you want with the word-sized Pattern parameter. Think of the Pattern parameter as a series of 16 bits; a 1 indicates that the pixel is on, and a 0 indicates that the pixel is off, as follows:

```
Solid       1111111111111111   $FFFF
Dotted      1010101010101010   $AAAA
Big dashes  1111111100000000   $FF00
Empty       1000000000000001   $F001
```

Hence, if LineStyle has been set to the value of UserBitLn, setting Pattern to $AAAA results in dotted lines, and setting Pattern to $FFFF results in solid lines.

This feature is demonstrated in GRID2 program in listing 11.11.

Listing 11.11

```
program Grid2;
uses Graph;
var
   GraphDriver, GraphMode : integer;
   Swath, Xmax, Yjump : word;
begin
   GraphDriver := Detect;
   InitGraph( GraphDriver, GraphMode, 'C:\TP' );
   Xmax   := GetMaxX;
   Yjump := GetMaxY div 17;
   for Swath := 1 to 16 do begin
      SetLineStyle( UserBitLn, ( 1 Shl Swath)-1, ThickWidth );
      Line( 0, Swath*Yjump, Xmax, Swath*Yjump );
   end;
   readln;
   CloseGraph;
end.
```

When GRID2 executes, it produces the image shown in figure 11.6.

The Pattern parameter used by GRID2 takes the form:

```
( 1 Shl Swath )-1
```

which is equivalent to the expression:

```
2Swath - 1
```

As Swath varies from 1 to 16, the SetLineStyle procedure changes the value of the Pattern parameter by increasing the number of set bits, as follows:

Fig. 11.6. Output produced by the GRID2 program.

```
21 - 1  =        1 :   00000000000000001
22 - 1  =        3 :   00000000000000011
23 - 1  =        7 :   00000000000000111
                       :
                       :
216 - 1 =  65,535 :   1111111111111111
```

Consequently, the length of each dash increases as the lines go lower on the screen.

Saving and Restoring Line Styles

If you need to switch frequently between two line styles, it's useful to be able to save and restore the current line settings. You can do this with the GetLineSettings procedure:

```
procedure GetLineSettings( var LineInfo : LineSettingsType );
```

GetLineSettings returns the current line style, pattern, and thickness within the fields of the LineInfo record. LineInfo is declared as being of the predefined type LineSettingsType, as follows:

```
LineSettingsType = record
                      LineStyle : word;
                      Pattern   : word;
                      Thickness : word;
                   end;
```

Call GetLineSettings when you want to save the current line style, pattern, and thickness. Later, you can restore these settings with the call

```
with LineInfo do
    SetLineStyle( LineStyle, Pattern, Thickness );
```

Lines and Solids

With the SetLineStyle procedure, you can increase the contrast among a set of lines by varying their width and style. But what happens if a line is drawn over a solid? Normally, the two images merge, and the line is invisible until (and unless) it exits the solid at the other end. You can change this with the following procedure:

```
procedure SetWriteMode( WriteMode : integer );
```

SetWriteMode sets the writing mode for drawing lines. The writing mode, determined by the WriteMode parameter, determines how a line is physically displayed. WriteMode can assume either of the values:

```
CopyPut         = Ø;
XORPut          = 1;
```

When WriteMode is set to CopyPut, the line is copied to the screen, the images blend together, and the line disappears. When WriteMode is set to XORPut, overlapping images are displayed by blanking the affected pixels; the line appears black against the background and can be distinguished easily.

SetWriteMode is best illustrated with an example. The LINETYPE program in listing 11.12 draws two lines through a solid rectangle—first with Write-Mode set to CopyPut, and then with WriteMode set to XORPut.

Listing 11.12

```
program LineType;
uses Graph;
var
    Width, Height : word;
    GraphDriver, GraphMode : integer;
begin
    GraphDriver := Detect;
    InitGraph( GraphDriver, GraphMode, 'C:\TP' );
    Width := GetMaxX div 3;
    Height := GetMaxY div 4;
    Bar( Ø, Height, GetMaxX, Height * 3 );
    SetWriteMode( CopyPut );
    Line( Width, Ø, Width, GetMaxY );
    SetWriteMode( XORPut );
    Line( Width*2, Ø, Width*2, GetMaxY );
    readln;
    CloseGraph;
end.
```

The *Bar* Procedure

You will be formally introduced to the Bar procedure shortly. For now, you've probably already figured out that its four parameters follow the (X1, Y1, X2, Y2) format. But instead of drawing a diagonal line, Bar uses the coordinates as the upper left and lower right corners of a solid rectangle.

When LINETYPE executes, it produces the drawing shown in figure 11.7. When WriteMode was set to CopyPut, the line wrote over whatever was on the screen. When WriteMode was set to XORPut, the screen was blank where the two shapes overlapped.

Fig. 11.7. Output produced by the LINETYPE program.

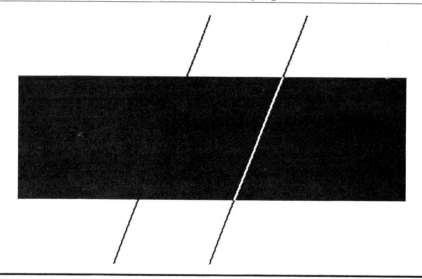

Viewports

In text mode, you could use the Window procedure to segregate a small region of the screen. Every subsequent screen instruction—except for another call to Window—was made relative to that region. Graphics mode has something similar: the viewport. This section discusses how to create—and manipulate—viewports.

Creating the Viewport

A graphics viewport is created with the SetViewPort procedure:

```
procedure SetViewPort( X1, Y1, X2, Y2 : integer; Clip : boolean );
```

The upper left corner is given by (X1, Y1) and the lower right corner by (X2, Y2). The X1 coordinate must be greater than or equal to 0 and less than or equal to X2. Similarly, the Y1 coordinate must be greater than or equal to 0 and less than or equal to Y2.

If the Clip parameter is set to True, you can output only to the area inside of the viewport. This restriction is called clipping. If the Clip parameter is set to False, no such restriction applies; you can output anywhere on the screen. Instead of using True or False for the Clip parameter, Turbo Pascal provides the following predefined constants:

```
ClipOn  = True;
ClipOff = False;
```

After SetViewPort establishes a viewport, the upper left corner of the viewport becomes the new coordinate (0, 0), as shown in figure 11.8.

All graphics screen commands—except for another call to SetViewPort —are relative to the viewport itself. The VIEWER program in listing 11.13 demonstrates this feature.

Listing 11.13

```
program Viewer;
uses Graph;
var
   GraphDriver, GraphMode : integer;
begin
   GraphDriver := Detect;
   InitGraph( GraphDriver, GraphMode, 'C:\TP' );
   SetViewPort( GetMaxX div 2,   { These lines reset the upper left of }
                GetMaxY div 2,   { the viewport to the center of the screen }
                GetMaxX, GetMaxY, ClipOff );
   Circle( 0, 0, GetMaxY div 4 );   { This circle will appear in }
                                     { the center of the screen   }

   readln;
   CloseGraph;
end.
```

VIEWER resets the viewport to the lower right corner of the screen. As a result, the (0, 0) coordinate is repositioned to the center of the display. When the Circle procedure is called, the circle—centered on (0, 0)—appears in the middle of the screen.

The effect of clipping can be seen in the CLIP program in listing 11.14.

Fig. 11.8. *Viewport coordinates before and after a call to SetViewPort.*

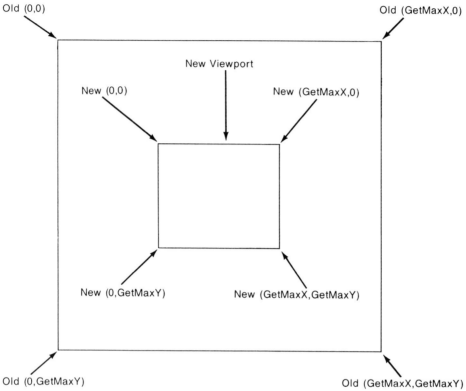

Listing 11.14

```
program Clip;
uses Graph;
var
   Height, Width : word;
   GraphDriver, GraphMode : integer;
begin
   GraphDriver := Detect;
   InitGraph( GraphDriver, GraphMode, 'C:\TP' );
   Height := GetMaxY div 5;
   Width := GetMaxX div 5;
   Rectangle( Width, Height, Width*2, Height*3 );
   SetViewPort( Width, Height, Width*2, Height*3, ClipOn );
   Line( Ø, Height, GetMaxX, Ø );
```

Listing 11.14 continues

***Listing 11.14** continued*

```
    SetViewPort( Ø, Ø, GetMaxX, GetMaxY, ClipOff );   { Resets the screen }
    Rectangle( Width*3, Height, Width*4, Height*3 );
    SetViewPort( Width*3, Height, Width*4, Height*3, ClipOff );
    Line( Ø, Height, GetMaxX, Ø );
    SetViewPort( Ø, Ø, GetMaxX, GetMaxY, ClipOff );   { Resets the screen }
    OutTextXY( Width, Height*4, 'CLIPPING IS ON' );
    OutTextXY( Width*3, Height*4, 'CLIPPING IS OFF' );
    readln;
    CloseGraph;
end.
```

When CLIP executes, it creates two viewports and draws two lines, producing the diagram shown in figure 11.9. Both lines start within a viewport and end outside it. When clipping is on, the line is confined to the viewport itself. When clipping is off, no such restrictions apply. Note that the calls to SetViewPort use coordinates relative to the entire screen while the coordinates passed to Line are relative to the viewport.

Fig. 11.9. *Output produced by the CLIP program.*

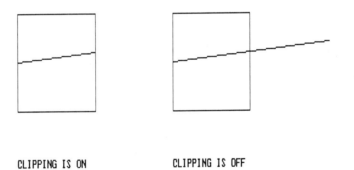

CLIPPING IS ON   CLIPPING IS OFF

The *Rectangle* Procedure

The Rectangle procedure is similar to Bar, except that Rectangle draws an empty shape. In this case, Rectangle draws a box around each viewport. The OutTextXY procedure positions—and then writes—a text message at the (X, Y) coordinates specified by its first two parameters.

Saving and Restoring Viewport Settings

If you need to switch between two graphics windows, it's useful to be able to save and restore each viewport setting quickly. You can do this with the GetViewSettings procedure:

```
procedure GetViewSettings( var ViewPort : ViewPortType );
```

GetViewSettings returns the current coordinates and clipping status within the fields of the ViewPort record. ViewPort is declared as being of the predefined type ViewPortType, as follows:

```
ViewPortType = record
                 X1, Y1, X2, Y2 : integer;
                 Clip           : boolean;
               end;
```

After you've used SetViewPort to create the first viewport—and before you use it again to create the second viewport—call GetViewSettings to save the current coordinates and clipping status. Later, you can restore these settings with the statement:

```
with ViewPort do
   SetViewPort( X1, Y1, X2, Y2, Clip );
```

Clearing the Viewport

There are two ways to erase the screen:

```
procedure ClearViewPort;
procedure ClearDevice;
```

ClearViewPort clears only the current viewport. ClearDevice clears the entire screen. Both procedures reset the current pointer to (0, 0), but neither affects the current viewport location.

The effects of ClearViewPort and ClearDevice can be seen in the CLEAR-VUE program in listing 11.15.

Listing 11.15

```
program ClearVue;
uses Graph;
var
   Radius : word;
   GraphDriver, GraphMode : integer;
begin
   GraphDriver := Detect;
   InitGraph( GraphDriver, GraphMode, 'C:\TP' );
```

Listing 11.15 continues

Listing 11.15 continued

```
    SetViewPort( GetMaxX div 2, GetMaxY div 2, GetMaxX, GetMaxY, ClipOff );
    for Radius := 1 to GetMaxY div 2 do
       Circle( 0, 0, Radius );
    readln;
    ClearViewPort;
    readln;
    ClearDevice;
    readln;
    for Radius := 1 to GetMaxY div 2 do
       Circle( 0, 0, Radius );
    CloseGraph;
  end.
```

When CLEARVUE executes, it creates a viewport in the lower right quarter of the screen. As a result, the origin—the (0,0) coordinate—is in the center of the screen. Next, circles are drawn around the origin. Because clipping is turned off, the circles appear mostly outside the viewport. After you press the Enter key, the ClearViewPort command clears the viewport and in the process erases the lower right quarter of the circle. At this point, the screen appears as shown in figure 11.10. After you press Enter again, ClearDevice clears the entire screen. Press the Enter key a final time, and the circle is redrawn once again—in the middle of the screen—proving that viewport settings were unchanged.

Fig. 11.10. *Output produced by the CLEARVUE program.*

Page Swapping Routines

By now you have noticed the time it takes to draw each graphics image. For most applications, the delay is noticeable, but acceptable. But some applications—animation, game, and training programs, for example—are more effective if they can immediately display a completed graphics screen, just as if the users were turning a page in a book.

In graphics terms, a *page* is an area of memory large enough to hold a single graphics screen. Ideally, if your program could access two graphics pages, it could be displaying the contents of one page while drawing graphics images on the second (invisible) page. Then your program could quickly switch the two pages, giving the impression that the images were drawn instantaneously.

EGA, VGA, and Hercules graphics cards all contain enough memory for more than one page; the exact number is given in the *Pages* column in table 11.2. If your PC uses a different graphics adapter (such as CGA), then your machine only has a single page available; and consequently, page swapping isn't available on your PC.

You can access the individual pages with the following routines:

```
procedure SetVisualPage( Page : word );
```

```
procedure SetActivePage (Page : word );
```

All graphics output is directed to the page selected by SetActivePage. The screen displays the contents of the page selected by SetVisualPage. If your PC doesn't support multiple pages, calling SetActivePage and SetVisualPage will have no effect on your program.

Paging routines are demonstrated by the ANIMATOR program in listing 11.16.

Listing 11.16

```
program Animator;    { EGA, VGA, or Hercules only }
uses Graph;
var
   Xmid, Ymid, Radius : word;
   GraphDriver, GraphMode : integer;
begin
   GraphDriver := Detect;
   InitGraph( GraphDriver, GraphMode, 'C:\TP' );
   Xmid := GetMaxX div 2;qqqqqqqq
   Ymid := GetMaxY div 2;
   SetVisualPage( Ø );
   SetActivePage( 1 );
   for Radius := 1 to GetMaxY div 2 do
      Circle( Xmid, Ymid, Radius );
   SetVisualPage( 1 );
   readln;
   CloseGraph;
end.
```

ANIMATOR begins by setting the visual page to 0 and setting the active page to 1. This means that while the screen is displaying the (empty) contents of page 0, all of the circles are drawn on page 1. When the final circle has been completed, the screen is switched to page 1, immediately displaying all of the circles at once.

This is one of the tricks used by demonstration programs in computer stores that make the graphics displays appear to change instantaneously.

The ANIMATE2 program in listing 11.17 shows a simple technique that you can include in your programs to take advantage of multiple pages whenever they're available. Calling the TurnThePage procedure at the beginning of the program and before each display makes the graphics images appear more dramatic.

Listing 11.17

```
program Animate2;    { EGA, VGA, or Hercules only }
uses Graph;
const
   PageCounter : word = Ø;
var
   Xmid, Ymid, Radius : word;
   GraphDriver, GraphMode : integer;
procedure TurnThePages;
begin
   Inc( PageCounter );
   if Odd( PageCounter ) then
      begin
         SetVisualPage( 1 );
         SetActivePage( Ø );
      end
   else
      begin
         SetVisualPage( Ø );
         SetActivePage( 1 );
      end;
end;
begin
   GraphDriver := Detect;
   InitGraph( GraphDriver, GraphMode, 'C:\TP' );
   Xmid := GetMaxX div 2;
   Ymid := GetMaxY div 2;
   TurnThePages;
   for Radius := 1 to GetMaxY div 2 do
      Circle( Xmid, Ymid, Radius );
   TurnThePages;
   readln;
   CloseGraph;
end.
```

Colors

The paint-by-number drawing sets that you find in toy stores include a collection of drawings and a set of paints. Each of the drawings is marked in such a way that every area on the page contains a number corresponding to a specific color of paint. Every part of every drawing that's supposed to be "green" might be marked, say, with the number 2, and every part of every drawing that's supposed to be "red" might be marked with the number 4. The set of paints, naturally enough, is marked the same way; the second paint is green, and the fourth paint is red. Match them up and you've got an attractive picture. Child's play!

Turbo Pascal works the same way. A *palette* is the set of available colors for your screen. Instead of globs of pigment, however, Turbo Pascal stores a palette as an array of numbers. The *index* of each element of the array corresponds to the reference on the paint-by-number diagram, and the actual value of the element corresponds to the color of the paint.

In other words, each pixel on the screen has a numeric color value associated with it. Turbo chooses the color of the pixel by using its color value as an index into the palette array.

Obviously, understanding the palette is as important for mastering the art of painting colors on the screen as it is for painting colors on the canvas. The remainder of this section explores the Turbo Pascal color routines.

Identifying Colors

Two procedures read the contents of the palette array.

```
procedure GetDefaultPalette( var Palette : PaletteType );
procedure GetPalette( var Palette : PaletteType );
```

GetDefaultPalette returns a copy of the *original* contents of the palette, just as it was immediately after InitGraph initialized the graphics system. GetPalette returns the *current* palette.

Both GetDefaultPalette and GetPalette take a single parameter consisting of a record of type PaletteType, which is predefined as follows:

```
const
  MaxColors = 15;
type
  PaletteType = record
                  Size   : byte;
                  Colors : array[0..MaxColors] of shortint;
                end;
```

The Size field isn't extremely important for now. It tells you how many entries there are in the Colors array. Because Turbo Pascal supports 16 colors (numbered 0 through 15), MaxColors is declared as a constant of 15; consequently, you already know that Size is 16.

Of greater concern is the *effective* size of the palette—that is, how many colors can *actually* be displayed for your graphics driver and mode. You can learn the effective palette size with the GetPaletteSize function. On a CGA adapter in mode C1, GetPaletteSize returns 3; consequently, although 16 array elements are defined, only elements 0 through 3 can be used.

A Special Note on CGA, MCGA, and AT&T Graphics

If your PC is equipped with a CGA, MCGA, or AT&T adapter, then you should be aware of some special restrictions that apply to the use of colors on your machine.

Refer back to table 11.2 for a summary of the Palette associated with each Mode. In the low-resolution modes C0 through C3, each pixel is represented in memory by two bits. These bits can take on the binary values for 0, 1, 2, or 3. In other words, each pixel can assume at most one of four colors. The first four elements of the Colors array correspond to the colors in table 11.3. Mode C0 (actually, mode CGAC0, MCGAC0, or ATT400C0) initializes Colors to palette C0, mode C1 (actually, mode CGAC1, MCGAC1, or ATT400C1) initializes Colors to palette C1, and so on. Only four colors can be used, so only the first four elements of the Colors array have any meaning.

In high-resolution mode, each pixel is controlled by a single bit; hence, its color can be either 0 (the background) or 1 (the drawing color itself). Notice that in table 11.2, high-resolution mode was shown to have a palette of 2 colors.

Figure 11.1 showed the output produced when the GRFINFO2 program (listing 11.2) is run on a PC with a CGA board. Notice how the default mode is the two-color 640 × 200 pixel high-resolution mode. In other words, if your PC uses a CGA, MCGA, or AT&T adapter, and you want to display the full four-color palette on your screen, then you must *select* a specific mode.

For example, instead of using the default code:

```
GraphDriver := Detect;
InitGraph( GraphDriver, GraphMode, 'C:\TP' );
```

you might use:

```
GraphDriver := CGA;
    { Assuming you have a CGA adapter }
GraphMode := CGAC0;
    { Palette 0 (LightGreen, LightRed, Yellow) }
InitGraph( GraphDriver, GraphMode, 'C:\TP' );
```

Of course, programs that don't use colors can continue to be run in one of the high resolution modes.

Selecting a Drawing Color

You can select the current drawing color with the SetColor procedure. For example, SetColor(2) selects the second palette color for the current drawing color. The color you choose may range from 0 through the maximum allowable for your adapter and the current mode. This maximum can be determined by calling the GetMaxColor function. For example, on a PC equipped with a CGA adapter and running in a low-resolution mode like CGAC0, GetMaxColor returns 3.

At any point in the program, you can use the GetColor function to learn the current drawing color.

Selecting a Background Color

In the Palette.Colors array, the first entry (element number 0) is the background color. You can select the current background color with the SetBkColor procedure. For example, SetBkColor(2) selects the second palette color for the current background color. Just as with the SetColor procedure, the color you choose must be within the range from 0 through GetMaxColor.

You can use the GetBkColor function to identify the current drawing color.

Changing Individual Palette Colors

To change the colors in your palette, use the following procedure:

```
procedure SetPalette( ColorNum : word; Color : shortint );
```

SetPalette changes palette color ColorNum to the color specified by Color. To change color 2 to Cyan, simply call

```
SetPalette( 2, Cyan );
```

There are a few restrictions to remember when you change palette colors. First, a CGA card will change only color 0 (the background). All other colors must remain as indicated in table 11.3. Second, SetPalette can't be used on an IBM® 8514. For that machine, you need to use the SetRGBPalette procedure.

Changing the Entire Palette

You can change every color of the EGA and VGA palettes with the routine:

```
procedure SetAllPalette( var Palette );
```

SetAllPalette takes a PaletteType variable as its parameter. Set-AllPalette is best explained with an example. Suppose that you want to change the first palette color to red and the third palette color to Green. When you call SetAllPalette, the first Palette.Size colors will be affected. Prepare the Palette variable as follows:

```
Palette.Size := 3;
Palette.Colors[ 1 ] := Red;
Palette.Colors[ 3 ] := Green;
```

To leave a particular palette color unchanged, set its value to –1. Finish the preparation of the Palette variable as follows:

```
Palette.Colors[ 0 ] := -1;
Palette.Colors[ 2 ] := -1;
```

Finally, call

```
SetAllPalette( Palette );
```

After SetAllPalette executes, every pixel on the screen that was painted with palette colors 1 and 3 is immediately changed. Note, however, that unless you plan on changing several colors frequently, SetPalette is almost always simpler and faster than SetAllPalette.

Again, remember the restrictions: CGA cards can only change color 0 (the background), and SetAllPalette can't be used on an IBM 8514.

Changing Colors on the VGA and the IBM-8514

A color television picture tube and a color PC display have one thing in common: both use only three primary colors (red, green, and blue) to produce every color, shade, and hue on the screen. In other words, every nuance of color is actually some combination of intensities of the three primaries.

In order to modify a palette entry for a VGA card or for an IBM 8514, you specify the relative intensities of red, green, and blue.

```
procedure SetRGBPalette( ColorNum,
              RedValue, GreenValue, BlueValue : integer );
```

You will find a complete list of colors in the adapter's technical manual. For a partial list, you can use the values in table 11.7.

Table 11.7. *VGA Color Hues*

Color	Red	Green	Blue
Black	$00	$00	$00
Blue	$00	$00	$FC
Green	$24	$FC	$24
Cyan	$00	$FC	$FC
Red	$FC	$14	$14
Magenta	$B0	$00	$FC
Brown	$70	$48	$00
White	$C4	$C4	$C4
Gray	$34	$34	$34
Lt. Blue	$00	$00	$70
Lt. Green	$00	$70	$00
Lt. Cyan	$00	$70	$70
Lt. Red	$70	$00	$00
Lt. Magenta	$70	$00	$70
Yellow	$FC	$FC	$24
Bright White	$FC	$FC	$FC

Hence, the command to change palette color number 7 to green is

```
SetRGBPalette( 7, $24, $FC, $24 );
```

Filling a Drawing

Line drawings are similar to stick figures of people: they get the idea across, but they don't offer any substance in the process. Quite simply, line drawings need to be "fleshed out" to increase their appeal. Here you will learn how to fill shapes with patterns and colors and in the process considerably increase the power and impact of your graphics displays.

Filling Solids

Normally when you use the FillPoly, Bar, Bar3D, and PieSlice procedures, the figures produced are solid and are painted with the maximum color of the palette (that is, Palette.Colors[GetMaxColor]). To change these defaults, use the routine:

```
procedure SetFillStyle( Pattern : word; Color : word );
```

SetFillStyle takes two parameters: a Color value that you can obtain from table 11.6 and a Pattern that you can obtain from table 11.8.

Table 11.8. *Fill patterns for* GetFillSettings *and* SetFillStyle

Constant	Value	Pattern
EmptyFill	0	The background color
SolidFill	1	A solid color
LineFill	2	Hyphens (---)
LtSlashFill	3	Thin slashes (///)
SlashFill	4	/// fill with thick lines
BkSlashFill	5	\\\ fill with thick lines
LtBkSlashFill	6	Thin backslashes (\\\)
HatchFill	7	Light hatch marks
XHatchFill	8	Heavy cross hatch marks
InterleaveFill	9	Interleaved lines
WideDotFill	10	Widely spaced dots
CloseDotFill	11	Closely spaced dots
UserFill	12	User-defined

User-Defined Fill Styles

When you pass SetFillStyle a Pattern parameter equal to UserFill, you are telling Turbo to customize the fill pattern. You can do this with the procedure:

```
procedure SetFillPattern( Pattern : FillPatternType; Color : word );
```

SetFillPattern takes two parameters: a word-sized Color specification and a parameter of type FillPatternType, which defines the pattern you want. FillPatternType is a predefined array of byte:

```
FillPatternType = array[1..8] of byte;
```

Recall that the default character size is an 8×8 matrix of pixels. Each byte of the FillPatternType array defines one row—top to bottom—in a custom character. The bits in each byte define the columns.

The use of SetFillPattern is demonstrated by the USERFILL program in listing 11.18.

Listing 11.18

```
program UserFill;
uses Graph;
const
    Shape : FillPatternType = ( $08,    { 00001000 }
                                $1C,    { 00011100 }
                                $3E,    { 00111110 }
                                $7F,    { 01111111 }
```

Listing 11.18 continues

Listing 11.18 *continued*

```
                              $3E,    { 00111110 }
                              $1C,    { 00011100 }
                              $08,    { 00001000 }
                              $00     { 00000000 } );
  var
     GraphDriver, GraphMode : integer;
     Height : word;
  begin
     GraphDriver := Detect;
     InitGraph( GraphDriver, GraphMode, 'C:\TP' );
     Height := GetMaxY div 3;
     SetFillPattern( Shape, 1 );
     Bar( 0, Height, GetMaxX, Height*2 );
     readln;
     CloseGraph;
  end.
```

When USERFILL executes, SetFillPattern changes the default color to Colors [1] and the default fill pattern to the one defined by the Shape array. Notice how the bits of the Shape array are arranged to form a diamond. The effect is visible in figure 11.11.

Fig. 11.11. *Output produced by the USERFILL program.*

Determining Patterns and Colors

With the GetFillSettings procedure, you can obtain a copy of the current fill pattern and color as set by SetFillStyle or SetFillPattern.

    procedure GetFillSettings(var FillInfo : FillSettingsType);

The FillSettingsType record is predefined as follows:

    FillSettingsType = record
                          Pattern : word;
                          Color   : word;
                       end;

If the Pattern parameter is equal to UserFill, you can obtain a copy of the custom character with the routine:

procedure GetFillPattern(var FillPattern : FillPatternType);

Using GetFillSettings and GetFillPattern, you can rapidly save information about the current fill pattern and color.

Flood Filling

You can only use SetFillStyle and SetFillPattern with the FillPoly, Bar, Bar3D, and PieSlice procedures. Other shapes require a different routine:

procedure FloodFill(X, Y : integer; Border : word);

FloodFill fills a bounded region with the current fill pattern determined by the most recent call to SetFillStyle or SetFillPattern. The coordinates (X, Y) must specify a point within an enclosed region that you want to fill. The boundaries must be lines of the color Border. If the position of (X, Y) lies outside the region, the exterior is filled.

The FloodFill procedure can be demonstrated with the GRID3 program in listing 11.19.

Listing 11.19

```
program Grid3;
uses Graph;
const
   Color : word = Green;
var
   GraphDriver, Graphmode : integer;
   Row, Column, Style,
   Swath, Xjump, Yjump, Xcenter, Ycenter : word;
begin
   GraphDriver := Detect;
   InitGraph( GraphDriver, Graphmode, 'C:\TP' );
   Xjump := GetMaxX div 10;
   Yjump := GetMaxY div 10;
   SetColor( Color );
   for Swath := 0 to 10 do begin
      SetLineStyle( SolidLn, 0, ThickWidth );
      Line( Swath*Xjump, 0, Swath*Xjump, 10*Yjump );
      Line( 0, Swath*Yjump, 10*Xjump, Swath*Yjump );
   end;
   for Row := 0 to 9 do
      for Column := 0 to 9 do begin
         Style := ( 10*Row +Column ) mod 12;
```

Listing 11.19 continues

Listing 11.19 *continued*

```
        Xcenter := Column*Xjump  + ( Xjump div 2 );
        Ycenter := Row*Yjump  + ( Yjump div 2 );
        SetFillStyle( Style, Color );
        FloodFill( Xcenter, Ycenter, Color );
      end;
    readln;
    CloseGraph;
end.
```

GRID3 draws 100 rectangles and "flood fills" them with changing patterns. The results of the GRID3 program can be seen in figure 11.12.

Fig. 11.12. *Output produced by the GRID3 program.*

Increasing Buffer Size

Flood filling relies on the presence of a 4K buffer on the heap, allocated as part of the `InitGraph` initialization process. In rare cases, you may need to slightly increase the buffer to avoid overflows. You can do this with the routine:

```
procedure SetGraphBufSize( BufSize : word );
```

Here, `BufSize` is the number of bytes you want to reserve.

An alternative use of the `SetGraphBufSize` procedure is to reduce the size of the buffer to free up space on the heap. In that case, call Set-GraphBufSize with a value less than 4K.

Note that `SetGraphBufSize` must be called before `InitGraph`.

Drawing Shapes

This section discusses how to draw complete figures: rectangles, bars, and polygons.

Rectangles and Bars

You have already used the `Rectangle` and `Bar` procedures described earlier in this chapter.

```
procedure Rectangle( X1, Y1, X2, Y2 : integer );
procedure Bar( X1, Y1, X2, Y2 : integer );
```

Both procedures draw from the upper left corner at (X1, Y1) to the lower right corner at (X2, Y2). The only functional difference is that `Rectangle` draws a hollow figure, whereas the image drawn with `Bar` is solid.

One use of the `Bar` procedure is to draw business-type bar graphs. You can achieve a three-dimensional effect with the procedure:

```
procedure Bar3D( X1, Y1, X2, Y2 : integer; Depth : word; Top : boolean );
```

The Depth parameter specifies the perceived depth of the bar. The Top parameter is a Boolean value that determines whether or not the bar has a top. You can use True or False, or the more understandable predefined constants:

```
TopOn  = True;
TopOff = False;
```

Use `TopOff` when you want to stack another bar on top of the current one.

Rectangles and bars are demonstrated with the BARS program in listing 11.20. BARS draws four shapes: a rectangle around the entire screen, a bar image, a three-dimensional bar with a top, and a three-dimensional bar without a top.

Listing 11.20

```
program Bars;
uses Graph;
var
   Width, Height : word;
   GraphDriver, GraphMode : integer;
begin
   GraphDriver := Detect;
   InitGraph( GraphDriver, GraphMode, 'C:\TP' );
   Rectangle( Ø, Ø, GetMaxX, GetMaxY );
   Width  := GetMaxX div 8;
   Height := GetMaxY div 4;
   Bar( Width, Height, Width*2, Height*3 );
   Bar3D( Width*3, Height, Width*4, Height*3, Width div 4, TopOn );
   Bar3D( Width*5, Height, Width*6, Height*3, Width div 4, TopOff );
   readln;
   CloseGraph;
end.
```

The output of the BARS program is shown in figure a11.13.

Fig. 11.13. *Output produced by the BARS program.*

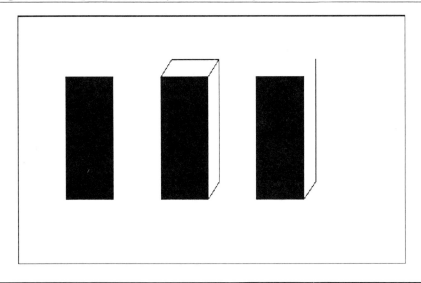

Polygons

A *polygon* is any enclosed shape drawn with straight lines. The sides of a polygon needn't all be the same length, but they aren't allowed to cross one another. Triangles, squares, pentagons, and hexagons are all examples of polygons.

To draw a polygon, specify its corners with the DrawPoly and FillPoly procedures.

```
procedure DrawPoly( NumPoints : word; var PolyPoints );
procedure FillPoly( NumPoints : word; var PolyPoints );
```

DrawPoly "connects the dots" and draws the outline of the polygon using the color selected by SetColor. FillPoly first draws the outline, then fills it in using the pattern and color determined by SetFillStyle.

PolyPoints is an untyped parameter that contains an array of the (X, Y) coordinates of the corners. Each coordinate consists of a record of the predefined type PointType, as follows:

```
PointType = record
                X, Y : integer;
            end;
```

For the DrawPoly procedure, NumPoints is the number of corners in the polygon plus 1. Both the beginning and ending corners must be specified; therefore, for a polygon with *N* corners, PolyPoints[1] must equal PolyPoints[N +1].

The FillPoly procedure doesn't need this repetition. NumPoints is simply the number of corners in the polygon, and PolyPoints contains only one element for each corner. Strangely, however, FillPoly will work correctly if the first and last elements of the PolyPoints array are repeated.

DrawPoly and FillPoly are demonstrated in the POLY program in listing 11.21. You will notice from the value of some of the X coordinates that POLY is intended to run in a high-resolution mode.

Listing 11.21

```
program Poly;
uses Graph;
const
   StopSign1 : array [ 1..7 ] of PointType =
       (  ( X :   50;   Y :   50 ),
          ( X :  150;   Y :   50 ),
          ( X :  200;   Y :   93 ),
          ( X :  150;   Y :  136 ),
          ( X :   50;   Y :  136 ),
```

Listing 11.21 continues

Listing 11.21 continued

```
            ( X :    Ø;    Y :   93 ),
            ( X :   50;    Y :   50 )   );
   StopSign2 : array [ 1..6 ] of PointType =
      (   ( X : 450;    Y :   50 ),
          ( X : 550;    Y :   50 ),
          ( X : 600;    Y :   93 ),
          ( X : 550;    Y :  136 ),
          ( X : 450;    Y :  136 ),
          ( X : 400;    Y :   93 )   );
var
   GraphDriver, Gr??? Mode : integer;
begin
   GraphDriver := Detect;
   InitGraph( GraphDriver, Gr??? Mode, 'C:\TP' );
   SetColor( Red );
   DrawPoly( 7, StopSign1 );
   SetColor( Green {Black} );
   SetFillStyle( CloseDotFill, Red );
   FillPoly( 6, StopSign2 );
   readln;
   CloseGraph;
end.
```

The output from the program is shown in figure 11.14.

Fig. 11.14. Output produced by the POLY program.

POLY uses the DrawPoly procedure to draw a stop sign (well, actually a hexagon) on the left side of the screen. On EGA and VAG adapters, the hexagon appears in red. POLY also uses the FillPoly procedure to draw a similar hexagon on the right side of the screen, but this time with a CloseDot-Fill interior.

To emphasize the difference between the border and the interior of the hexagon on the right, we used green for the boundary and red for the center. If you don't want a boundary line to appear, you can call SetColor with black.

Note how DrawPoly is passed seven coordinates, whereas FillPoly only receives six. You may want to experiment with the number of corners. For example, if you omit the last coordinate when you call DrawPoly, the hexagon will be drawn with one open side. You should also notice that if Shapes is an array of PointType, the statements

```
DrawPoly( SizeOf( Shapes ) div SizeOf( PointType ), Shapes );
```

and

```
FillPoly( SizeOf( Shapes ) div SizeOf( PointType ), Shapes );
```

enable you to vary the number of corners in the Shapes array itself without worrying about modifying any code in the body of the program.

Parameters with DrawPoly and FillPoly

Before you continue to the next section, consider for a moment how cleverly the DrawPoly and FillPoly procedures handled parameters. With few exceptions (such as write and writeln), Turbo Pascal doesn't allow procedures or functions to have a variable number of parameters. (Certainly no user-defined procedure or function is allowed such a luxury!)

Because polygons can have any number of sides, the DrawPoly and FillPoly procedures couldn't be written with a fixed number of parameters. By defining a PointType parameter and letting PointType be user-defined, this restriction was circumvented. You might find this trick useful in your own programs.

Curves

This section discusses the Turbo Pascal routines for generating curved images.

The Aspect Ratio

At the beginning of the chapter, I said that the monochrome screen is 350 pixels high by 750 pixels wide. If you take a quick glance at your screen, it probably seems relatively square. It's reasonable to assume, then, that pixels are packed together more closely in the horizontal direction.

The *aspect ratio* is a measure of the relative height and width of a pixel, as follows:

(Display Width) ÷ (Display Height)

On a screen with an aspect ratio of 0.5, each pixel is half as wide as it is tall. Consequently, 100 horizontal pixels are exactly as long as 50 vertical pixels.

You can determine the aspect ratio for your screen with the routine:

procedure GetAspectRatio(var Xasp, Yasp : word);

GetAspectRatio returns two word-type variables from which the aspect ratio can be computed. If you call GetAspectRatio on a COMPAQ PLUS in high-resolution CGA 640 × 350 mode, you get:

Xasp = 4167
Yasp = 10000

This gives an aspect ratio of 0.4167, indicating that the width of a pixel is only 41.67 percent of its height.

Turbo Pascal uses the aspect ratio to compensate for the shape of a screen when your program draws circles, arcs, and pie slices. If you are not happy with the default, you can change the aspect ratio of your screen with the SetAspectRatio procedure.

procedure SetAspectRatio(Xasp, Yasp : word);

The use of SetAspectRatio is demonstrated in the ASPECT program in listing 11.22.

Listing 11.22

```
program Aspect;
uses Graph;
var
   Height, Width, Radius : word;
   Xasp, Yasp : word;
   GraphDriver, GraphMode : integer;
begin
   GraphDriver := Detect;
   InitGraph( GraphDriver, GraphMode, 'C:\TP' );
   Height := GetMaxY div 2;
   Width := GetMaxX div 3;
   Radius := GetMaxY div 4;
   Circle( Width, Height, Radius );      { Good circle }
   GetAspectRatio( Xasp, Yasp );
   SetAspectRatio( 4*Xasp, Yasp );
   Circle( Width*2, Height, Radius );    { Distorted circle }
   readln;
   CloseGraph;
end.
```

The ASPECT program draws two circles, as shown in figure 11.15. The circle on the left uses the default aspect ratio and appears acceptably round.

The circle on the right uses an aspect ratio in which the default Xasp parameter is increased by a factor of four. The compiler now thinks the width is four times larger than it really is, and it tries to compensate by increasing the circle's vertical size, resulting in an extremely tall ellipse.

Fig. 11.15. *Output produced by the ASPECT program.*

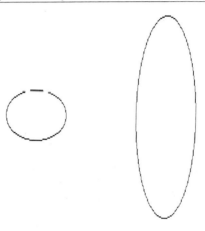

Because Turbo corrects only the circle, arc, and pie slice procedures, other figures must be adjusted manually. In general, you can do this by dividing the X coordinate of your drawings by the aspect ratio, as shown in the TANLINE3 program in listing 11.23.

Listing 11.23

```
program TanLine3;
uses Graph;
var
    Xasp, Yasp : word;
    GraphDriver, GraphMode : integer;
    Y, Ymax : word;
    Ratio : real;
begin
    GraphDriver := Detect;
    InitGraph( GraphDriver, GraphMode, 'C:\TP' );
    YMax := GetMaxY;
    GetAspectRatio( Xasp, Yasp );
    Ratio := Yasp / Xasp;    { inverse aspect ratio }
    for y := 1 to YMax do
```

Listing 11.23 continues

Listing 11.23 *continued*

```
    Line( Max-y, Ø, Ø, y );
  SetViewPort( Ymax, Ø, GetMaxX, GetMaxY, ClipOn );
  for Y := 1 to Ymax do
    Line( Round( Ratio * ( Ymax - Y ) ), Ø, Ø, Y );
  readln;
  CloseGraph;
end.
```

TANLINE3 is a modification of the TANLINES program, in which tangents are drawn to give the illusion of a circle. The output of TANLINE3 is shown in figure 11.16. Two separate arcs are displayed. The drawing on the right compensates for the screen's aspect ratio. Notice how TANLINE3 uses the SetViewPort procedure to change the screen coordinates.

Fig. 11.16. *Output produced by the TANLINE3 program.*

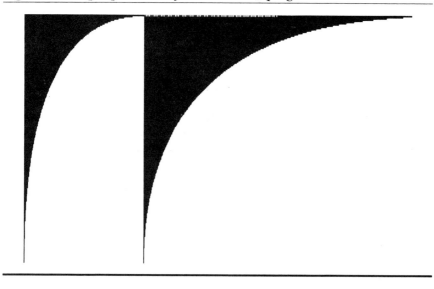

Circles and Ellipses

You have seen the Circle procedure several times already in this chapter.

```
procedure Circle( X, Y : integer; Radius : word );
```

Circle draws a complete circle centered at (X, Y) with a radius of Radius. The interior of the circle is left untouched.

In the last section, you saw how to distort the aspect ratio to force the Circle procedure to draw an ellipse. There is, fortunately, an easier way to accomplish the same thing using the Ellipse and FillEllipse procedures.

An *ellipse* is any oval shape—including a circle—that enables you to control its width and height independently.

```
procedure Ellipse( X, Y : integer;
                   StAngle, EndAngle : word;
                   XRadius, YRadius  : word );
```

Ellipse draws an elliptical arc, centered at (X,Y), from the starting angle StAngle to the ending angle EndAngle. XRadius and YRadius are the horizontal and vertical axes, respectively. Figure 11.17 explains these parameters graphically. Notice that angles are measured counterclockwise, in degrees, with 0 degrees in the three o'clock position.

Fig. 11.17. *The parameters used by the Ellipse procedure.*

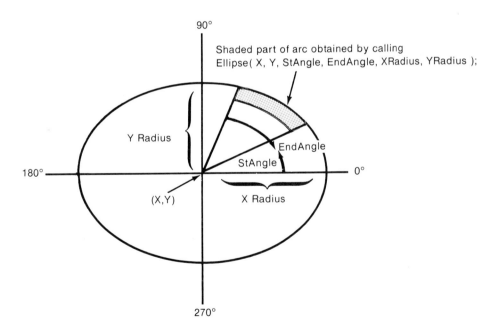

Just as with the Circle procedure, Ellipse only draws the arc itself; the center of the ellipse is unaffected. However, unlike the Circle procedure, Ellipse doesn't adjust its shape to compensate for the aspect ratio of your screen. Hence, even if XRadius and YRadius are equal, the ellipse still appears to be oval.

To draw a filled ellipse or a filled circle, use the FillEllipse procedure.

```
procedure FillEllipse( X, Y : integer;
                       XRadius, YRadius  : word );
```

FillEllipse draws an ellipse centered at (X, Y). XRadius and YRadius are the horizontal and vertical axes, respectively.

The FillEllipse procedure is demonstrated in the BUG program in listing 11.24.

Listing 11.24

```
program Bug;
uses Graph;
var
   Xpos, Ypos, Xinc, grDriver, grMode : integer;
   Width, Height, Xradius, Yradius, i : word;
begin
   grDriver := Detect;
   InitGraph( grDriver, grMode, 'C:\TP' );
   GetAspectRatio( Width, Height );
   Ypos := GetMaxY div 2;
   Xinc := GetMaxX div 20;
   Xradius := Xinc div 2;
   Yradius := Round( Xradius * Width / Height );
   for i := 2 to 18 do begin
      SetColor( Random( GetMaxColor - 1 ) + 1 );    { Never set to background }
      SetFillStyle( ( i - 2 ) mod 13, i - 2 );
      FillEllipse( Xinc * i, Ypos, Xradius, Yradius );
      if i < 18 then OutTextXY( Xinc * i, Ypos + Yradius, 'L' );
   end;
   OutTextXY( Xinc * 18, Ypos - 2*Yradius, 'V' );
   write( 'The Turbo Bug' );
   readln;
   CloseGraph;
end.
```

The results of the BUG program are shown in figure 11.18. The caterpillar is created by several calls to the FillEllipse procedure. Notice how BUG uses the aspect ratio to force each ellipse into a circle.

Fig. 11.18. Output produced by the BUG program.

The Turbo Bug

Arcs

An *arc* is a portion of a circle.

```
procedure Arc( X, Y : integer; StAngle, EndAngle, Radius : word );
```

The Arc procedure is similar to Circle, except that it draws only from the starting angle, StAngle, to the ending angle, EndAngle. Angles are measured counterclockwise, in degrees, with 0 degrees in the three o'clock position.

With most graphics routines, if you know the coordinates of the current pointer prior to calling the routine, you can calculate the location of the CP after the routine finishes. The same, of course, is true for the Arc procedure, but the trigonometry can be somewhat involved, especially because the compiler compensates for the aspect ratio of your screen. To simplify the effort, Turbo Pascal offers the procedure:

```
procedure GetArcCoords( var ArcCoords : ArcCoordsType );
```

GetArcCoords returns the coordinates of the last Arc command within a record of the predefined type ArcCoordsType, defined as follows:

```
ArcCoordsType = record
                X, Y         : integer;
                Xstart, Ystart : integer;
                Xend, Yend   : integer;
            end;
```

The ArcCoords record returns the coordinates of the center point of the arc (X, Y), plus the coordinates of its starting point (Xstart, Ystart) and ending point (Xend, Yend).

Pie Slices and Sectors

You can draw partially filled circles and ellipses with the `PieSlice` and Sector procedures.

```
procedure PieSlice( X, Y : integer; StAngle, EndAngle, Radius : word );
procedure Sector( X, Y : Integer;
                  StAngle, EndAngle,
                  XRadius, YRadius : word );
```

The `PieSlice` procedure draws and fills a pie slice, using (X, Y) as its center point and Radius as its radius, and drawing from starting angle StAngle to ending angle EndAngle. The Sector procedure draws and fills an elliptical sector. Sector has the same parameters as PieSlice except that the width and height are controlled individually by XRadius and YRadius, respectively. Angles are measured counterclockwise, in degrees, with 0 degrees in the three o'clock position.

The WEDGE program in listing 11.25 demonstrates how PieSlice and Sector are used.

Listing 11.25

```
program Wedge;
uses Graph;
var
   Xmid, Ymid : word;
   GraphDriver, GraphMode : integer;
begin
   GraphDriver := Detect;
   InitGraph( GraphDriver, GraphMode, 'C:\TP' );
   Xmid := GetMaxX div 4;
   Ymid := GetMaxY div 2;
   Arc( Xmid, Ymid, 55, 350, Xmid div 2 );
   PieSlice( Xmid, Ymid, 0, 45, Xmid );
   Sector( Xmid*3, Ymid, 90, 360, Xmid div 2, Ymid );
   readln;
   CloseGraph;
end.
```

The results of the WEDGE program are shown in figure 11.19. Notice that both the Arc and PieSlice figures have automatically been adjusted for the aspect ratio of the screen.

Fig. 11.19. *Output produced by the WEDGE program.*

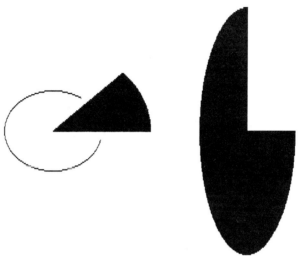

Saving and Restoring Graphics Screens

Chapter 10 discussed how to save and restore text windows. You recall that to save the display, you copy the 2,000 word video memory to a special buffer. You restored the screen by copying the buffer back to video memory.

Admittedly, manipulating an entire text screen is a brute-force approach, especially because most of the time you want to save only a small portion of the display. The technique is simple to code, however, and it isn't difficult to find space on the heap for 2,000 words.

On the other hand, a single graphics screen can take up to 16K of the PC's internal memory plus additional memory on the graphics adapter board itself. Saving one or more complete graphics screens rapidly consumes space on the heap. For practical reasons, you have to limit yourself to dealing with only a small portion of a screen at one time.

Turbo Pascal provides the `ImageSize` function, the `GetImage` function, and the `PutImage` procedures to simplify this task.

```
function ImageSize( X1, Y1, X2, Y2 : integer ) : word;
procedure GetImage( X1, Y1, X2, Y2 : integer; var BitMap );
procedure PutImage( X, Y : integer; var BitMap; BitBlt : word );
```

The GetImage procedure saves an area of the screen—the rectangle defined by the upper left coordinates of (X1, Y1) and lower right coordinates of (X2, Y2)—by locating its video memory and copying it into a buffer identified by the untyped variable BitMap. The width and height of the rectangle are also saved. Use the GetMem procedure to allocate the buffer and FreeMem to return it to the heap when you are done. The ImageSize function calculates the number of bytes you need to reserve.

The PutImage procedure returns the contents of the buffer to the screen. Because GetImage stored the dimensions of the rectangle as part of the BitMap buffer, PutImage needs only the upper left starting coordinates.

The BitBlt parameter enables you to choose how PutImage redisplays the rectangle. Turbo Pascal defines the following five constants for you to use as options:

- ❏ CopyPut   0   { MOV }
- ❏ XORPut   1   { XOR }
- ❏ OrPut   2   { OR }
- ❏ AndPut   3   { AND }
- ❏ NotPut   4   { NOT }

CopyPut indicates a complete replacement; the buffer image writes over whatever was already on the screen. NotPut returns the inverse image. The remaining options determine the final display by logically comparing each pixel on the screen with the corresponding pixel in the buffer: XORPut performs a logical exclusive OR; OrPut performs a logical inclusive OR; and AndPut performs a logical AND.

These techniques are demonstrated in the BITGRAPH program, shown in listing 11.26.

Listing 11.26

```
program BitGraph;
uses Graph;
var
    Image                     : pointer;
    i, Width, Height, Storage : word;
    GraphDriver, GraphMode    : integer;
begin
```

Listing 11.26 continues

Listing 11.26 *continued*

```
        GraphDriver := Detect;
        InitGraph( GraphDriver, GraphMode, 'C:\TP' );
        Width := GetMaxX div 5;
        Height := GetMaxY div 4;
        for i := 1 to 100 do begin
            SetColor( Random( GetMaxColor ) + 1 );
            Circle( Random( Width ), Random( GetMaxY ), Random( Width div 4 ) );
        end;
        Storage : ImageSize( 0, 0, Width, GetMaxY );
        GetMem( Image, Storage );
        GetImage( 0, 0, Width, GetMaxY, Image^ );
        readln;
        ClearDevice;
        Bar( 0, Height, GetMaxX, Hoight * 3 );
        readln;
        for i := 0 to 4 do
            PutImage( i*Width, 0, Image^, i );
        FreeMem( Image, Storage );
        readln;
        CloseGraph;
end.
```

BITGRAPH divides the screen into five vertical sections. It begins by randomly displaying 100 circles in the section on the far left, as shown in figure 11.20.

Fig. 11.20. *Output produced by BITGRAPH: 100 random circles.*

After you press the Enter key, BITGRAPH stores the left section in a buffer named Image^. Then it displays a large rectangle, horizontally across the middle of the screen, as shown in figure 11.21.

Fig. 11.21. Output produced by BITGRAPH: a solid rectangle.

After you press Enter once again, BITGRAPH returns the original image to the screen in each of the five sections, using a different BitBlt option each time. Figure 11.22 compares the effects of using CopyPut, XORPut, OrPut, AndPut, and NotPut.

Fig. 11.22. Output produced by BITGRAPH: five display options.

Displaying Text

The `write` and `writeln` statements operate the same in graphics mode as they do in text mode. Unfortunately, the Graph unit doesn't include a way to freely position `write` and `writeln` output. No matter where the current pointer is located, the first occurrence of `write` or `writeln` appears in the upper left corner of the screen. Every subsequent occurrence begins immediately to the right of the previous message, or, if the previous call was to a `writeln`, in the first position of the next line.

A Note about Using the Crt Unit

If you use the Crt unit in your program, `write` and `writeln` switch to the special display routines that output directly to text video memory. In order to redirect `write` and `writeln` to the graphics screen, set the `DirectVideo` variable to False, as follows:

```
DirectVideo := False;
```

This enables you to use the other features of the Crt unit without losing the use of `write` and `writeln` in the process.

The Graph unit provides its own means of displaying text:

```
procedure OutText( TextString : string );
procedure OutTextXY( X, Y : integer; TextString : string );
```

The `OutText` procedure displays a string beginning at the current pointer. After `OutText` is finished, the CP is moved to the first position after the last string character. The `OutTextXY` procedure displays a string at (X, Y). The CP remains at (X, Y) after `OutTextXY` is run.

Text Style

The default graphics character set is called a *bit-mapped font*. The shape of each of the 256 standard ASCII characters is stored as an 8×8 matrix of pixels. When a bit-mapped character is enlarged, it appears jagged, and its block-like structure is clearly evident.

In addition, Turbo Pascal provides four stroked fonts: Triplex, Small, Sans-Serif, and Gothic. With a *stroked font*, each character is defined by a set of reference points similar to those you used earlier in the chapter to draw polygons. Consequently, a stroked font is able to retain its appearance as the character is enlarged or compressed.

You can select the font you want with the SetTextStyle procedure.

```
procedure SetTextStyle( Font, Direction : word; CharSize : word );
```

SetTextStyle controls not only the text font but also the direction (horizontal or vertical) in which the text should be written and the size of the characters.

Select the text font by specifying a value from 0 through 4 or by using one of the predefined constants shown in table 11.9.

Table 11.9. *Text Fonts*

Constant	Value	File
DefaultFont	0	GRAPH.TPU
TriplexFont	1	TRIP.CHR
SmallFont	2	LITT.CHR
SansSerifFont	3	SANS.CHR
GothicFont	4	GOTH.CHR

DefaultFont is the default 8 × 8 bit-mapped font. All others are stroked fonts. Each stroked font is physically stored in a separate file with a .CHR extension. To use a stroked font, be sure its file resides in the same directory as the one you specified in the InitGraph procedure.

The Direction parameter enables you to choose between displaying text horizontally (left to right) or vertically (bottom to top). You can use either the values 0 or 1, respectively, or one of the predefined constants:

```
HorizDir   = 0;
VertDir    = 1;
```

Unlike text mode, the graphics mode features of Turbo Pascal help you to scale the character fonts to any size. The CharSize parameter is a word value containing the multiplication factor. A value of 1 indicates normal-sized characters, 2 indicates characters twice the normal size, and so on.

The use of SetTextStyle is demonstrated in the EYECHART program in listing 11.27.

Listing 11.27

```
program EyeChart;
uses Graph;
var
   Alphabet : byte;
   Height, Width, FontType, FontSize : word;
   GraphDriver, GraphMode : integer;
```

Listing 11.27 continues

Listing 11.27 *continued*

```
begin
    GraphDriver := Detect;
    InitGraph( GraphDriver, GraphMode, 'C:\TP' );
    Height := GetMaxY div 5;
    Width := GetMaxX div 10;
    for FontType := 0 to 4 do begin
        writeln( 'Font ', FontType );
        Alphabet := 84;
        MoveTo( GetMaxX div 5, FontType*Height );
        for FontSize := 1 to 6 do begin
            SetTextStyle( FontType, HorizDir, FontSize );
            Inc( Alphabet );
            OutText( Chr( Alphabet ) );
            MoveRel( Width, 0 );
        end;
    end;
    readln;
    CloseGraph;
end.
```

When EYECHART executes, it produces the output shown in figure 11.23.

Fig. 11.23. *Output produced by the EYECHART program.*

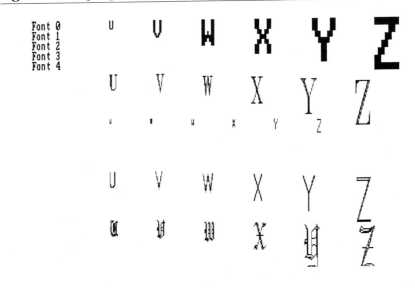

Vertical text is demonstrated in the CHART2 program in listing 11.28.

Listing 11.28

```
program Chart2;
uses Graph;
var
   Width, Height, FontType, Letter : word;
   GraphDriver, GraphMode : integer;
begin
   GraphDriver := Detect;
   InitGraph( GraphDriver, GraphMode, 'C:\TP' );
   Width := GetMaxX div 6;
   Height := GetMaxY div 5;
   for FontType := 0 to 4 do begin
      MoveTo( Width*( FontType +1 ), 0 );
      SetTextStyle( FontType, VertDir, 8 );
      OutText( 'abcdefghijklmnopqrstuvwxyz' );
   end;
   readln;
   CloseGraph;
end.
```

CHART2 produces the output shown in figure 11.24. Notice that the end of the string in the OutText procedure is positioned at the top of the screen.

Fig. 11.24. Output produced by the CHART2 program.

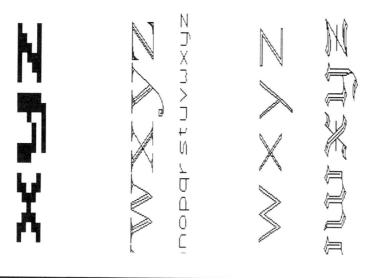

Text Justification

In figures 11.23 and 11.24, you probably noticed that even though the programs attempted to position the characters evenly, their actual locations appeared somewhat haphazard. The SetTextJustify procedure helps you to justify the characters—horizontally and vertically—relative to the current pointer.

```
procedure SetTextJustify( Horiz, Vert : word );
```

For the Horiz(ontal) parameter, use one of the constants:

LeftText   = 0;
CenterText   = 1;
RightText   = 2;

For the Vert(ical) parameter, use one of the constants:

BottomText   = 0;
CenterText   = 1;
TopText   = 2;

The JUSTTEXT program in listing 11.29 demonstrates how the SetText-Justify procedure operates.

Listing 11.29

```
program JustText;
uses Graph;
var
   i, Height, Width,
   Horizontal, Vertical : word;
   GraphDriver, GraphMode : integer;
begin
   GraphDriver := Detect;
   InitGraph( GraphDriver, GraphMode, 'C:\TP' );
   Height := GetMaxY div 4;
   Width := GetMaxX div 4;
   SetTextStyle( DefaultFont, HorizDir, 6 );
   for i := 1 to 3 do begin
      Line( 0, Height*i, GetMaxX, Height*i );
      Line( Width*i, 0, Width*i, GetMaxY );
   end;
   for Horizontal := 0 to 2 do
      for Vertical := 0 to 2 do begin
      ??? MoveTo( ( Horizontal +1 )*Width, ( Vertical +1 )*Height );
         SetTextJustify( Horizontal, Vertical );
         OutText( '0' );
      end;
   readln;
   CloseGraph;
end.
```

When JUSTTEXT executes, it produces the results shown in figure 11.25. All nine possible combinations are presented. The vertical justification options are shown top to bottom, whereas the horizontal justification options are shown left to right.

Fig. 11.25. *Output produced by the JUSTTEXT program.*

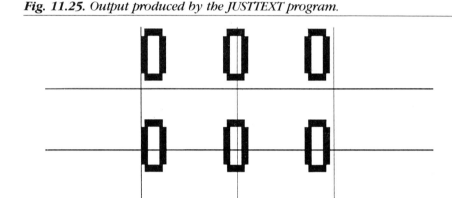

Determining Text Settings

If your program switches between two or more text character styles, you can use the GetTextSettings procedure to obtain and store the current text font, direction, size, and justification.

```
procedure GetTextSettings( var TextInfo : TextSettingsType );
```

GetTextSettings uses a single variable parameter of type TextSettings-Type, which is defined as follows:

```
TextSettingsType = record
              Font      : word;
              Direction : word;
              CharSize  : word;
              Horiz     : word;
              Vert      : word;
            end;
```

Assuming that you defined a variable TextInfo as type TextSettingsType, you can retrieve the current settings with the call

```
GetTextSettings( TextInfo );
```

Later, to return to the original settings, use the contents of TextInfo as inputs to SetTextStyle and SetTextJustify.

```
with TextInfo do begin
   SetTextStyle( Font, Direction, CharSize );
   SetTextJustify( Horiz, Vert );
end;
```

Controlling Text Size

The SetTextStyle procedure restricts you to integral multiples of the standard font sizes. If you want to shrink the size of a stroked font or change its proportions, you can use the SetUserCharSize procedure.

```
procedure SetUserCharSize( MultX, DivX, MultY, DivY : word );
```

The width and height of any stroked font used after SetUserCharSize is called will be adjusted by factors of:

$$\frac{MultX}{DivX} \quad \text{and} \quad \frac{MultY}{DivY}$$

respectively. To use SetUserCharSize, you must first call the SetTextStyle procedure with the following for its CharSize parameter:

```
UserCharSize = Ø;
```

Using the predefined constant UserCharSize tells the compiler that you want to modify the proportions of a stroked font. Next, call SetUserCharSize.

This technique is demonstrated in the TEXTSIZE program in listing 11.30.

Listing 11.30

```
program TextSize;
uses Graph;
var
   GraphDriver, GraphMode : integer;
   Width, Height : word;
begin
   GraphDriver := Detect;
   InitGraph( GraphDriver, GraphMode, 'C:\TP' );
   Width := GetMaxX div 2;
   Height := GetMaxY div 4;
   SetTextJustify( CenterText, CenterText );
```

Listing 11.30 continues

Listing 11.30 *continued*

```
SetUserCharSize( 4, 1, 2, 1 );
SetTextStyle( SansSerifFont, HorizDir, UserCharSize );
OutTextXY( Width, Height, 'CONTRACT' );
SetUserCharSize( 1, 1, 1, 1 );
SetTextStyle( SansSerifFont, HorizDir, UserCharSize );
OutTextXY( Width, 2*Height, 'THIS IS THE BODY OF THE AGREEMENT...' );
SetUserCharSize( 1, 2, 1, 2 );
SetTextStyle( SansSerifFont, HorizDir, UserCharSize );
OutTextXY( Width, 3*Height, 'THIS IS THE FINE PRINT...' );
readln;
CloseGraph;
end.
```

When TEXTSIZE executes, it produces the results shown in figure 11.26. Note that the `SetUserCharSize` procedure allowed TEXTSIZE independently to vary the character width and height.

Fig. 11.26. *Output produced by the TEXTSIZE program.*

Determining Text Size

On a text screen, the size of a string is easy to determine. Its height is one twenty-fifth (four percent) of the size of the screen, and its length can be found with the Length function.

The size of a string on a graphics screen is more difficult to ascertain, especially after selecting and scaling a font. Fortunately, Turbo Pascal provides two functions that return the height and width of a graphics string:

```
function  TextHeight( TextString : string ) : word;
```

```
function  TextWidth (TextString : string ) : word;
```

The TextHeight function returns the height of a string in pixels. The TextWidth function returns the width of a string in pixels.

The TEXTRING program in listing 11.31 uses TextHeight and TextWidth to determine the size of a string, then calculates the radius of a circle to enclose it.

Listing 11.31

```
program TextRing;
uses Graph;
var
    GraphDriver, GraphMode : integer;
    StartX, StartY, Radius : word;
    Height, Width : LongInt;
    Message : string[ 20 ];
begin
    GraphDriver := Detect;
    InitGraph( GraphDriver, GraphMode, 'C:\TP' );
    Message := 'Press the ENTER key.';
    SetTextJustify( CenterText, CenterText );
    SetTextStyle( SansSerifFont, HorizDir, 4 );
    StartX := GetMaxX div 2;
    StartY := GetMaxY div 2;
    OutTextXY( StartX, StartY, Message );
    Height := TextHeight( Message );
    Width := TextWidth( Message );
    Radius := Round( 1.1*( Sqrt( Height*Height + Width*Width ) / 2 ) );
    Circle( StartX, StartY, Radius );
    readln;
    CloseGraph;
end.
```

When TEXTRING executes, it produces the results shown in figure 11.27. You can experiment with different font sizes and string lengths; the circle produced will adapt as needed.

Graphics Defaults

The GraphDefaults procedure resets the graphics parameters to the values they had immediately after the graphics system was initialized with InitGraph.

```
procedure GraphDefaults;
```

GraphDefaults resets all system default values, as follows:

❏ The current pointer is moved to the upper left corner of the screen.

❏ The viewport is returned to the full screen.

Fig. 11.27. *Output produced by the TEXTSTRING program.*

- [ ] The palette, drawing, and background colors are returned to the defaults.
- [ ] The line style and pattern are restored.
- [ ] The fill style, color, and pattern are restored.
- [ ] The active font, text style and justification, and user character size are all restored.

Interestingly, though, GraphDefaults does not clear the screen. If you want that done as well, follow the call to GraphDefaults with a call to ClearDevice.

Including Drivers and Fonts with Your Programs

Generally, it's not inconvenient to have the .BGI device driver files and the .CHR stroked character font files reside somewhere on your disk. After all, your program loads and runs successfully as long as you can reference the location of the files when you initialize the graphics system, as follows:

```
GraphDriver := Detect;
InitGraph( GraphDriver, GraphMode, 'C:\TP' );
```

Now suppose that you like your graphics program so much that you want to give a copy to a friend. Or you've developed a business graphics application at work and need to run it on five other PCs. Or you want to make your program available through public domain groups—or even sell it commercially.

Suddenly, you have a problem. Unless every machine that runs your program has a directory named C:\TP that contains the appropriate .BGI device driver and .CHR character font files, your program won't operate.

The immediate solution is to change the path in the InitGraph call to a null string (indicating the current directory) and include all of the .BGI and .CHR files when you distribute your program. But even this is only temporary relief. If your program has any value at all, people will want to run it outside of the directory in which it's stored by including its location as part of their PC's PATH command. Again, your program won't operate, because the .BGI and .CHR files aren't where InitGraph searches. So, you include a line in your documentation: "These files must always reside in the current directory." It works, of course, but it just doesn't seem professional.

A completely different problem arises when you use several stroked fonts. By default, your program only keeps one character set in its memory at a time. Consequently, if you switch back and forth between two (or more) character fonts, your program must reload each font from the disk every time it's used. It doesn't take long before even your more patient users complain about the performance delays and the grinding noises during disk access.

The answer to all these troubles is to include the .BGI and .CHR files within your program itself. In other words, if all of the device drivers and fonts you need could be compiled along with your program, you wouldn't need to worry about their physical location on disk, nor would your users experience noticeable delays when switching among several character fonts.

In this section, you learn how this can be done.

Loading Drivers and Fonts

There are two ways to combine drivers and fonts with your programs.

1. The Heap Memory method. Normally, InitGraph places the selected driver and font on the heap. You can do this directly. Read all the .BGI and .CHR files you want, place them on the heap, and give their locations to InitGraph so that it can bypass the loading process.

2. The External Procedure method. Convert the .BGI and .CHR files into object files with the BINOBJ.EXE program, then link the object files into your program. Tell InitGraph that the code for the drivers and fonts can be found in procedures within the program.

Both approaches work, but the first method suffers from the same drawback discussed before, namely that the .BGI and .CHR files must accompany your program and must reside in a predetermined directory. The Turbo Pascal *Reference Guide* describes how this technique can be implemented.

The second technique is cleaner and more efficient. It's the one described here. No matter which method you use, you are registering the drivers and fonts with InitGraph when you specify their memory locations. (In this context, *registering* means "signing up" as in registering to vote, registering for school, and registering for the draft.) Registering is performed with the following functions:

```
function RegisterBGIdriver( Driver : pointer ) : integer;
function RegisterBGIfont( Font : pointer ) : integer;
```

RegisterBGIdriver and RegisterBGIfont register a driver file and a font, respectively, with the graphics system. Both take a pointer as their single parameter. If you use the Heap Memory method, the pointer points to the starting location of the driver or font on the heap. If you use the External Procedure method, the pointer points to the linked-in procedure.

Creating Object Files with BINOBJ.EXE

Locate the BINOBJ.EXE program that was supplied with your Turbo Pascal distribution disks. If you've installed Turbo on a hard drive, you will probably find the program in the C:\TP subdirectory, next to the compiler itself.

The BINOBJ.EXE program converts the binary versions of the .CHR character file and the .BGI driver file to object file format. A *binary file* is nothing other than data. An *object file* contains either code or data that a Turbo Pascal program can use. An object file, which has .OBJ as its extension, can be linked with your program by using the {$L} compiler directive.

BINOBJ.EXE takes three parameters, as follows:

```
BINOBJ   <source[.BIN]>   <destination[.OBJ]>   <public??? Me>
```

The source file is the binary file you want to convert. It assumes .BIN as its default extension. The destination file is the .OBJ file you want to produce. The public name is the name of the procedure you will use in your program.

Before you proceed, remember: you are about to create new object files based on the .BGI and .CHR files; the original drivers and fonts won't be modified in any way.

The easiest way to use BINOBJ.EXE is in the form of a batch file. The PORTABLE.BAT file in listing 11.32 contains batch instructions that create object files for every driver and font.

Listing 11.32

```
BINOBJ  C:\TP\GOTH.CHR     GOTH     GOTHfont
BINOBJ  C:\TP\LITT.CHR     LITT     LITTfont
BINOBJ  C:\TP\SANS.CHR     SANS     SANSfont
BINOBJ  C:\TP\TRIP.CHR     TRIP     TRIPfont
BINOBJ  C:\TP\ATT.BGI      ATT      ATTDriver
BINOBJ  C:\TP\CGA.BGI      CGA      CGADriver
BINOBJ  C:\TP\EGAVGA.BGI   EGAVGA   EGAVGADriver
BINOBJ  C:\TP\HERC.BGI     HERC     HerculesDriver
BINOBJ  C:\TP\IBM8514.BGI  IBM8514  IBM8514Driver
BINOBJ  C:\TP\PC3270.BGI   PC3270   PC3270Driver
```

To use the file, simply enter the following command from the DOS prompt:

PORTABLE

DOS will respond by running the BINOBJ.EXE program for every driver and font. (Of course, you could have typed in each line individually, but the odds are fairly high that you will want to use this technique again some time.) You can confirm that the batch file operated correctly by verifying the presence of the object files with the command:

DIR *.OBJ

DOS responds with a listing of the 10 files:

GOTH.OBJ
LITT.OBJ
SANS.OBJ
TRIP.OBJ
ATT.OBJ
CGA.OBJ
EGAVGA.OBJ
HERC.OBJ
IBM8514.OBJ
PC3270.OBJ

Each instruction in the batch file performed a similar conversion for every driver and font. For example, the command:

```
BINOBJ  C:\TP\GOTH.CHR     GOTH     GOTHfont
```

took the binary data file GOTH.CHR residing in the C:\TP subdirectory and created an object file version, GOTH.OBJ, in the current subdirectory. This object file can now be referenced as a procedure in a Turbo Pascal program using the name GOTHfont. Of course, even though it's declared as a procedure, GOTHfont doesn't contain any executable code. Fortunately, Init-Graph doesn't care; it expects data, so it will treat GOTHfont as data.

Incorporating Drivers and Fonts in Your Programs

The process of linking an object file into your program is demonstrated in the ALLSTUFF program, shown in listing 11.33.

The drivers and character fonts are declared as external procedures. Each procedure name corresponds to the third parameter in the BINOBJ.EXE command: the public name. By declaring a procedure as external, you are simply telling the compiler that its contents can be found in another file—specifically, the one you name with the {$L} compiler directive. During compilation, Turbo reads each external file and physically includes it with the main program. The .OBJ files won't be needed after the compilation is completed, but you will probably want to keep them around for next time.

Listing 11.33

```
program AllStuff;
uses Graph;
var
   FontStyle, Height : word;
   GraphDriver, GraphMode : integer;
procedure GOTHfont;          external;    {$L GOTH.OBJ }
procedure LITTfont;          external;    {$L LITT.OBJ }
procedure SANSfont;          external;    {$L SANS.OBJ }
procedure TRIPfont;          external;    {$L TRIP.OBJ }
procedure ATTDriver;         external;    {$L ATT.OBJ }
procedure CGADriver;         external;    {$L CGA.OBJ }
procedure EGAVGADriver;      external;    {$L EGAVGA.OBJ }
procedure HerculesDriver;    external;    {$L HERC.OBJ }
procedure IBM8514Driver;     external;    {$L IBM8514.OBJ }
procedure PC3270Driver;      external;    {$L PC3270.OBJ }
procedure LoadTheFont( ProcedurePointer : pointer );
begin
   if RegisterBGIfont( ProcedurePointer ) < 0 then begin
      writeln( 'Error registering font: ', GraphErrorMsg( GraphResult ) );
      Halt( 1 );
   end;
end;
procedure PrepareTheFonts;
begin
   LoadTheFont( @GOTHfont );
   LoadTheFont( @LITTfont );
   LoadTheFont( @SANSfont );
   LoadTheFont( @TRIPfont );
```

Listing 11.33 continues

Listing 11.33 continued

```
   end;
procedure LoadTheDriver( ProcedurePointer : pointer );
begin
   if RegisterBGIdriver( ProcedurePointer )  < Ø then begin
      writeln( 'Error registering driver: ', GraphErrorMsg( GraphResult ) );
      Halt( 1 );
   end;
end;
procedure PrepareTheDrivers;
begin
   LoadTheDriver( @ATTDriver );
   LoadTheDriver( @CGADriver );
   LoadTheDriver( @EGAVGADriver );
   LoadTheDriver( @HerculesDriver );
   LoadTheDriver( @IBM8514Driver );
   LoadTheDriver( @PC327ØDriver );
end;
begin
   PrepareTheFonts;
   PrepareTheDrivers;
   GraphDriver := Detect;
   InitGraph( GraphDriver, GraphMode, '' );
   Height := GetMaxY div 6;
   SetTextJustify( CenterText, CenterText );
   for  FontStyle := DefaultFont to GothicFont do begin
      SetTextStyle( FontStyle, HorizDir, 4 );
      OutTextXY( GetMaxX div 2, Height*( FontStyle +1 ), 'Greetings!' );
   end;
   readln;
   CloseGraph;
end.
```

The `RegisterBGIdriver` and `RegisterBGIfont` functions register each of the external files with the GRAPH.TPU unit as a potential driver or font. `InitGraph`, which is called here with a null string for its search path, looks first to the GRAPH.TPU internal driver and font tables, locates the names of the procedures, and looks no further. All drivers and fonts are already available within the program, so no disk access is required.

When ALLSTUFF executes, it produces five `Greetings!` messages, as shown in figure 11.28.

Admittedly, ALLSTUFF isn't a fancy program, but consider: it can run on any graphics adapter on any PC that supports Turbo Pascal, and it runs without the need for separate .BGI or .CHR files! You can use ALLSTUFF as a template for making your own applications independent of separate drivers and fonts.

Of course, ALLSTUFF is the "full-size" version. In your program, you should remove all references to unused fonts. Similarly, if you know your program

---

Fig. 11.28. *Output produced by the ALLSTUFF program.*

Greetings!

Greetings!

Greetings!

Greetings!

Greetings!

---

won't need to run on a PC equipped with a specific graphics adapter, you should eliminate unnecessary driver references as well. The difference between an .EXE file that runs on all graphics cards with all fonts and an .EXE file that uses one font on one card is about 45,000 bytes.

Installing New Fonts and Drivers

It's quite likely that software firms and public domain groups will soon begin to offer additional .CHR character font files. It's even more likely that if a new graphics adapter board is introduced to the market, it will come complete with its own .BGI (or comparable) driver file. In both cases, installation instructions will probably be provided with the product. However, just in case, you should know that there are two ways to incorporate new font and driver files in your programs.

1. Convert the new font or driver file to object format with the BIN-OBJ.EXE program and link the object file to your program. This method was demonstrated earlier.

2. Use two special functions: `InstallUserFont` and `InstallUserDriver`.

Now you will see how to use `InstallUserFont` and `InstallUserDriver` to install new fonts and drivers.

Installing a New Font

To install a new stroked character font, use the procedure:

```
function InstallUserFont( FontFileName : string ) : integer;
```

InstallUserFont takes the name of the font file as its single parameter, loads the font into heap memory, and returns an identification number that can be used by SetTextStyle to reference the font.

Assuming that you have defined an integer variable NewFont, perform the installation with the command:

```
NewFont := InstallUserFont( 'FontFile.CHR' );
```

You should call GraphResult immediately afterward to test for an error. If the font table was full when you called InstallUserFont, NewFont will have a value of zero. Otherwise, NewFont contains a positive integer that can be used to reference the new font, as follows:

```
SetTextStyle( NewFont, HorizDir, 1 );
```

All subsequent OutText and OutTextXY statements use the new font design.

Additional information on installing character fonts can be found in the Turbo Pascal *Reference Guide*.

Installing a New Driver

When you open the box of your new graphics board, you will probably find three items:

1. The board itself.

2. An instruction manual.

3. A diskette, containing a .BGI device driver file and (optionally) code for a Turbo Pascal autodetection function that returns True if it determines that the new board is installed and False if the board isn't present.

Autodetection is what enables you to call

```
GraphDriver := Detect;
InitGraph( GraphDriver, GraphMode, '' );
```

and trust that InitGraph will correctly identify the graphics card in your machine and install the appropriate driver.

To add the new device driver to the BGI device driver table, use the procedure:

```
function InstallUserDriver( DriverFileName : string;
                  AutoDetectPtr : pointer ) : integer;
```

`InstallUserDriver` takes two parameters. `DriverNameFile` is the name of the file containing the new device driver. `AutoDetectPtr` is a pointer to the autodetection function. If no function was included, `AutoDetectPtr` is set to Nil.

Assuming that you have defined an integer variable `NewDriver`, perform the installation with the command:

```
NewDriver := InstallUserDriver( 'DrvFile.BGI', Nil );
```

or

```
NewDriver := InstallUserDriver( 'DrvFile.BGI', @AutoDetect );
```

You should call `GraphResult` immediately afterward to test for an error. If the internal driver table is full, `NewDriver` will have a value of zero. Otherwise, `NewDriver` can serve as an identifier to reference the new driver. For example, if no autodetection function was included, you can initiate graphics as follows:

```
GraphDriver := NewDriver;
GraphMode := ???;                         { Read the handbook!! }
InitGraph( GraphDriver, GraphMode, '' );
```

Of course, if the autodetection function was included, you could initiate graphics more traditionally:

```
GraphDriver := Detect;
InitGraph( GraphDriver, GraphMode, '' );
```

Additional information on installing device drivers can be found in the Turbo Pascal *Reference Guide*.

A Note on Autodetection

Autodetection isn't always possible. Remember that the IBM 8514 graphics adapter appears to the `DetectGraph` procedure just like a VGA card.

Advanced Topic: User Heap Management

The Graph unit includes two internal heap management routines: the `GraphGetMem` procedure allocates heap memory for graphics, and the `GraphFreeMem` procedure frees the heap after graphics is shut down.

Neither `GraphGetMem` nor `GraphFreeMem` are directly accessible to your program. However, Turbo Pascal provides two predefined procedure pointer variables.

1. The `GraphGetMemPtr` variable points to the `GraphGetMem` procedure. You can use `GraphGetMemPtr` to point to your own heap allocation procedure.

2. The `GraphFreeMemPtr` variable points to the `GraphFreeMem` procedure. You can use `GraphFreeMemPtr` to point to your own heap deallocation procedure.

The Turbo Pascal *Reference Guide* contains specifics on how to use `GraphGetMomPtr` and `GraphFreeMemPtr` to develop your own heap management routines.

You should note, however, that in almost every application, the Turbo Pascal defaults are more than adequate.

Summary

In this chapter, you have learned how to use Turbo Pascal's graphics procedures and functions. You have learned the performance characteristics of the most common graphics adapters, and you have learned how individual drivers (in the form of .BGI files) and fonts (in the form of .CHR files) are used by your programs.

You have seen how Turbo Pascal can automatically select an optimal graphics mode based on the equipment installed in your PC. You have learned how to initiate and terminate a graphics session, how to switch between text and graphics modes, and how to handle errors arising in graphics operations.

You have learned about the graphics window, called a *viewport*, and you have seen how viewports can be created, saved, restored, and cleared.

You have learned how color palettes are used in Turbo Pascal, and you have learned how individual colors are selected and changed.

You have learned how to plot an individual point, called a *pixel*. You have learned how to draw lines in a variety of styles and widths. You have learned how to draw a variety of polygons, arcs, circles, and ellipses in both outline and solid form.

You have learned how to combine text with your graphics displays, and you have seen how to control text size, justification, and direction.

You have learned how to incorporate .BGI and .CHR files *within* your programs, and you have seen how new drivers and fonts can be added to those already available.

CHAPTER 12

Accessing DOS

A common statement in microcomputer literature is "Programs run under the control of DOS." On a practical level, this is not strictly true. The 8086-family processor can perform only one task at a time. When a program is executing, the program itself tells the CPU what to do next; the operating system is sitting idly by in another part of memory. Nevertheless, linkages or potential linkages exist between the program and the operating system.

Your program interacts with DOS in three ways. First, all DOS services and functions remain—on an individual basis—available for use throughout program execution. Second, when DOS initiates a program, it stores useful information in an accessible area of memory known as the Program Segment Prefix (PSP). Third, when a program terminates, it triggers a sequence of DOS calls that can be affected by the program itself.

This chapter discusses some of the various Turbo Pascal procedures and functions that allow direct interaction with DOS operations.

System Date and Time

The system date and time can be accessed with the Turbo Pascal procedures GetDate and GetTime, respectively. The opposite procedures, SetDate and SetTime, enable you to reset the system date and time to any legal settings.

These procedures access only the DOS software system clock and calendar. If your machine has an internal hardware clock (such as AST's SixPak Plus®), the clock can be changed only with the routines provided by the manufacturer.

361

The date and time procedures are called in the following format:

```
GetDate( Year, Month, Day, DayofWeek );
GetTime( Hour, Minute, Second, Sec100 );
SetDate( Year, Month, Day );
SetTime( Hour, Minute, Second, Sec100 );
```

Year may be any year from 1980 through 2099. Hour is expressed in military fashion (24-hour clock format) from 0 through 23. Minute and Second must be within the range 0 through 59. Sec100, which represents hundredths of a second and ranges from 0 through 99, is inaccurate and should not be trusted for critical time calculations. DayofWeek ranges from 0 through 6, corresponding to Sunday through Saturday.

Retrieving the Date and Time

The DATE1 program (listing 12.1) demonstrates how to use GetDate and GetTime to create strings that can be included as part of your screen and printer headings.

Listing 12.1

```
program Date1;
uses Dos;
const
   DayNames : array [ 0..6 ] of string[ 4 ] =
             ( 'Sun ', 'Mon ', 'Tue ', 'Wed ', 'Thu ', 'Fri ', 'Sat ' );
   MonNames : array [ 1..12 ] of string[ 4 ] =
             ( 'Jan ', 'Feb ', 'Mar ', 'Apr ', 'May ', 'Jun ',
               'Jul ', 'Aug ', 'Sep ', 'Oct ', 'Nov ', 'Dec ' );
type
   String2  = string[ 2 ];
   String4  = string[ 4 ];
   String8  = string[ 8 ];
   String16 = string[ 16 ];
var
   Year,          { 1980..2099 }
   Month,         { 1..12 }
   Day,           { 1..31 }
   DayofWeek,     { 0 (Sunday) .. 6 (Saturday) }
   Hour,          { 0..23 }
   Minute,        { 0..59 }
   Second,        { 0..59 }
   Sec100         { 0..99 }
                              : word;
   DateString   : String16;   { DayofWeek Mon Day Year }
   TimeString1,               { Hour:Minute:Second }
   TimeString2  : String8;    { Hour:Minute AM/PM }
```

Listing 12.1 continues

Listing 12.1 continued

```
function DString2( DateIn : word ) : String2;
begin
    DString2 := chr( 48 + DateIn div 10 ) + chr( 48 + DateIn mod 10 );
end;
function DString4( YearIn : word ) : String4;
begin
    DString4 := DString2( YearIn div 100 ) + DString2( YearIn mod 100 );
end;
begin
    GetDate( Year, Month, Day, DayofWeek );
    DateString := DayNames[ DayofWeek ] +
                  MonNames[ Month ] +
                  DString2( Day ) + ', ' +
                  DString4( Year );
    writeln( DateString );
    GetTime( Hour, Minute, Second, Sec100 );
    TimeString1 := DString2( Hour ) + ':' +
                   DString2( Minute ) + ':' +
                   DString2( Second );
    writeln( TimeString1 );
    TimeString2 := DString2( Hour mod 12 ) + ':' +
                   DString2( Minute ) + ' ' +
                   chr( ord( 'A' ) + 15*( Hour div 12 ) ) + 'M';
    writeln( TimeString2 );
end
```

When the program is executed, it produces one standard date and two standard time formats.

```
Mon Aug 01, 1988
22:17:09
10:17 PM
```

Changing the Date

When you use SetDate and GetDate together, you can have DOS calculate which day of the week a certain date falls on. The program DATE2 (listing 12.2) exploits this feature by creating a calendar for any given month and year.

Listing 12.2

```
program Date2;
uses Dos;
var
   OldYear,        Year,       { 1980..2099 }
   OldMonth,       Month,      { 1..12 }
   OldDay,         Day,        { 1..31 }
   OldDayofWeek,   DayofWeek   { 0 (Sunday) .. 6 (Saturday) }
                   : word;
   DayCount        : byte;
   i               : byte;
begin
   repeat
      write( 'Enter month, year: ' );
      readln( Month, Year );
   until (Year>1979) and (Year <2100) and (Month in [ 1..12 ]);
   Day := 1;
   GetDate( OldYear, OldMonth, OldDay, OldDayofWeek );
   SetDate( Year, Month, Day );
   GetDate( Year, Month, Day, DayofWeek );
   SetDate( OldYear, OldMonth, OldDay );
   case Month of      { How many days are in the month? }
      1, 3, 5, 7, 8, 10, 12 : DayCount := 31;
      4, 6, 9, 11 : DayCount := 30;
      2 : if Year mod 4 = 0 then DayCount := 29 else DayCount := 28;
   end;
   writeln;
   writeln( ' Sun Mon Tue Wed Thu Fri Sat' );
   for i := 1 to DayCount  + DayofWeek do begin
      if i mod 7 = 1 then writeln;
      if i  <= DayofWeek then write( '    ' ) else write( (i - DayofWeek):4 );
   end;
   writeln;
end.
```

If you run the program for February 1988 and January 2000, the program produces the following output:

```
Enter month, year: 2 1988

Sun Mon Tue Wed Thu Fri Sat
         1   2   3   4   5   6
 7   8   9  10  11  12  13
14  15  16  17  18  19  20
21  22  23  24  25  26  27
28  29

Enter month, year: 1 2000

Sun Mon Tue Wed Thu Fri Sat
                         1
 2   3   4   5   6   7   8
 9  10  11  12  13  14  15
16  17  18  19  20  21  22
23  24  25  26  27  28  29
30  31
```

Essentially, the program calculates how far to shift over before beginning to write the days of the month. Note that the original system date is restored as soon as possible. If SetDate is called with invalid parameters, no action results.

Timing Program Operations

SetTime can be used to determine the duration of execution. The program DATE3 (listing 12.3) compares the execution speed of half a million repeat loops with the same number of for loops. At the beginning of each process, SetTime resets the system clock to all zeros; at the end, GetTime directly obtains the amount of time passed.

Listing 12.3

```
program Date3;
uses Dos;
var
   Hour,        { Ø..23 }
   Minute,      { Ø..59 }
   Second,      { Ø..59 }
   Sec1ØØ       { Ø..99 }
                : word;
   i            : longint;
procedure StartTheTimer( Message : string );
begin
   writeln;
   writeln( Message );
   SetTime( Ø, Ø, Ø, Ø );
end;
procedure EndTheTimer;
begin
   GetTime( Hour, Minute, Second, Sec1ØØ );
   writeln( 'Time elapsed:' );
   writeln( Hour:5,    ' hours' );
   writeln( Minute:5, ' minutes' );
   writeln( Second:5, ' seconds' );
   writeln;
end;
begin
   StartTheTimer( 'The "repeat" loop' );
      i := Ø;
      repeat
         i := i + 1;
      until i = 5ØØØØØ;
   EndTheTimer;
   StartTheTimer( 'The "for" loop' );
      for i := 1 to 5ØØØØØ do begin end;
   EndTheTimer;
end.
```

Not surprisingly, the comparison reveals that the for loop is slightly faster than the repeat loop.

```
The "repeat" loop
Time elapsed:
     Ø hours
     Ø minutes
    18 seconds
The "for" loop
Time elapsed:
     Ø hours
     Ø minutes
    14 seconds
```

The problem with this method, however, is that the system clock now must be reset. A better method of calculating duration is to compare the parameters from two successive GetTime calls, as shown in DATE4 (listing 12.4).

Listing 12.4

```pascal
program Date4;
uses Dos;
var
   Hour,          OldHour,     { Ø..23 }
   Minute,        OldMinute,   { Ø..59 }
   Second,        OldSecond,   { Ø..59 }
   Sec1ØØ,        OldSec1ØØ    { Ø..99 }
                               : word;
   HoursPassed,
   MinutesPassed,
   SecondsPassed               : integer;
   i : longint;
procedure StartTheTimer( Message : string );
begin
   writeln;
   writeln( Message );
   GetTime( OldHour, OldMinute, OldSecond, OldSec1ØØ );
end;
procedure EndTheTimer;
begin
   GetTime( Hour, Minute, Second, Sec1ØØ );
   HoursPassed   := Hour - OldHour;
   MinutesPassed := Minute - OldMinute;
   SecondsPassed := Second - OldSecond;
   if Hour  < OldHour then
      HoursPassed := HoursPassed  + 24;
   if Minute  < OldMinute then begin
      MinutesPassed := MinutesPassed  + 6Ø;
      HoursPassed   := HoursPassed - 1;
   end;
```

Listing 12.4 continues

Listing 12.4 continued

```
      if Second < OldSecond then begin
         SecondsPassed := SecondsPassed + 60;
         MinutesPassed := MinutesPassed - 1;
      end;
      writeln( 'Time elapsed:' );
      writeln( HoursPassed:5,   ' hours' );
      writeln( MinutesPassed:5, ' minutes' );
      writeln( SecondsPassed:5, ' seconds' );
      writeln;
   end;
   begin
      StartTheTimer( 'The "repeat" loop' );
         i := 0;
         repeat
            i := i + 1;
         until i = 500000;
      EndTheTimer;
      StartTheTimer( 'The "for" loop' );
         for i := 1 to 500000 do begin end;
      EndTheTimer;
   end.
```

The same output is obtained, but the system clock hasn't been corrupted.

By the way, as proof that you should use the increment function whenever possible, if you change the code in the repeat loop from

```
   i := i + 1;
```

to

```
   Inc( i );
```

you will be able to see a significant improvement in performance.

Creating Tones

Every programmer with more than two minutes of experience is familiar with the beep sound produced by the PC. Although a few particularly obnoxious programs beep every time a key is pressed, most applications quite properly use the sound as part of a warning or error message.

Sound generation is not limited to warning beeps; the sound capabilities are part of the tool kit you have available to develop user interfaces. The same hardware that produces the beep can also be used to produce a far wider range of tones.

The beep is nothing more than ASCII character 7. To generate it, all you need do is write the following:

```
program Sound1;
begin
   writeln( chr( 7 ));   { or writeln( #7 ); }
end.
```

When used sparingly, beeps are an excellent way of drawing the user's attention. When used excessively, they detract from the quality of a program, no matter how valuable it may otherwise be.

The Turbo Pascal procedure Sound causes the speaker to emit a tone that continues until disabled with the NoSound procedure. Sound is called with a single word-sized parameter specifying the desired frequency in Hertz (cycles per second).

If Sound is immediately followed by NoSound, the speaker in your PC won't be able to respond fast enough to generate any noise. The Delay procedure is usually used to allow the speaker enough time to react. Delay takes a single word-sized parameter that specifies the delay in milliseconds (1,000 milliseconds equals 1 second).

By selecting the right combination of frequencies and delays, you can produce a pleasant set of musical tones. In the SOUND2 program (listing 12.5), the numbers 1 through 7 correspond to the notes of an electronic organ. The program terminates when any other key is pressed.

Listing 12.5

```
program Sound2;
uses Crt;
const
   C = 523;
   D = 587;
   E = 659;
   F = 699;
   G = 784;
   A = 880;
   B = 988;
var
   Key : char;
   OffBoard : boolean;
   Note : word;
begin
   OffBoard := False;
   repeat
      Key := ReadKey;
      case Key of
         '1' : Note := C;
         '2' : Note := D;
```

Listing 12.5 continues

Listing 12.5 continued

```
        '3' : Note := E;
        '4' : Note := F;
        '5' : Note := G;
        '6' : Note := A;
        '7' : Note := B;
        else  OffBoard := True;
    end;
    if not OffBoard then begin
        write( Key:2 );     { Displays each note }
        Sound( Note );
        Delay( 100 );       { 100 milliseconds = 0.1 second }
        NoSound;
    end;
    until OffBoard = True;
    writeln;
end.
```

The DOS Environment Table

The *environment* is a collection of strings that programs can locate and use as a reference. Each string is established with the DOS SET instruction and stored by the operating system. Most environment variables are established as part of the AUTOEXEC.BAT start-up file.

Each string is in the form

```
EnvironmentVariable = EnvironmentString
```

The most common environment variables are COMSPEC, which is usually set to the exact location of the COMMAND.COM program, and PATH, which defines the preferred sequence of directories to search when you look for a file that isn't completely defined. Environment strings are stored in an area of memory called the environment *table*, which can be as large as 32K.

Using the Environment Table

To examine the contents of your environment table, execute the DOS SET command—without parameters—as follows:

C>set
COMSPEC =C:\COMMAND.COM
PATH =C:\DOS;C:\WORD;C:\TURBOC;C:\TP

Although some variables, such as COMSPEC and PATH, have clearly defined uses, any variable name and assignment is allowed. For example, the variable `favorite_show` can be defined as follows:

C>set favorite_show ="My Fair Lady"

The new entry can be confirmed by inspecting the environment table again.

C>set
COMSPEC =C:\COMMAND.COM
PATH =C:\DOS;C:\WORD;C:\TURBOC;C:\TP
FAVORITE_SHOW ="My Fair Lady"

If you now want to remove this variable, simply set it to "nothing", and test the results, as follows:

C>set favorite_show =
C>set
COMSPEC =C:\COMMAND.COM
PATH =C:\DOS;C:\WORD;C:\TURBOC;C:\TP

There is no magic about the use of environment variables. Although some DOS functions expect certain names to have certain meanings, you can use any convenient environment name to reference any data you wish.

For example, suppose that you work in an office that has PCs in several departments. Each PC could be configured with a unique AUTOEXEC.BAT file, which might include lines like the following:

set pc_id =004
set dept =Finance

This PC now includes two unique environment entries.

C>set
COMSPEC =C:\COMMAND.COM
PATH =C:\DOS;C:\WORD;C:\TURBOC;C:\TP
PC_ID =004
DEPT =Finance

If programs running on this PC could access this information, department-specific and user-specific applications could be developed without the hassle of recompiling software for each machine.

Changing the Environment Table

Any changes made to the environment table must be made directly from DOS, not from within the *File/OS shell* option of the Turbo Pascal integrated environment.

Accessing Environment Strings

EnvCount returns the number of strings contained in the DOS environment table. The EnvStr function returns the entire string, whereas GetEnv returns only the value of a specified environment variable. Therefore, the ENV1A program (listing 12.6) lists the contents of the environment table.

Listing 12.6

```
program Env1A;
uses Dos;
var
    i : byte;
begin
    for i := 1 to EnvCount do
        writeln( EnvStr(i) );
end.
```

When executed, ENV1A might produce the following:

```
COMSPEC=C:\COMMAND.COM
PATH=C:\DOS;C:\WORD;C:\TURBOC;C:\TP
PC_ID=004
DEPT=Finance
```

Normally, to find the contents of the PC_ID variable, you would have to read through the environment table until you found PC_ID in the first five characters of a string, then extract the seventh through the last character in the string. With the GetEnv function you can do this directly. The ENV1B program (listing 12.7) demonstrates GetEnv:

Listing 12.7

```
program Env1B;
uses Dos;
begin
    writeln( GetEnv( 'pc_id' ) );
end.
```

When the ENV1B program executes, it displays the single line:

```
004
```

The Val procedure could be used to convert the string to numeric format. Notice that the GetEnv function ignores cases and treats pc_id and PC_ID identically.

The Program Segment Prefix

Before DOS loads an .EXE file for execution, it first creates and then loads a 256-byte area called the *Program Segment Prefix* (PSP). The PSP is where DOS stores the information it needs to regain control of the PC when the program terminates. Some of the more useful fields in the PSP are listed in figure 12.1. Areas marked "Reserved" contain data useful only to the operating system.

Although these fields are freely accessible to your program, under no circumstances should you attempt to modify any of them. The following sections discuss how these PSP fields can be accessed and used.

Table 12.1. *Contents of the Program Segment Prefix.*

Offset			
Hex	Decimal	Length	Contents
$00	0	2	Reserved
$02	2	2	Top of memory (that is, the last paragraph allocated to the program)
$04	4	6	Reserved
$0A	10	2	Offset, previous contents of the termination handler
$0C	12	2	Segment, interrupt vector (Int $22)
$0E	14	2	Offset, previous contents of the Ctrl-C/Ctrl-Break
$10	16	2	Segment, interrupt vector (Int $23)
$12	18	2	Offset, previous contents of the critical-error handler
$14	20	2	Segment, interrupt vector (Int $24)

Table 12.1 continues

Table 12.1 *continued*

| | Offset | | |
Hex	Decimal	Length	Contents
$16	22	22	Reserved
$2C	44	2	Segment address of the environment table
$2E	46	82	Reserved
$80	128	128	Buffer for both the command line and the Disk Transfer Area (DTA)

Accessing the Program Segment Prefix

You can access any field in the PSP by using pointers. The segment address of the PSP is given by the predeclared variable PrefixSeg. The PSP1 program (listing 12.8) demonstrates how the *top-of-memory* information can be obtained.

Listing 12.8

```
program PSP1;
var
    TopOfMemory : ^word;
    LongTopOfMemory,
    Bytes,
    KBytes : longint;
begin
    TopOfMemory := Ptr( PrefixSeg, 2 );        { Access top of memory info }
    LongTopOfMemory := TopOfMemory^ + 1;       { Reference starts at zero  }
    Bytes := 16 * LongTopOfMemory;             { Size is in paragraphs     }
    KBytes := Bytes div 1024;
    writeln( 'System memory is as follows:' );
    writeln( LongTopOfMemory:10, ' paragraphs' );
    writeln( Bytes:10, ' bytes' );
    writeln( KBytes:9, 'K bytes' );
end.
```

The top-of-memory field in the PSP contains the number of the highest paragraph used by the program. Since, by default, Turbo allocates all remaining internal memory, the top-of-memory for the program is the same as the top-of-memory paragraph for the PC itself. Executing this program gives the following:

```
System memory is as follows:
     40960 paragraphs
    655360 bytes
      640K bytes
```

Note, though, that the program obtains this result through trickery. If the program's memory usage had been reduced with the {$M} compiler directive, the program would have obtained a lower number. Either way, the PSP contains the highest memory location used by the program.

Interrupt Vectors

Beginning at offset $0A (10 decimal), three addresses, called *interrupt vectors*, can be found.

The first one, the termination handler, contains the memory address to go to when the current program ends execution. Typically, this address would contain the start of the code DOS needs to regain control of the PC from the spent program.

The second address points to the location of the code that executes if, during the running of the program, an operator presses the Ctrl-C or Ctrl-Break key combination. Without the availability of this address, the CPU might know to suspend program execution, but it wouldn't know what to do next.

The third address, the critical-error handler, is the start of the code the CPU will execute if an unrecoverable run-time error is encountered.

By placing these addresses in a convenient location, the operating system creates a safety net the CPU can use to return control to DOS if a program experiences an "exception" condition.

All three addresses contain the previous (that is, original) memory locations. Nothing stops your program from establishing its own error-handling or interrupt-handling routines, but DOS needs to be restored to the condition it was in prior to the program's run. These addresses, then, represent a scratch pad for DOS to use to keep track of information it needs.

The Environment Table Address

The PSP contains the segment address of the environment table. The table consists of ASCIIZ strings terminated by a null character (that is, a byte set to zero). An *ASCIIZ string* itself consists of a series of characters followed by a null character.

The ENV1 program (listing 12.9) displays the contents of the environment table:

Listing 12.9

```
program Env1;
var
   i,j,
   EnvSegment : word;
   EnvString  : string[ 80 ];
begin
   EnvSegment := MemW[ PrefixSeg : $2C ];   { Get segment from PSP   }
   i := 0;                                  { The offset begins at 0 }
   repeat                                   { For the entire table   }
      j := 0;
      repeat                                { Just the current entry }
         j := j + 1;
         EnvString[ j ] := chr( Mem[ EnvSegment : i ] );
         i := i + 1;
      until EnvString[ j ] = chr( 0 );      { Test for null character }
      EnvString[ 0 ] := chr( j - 1 );       { Chop null from string   }
      writeln( EnvString );                 { Write the Env string    }
   until Mem[ EnvSegment : i ] = 0;         { Stop if two nulls found }
   writeln;
   writeln( 'End' );
end.
```

When executed, ENV1 produces the following:

```
COMSPEC=C:\COMMAND.COM
PATH=C:\DOS;C:\WORD;C:\TURBOC;C:\TP
PC_ID=004
DEPT=Finance

End
```

Fortunately, as you saw earlier in the chapter, Turbo Pascal provides the EnvCount, EnvStr, and GetEnv functions to simplify the use of environment strings.

Accessing the Command Line

A string containing a copy of the command line is stored in the PSP beginning at offset $80. This string has the same format as an ordinary Turbo Pascal string. Byte $80 contains its dynamic length, and byte $81 contains its first character.

To access the command line within your program, simply define a string pointer variable such as the following:

```
type
   CmdArray = string[ 127 ];
var
   CmdLine : ^CmdArray;
```

Next, within the body of the program, assign the address of the PSP command-line string to the pointer variable.

```
CmdLine := Ptr( PrefixSeg, $80 );
```

The contents of the command line can now be accessed with the `CmdLine^` variable. An example of this technique is found in the EXEC2 program (listing 12.13) later in this chapter.

Note that this particular area of the PSP doubles as a buffer for any file input or output. Consequently, if your program needs to process the command-line field, it should do so before any disk I/O is performed.

Program Termination

For all the good words and posturing about writing only structured code, programmers sometimes find themselves in a situation where they want to terminate a program *immediately*. In pure, structured form, if a program needs four files to be successfully opened before it can begin its main processing, its skeleton might look like the following:

```
begin
    OpenFileA;
    if A_WasOpenedWithoutIncident then begin
        OpenFileB;
        if B_WasOpenedWithoutIncident then begin
            OpenFileC;
            if C_WasOpenedWithoutIncident then begin
                OpenFileD;
                if D_WasOpenedWithoutIncident then begin
                    GoAheadAndRunTheProgram;
                end;
            end;
        end;
    end;
end;
```

By the time the programmer has included the `else` statements to display error messages, he or she begins to feel that the religion of structure has found its first martyr.

As the example shows, testing for fatal error conditions usually requires a disproportionate amount of code. Fortunately, Turbo Pascal provides the `Halt` procedure to safely terminate execution at any point within a program.

Termination with *Halt*

The Halt procedure terminates a program no matter where the procedure is located. For example, a program could be designed to terminate if either of two parameters is invalid:

```
case Opt1 of
    1 : Opt1is1;
    2 : Opt1is2;
    3 : Opt1is3;
    else begin
            writeln( 'Option 1 is invalid' );
            Halt;
         end;
end;
case Opt2 of
    1 : Opt2is1;
    2 : Opt2is2;
    3 : Opt2is3;
    else begin
            writeln( 'Option 2 is invalid' );
            Halt;
         end;
end;
```

It might not be "structured," but it's efficient. Using the Halt procedure unquestionably saves you from writing and debugging many longer lines of code.

Termination within a Batch File

Presumably, when your programs encounter an error, they will do everything possible to terminate the program smoothly (close files, display messages, ask for help, and so on). Sometimes, you also have to worry about the bigger picture. If you terminate a program that's being run within a batch file, you should let the batch file itself know what happened.

To provide this feature, Halt can optionally accept a word-sized parameter (for example, Halt(5);) and pass that parameter to the program or batch file that called the terminated program. Halt without a parameter is equivalent to Halt(Ø).

The HALT1 program (listing 12.10) terminates with a Halt procedure call when the user tries to calculate the square root of a negative number.

Listing 12.10

```
program Halt1;
var
    Selection : real;
begin
    repeat
        write( 'Enter a number: ' );
        readln( Selection );
        if Selection > Ø then
            writeln( 'The square root of ', Selection:1:1,
                     ' is ', Sqrt( Selection ):1:5 )
        else
            if Selection  < Ø then begin
                writeln( 'I can''t handle negative numbers!' );
                Halt( 1 );
            end;
    until Selection = Ø;
    writeln( 'Good-bye' );
end.
```

This program is designed to be executed under the control of the BATCH1.BAT batch file:

```
echo off
echo BATCH1.BAT:  Executing the HALT1.EXE program.
halt1
if errorlevel 1 goto problems
goto finished
:problems
echo The program terminated with an error.
:finished
```

Admittedly, an interactive square root program isn't the type of application you ordinarily design to run within a batch file, but it does enable you to directly control whether the program terminates normally or with an error.

Within a batch file, an if errorlevel n test is true if the actual error level (the parameter passed by the Halt procedure) is greater than or equal to n.

Compare the following two runs of BATCH1.

```
C>batch1

C>echo off
BATCH1.BAT:  Executing the HALT1.EXE program.
Enter a number: 234
The square root of 234.Ø is 15.29706
Enter a number: 23.9
The square root of 23.9 is 4.88876
Enter a number: Ø
Good-bye
```

```
C>batch1

C>echo off
BATCH1.BAT:  Executing the HALT1.EXE program.
Enter a number: 234
The square root of 234.0 is 15.29706
Enter a number: 23.9
The square root of 23.9 is 4.88876
Enter a number: -5
I can't handle negative numbers!
The program terminated with an error.
```

The first run terminated normally with the Good-bye sign-off message. The default value of *zero* was passed to the batch file. During the second run, the entry of a negative number triggered the Halt procedure to pass an error code of *one* to the batch file. Both the program and the batch file generated error messages.

Using Halt To Pass Parameters

Programs frequently use different error codes to indicate the type of error encountered. For example, the DosError variable uses the following codes:

0	No error
2	File not found
3	Path not found
5	Access denied
6	Invalid handle
8	Not enough memory
10	Invalid environment
11	Invalid format
18	No more files

Instead of treating the parameter as an *error* code, some programs use the parameter to indicate a *condition* that can be tested within the batch file. For example, the HALT2 program (listing 12.11) deliberately passes a 1, 2, or 3 *condition code* to its controlling batch file.

Listing 12.11

```
program Halt2;
var
   Selection : word;
begin
   repeat
      write( 'Choose an application: ' );
      readln( Selection );
   until Selection in [ 1, 2, 3 ];
   Halt( Selection );
end.
```

The parameter could be read by the DOS variable errorlevel to select a specific application, as in the BATCH2.BAT file.

```
echo off
echo BATCH2.BAT:  Executing the HALT2.EXE program.
halt2
if errorlevel 3 goto menu3
if errorlevel 2 goto menu2
if errorlevel 1 goto menu1

:menu1
echo Menu1 program goes here
goto finished

:menu2
echo Menu2 program goes here
goto finished

:menu3
echo Menu3 program goes here

:finished
```

Together, these files patiently await a valid user response, as illustrated here:

```
C>batch2

C>echo off
BATCH2.BAT:  Executing the HALT2.EXE program.
Choose an application: 9
Choose an application: -45
Choose an application: 78
Choose an application: 2
Menu2 program goes here
```

Forcing a Run-Time Error

Using the Halt procedure, a program can terminate without causing a run-time error. If you *do* want to generate a run-time error, Turbo Pascal offers the RunError procedure. For example, to terminate the program with a run-time error of 152, Drive not ready, the command is

```
RunError( 152 );
```

If no parameter is given, RunError(∅) is assumed.

Running a Program within Another Program

Although batch files are useful for segmenting large applications into smaller units, it's sometimes more convenient to have one program call another program directly.

In Turbo Pascal, this is accomplished with the Exec procedure. One program (the *parent*) can call another program (the *child*). After the child program is finished, control returns to the parent. This action is usually referred to as *process handling*.

Running the Exec Procedure

The Exec procedure takes two parameters, as follows:

```
Exec( FileName, CommandTail : string );
```

FileName is the complete file name of the program you wish to execute, including the extension. If the program isn't in the current directory, the complete path name must also be specified. The CommandTail is a string containing command-line parameters (if any) required to run the *child* program. Any problems encountered in using the procedure can be identified by accessing the DosError variable.

Any program can be executed in this manner, running just as if it were the program originally invoked. DOS even creates a separate PSP for it.

The memory directive {$M} should be used to minimize the memory consumed by the parent. In the absence of this directive, the parent would be allocated all available memory, leaving no room for the child program to run. Because you can't adjust the memory already assigned to the TURBO.EXE integrated environment, always compile Exec programs to disk and run them from the DOS prompt.

To better isolate the parent and child processes, the SwapVectors procedure should be called immediately before and after the Exec procedure. In so doing, SwapVectors alternately stores and restores the contents of the interrupt vector table, discussed in Chapter 18.

The EXEC1 program (listing 12.12) calls EXEC2.EXE (listing 12.13), which happens to be in the same directory. EXEC2 does nothing more than display command-line parameters, which here consist of three arbitrarily chosen file names.

Listing 12.12

```
program Exec1;
{$M 1024,0,0  Sets all memory usage to minimum levels}
uses Dos;
begin
   writeln( 'You are in the parent program.' );
   SwapVectors;
   Exec( 'Exec2.exe', 'file1.pas file2.pas file3.pas' );
   SwapVectors;
   writeln( 'You are in the parent program.' );
end.
```

Listing 12.13

```
program Exec2;
type
   CmdArray = string[ 127 ];
var
   CmdLine : ^CmdArray;
begin
   CmdLine := Ptr( PrefixSeg, $80 );
   writeln( 'We''re in the child program.' );
   writeln( 'The command tail is: ', CmdLine^ );
end.
```

When you run EXEC1, it generates the following results:

```
C>exec1
You are in the parent program.
You are in the child program.
The command tail is: file1.pas file2.pas file3.pas
You are in the parent program.
```

Accessing the Termination Parameter

If the child program terminates with the Halt procedure, the parent can access the exit code with the DosExitCode function. DosExitCode returns a word-sized value; its low byte is the low byte of the exit code, and its high byte indicates the cause of the termination, as summarized in table 12.2.

Table 12.2. *Causes of Program Termination Given by* DosExitCode

High Byte of DosExitCode	Reason the Child Program Terminated
0	Normal termination
1	Ctrl-C
2	Device error
3	Keep procedure executed

After DosExitCode is called, the error/condition code is reset to zero. The EXEC3 and EXEC4 programs (listings 12.14 and 12.15) demonstrate its use.

Listing 12.14

```
program Exec3;
{$M 1024,0,0 }
uses Dos;
var
   Message : word;
begin
   writeln( 'You are in the parent program.' );
   SwapVectors;
   Exec( 'Exec4.exe', '' );
   SwapVectors;
   Message := DosExitCode;
   write( 'The child terminated ' );
   case Hi( Message ) of
      0 : writeln( 'normally.' );
      1 : writeln( 'by Ctrl-C.' );
      2 : writeln( 'because of a device error.' );
      3 : writeln( 'by the Keep procedure.' );
   end;
   writeln( 'The child wants the parent to know: ', Lo( Message ) );
end.
```

Listing 12.15

```
program Exec4;
var
   ConditionCode : word;
begin
   writeln( 'You are in the child program.' );
   repeat
      write( 'What do you want to tell the parent? ' );
      readln( ConditionCode );
   until ConditionCode in [ 0..255 ];
   writeln( 'We need to tell the parent: ', ConditionCode );
   Halt( ConditionCode );
end.
```

Executing the EXEC3 program (and selecting 173 as the message to be passed) results in the following output:

```
C>exec3
You are in the parent program.
You are in the child program.
What do you want to tell the parent? 173
We need to tell the parent: 173
The child terminated normally.
The child wants the parent to know: 173
```

When EXEC3 called the DosExitCode function, it obtained the value $00AD. The high byte ($00) indicated normal termination while the low byte ($AD or 173) contained the message itself.

Executing DOS Utilities

Although any program can be executed with the Exec procedure, some care must be taken when using it to run DOS utilities.

Only a few DOS commands (such as FORMAT and SORT) are stand-alone programs. Most of the common instructions (including DIR and COPY) are actually options of the COMMAND.COM program. When you type a file name at the DOS prompt, it's COMMAND.COM that actually executes, checking first to see if one of its intrinsic functions (such as DIR) is being requested. If the name isn't recognized, COMMAND.COM assumes that you want to execute a stand-alone program.

The EXEC5 program (listing 12.16) demonstrates how to list a directory from within a Turbo Pascal program. Note that the COMMAND.COM file is assumed to reside in the root directory.

Listing 12.16

```
program Exec5;
{$M 1024,0,0}
uses Dos;
procedure RunDirectory;
begin
    SwapVectors;
    Exec( 'c:\command.com', '/c dir *.*' );
    SwapVectors;
end;
begin
    writeln( 'The directory follows:' );
    RunDirectory;
    writeln( 'End of directory' );
end.
```

Just as in the previous uses of the Exec procedure, Turbo Pascal is being directed to run a program with certain specified options. In this case, however, the desired program is a copy of COMMAND.COM. The /C code is an option of COMMAND.COM itself; in DOS versions before 3.3, /C is used to indicate that the remainder of the line (dir *.*) is an *intrinsic* option.

Of course, you may not know where the COMMAND.COM file resides on your disk. Further, different PCs are configured differently. Instead of assuming that COMMAND.COM is always in the root directory, you could use the GetEnv function to locate it automatically, as follows:

```
Exec( GetEnv( 'comspec' ), '/c dir *.*' );
```

If you want to run a stand-alone DOS program such as the CHKDSK utility, COMMAND.COM isn't needed. The procedure call would simply be

```
Exec( 'c:\dos\chkdsk.com', 'c:' );
```

If your program doesn't need command-line parameters, the second string in Exec can be null. For example, to run CHKDSK on the current drive, all you need is:

```
Exec( 'c:\dos\chkdsk.com', '' );
```

Note that in later versions of DOS, the CHKDSK utility is an .EXE file.

Exit Procedures

So far you have seen that when a program terminates, DOS restores the value of the major interrupt vectors by copying the addresses from the PSP, and it passes along any generated error/condition code to the calling program.

Turbo itself provides a few additional program termination services. For example, it closes the standard input and output files, and, if the program ended because of a run-time error, it displays a run-time error message.

These concluding routines are called *exit* procedures. They represent a well-defined sequence of procedure calls—both within Turbo and within DOS—triggered by any program termination event. Normal termination, a Ctrl-C break, and run-time errors all cause the program to jump to the first procedure in the chain, the address of which is stored in the pointer variable ExitProc.

Developing Custom Exit Procedures

Although it isn't a good idea to affect the internal flow of these calls, with Turbo Pascal you can create your own exit procedures and insert them on the *top* of the chain. To do this, set the ExitProc pointer to the address of your exit procedure, then restore ExitProc to its original value after your procedure finishes.

Customized exit procedures offer you a means to control—but not prevent—program termination. If your program uses a printer, the final page eject command could be issued. In a communications program, you can ensure that you sign off and hang up the phone. In a word processing or spreadsheet program, you can save the current work file.

The basic technique can be demonstrated in the EXIT1 program (listing 12.17).

Listing 12.17

```
program Exit1;
var
   ExitAddress : pointer;
{$F +}
procedure CustomizedExit;
{$F-}
begin
   { Any user-defined termination code could go here }
   writeln( 'Program is terminating...' );
   ExitProc := ExitAddress;      { Restore original exit routine }
end;
begin
   ExitAddress := ExitProc;      { Save original exit address }
   ExitProc := @CustomizedExit;  { New exit is "CustomizedExit" }
   { The rest of the program is written normally }
end.
```

The global ExitAddress variable is used to save the value of ExitProc, which contains the address of the first default exit procedure. ExitProc is then set to the address of your own exit procedure, here called Customized-Exit. At the end of CustomizedExit, ExitProc is reset to its original value, beginning the default termination sequence.

Although CustomizedExit isn't explicitly called, it is the first logical procedure invoked when the program terminates. Running the program results in the display:

Program is terminating...

Notice that the Force Far Calls directive {$F} was used to force Turbo to treat CustomizedExit as a far procedure. This is because the code for the default exit procedure chain resides in the run-time library, which, as explained in Chapter 6, sits in a different code segment from the main program. Consequently, saving, modifying, and restoring the ExitProc pointer require accessing both the segment and offset address components.

Determining the Cause of Program Termination

Table 12.3 shows how the ExitCode and ErrorAddr variables can be used to determine what caused your program to terminate.

Table 12.3. *Contents of Variables*

Termination Type	ExitCode	ErrorAddr
Normal	0	Nil
Halt(n);	n	Nil
Run-Time Error	error code	The address of the statement causing the error

If the program terminated normally, ExitCode is zero, and ErrorAddr is Nil. If termination resulted from the execution of the Halt procedure, ExitCode contains the value of the Halt parameter and ErrorAddr is Nil. Remember that Halt without a parameter is equivalent to Halt(∅).

If program termination resulted from a run-time error, ExitCode contains the number of the error. ErrorAddr points to the code generating the error. ErrorAddr is the variable that Turbo tests to determine if a run-time error message should be displayed. When ErrorAddr is set to Nil, no message appears.

By testing the ExitCode and ErrorAddr variables, your customized exit procedures can appropriately react to both normal and abnormal termination, as demonstrated in the EXIT2 program (listing 12.18).

Listing 12.18

```
Program Exit2;
var
   ExitAddress : pointer;
   Selection : longint;
{$F +}
procedure CustomizedExit;
{$F-}
begin
   if ErrorAddr  <> Nil then begin
      writeln;
      writeln( 'This program is terminating as a result ' );
      writeln( 'of run-time error number ', ExitCode:3, '.  It was' );
      writeln( 'encountered at:' );
```

Listing 12.18 continues

Listing 12.18 continued

```
      writeln;
      writeln( '   Segment: ', seg( ErrorAddr ):5 );
      writeln( '   Offset:  ', ofs( ErrorAddr ):5 );
      writeln;
      ErrorAddr := Nil;              { Prevents Turbo from generating }
                                     { another error message }
   end;
   ExitProc := ExitAddress;         { Restore original exit routine }
end;
begin
   ExitAddress := ExitProc;         { Save original exit address }
   ExitProc := @CustomizedExit;     { New exit is "CustomizedExit" }
   repeat
      write( 'Please enter an integer: ' );
      readln( Selection );
      writeln( 'The square of ', Selection, ' is ', Sqr( Selection ) );
   until Selection = Ø;
end.
```

This program is designed to calculate integer squares. It ends when a zero is entered. The CustomizedExit procedure is always executed; however, if the program terminates normally, ErrorAddr is Nil, and no error message is produced.

```
Please enter an integer: 43
The square of 43 is 1849
Please enter an integer: 11
The square of 11 is 121
Please enter an integer: Ø
The square of Ø is Ø
```

If a nonintegral entry is made, the customized error message is displayed.

```
Please enter an integer: 4
The square of 4 is 16
Please enter an integer: 76
The square of 76 is 5776
Please enter an integer: 2.3

This program is terminating as a result
of run-time error number 1Ø6.  It was
encountered at:

   Segment: 27815
   Offset:    546
```

Note that the segment and offset values will probably differ on your machine.

The error code of 106 corresponds to the run-time error Invalid numeric format. You will probably agree that this message is much more polite than the standard run-time error. In a professionally written program, you might also include a brief apology and the name and phone number of the customer support person to be contacted.

Customized Exit Procedures for Units

In addition to the main program, each module can have its own customized exit procedure. Procedures on the exit chain are executed in the reverse order from the one in which they were installed. Therefore, if the code establishing a customized exit procedure is placed in the initialization section of each unit, then the exit procedures will be executed in the reverse order in which the units are declared in the uses clause. Turbo continues to call exit procedures until the ExitProc pointer becomes Nil. Because ExitProc is set to Nil every time it's called, you must ensure that the pointer is properly restored after each use. Otherwise, the default routines will not execute, and the program will terminate abnormally.

The next example illustrates how customized exit code can be used in a unit. In the event of an abnormal termination, the EXIT3 module (listing 12.19) is designed to display the system variables defined in the System unit.

Listing 12.19

```
unit Exit3;
interface
implementation
type
   HexFormat = string[ 5 ];    { $xxxx }
var
   ExitAddress : pointer;
function Hex( HexWord : word ) : HexFormat;
const
   HexDigits : array[ 0..15 ] of char = '0123456789ABCDEF';
begin
   Hex := '$'  + HexDigits[ hi( HexWord ) div 16 ] +
               HexDigits[ hi( HexWord ) mod 16 ] +
               HexDigits[ lo( HexWord ) div 16 ] +
               HexDigits[ lo( HexWord ) mod 16 ];
end;
procedure writeWord( Wname : word );
begin
   write( Hex( Wname ), '            ' );
   writeln( Wname );
end;
procedure writePntr( Pname : pointer );
begin
   write( Hex( seg( Pname ) ), ':', Hex( ofs( Pname ) ) );
   write( '    ' );
   writeln( seg( Pname ):5, ':', ofs( Pname ):5 );
```

Listing 12.19 continues

Listing 12.19 continued

```
end;
{$F +}
procedure TerminationData;
{$F-}
begin
   write( 'Program segment prefix  ' );   writeWord( PrefixSeg );
   write( 'Stack pointer low limit ' );   writeWord( StackLimit );
   write( 'Overlay buffer origin   ' );   writeWord( OvrHeapOrg );
   write( 'Overlay buffer pointer  ' );   writeWord( OvrHeapPtr );
   write( 'Overlay buffer end      ' );   writeWord( OvrHeapEnd );
   write( 'Heap origin             ' );   writePntr( HeapOrg );
   write( 'Heap pointer            ' );   writePntr( HeapPtr );
   write( 'Free list pointer       ' );   writePntr( FreePtr );
   write( 'Minimum free list size  ' );   writeWord( FreeMin );
   write( 'Heap error function     ' );   writePntr( HeapError );
   write( 'Exit procedure          ' );   writePntr( ExitAddress ); {!}
   write( 'Exit code               ' );   writeln( ExitCode );
   write( 'Runtime error address   ' );   writePntr( ErrorAddr );
   write( 'Random seed             ' );   writeln( RandSeed );
   write( 'File open mode          ' );   writeln( FileMode );
   write( '8087 test result        ' );   writeln( Test8087 );
   ExitProc := ExitAddress;
end;
begin
   ExitAddress := ExitProc;
   ExitProc := @TerminationData;
end.
```

The EXIT4 program (listing 12.20) demonstrates how easy it is to use this
"mini-debugger" unit. The only modification required is the addition of a uses
Exit3; clause.

Listing 12.20

```
program Exit4;
uses Exit3;    { The mini-debugger }
var
   Selection : longint;
begin
   repeat
      write( 'Please enter an integer: ' );
      readln( Selection );
      writeln( 'The square of ', Selection, ' is ', Sqr( Selection ) );
   until Selection = Ø;
end.
```

Any run-time error immediately triggers the execution of the termination procedure from the EXIT3 unit.

```
Please enter an integer: 12
The square of 12 is 144
Please enter an integer: 17
The square of 17 is 289
Please enter an integer: CAT
Program segment prefix  $3AØ8              14856
Stack pointer low limit  $ØØØØ              Ø
Overlay buffer origin    $3FCØ              1632Ø
Overlay buffer pointer   $3FCØ              1632Ø
Overlay buffer end       $3FCØ              1632Ø
Overlay buffer end       $3FCØ              1632Ø
Heap origin              $3BCØ:$3FF4        15296:16372
Heap pointer             $3BCØ:$3FF4        15296:16372
Free list pointer        $3BCØ:$3FF4        15296:16372
Minimum free list size   $ØØØØ              Ø
Heap error function      $3BCØ:$3FF4        15296:16372
Exit procedure           $3BCØ:$3FF4        15296:16372
Exit code                1Ø6
Runtime error address    $3BCØ:$3FF4        15296:16372
Random seed              Ø
File open mode           2
8Ø87 test result         Ø
Runtime error 1Ø6 at ØØØØ:ØØ82.
```

Note that the segment and offset values will probably differ on your machine.

Additional debugging information can be included, if desired. For example, by adding the lines

```
write( 'Code segment           ' );   writeWord( CSeg );
write( 'Data segment           ' );   writeWord( DSeg );
write( 'Stack segment          ' );   writeWord( SSeg );
write( 'Stack pointer          ' );   writeWord( SPtr );
```

you can display segment information.

Summary

In this chapter, you learned about the various Turbo Pascal procedures and functions that allow direct interaction with DOS operations.

You have learned how your programs can read and set the system date and time. You have seen—and heard—how to produce the common beep effect and how to produce tones of any desired frequency. You have learned about the DOS environment table, how environment strings can be added or removed from it, and how the strings can be accessed by your programs. You have learned about the Program Segment Prefix (PSP) and the useful information DOS stores in it. You have learned how to control the termination of a Turbo Pascal program, and how to pass parameters between programs. You have seen how your programs can be run within batch files. You have learned how your programs can activate and control the execution of a second program and how your programs can execute DOS utilities. You have learned how to write customized exit routines for programs and units.

You will find that you utilize the topics presented in this chapter in a wide variety of programming applications. They are powerful tools that will help you solve many frequently encountered problems.

CHAPTER 13

File Handling

The electronics in your PC make it incredibly fast. The reaction times of the individual logic circuits in the CPU are measured in nanoseconds; that's *billionths* of a second. To try to grasp how fast that really is, consider: electricity travels at the speed of light. In one second, a beam of light travels 186,000 miles—more than seven times around the equator of the Earth. Yet in one nanosecond that same beam of light moves *less than 12 inches*! (You can see why the early room-full-of-vacuum-tubes computers couldn't offer anywhere near the speed of the machine that now fits comfortably on top of your desk.)

On the flip side, disk drives are incredibly slow. Few PC users haven't complained at some time or other about the time "wasted" as they waited for the drive's grinding noises to stop and the red light to go out.

Yet disk drives—and the files they contain—are critical to program development. The *file* is Turbo Pascal's principal means of communicating with data outside the main memory of the PC. Programming applications often need to store large volumes of data. Further, because files are independent of any one program, they provide an excellent means of sharing common data among several programs.

In this chapter, you will learn about the three different types of files supported by Turbo Pascal, and you will learn about the procedures and functions that allow files to be used in your program.

393

File Handling in Turbo Pascal

There has always been a (mostly) friendly battle between hardware and software enthusiasts. Hardware people delight in cramming more bits into smaller amounts of silicon, installing more memory capacity in their PCs, and acquiring the latest in graphics displays and laser printers. Software people like nothing better than developing an elegant algorithm and generally making their programs faster, larger, and more sophisticated.

Fortunately, these preferences are compatible. A computer does, after all, consist of a blend of hardware and software technologies. Some concepts, such as a file, even overlap the two worlds.

In the hardware arena, a file is a *physical* device on which you store and retrieve information. The Turbo Pascal distribution disks that contain the compiler and its supporting programs and files are either 5 1/4-inch or 3 1/2-inch floppy disks. Your PC may have a hard disk that can hold 5, 10, 20, 40, or more megabytes. Storage media range from the primitive, such as cassette tapes, to the advanced, such as optical disks.

Turbo Pascal regards all of these physical forms of file storage to be identical. In fact, when you first learn about files, it's better to completely ignore their physical form. Instead, think of a file as having two components:

❏ A name, which may or may not include a physical drive and/or directory reference

❏ A continuous stream of characters containing data

A file contains data, so a *logical* file is simply another data type, just like byte, integer, record, and array. Turbo Pascal hides the underlying complexity.

File names in Pascal, as in DOS, are up to eight characters long, optionally followed by a period and an extension of up to three characters. Both DOS and Turbo Pascal make assumptions about the contents of a file based on its extension. For example, .PAS is assumed to be a Turbo Pascal source program, and .EXE is assumed to be an executable file.

The only impact the physical medium has on your programming is that your file name should help the system find the file. When you reference a file that doesn't reside in the current drive and directory (or *may not* the next time you run the program), include the drive and directory as part of the file's name. For example, the full name of file EDITOR.PAS on drive C: in subdirectory \TURBO\SOURCE is C:\TURBO\SOURCE\EDITOR.PAS. Otherwise, all Turbo Pascal file programming is the same, regardless of where or how a file is stored.

File Variable Types

Although there is only one type of *physical* disk file, the Turbo Pascal compiler supports three types of *logical* files, named for the syntax of their declarations: text, typed, and untyped.

```
var
    FileName1 : file of DataRecord;    { Typed file   }
    FileName2 : file;                  { Untyped file }
    FileName3 : Text;                  { Text file    }
```

A *typed file* contains *only* data of the one particular type named in the declaration.

An *untyped file* is completely unstructured. It may contain any data in any format in any length. The most common reason to declare a file as untyped is to manipulate its contents in large blocks, not as individual characters.

Unfortunately, the names *typed* and *untyped* imply complete definition. In reality, a third file type also exists. A *text file* contains lines of characters (that is, data of type char) terminated by a carriage return (#13) and, usually, a line feed (#10) as well. Lines may vary in length. Note that a text file is *not* the same as a file of type char.

Text Files

A text file is the most commonly used file type. Even if Turbo Pascal is the first software package you have ever used, you have already been using text files extensively without realizing it. All Turbo Pascal source code is stored in text files that have .PAS as their extension. Therefore, if you have tried out any of the examples that accompany this text, you used text files to store the program code.

In addition, all of the unit header files on the Turbo Pascal distribution disks (such as SYSTEM.DOC, GRAPH.DOC, DOS.DOC, and so on) are text files. You can list them out on your printer using a word processor or simply by entering a DOS command such as the following:

TYPE SYSTEM.DOC > PRN

In general, whenever you use a file that contains *lines* of ASCII characters, you should declare a file as type text.

Comparison to Other File Types

Turbo Pascal treats each text file as if it contains a series of lines. Each *line* is composed of a sequence of characters terminated by an end-of-line marker, which consists of either a carriage return (#13) or a carriage-return and line-feed combination (#13#10). Text files offer special subroutines for detecting and manipulating end-of-line markers. A line may have any number of characters, including no characters at all.

It's natural to envision a text file as something that holds letter and number patterns that form English language phrases. After all, when you hear a file described as "text" and you are presented with examples that include program source code and documentation, you expect a text file to contain—well, to contain *text*.

In practice, the reason that a text file is so frequently used is that *any* file can be declared as Text—including a file such as TURBO.EXE, which contains nothing but illegible, unreadable, and unpronounceable hexadecimal!

Remember the original definition of a file: a data structure that consists of a sequence of ASCII characters. Suppose that you find a strange file on your disk. (Actually, this happens more often than most programmers like to admit.) Suppose further that you want to examine it with Turbo Pascal. Your first consideration is how the file should be declared. Your reasoning would proceed as follows:

1. Because you don't know what data types the file might contain, you wouldn't consider declaring it as a *typed* file. Of course, you could declare it as a *file of byte*, but that assumes that the file exclusively contains numbers. (The three hexadecimal characters $44, $6F, and $67 would be interpreted as the decimal values 68, 111, and 103—not as the intended character string *Dog*.) Similarly, a *file of char* assumes that the file holds nothing but characters, and gives no special importance to the end-of-line markers.

2. You could declare the file as *untyped*, but untyped files, as you will see, typically deal in large groups of bytes called *blocks*. Untyped files don't offer an easy way to process their contents on a character-by-character basis.

3. Therefore, you really have no other alternative; you are forced to treat the file in the most general way possible—as type Text.

Of course, once you have determined what the file contains, you may decide to go back and declare it as a typed or untyped file.

Declaring a Text File

The first step in using a text file is to declare an identifier as type Text, as follows:

```
var
    InFile         : Text;
    OutputDetails  : Text;
    WorkFile       : Text;
```

Note that the format of a text file declaration is identical to that of any other declaration. A text file is—quite properly—considered its own data type.

Identifying the Physical File

To relate the *internal* file data structure with the *external* physical data file, you use the Assign procedure. In the following example, the identifier Output-putDetails, previously declared as a text file, is defined to refer to the DOS file DATAFILE.TXT in the current drive and directory.

```
Assign( OutputDetails, 'DATAFILE.TXT' );
```

The DOS drive and path may be included as part of the file name. The Assign procedure must be called before any other file-related procedure or function that uses the OutputDetails identifier. The Assign procedure is the only time your program calls a file by its DOS name; all future references to DATAFILE.TXT will be made by the identifier OutputDetails.

Opening a Text File

After you use Assign for an identifier to an external file, the next step is to physically *open* it with one of these: Reset, Rewrite, or Append.

❏ The Reset procedure opens an existing text file for input, starting at the beginning of the file. The syntax is

```
Reset( TextFileIdentifier );
```

If the file specified in the Assign procedure doesn't exist, a run-time error is generated. If the file is already open (the result of a previous Reset, Rewrite, or Append operation), then Reset first *closes* the file and moves the file pointer back to its beginning and then reopens the file so that the next input command will read its first record. (The Close procedure is discussed in the next section.)

❏ The Rewrite procedure opens a text file for output. The syntax is

```
Rewrite( TextFileIdentifier );
```

The Rewrite procedure first searches for the DOS file specified in the Assign procedure. If the file already exists, Rewrite deletes it. If the file doesn't exist, Rewrite creates it. This ensures that the file is always empty and that output starts at the *beginning* of the file.

❑ The Append procedure opens an existing text file for output, starting at the *end* of the file. The syntax is

```
Append( TextFileIdentifier );
```

The Append procedure first searches for the DOS file specified in the Assign procedure. A run-time error is generated if the file cannot be found. Note that if the file doesn't already exist, you must use Rewrite to create it.

A text file can be opened for either input or output, but not for both. You can, however, switch between input and output modes simply by issuing a new Reset, Rewrite, or Append procedure anytime you wish. You need not call the Assign procedure more than once, however. For example, the body of a program that creates a file, reads information from it, and then adds new data to the file would have the following form:

```
Assign( WorkFile, 'Data.DAT' );
Rewrite( WorkFile );
:
:    { Statements that create new records }
:
Reset( WorkFile );
:
:    { Statements that read the new records }
:
Append( WorkFile );
:
:    { Statements that write new records after the end of the file }
```

Closing a File

Every file must be *closed* when your program finishes using it. The syntax is:

```
Close( TextFileIdentifier );
```

If, in this example, the TextFileIdentifier file had been opened for output with Rewrite or Append, then Close would write out any data that might still remain in the buffer. (Buffers are discussed in more detail later in this chapter.) Therefore, failure to Close an output file may result in lost data! In addition, Close updates an output file's DOS disk directory entry to reflect the new size and the last date and time the file was modified.

Closed files must be reopened with Reset, Rewrite, or Append before any further input or output operations can take place. However, because Turbo Pascal doesn't forget the relationship between the logical and physical file names, it isn't necessary to issue another Assign procedure.

Now, the truth is that Turbo Pascal automatically closes all files when your program terminates. Consequently, it isn't *really* necessary for you to explicitly Close a file, but you should do so for the following reasons:

❏ DOS only allows 15 Turbo Pascal files to be opened at any one time. It isn't difficult for some file-intensive programs with sloppy housekeeping to exceed that number.

❏ The Close procedure deallocates any memory buffer space assigned to the file. Therefore, Close frees up memory.

❏ Keeping a file open longer than necessary increases the chance (however slight) of accidental file damage or loss. For example, if a power failure strikes, the data in the buffer of an open output file may not have been saved. In addition, because the DOS directory entry hasn't been updated, the disk itself may need to be repaired with the CHKDSK utility.

❏ Other Pascal compilers probably don't offer such a feature, so your program's "portability" is reduced.

❏ Future versions of Turbo Pascal may not be so forgiving.

❏ It's simply good, professional practice.

Reading from a Text File

If you have been reading this book from the beginning, you have already seen several dozen examples of programs that use read and readln for keyboard input. Except for the addition of a text file identifier as their first parameter, the two procedures operate similarly when they are applied to text files.

The read procedure

```
read( TextFile, Var1 { , Var2, Var3, ... } );
```

inputs data items from TextFile and assigns them to the variables listed as parameters. The file pointer is then set so that the next read will begin with the data item that follows on the same line.

The readln procedure

```
readln( TextFile, Var1 { , Var2, Var3, ... } );
```

inputs data just like a read, except that it then advances the file pointer to the beginning of the *next* line in the file. In other words, readln *skips over* any remaining characters in the current line through the end-of-line marker.

For both read and readln, the data items input from the file must be compatible with the types of the corresponding variables. Each data item can be read only once.

The properties of the read and readln procedures can best be illustrated with an example. The text file you will use—NUMARRAY.DAT, shown in listing 13.1—consists of 10 rows of digits enclosed in brackets and separated by periods. Each row is terminated with a carriage return and line feed (#13#10).

Listing 13.1

```
[Ø1].[Ø2].[Ø3].[Ø4].[Ø5].[Ø6].[Ø7].[Ø8].[Ø9]
[11].[12].[13].[14].[15].[16].[17].[18].[19]
[21].[22].[23].[24].[25].[26].[27].[28].[29]
[31].[32].[33].[34].[35].[36].[37].[38].[39]
[41].[42].[43].[44].[45].[46].[47].[48].[49]
[51].[52].[53].[54].[55].[56].[57].[58].[59]
[61].[62].[63].[64].[65].[66].[67].[68].[69]
[71].[72].[73].[74].[75].[76].[77].[78].[79]
[81].[82].[83].[84].[85].[86].[87].[88].[89]
[91].[92].[93].[94].[95].[96].[97].[98].[99]
```

The READSTR program in listing 13.2 inputs the NUMARRAY.DAT text file twice: the first time with read and, after the file is reset, the second time with readln.

Listing 13.2

```
program ReadStr;
uses Crt;
var
    StrChars : Text;
    Str5A,    Str5B,    Str5C,   Str5D    : string[ 5 ];
    Str15A,   Str15B,   Str15C, Str15D : string[ 15 ];
    Str1ØØA, Str1ØØB, Str1ØØC           : string[ 1ØØ ];
begin
    ClrScr;
    Assign( StrChars, 'NumArray.DAT' );

    writeln;
    writeln( '====================================================' );
    writeln( 'Using Read:' );
    writeln;

    Reset( StrChars );

    Read( StrChars, Str5A, Str5B, Str5C, Str5D );
    writeln( Str5A, '*', Str5B, '*', Str5C, '*', Str5D, '*' );
    Read( StrChars, Str15A, Str15B, Str15C, Str15D );
    writeln( Str15A, '*', Str15B, '*', Str15C, '*', Str15D, '*' );
    Read( StrChars, Str1ØØA, Str1ØØB, Str1ØØC );
    writeln( Str1ØØA, '*', Str1ØØB, '*', Str1ØØC, '*' );
```

Listing 13.2 continues

Listing 13.2 continued

```
      writeln;
      writeln( '===================================================' );
      writeln( 'Using Readln:' );
      writeln;

      Reset( StrChars );

      Readln( StrChars, Str5A, Str5B, Str5C, Str5D );
      writeln( Str5A, '*', Str5B, '*', Str5C, '*', Str5D, '*' );
      Readln( StrChars, Str15A, Str15B, Str15C, Str15D );
      writeln( Str15A, '*', Str15B, '*', Str15C, '*', Str15D, '*' );
      Readln( StrChars, Str100A, Str100B, Str100C );
      writeln( Str100A, '*', Str100B, '*', Str100C, '*' );

      writeln;
      writeln( '===================================================' );
      writeln;

      Close( StrChars );
end.
```

Figure 13.1 contains the output from the READSTR program. The results of the input with read are displayed at the top. The readln results are at the bottom. READSTR outputs an asterisk after each variable to show it more easily.

Fig. 13.1. The output produced by the READSTR program.

```
===================================================
Using Read:

,[01]*,[02]*,[03]*,[04]*
,[05],[06],[07]*,[08],[09]***
***


===================================================
Using Readln:

,[01]*,[02]*,[03]*,[04]*
,[11],[12],[13]*,[14],[15],[16]*,[17],[18],[19]**
,[21],[22],[23],[24],[25],[26],[27],[28],[29]***


===================================================
```

The read procedure fills each variable with the maximum number of characters until it reaches the end-of-line marker. No read can proceed past the end-of-line marker in the first line; all subsequent read attempts return only empty strings.

Like read, each readln procedure assigns characters until it reaches an end-of-line marker, and thereafter returns only empty strings. But unlike read, after each readln finishes, the file pointer is advanced to the first character of the next line.

Clearly, you need a means to both detect and bypass the end-of-line markers in a text file.

Detecting the End of a File and the End of a Line

Turbo Pascal provides two Boolean functions, Eof and Eoln, that smooth the process of reading data from files.

Eof returns True when the end of the file has been reached. Eoln also returns True when no more data items remain and the character about to be input is an end-of-line marker.

Eof and Eoln are demonstrated in the READSTR1 program in listing 13.3.

Listing 13.3

```
program ReadStr1;
uses Crt;
var
   StrChars : Text;
   Str5A    : string[ 5 ];
begin
   ClrScr;
   Assign( StrChars, 'NumArray.DAT' );

   writeln;
   writeln( '=====================================================' );
   writeln( 'Using Eoln:' );
   writeln;

   Reset( StrChars );
   while not Eoln( StrChars ) do begin
      Read( StrChars, Str5A );
      Write( Str5A, '*' );
   end;
```

Listing 13.3 continues

Listing 13.3 continued

```
    writeln;
    writeln;
    writeln( '====================================================' );
    writeln( 'Using Eof:' );
    writeln;

    Reset( StrChars );
    while not Eof( StrChars ) do begin
        Read( StrChars, Str5A );
        Write( Str5A, '*' );
    end;

    writeln;
    writeln( '====================================================' );
    writeln;

    Close( StrChars );
  end.
```

READSTR1 produces the output shown in figure 13.2. Note that after Eoln correctly detects the first end-of-line marker, the first while loop concludes, the text file is Reset, and the program proceeds to the test for Eof.

Fig. 13.2. Output produced by the READSTR1 program.

```
====================================================
Using Eoln:

,[01]*,[02]*,[03]*,[04]*,[05]*,[06]*,[07]*,[08]*,[09]*


====================================================
Using Eof:

,[01]*,[02]*,[03]*,[04]*,[05]*,[06]*,[07]*,[08]*,[09]*****************************
**********************************************************************
**********************************************************************
**********************************************************************
**********************************************************************
**********************************************************************
**********************************************************************
**********************************************************************
**********************************************************************
**********************************************************************
**********************************************************************
**********************************************************************
*******
```

The only way READSTR1 can terminate is by interrupting it with Ctrl-Break. Because the read procedure can't proceed beyond the end-of-line marker, the while loop will never encounter the end-of-file. As READSTR1 is currently written, Eof can never return True.

You can use Eof and Eoln in combination if you don't know how many data items are in a line, or if you don't know how many lines are in a file. The process is as follows:

1. Use read for data items until Eoln returns True.

2. Use readln to bypass the end-of-line marker and move the file pointer to the beginning of the next line. This also has the effect of resetting Eoln to False.

3. Repeat steps 1 and 2 until Eof returns True.

This technique is demonstrated in the READSTR2 program in listing 13.4.

Listing 13.4

```
program ReadStr2;
   uses CRT;
var
   StrChars : Text;
   Str5A    : string[ 5 ];
begin
   ClrScr;
   Assign( StrChars, 'NumArray.DAT' );
   Reset( StrChars );
   while not Eof( StrChars ) do begin
      while not Eoln( StrChars ) do begin
         read( StrChars, Str5A );
         write( Str5A, '*' );
      end;
      readln( StrChars );
      writeln;
   end;
   Close( StrChars );
end.
```

READSTR2 produces the output shown in figure 13.3.

Notice the similarity between the output of READSTR2 and the NUMAR-RAY.DAT text file itself. This resemblance is deliberate. If you remove the single writeln procedure, READSTR2 correctly returns all of the data in the text file in a single, continuous stream.

Fig. 13.3. *Output produced by the READSTR2 program.*

```
,[01]*,[02]*,[03]*,[04]*,[05]*,[06]*,[07]*,[08]*,[09]*
,[11]*,[12]*,[13]*,[14]*,[15]*,[16]*,[17]*,[18]*,[19]*
,[21]*,[22]*,[23]*,[24]*,[25]*,[26]*,[27]*,[28]*,[29]*
,[31]*,[32]*,[33]*,[34]*,[35]*,[36]*,[37]*,[38]*,[39]*
,[41]*,[42]*,[43]*,[44]*,[45]*,[46]*,[47]*,[48]*,[49]*
,[51]*,[52]*,[53]*,[54]*,[55]*,[56]*,[57]*,[58]*,[59]*
,[61]*,[62]*,[63]*,[64]*,[65]*,[66]*,[67]*,[68]*,[69]*
,[71]*,[72]*,[73]*,[74]*,[75]*,[76]*,[77]*,[78]*,[79]*
,[81]*,[82]*,[83]*,[84]*,[85]*,[86]*,[87]*,[88]*,[89]*
,[91]*,[92]*,[93]*,[94]*,[95]*,[96]*,[97]*,[98]*,[99]*
```

SeekEof and *SeekEoln*

You can use the Eof and Eoln functions to determine if the *current* position of the file pointer is at the end of a line or the end of a file. Two other text file procedures—SeekEof and SeekEoln—can be used to detect if the *next* input will result in Eof and Eoln being True.

SeekEof acts just like Eof, except it looks ahead, skipping over all blanks, tabs, line feeds, and carriage returns before it returns the end-of-file status. Using SeekEof to search for the next significant character enables you to ignore blank lines.

SeekEoln is similar to SeekEof except that it skips over all blanks and tabs while it searches for the next end-of-line marker. Using SeekEoln enables you to ignore blanks at the end of a line.

The READSTR3 program in listing 13.5 uses SeekEof to read the NUMAR-RAY.DAT file.

Listing 13.5

```
program ReadStr3;
   uses CRT;
var
   StrChars : Text;
   Str5A    : string[ 5 ];
begin
   ClrScr;
   Assign( StrChars, 'NumArray.DAT' );
   Reset( StrChars );
   while not seekEof( StrChars ) do begin
      read( StrChars, Str5A );
      write( Str5A, '*' );
   end;
   Close( StrChars );
end.
```

The output from READSTR3 is shown in figure 13.4. Notice how SeekEof ignored the line feeds and carriage returns, making it unnecessary to perform a separate end-of-line test. Using SeekEof enables you to avoid the more complicated logic of the earlier READSTR2 program.

Fig. 13.4. Output produced by the READSTR3 program.

```
,[01]*,[02]*,[03]*,[04]*,[05]*,[06]*,[07]*,[08]*,[09]*,[11]*,[12]*,[13]*,[14]*,[
15]*,[16]*,[17]*,[18]*,[19]*,[21]*,[22]*,[23]*,[24]*,[25]*,[26]*,[27]*,[28]*,[29
]*,[31]*,[32]*,[33]*,[34]*,[35]*,[36]*,[37]*,[38]*,[39]*,[41]*,[42]*,[43]*,[44]*
,[45]*,[46]*,[47]*,[48]*,[49]*,[51]*,[52]*,[53]*,[54]*,[55]*,[56]*,[57]*,[58]*,[
59]*,[61]*,[62]*,[63]*,[64]*,[65]*,[66]*,[67]*,[68]*,[69]*,[71]*,[72]*,[73]*,[74
]*,[75]*,[76]*,[77]*,[78]*,[79]*,[81]*,[82]*,[83]*,[84]*,[85]*,[86]*,[87]*,[88]*
,[89]*,[91]*,[92]*,[93]*,[94]*,[95]*,[96]*,[97]*,[98]*,[99]*
```

Because SeekEof and SeekEoln ignore blanks and tabs, they are ideal for extracting information from text files. We can demonstrate this with the data file LINEDATA.DAT, shown in figure 13.5. The dots represent blank spaces. As you can see, LINEDATA.DAT contains frequent occurrences of leading and trailing blank characters. Lines 4, 6, 16, 19, and 23 contain only blanks. Lines 12, 13, and 22 are completely empty. In short, LINEDATA.DAT is not the type of file you would normally want to encounter.

Fig. 13.5. The contents of the LINEDATA.DAT file.

```
 1    ·1··2··3····4····5·······
 2    ··2··4··6····8····10······
 3    ···3··6····9····12·······15
 4    ·······················
 5    ···4····8····12·····16·······20
 6    ··············································
 7    ····5····10·····15·······20··25·······
 8    ······6·······12·······18·24···30···
 9    ·······7····14··21··28···35·····
10    ·8··16··24···32·····40·······
11    ··9···18···27····36······45··
12
13
14    ···10····20··30·····40······50·
15    ····11···22··33······44·55······
16    ·
17    ·····12·····24··36··48··60······
18    ······13·····26·39··52···65·········
19    ·······
20    ·······14··28··42···56····70······
21    ·15··30···45····60·····75·········
22
23    ·····
```

The LINECNT program in listing 13.6 reads and displays the LINE-DATA.DAT file three times. First, LINECNT uses Eof to test for the end of the file, displaying each line as it goes. Second, LINECNT repeats the process with SeekEof. Finally, LINECNT uses a combination of SeekEof and SeekEoln. Note that LINECNT processes each line in its entirety as a single string.

Listing 13.6

```
program LineCnt;
uses Crt;
var
    InFile   : Text;
    Contents : string;
    LineNo   : word;
begin
    Assign( InFile, 'LineData.DAT' );
    ClrScr;
    Reset( InFile );
    LineNo := Ø;
    while not Eof( InFile ) do begin
        readln( InFile, Contents );
        Inc( LineNo );
        writeln( LineNo:6, '    ', Contents, '*' );
    end;
    readln;
    ClrScr;
    Reset( InFile );
    LineNo := Ø;
    while not SeekEof( InFile ) do begin
        readln( InFile, Contents );
        Inc( LineNo );
        writeln( LineNo:6, '    ', Contents, '*' );
    end;
    readln;
    ClrScr;
    Reset( InFile );
    LineNo := Ø;
    while not SeekEof( Infile ) do begin
        while not SeekEoln( InFile ) do begin
            readln( InFile, Contents );
            Inc( LineNo );
            writeln( LineNo:6, '    ', Contents, '*' );
        end;
    end;
    readln;
    Close( InFile );
end.
```

The results of LINECNT's first pass of the file are shown in figure 13.6. The LINEDATA.DAT file is displayed in its entirety. Asterisks mark the end of each line. The second and third passes produce identical results, shown in figure 13.7.

Fig. 13.6. Output produced by the first part of the LINECNT program.

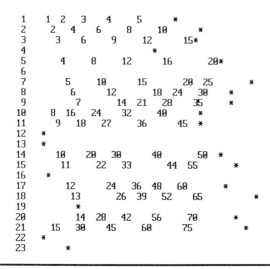

Fig. 13.7. Output produced by both the second and third parts of the LINE-CNT program.

In processing the text file as a series of strings, SeekEof and SeekEoln eliminated all blank lines, empty lines, and even leading blanks. If, instead, you process the text file as a series of individual variables of type char, you can eliminate *every* unnecessary character. The LINECNT1 program (listing 13.7) does just that.

Listing 13.7

```
program LineCnt1;
   uses CRT;
var
   InFile   : Text;
   LineNo   : word;
   AlphaNum : char;
begin
   ClrScr;
   Assign( InFile, 'LineData.DAT' );
   Reset( InFile );
   LineNo := 0;
   while not SeekEof( Infile ) do begin
      Inc( LineNo );
      write( LineNo:6, '   ' );
      while not SeekEoln( InFile ) do begin
         read( InFile, AlphaNum );
         write( AlphaNum );
      end;
      writeln;
   end;
   Close( InFile );
end.
```

The output from LINECNT1 is shown in figure 13.8. All of the blank spaces have been completely eliminated.

Fig. 13.8. *Output produced by the LINECNT1 program.*

```
 1    12345
 2    246810
 3    3691215
 4    48121620
 5    510152025
 6    612182430
 7    714212835
 8    816243240
 9    918273645
10    1020304050
11    1122334455
12    1224364860
13    1326395265
14    1428425670
15    1530456075
```

Since SeekEof and SeekEoln ignore major portions of a text file while searching for significant characters, they have limited appeal when you use them to input character or string data. However, SeekEof and SeekEoln are ideal for processing the *numeric* contents of a text file.

The LINECNT2 program, shown in listing 13.8, is designed to extract the numbers contained in the LINEDATA.DAT text file.

Listing 13.8

```
program LineCnt2;
uses Crt;
var
   InFile    : Text;
   i, LineNo : word;
begin
   Assign( InFile, 'LineData.DAT' );
   ClrScr;
   Reset( InFile );
   while not Eof( InFile ) do begin
      while not Eoln( InFile ) do begin
         read( InFile, i );
         write( i:3 );
      end;
      readln( InFile );
      writeln;
   end;
   readln;
   ClrScr;
   Reset( InFile );
   LineNo := Ø;
   while not SeekEof( Infile ) do begin
      Inc( LineNo );
      write( LineNo:6, '    ' );
      while not SeekEoln( InFile ) do begin
         read( InFile, i );
         write( i:3 );
      end;
      writeln;
   end;
   readln;
   Close( InFile );
end.
```

LINECNT2 processes the text file twice, the first time with Eof and Eoln (see fig. 13.9), and the second time with SeekEof and SeekEoln (see fig. 13.10).

Fig. 13.9. Output produced by the first part of the LINECNT2 program.

```
 1  2  3  4  5  2  4  6  8 10  3  6  9 12 15
 4  8 12 16 20
 5 10 15 20 25  6 12 18 24 30  7 14 21 28 35  8 16 24 32 40  9 18 27 36 45 10 2
 0 30 40 50 11 22 33 44 55 12 24 36 48 60 13 26 39 52 65 14 28 42 56 70 15 30 45
60 75  0
```

Fig. 13.10. Output produced by the second part of the LINECNT2 program.

```
 1      1  2  3  4  5
 2      2  4  6  8 10
 3      3  6  9 12 15
 4      4  8 12 16 20
 5      5 10 15 20 25
 6      6 12 18 24 30
 7      7 14 21 28 35
 8      8 16 24 32 40
 9      9 18 27 36 45
10     10 20 30 40 50
11     11 22 33 44 55
12     12 24 36 48 60
13     13 26 39 52 65
14     14 28 42 56 70
15     15 30 45 60 75
```

As you can see in figure 13.9, Eof and Eoln are not capable of directly handling blank lines. In fact, notice how the trailing blank line was actually input as a zero! SeekEof and SeekEoln are far cleaner, because they jump over every non-numeric character.

A Note on SeekEof and SeekEoln

Strictly speaking, SeekEof and SeekEoln skip over more than just blanks and tabs.

SeekEof bypasses all characters from ASCII 0 through ASCII 32 (#0 through #32), with the exception of #26. This range includes blanks (#32) and ASCII control characters such as tabs (#9), line feeds (#10), and carriage returns (#13). The single exception, #26, is also called Ctrl-Z; SeekEof can't ignore it because it's the character Turbo Pascal uses to indicate the presence of an end of file.

SeekEoln is identical to SeekEof except, of course, for also not being able to ignore the line feed (#10) and carriage return (#13).

Writing Data

You can output to a text file after opening it with Rewrite or Append, as we discussed earlier in the chapter. The write and writeln procedures perform the actual data transfer.

Except for the addition of a text file identifier as their first parameter, write and writeln operate the same way with text files as they do when outputting to the screen. Both procedures accept any number of parameters.

The syntax of write and writeln is as follows:

```
write( TextFile, Var1 { , Var2, Var3, ... } );
writeln( TextFile, Var1 { , Var2, Var3, ... } );
```

After you call a write procedure, the next write or writeln begins its output wherever the original write procedure ended. After you call a writeln, the next write or writeln begins its output on a new line. In other words, writeln always terminates with an end-of-line marker (#13#10). You can generate a blank line in the file by using a writeln with no data item parameters.

Formatting Text File Output

When you output a string to a text file, the field width equals the number of bytes *actually in* the string, not the size of the string itself. No leading or trailing spaces are generated. All numeric data are written as a continuous sequence of digits, broken only by an occasional decimal point or plus or minus sign. Real numbers are output in scientific notation.

In short, text file output can easily appear cluttered. You can see this for yourself with the UNFORMED program in listing 13.9.

Listing 13.9

```
program Unformed;
var
   i : LongInt;
   r : real;
   s : string[ 100 ];
   c : char;
   F : Text;
begin
```

Listing 13.9 continues

Listing 13.9 continued

```
Assign( F, 'DataForm.DAT' );
Rewrite( F );
s := 'abc';
c := 'X';
for i := 1 to 5 do
   write( F, i );
for i := 1 to 5 do begin
   r := Sqrt( i );
   write( F, r );
end;
for i := 1 to 5 do
   write( F, s );
for i := 1 to 5 do
   write( F, c );
Close( F );
end.
```

When it executes, UNFORMED creates the DATAFORM.DAT file. To see what it contains, you will have to use a special program such as your Turbo Pascal editor or the DOS TYPE utility.

You can also use the DUMP program, which is discussed in greater detail at the end of this chapter. When DUMP is used on DATAFORM.DAT, it produces the display shown in figure 13.11.

Fig. 13.11. A dump of the DATAFORM.DAT file, produced by the UNFORMED program.

```
dataform.dat                    Page  1 of 1                    110 bytes

31323334 3520312E 30303030 30303030 3030452B 30302031  12345 1.0000000000E+00 1
2E343134 32313335 36323445 2B303020 312E3733 32303530  .4142135624E+00 1.732050
38303736 452B3030 20322E30 30303030 30303030 30452B30  8076E+00 2.0000000000E+0
3020322E 32333630 36373937 3735452B 30306162 63616263  0 2.2360679775E+00abcabc
61626361 62636162 63585858 5858                        abcabcabcXXXXX
```

DUMP displays the contents of a file in both hexadecimal and character form. The first six columns each contain four hexadecimal values. The corresponding 24 characters are in the column on the far right.

Notice how all of the data items output by UNFORMED run together. The only spaces represent the positive signs of the five real numbers.

Now, obviously, data stored in this form is difficult to process. Fortunately, there is a simple solution. If, within a write or writeln procedure, you follow a data item with a colon and a positive number, Turbo Pascal will interpret the number as the minimum desired width of the data item. This number can be written as a constant, a variable, or an expression.

The complete format for a real number is a bit more complicated: a colon followed by a positive number specifying the field width, followed by another colon and another positive number specifying the number of characters to follow the decimal point. If necessary, the compiler automatically rounds the number.

If the specified field width is larger than the data item, then the data item is right-justified and given one or more leading spaces. On the other hand, if the data item is larger than the specified width, the compiler will automatically expand the width of the field; the data item will not be truncated.

The FORMED program (listing 13.10) outputs the same data items as the UNFORMED program. This time, however, the write procedures use the formatting techniques just described.

Listing 13.10

```
program Formed;
var
    i : LongInt;
    r : real;
    s : string[ 100 ];
    c : char;
    F : Text;
begin
    Assign( F, 'DataForm.DAT' );
    Rewrite( F );
    s := 'abc';
    c := 'X';
    for i := 1 to 5 do
        write( F, i:3 );
    for i := 1 to 5 do begin
        r := Sqrt( i );
        write( F, r:8:4 );
```

Listing 13.10 continues

Listing 13.10 continued

```
    end;
    for i := 1 to 5 do
        write( F, s:5 );
    for i := 1 to 5 do
        write( F, c:3 );
    Close( F );
end.
```

Once again, you can use the DUMP program to see what FORMED output to the DATAFORM.DAT file. DUMP produces the display shown in figure 13.12.

Fig. 13.12. *A dump of the DATAFORM.DAT file, produced by the FORMED program.*

```
dataform.dat                      Page  1 of 1                        95 bytes

20203120 20322020 33202034 20203520 20312E30 30303020    1  2  3  4  5  1.0000
20312E34 31343220 20312E37 33323120 20322E30 30303020    1.4142  1.7321  2.0000
20322E32 33363120 20616263 20206162 63202061 62632020    2.2361  abc  abc  abc
61626320 20616263 20205820 20582020 58202058 202058      abc  abc  X  X  X  X  X
```

Disk Files and Buffers

Now you are ready to take a quick tour through a diskette. Because it's the most common type around, let's focus on a 5 1/4-inch double-sided double-density (DSDD) floppy diskette. This floppy diskette is so common, in fact, that it's probably the format of your Turbo Pascal distribution diskettes. Other diskettes have different physical characteristics, but the principles are the same.

A diskette stores data in concentric rings centered around its hub. A *double-sided* diskette has ring patterns on both sides. A *double-density* diskette has 40 such rings on each side. Each ring is called a *track*. Track 0, which contains DOS booting information, is on the outside while Track 39 is closest to the center. Each track consists of 9 *sectors* of 512 bytes. The sector is the *smallest* amount of data that DOS allows the computer to read at one time.

With a little arithmetic, you can calculate the storage capacity of a double-sided double-density diskette as follows:

2 sides × 40 tracks/side × 9 sectors/track × 512 bytes/sector

This equation yields 368,640 bytes.

DOS groups pairs of sectors into *clusters*. Cluster 0 is Sector 0 and Sector 1, Cluster 1 is Sector 2 and Sector 3, and so on. Rather than keep track of all 720 individual sectors, DOS chooses instead to keep track of the 360 clusters. Therefore, file space is always allocated in multiples of 1,024 byte clusters. This is why erasing a file that contains a single byte adds 1,024 bytes of available space to your disk, and this is also why the number of free bytes returned by the DIR command is always a multiple of 1,024.

To understand why a disk drive is so slow, you have to remember that there are two actions that must be taken before data transfer is complete.

1. The disk head (the actual electronic read-write device) must be positioned to the correct track. The time it takes for this physical movement is usually measured in milliseconds.

2. Once over the correct track, the spinning action of the diskette moves every byte in the track under the disk head every few hundredths of a second.

If a file is larger than 1,024 bytes, its next cluster may be located on another track, which means that these two steps must be repeated. Large files are only rarely stored in contiguous clusters. In fact, as a diskette fills up, its available clusters can become widely scattered. You have probably noticed that even the DOS COPY utility seems to take forever on a well-used diskette. Clearly, minimizing disk head movement could save a great deal of time.

Controlling Buffer Size

So what does all this have to do with Turbo Pascal? Well, suppose that you have an array of bytes, as follows·

```
var
    ByteArray : array [ 1..1000 ];
```

Further suppose that you want to input data into ByteArray from a text file. You would probably use code like the following:

```
for i := 1 to 1000 do
    read( TextFileId, ByteArray[ i ] );
```

From the previous discussion, you know that 1,000 separate diskette accesses would need to be performed—a process requiring several seconds at best.

Fortunately, Turbo Pascal automatically provides a text file *buffer* of 128 bytes. When your program processes the first read procedure, it stores 128 bytes (one quarter of a sector) in this buffer. Every subsequent read procedure gets its data electronically from the buffer, not mechanically from the disk. The next physical diskette access occurs only when all of the bytes in the buffer have been assigned.

The compiler *always* uses a buffer when it processes a text file. Because DOS transfers data in complete sectors of 512 bytes, storing 128 of them is far from wasteful or time consuming. After all, even if you only wanted to input a *single* byte, DOS would still try to send you 512!

The buffer size was set at 128 bytes because of historical reasons relating to early versions of DOS. However, it turns out that 128 bytes is an excellent compromise for most file processing operations.

Of course, if your program needs to manipulate larger chunks of data (such as when reading a word processing file or a spreadsheet data file into memory), the default size of 128 bytes is far smaller than you would really like. It would be helpful, for example, to reduce disk head movement by storing an entire 1,024 byte cluster in the buffer, because you know that your program will need to use it shortly anyway.

Turbo Pascal provides the SetTextBuf procedure for just such a situation. The syntax is as follows:

```
SetTextBuf( var TextFileIdentifier : Text;  BufferVar   { ; Size : word } );
```

TextFileIdentifier is the text file variable. BufferVar is the name of the variable that you want to use as the new buffer. The optional Size field determines the size of the buffer. If Size is omitted, SizeOf(BufferVar) will be used.

You should call SetTextBuf *after* you have performed the file Assign but *before* you have opened it with Reset, Rewrite, or Append.

The NEWTYPE program (listing 13.11) demonstrates how SetTextBuf is used. NEWTYPE operates just like the DOS TYPE utility, except that while TYPE continuously scrolls the screen, NEWTYPE pauses after each screen is filled and waits for you to press the Enter key. This enables you to examine a file one page at a time.

Listing 13.11

```
program NewType;
uses Crt;
var
   TextFile            : Text;
   IndividualCharacter : char;
   Buffer              : array [ 1..1024 ] of char;    { A full cluster }
begin
   if ParamCount = 1 then begin
      Assign( TextFile, ParamStr( 1 ) );
      SetTextBuf( TextFile, Buffer );      { Assumes all 1,024 characters }
      Reset( TextFile );
      while not Eof( TextFile ) do begin
         ClrScr;
         while (WhereY <> 24) and (not Eof( TextFile )) do begin
            read( TextFile, IndividualCharacter );
            write( IndividualCharacter );
         end;
         readln;
      end;
   end;
end.
```

Flushing a File

So far, you have seen how Turbo Pascal uses the buffer to store data being input *from* a text file. In a similar fashion, write and writeln procedures transfer program data *to* the buffer. The buffer is physically output to the disk only when it becomes full.

Earlier, the chapter stressed how important it is to close a file as soon as your program finishes with it. Unfortunately, some programs—like word processors and spreadsheets—don't have this luxury. They must keep a file open until the user closes it—often after a long period of time has passed.

To minimize the risk of lost data, you can *flush* the text file's buffer—causing whatever data is in the buffer to be immediately saved to disk—by using the Turbo Pascal Flush procedure. The syntax is simply:

```
Flush( TextFileIdentifier );
```

Although you can call `Flush` whenever you want, the best time to use it is just before input in an interactive program. Waiting for a user response is frequently the longest period of program inactivity.

I/O Error Checking

Normally, Turbo Pascal treats all run-time errors as fatal. It believes that it's doing you a favor by aborting the program immediately whenever an error is encountered.

Sometimes, however, Turbo's well intentioned desire to protect you can prove more bothersome than benevolent. For example, suppose that you want to append data to a text file. If the file already exists, it should be opened with `Append`. If it doesn't exist, it should be opened with `Rewrite`. Unfortunately, if you begin with `Append`, your program will generate a fatal run-time error if the file can't be found. Similarly, if you begin with `Rewrite`, the current contents of the file will be lost.

Turbo Pascal helps you avoid problems like this. You can disable I/O error checking with the {$I-} compiler directive. I/O error checking can later be turned back on by using the {$I +} directive.

While I/O error checking is off, no I/O error will fatally abort the program. Instead, your program must test the success or failure of every critical I/O operation with the `IOResult` function. In fact, until you do call `IOResult`, every subsequent I/O procedure or function call will be ignored!

`IOResult` returns zero for a successful operation; a nonzero value indicates an error has occurred. The possible return codes are given in table 13.1.

Table 13.1. *Possible Return Codes of* IOResult

Category	Value	Meaning
DOS Errors	0	NO ERROR
	2	File not found
	3	Path not found
	4	Too many open files
	5	File access denied
	6	Invalid file handle
	12	Invalid file access code
	15	Invalid drive number
	16	Cannot remove current directory
	17	Cannot rename across drives

Table 13.1 continues

Table 13.1 *continued*

Category	Value	Meaning
I/O Errors	100	Disk read error
	101	Disk write error
	102	File not assigned
	103	File not open
	104	File not open for input
	105	File not open for output
	106	Invalid numeric format
Critical Errors	150	Disk is write-protected
	151	Unknown unit
	152	Drive not ready
	153	Unknown command
	154	CRC error in data
	155	Bad drive request structure length
	156	Disk seek error
	157	Unknown media type
	158	Sector not found
	159	Printer out of paper
	160	Device write fault
	161	Device read fault
	162	Hardware failure

Your DOS programmer's reference manual and Appendix D of the Turbo Pascal *Reference Guide* contain more information on the actual causes of these errors. But don't despair. Unless you are trying to detect a specific type of error, it's usually enough to test for a nonzero value. For example, to append to an existing file or, alternatively, to create a new file, you can use the following code:

```
      Assign( InfoFile, FileName );
{$I-} Append( InfoFile ); {$I +}
      if IOResult <> Ø then
         Rewrite( InfoFile );
```

Here, any error that results from a failure of the Append procedure is *most likely* a nonexistent file. Of course, if the file does exist but is write protected, the Rewrite procedure *will* generate a fatal run-time error. Similarly, if you perform I/O checking after both the Append and the Rewrite procedures but don't test each subsequent write or writeln, a fatal run-time error will result from using up all remaining space on the disk. Obviously, you have to use some judgment.

Note that once IOResult is called, the error code is reset to zero. If you need to use the same value of IOResult in more than one place, you should first assign it to an integer variable, as follows:

```
ErrorCode := IOResult;
if ErrorCode = 2 then
   writeln( 'File not found.' )
else if ErrorCode = 3 then
   writeln( 'Path not found.' );
```

The most common use of IOResult is simply to ensure that a file is successfully opened. The NEWTYPE2 program in listing 13.12 slightly modifies the NEWTYPE program to terminate gracefully if the specified file can't be found.

Listing 13.12

```
program NewType2;
uses Crt;
var
   TextFile          : Text;
   IndividualCharacter : char;
   Buffer            : array [ 1..1024 ] of char;    { A full cluster }
begin
   if ParamCount = 1 then begin
      Assign( TextFile, ParamStr( 1 ) );
      SetTextBuf( TextFile, Buffer );       { Assumes all 1,024 characters }
{$I-}
      Reset( TextFile );
{$I +}
      if IOResult <> 0 then
         writeln( ParamStr( 1 ), ' wasn''t found.' )
      else begin
         while not Eof( TextFile ) do begin
            ClrScr;
            while (WhereY <> 24) and (not Eof( TextFile )) do begin
               read( TextFile, IndividualCharacter );
               write( IndividualCharacter );
            end;
            readln;
         end;
      end;
   end;
end.
```

> **The IOResult Function**
>
> You will notice from the contents of table 13.1 that IOResult can detect more than just file errors. The function is described more extensively in the next chapter, which discusses directory operations.
>
> Most of the programs in this book don't use I/O checking in order to save space. However, you should remember that IOResult could be used in *any* program that contains input or output. See the discussion of the {$I} compiler directive in the reference section of this book for further examples.

Typed Files

A *typed* file contains data of the type named in the file declaration. In the following example, the files F1, F2, F3, and F4 are all declared as typed files.

```
type
    CustomerRecord = record
                        Name        : string[ 3Ø ];
                        AcctNumber  : longint;
                        CreditLimit :  real;
                    end;
var
   F1 : file of byte;
   F2 : file of CustomerRecord;
   F3 : file of char;
   F4 : file of real;
```

Accessing a typed file is extremely fast because the compiler can assume that its contents consist entirely of data of the declared type. Specifically, Turbo Pascal assumes that all data items in a typed file are stored in *exactly* the same format as when they're stored in RAM.

Reading from Typed Files

The data elements in a typed file are not stored with any separating end-of-line characters. Consequently, the readln and writeln procedures can't be used; read and write must be used exclusively.

This is an example of how a Text file differs from a *file of char*.

Writing to Typed Files

The best way to see the difference between text and typed files is with examples. The FILECMP program in listing 13.13 writes a single word to both a text file and a typed file.

Listing 13.13

```
program FileCmp;
var
   TextFile  : text;
   TypedFile : file of word;
   Value     : word;
begin
   Assign( TextFile, 'File1.txt' );
   Rewrite( TextFile );
   Assign( TypedFile, 'File1.typ' );
   Rewrite( TypedFile );
   Value := $9AE5;
   write( Value );
   write( TextFile, Value );
   write( TypedFile, Value );
   Close( TextFile );
   Close( TypedFile );
end.
```

The characters $9AE5 translate to 39,653 in decimal. If, after FILECMP executes, you use the DUMP program to view the contents of the FILE1.TXT file, you see the display shown in figure 13.13. In a text file, the number is stored as the five ASCII characters for *3, 9, 6, 5,* and *3*—that is, bytes $33, $39, $36, $35, and $33.

Next, if you apply the DUMP program to view the contents of the FILE1.TYP file, you obtain the display in figure 13.14. (Remember that DOS swaps the high and low bytes in a word.)

A time-consuming conversion process must take place before data items can be exchanged between text files and internal memory. Data from typed files avoid this time and effort.

If you are familiar with the BASIC programming language, you can follow this comparison: Pascal's text files correspond to BASIC's ASCII files, and Pascal's typed files correspond to BASIC's binary files.

Now look at what happens with string variables. The FILECMP1 program in listing 13.14 compares string output in text and typed files.

Fig. 13.13. A dump of the FILE1.TXT file, produced by the FILECMP program.

```
 file1.txt                  Page  1 of  1                      5 bytes

33393635 33                                        39653
```

Fig. 13.14. A dump of the FILE1.TYP file, produced by the FILECMP program.

```
 file1.typ                  Page  1 of  1                      2 bytes

E59A                                         σü
```

Listing 13.14

```
program FileCmp1;
var
   TextFile  : text;
   TypedFile : file of string;
   Message   : string;
begin
   Assign( TextFile, 'File1.txt' );
   Rewrite( TextFile );
   Assign( TypedFile, 'File1.typ' );
   Rewrite( TypedFile );
   Message := 'This message is 35 characters long.';
   write( Message );
   write( TextFile, Message );
   write( TypedFile, Message );
   Close( TextFile );
   Close( TypedFile );
end.
```

After FILECMP1 executes, the new contents of the FILE1.TXT file can be examined with DUMP. As shown in figure 13.15, the text file contains only the 35 characters representing the *contents* of the string. The new FILE1.TYP file is shown in figure 13.16. The typed file holds the *entire* string: the leading byte containing the size of the active portion (hexadecimal $23 is decimal 35); the 35 character message itself; and, finally, 220 bytes of garbage.

Fig. 13.15. *A dump of the FILE1.TXT file, produced by the FILECMP1 program.*

```
 file1.txt                        Page  1 of 1                  35 bytes

54686973 206D6573 73616765 20697320 33352063 68617261  This message is 35 chara
63746572 73206C6F 6E672E                               cters long.
```

Fig. 13.16. *A dump of the FILE1.TYP file, produced by the FILECMP1 program.*

```
┌────────────────────────────────────────────────────────────────────┐
│ file1.typ                    Page  1 of 1                256 bytes  │
├────────────────────────────────────────────────────────────────────┤
│23546869 73206D65 73736167 65206973 20333520 63686172 #This message is 35 char│
│61637465 7273206C 6F6E672E 00000000 00000000 00000000 acters long.   │
│00000000 00000000 00000000 00000000 00000000 00000000                │
│00000000 00000000 00000000 00000000 00000000 00000000                │
│00000000 00000000 00000000 00000000 00000000 00000000                │
│00000000 00000000 00000000 04B09C5B 110C4649 4C45434D    ♦▌£[◄♀FILECM │
│50312E50 41530000 00000000 00000000 00000000 00000000 P1.PAS         │
│00000600 38000700 40000800 4F000A00 5E000B00 6D000D00    ♠ 8  @  0  ^ δ m│
│00000F00 93001000 AF001100 CB001300 E2001400 F1001500 ç * ô ► » ◄ ╥ ‼ Γ ¶ ± § ▌│
│0001672E 9A000000 005589E5 BF00001E 57BF0000 0E579A00 ☺g.ü  Uëσ┐  ▲W┐ ╥Wü│
│000000BF 00001E57 9A000000 009A0000                      ┐  ▲Wü  ü    │
└────────────────────────────────────────────────────────────────────┘
```

Untyped Files

A file is declared *untyped* when you absolutely don't care about its contents. Data from an untyped file can be input directly into any variable of any type. Similarly, you can output to an untyped file from any variable of any type.

It might seem initially as though an untyped file has the same properties as a text file, but there are three major differences between them:

❑ The text file input and output procedures read, readln, write, and writeln can't be used on untyped files. Instead, two new procedures—BlockRead and BlockWrite, discussed in the next section —must be used.

❑ By default, text files use a 128 byte buffer for transferring data between main memory and disk. If you use the SetTextBuf procedure, you can specify your own buffer area. Untyped files don't use any buffers at all. All data transfers are made directly between the disk and a specified memory area. This saves memory space, as well as the time it takes to move data to and from the buffer.

❑ When writing data from memory to a text file, data items are converted from binary to ASCII format. Similarly, when reading data from a text file to memory, data items are converted from ASCII format to binary. No such conversion process is performed on an untyped file. In fact, no type checking of any kind is performed.

Declaring and Opening an Untyped File

An untyped file is declared with the reserved word File and nothing more. For example:

```
var
    UnTypedFile : File;
```

Untyped files can be opened only with Reset or Rewrite.

Blocking Data

The BlockRead and BlockWrite procedures are designed to transfer data in large chunks, more properly called *blocks*. A block can be any size, but defaults to 128 bytes. The syntax of BlockRead and BlockWrite is as follows:

```
BlockRead( var F: file; var Buffer; Count: word; [; var Result: word] );
BlockWrite( var F: file; var Buffer; Count: word; [; var Result: word] );
```

BlockRead inputs Count blocks from the untyped file F. The data is assigned to the variable specified by Buffer. The actual number of blocks read is returned in the optional parameter Result.

BlockWrite outputs Count blocks to the untyped file F. The data is read from the variable specified by Buffer. The actual number of blocks output is returned in the optional parameter Result.

If Result isn't specified, the compiler generates an I/O error if the actual number of blocks transferred was less than Count. Therefore, if Result is equal to Count, all of the blocks were processed successfully.

Setting the Size of a Block

BlockRead and BlockWrite can handle only *complete* blocks. Partially filled blocks will not be transferred. Consequently, it's important to choose a block size that divides evenly into the size of the data you are working with.

Because few files are obliging enough to contain exact multiples of the default block size of 128 bytes, it would be helpful to reset the block size to something more general, such as 1. Fortunately, the Reset and Rewrite procedures offer a record size parameter that enables you to choose the length of a block in an untyped file.

The syntax for untyped files is:

```
Reset( UntypedFileIdentifier, RecSize );
Rewrite( UntypedFileIdentifier, RecSize );
```

Although RecSize can be any value from 1 up through 65,535, using 1 is the safest choice for most applications.

Block versus Record

For untyped files, the terms *block* and *record* are sometimes used interchangeably. *Block* is more precise, because it refers to a *chunk* of a file without regard for its content. *Record* implies that the data has the same structure as found in a Pascal Record type. Unfortunately, *record* is one of those words with multiple meanings. Computer people have always referred to any group of bytes read from or written to a file at the same time as a *logical record*.

The QUIKCOPY program in listing 13.15 demonstrates how BlockRead and BlockWrite are used. QUIKCOPY is a simpler version of the DOS COPY utility. Two file names are read from the command line; the contents of the first file are copied to the second.

Listing 13.15

```
program QuikCopy;
var
    InFile, OutFile : file;
    Buffer          : array [ 1..512 ] of char;
    NumberRead, NumberWritten : word;
begin
    if ParamCount  <> 2 then Halt( 1 );
    Assign( InFile, ParamStr( 1 ) );
    Reset( InFile, 1 );
    Assign( OutFile, ParamStr( 2 ) );
    Rewrite( OutFile, 1 );
    repeat
        BlockRead( InFile, Buffer, SizeOf( Buffer ), NumberRead );
        BlockWrite( OutFile, Buffer, NumberRead, NumberWritten );
    until (NumberRead = 0) or (NumberRead <> NumberWritten);
    Close( InFile );
    Close( OutFile );
end.
```

Notice how both the Reset and Rewrite procedures open files with a block size equal to 1 byte. The test

```
until (NumberRead = Ø) or (NumberRead <> NumberWritten);
```

serves several purposes. After the first loop, NumberRead would be equal to zero only if no block had been successfully read—a situation that could occur only if the input file was empty. Similarly, later in the program, NumberRead equals zero when no more records remain—that is, when the file is empty. The second condition, NumberRead <> NumberWritten, can be true only if a disk write error occurred.

Moving Data to Internal Memory

One of the most common uses of the block transfer commands is to move data rapidly between internal memory and the disk. Here are two programs that demonstrate how this is done.

The SEE program in listing 13.16 uses BlockRead to transfer a selected file onto the heap. Once there, its contents can be scanned conveniently and displayed to the screen a page at a time. Unlike the NEWTYPE and NEWTYPE2 programs presented earlier in the chapter, SEE actually enables you to page *backward* and even provides for directly returning to the first page.

Listing 13.16

```
program See;
uses Crt, Dos;
const
   EndProg    : Boolean = False;
   PageIndex : word = 1;
var
   InFile                   : file;
   FileArea                 : pointer;
   Size, Result, MemSeg, i : word;
   Pages                    : array[ 1..2ØØ ] of word;
   ch                       : char;
begin
   if ParamCount = Ø then Halt( 1 );
   Assign( InFile, ParamStr( 1 ) );
   Reset( InFile, 1 );
   Size := FileSize( InFile );
   GetMem( FileArea, Size );
   MemSeg := Seg( FileArea^ );
```

Listing 13.16 continues

Listing 13.16 continued

```
   BlockRead( InFile, FileArea^, Size, Result );
   FillChar( Pages, SizeOf( Pages ), Ø );
   repeat
     ClrScr;
     i := Pages[ PageIndex ];
     repeat
       write( Chr( Mem[ MemSeg:i ] ) );
       Inc( i );
     until (i = Size) or (WhereY = 25);
     repeat
       ch := ReadKey;
       if ch = #27 then
          EndProg := True
       else if ch = #Ø then
          case ReadKey of
              #71 : PageIndex := 1;              { Home }
              #73 : if PageIndex > 1 then        { PgUp }
                       Dec( PageIndex );
              #81 : if i < Size then begin       { PgDn }
                       Inc( PageIndex );
                       Pages[ PageIndex ] := i;
                     end;
            else ch := #255;
          end;
     until (ch = #Ø) or EndProg;
   until EndProg;
   Close( InFile );
 end.
```

The FileSize function (discussed in greater detail in the next chapter) returns the number of bytes in the input file. Knowing this, SEE is able to reserve a suitable area on the heap. After the file is transferred, its first page is displayed on the screen. The Home, PgUp, and PgDn keys control the next screen to be displayed. You can terminate the program by pressing the Esc key.

SEE is designed principally for viewing text files such as program source code. Lines longer than 80 characters are wrapped around to the next line. Because of this feature, SEE doesn't know in advance how many lines of text will fill a screen; consequently, the WhereY = 25 test determines page breaks.

The DUMP program in listing 13.17 expands on these ideas. DUMP is the program we used earlier in the chapter to view the contents of both text and binary files. The program displays data in both hexadecimal and character format.

Listing 13.17

```
program Dump;
uses Crt, Dos;
const
    EndProg    : Boolean = False;
    PageIndex : word = 1;
    Displayed : word = 456;
var
    InFile                    : file;
    FileArea                  : pointer;
    Size, Result, MemSeg, i, j,
    DisplaySize, LineSize,
    MaxPages                  : word;
    Pages                     : array[ 1..200 ] of word;
    ch                        : char;
    FileName                  : string;
    DisplayLine               : array [ 1..24 ] of byte;
function CreateHex( binary_form : byte ) : char;
begin
    case binary_form of
        0..9   : CreateHex := chr( binary_form + 48 );
        10..15 : CreateHex := chr( binary_form + 55 );
    end;
end;
procedure horizon( left, right : char );
begin
    write( left );
    for i := 1 to 78 do write( #205 );
    write( right );
end;
procedure MakeBorder;
begin
    ClrScr;
    horizon( #201, #187 );
    write( #186, ' ' );
    write( FileName );
    GotoXY( 67, 2 ); write( Size:6, ' bytes' );
    GotoXY( 80, 2 ); write( #186 );
    horizon( #204, #185 );
    for i := 4 to 23 do begin
        GotoXY(  1, i );  write( #186 );
        GotoXY( 80, i );  write( #186 );
    end;
    GotoXY( 1, 24 );
    horizon( #200, #188 );
end;
begin
    if ParamCount = 0 then Halt( 1 );
    FileName := ParamStr(  1 );
```

Listing 13.17 continues

```
Assign( InFile, FileName );
Reset( InFile, 1 );
Size := FileSize( InFile );
MakeBorder;
GetMem( FileArea, Size );
MemSeg := Seg( FileArea^ );
BlockRead( InFile, FileArea^, Size, Result );
MaxPages := (Size div Displayed) + 1;
for i := 1 to MaxPages do
   Pages[ i ] := (i - 1) * Displayed;
GotoXY( 33, 2 );
write( 'Page  1 of ', MaxPages );
Window( 2, 4, 79, 23 );
repeat
   ClrScr;
   i := Pages[ PageIndex ];
   repeat
      LineSize := 0;
      repeat
         Inc( LineSize );
         DisplayLine[ LineSize ] := Mem[ MemSeg:i ];
         Inc( i );
      until (LineSize = 24) or (i = Size);
      for j := 1 to LineSize do begin
         write( CreateHex( DisplayLine[ j ] div 16 ),
               CreateHex( DisplayLine[ j ] mod 16 )  );
         if j mod 4 = 0 then write( ' ' );
      end;
      for j := LineSize + 1 to 24 do begin
         write( '  ' );
         DisplayLine[ j ] := ord( ' ' );
         if j mod 4 = 0 then write( ' ' );
      end;
      for j := 1 to 24 do
         if DisplayLine[ j ] in [ 7, 8, 10, 13 ] then
            write( ' ' )
         else
            write( chr( DisplayLine[ j ] ) );
   until (i=Size) or (i >= Pages[ PageIndex + 1 ]);
   repeat
      ch := ReadKey;
      if ch = #27 then
         EndProg := True
      else if ch = #0 then
         case ReadKey of
```

Listing 13.17 continues

Listing 13.17 continued

```
                #71 : PageIndex := 1;              { Home }
                #73 : if PageIndex > 1 then        { PgUp }
                         Dec( PageIndex );
                #81 : if i  < Size then            { PgDn }
                         Inc( PageIndex );
                #79 : PageIndex := MaxPages;       { End }
                else ch := #255;
              end;
              Window( 1, 1, 80, 25 );
              GotoXY( 37, 2 );
              write( PageIndex:3 );
              Window( 2, 4, 79, 23 );
          until (ch = #0) or EndProg;
        until EndProg;
        Window( 1, 1, 80, 25 );
        GotoXY( 1, 25 );
      end.
```

Here again, BlockRead is used to copy a file to the heap. But this time, the program displays the contents continuously, without starting new lines after each carriage return. You know at once how many screens will be needed. Consequently, in addition to the Home, PgUp, and PgDn keys, the End key is also available. You can terminate the program by pressing the Esc key.

Using DUMP on its own source file, with the command:

DUMP DUMP.PAS

produces the screen shown in figure 13.17.

Both SEE and DUMP are extremely useful programming utilities.

Random Access Files

Files can be processed either sequentially or randomly. In a *sequential* file, you can only read characters starting from the beginning of the file, and you can only write characters after the current position of the file pointer. In a *random* file, each record may be read from or written to without regard for its position in the file.

Sequential files are used when their data will always be processed in a specific order or when (as with SEE and DUMP) the file needs to be manipulated in its entirety. However, random processing is essential when information must be rapidly retrieved from or stored to the middle of a large file; sequential processing would simply take too much time.

Fig. 13.17. *A dump of the DUMP program itself.*

```
┌─────────────────────────────────────────────────────────────────────────┐
│ dump.pas                    Page   1 of 8                    3418 bytes   │
├─────────────────────────────────────────────────────────────────────────┤
│70726F67 72616D20 44756D70 3B0D0A75 73657320 4372742C  program Dump;  uses Crt,│
│20446F73 3B0D0A63 6F6E7374 0D0A2020 20456E64 50726F67  Dos;  const      EndProg│
│2020203A 20426F6F 6C65616E 203D2046 616C7365 3B0D0A20     : Boolean = False;   │
│20205061 6765496E 64657820 3A20776F 7264203D 20313B0D    PageIndex : word = 1; │
│0A202020 44697370 6C617965 64203A20 776F7264 203D2034    Displayed : word = 4  │
│35363B0D 0A766172 0D0A2020 20496E46 696C6520 20202020  56; var    InFile       │
│20202020 20202020 20202020 203A2066 696C653B           : file;│
│0D0A2020 2046696C 65417265 61202020 20202020 20202020        FileArea          │
│20202020 20202020 203A2070 6F696E74 65723B0D 0A202020                : pointer; │
│53697A65 2C205265 73756C74 2C204D65 6D536567 2C20692C  Size, Result, MemSeg, i,│
│206A2C0D 0A202020 44697370 6C617953 697A652C 204C696E   j,   DisplaySize, Lin│
│6553697A 652C0D0A 2020204D 61785061 67657320 20202020  eSize,    MaxPages      │
│20202020 20202020 20202020 203A2020 20776F72 643B0D0A              :   word;│
│20202020 61676573 20202020 20202020 20202020 20202020      Pages             │
│20202020 2020203A 20617272 61795B20 312E2E32 3030205D          : array[ 1..200 ]│
│206F6620 776F7264 3B0D0A20 20206368 20202020 20202020  of word;    ch          │
│20202020 20202020 20202020 20202020 20203A20 63686172                   : char │
│3B0D0A20 20204669 6C654E61 6D652020 20202020 20202020  ;    FileName           │
│20202020 20202020 20203A20 73747269 6E673B0D 0A202020            : string;│
└─────────────────────────────────────────────────────────────────────────┘
```

Text files are strictly sequential. Because each line in a text file may be a different length, you couldn't guarantee that a new line written to the middle of the file would have exactly the same length as the line it replaced. If the new line was longer, the overlap would corrupt other lines around it. If the new line was shorter, part of the original line would be unaffected.

On the other hand, typed and untyped files always process identically sized records. By positioning the file pointer to any desired record, you can read from or write to the file in any order you wish.

Typed files and untyped files can always be both read and written to regardless of whether they were opened with Reset or Rewrite.

Accessing Records Randomly

The Seek procedure is used to position the file pointer to a specific record. This procedure accepts as a parameter the desired record number. The first record number in the file is zero.

(If you ever need to know where you are in a file, you can use the FilePos function to learn the record number of the current file position.)

The MAKERAND program (listing 13.18) demonstrates how random file accessing works.

Listing 13.18

```
program MakeRand;
uses Crt;
type
    String20 = string[ 20 ];
    PassengerRecord = record
                        LastName : String20;
                        FlightNo : word;
                        AirFare  : real;
                      end;

var
    Passenger   : PassengerRecord;
    PassFile    : file of PassengerRecord;
    Who, Change : char;
procedure ClearBottomLines;
begin
    GotoXY( 1, 23 );    ClrEol;
    GotoXY( 1, 24 );    ClrEol;
    GotoXY( 1, 25 );    ClrEol;
    GotoXY( 1, 24 );
end;
procedure MakeReservation( LastNameIn : String20;
                           FlightNoIn : word;
                           AirFareIn  : real );

begin
    with Passenger do begin
        LastName := LastNameIn;
        FlightNo := FlightNoIn;
        AirFare  := AirFareIn;
        write( PassFile, Passenger );
    end;
end;
procedure ConfirmReservation;
begin
    ClrScr;
    Seek( PassFile, Ord( UpCase( Who ) ) - 65 );
    read( PassFile, Passenger );
    with Passenger do begin
        GotoXY( 20, 10 );    write( '   Last Name : ', LastName );
        GotoXY( 20, 12 );    write( 'Flight Number : ', FlightNo );
        GotoXY( 20, 14 );    write( '    Air Fare : ', AirFare:0:2 );
    end;
    ClearBottomLines;
end;
procedure ChangeReservation;
var
    Modifier : byte;
begin
    ClearBottomLines;
```

Listing 13.18 continues

Listing 13.18 continued

```pascal
            write( 'Change:  (1) Flight Number   (2) AirFare   (3) No change  ' );
            readln( Modifier );
            with Passenger do begin
                case Modifier of
                    1 : begin
                            GotoXY( 36, 12 );
                            readln( FlightNo );
                        end;
                    2 : begin
                            GotoXY( 36, 14 );
                            readln( AirFare );
                        end;
                end;
                if Modifier - 1  < 2 then begin
                    Seek( PassFile, Ord( UpCase( Who ) ) - 65 );
                    write( PassFile, Passenger );
                    ConfirmReservation;
                end;
            end;
            ClearBottomLines;
    end;
begin
    Assign( PassFile, 'PassData.Dat' );
    Rewrite( PassFile );
    MakeReservation( 'Adams',    174,    456.72 );
    MakeReservation( 'Baker',    392,    893.21 );
    MakeReservation( 'Charles', 263,    765.38 );
    MakeReservation( 'Dover',    551, 1298.43 );
    MakeReservation( 'Edwards', 290,     99.99 );
    MakeReservation( 'Finch',    327,    223.64 );
    Reset( PassFile );
    ClrScr;
    repeat
        repeat
            GotoXY( 1, 1 );
            writeln( 'Enter the first letter of the last name' );
            write( 'or enter ''X'' to exit the program: ' );
            readln( Who );
        until UpCase( Who ) in [ 'A'..'F', 'X' ];
        if UpCase( Who ) <> 'X' then begin
            ConfirmReservation;
            repeat
                write( 'Change (Y/N)? ' );
                readln( Change );
                ClearBottomLines;
            until UpCase( Change ) in [ 'Y', 'N' ];
            if UpCase( Change ) = 'Y' then
                ChangeReservation;
        end;
    until UpCase( Who ) = 'X';
end.
```

MAKERAND uses the MakeReservation procedure to create a typed file containing airline reservation records. The six people supported conveniently have last names starting with unique letters of the alphabet. The ChangeReservation procedure contains code to retrieve a record at random, change its contents, and replace the new record back in the file. Notice how the Seek procedure uses the last name of the passenger to automatically determine which record to access.

The opening screen is shown in figure 13.18. Requesting B (for Baker) results in the display shown in figure 13.19.

Fig. 13.18. *The opening screen of the MAKERAND program.*

```
        Enter the first letter of the last name
        or enter 'X' to exit the program:
```

Fig. 13.19. *The contents of the second record in the PASSDATA.DAT file as displayed by the MAKERAND program.*

```
                              Last Name : Baker
                          Flight Number : 392
                               Air Fare : 893.21




        Change (Y/N)?
```

The contents of the record can be changed at will, then recalled to confirm that the modification actually took place.

Although MAKERAND uses a typed file of records, other useful applications can be created, for example, from files of bytes, reals, and Booleans.

Appending and Truncating Typed and Untyped Files

Although typed and untyped files opened with Reset or Rewrite can be read from or written to at your discretion, they cannot be opened for Append. Instead, a small trick is required.

The command

```
Seek( FileID, FileSize( FileID ) );
```

positions the file pointer one record *beyond* the end of the file. Using this line causes all subsequent write or BlockWrite procedures to append their data to the existing file.

You can use the Truncate procedure to truncate a typed or untyped file past the current position of the file pointer.

Summary

In this chapter, you have learned that the Turbo Pascal compiler supports three *logical* file types, named for the syntax of their declarations: text, typed, and untyped. A *text file* contains lines of characters terminated by a carriage return and a line feed. A *typed file* contains only data of the one particular type named in its declaration. An *untyped file* is completely unstructured and may contain any data in any format in any length. You have seen examples of how each of these three file types are used.

You have learned how to relate a *logical* file in your program with a *physical* file on disk. You have seen how to open a file for input or output and how to close a file when your program is finished with it. You have learned a variety of ways to exchange formatted and unformatted data between your program and the disk. You have learned how to bypass separators in text files, and you have seen how records in typed and untyped files can be processed randomly.

You have learned how to test for I/O errors and how to recover from them.

Table 13.2 contains the procedures and functions presented in this chapter together with a summary of the file types with which the subroutines can be used.

Table 13.2. Turbo Pascal File Subroutines

Category	Subroutine	Text	Typed	Untyped
File Opening	Append	Yes	No	No
	Assign	Yes	Yes	Yes
	Reset	Yes	Yes	Yes
	Rewrite	Yes	Yes	Yes
	Close	Yes	Yes	Yes
File Input	BlockRead	No	No	Yes
	Read	Yes	Yes	No
	Readln	Yes	No	No
File Output	BlockWrite	No	No	Yes
	Write	Yes	Yes	No
	Writeln	Yes	No	No
Location Tests	Eof	Yes	Yes	Yes
	Eoln	Yes	No	No
	SeekEof	Yes	No	No
	SeekEoln	Yes	No	No
Random Access	FilePos	No	Yes	Yes
	FileSize	No	Yes	Yes
	Seek	No	Yes	Yes
	Truncate	No	Yes	Yes

This chapter presented many of these subroutines in the form of utilities that you will find yourself using throughout the remainder of the book.

CHAPTER 14

Directory Handling

M any problems can arise when you work with files. A program and its data file can be stored in different directories or on completely different drives; both need to be located, no matter where they are. Programs can crash when you run out of disk space. Files might need to be created in or erased from a particular subdirectory. You may want to create new file names automatically.

In the last chapter, you saw how to use files to store and retrieve information. This chapter approaches files from the other direction—as residents of disk drives and directories.

Disk Drive Specifications

The DiskSize function returns the total number of bytes that can be stored on the specified drive. The disk may be any type, from a microfloppy through a mammoth hard disk. DiskFree returns its free space (that is, the number of unused bytes available for use).

Both functions take a single, byte-sized parameter to indicate the drive: 1 for drive A:, 2 for drive B:, and so on. The default drive is specified by setting the parameter to 0.

The DISK1 program (listing 14.1) describes space usage on the default drive.

Listing 14.1

```
program Disk1;
uses Dos;
var
   BytesFree,
   TotalSize,
   Utilization : longint;
begin
   BytesFree := DiskFree( Ø );
   TotalSize := DiskSize( Ø );
   Utilization := 1ØØ - (BytesFree * 1ØØ div TotalSize);
   writeln( 'The default drive has ',
            BytesFree, ' bytes free out of ',
            TotalSize, ' for ',
            Utilization, '% utilization.' );
end.
```

If the specified drive is invalid (if you specify drive 45, for example) or unavailable (such as when drive 1 is specified, but no floppy is inserted), the functions return –1. Program DISK2 (listing 14.2) uses this property to develop a simple drive availability function.

Listing 14.2

```
program Disk2;
uses Dos;
function DriveInUse( DriveNumber : byte ) : boolean;
begin
   DriveInUse := DiskSize( DriveNumber ) > Ø;
end;
begin
   if DriveInUse( 1 ) then
      writeln( 'Begin processing.' )
   else
      writeln( 'Please insert a formatted floppy disk.' );
end.
```

Directories

It's common for programs to access files on other drives and directories. A program may, for example, reside in a utility directory accessed through your system path, whereas your data files are in the current directory. Conversely, you may restrict an application to executing in only one directory or to direct all of its output to a single directory.

Turbo Pascal provides several directory management functions to completely control directory access.

Determining the Current Directory

The Turbo Pascal GetDir procedure enables you to determine the currently active directory for any drive. GetDir accepts two parameters, the drive number (again, 0 for the default, 1 for drive A:, 2 for drive B:, and so on) and a string to contain the directory name when the procedure is finished. Because an I/O error can result if GetDir is unsuccessful, IOResult should be tested. Program DIR1 (listing 14.3) returns the name of the active directory on the disk drive specified in the command line. Compile the program to disk and execute it from DOS.

Listing 14.3

```
program Dir1;
{$I- I/O error checking is now disabled }
var
    CurrentDirectory : string;
    Drive : byte;
    CmdCode : integer;
begin
    if ParamCount = Ø then
        Drive := Ø
    else
        Val( ParamStr( 1 ), Drive, CmdCode );
    if CmdCode <> Ø then
        writeln( 'A drive number must be specified' )
    else begin
        GetDir( Drive, CurrentDirectory );
        if IOResult = Ø then
            writeln( 'The current directory is ', CurrentDirectory )
        else
            writeln( 'Directory not found' );
    end;
end.
```

When executed, DIR1 may return the following:

The current directory is C:\payroll\data

Notice that the letter of the drive is always included as the first character of the path name. As a consequence, you can identify the current drive by calling GetDir for drive Ø.

Changing the Current Directory

When a program is executing, it resides entirely in internal memory, completely independent of the current drive or directory. Consequently, a program can change both the default drive and directory without adversely affecting its execution. In Turbo Pascal, this is accomplished with the ChDir procedure.

ChDir is called with a string containing the complete name of the new path. The letter of the drive must be included. Because an I/O error results if ChDir is unsuccessful, IOResult should be used to test that the change has occurred.

The DIR2 program (listing 14.4) is a useful routine that uses GetDir to determine the current directory, then changes the default to the directory one level up.

Listing 14.4

```
program Dir2;
var
   CurrentDirectory : string;
   i : byte;
begin
   GetDir( Ø, CurrentDirectory );
   writeln( 'The current directory is ', CurrentDirectory );
   i := Length( CurrentDirectory );
   while CurrentDirectory[ i ] <> '\' do i := i - 1;
   if i > 3 then
      begin
         CurrentDirectory[ Ø ] := chr( i - 1 );
         ChDir( CurrentDirectory );
         writeln( 'The new directory is ', CurrentDirectory );
      end
   else
      writeln( 'Already at root directory!' );
end.
```

For example, the directory may change as follows:

```
The current directory is C:\finance\payroll\data
The new directory is C:\finance\payroll
```

Because you knew that the requested directory existed, you didn't bother to perform the IOResult test.

Creating a New Directory

Sometimes, however, a directory doesn't already exist and must be created. The MkDir procedure can solve this problem. MkDir is called with a string containing the complete path name of the directory to be made, including the letter of the drive. An I/O error will result if the procedure is unsuccessful. You can test IOResult to see if the new directory has been successfully created, and you can use the ChDir procedure to enter it.

The DIR3 program (listing 14.5) creates and then enters a temporary directory one level lower than the current directory. If such a directory already exists, an error message is produced.

Listing 14.5

```
program Dir3;
{$I- I/O checking is disabled}
var
   CurrentDirectory : string;
begin
   GetDir( 0, CurrentDirectory );
   writeln( 'The current directory is ', CurrentDirectory );
   CurrentDirectory := CurrentDirectory + '\TEMP';
   MkDir( CurrentDirectory );
   if IOResult <> 0 then
      writeln( CurrentDirectory, ' already exists.' )
   else begin
      ChDir( CurrentDirectory );
      writeln( 'The new directory is ', CurrentDirectory );
   end;
end.
```

For example, executing DIR3 in the C:\FINANCE\PAYROLL directory results in the following:

```
The current directory is C:\FINANCE\PAYROLL
The new directory is C:\FINANCE\PAYROLL\TEMP
```

Removing a Directory

The Turbo Pascal RmDir procedure can remove the temporary directory once you are finished with it. (Actually, you may want to remove several levels of temporary directories, depending on how many times you ran DIR3.)

Just like its DOS equivalent, RmDir requires that the directory be completely empty with no files or subordinate directories. Also, the directory to be removed can't be the current directory. RmDir is called with a string containing the complete path name and, like ChDir and MkDir, can result in an I/O error if unsuccessful.

You can use the DIR4 program (listing 14.6) to bump up your current directory by one level and to remove the original directory, provided it doesn't contain any files.

Listing 14.6

```
program Dir4;
{$I- I/O checking is disabled}
var
   OldDirectory,
   CurrentDirectory : string;
   i : byte;
begin
   GetDir( 0, CurrentDirectory );
   writeln( 'The current directory is ', CurrentDirectory );
   i := Length( CurrentDirectory );
   if i = 3 then    { Only remove if not the root directory }
      writeln( 'Can''t remove root directory!' )
   else begin
      OldDirectory := CurrentDirectory;
      while CurrentDirectory[ i ] <> '\' do i := i - 1;
      CurrentDirectory[ 0 ] := chr( i - 1 );
      ChDir( CurrentDirectory );
      RmDir( OldDirectory );
      if IOResult = 0 then
         writeln( 'The new directory is ', CurrentDirectory )
      else begin
         writeln( 'Directory not empty!' );
         ChDir( OldDirectory );
      end;
   end;
end.
```

Accessing File Information

Programmers tend to be spoiled by the efficiency of Turbo Pascal. For each use of a file management procedure such as Reset or Rewrite, Turbo must generate instructions to locate the file, reserve buffer space for it, establish pointers, and so on. One Pascal procedure can trigger a dozen tasks.

In fact, these detailed file access instructions are so common at the DOS level that whenever a program looks up an entry in the disk directory, a special record is automatically created in internal memory. This record—called a *file control block (FCB)*—contains such file information as the file's name, total size, time and date of creation, and attribute (discussed later in this chapter).

The file control block has been slightly restructured by Turbo Pascal into the predefined record SearchRec, which allows access to several useful fields.

```
SearchRec = record
              Fill: array[1..21] of Byte;
              Attr: Byte;
              Time: Longint;
              Size: Longint;
              Name: string[12];
            end;
```

The 21-byte filler contains technical details needed by DOS; you should *never* allow your programs to modify it. You will learn about each of the other fields in detail.

Accessing a Directory Entry

The FCB is a record created by DOS and placed as a *reference* in internal memory to provide easy access to directory data. Changing a field in the FCB has no effect on the characteristics of the underlying file, but the change may sufficiently confuse DOS to provoke a run-time error. In order to modify any file characteristics (that is, to change a file's name, attribute, or time stamp) you need special procedures that are discussed in the next section. Reading from or writing to an individual file still requires the use of the Assign, Reset, and Rewrite procedures.

Turbo Pascal provides the FindFirst and FindNext procedures to access the information contained in the FCB. The primary purpose of these procedures is to quickly scan through an entire directory and identify files with certain characteristics.

FindFirst takes three parameters: a target file name, the desired attribute, and the output record of type SearchRec. The target file name is in the same format you would use in a DOS directory call, with wild-card characters permitted. For example, to find all Pascal source files in the current directory, the target file string *.PAS is used. The attribute field is discussed in greater detail in the next section; for now, specify the predefined constant AnyFile.

FindNext uses the output record from the most recent FindFirst call to search for the *next* FCB entry that matches the name and attribute.

Accessing the Name and Size of a File

Within the SearchRec record, the Name field is the DOS file name and extension, separated by a period, without the path or drive designator. The Size field is the size of the file in bytes.

To see how these fields are used, retrieve a set of file control blocks using the FindFirst and FindNext procedures, as demonstrated in the DIR5 program (listing 14.7).

Listing 14.7

```
program Dir5;
uses Dos;
var
   FileInfo : SearchRec;
begin
   FindFirst( 'DIR*.PAS', AnyFile, FileInfo );
   while DosError = Ø do
      begin
         with FileInfo do writeln( Name:14, Size:8 );
         FindNext( FileInfo );
      end;
end.
```

When executed, DIR5 produces a primitive directory listing similar to the following:

```
DIR1.PAS      541
DIR5.PAS      254
DIR2.PAS      514
DIR4.PAS      8Ø4
DIR6.PAS      537
DIR7.PAS      913
DIR8.PAS     1Ø44
DIR9.PAS      376
```

Notice that the `FileInfo` record of type `SearchRec` is used to provide, store, and pass information. It should not be modified in any way.

Accessing the Attribute Byte

Files come in several flavors. A *read-only* file, as the name implies, can only be read; you cannot write to or erase it. A *hidden* file is one that is skipped in normal directory searches (that is, a search that doesn't specifically request that hidden files be included). A *system* file, like a hidden file, is used by DOS and is also skipped in normal directory searches. A file name may be the *volume* name of the disk on which it resides, or it may be the name of a *subdirectory*.

The *attribute byte* describes the type of file and how it can be processed. Each of its bits corresponds to a particular characteristic. More than one of the bits can be set at the same time. The structure of the attribute byte is shown in figure 14.1.

***Fig. 14.1.** The structure of the File Attribute Byte.*

7	6	5	4	3	2	1	0
Reserved for System Use		Archive	Directory Name	Volume Label	System File	Hidden File	Read Only

---

In addition to identifying file types, the attribute byte also tracks a file's archival status. Whenever a file is created or modified, the *archive* bit is set. The bit is set to zero only after a DOS BACKUP operation is performed. Therefore, subsequent BACKUPs can ignore unmodified files.

To help with the process of testing, setting, and clearing the file attribute byte, Turbo predefines several constants that reflect the various bit patterns. Table 14.1 summarizes the constants and their patterns.

***Table 14.1.** File Attribute Constants*

Predefined Constant	Value (Hex)	Bit Pattern
ReadOnly	$01	0000 0001
Hidden	$02	0000 0010
SysFile	$04	0000 0100
VolumeID	$08	0000 1000
Directory	$10	0001 0000
Archive	$20	0010 0000
AnyFile	$3F	0011 1111

For example, to learn the names of all subordinate directories within the current directory, you simply read every FCB and test for the presence of a 1 in bit four (starting from zero) of the attribute byte. In other words, you test if the attribute byte is equal to the predefined variable `Directory`, as shown in program DIR1A (listing 14.8).

Listing 14.8

```
program Dir1A;
uses Dos;
var
   level    : byte;
procedure GetFileData( Path : string );
var
   Path2    : string;
   FileInfo : SearchRec;
   i        : byte;
begin
   level := level + 1;
   FindFirst( Path + '\*.*', Directory, FileInfo );
   while DosError = Ø do
      begin
         if (FileInfo.Attr = Directory ) and
            (FileInfo.Name[ 1 ] <> '.') then begin
            for i := 1 to 12*(level - 1) do write( ' ' );
            writeln( FileInfo.Name );
            Path2 := Path + '\' + FileInfo.Name;
            GetFileData( Path2 );
         end;
         FindNext( FileInfo );
      end;
   level := level - 1;
end;
begin
   level := Ø;
   GetFileData( 'c:' );
end.
```

The DIR1A program uses recursion to produce an indented tree diagram of all directories on drive C: (see fig. 14.2).

When doing comparisons, the Turbo procedures FindFirst and FindNext test whether the *logical AND* of the attribute byte and the predefined constant is nonzero; in other words, the constants are additive. Therefore, to test for *either* a hidden file *or* an archive file, the parameter you pass is (Hidden + Archive). Similarly, if you want every entry except a directory name, you can use (AnyFile - Directory).

Accessing the Time Field

The long integer *Time* contains the packed format of the time and date of the last write operation on the file.

The high-order word is the *date stamp*, which is stored in the format shown in figure 14.3.

Fig. 14.2. Sample output produced by DIR1A.

```
123
TP
            DOC
            EXAMPLES
            TURBO3
TURBOC
            LIB
            LIBRARY
                          INCLUDE
                          CLIB
                          MATH
                          EMU
QUE
            TEXT
                          PIX
            PROGRAMS
WORD
            SAVE

C>
```

Fig. 14.3. The structure of the Date Stamp word.

Bit:	15	14	13	12	11	10	9	8	7	6	5	4	3	2	1	0
Content:	Y	Y	Y	Y	Y	Y	Y	Y	M	M	M	M	D	D	D	D

The parameters of the date stamp are listed in table 14.2.

Table 14.2. Date Stamp Parameters

Code	Bits	Contents	Value
D	0–4	Day of month	1 to 31
M	5–8	Month	1 to 12
Y	9–15	Year	(Year, such as 1980)

The low-order word is the *time stamp*, which is stored in the format shown in figure 14.4.

Fig. 14.4. *The structure of the Time Stamp word.*

Bit:	15	14	13	12	11	10	9	8	7	6	5	4	3	2	1	0
Content:	H	H	H	H	H	M	M	M	M	M	M	S	S	S	S	S

The parameters of the time stamp are listed in table 14.3.

Table 14.3. *Time Stamp Parameters*

Code	Bits	Contents	Value
S	0–4	Number of 2-second increments	0 to 29
M	5–10	Minutes	0 to 59
H	11–15	Hours	0 to 23

Notice that the data are stored in the order of significance. Even without unpacking the fields, two Time variables can be directly compared to determine chronological sequence.

In addition to the FindFirst and FindNext procedures, the *Time* field of a file can be accessed with the GetFTime procedure. Similarly, it can be reset with the SetFTime procedure. Both GetFTime and SetFTime are discussed later in this chapter.

Fortunately, Turbo provides the PackTime procedure to create the packed date and time format from ordinary word-sized variables. Similarly, the packed format can be converted to more manageable word-sized variables with the UnpackTime procedure. PackTime and UnpackTime both expect one long integer parameter and one parameter of the predefined record type DateTime.

```
DateTime = record
        Year,Month,Day,Hour,Min,Sec: Word;
     end;
```

By adding the GetFTime and UnpackTime procedures to the DIR5 program to create DIR6 (listing 14.9), you can test each returned FCB record to find only the files created today. Note that the program assumes that the COM-MAND.COM file is in the root directory on drive C:.

Listing 14.9

```
program Dir6;
{$M 1024,0,0      Minimum memory so Exec can work }
uses Dos;
var
   Year,
   Month,
   Day,
   DayofWeek : word;
   FileInfo  : SearchRec;
   FileDate  : DateTime;
   CmdString : string;
begin
   GetDate( Year, Month, Day, DayofWeek );
   FindFirst( '* *', Archive, FileInfo );
   while DosError = 0 do
      begin
         UnpackTime( FileInfo.Time, FileDate );
         if ( FileDate.Year = Year ) and
            ( FileDate.Month = Month ) and
            ( FileDate.Day = Day ) then
            begin
               write( 'Now copying ', FileInfo.Name );
               CmdString := '/C copy ' + FileInfo.Name + ', a:';
               exec( 'C:\command.com', CmdString );
            end;
         FindNext( FileInfo );
      end;
end.
```

DIR6 is a backup program designed to identify the files created today and copy them to a diskette for safekeeping. When it executes, it copies each file to drive A: and displays progress messages as follows:

```
Now copying DIR10.PAS
        1 File(s) copied
Now copying DISK2.PAS
        1 File(s) copied
Now copying DIR3.EXE
        1 File(s) copied
Now copying DIR3.PAS
        1 File(s) copied
Now copying DIR5.BAK
        1 File(s) copied
Now copying DIR5.PAS
        1 File(s) copied
Now copying DIR6.PAS
        1 File(s) copied
```

Managing Individual Files

In the discussion of the date-and-time stamps, you saw how the FindFirst and FindNext procedures use the file control block to scan a directory and quickly obtain information about several major file characteristics.

Although FindFirst and FindNext are extremely useful for *locating* a set of files, they aren't intended to *manipulate* individual files. Again, information in the FCB is only a reference copy; directory data can be accessed, but none of it can be changed. Furthermore, because most of the time you already know the name of the file you wish to modify, FindFirst and FindNext are unnecessary.

The fields in the FCB were copied from the *disk directory*, the official source of all disk data. The disk directory contains the file name and extension, attribute, date-and-time stamp, and file size. In addition, it contains the technical data DOS needs to physically find the file on the disk.

This section discusses the procedures Turbo Pascal provides to modify the key file characteristics (name, attribute, and date-and-time stamp) found in the disk directory.

Modifying the Time Field

By maintaining the time and date of the last write operation on a file, DOS provides one of the most useful pieces of identifying information next to the file name itself. There is, consequently, only one good reason to change a file's time and date fields: when another program will produce an undesirable result unless the time and date have been modified.

The DIR6 backup program presented in listing 14.9 uses the date of the file to determine whether it should be saved on a floppy disk. To save even more files (and increase your peace of mind), it would be useful to be able to reset the date stamp of selected files to today's date so that DIR6 can capture them as well.

The DIR8 program (listing 14.10) uses PackTime and SetFTime to do just that. First, a comparison date of one month ago is stored in the variable FileTimeCutoff. As each file name is read, its date is tested. If the file was created within the last month, its date and time are reset.

Compile DIR8 to disk and execute it directly from DOS. Entering the command

    DIR8 dir*.pas

ensures that all files created within the last month that match the template dir*.pas will have their date-and-time stamps reset to the current PC clock setting.

Listing 14.10

```
program Dir8;
uses Dos;
var
    Year, Month, Day, DayofWeek  : word;     { GetDate }
    Hour, Minute, Second, Sec100 : word;     { GetTime }
    FileInfo            : SearchRec;
    TimeNow             : DateTime;
    FileTimeThen,
    FileTimeCutoff,
    FileTimeNow         : longint;
    FileReference       : file;
begin
    if ParamCount <> 1 then
        writeln( 'Improper file format' )
    else begin
        GetDate( Year, Month, Day, DayofWeek );
        GetTime( Hour, Minute, Second, Sec100 );
        TimeNow.Year := Year;
        TimeNow.Month := Month;
        TimeNow.Day := Day;
        TimeNow.Hour := Hour;
        TimeNow.Min := Minute;
        TimeNow.Sec := Second;
        PackTime( TimeNow, FileTimeNow );
        if Month = 1 then
            TimeNow.Month := 12
        else
            TimeNow.Month := Month - 1;
        PackTime( TimeNow, FileTimeCutoff );
        FindFirst( ParamStr( 1 ), AnyFile, FileInfo );
        while DosError = 0 do
            begin
                Assign( FileReference, FileInfo.Name );
                Reset( FileReference );
                GetFTime( FileReference, FileTimeThen );
                if FileTimeCutoff < FileTimeThen then begin
                    SetFTime( FileReference, FileTimeNow );
                    writeln( FileInfo.Name:12, ' being modified' );
                end;
                Close( FileReference );
                FindNext( FileInfo );
            end;
    end;
end.
```

Although FindFirst and FindNext were used to identify the desired files, each file had to be individually opened (assigned and reset) before GetFTime and SetFTime could be used. FindFirst and FindNext access the file control block, which is copied from the disk directory; GetFTime and SetFTime access the disk directory itself.

The PackTime and UnpackTime procedures don't perform a range check on the dates you supply them. Similarly, GetFTime and SetFTime don't test the validity of their time-and-date parameters. This means that if you don't care about the details of when a file was created, you have four extra bytes to use at your discretion. You may, for example, have a budgeting application in which several departments send you data for consolidation. Each file on each diskette could have the same name, but you could use the two bytes of the time field to track the number of the originating PC.

Erasing and Renaming a File

Two Turbo Pascal procedures operate directly on the file-name field in the disk directory: Rename and Erase. As their names imply, Rename changes the name of a file; Erase deletes it. Files can be renamed or erased only if the read-only bit of their attribute byte isn't set. Rename and Erase have no effect on directory names.

Renaming is a straightforward action. If the new name isn't already assigned to a file in the directory, DOS writes over the original name field.

Erasing is more subtle. A file is *erased* when the first byte of its name in the directory entry is changed to the special character $E5. Figure 14.5 shows how the name of the PAYROLL.DAT file changes when the file is erased.

Fig. 14.5. *The effect on the directory entry after deleting the PAYROLL.DAT file.*

Before the deletion:

P	A	Y	R	O	L	L		D	A	T

After the deletion:

$E5	A	Y	R	O	L	L		D	A	T

In addition, the file allocation table (FAT) is told that the clusters used by the file are now available for reassignment.

Erasing a File

The Turbo Pascal Erase procedure requires that a file be assigned but doesn't allow it to be opened at the time the erase occurs. You can call Erase within a FindFirst/FindNext loop without affecting the search. The DIR9 program (listing 14.11) erases—perhaps unwisely—all backup files in the current directory.

Listing 14.11

```
program Dir9;
uses Dos;
const
    FileCounter    : word = Ø;
var
    FileInfo      : SearchRec;
    FileReference : file;
begin
    FindFirst( '*.BAK', (AnyFile - Directory), FileInfo );
    while DosError = Ø do
        begin
            writeln( 'Erasing ', FileInfo.Name );
            Assign( FileReference, FileInfo.Name );
            Erase( FileReference );
            Inc( FileCounter );
            FindNext( FileInfo );
        end;
    if FileCounter = Ø then
        writeln( 'No backup files were found.' )
    else
        writeln( FileCounter, ' backup file(s) erased.' );
end.
```

Wiping a File Clean

When DOS scans the disk directory and encounters a file name with $E5 in the first position, it simply ignores it. "Undelete" programs (most notably, the undelete feature of the Norton Utilities™ package) access the disk directory and identify file names with $E5 in their first byte. The file is restored by replacing the first byte with a valid character and telling the FAT that the clusters are again in use.

Therefore, when a file is erased, its contents become *available* for reuse; but until they *are* reused, the contents remain untouched. If the file contains confidential, sensitive, or embarrassing information, it should first be overwritten, then erased. The DIR9A program (listing 14.12) performs such a service. DIR9A takes the complete file name as its only parameter, reads the file byte-by-byte to determine its size, overwrites the file with asterisks, and only then erases it.

Listing 14.12

```
program Dir9A;
{$I- Disable I/O checking}
uses Dos;
var
   FileReference : file of byte;
   DummyByte      : byte;
   i,
   NumberOfBytes : longint;
   Attribute      : word;
begin
   if ParamCount = 0 then
      writeln( 'No file specified' )
   else begin
      Assign( FileReference, ParamStr( 1 ) );
      Reset( FileReference );
      if IOResult <> 0 then
         writeln( 'File not found' )
      else begin
         GetFAttr( FileReference, Attribute );
         if Attribute and ReadOnly <> 0 then
            writeln( 'File is read only.  Cannot erase.' )
         else begin
            NumberOfBytes := 0;
            while not eof( FileReference ) do begin
               NumberOfBytes := NumberOfBytes + 1;
               read( FileReference, DummyByte );
            end;
            Close( FileReference );
            if NumberOfBytes > 0 then begin
               Rewrite( FileReference );
               DummyByte := ord( '*' );
               for i := 1 to NumberOfBytes do
                  write( FileReference, DummyByte );
               writeln( NumberOfBytes, ' bytes were overwritten' );
               Close( FileReference );
            end;
            Erase( FileReference );
            writeln( 'The file has been erased' );
         end;
      end;
   end;
end.
```

Renaming a File

The Turbo Pascal Rename procedure has restrictions similar to Erase: The file must be assigned but unopened. In addition, it's the programmer's responsibility to test whether the new file name already exists in the directory. The DIR10 program (listing 14.13) demonstrates how Rename can be used to modify a single file.

Listing 14.13

```
program Dir10;
uses Dos;
var
   OldFileName,
   NewFileName    : string;
   FileReference,
   FileReference2 : file;
begin
   write( 'Old file name: ' );
   readln( OldFileName );
   Assign( FileReference, OldFileName );
{$I-}
   Reset( FileReference );
{$I+}
   if IOResult <> 0 then
      writeln( 'Old file not found.  Request ignored.' )
   else begin
      write( 'New file name: ' );
      readln( NewFileName );
      Assign( FileReference2, NewFileName );
{$I-}
      Reset( FileReference2 );
{$I+}
      if IOResult = 0 then
         writeln( 'New file in use.  Request ignored.' )
      else
         Rename( FileReference, NewFileName );
   end;
end.
```

Notice that the program checks for the existence of *both* the original and the new files.

Determining the Size of a File

The DIR9A program in listing 14.12 reads a file one byte at a time to learn the total file size. Of course, a separate file-size field is included as part of the FCB record, but unless the file was originally accessed with FindFirst and FindNext, that information isn't readily available. To remedy this deficiency, Turbo Pascal provides the FileSize procedure, which returns the *number of records* in a file.

Record size is measured from the perspective of the operating system. If the file was created as a file of a specific type (for example, file of InfoRecord or file of longint), the record size is the size of the typed field. Untyped files and text files are assumed to have record sizes equal to the default buffer size of 128 bytes.

You can circumvent this problem by declaring a file to be a `file of byte` and in the process force the record size to be one byte long. In so doing, you make the number of records equal to the size of the file. The DIR7B program (listing 14.14) demonstrates this trick by determining its own length.

Listing 14.14

```
program Dir7B;
var
   FileName      : string;
   FileReference : file of byte;
begin
   FileName := 'Dir7B.pas';
   Assign( FileReference, FileName );
   Reset( FileReference );
   writeln( FileName, ' is ', FileSize( FileReference ), ' bytes long' );
end.
```

When executed, you see

`Dir7B.pas is 268 bytes long`

Sometimes you need to know not only if a file exists but also if it contains data as well. You could obtain this information directly by opening the file and seeing if the first read operation results in an end of file. Alternatively, you can use the `FileSize` function, as shown in program DIR7C (listing 14.15).

Listing 14.15

```
program Dir7C;
var
   FileToCheck : string;

function FileHasContent( FileName : string ) : boolean;
var
   FileReference : file of byte;
begin
   Assign( FileReference, FileName );
{$I- Disable I/O checking}
   Reset( FileReference );
{$I + Reinstate I/O checking}
   if IOResult  <> 0 then
      FileHasContent := False
   else
      FileHasContent := FileSize( FileReference ) > 0;
end;

begin
   FileToCheck := 'Dir7C.pas';
   if FileHasContent( FileToCheck ) then
      writeln( FileToCheck, ' exists!' )
   else
      writeln( FileToCheck, ' wasn''t found' );
end.
```

Applying `FileSize` to yet another directory list, you obtain the closest program yet to the DOS utility DIR. Program DIR7A (listing 14.16) demonstrates its use. Again, the file variable is defined as a `file of byte`, so `FileSize` will directly return the correct result.

Listing 14.16

```
program Dir7A;
uses Dos;
var
   FileInfo       : SearchRec;
   TimeNow        : DateTime;
   FileTimeStamp  : longint;
   FileReference  : file of byte;
   StartString    : string;
begin
   if ParamCount <> 1 then
      StartString := '*.*'
   else
      StartString := ParamStr( 1 );
   FindFirst( StartString, (AnyFile - Directory), FileInfo );
   while DosError = Ø do
      begin
         Assign( FileReference, FileInfo.Name );
         Reset( FileReference );
         GetFTime( FileReference, FileTimeStamp );
         UnpackTime( FileTimeStamp, TimeNow );
         write( FileInfo.Name:12, FileSize( FileReference ):9 );
         with TimeNow do writeln( Month:4, '-', Day:2, '-', Year:2,
                                  Hour:4, ':', Min:2, ':', Sec:2 );
         Close( FileReference );
         FindNext( FileInfo );
      end;
end.
```

Executing the program with the command

`DIR7A ex*.pas`

results in the following:

```
     EXEC2.PAS     242    7-29-1988   16:48: Ø
     EXEC5.PAS     234    7-29-1988   2Ø:29:44
     EXEC1.PAS     216    7-29-1988   16:53:44
     EXEC3.PAS     499    7-29-1988   17:48:48
     EXIT2.PAS    1Ø32    7-3Ø-1988   16:51:56
     EXEC4.PAS     334    7-29-1988   17:43:14
     EXIT4.PAS     277    7-3Ø-1988   17:19:58
     EXEC6.PAS     234    7-29-1988   2Ø:31:22
     EXIT1.PAS     474    7-27-1988   12:25: 2
     EXIT3.PAS    3455    7-3Ø-1988   17:22: 6
     EXEC7.PAS      93    7-29-1988   21:24: 2
```

Modifying the Attribute Byte

You have already seen how useful a file's attribute byte can be. Not only does it identify the basic nature of a disk directory entry, but it can also serve to provide an added measure of security by preventing a file from being deleted. For example, it's not uncommon for a program to remove the read-only status on an important file at the beginning of its run and to reinstate read-only status upon program termination.

The GetFAttr and SetFAttr procedures can be used to retrieve and reset the attribute byte, respectively. Both procedures take two parameters: an assigned but unopened file name and a word-sized variable representing the attribute itself.

The DIR11 program (listing 14.17) offers a means of changing the settings of the attribute byte in a group of files. It is executed with the following command:

    DIR11 <file-spec> <original> <new>

The <file-spec> parameter may include wild-card characters. The <original> and <new> parameters represent the archive, hidden, and read-only bits. In the following sample command line and in listing 14.17, the capitals A, H, and R represent set bits; the lowercase a, h, and r indicate cleared bits. For example, to set the read-only bit in all files of the form dir*.pas enter the command

    DIR11 dir*.pas r R

The bits can later be cleared with the command

    DIR11 dir*.pas R r

Notice that to test whether a bit is set, the attribute byte is logically ANDed with one of the predefined constants Archive, Hidden, or ReadOnly. The result is zero when the bit is set and nonzero otherwise. Bits are turned on by logically ORing the attribute byte with one of the predefined constants; they are cleared by ANDing the attribute byte with another byte (the logical NOT of a predefined constant) in which every bit is set except for the one you want to switch off.

Listing 14.17

```pascal
program Dir11;
uses Dos;
var
    FileInfo      : SearchRec;
    Match         : boolean;
    OldAttr,
    NewAttr       : word;
    Old,
    New           : string;
    FileReference : file;
begin
    if ParamCount <> 3 then
        writeln( 'Improper parameters' )
    else begin
        Old := ParamStr( 2 );
        New := ParamStr( 3 );
        if (Old[ 1 ] in [ 'a', 'A', 'h', 'H', 'r', 'R' ]) and
           (New[ 1 ] in [ 'a', 'A', 'h', 'H', 'r', 'R' ]) then begin
            FindFirst( ParamStr( 1 ), (AnyFile - Directory), FileInfo );
            while DosError = 0 do
              begin
                Assign( FileReference, FileInfo.Name );
                GetFAttr( FileReference, OldAttr );
                case Old[ 1 ] of
                    'a' : Match := (OldAttr and Archive ) = 0;
                    'A' : Match := (OldAttr and Archive ) <> 0;
                    'h' : Match := (OldAttr and Hidden  ) = 0;
                    'H' : Match := (OldAttr and Hidden  ) <> 0;
                    'r' : Match := (OldAttr and ReadOnly) = 0;
                    'R' : Match := (OldAttr and ReadOnly) <> 0;
                    else  Match := False;
                end;
                if Match then begin
                    case New[ 1 ] of
                        'a' : NewAttr := OldAttr and $DF;    { Not Archive  }
                        'A' : NewAttr := OldAttr or $20;     { Archive      }
                        'h' : NewAttr := OldAttr and $FD;    { Not Hidden   }
                        'H' : NewAttr := OldAttr or $02;     { Hidden       }
                        'r' : NewAttr := OldAttr and $FE;    { Not ReadOnly }
                        'R' : NewAttr := OldAttr or $01;     { ReadOnly     }
                        else  NewAttr := OldAttr;
                    end;
                    SetFAttr( FileReference, NewAttr );
                    writeln( FileInfo.Name, ' has been modified' );
                end else
                    writeln( FileInfo.Name, ' hasn''t been modified' );
                FindNext( FileInfo );
              end;
        end else
            writeln( 'Improper attribute selections' );
    end;
end.
```

Examining File Names

If a file doesn't reside in the current directory, Turbo Pascal procedures such as Assign require a complete file path. For example, a file identified as WORKFILE.DAT is assumed to belong to the current drive and directory. If the file isn't found, an error is generated; no attempt is made to locate it elsewhere. To avoid this problem, the file must be referenced in its complete form, such as C:\PASCAL\CODE\WORKFILE.DAT. This complete specification is called the *fully qualified file name*.

Turbo Pascal never modifies the name, drive, or directory of a declared file. Every file name is passed to the operating system precisely as it's defined in the program. However, a well-designed program should be able to find a required file wherever it is saved or, alternatively, should help the user to find the file.

This section discusses the procedures offered by Turbo Pascal to create, modify, and locate fully qualified files.

Expanding the File Name

The Turbo Pascal function FExpand will create a fully qualified file name using the current drive and directory as defaults. The FEXP1 program (listing 14.18) demonstrates its use.

Listing 14.18

```
program FExp1;
uses Dos;
var
   FileString : string;
begin
   repeat
      readln( FileString );
      writeln( FExpand( FileString ) );
      writeln;
   until Length( FileString ) = Ø;
end.
```

FEXP1 enables you to experiment with FExpand. When the function is applied to a fully qualified file name, it simply returns the parameter itself. When the function is applied to any other file name, it uses the currently active drive and directory as a basis for creating a fully qualified file name. The following is an example of output from FEXP1.

```
fexp1.pas
C:\QUE\PROGRAMS\FEXP1.PAS
fexp1.pas
C:\QUE\PROGRAMS\FEXP1.PAS
```

```
fexp1.*
C:\QUE\PROGRAMS\FEXP1.*
.\progdata.dat.
C:\QUE\PROGRAMS\PROGDATA.DAT
..\progdata.dat
C:\QUE\PROGDATA.DAT
c:\turbo\code\progdata.dat
C:\TURBO\CODE\PROGDATA.DAT
a:*.*
A:\*.*
```

FExpand isn't needed if your program uses only the current directory. However, if you access more than one directory (especially if you call the ChDir procedure), the FExpand function enables you to preserve the original drive and directory names.

Searching Several Directories

Usually, the search for a file can be narrowed to a few directories. You are probably using a PATH environment variable in your own PC for just such a purpose. If you enter the name of a program that doesn't reside in the current directory, DOS automatically searches for the program in each of the directories specified by the PATH variable.

Similarly, in Turbo Pascal, the FSearch function can be used to search for a file within a given set of directories. FSearch takes two parameters: the name of the file you want to find and a string containing the directories to search. If it finds the file in one of the directories, FSearch returns the fully qualified file name; otherwise, it returns a null string.

You will probably want to limit your search to the same directories you identified in the PATH entry of your PC's environment table. For example, if your PC is configured with the following environment table entry:

PATH =C:\DOS;C:\WORD;C:\TURBOC;C:\TP

the FEXP2 program (listing 14.19) will search for the TURBO.EXE file in the current directory of the current drive. If unsuccessful, the program will continue the search in C:\DOS, then C:\WORD, then C:\TURBOC, and then C:\TP.

Listing 14.19

```
program FExp2;
uses Dos;
var
   FileName,
   FileString : string;
begin
   FileName := 'turbo.exe';
   FileString := FSearch( FileName, GetEnv( 'path' ) );
   if Length( FileString ) = Ø then
      writeln( FileName, ' not found' )
   else
      writeln( FExpand( FileString ) );
end.
```

When the file is found (in the C:\TP directory), the following string is displayed:

```
C:\TP\TURBO.EXE
```

Creating a New File Name

Frequently, you will encounter the opposite situation. You may have an application that requires you to develop a variation of the original file name.

For example, suppose that you want to create a listing file for a Pascal source program. You would begin by prompting for the name of the original file, with .PAS as its default extension. Your output file might be the same name but would have .LST as its default extension.

In Turbo Pascal, the FSplit procedure can break a fully qualified file name into its three main components: the directory, name, and extension. In the FEXP3 program (listing 14.20), the user is prompted first for the name of a Pascal program, then for the names of the object and listing files. The default extensions of the object and listing files are .OBJ and .LST, respectively. The name may also be changed if the user wants to change it.

Listing 14.20

```
program FExp3;
uses Dos;
var
   FileSource, FileObject, FileList : string;
   PathName    : PathStr;
   DirectoryØ,
   Directory   : DirStr;
```

Listing 14.20 continues

Listing 14.20 continued

```
      FileNameØ,
      FileName   : NameStr;
      Extension  : ExtStr;
      FileString : string;
  begin
    Repeat
       write( 'Source file name (*.pas): ' );
       readln( FileString );
       FSplit( FileString, DirectoryØ, FileNameØ, Extension );
       if Extension = '' then    { Default extension requested }
          FileString := DirectoryØ + FileNameØ + '.pas';
       PathName := FSearch( FileString, GetEnv( 'path' ) );
       FSplit( PathName, DirectoryØ, FileNameØ, Extension );
    until PathName <> '';  { Source file must exist }
    FileSource := PathName;

    write( 'Object file name (', FileNameØ, '.obj): ' );
    readln( FileString );
    FSplit( FileString, Directory, FileName, Extension );
    if Directory = '' then Directory := DirectoryØ;
    if FileName  = '' then FileName  := FileNameØ;
    if Extension = '' then Extension := '.obj';
    FileObject := Directory + FileName + Extension;

    write( 'Listing file name (', FileNameØ, '.lst): ' );
    readln( FileString );
    FSplit( FileString, Directory, FileName, Extension );
    if Directory = '' then Directory := DirectoryØ;
    if FileName  = '' then FileName  := FileNameØ;
    if Extension = '' then Extension := '.lst';
    FileList := Directory + FileName + Extension;

    writeln;
    writeln( 'Source: ', FileSource );
    writeln( 'Object: ', FileObject );
    writeln( 'Listing: ', FileList );
  end.
```

Note that some duplication could have been avoided using a procedure or a function, but presented in this manner the code more clearly demonstrates the program flow.

In the following output example, WORKPROG.PAS was identified as the source file. The default object and listing file names were then displayed; only the changes had to be entered.

```
Source file name (*.pas): workprog
Object file name (workprog.obj): .ob2
Listing file name (workprog.lst): w2
```

```
Source:  workprog.pas
Object:  workprog.ob2
Listing: w2.lst
```

Summary

In this chapter, you have learned how to use the Turbo Pascal procedures and functions that manage files and directories.

You have learned how to obtain the total size of any disk, and you have seen how to determine the amount of free space it contains.

You have learned how your programs can determine the current directory, change to a different directory, create a new directory, and remove an empty directory.

You have learned how to access the information kept by the disk directory itself. For each file, this information includes the file name, size, attribute byte, and date-and-time stamp. You have learned that the bits in the attribute byte describe the type of file and how it can be processed. You have seen how to rename or completely erase a file, how to modify the date-and-time stamp, and how to modify the attribute byte.

Several directory programs were presented, including utilities you can use to search the disk for files that have common, user-specified characteristics. You have learned how to search for a file in several directories, including the directory specified by the DOS system path.

You have also learned several useful routines to expand the name of a file into its component parts and to create a new file name.

Part III

Advanced Programming

CHAPTER 15

Overlays

I n the early days of mainframe computers, memory size was a serious constraint. 4K, 8K, and 16K memories were considered huge! What little memory was available had to be used sparingly.

Few applications—then or now—could fit entirely within such a small space, so programs were written in modules that could be called into memory for only as long as they were needed, then exchanged for another module containing code for a different, independent purpose. A payroll report program, for example, might have one module to print the headings on each page and another module to print the lines of data. Only the code controlling the running totals (subtotals and totals of wages and withholdings, page numbers, and so on) remained in memory at all times.

In the 1960s, the Cobol programming language gained immense popularity in business circles because it simplified the development of these overlaying modules (or more simply, *overlays*). Cobol forced programmers to write data and procedures in separate sections and encouraged programmers to construct collections of subroutines rather than one big program.

The early days of personal computers weren't much different. Although today programmers tend to think of 64K as only one row of chips on a board, originally even 64K was the upper limit of memory in most machines. However, having learned the lessons of history, programmers knew that if they were able to set aside a section of memory and overlay it with independent code modules, the effective size of a program would be unlimited. The Pascal language, which combined the best elements of Cobol with greater ease of use, emerged as the most convenient tool for that purpose.

As PC memory became less expensive, it became less of a programming restriction. Version 4.0 of Turbo Pascal enabled programs to use units and consequently to break the 64K barrier; the support of overlays was temporarily discontinued. However, two problems remained. On one end, the absence of overlays meant that smaller machines (and there are still lots of them around) no longer had a way to support larger programs. On the other end, programs could be large, but their effective size was now limited by the size of the machine on which they ran.

In Version 5.0, Turbo Pascal reintroduced overlays. Their availability, coupled with the capability of executable programs to exceed the 64K size limit, now provides almost unlimited memory management power.

This chapter introduces five rules to follow when creating overlays and demonstrates those rules through a simple programming exercise. In the process, the chapter discusses what overlays are, how to use them, and what situations you should avoid.

What Is an Overlay?

Overlays are parts of a program (really, collections of subroutines) that can share the same physical memory. In Turbo Pascal, the smallest collection of overlay subroutines is the unit. Each unit, in its entirety, is swapped into the common memory area before a routine is called within the unit.

When an overlay program is compiled, Turbo creates two files. The executable .EXE file contains that portion of the code that remains in memory throughout program execution. In addition, Turbo places all the overlay units into a separate .OVR file, where they remain available for the resident program to access. The .OVR file either remains in a convenient location on disk or can be loaded into expanded memory (EMS) for faster access.

Saving Memory Space

Through overlays, Turbo ensures that a program uses the minimum amount of internal memory. The total size of a program that uses overlays consists of a resident section that remains in memory throughout the execution of the program and a buffer big enough to accommodate the largest of the overlay units.

For example, if the resident portion of the program requires 20K of memory and has five units, as follows:

Unit	Size
A	10K
B	10K
C	40K
D	5K
E	3K

then the overlay buffer must be allocated 40K of memory to contain Unit C. Therefore, adding the 20K requirement for the resident portion, the total size of the program is 60K. Without the use of overlays, every unit would need to reside in memory at a total cost of 88K (ignoring the overlay code itself).

Loading Units into the Buffer

Whenever a subroutine in one of the overlay units is called, Turbo Pascal checks to see if the unit is already in the buffer. If the unit isn't there, the entire overlay unit is loaded.

More than one unit may reside in the overlay buffer. If the buffer contains unused space, the unit is loaded into the open section. If the unit to be loaded is larger than the space available, it overwrites any units already in the buffer. In the previous example, in which the overlay buffer was set to 40K, Units A, B, D, and E together require 28K of space; therefore, they may all be in the overlay buffer at the same time.

A Programming Example

To see how Turbo Pascal uses overlays, consider an example of their use. The following program, called OVRMST1, is designed to produce a billing summary for a small law office.

The four attorneys (Fred, Wilma, Barney, and Betty) commonly handle five types of cases (divorce, criminal, bankruptcy, corporate, and probate). OVR-MST1 summarizes the total billings by lawyer and by specialty. The firm's actual billings are shown in Table 15.1.

Table 15.1. Billings Used for OVRMST1.

	Divorce	Criminal	Bnkrptcy	Corp	Probate	Total
Fred	8000	1000	500	0	0	9500
Wilma	0	25000	250	0	0	25250
Barney	0	0	0	0	12000	12000
Betty	1000	0	0	25000	250	26250
Total	9000	26000	750	25000	12250	73000

The OVRMST1 program consists principally of a two-dimensional array and two independent addition routines.

Developing the Program

The OVRMST1 program (listing 15.1) is fairly straightforward. Ordinarily, the raw billing data would be read from a separate file, but to make the operation of the program easier to follow here, you can enter the data directly in the form of a typed constant array.

Listing 15.1

```
program OvrMst1;
type
   Attorneys = ( Fred, Wilma, Barney, Betty );
   Cases     = ( Divorce, Criminal, Bankruptcy, Corporate, Probate );
   Billings  = array [ Attorneys ] of array [ Cases ] of real;
const
                                { Div    Crim   Bkrp   Corp   Prob }
   Revenue : Billings = ( { Fred }  ( 8000,  1000,   500,    0,     0 ),
                          { Wilma }  (    0, 25000,   250,    0,     0 ),
                          { Barney } (    0,     0,     0,    0, 12000 ),
                          { Betty }  ( 1000,     0,     0, 25000,   250 ) );
   Names   : array [ Fred..Betty ] of string[ 8 ] =
           ( 'Fred    ', 'Wilma   ', 'Barney  ', 'Betty   ' );
   Source  : array [ Divorce..Probate ] of string[ 6 ] =
           ( '  Div', '  Crim', '  Bkrp', '  Corp', '  Prob' );
var
   Lawyer    : Attorneys;
   Specialty : Cases;
   Tally     : real;
   Total     : real;
begin
   writeln( 'This section is where you would read data from a file.' );

   Total := 0.0;
   for Lawyer := Fred to Betty do begin
      write( Names[ Lawyer ] );
      Tally := 0.0;
      for Specialty := Divorce to Probate do
         Tally := Tally + Revenue[ Lawyer, Specialty ];
      writeln( Tally:8:0 );
      Total := Total + Tally;
   end;
   writeln( Total:16:0 );
   writeln;
```

Listing 15.1 continues

Listing 15.1 continued

```
    Total := Ø.Ø;
    for Specialty := Divorce to Probate do begin
        write( Source[ Specialty ] );
        Tally := Ø.Ø;
        for Lawyer := Fred to Betty do
            Tally := Tally + Revenue[ Lawyer, Specialty ];
        writeln( Tally:10:Ø );
        Total := Total + Tally;
    end;
    writeln( Total:16:Ø );
    writeln;
end.
```

Accountants use the term *foot* to mean the calculation of totals for each column. Similarly, the term *crossfoot* means the calculation of totals for each line. To *foot and crossfoot* a report means to independently add the numbers down and across; if the totals don't match, an error was made.

The OVRMST1 program foots and crossfoots the billing report. When run, it produces the following:

```
This section is where you would read data from a file.
Fred        95ØØ
Wilma      2525Ø
Barney     12ØØØ
Betty      2625Ø
           73ØØØ


   Div      9ØØØ
   Crim    26ØØØ
   Bkrp      75Ø
   Corp    25ØØØ
   Prob    1225Ø
           73ØØØ
```

The message is included to indicate the normal sequence of events. Again, the revenue array would normally be read from a file, not entered as a typed constant, as in this example.

Converting to Units

Now you can modify the program by creating units: one for the footing calculation and another for the crossfooting calculation.

Because both the footing and crossfooting units require access to the global data, a third unit, OvrSubØ, is created as shown in listing 15.2.

Listing 15.2

```
unit OvrSub0;
interface
type
   Attorneys = ( Fred, Wilma, Barney, Betty );
   Cases    = ( Divorce, Criminal, Bankruptcy, Corporate, Probate );
   Billings = array [ Attorneys ] of array [ Cases ] of real;
const
                              { Div    Crim   Bkrp   Corp    Prob }
   Revenue : Billings = ( { Fred }   ( 8000,  1000,  500,    0,     0 ),
                          { Wilma }  (    0, 25000,  250,    0,     0 ),
                          { Barney } (    0,     0,    0,    0, 12000 ),
                          { Betty }  ( 1000,     0,    0, 25000,  250 ) );
   Names   : array [ Fred..Betty ] of string[ 8 ] =
             ( 'Fred    ', 'Wilma   ', 'Barney  ', 'Betty   ' );
   Source  : array [ Divorce..Probate ] of string[ 6 ] =
             ( '   Div', '  Crim', '  Bkrp', '  Corp', '  Prob' );
var
   Lawyer    : Attorneys;
   Specialty : Cases;
   Tally     : real;
implementation
end.
```

The crossfooting unit, OvrSub1, and the footing unit, OvrSub2, are defined in listing 15.3.

Listing 15.3

```
unit OvrSub1;
interface
uses OvrSub0;
   procedure CrossFoot;
implementation
   procedure CrossFoot;
   var
      Total : real;
   begin
      Total := 0.0;
      for Lawyer := Fred to Betty do begin
         write( Names[ Lawyer ] );
         Tally := 0.0;
         for Specialty := Divorce to Probate do
            Tally := Tally + Revenue[ Lawyer, Specialty ];
         writeln( Tally:8:0 );
         Total := Total + Tally;
      end;
      writeln( Total:16:0 );
      writeln;
   end;
end.
```

Listing 15.3 *continues*

Listing 15.3 *continued*

```
unit OvrSub2;
interface
uses OvrSub0;
   procedure Foot;
implementation
   procedure Foot;
   var
      Total : real;
   begin
      Total := 0.0;
      for Specialty := Divorce to Probate do begin
         write( Source[ Specialty ] );
         Tally := 0.0;
         for Lawyer := Fred to Betty do
            Tally := Tally + Revenue[ Lawyer, Specialty ];
         writeln( Tally:10:0 );
         Total := Total + Tally;
      end;
      writeln( Total:16:0 );
      writeln;
   end;
end.
```

Almost all of the data and code are now contained in the three units, so the OVRMST2 program can be fairly short.

Listing 15.4

```
program OvrMst2;
uses OvrSub1, OvrSub2;
begin
   writeln( 'This section is where you would read data from a file.' );
   CrossFoot;
   Foot;
end.
```

The OvrSub0 module is compiled to disk first, followed by OvrSub1, Ovr-Sub2, and finally the main OVRMST2 program. When OVRMST2 is executed, it produces results identical to OVRMST1.

Creating Overlays from the Units

It's probably fairly obvious that your PC contains enough internal memory to run OVRMST2 without any trouble. Assume, however, that you now want to turn OvrSub1 and OvrSub2 into overlays.

Preparing Each Unit

Because a unit must operate differently when it becomes an overlay, you should alert the compiler to your intentions as soon as possible.

Rule 1: Turbo Pascal must know immediately whether you intend to use a unit as an overlay. Therefore, every overlay unit must be compiled with the {$O +} directive.

The presence of {$O +} at the beginning of a unit doesn't *force* the unit to be used as an overlay. This directive just instructs Turbo Pascal to ensure that the units *can* be used as overlays, if so desired. If you develop units you plan to use in overlay as well as nonoverlay applications, then compiling them with {$O +} ensures that you can indeed do both with just one version of the unit.

Using Far Calls

When overlays are not used, Turbo Pascal places the main program and each unit in its own memory segment. Therefore, all subroutine calls across segments require far calls (that is, calls that specify both the segment and offset). Similarly, when parameters are passed across segments, far pointers must be used. The compiler handles this automatically.

For example, suppose that UnitA contains the following procedure:

```
procedure DisplayProgress( Message : string );
begin
   GotoXY( 1, 25 );
   write( Message );
end;
```

and UnitB contains the following call:

```
DisplayProgress( 'Now sorting file. Please wait.' );
```

Turbo Pascal places the constant string 'Now sorting file. Please wait.' in UnitB's code segment, passes a far pointer to its location to the Display-Progress procedure in UnitA, and invokes DisplayProgress from UnitB with a far call.

Now suppose that UnitA and UnitB are overlays. Both the message and the procedure that displays it will reside in the same segment (although at different times), so the compiler no longer regards a far procedure call as necessary. In addition, the compiler passes the message string with a near pointer.

This can't be allowed. Somehow, you must tell the compiler that even though the two units are in the same physical segment, they're really overlays. Otherwise, the compiler won't be able to differentiate between the unit that contains the string and the unit that contains the procedure and won't know which unit to place in memory. To complicate the situation further, when UnitB calls the `DisplayProgress` procedure in UnitA, then UnitA is moved into memory, overwriting the memory location where the constant string was stored!

Turbo Pascal solves these problems in a simple and clever way.

Rule 2: Every subroutine and every pointer used by a program containing overlays should be far, with both the segment and offset specified. Therefore, every unit (in addition to the main program itself) should be compiled with the `Force Far Calls` directive.

Note that the easiest way to satisfy the far call requirement is to place the {$F +} directive at the beginning of the main program and each unit. Alternatively, you can change the default {$F } setting to {$F +} using a /$F + command-line directive for the TPC.EXE command-line compiler, or you can change the /O/C/Force Far Calls menu command in the interactive environment.

Technically, only a near pointer is required, but compiling the program with the `Force Far Calls` directive enables the compiler to use the segment half of each pointer to identify the desired overlay unit. Whenever Turbo Pascal detects a call from one unit compiled with {$O +} to another unit compiled with {$O +}, the compiler is certain to copy parameters to the stack before passing pointers to them. Next, Turbo determines whether the unit being called is currently in memory. If the unit resides in memory, the call proceeds normally; if it doesn't, the required unit is first brought into memory, then the call proceeds.

Turbo makes no other changes to the code generated by the overlay unit. In fact, overlays are so similar to units, you don't have to make any other modifications to a unit when you use it as an overlay.

Creating the Overlay Units

You can combine the first two rules into a single modification: add the {$O +,F +} directive pair immediately after the unit declaration. The {$O +} directive tells the compiler to treat the units as overlays. The {$F +} directive ensures that all procedures, functions, and pointers will be called with the far calling model.

The revised files OvrSub1A and OvrSub2A (listings 15.5 and 15.6 respectively) now appear as follows:

Listing 15.5

```
unit OvrSub1A;
{$O +,F +}
interface
uses OvrSub0;
   procedure CrossFoot;
implementation
   procedure CrossFoot;
   var
      Total : real;
   begin
      Total := 0.0;
      for Lawyer := Fred to Betty do begin
         write( Names[ Lawyer ] );
         Tally := 0.0;
         for Specialty := Divorce to Probate do
            Tally := Tally  + Revenue[ Lawyer, Specialty ];
         writeln( Tally:8:0 );
         Total := Total  + Tally;
      end;
      writeln( Total:16:0 );
      writeln;
   end;
end.
```

Listing 15.6

```
unit OvrSub2A;
{$O +,F +}
interface
uses OvrSub0;
   procedure Foot;
implementation
   procedure Foot;
   var
      Total : real;
   begin
      Total := 0.0;
      for Specialty := Divorce to Probate do begin
         write( Source[ Specialty ] );
         Tally := 0.0;
         for Lawyer := Fred to Betty do
            Tally := Tally  + Revenue[ Lawyer, Specialty ];
         writeln( Tally:10:0 );
         Total := Total  + Tally;
      end;
      writeln( Total:16:0 );
      writeln;
   end;
end.
```

No change is made to the OvrSub0 unit containing the global declarations.
Only the units being transformed to overlays are affected.

A Note on Initialization Sections in Overlay Units

Whenever any subroutine in an overlay unit is called, the entire unit is brought into memory. If each unit contains initialization code, then that code is also moved, even though it was only designed to be executed once.

Depending on the size of the initialization code and the number of times the overlay unit is swapped into memory, you may note some performance degradation. Further, because the overlay buffer must be large enough to accommodate the largest unit, the presence of initialization code may increase the buffer size.

To avoid these situations, try to combine all initialization code into a single, small overlay unit. You may even have a separate overlay unit containing nothing but initialization code. This should reduce the size of the other individual units, decrease the time it takes to move them in memory, and decrease the size of the overlay buffer.

Modifying the Main Program

You already saw from Rule 2 that the main program must be recompiled with the Force Far Calls directive. A few other changes must also be made. The main program controls overall execution, so the OVRMST2 program will undergo more modifications than the units.

Including Run-Time Code Support

When the {$O +} directive was included in the overlay units, Turbo Pascal was being informed that the compilation process (at least for those units) would be different from normal. However, as you might expect, the overlay process itself requires additional run-time support.

Rule 3: The main program must include the Overlay unit in the *first* position of the uses statement.

The uses statement in the main program will be modified as follows:

```
uses Overlay, OvrSub1A, OvrSub2A;
```

Including the Overlay unit ensures that run-time support is made available to the compiled code.

Identifying the Overlays

A program may use both overlay and nonoverlay units. Therefore, the overlay units must be specifically identified.

Rule 4: Turbo Pascal must know immediately which units are to be treated as overlays. Therefore, the main program must specify every overlay unit with the {$O filename} directive.

The {$O filename} directive tells the compiler which of the units in the uses clause are to be treated as overlays; consequently, the directive must appear *after* the units are named.

```
uses Overlay, OvrSub1A, OvrSub2A;
{$O OvrSub1A }
{$O OvrSub2A }
```

Remember that the {$O +} directive in the individual units alerted the compiler only to the *possibility* that they would be used as overlays; the {$O filename} directive in the main program makes the formal request.

Initializing Run-Time Support

The Overlay standard unit is declared first in the uses statement, so any initialization code it contains will be run *before* the initialization code of any other unit and *before* the main program begins. However, this also means that the Overlay unit initialization code is executed *before* you identify which other units are to be treated as overlays. Therefore, the remaining run-time overlay support must be initialized within the main program itself through a call to the OvrInit procedure.

Rule 5: The run-time overlay support must be initialized before its use. Therefore, the OvrInit overlay initiation procedure must be executed before any procedure or function calls are made to subroutines defined in the overlay units.

The OvrInit procedure ideally should be called as early as possible. OvrInit initializes the overlay manager and opens the .OVR overlay file. If the filename parameter does not specify a drive or a subdirectory, the overlay manager searches for the file in the current directory, in the directory that contains the .EXE file (if running under DOS Version 3.x), and in the directories specified by the DOS PATH environment variable.

Final Version of the Main Program

Incorporating these rules, the new main program is structured as follows in listing 15.7:

Listing 15.7

```
program OvrMst3;
{$F + Forces a Far call for all procedures and functions }
uses Overlay, OvrSub1A, OvrSub2A;
{$O OvrSub1A }
{$O OvrSub2A }
begin
    OvrInit( 'OvrMst3.OVR' );
    writeln( 'This section is where you would read data from a file.' );
    CrossFoot;
    Foot;
end.
```

After OvrSub1A, OvrSub2A, and OVRMST3 are compiled, the new program produces the same output as the original program. Footing and crossfooting produce the same totals by different means, so the two units are able to compute the same totals independently.

This shouldn't be too surprising, because the code hasn't really undergone much of a change. Three new directives and one new procedure call were added, and one line of code was modified.

With just a few exceptions, the five rules that have been presented are sufficient to convert any unit to overlay form.

Using Overlay Routines

The Overlay standard unit defines the procedures OvrInit, OvrInitEMS, OvrSetBuf, and OvrClearBuf, and the function OvrGetBuf. Any errors occurring from executing these routines may cause your program to terminate with a run-time error.

You can test the result of each subroutine call by examining the predefined integer variable OvrResult. Any nonzero value indicates an error and requires immediate remedy. Table 15.2 shows the possible return values, together with several predefined constants that you can use to make the test of OvrResult easier to understand.

Table 15.2. *Results Returned by OvrResult*

Predefined Constant	Value	Typical Error Messages
ovrOk	0	NO ERROR
ovrError	−1	No overlays/Buffer too small/Heap not empty
ovrNotFound	−2	.OVR file was not found
ovrNoMemory	−3	Not enough available heap space
ovrIOError	−4	I/O error reading overlay file
ovrNoEMSDriver	−5	EMS driver not installed
ovrNoEMSMemory	−6	Not enough free EMS memory

Your programs can use OvrResult to recover from almost any situation. Use of the constants will be discussed in greater detail throughout the rest of the chapter.

Initiating the Overlay Manager

As stated in Rule 5, the initialization code must be placed before the first call to an overlay routine. The following code actually initialized the overlay manager:

```
OvrInit( 'OvrMst3.OVR' );
```

Essentially, the OvrInit procedure either works or it doesn't. If unsuccessful, the first call to any routine in an overlay unit aborts the program and produces run-time error 208, Overlay manager not installed.

This is the basis for the advice that OvrInit should be called as soon as possible after the program begins. Imagine the disgruntled user who works with your program—say a spreadsheet—for several hours, only to have it abort before the session can be saved to disk!

Nothing can be done within the program to recover from the error. However, you can include the following code immediately after the OvrInit call to help the user understand its cause:

```
if OvrResult <> ovrOk then begin
    case OvrResult of
        ovrError    { -1 } : writeln( 'Program doesn''t have overlays' );
        ovrNotFound { -2 } : writeln( '.OVR file wasn''t found' );
    end;
    Halt( 1 );
end;
```

Using Expanded Memory

If EMS, named for the Lotus/Intel/Microsoft Expanded Memory Specification, is available on your PC and if an EMS driver is detected, a call to the OvrInitEMS procedure loads the .OVR file into memory and closes the .OVR file on disk. Storing the .OVR file in memory significantly reduces the time required to access each overlay.

If OvrInitEMS isn't successful, the program continues to use the disk-based .OVR file. Consequently, unless you know that your program will never run on a machine with EMS, including a call to OvrInitEMS offers a considerable potential increase in execution speed with little increase in the size of the executable file.

OvrInitEMS should be called immediately after OvrInit, as follows:

```
OvrInit( 'OvrMst3.ovr' );
OvrInitEMS;
```

After OvrInitEMS is called, OvrResult can be tested as follows:

```
if OvrResult <> ovrOk then
   case OvrResult of
      ovrIOError       { -4 } : writeln( 'I/O error reading overlay file' );
      ovrNoEMSDriver   { -5 } : writeln( 'EMS driver not installed' );
      ovrNoEMSMemory   { -6 } : writeln( 'Not enough free EMS memory' );
   end;
```

Changing the Size of the Overlay Buffer

When the OvrInit procedure is called, the size of the overlay buffer is initialized to the size of the largest overlay plus a small allowance for some interfacing information. At any time during the execution of the program, you can use the OvrGetBuf function to obtain the current size of the overlay buffer. For example:

```
writeln( 'The overlay buffer now contains ', OvrGetBuf, ' bytes' );
```

Although the default size of the overlay buffer is adequate for most applications, in some situations you might find a larger buffer useful. For example, suppose that your program needs frequent access to two different overlay units. If the combined size of the units exceeds the current size of the buffer, then both units cannot be available at the same time. You can remedy this by using the OvrSetBuf procedure to increase the size of the overlay buffer to contain both overlay units.

The overlay buffer physically resides at the bottom of heap memory. Therefore, the single parameter of OvrSetBuf, a long integer containing the desired size, must be greater than or equal to the initial size of the overlay buffer and less than or equal to (MemAvail + OvrGetBuf). Any additional buffer allocation is obtained from the beginning of the heap. If OvrSetBuf decreases the size of the buffer, the extra space becomes available to the heap.

The size of the heap can be adjusted only when it's empty. Consequently, OvrSetBuf must be executed *before* any dynamic variables are allocated with New or GetMem and *before* the InitGraph procedure allocates heap space for any graphics operations. Further, if you need to increase the size of the overlay buffer, you should first use the {$M} compiler directive to increase the minimum size of the heap (listing 15.8).

Listing 15.8

```
{$M 16384,65536,655360  Increase HeapMin from Ø to 64K! }
uses Overlay,....
const
   OvrExtra = 8192;   { 8K }
begin
   OvrInit( 'OvrMst3.ovr' );
   OvrInitEMS;
   OvrSetBuf( OvrGetBuf + OvrExtra );   { Bump up by 8K }
   :
   :
end;
```

The success or failure of the call to OvrSetBuf can be tested as follows in listing 15.9:

Listing 15.9

```
if OvrResult <> ovrOk then begin
   case OvrResult of
      ovrError     { -1 } :
         writeln( 'Requested buffer size too small or heap not empty' );
      ovrNotFound { -2 } : writeln( '.OVR file wasn''t found' );
      ovrNoMemory { -3 } : writeln( 'Not enough available heap space' );
   end;
   Halt( 1 );
end;
```

The overlay manager will continue to function if OvrSetBuf returns an error, but the size of the overlay buffer will remain unchanged.

Clearing the Overlay Buffer

The OvrClearBuf procedure completely clears the overlay buffer. Any subsequent call to a routine in an overlay unit causes that unit to be reloaded.

The overlay manager never *requires* you to call OvrClearBuf; in fact, doing so considerably decreases your application's performance.

Summary

In this chapter, you have learned that overlays can be used to minimize the internal memory required to execute a Turbo Pascal program, and you have seen how any user-written unit can be converted to overlay format. Specifically, you have learned five rules to follow to transform normal units into overlays:

❏ Every overlay unit must be compiled with the {$O +} directive.

❏ Every overlay unit and the main program itself should be compiled with the /{$F +} directive.

❏ The main program must include the Overlay standard unit in the first position of the uses statement.

❏ The main program must specify every overlay unit with the {$O filename} directive.

❏ The main program must execute the OvrInit overlay initiation procedure as soon as possible.

You have learned how to apply these rules through working with a simple case study. In the process, you have seen how the main program and the individual units are prepared, and you have learned how the run-time support for the Turbo Pascal overlay manager is initialized.

Finally, you have learned some advanced overlay features, such as the use of expanded memory (EMS), how to change the size of the overlay buffer, and how the overlay buffer can be cleared.

16

BIOS, DOS, and Assembly Language

Programmers are traditionally concerned only with the final success or failure of their efforts. In fact, most judge the quality of software by its transparency; that is, the degree to which the product hides its inner workings and the details of its output. As a result, programming languages strive to be "user friendly." Turbo Pascal is probably the greatest such success story. It gracefully balances the need to protect the user from the complexities of the PC with the need to protect the microprocessor from poor coding practices.

One consequence of this benevolent protection is that programmers don't often need to get close to the CPU. Most of the time, of course, this is more of a blessing than a problem. Yet, both fortunately and unfortunately, the programmer can only realize the potential and flexibility of the PC by understanding what software choices are available and when each choice is the most appropriate.

Every microprocessor has its own set of low-level subroutines that can be accessed to perform certain basic input and output functions. These subroutines are hard-coded in ROM (read-only memory) and can be accessed immediately by any program. Collectively, they are called the Basic Input/Output System (BIOS). They primarily serve as the interface between the operating system and the hardware of the PC.

DOS itself relies on BIOS services. BIOS routines are custom designed for the specific hardware configuration of a PC. COMPAQ portables, IBM ATs, the

PCjr™, and the latest laptops may all have different hardware internals, yet the BIOS routines they contain can all understand and appropriately react to the same DOS commands. When referring to the *operating system* of the PC, a programmer is usually talking about the way DOS and BIOS services are teamed together.

BIOS and DOS services are prewritten, pretested subroutines that together form one of the most powerful languages available on the PC. When a Turbo Pascal program executes, it runs on top of—not in place of—the operating system. As a consequence, the full power of the PC is immediately available—just one layer down.

Turbo Pascal provides several tools to bring DOS and BIOS services within reach. Because these routines are the most fundamental commands available on your PC, accessing these services is useful for those applications requiring special hardware access, increased speed, or smaller code size. By taking advantage of these tools, your programs can often obtain more than a tenfold improvement in speed—about the difference between a fast car and a jet.

This chapter demonstrates how you can use Turbo Pascal to directly access BIOS and DOS services as easily as you would access a standard procedure or function. In addition, for those infrequent occasions when you need even greater processing speed, you will see how Turbo Pascal enables you to directly incorporate assembly language in your programs.

Communicating with BIOS and DOS Services

In most ways, BIOS and DOS services behave just like ordinary Turbo Pascal procedures. A routine is called, it performs its tasks, and it returns control to the calling program when it finishes.

In Chapter 6, you saw how the CPU uses its segment and pointer registers to manipulate information stored in internal memory. Although most of the individual processor instructions have options that allow operations directly on data in memory, you can achieve even greater speed by placing the data in one of four general-purpose registers.

In fact, the only real functional difference between BIOS and DOS routines and ordinary Turbo Pascal procedures is in how parameters are passed. A Turbo Pascal program uses internal memory (specifically, the stack) to exchange information with its subroutines. BIOS and DOS routines, on the other hand, pass parameters in the registers themselves.

Using the Registers

Whenever you call a BIOS or DOS routine, you pass a set of variable parameters that correspond to the contents of the most frequently used registers. To simplify this process, Turbo Pascal predefines a variant record type, as follows:

```
Registers = record
              case Integer of
                0 : (AX, BX, CX, DX, BP, SI, DI, DS, ES, Flags : Word);
                1 : (AL, AH, BL, BH, CL, CH, DL, DH : Byte);
            end;
```

The AX, BX, CX, and DX registers are word-sized, *general-purpose* registers. Each one can be accessed either as two 8-bit registers or as a single 16-bit register. The AH, BH, CH, and DH registers represent the high-order bytes of the corresponding registers. Similarly, the AL, BL, CL, and DL registers represent the low-order bytes.

The BP, SI, and DI registers are the base pointer, source index, and destination index registers, respectively. The BP register contains the current working offset of the stack segment. The SI and DI registers hold the offsets of items in the data segment. For example, when a string is copied from memory location *A* to memory location *B*, SI holds the offset of *A* and DI holds the offset of *B*. Unless you write code that relies heavily on assembly language, you will have little or no practical interest in the contents of the BP, SI, and DI registers.

The flags register consists of 16 bits, each of which indicates a characteristic or result of an arithmetic or logical operation.

The general-purpose registers most often pass parameters between your program and the BIOS and DOS services. The success or failure of the service can usually be determined by examining the contents of the flags register. Because these are the registers used most frequently, I will examine each of them in more detail.

The General-Purpose Registers

The general-purpose registers are the workhorses of the CPU. All of them can be used to store temporary data. However, to increase processing speed even further, each general-purpose register is designed with its own particular set of specialties.

The AX (accumulator) register is the primary accumulator register. Most arithmetic instructions are optimized to work slightly faster (and require less code) when using it. As you will see shortly, the accumulator register is also used to hold the specific *function* of the BIOS or DOS service you want to execute.

The BX (base) register is the only general-purpose register that can be used as a memory pointer. Ultrafast memory operations store addresses here.

The CX (count) register holds the count for several of the instructions that do looping or other repeated operations, such as the shift and rotate instructions. Other constants, such as the row and column numbers of a screen, are also often stored here.

The DX (data) register, as its name implies, is most often used for storing data. Whereas the BX register is often used to store a pointer to some data item, the DX register stores the value itself.

Table 16.1 summarizes the most common uses of the general purpose registers.

Table 16.1. *Typical Register Uses*

Register	Typical Operation
AX	Word multiply, divide, I/O
AL	Byte multiply, divide, I/O, translate, decimal arithmetic
AH	Byte multiply, divide
BX	Translation and data area addressing
CX	String operations, loops, and repeats
CL	Shift and rotate counts
DX	Word multiply, divide, indirect I/O

The Flags Register

The flags register consists of 16 bits that either control various conditions or reflect the current status of the processor. A diagram of the flags register is shown in figure 16.1. All of these bits are intended to indicate the results of an operation. Changing their settings before a service is called has no effect.

The individual bits have the following meanings.

❑ Carry. The *carry* flag is set if an operation between two 16-bit numbers generates a *carry* as a result of an addition, or a *borrow* as a result of a subtraction.

❑ Parity. The *parity* flag is set if the low-order byte of the result of an operation contains an even number of set (one) bits. This flag is primarily used for data communication programs.

***Fig. 16.1.** The contents of the flags register.*

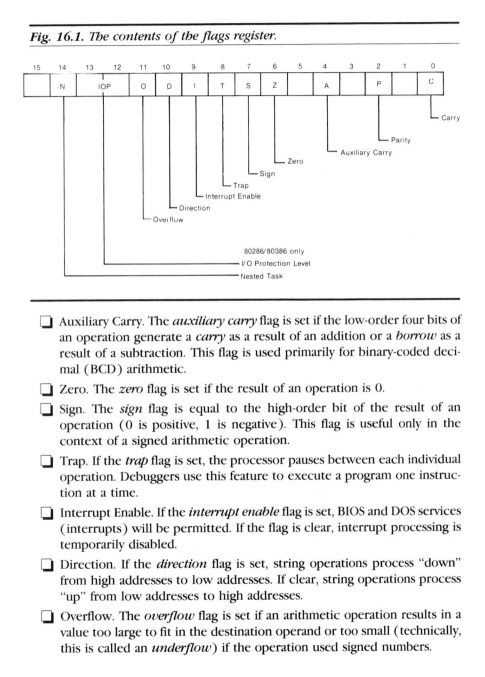

❏ Auxiliary Carry. The *auxiliary carry* flag is set if the low-order four bits of an operation generate a *carry* as a result of an addition or a *borrow* as a result of a subtraction. This flag is used primarily for binary-coded decimal (BCD) arithmetic.

❏ Zero. The *zero* flag is set if the result of an operation is 0.

❏ Sign. The *sign* flag is equal to the high-order bit of the result of an operation (0 is positive, 1 is negative). This flag is useful only in the context of a signed arithmetic operation.

❏ Trap. If the *trap* flag is set, the processor pauses between each individual operation. Debuggers use this feature to execute a program one instruction at a time.

❏ Interrupt Enable. If the *interrupt enable* flag is set, BIOS and DOS services (interrupts) will be permitted. If the flag is clear, interrupt processing is temporarily disabled.

❏ Direction. If the *direction* flag is set, string operations process "down" from high addresses to low addresses. If clear, string operations process "up" from low addresses to high addresses.

❏ Overflow. The *overflow* flag is set if an arithmetic operation results in a value too large to fit in the destination operand or too small (technically, this is called an *underflow*) if the operation used signed numbers.

The *I/O protection level* and *nested task* flags are used for systems programming functions not described in this book.

Table 16.2 contains several predefined constants that you can use to test the settings of the various flags. For example, if you use a Registers variable named Regs and you want to determine if the parity flag is set, simply test whether (Regs.Flags and FParity) is nonzero.

Table 16.2. *Bit Settings in the Flags Register*

Constant	Value
FCarry	$0001
FParity	$0004
FAuxiliary	$0010
FZero	$0040
FSign	$0080
FOverflow	$0800

Calling BIOS Services

The Intr procedure can be used to call any of the BIOS services.

```
Intr( IntNo : byte;  var Regs : Registers )
```

IntNo is the number of the BIOS service, and Regs is a variable parameter of the type Registers.

Unlike Turbo Pascal, in which all standard procedures and functions have specific names, BIOS services are always referenced by number. Theoretically, 256 BIOS services are available (numbered from 0 through 255), but on a practical level, most of these slots aren't used, and of the ones that are taken, only about 10 are useful for Pascal programming.

The word *service* recurs in discussions of BIOS operations because each BIOS number can represent a collection of individual subroutines called *functions*. This is similar to the way a single Turbo Pascal unit can contain dozens of procedures and functions. For example, to move the cursor to a specific screen location, your Turbo Pascal program includes the statement uses Crt and you execute a GotoXY operation; to do the same thing with BIOS code, you execute BIOS service number $10, function number $02. (I will identify the individual services and functions shortly.) The function number is always placed in the AH register prior to executing the Intr procedure.

Calling DOS Services

A DOS service is called with the MsDos procedure.

```
MsDos( var Regs : Registers )
```

Here again, Regs is a variable parameter of the type Registers.

The similarity between the syntax of the Intr and MsDos procedures isn't accidental. Like the BIOS services, DOS services are also referenced only by number. But unlike the BIOS services, only one DOS service is useful to Pascal programmers: number $21. Because DOS uses some of the available BIOS slots to store its code in the PC's memory, DOS service $21 is *functionally* the same as BIOS service $21. Hence, the following statements are equivalent:

```
Intr( $21, Regs )
```

and

```
MsDos( Regs )
```

There are dozens of individual DOS functions available within DOS service $21. Place the number of the desired function in the AH register prior to executing the MsDos procedure.

A Note on BIOS and DOS Service Numbers

Remember that all of the BIOS routines were developed by the hardware manufacturer and stored in ROM. When the PC is booted, the ROM addresses of the BIOS services are placed in a special 256-element array called the *interrupt vector table*. When your program calls a specific BIOS service, Turbo Pascal simply looks up its address in the interrupt vector table and then executes it.

DOS services are stored on disk, then loaded into memory when the PC boots. Individual DOS services also store their addresses in the interrupt vector table.

In a real sense, understanding how the interrupt vector table works—the subject of Chapter 18—is the same as understanding how the operating system itself works.

Accessing BIOS Services

Ten BIOS services are useful for Turbo Pascal programming. The number of these services (in hex), together with the numbers of their individual functions (in hex), are listed in Table 16.3.

This section briefly discusses each of these categories.

Table 16.3. BIOS Services of IBM-Compatible Personal Computers

Category	Interrupt Number	Function	Description
Print-Screen	05	—	Print the Screen Display
Video	10	00	Set Video Mode
		01	Set Cursor Size
		02	Set Cursor Position
		03	Read Cursor Position and Size
		04	Read Light Pen Position
		05	Select Active Display Page (Text Mode)
		06	Scroll Window Up
		07	Scroll Window Down
		08	Read Character and Attribute at Cursor
		09	Write Character and Attribute at Cursor
		0A	Write Character
		0B	Set Color Palette
		0C	Write a Pixel
		0D	Read a Pixel
		0E	Teletype Style Character Output
		0F	Get Current Video State
		13	Write String (AT and EGA Only)
Equipment List	11	—	Identify PC Hardware Configuration
Memory Size	12	—	Determine Internal Memory Size
Disk	13	00	Reset Disk Drive
		01	Get Diskette Status
		02	Read Disk Sectors
		03	Write Disk Sectors
		04	Verify Sectors
		05	Format Diskette Track
		08	(AT only) Return the Current Drive Parameters
		09	(AT only) Initialize the Fixed Disk Table
		0A	(AT only) Read Long Sectors
		0B	(AT only) Write Long Sectors
		0C	(AT only) Seek a Cylinder
		0D	(AT only) Alternate Disk Reset
		15	(AT only) Read Disk Type
		16	(AT only) Read Disk Change Line Status
		17	(AT only) Set Disk Type for Format

Table 16.3 continues

Table 16.3 continued

Category	Interrupt Number	Function	Description
Communications	14	00	Initialize Communications Port
		01	Send Character to Communications Port
		02	Receive Character from Communications Port
		03	Get Communications Port Status
Cassette I/O	15	00	Turn Cassette Motor On
		01	Turn Cassette Motor Off
		02	Read 256-Byte Blocks from Cassette
		03	Write 256-Byte Blocks to Cassette
Extended PC/AT Support	15	80	Device Open
		81	Device Close
		82	Device Program Terminate
		83	Event Wait
		84	Get Joystick Switch Settings/Read Inputs
		85	Systems Request Key Pressed
		86	Delay
		87	Move Block of Words
		88	Get Size of Extended Memory
		89	Go to Virtual Mode
		90	Device Busy Loop
		91	Set Flag/Complete Interrupt
Keyboard	16	00	Return Next Character from Keyboard
		01	Test Next Keyboard Character
		03	Return Current Keyboard Shift Status
Printer	17	00	Print Character
		01	Initialize the Printer
		02	Get Printer Status
Time-of-Day	1A	00	Read Clock Counter
		01	Set Clock Counter
		02	Read Real-Time Clock (AT Only)
		03	Set Real-Time Clock (AT Only)
		04	Read Date from Real-Time Clock (AT Only)
		05	Set Date of Real-Time Clock (AT Only)
		06	Set Alarm (AT Only)
		07	Reset Alarm (AT Only)

Print Screen (Interrupt $05)

Whenever you press the Shift and the PrtSc keys simultaneously, you cause the current contents of the screen (actually, of course, the characters in video memory) to be output to the printer.

The software routine that controls this process is contained in BIOS service number 5. The INT05 program in listing 16.1 demonstrates how to print the screen from within a Turbo Pascal program. No options are available, so no function number needs to be specified. Nevertheless, the syntax of the Intr procedure must be obeyed; a dummy Registers record must still be included as a parameter.

Listing 16.1

```
program Int05;
uses Dos;
procedure PrintScreen;
var
   Regs : Registers;
begin
   Intr( 5, Regs );
end;
begin
   PrintScreen;
end.
```

Video Services (Interrupt $10)

The Video Services BIOS is extensively used by the Crt and Graphics standard units. ClrScr, GotoXY, and Window are all examples of Turbo Pascal procedures that rely on these functions, as well as almost all color, high-resolution graphics, and screen highlighting routines.

Most of the Video Services BIOS functions are available in more convenient packages within standard Turbo Pascal subroutines. Those few features that are not supported, such as reading the light pen, are not likely to be missed.

The ClrScr procedure in the Crt unit can be thought of as the combination of erasing the screen and repositioning the cursor. The INT10A program in listing 16.2 shows how these actions can be separated.

Listing 16.2

```
program Int1ØA;
uses Crt, DOS;
var
   i : integer;
procedure EraseScreen;
var
   Regs : registers;
begin
   with Regs do begin
      AH := $Ø6;
      CH := Ø;          { Row of upper left-hand corner }
      CL := Ø;          { Column of upper left-hand corner }
      DH := 25-1;       { Row of bottom right-hand corner }
      DL := 8Ø-1;       { Column of bottom right-hand corner }
      BH := 7;          { Attribute byte for blank lines }
      Intr( $1Ø, Regs );
   end;
end;
procedure ReturnCursor;
var
   Regs : registers;
begin
   with Regs do begin
      AH := 2;
      BH := Ø;          { Page }
      DH := Ø;          { Row }
      DL := Ø;          { Column }
      Intr( $1Ø, Regs );
   end;
end;
begin
   ClrScr;
   for i := 1 to 3ØØ do
      write( i );
   GotoXY( 4Ø, 5 );
   Delay( 1ØØØ );
   EraseScreen;
   write( '*' );    { Output an asterisk at the cursor location }
   Delay( 1ØØØ );
   ReturnCursor;
   readln;
end.
```

The EraseScreen procedure, like its name implies, erases the screen but *doesn't* change the current cursor position in the process. When the program executes, the top half of the screen fills with numbers, and the cursor is placed in the center of the display. Notice that the cursor doesn't move when the screen is erased. The ReturnCursor procedure is what finally resets the cursor to the upper left corner.

One other potentially useful application of the Video Services BIOS can be found in Function 01, which sets the size of the cursor.

Recall that the monochrome and EGA displays use text characters that are 14 pixels high, and that the default CGA text is 8 pixels high. Most of the time, the cursor appears as an underline, using only the bottom two pixel rows. Function 01 reshapes the cursor by changing its top and bottom rows. If, for example, you use it on a system with a monochrome screen and you set the top line to zero and the bottom line to 13, the cursor changes to a solid block.

To use Function 01, set the CH and CL registers to the desired upper and lower lines, respectively. The parameters are small, so only the bottom four bits of each register are needed to contain the selected values. Interestingly, if you set the sixth bit in the CH register, you can make the cursor disappear completely. The INT10B program in listing 16.3 does just that.

Listing 16.3

```
program Int1ØB;
uses Crt, DOS;
procedure SetCursorType( StartingLine, StoppingLine : byte );
var
   Regs : registers;
begin
   with Regs do begin
      AH := $Ø1;
      CH := StartingLine;
      CL := StoppingLine;
      Intr( $1Ø, Regs );
   end;
end;
begin
   ClrScr;
   SetCursorType( $2Ø, $ØØ );
   readln;
end.
```

By itself, INT10B isn't exciting. It erases the screen, blanks out the cursor, and waits for you to press the Enter key. Consider, however, that in some applications (such as displaying a help screen) you can improve the quality of the display by temporarily erasing the cursor.

Of course, in order to reset the cursor, you should have first saved its original shape. The INT10C program (listing 16.4) demonstrates how to obtain this information by using Function 3.

Listing 16.4

```
program Int10C;
uses Crt, DOS;
var
    StartingLine,
    StoppingLine,
    WhereIsY,
    WhereIsX    : word;

procedure GetCursorInfo;
var
    Regs : registers;
begin
    with Regs do begin
        AH := $03;            { Read cursor position and size }
        BH := $00;            { Default page number           }
        Intr( $10, Regs );    { BIOS interrupt $10            }
        StartingLine := CH;   { Top line in cursor            }
        StoppingLine := CL;   { Bottom line in cursor         }
        WhereIsY     := DH + 1;  { WhereY                     }
        WhereIsX     := DL + 1;  { WhereX                     }
    end;
end;

begin
    GotoXY( 38, 12 );    { Initial position for test }
    GetCursorInfo;
    ClrScr;
    writeln( 'The top line of the cursor is at:    ', StartingLine );
    writeln( 'The bottom line of the cursor is at: ', StoppingLine );
    writeln;
    writeln( '(X, Y) position:  (', WhereIsX, ', ', WhereIsY, ')' );
    readln;
end.
```

When INT10C executes, it produces the following output:

```
The top line of the cursor is at:    6
The bottom line of the cursor is at: 7

(X, Y) position:  (38, 12)
```

Notice that function 3 returns the top and bottom cursor lines in the CH and CL registers, respectively. In addition, the DH register contains the current cursor row, and the DL register contains the current cursor column. Hence, Function 3 is the equivalent of calling both WhereX and WhereY!

Equipment List (Interrupt $11)

The Equipment Service BIOS is a convenient way to determine which peripherals are installed in your PC. It reports the number of printers, serial ports, and diskettes; whether a game adapter or math coprocessor is installed;

the initial video mode of the system; and the size of the memory on the PC's motherboard.

No individual functions are available within the Equipment Service BIOS, so the initial value of the AH register is ignored.

The INT11A program in listing 16.5 is designed to report on the configuration of the PC that runs it. All information is returned in the AX register; the large comment within the program explains how the individual bits can be interpreted.

Listing 16.5

```
program Int11A;
uses Dos;
var
   GamePort,
   Coprocessor      : Boolean;
   PrinterCount,
   RS232PortCount,
   DisketteCount,
   StartMode,
   Kbytes_RAM       : byte;
procedure EquipmentData( var NumberOfPrinters      : byte;
                         var GamePortAvailable     : Boolean;
                         var NumberOfRS232Ports     : byte;
                         var NumberOfDiskettes      : byte;
                         var InitialVideoMode       : byte;
                         var MotherboardRAM         : byte;
                         var CoprocessorAvailable : Boolean  );
var
   Regs : Registers;
begin
   Intr( $11, Regs );
{
   Bits returned in the AX register:
        ***AH*** ***AL***
        76543210 76543210
        -------- --------
   AX = PPUGRRRU FFVVMMCI
   U    Unused
   PP   Number of printers installed
   G    1 if a game adapter is installed, else Ø
   RRR  Number of RS-232 ports installed
   FF   Number of floppy-disk drives minus 1 (Ø = one drive)
   VV   Initial video mode
        Ø1 = 4Ø x 25 color
        1Ø = 8Ø x 25 color
        11 = 8Ø x 25 monochrome
```

Listing 16.5 continues

Listing 16.5 *continued*

```
    MM   RAM on motherboard (Ø = 16K, 1 = 32K, 2 = 48K, 3 = 64K)
    C    1 if a math coprocessor is installed, else Ø
    I    1 if diskette installed, else Ø
}
    with Regs do begin
        NumberOfPrinters       := (AH and $CØ) shr 6;
        GamePortAvailable      := (AH and $1Ø) = $1Ø;
        NumberOfRS232Ports     := (AH and $ØE) shr 1;
        if Odd( AL ) then
            NumberOfDiskettes  := ((AL and $CØ) shr 6) + 1
        else
            NumberOfDiskettes  := Ø;
        InitialVideoMode       := (AL and $3Ø) shr 4;
        CoprocessorAvailable   := (AL and $Ø2) = $Ø2;
        MotherboardRAM         := (((AL and $ØC) shr 2) + 1) * 16;
    end;
end;
begin
    EquipmentData( PrinterCount, GamePort, RS232PortCount,
                   DisketteCount, StartMode,
                   Kbytes_RAM, Coprocessor );
    writeln( 'Equipment Status Report' );
    writeln( '=======================' );
    writeln;
    writeln( 'Game port available?     ', GamePort );
    writeln( 'Number of printers:      ', PrinterCount );
    writeln( 'Number of RS232 ports:   ', RS232PortCount );
    writeln( 'Number of floppy drives: ', DisketteCount );
    writeln( 'Initial video mode:      ', StartMode );
    writeln( 'RAM on motherboard:      ', Kbytes_RAM, 'K' );
    writeln( 'Coprocessor available?   ', Coprocessor );
end.
```

Of course, the EquipmentData procedure is clumsy to use. A more practical application of the Equipment Service BIOS can be found in the INT11B program in listing 16.6. Here, the DisketteCount function returns the number of floppy diskettes, and the Coprocessor function returns a Boolean value to indicate whether a math coprocessor is installed.

Listing 16.6

```
program Int11B;
uses Dos;
function DisketteCount : byte;
var
    Regs : Registers;
begin
```

Listing 16.6 *continues*

Listing 16.6 continued

```
     Intr( $11, Regs );
     with Regs do begin
        if Odd( AL ) then
           DisketteCount := ((AL and $C0) shr 6) + 1
        else
           DisketteCount := 0;
     end;
end;
function Coprocessor : Boolean;
var
   Regs : Registers;
begin
   Intr( $11, Regs );
   Coprocessor := (Regs.AL and $02) = $02;
end;
begin
   writeln( 'Equipment Status Report' );
   writeln( '========================' );
   writeln;
   writeln( 'Number of floppy drives: ', DisketteCount );
   writeln( 'Coprocessor available?   ', Coprocessor );
end.
```

Memory Size (Interrupt $12)

The Memory Size Service BIOS reports how many contiguous 1K byte blocks of memory are installed in your PC. No individual functions are available, so the initial value of the AH register is ignored.

The INT12 program in listing 16.7 reveals the amount of internal memory in your PC.

Listing 16.7

```
program Int12;
uses Dos;
function MemorySize : word;
var
   Regs : Registers;
begin
   Intr( $12, Regs );
   MemorySize := Regs.AX;
end;
begin
   writeln( 'The internal memory of your PC is ',
           MemorySize, 'K bytes.' );
end.
```

> On the PC AT, BIOS service $15, function $88 returns in the AX register the amount of *extended* memory, in 1K bytes.

Disk Services (Interrupt $13)

The Disk Service BIOS contains a variety of functions that transfer data between the CPU and the disks.

These functions are decidedly *not* trivial. Don't even *think* about executing them directly; even one mistake can cause a disastrous loss of data.

Communications Services (Interrupt $14)

The Communications Service BIOS contains functions that enable your PC to transfer data serially. This is the software that supports modems on the COM1 and COM2 ports.

Cassette I/O and Extended PC/AT Support Services (Interrupt $15)

BIOS service number $15 contains the routines that support cassette tape I/O on the PC. For obvious reasons, these functions have no value for most programmers; in fact, some later model PCs no longer bother to include them.

Of considerably greater interest, however, is the fact that IBM also uses service $15 for specialized AT support routines. Consult the *PC/AT Technical Reference Manual* for further information.

Keyboard Services (Interrupt $16)

The Keyboard Service BIOS is used to manage input from the console. Function 00 returns the *first* character in the input buffer. Function 01 returns the *next* character but doesn't remove it from the buffer. Function 03 copies the keyboard status byte in $0040:$0017 to the AL register.

In some ways, Function 01 corresponds to the Turbo Pascal KeyPressed function. If a keystroke is available, the zero flag is cleared, the ASCII value of the keystroke is returned in AL, and the scan code is returned in AH. The INT16 program in listing 16.8 shows how it can be used.

Listing 16.8

```
program Int16;
uses Dos;
var
    i : byte;
    S : string;
    ch : char;
    ScanCode, ASCIIcode : byte;
function CharacterReady : Boolean;
var
    Regs : Registers;
begin
    Regs.AH := $Ø1;
    Intr( $16, Regs );
    CharacterReady := Regs.Flags and FZero = Ø;
end;
procedure NextCharacter( var ScanCodeValue, ASCIIcodeValue : byte );
var
    Regs : Registers;
begin
    Regs.AH := $Ø1;
    Intr( $16, Regs );
    if Regs.Flags and FZero = Ø then begin
        ScanCodeValue  := Regs.AH;
        ASCIIcodeValue := Regs.AL;
    end else begin
        ScanCodeValue  := Ø;
        ASCIIcodeValue := Ø;
    end;
end;
begin
    while not CharacterReady do;    { Waiting for keystroke }
    NextCharacter( ScanCode, ASCIIcode );
    read( ch );
    writeln( 'I read "', ch, '"' );
    writeln( 'Scan code: ', ScanCode, '  ASCII code: ', ASCIIcode );
end.
```

INT16 uses Function 01 twice—the first time to wait patiently for a keystroke, and the second time to learn which key was pressed. Note that the NextCharacter procedure can correctly identify the key *before* it is read.

Printer Services (Interrupt $17)

The Printer Service BIOS allows Turbo Pascal to interface with the printers attached to the PC.

Three functions are available. Function 00 prints a single character. Function 01 initializes the printer. Neither of these is particularly interesting.

Function 02, however, is a different matter. It tests the *availability* of a printer. With it, you can avoid those annoying delays caused by not knowing whether a printer is on-line. The INT17 program in listing 16.9 demonstrates how to test the status of a printer.

Listing 16.9

```
program Int17;
uses Dos;

function PrinterReady( Printer : byte ) : Boolean;
var
   Regs : Registers;
begin
   Regs.AH := $02;
   Regs.DX := Printer;    { 0=LPT1, 1-LPT2, 2-LPT3 }
   Intr( $17, Regs );
   PrinterReady := (Regs.AH and $80 = $80) and    { Test if ready      }
                   (Regs.AH and $10 = $10) and    { Test if selected   }
                   (Regs.AH and $08 = $00);       { Test if I/O error  }
end;

function PrinterOutOfPaper( Printer : byte ) : Boolean;
var
   Regs : Registers;
begin
   Regs.AH := $02;
   Regs.DX := Printer;    { 0=LPT1, 1=LPT2, 2=LPT2 }
   Intr( $17, Regs );
   PrinterOutOfPaper := Regs.AH and $20 = $20;
end;

begin
   if PrinterReady( 0 ) then    { Check LPT1 }
      begin
         writeln( 'LPT1 is online' );
         if PrinterOutOfPaper( 0 ) then
            writeln( '...but it''s out of paper' );
      end
   else
      writeln( 'Printer not ready' );
end.
```

Of course, if `PrinterReady` returns `False`, the `PrinterOutOfPaper` test is undefined.

Strangely, as simple as these functions are, they are probably the two most useful BIOS routines you will ever use directly.

> **A Precaution about INT17**
>
> Note that because of the absence of standards in the printer industry, Function $02 of BIOS service $17 may return different values for different printers even though they have the same status. If the INT17 program doesn't work correctly on your system, check the technical manual for your printer and adjust the program accordingly.

Time-of-Day Services (Interrupt $1A)

The Time-of-Day Service BIOS is used primarily to control the settings of the real-time clock in the AT. See the *PC/AT Technical Reference Manual* for further information.

A Note on Other BIOS Services

There are, of course, many other BIOS services not mentioned here, but unless you are an experienced systems programmer, you will never need (or want) to access them.

You should *never* randomly call an interrupt. However, accidents—in the form of typographical errors—occur frequently, so you should know something about what might happen so that you can figure out how to prevent recurring problems.

Whenever you write a program that uses interrupts, save it to disk before you run it. As obvious as that sounds, it's the best way to generate an "audit trail" you can later follow to discover your mistake.

If you do make an error, the odds are that nothing bad will happen. Most of the 256 possible slots in the interrupt vector table aren't used; because no subroutine exists, calling a nonexistent service will "hang" your system until you reboot—probably by turning the machine completely off.

Other interrupts can cause bizarre results. In early version of the BIOS, service $18 brings up the PC's ROM BASIC program—the particular version of BASIC that runs when DOS hasn't yet been loaded. Enjoy the session while it lasts; you will have to reboot to terminate it.

BIOS service $19 is a "warm" reboot—an annoying but harmless event. Consider, however, what might happen if you make a mistake while trying to run it yourself. If you forget to type the dollar sign in front of the number $19, then *hexadecimal* 19 (which is decimal 25) becomes *decimal* 19 (which is hexadecimal $13). This simple error causes the Disk Service BIOS to execute, and—depending on the initial contents of the registers—can result in the need to reformat your hard disk.

Accessing DOS Services

Recall that the *number* of a BIOS service is actually a reference to the element of an array of addresses called the interrupt vector table. The disk operating system—commonly called *DOS*—also stores addresses in the interrupt vector table. Although IBM reserves all of the vectors from $20 through $3F for DOS, only a few of these are actually used. Table 16.4 summarizes how these interrupts are currently employed.

Table 16.4. MS-DOS Interrupt Services

Interrupt Number	Description
20	Terminate Program
21	PRIMARY DOS FUNCTIONS
22	Terminate Routine Address
23	Control-C Handler Address
24	Critical Error Handler Address
25	Absolute Disk Read
26	Absolute Disk Write
27	Terminate and Stay Resident
2F	Print Spooling
28 to 2E	Unused but Reserved
30 to 3F	Unused but Reserved

This section explains what these services offer and how they can be used.

The DOS Services

Only nine DOS services are currently available through the interrupt vector table.

Interrupt $20 was the original program termination service. However, since DOS Version 2.0, the preferred method is to use DOS Service $21, Function $4C.

Interrupts $22, $23, and $24 aren't ordinary DOS routines and aren't intended to be called directly. Rather, they serve as convenient pigeon holes for storing addresses. DOS fills them before it runs a program. $22 is the address of the next routine to run after the program terminates normally. $23 is the address of the routine to run if Ctrl-C is pressed while the program runs. $24 is the address of the routine to run in case the program terminates because of a run-time error. By keeping these three addresses in one convenient place, DOS ensures that it can regain control of the PC after a program ends.

Interrupts $25 and $26 directly access individual disk sectors. They aren't intended to be used by ordinary applications programs.

Interrupt $27 is used by terminate-and-stay-resident (TSR) programs.

Interrupt $2F is primarily designed to support the PRINT.COM utility under DOS 3.X, but it can actually handle almost every other print spooler as well.

None of these DOS services contains more than a single function, yet over 80 individual DOS functions exist. All of the rest are found within the one major service accessed through Interrupt $21. In fact, so many functions are contained within service $21 that Turbo Pascal provides a separate procedure for using it: MsDos.

The DOS services are documented in the IBM *PC-DOS Technical Reference Manual.* Table 16.5 contains a listing of all DOS services and component functions by category. Table 16.6 reorganizes the same list into numeric sequence.

Table 16.5. *MS-DOS Services by Category*

Category	Interrupt	Function	Description
Character	21	01	Character Input with Echo
Input	21	03	Auxiliary Input
	21	07	Direct Character Input without Echo
	21	08	Character Input without Echo
	21	0A	Buffered Input
	21	0B	Check whether Character Waiting
	21	0C	Flush Buffer, Then Read Input
Character	21	02	Character Output
Output	21	04	Auxiliary Output
	21	05	Printer Output
	21	06	Direct Console I/O
	21	09	Output a Character String
Disk	21	0D	Disk Reset
Management	21	0E	Select Default Drive
	21	19	Get Current Drive

Table 16.5 continues

Table 16.5 *continued*

Category	Interrupt	Function	Description
	21	1B	Get File Allocation Table for Default Drive
	21	1C	Get File Allocation Table for Specified Drive
	21	2E	Set/Reset Verify Flag
	21	36	Get Disk Free Space
	21	54	Get Verify Flag
	21	68	Flush Buffer
File Management	21	0F	Open File with File Control Block (FCB)
	21	10	Close File with File Control Block (FCB)
	21	11	Find First File
	21	12	Find Next File
	21	13	Delete File
	21	16	Create File with File Control Block (FCB)
	21	17	Rename File
	21	1A	Set Disk Transfer Area (DTA) Address
	21	23	Get File Size
	21	2F	Get Disk Transfer Area (DTA) Address
	21	3C	Create File
	21	3D	Open File
	21	3E	Close File
	21	41	Delete File
	21	43	Get/Set File Attributes
	21	45	Duplicate File Handle
	21	46	Force Duplication of File Handle
	21	4E	Find First File
	21	4F	Find Next File
	21	56	Rename File
	21	57	Get/Set Date/Time of File
	21	5A	Create Temporary File
	21	5B	Create New File
	21	5C	Lock/Unlock File Region
Information Management	21	14	Sequential Read
	21	15	Sequential Write
	21	21	Random Read
	21	22	Random Write
	21	24	Set Random Record
	21	27	Random Block Read
	21	28	Random Block Write

Table 16.5 *continues*

Table 16.5 *continued*

Category	Interrupt	Function	Description
	21	3F	Read File or Device
	21	40	Write File or Device
	21	42	Move File Pointer
	25		Absolute Disk Read
	26		Absolute Disk Write
Directory	21	39	Create Subdirectory
Management	21	3A	Remove Subdirectory
	21	3B	Change Current Directory
	21	47	Get Current Directory
Process	21	00	Terminate Program
Management	21	31	Terminate and Stay Resident
	21	4B	Load and Execute a Program
	21	4C	Terminate Process with Return Code
	21	4D	Get Return Code of Child Process
	21	59	Get Extended Error Information
	20		Terminate Program
	27		Terminate and Stay Resident
Memory	21	48	Allocate Memory Block
Management	21	49	Free Memory Block
	21	4A	Resize Memory Block
Miscellaneous	21	25	Set Interrupt Vector
System	21	26	Create New Program Segment Prefix
Management			(PSP)
	21	29	Parse File name
	21	2A	Get System Date
	21	2B	Set System Date
	21	2C	Get System Time
	21	2D	Set System Time
	21	30	Get DOS Version Number
	21	33	Get/Set Control-Break Check Flag
	21	35	Get Interrupt Vector
	21	38	Get/Set Current Country
	21	44	Device I/O Control
	21	5E	Get Network Machine/Printer Name
	21	5F	Get/Make Assign List Entry
	21	62	Get Program Segment Prefix Address
	21	65	Get Extended Country Information
	21	66	Get/Set Global Code Page
	21	67	Change Handle Count
	22		Terminate Routine Address
	23		Control-C Handler Address
	24		Critical Error Handler Address

Table 16.6. *MS-DOS Services in Numerical Order*

Interrupt Number	Function Number	Description
20		Terminate Program
21	00	Terminate Program
21	01	Character Input with Echo
21	02	Character Output
21	03	Auxiliary Input
21	04	Auxiliary Output
21	05	Printer Output
21	06	Direct Console I/O
21	07	Direct Character Input without Echo
21	08	Character Input without Echo
21	09	Output a Character String
21	0A	Buffered Input
21	0B	Check whether Character Waiting
21	0C	Flush Buffer, Then Read Input
21	0D	Disk Reset
21	0E	Select Default Drive
21	0F	Open File with File Control Block (FCB)
21	10	Close File with File Control Block (FCB)
21	11	Find First File
21	12	Find Next File
21	13	Delete File
21	14	Sequential Read
21	15	Sequential Write
21	16	Create File with File Control Block (FCB)
21	17	Rename File
21	19	Get Current Drive
21	1A	Set Disk Transfer Area (DTA) Address
21	1B	Get File Allocation Table for Default Drive
21	1C	Get File Allocation Table for Specified Drive
21	21	Random Read
21	22	Random Write

Table 16.6 continues

Table 16.6 *continued*

Interrupt Number	Function Number	Description
21	23	Get File Size
21	24	Set Random Record
21	25	Set Interrupt Vector
21	26	Create New Program Segment Prefix (PSP)
21	27	Random Block Read
21	28	Random Block Write
21	29	Parse File name
21	2A	Get System Date
21	2B	Set System Date
21	2C	Get System Time
21	2D	Set System Time
21	2E	Set/Reset Verify Flag
21	2F	Get Disk Transfer Area (DTA) Address
21	30	Get DOS Version Number
21	31	Terminate and Stay Resident
21	33	Get/Set Control-Break Check Flag
21	35	Get Interrupt Vector
21	36	Get Disk Free Space
21	38	Get/Set Current Country
21	39	Create Subdirectory
21	3A	Remove Subdirectory
21	3B	Change Current Directory
21	3C	Create File
21	3D	Open File
21	3E	Close File
21	3F	Read File or Device
21	40	Write File or Device
21	41	Delete File
21	42	Move File Pointer
21	43	Get/Set File Attributes
21	44	Device I/O Control
21	45	Duplicate File Handle
21	46	Force Duplication of File Handle
21	47	Get Current Directory
21	48	Allocate Memory Block

Table 16.6 *continues*

Table 16.6 *continued*

Interrupt Number	Function Number	Description
21	49	Free Memory Block
21	4A	Resize Memory Block
21	4B	Load and Execute a Program
21	4C	Terminate Process with Return Code
21	4D	Get Return Code of Child Process
21	4E	Find First File
21	4F	Find Next File
21	54	Get Verify Flag
21	56	Rename File
21	57	Get/Set Date/Time of File
21	59	Get Extended Error Information
21	5A	Create Temporary File
21	5B	Create New File
21	5C	Lock/Unlock File Region
21	5E	Get Network Machine/Printer Name
21	5F	Get/Make Assign List Entry
21	62	Get Program Segment Prefix Address
21	65	Get Extended Country Information
21	66	Get/Set Global Code Page
21	67	Change Handle Count
21	68	Flush Buffer
22		Terminate Routine Address
23		Control-C Handler Address
24		Critical Error Handler Address
25		Absolute Disk Read
26		Absolute Disk Write
27		Terminate and Stay Resident

Using DOS Services

Turbo Pascal provides *over 200* predefined procedures and functions—considerably more than the 80 or so provided by DOS itself.

In fact, the list of DOS functions in table 16.5 reads like the index of the Turbo Pascal *Reference Guide*. Because compilers, like all programs designed to run on the PC, must rely heavily on DOS services, it's no surprise that almost all of the DOS functions have found their way into Turbo routines.

When Borland first introduced Turbo Pascal, the MsDos procedure was a necessary part of almost every major programming application. Today, it's used principally in those few situations when execution speed is more important than programming convenience.

Calling DOS Services from Turbo Pascal

The rules for using MsDos are the same as those for Intr. The specific function number is placed in the AH register prior to calling the procedure. Any necessary parameters are placed in the appropriate registers. Any results generated by the procedure are returned in the registers. A few examples will illustrate how MsDos operates.

The INT21_9 program in listing 16.10 shows how Function 09 of DOS Service $21 can be used. Function 09 displays a string of characters beginning at the current cursor location. However, rather than using an ordinary Turbo Pascal string type, Function 09 can only handle a sequence of char-type characters, the last of which must be a dollar sign.

Listing 16.10

```
program Int21_9;
uses Dos;
var
   S : string;
procedure ShowString( var DisplayString : string );
var
   Regs : Registers;
begin
   Regs.AH := $09;
   Regs.DS := Seg( DisplayString );
   Regs.DX := Ofs( DisplayString ) + 1;
   MsDos( Regs );
end;
begin
   S := 'Hello, world!' + '$';
   ShowString( S );
end.
```

As you can tell from a quick examination of the ShowString procedure, the DS and DX registers must contain the segment and offset, respectively, of the first character in the string. ShowString adds 1 to the offset of DisplayString to bypass the string's size byte. When INT21_9 executes, the dollar sign is *not* displayed.

The INT21_2A program in listing 16.11 performs the same DOS call (Function $2A) as the GetDate procedure. After Function $2A is invoked, the DH register contains the month, the DL register contains the day, and the CX register contains the year.

Listing 16.11

```
program Int21_2A;
uses Dos;
procedure TodayIs;
var
   Regs : Registers;
begin
   Regs.AH := $2A;
   MsDos( Regs );
   with Regs do begin
      write( 'Current date:   ' );
      if DH < 10 then write( '0' );
      write( DH, '/' );
      if DL < 10 then write( '0' );
      writeln( DL, '/', CX - 1900 );
   end;
end;
begin
   TodayIs;
end.
```

The INT21_30 program in listing 16.12 duplicates the workings of the DosVersion function.

Listing 16.12

```
program Int21_30;
uses Dos;
procedure IdentifyVersion;
var
   Regs : Registers;
begin
   Regs.AH := $30;
   MsDos( Regs );
   writeln( 'Now running DOS Version ', Regs.AL, '.', Regs.AH );
end;
begin
   IdentifyVersion;
end.
```

The INT21_36 program in listing 16.13 uses Function $36 to obtain information about the formatting characteristics of a specified disk.

Listing 16.13

```
program Int21_36;
uses Dos;
procedure DiskFreeSpace( DriveCode : byte );
var
   Regs                  : Registers;
   SectorsPerCluster,
   AvailableClusters,
   BytesPerSector,
   ClustersPerDrive,
   Capacity,
   Free                  : LongInt;
begin
   Regs.AH := $36;
   Regs.DL := DriveCode;
   MsDos( Regs );
   SectorsPerCluster := Regs.AX;    { If bad DriveCode, AX = -1 ($FFFF) }
   AvailableClusters := Regs.BX;
   BytesPerSector    := Regs.CX;
   ClustersPerDrive  := Regs.DX;
   writeln( 'Sectors Per Cluster = ', SectorsPerCluster:10 );
   writeln( 'Available Clusters  = ', AvailableClusters:10 );
   writeln( 'Bytes Per Sector    = ', BytesPerSector:10   );
   writeln( 'Clusters Per Drive  = ', ClustersPerDrive:10   );
   Capacity := SectorsPerCluster * BytesPerSector * ClustersPerDrive;
   Free     := SectorsPerCluster * AvailableClusters * BytesPerSector;
   writeln( 'Capacity            = ', Capacity:10          );
   writeln( 'Free                = ', Free:10              );
end;
begin
   DiskFreeSpace( 0 );
end.
```

Using Assembly Language in Turbo Pascal

There is one final means of exploiting the power and speed of the PC: through assembly language programming.

And, like all "final" means, assembly language is to be used only as a last resort.

Using Assembly Language with the Inline Procedure

The most direct way of using assembly language is to insert it into a Turbo Pascal program using the Inline procedure. Inline accepts any number of parameters, each of which corresponds to a hexadecimal value representing the results of the assembly operation—that is, the final 8086 machine code itself. A few examples will illustrate how to use `Inline`.

The INT05 program in listing 16.1 used the `Intr` procedure to execute the Print Screen Service BIOS. To achieve the same results with the `Inline` procedure, you would use the following code:

```
procedure PrintScreen;
begin
  Inline
    ($CD/$Ø5);
end;
```

The two hex characters $CD and $05 are the *actual 8086 machine code instructions* that trigger an Interrupt 05.

A slightly more complicated situation arises when a value must be returned as a result of the execution of a procedure or function. The INT12 program in listing 16.7 used the `Intr` procedure to determine the size of internal memory in 1K blocks. To implement this interrupt in the form of an assembly language function, you would use the following code:

```
function MemorySize : integer;
  Inline
    ($CD/$12/       { int  12h        ; BIOS Equip Service }
     $89/$46/$Ø4);  { mov  [bp+4],ax  ; Return size (x 1K) }
```

Here, five hexadecimal machine language instructions must be sent to the CPU. The equivalent assembly language source statements are shown in the comments on the right-hand side. Recall that the BP register contains the current working offset of the stack segment. Hence, the instruction

```
mov   [bp +4],ax
```

copied the contents of the AX register (the result of the BIOS call) to the top of the stack—something that Turbo Pascal manages for you automatically.

These two examples show that a relatively trivial operation in Turbo Pascal can be excruciatingly painful to perform in assembly language. After all, not only do you need to understand how to translate your commands from Turbo Pascal to assembly language, but you also need to know how to translate assembly language to machine code.

It's impossible to teach assembly language in the space of a few pages. It's equally challenging to explain how to write machine-code instructions. Just to illustrate the difficulties, consider the following example. The single assembly language instruction MOV (short for *move*) corresponds to a simple assignment operation in Turbo Pascal. While the two characters := achieve the desired result in Turbo Pascal, you need to choose among *22 unique hexadecimal machine code formats!* Either two or three bytes would need to be generated; thankfully, the exact rules don't matter for now.

Other Ways of Incorporating Assembly Language

While the inline statement itself is usually used to replace a few lines of Turbo Pascal code, the inline directive format is used to replace an entire procedure or function, similar to the way macros are implemented in assembly language.

Separate assembly language programs can be combined with Turbo Pascal by a process called *linking*, similar to the way the Turbo Pascal run-time libraries are linked with your program during compilation. The assembly language source program must first be assembled into object file (.OBJ) format with an assembler. The object file is then linked with your Turbo Pascal program using the {$L} compiler directive. After the assembled routines are declared in your Turbo program with the reserved word external, they can be used like ordinary Turbo Pascal routines.

When To Use Assembly Language

Because Turbo Pascal provides the Intr and MsDos procedures, as well as the Port, PortW, Mem, MemW, and MemL arrays, there is really only one reason to consider using assembly language in a Turbo Pascal program: speed. Even then, assembly language provides only a minor improvement—often on the order of just a few clock cycles.

Although a full discussion of the use of assembly language is beyond the scope of this book, remember: Turbo Pascal is—in and of itself—fast enough and powerful enough for almost every possible programming application.

Summary

In this chapter, you have learned how Turbo Pascal allows you to directly access the BIOS and DOS services of your PC, and, in addition, you have seen how to directly incorporate assembly language instructions in your programs.

You have learned that BIOS and DOS services are called just like ordinary Turbo Pascal procedures. The Intr procedure is used to call BIOS services, and the MsDos procedure is used to call DOS services. Many of the more useful BIOS and DOS routines were demonstrated.

You have learned that the rules for using Intr and MsDos are the same. The specific function number is placed in the AH register prior to calling the procedure. Registers are used to pass parameters to the BIOS and DOS services, and any results are returned in the registers.

You have learned that assembly language may be incorporated in your Turbo Pascal programs through the use of the Inline procedure. Inline accepts any number of parameters, each of which corresponds to an actual machine code instruction. You have seen that in order to use Inline, you need to understand how to translate your commands from Turbo Pascal to machine code. You now know that even a simple inline operation is difficult to implement and only rarely worth the effort.

You have also learned that external object files can be linked with Turbo Pascal through the use of the {$L} compiler directive. After the assembled routine is declared in your Turbo program with the reserved word external, it can be used like an ordinary Turbo Pascal procedure or function.

CHAPTER 17

The 8087 and External Devices

Long before IBM sold the first Personal Computer, the corporation had already taken the unprecedented step of publishing its technical specifications. IBM's design philosophy was called *open architecture*. IBM believed that if you knew how its new machine worked, you could more rapidly design, develop, and market products that relied on the PC and consequently increase the sales potential of the PC itself. Early editions of the *Technical Reference Manual* even contained the complete listing of the BIOS software.

IBM's open architecture is probably the biggest reason why the PC enjoys its current popularity. Other manufacturers were quickly able to introduce high-quality, competitively priced add-on memories, peripherals, and software. Today's PC supports such diverse products as modems, graphics plotters, laser printers, compact disk storage devices, and local area networks. PCs are connected to robots on assembly lines, laboratory equipment, and speech generation and recognition equipment.

Yet, even the engineers who designed the PC couldn't have predicted the range of products that emerged and flourished in the years since. The twofold question is: How were the new products able to adapt themselves to the PC, and how was the PC itself able to cope with them?

The answer is that both the computer's internal architecture and the operating system *expect* to support a generic piece of equipment called a *device*. Anything that can conform to the definition of a device can successfully interface with the PC.

In this chapter, you will learn how Turbo Pascal can access these strange machines through data ports and special software.

Accessing Data Ports

Turbo Pascal provides the predefined arrays Port and PortW so that you can access the computer's input and output data ports. Reading from or assigning to the Port and PortW arrays has the same effect as reading from or assigning to the I/O ports themselves.

A *port* is a special channel used by the CPU to communicate with its support circuitry. Each port is identified by a 16-bit value called the *port address*. Almost all of the PC's peripherals (including everything from fixed disks through any installed game adapter cards) communicate with the CPU through one or more ports. Therefore, by accessing the ports individually, you can directly communicate with any external hardware device.

Transferring Data

When Port or PortW appears on the left side of an assignment statement, the compiler assumes that you want to *move* data to the specified port. At all other times, the compiler assumes that you want to *read* data from the specified port. The Port and PortW array index corresponds to the port address.

The Port array transfers one byte of data at a time. PortW transfers a full word. Because most peripheral devices are designed to accommodate the 8-bit data bus of the PC, it's unlikely that you will ever use PortW.

The VANISH program in listing 17.1 uses the Port array to send instructions directly to the adapter card—either color or monochrome—and disable the PC's screen. The Color constant is set to either True or False, depending on whether your PC uses a color or monochrome adapter.

Listing 17.1

```
program Vanish;
uses Crt;
const
   Color = True;
var
   ch : char;
begin
   if Color then begin          {********* COLOR **********}
      Port[ $3D8 ] := $25;      {*   Disable the screen    *}
      repeat until KeyPressed;   {*   Wait for key press    *}
      Port[ $3D8 ] := $2D;      {*   Restore the screen    *}
   end else begin               {****** MONOCHROME *******}
      Port[ $3B8 ] := $21;      {*   Disable the screen    *}
      repeat until KeyPressed;   {*   Wait for key press    *}
      Port[ $3B8 ] := $29;      {*   Restore the screen    *}
   end;                         {*************************}
   ch := ReadKey;               {* Clear keyboard buffer   *}
end.                            {*************************}
```

The VANISH program blanks the screen until a key is pressed. Blanking isn't the same as erasing; a blanked screen is *prevented* from displaying the contents of video memory, but the video memory itself is unaffected. When the screen is restored, the original screen image returns.

Blanking has its practical applications. For example, some graphics programs blank the screen while images are drawn. Restoring the screen has the effect of making the graphics display appear instantaneous.

The Danger of Accessing Ports

Never randomly experiment with a port! Some ports, for example, activate events when *read*, not just when *written*. The PORT1 program in listing 17.2 accesses port $3D9, which controls the background color of text mode. Even though the program only *reads* the value of the port, it's possible that the background color will change as a consequence.

Listing 17.2

```
program Port1;
begin
   writeln( Port[ $3D9 ] )
end.
```

Similar side-effects exist with other ports. Unless you are careful, you can easily destroy data on your disks. For a complete list of ports, the devices they service, and the values they return, consult the *IBM PC Technical Reference Manual*.

Eliminating Snow on the Screen

When you write directly to the video memory of a CGA color adapter card, you are liable to see *snow* on the screen. Snow is the result of the competition between two screen output instructions—in this case, the "normal" display signal and your own direct memory write.

All images appearing on the screen must constantly be updated, or *refreshed*, 60 times per second. On a monochrome screen, a single beam moves in a left-to-right and top-to-bottom motion, establishing the content of each pixel. A color screen uses three beams—one for each primary color.

When the beam reaches the right side of a line, the beam is temporarily turned off while it moves to the left side of the next line. Similarly, when the beam reaches the bottom right corner of the screen, it is temporarily disabled while it resets itself to the upper left corner. These periods of inactivity are called horizontal and vertical *blanking*, respectively. A blanking interval is also known as a *retrace*. Direct video writes occurring during the horizontal and vertical blanking periods won't conflict with the normal screen update process. As a result, no snow appears.

To detect a retrace, access port $3DA. If bit 0 is set, the screen is in horizontal blanking. If bit 3 is set, the screen is in vertical blanking. By continuously testing this port and examining these bits, you can tell when your direct video write should begin.

The NOSNOW1 program in listing 17.3 performs a direct write to video memory for all of the characters in a string. Each character is written only after the horizontal retrace is complete.

Listing 17.3

```
program NoSnow1;
const
    VideoSegment = $B800;
    Blank        = 1;      { 1 = Horizontal (Bit 0), 8 = Vertical (Bit 3) }
var
    Position : byte;
procedure FlickerFree( Column, Row : word;  Message : string );
var
    i : byte;
    Offset : word;
```

Listing 17.3 continues

Listing 17.3 continued

```
begin
   Offset := (160 * Row) + (2 * Column);
   for i := 1 to Length( Message ) do begin
      while (Port[ $3DA ] and Blank =  Blank) do;   { Wait until clear }
      while (Port[ $3DA ] and Blank  <> Blank) do;   { Wait until set }
      Mem[ VideoSegment : Offset ] := ord( Message[ i ] );
      Inc( Offset, 2 );
   end;
end;
begin
   for Position := 5 to 20 do
      FlickerFree( Position, Position, 'Hello, world!' );
end.
```

The `FlickerFree` procedure writes a single character at the beginning of a horizontal blanking period. The statement

```
while (Port[ $3DA ] and Blank = Blank) do;
```

prevents the program from proceeding until one horizontal blanking period ends (that is, until bit 0 is cleared). Similarly, the statement

```
while (Port[ $3DA ] and Blank <> Blank) do;
```

waits for the next horizontal blanking to begin (when bit 0 is set).

Because horizontal blanking lasts only 18.5 microseconds, you barely have time to write one character. In fact, because the blanking interval is so brief, this technique might not work at all unless the code is written in assembly language. Consequently, it may be necessary to use the vertical blanking interval by changing the `Blank` constant to 8. Because by comparison vertical blanking lasts an incredibly long time (1,500 microseconds), you can further modify the program to allow several characters to be written during a *single* vertical blanking interval.

In the NOSNOW2 program in listing 17.4, the `FlickerFree` procedure waits for the vertical retrace to begin, then writes out the entire string.

Listing 17.4

```
program NoSnow2;
const
   VideoSegment = $B800;
   Blank        = 8;      { 1 = Horizontal (Bit 0), 8 = Vertical (Bit 3) }
var
   Position : byte;
procedure FlickerFree( Column, Row : word;  Message : string );
var
   i : byte;
   Offset : word;
```

Listing 17.4 continues

Listing 17.4 *continued*

```
begin
   Offset := (160 * Row) + (2 * Column);
   while (Port[ $3DA ] and Blank =  Blank) do;   { Wait until clear }
   while (Port[ $3DA ] and Blank <> Blank) do;   { Wait until set }
   for i := 1 to Length( Message ) do begin
      Mem[ VideoSegment : Offset ] := ord( Message[ i ] );
      Inc( Offset, 2 );
   end;
end;
begin
   for Position := 5 to 20 do
      FlickerFree( Position, Position, 'Hello, world!' );
end.
```

If coordinating direct memory writes with the vertical blanking interval still isn't sufficient to remove flicker, one other trick remains for you to try.

1. Using the techniques in NOSNOW1 and NOSNOW2 (listings 17.3 and 17.4), wait for a blanking interval to begin.

2. Blank the entire screen, as shown in the VANISH program (listing 17.1).

3. Execute all of your direct memory write statements.

4. Wait for another blanking interval to begin.

5. Redisplay the screen.

With a little experimenting, you can create fast screen updates with no annoying snow.

Using Devices

To DOS, anything outside the main memory is a *device*. The keyboard, screen, disk drives, modem, and printer are all examples of devices. If your PC has an internal clock (such as on an AST SixPak Plus memory card), the clock itself is considered a device. Optical disks, network connector cards, and graphics plotters are also devices.

A device isn't limited to external hardware that's physically connected to your PC. If your machine is configured for a RAM disk (that is, if you use internal memory to *imitate* a disk drive), the RAM disk is a device.

There are two broad categories of devices. *Block* devices are disks. Everything else is a *character* device. Disks, files, and directories were discussed in Chapters 13 and 14. In this section, you will learn how to develop Turbo Pascal programs that access the character devices installed in your PC.

DOS Devices

Normally, when you use DOS, you access the devices attached to your PC with the reserved file names shown in table 17.1.

Table 17.1. *DOS Device File Names*

Name	Description
AUX	(Same as COM1) The first asynchronous communications port
COM1	(Same as AUX) The first asynchronous communications port
COM2	The second asynchronous communications port
CON	For input, CON is to the keyboard For output, CON is the screen
LPT1	(Same as PRN) The first parallel printer port
LPT2	The second parallel printer port
LPT3	The third parallel printer port
PRN	(Same as LPT1) The first parallel printer port

You are probably intimately familiar with DOS devices already. For example, to change the system printer (LPT1) from its default setting of 80 columns to the larger size of 132 columns, you would use the DOS command:

MODE LPT1: 132

Similarly, to display a text file on the screen, you could redirect output from the console (CON) to the printer (PRN), as follows:

TYPE TEXTFILE.TXT > PRN

Although it isn't shown in table 17.1, DOS also provides for a *nonexistent* device called NUL. The NUL device, which is rarely used, is handy only in those unusual circumstances when you *don't* want a real device to be used. For example, if you have a batch file that contains the instruction:

TYPE TEXTFILE.TXT > PRN

but you don't want printer output, you can either delete the line or change it to

TYPE TEXTFILE.TXT > NUL

DOS Device Drivers

Obviously, each physical device is different and requires a unique set of control commands. Yet, under DOS, all of these devices can be accessed identically.

For each device configured in your PC, the operating system includes a separate piece of controlling software called a *device driver* that serves as an interface between DOS and the peripheral. A device driver includes all the low-level, machine-specific code that manages the actual piece of hardware, but it also allows DOS to control the device with just a few standardized commands.

An individual device driver may be stored in a separate file on disk, but is loaded into memory after the system is running but before COMMAND.COM is loaded. Hence, a device driver may be part of the operating system, but it isn't necessarily part of the DOS files.

Because of the existence of device drivers, DOS provides the same input and output software services for all external devices. Because Turbo Pascal uses DOS extensively, it must follow along. Consequently, the compiler itself interfaces with every device in the same way and can't differentiate the exact *type* of physical device it's accessing.

Devices in Turbo Pascal

One of the reasons that DOS character devices can be treated so similarly is because of the common way they transfer data. All devices communicate with the CPU one byte at a time, sending and receiving their data in ASCII format. Suppose, for example, that you want to output the number $9AE5 to the printer. Even though $9AE5 is stored internally in binary format, you would probably want the number to list out as the string

39653

Consequently, the two-byte binary value is converted to the five individual ASCII characters for *3, 9, 6, 5*, and *3*—that is, bytes $33, $39, $36, $35, and $33.

Similarly, when you use a modem to receive data over a phone line, you probably use a protocol that groups every nine bits into one ASCII byte and one parity bit. If the parity test is successful, the ASCII data from the modem is converted to binary form for internal storage and later processing by the PC.

Not surprisingly, the ASCII-binary conversion that occurs when your program communicates with a device is identical to the conversion that occurs when you are processing text files. In fact, the text file is Turbo Pascal's mechanism for communicating with devices. You use `write` and `writeln` as the principal output procedures, and `read` and `readln` are the principal input procedures.

A *physical* character device may be any piece of hardware you can imagine. But to Turbo Pascal, it will always be a text file.

Using Devices as Turbo Pascal Text Files

Turbo Pascal provides predefined file names that correspond to the standard DOS devices. For the sake of simplicity, the file names used by the compiler correspond closely with those used by DOS itself.

To use one of the devices, declare a text file identifier, `Assign` it to one of the file names listed in table 17.2 and open it for input or output with `Reset` or `Rewrite`.

Table 17.2. *Turbo Pascal Device File Names*

Name	Description
AUX	(Same as COM1) The first asynchronous communications port
COM1	(Same as AUX) The first asynchronous communications port
COM2	The second asynchronous communications port
CON	Keyboard or screen
LPT1	(Same as PRN) The first parallel printer port
LPT2	The second parallel printer port
LPT3	The third parallel printer port
NUL	The nonexistent device
PRN	(Same as LPT1) The first parallel printer port
"	Standard input or output

For example, to open one file as the printer and another file as the keyboard, you can use the code demonstrated in the DEVICE1 program in listing 17.5. Be sure your printer is on line before running the program.

Listing 17.5

```
program Device1;
var
   Printer, Console : Text;
   S : string;
begin
   Assign( Printer, 'PRN' );
   Rewrite( Printer );
   Assign( Console, 'CON' );
   Reset( Console );
   readln( Console, S );    { This is coming from the keyboard }
   writeln( Printer, 'This is going to the printer.' );
   writeln( Printer, S );
   Close( Printer );
   Close( Console );
end.
```

The Printer Standard Unit

Remember that the Printer standard unit declares the Lst variable as a text file, assigns Lst to the PRN device with the Assign procedure, and opens the file for output with Rewrite. Consequently, if your program includes a uses Printer; declaration, you can output to the printer by writing directly to the Lst file.

The CON device can be used for either input or output, as demonstrated in the DEVICE2 program in listing 17.6.

Listing 17.6

```
program Device2;
var
   Keyboard, Screen : Text;
   S : string;
begin
   Assign( Keyboard, 'CON' );
   Reset( Keyboard );
   Assign( Screen, 'CON' );
   Rewrite( Screen );
   readln( Keyboard, S );
   writeln( Screen, S );
   Close( Keyboard );
   Close( Screen );
end.
```

With only a few obvious exceptions (not being able to read from the printer, for example) DOS devices behave exactly like files. In fact, the procedures, functions, and syntax of Turbo Pascal is the same for a DOS device as it is for any normal text file.

Standard Input and Output

The System unit includes the two predefined text files Input and Output. You will find them declared in the SYSTEM.DOC unit header file that came with your Turbo Pascal distribution disks.

Input and Output are called the *standard* input and output files, respectively. These files are automatically opened and available throughout the execution of a Turbo Pascal program. The two file identifiers are both Assigned to CON, but Input is opened with Reset, and Output is opened with Rewrite.

Whenever a file parameter is omitted from a read or write procedure, the compiler assumes that you are referring to Input or Output. For example, the following instructions are equivalent:

```
readln( x )   =   readln( Input, x )
writeln( x )  =   writeln( Input, x )
```

Note that every time one of your programs accessed the keyboard or the screen, Turbo Pascal processed the instructions invisibly as text files!

You can *specifically* open Input and Output by referencing the null file in an assignment statement. For example, the following code opens Output as the text file StdOut:

```
Assign( StdOut, '' );
Rewrite( StdOut );
```

All data written to the StdOut file will now be sent to Output. The CRTR1 program in Chapter 10 (listing 10.4) demonstrates the advantages of this technique.

DOS File Handles

When a Reset, Rewrite, or Append procedure is executed, the compiler passes DOS the name of the physical file identified in the Assign procedure. After DOS successfully opens a file, it returns a 16-bit number called a *file handle*. From that point forward, DOS always references the open file by its handle. (An unopened file always has a handle of –1.) Consequently, when the compiler wants to access a file, it must communicate with DOS using the handle rather than the file name.

In effect, the DOS file handle acts like the Turbo Pascal file identifier variable. Your program can use the same identifier to access several physical files (after each is appropriately closed and reopened, of course). Similarly, DOS can use the same handle to reference several physical files, although, like Pascal, DOS must also close and reopen a file before the handle can be reused.

By default, DOS only allows eight file handles to be active at a time. To change this value, include the instruction:

FILES =nn

in the CONFIG.SYS file. Under MS-DOS Version 3.0, the maximum number of file handles is 255. In Chapter 1, you learned that Turbo Pascal requires 20 files to be configured (that is, FILES =20).

Turbo Pascal *always* opens five standard DOS character devices. Each of these devices, together with their associated file handles, is listed in table 17.3.

Table 17.3 *Standard Files*

Handle	Device Name	Opened to
0	Standard input	CON
1	Standard output	CON
2	Console device	CON
3	Communications	COM1/AUX
4	Printer	LPT1/PRN

DOS allows Turbo Pascal to have only 15 files open simultaneously. These 15 files are the difference between the system configuration total of 20 files and the 5 standard files shown in the table.

Typed and Untyped File Variables

Whenever a file is opened in a Turbo Pascal program, the compiler creates a data record containing the information it needs to manage the file. If the Turbo Pascal file identifier variable is FilVar, the data record for the file can be found at the memory location @FilVar.

This data record takes one of two forms. The form of records for text files is slightly different than one created for typed and untyped files. While more interesting, text file data records are also more complicated; they are covered a bit later in the chapter. The data records for typed and untyped files are smaller and less complicated, so I will begin with them.

Every open typed and untyped file has an associated 128-byte data record defined as FileRec in the Dos standard unit. FileRec is laid out as shown here.

```
FileRec = record
            Handle   : Word;
            Mode     : Word;
            RecSize  : Word;
            Private  : array[1..26] of Byte;
            UserData : array[1..16] of Byte;
            Name     : array[0..79] of Char;
          end;
```

The Handle field contains the file handle assigned by DOS. Remember that its value is –1($FFFF) until the file is opened. The Mode field contains one of the four values listed in table 17.4.

Table 17.4 *File Mode Constants*

Constant	Value	Hex Value	Decimal Meaning
fmClosed	$D7B0	55,216	File is closed.
fmInput	$D7B1	55,217	File is a text file open for input.
fmOutput	$D7B2	55,218	File is a text file open for output.
fmInOut	$D7B3	55,219	File is open for both input and output.

The Turbo Pascal *Reference Guide* colorfully describes these numbers as "magic" values. The Mode field of typed and untyped files may be either fmClosed or fmInOut. As you will see shortly, the Mode field of a text file can be fmClosed, fmInput, or fmOutput. If the Mode field contains any other number, then the file variable hasn't yet been initialized.

RecSize equals the size of each data element in the file—in bytes. Although the Private field is currently unused, future releases of the compiler will probably need it. The UserData field is available if you want to store any file-specific data. You can use it to store one or more pointers in case you need more than 16 bytes.

The Name field contains the file name in ASCIIZ format. In other words, Name isn't a Turbo Pascal string data type, but rather a sequence of ASCII characters ending with a null character (#0).

To show you how a file record is used, the FILE0 program in listing 17.7 creates a small data file.

Listing 17.7

```
program Fileط;
type
   TestRecord = record
                   A : real;        { 6 bytes }
                   B : integer;     { 2 bytes }
                   C : byte;        { 1 byte  }
               end;                 { 9 bytes total }
var
   TestFile : file of TestRecord;
   TestData : TestRecord;
   i : byte;
begin
   Assign( TestFile, 'FileData.Tst' );
   Rewrite( TestFile );
   with TestData do begin
     A := 1طط.ط;
     B := 1طط;
     C := 1طط;
   end;
   for i := 1 to 2ط do
     write( TestFile, TestData );
   Close( TestFile );
end.
```

When FILE0 executes, it creates the file FILEDATA.TST consisting of 20 records of nine bytes each. You can examine the file record for FILEDATA.TST using the FILE1 program in listing 17.8.

Listing 17.8

```
program File1;
uses Dos;
type
   TestRecord = record
                   A : real;
                   B : integer;
                   C : byte;
               end;
var
   InFile : file of TestRecord;
   InRec  : ^FileRec;
   i : byte;
begin
   Assign( InFile, 'FileData.Tst' );
   Reset( InFile );
   InRec := @InFile;
   with InRec^ do begin
     write( 'File name:    ' );
     i := ط;
     while Name[i] <> #ط do begin    { Process an ASCIIZ string }
       write( Name[i] );
       Inc(i);
```

Listing 17.8 continues

Listing 17.8 continued

```
            end;
         writeln;
         writeln( 'Handle:        ', Handle );
         writeln( 'Record size:  ', RecSize );
         write( 'Mode:          ' );
         case Mode - $D700 of   { Selectors can't exceed value of MaxInt }
            $B0 : writeln( 'Closed' );
            $B1 : writeln( 'Open for input' );
            $B2 : writeln( 'Open for output' );
            $B3 : writeln( 'Open for both input and output' );
         end;
         write( 'Private area: ' );
         for i := 1 to 26 do write( Chr( Private[ i ] ) );   writeln;
         write( 'User area:    ' );
         for i := 1 to 16 do write( Chr( UserData[ i ] ) );   writeln;
      end;
      Close( InFile );
end.
```

FILE1 produces the following output:

```
File name:    FileData.Tst
Handle:       5
Record size:  9
Mode:         Open for both input and output
Private area:
User area:
```

The Name field contains the file name just as it appeared in the Assign statement, complete with the same pattern of upper- and lowercase letters. The Handle field is 5, the first available value after the standard devices are opened and their handles (0 through 4) are assigned. The 9-byte record size corresponds to SizeOf(TestRecord). Both the Private and UserData fields are blank.

How the File Data Type Record Is Used

Assume that DataRecs is a file identifier variable. When you use DataRecs in an input or output statement, such as

```
Read( DataRecs, x, y, z )   or   Write( DataRecs, x, y, z )
```

what you are really doing is passing the file identifier variable to the read and write procedures as one of the parameters. The read and write procedures can access the file record at @DataRecs to obtain information such as the following:

❑ The file handle, to pass along to DOS

❑ The file mode, to ensure that a read or write is a legal operation on the file

❏ The record size, to determine how many characters should be input or output at one time

❏ The file name, to pass along to any error messages

All things considered, you are really passing along a rather impressive amount of information. And as you will see next, a text file record type contains even more data.

Text File Variables

When a text file is opened in a Turbo Pascal program, the compiler creates a 256-byte data record defined as TextRec in the Dos standard unit. TextRec is laid out as shown here.

```
TextBuf = array[0..127] of Char;
TextRec = record
            Handle    : Word;
            Mode      : Word;
            BufSize   : Word;
            Private   : Word;
            BufPos    : Word;
            BufEnd    : Word;
            BufPtr    : ^TextBuf;
            OpenFunc  : Pointer;
            InOutFunc : Pointer;
            FlushFunc : Pointer;
            CloseFunc : Pointer;
            UserData  : array[1..16] of Byte;
            Name      : array[0..79] of Char;
            Buffer    : TextBuf;
          end;
```

The Handle, Mode, UserData, and Name fields are the same for a text file as for typed and untyped files. The Private field also has the same purpose, except that here it's defined as a word instead of an array.

Several additional fields are also evident. The BufSize, BufPos, BufEnd, BufPtr, and Buffer fields manage the text file buffering process. By default, the text file buffer is contained in the Buffer field. BufPtr points to a buffer whose size is given by BufSize. BufPos is the buffer location of the next character to be processed. BufEnd holds the number of characters in the buffer. If the SetTextBuf procedure is used to designate a different text file buffer, these fields change accordingly.

OpenFunc, InOutFunc, FlushFunc, and CloseFunc point to the DOS device driver software. These fields are discussed in more detail next.

The FILE3 program in listing 17.9 can be used to examine its own text file record.

Listing 17.9

```pascal
program File3;
uses Crt, Dos;
var
   InFile : Text;
   InRec  : ^TextRec;
   Data   : string;
   i : byte;
begin
   Assign( InFile, 'File3.PAS' );
   Reset( InFile );
   InRec := @InFile;
   with InRec^ do repeat
      ClrScr;
      readln( InFile, Data );
      write( 'File name:    ' );
      i := 0;
      while Name[i] <> #0 do begin
         write( Name[i] );
         Inc(i);
      end;
      writeln;
      writeln( 'Handle:      ', Handle );
      write( 'Mode:        ' );
      case Mode - $D700 of
         $B0 : writeln( 'Closed' );
         $B1 : writeln( 'Open for input' );
         $B2 : writeln( 'Open for output' );
         $B3 : writeln( 'Open for both input and output' );
      end;
      writeln( 'Private area: ', Private );
      write( 'User area:   ' );
      for i := 1 to 16 do write( Chr( UserData[ i ] ) );   writeln;
      writeln( 'Buffer size: ', BufSize );
      writeln( 'Buffer pos:  ', BufPos );
      writeln( 'Buffer end:  ', BufEnd );
      writeln( 'Buffer:      ' );
      writeln( '=========================================' );
      for i := 0 to 127 do write( Buffer[ i ] );   writeln;
      writeln( '=========================================' );
      readln;
   until Eof( InFile );
   Close( InFile );
end.
```

FILE3 displays the contents of the text file record as each data record is read. The first display is shown in figure 17.1.

Fig. 17.1. Output produced by the FILE3 program.

```
File name:     File3.PAS
Handle:        5
Mode:          Open for input
Private area:  0
User area:
Buffer size:   128
Buffer pos:    16
Buffer end:    128
Buffer:
==============================================
program File3;
uses Dos;
var
   InFile : Text;
   InRec  : ^TextRec;
   Data   : string;
   i : byte;
begin
   Assign( I
==============================================
```

Pressing the Enter key causes the next record to be read and a new screen to be displayed. With each new record, notice that the BufPos value increases until all of the characters in the buffer are assigned to the Data string. Then, the next 128 bytes from the file are placed in the buffer, and the BufPos field is reset.

Text File Device Drivers

Although the set of built-in device drivers is more than adequate for most programming applications, new drivers are frequently needed as a result of special hardware and software requirements.

For example, in Chapter 11, the Borland Graphics Interface (BGI) files are used as device drivers for the graphics adapter cards. Other peripherals that usually require their own device driver include:

❏ RAM disks

❏ Mouse drivers

❏ Expanded memory managers

❏ Joysticks

❏ Modems and other communications hardware

Similarly, new device drivers may be required to support special software applications. For example, in the configuration instructions of Chapter 1, you are told to include the line

DEVICE = ANSI.SYS

in your CONFIG.SYS file. ANSI.SYS is actually a device driver that offers more sophisticated keyboard and screen management capabilities than does the standard console driver. You also recall that when Chapter 10 discussed the text screen, I noted that the Crt standard unit contains its own customized screen and keyboard interface routines—actually, device drivers in disguise.

Turbo Pascal enables you to develop your own text-file device drivers. For ordinary disk files and the predefined devices listed in table 17.2, the four pointer fields in the text file record (OpenFunc, InOutFunc, FlushFunc, and CloseFunc) reference the built-in subroutines that manage the file opening, closing, and I/O processes—in other words, the DOS device drivers. By redirecting these pointers to functions of your own design, Turbo Pascal enables you to implement your own device drivers.

Developing the Customized Device Driver

Your device driver will need at least five major subroutines: one routine each for OpenFunc, InOutFunc, FlushFunc, and CloseFunc to point to, plus a customized assignment procedure that actually initiates the driver. Although your program can call them any name you want, here I adopt the generic names used by the Turbo Pascal *Reference Guide*: Open, InOut, Flush, Close, and Assign.

Except for Assign, each function should be compiled in the Force Far Calls state; that is, with the {$F +} compiler directive active.

Each of these five subroutines is explained in turn. Just reading about them can be rather confusing at first, so you should probably look ahead to see how they are implemented in the generalized device driver program in listing 17.10.

When you access the standard DOS device drivers, you always use the Assign procedure. This action associates a file identifier variable with one of the *reserved* file names such as CON, PRN, and LPT1. Because the compiler won't accept new reserved words, your customized device driver will have to operate a bit differently—specifically, with a *customized assign* procedure, similar to the way the CRT device driver is accessed with the AssignCrt procedure.

Here, the customized assign procedure is shown as AssignDriver in listing 17.10.

The Assign Procedure

This customized assign procedure must perform the following tasks:

1. Accept the name of the text file identifier variable.

2. Set the OpenFunc and CloseFunc pointer variables to the address of your customized Open and Close functions, respectively.

3. Because the file hasn't yet been opened, the Mode field should be set to fmClosed and the Handle field should be set to –1 ($FFFF).

4. Establish the text file buffer. Any memory region can be used, but be sure to identify it to the compiler by assigning a pointer to the buffer to the BufPtr field and assigning the size of the buffer to the BufSize field.

5. Since run-time error messages might try to reference the text file by name, the Name field should be cleared. Remember that Name is an ASCIIZ string; consequently, all you have to do is set its first character to the null character (#0).

The *Open* Function

This is shown as DriverOpen in listing 17.10. The Open function is called by the Reset, Rewrite, and Append procedures. Remember, though, that although Append is a valid text-file opening procedure, most peripheral devices are either read only or write only.

The customized Open function should perform the following tasks:

1. The Mode field should be set to either fmInput or fmOutput, depending on whether the file was opened with Reset or Rewrite. If the file was opened with Append, it initially has a mode of fmInOut and should be handled as follows:

    a. If "appending" has a special meaning for the physical device, then the device should be positioned to its current end of file. Normally, however, you assume that files opened with Append will be used exclusively for output.

    b. Because text files can't have a mode of fmInOut, Mode should be reset to fmOutput.

2. The InOutFunc and FlushFunc pointer variables should be set to reference functions that depend on whether the file was opened for input or output.

3. If no errors occurred during the execution of the function, Open should return a value of zero.

The *InOut* Function

This is shown as DriverInput and DriverOutput in listing 17.10. The InOut function is called by the read, readln, write, writeln, Eof, Eoln, SeekEof, SeekEoln, and Close procedures.

Of course, you probably won't use the same InOut function for *both* input and output. The Open function selects an appropriate function when it sets the InOutFunc pointer variable. Each input and output function should be designed to transfer one byte at a time between the buffer and the text file itself.

If no errors occurred during the execution of the function, InOut should return a value of zero.

The *Flush* Function

This is not shown in listing 17.10. The Flush function is called by the Flush procedure after each read, readln, write, and writeln. You probably won't need a separate Flush function. It has little or no value during input operations and can probably be replaced with InOut for output operations. This is demonstrated in the sample programs that follow.

The *Close* Function

This is shown as DriverClose in listing 17.10. The Close function is called by the Close procedure. Close can also be called by Reset, Rewrite, and Append if the file they reference is currently open.

Close should execute any and all appropriate file cleanup routines. If no errors occurred during execution of the function, Close should return a value of zero.

A General Text File Device Driver

The Driver unit in listing 17.10 is a model you can use for your own device driver file. All necessary control code is shown, and all areas that either expect or allow your customized code are identified.

Listing 17.10

```
unit Driver;
    {**************************************************
    *    General Turbo Pascal text file device driver    *
    **************************************************}
interface
    uses Dos;
    procedure AssignDriver( var DriverFile : Text;
                                FileName    : string );
implementation
{$R-,S-    Disable range and stack checking }
    {************************************
    *    All unit-wide types, constants,    *
    *    and variables are defined here     *
    ************************************}
    const
        MoreInputAvailable : Boolean = True;    { An end-of-file test }
    function DriverCharacterInput : char;
    begin
        {******************************
        *    Return the next character    *
        ******************************}
    end;
    procedure DriverCharacterOutput( ch : char );
    begin
        {******************************
        *    Output the next character    *
        ******************************}
    end;
{$F +}
    function DriverInput( var DriverFile : TextRec ) : integer;
    var
        BufIndex : word;
    begin
        with DriverFile do begin
            BufIndex := 0;
            while MoreInputAvailable and (BufIndex < BufSize) do begin
                BufPtr^[ BufIndex ] := DriverCharacterInput;
                Inc( BufIndex );
            end;
            BufPos := 0;
            BufEnd := BufIndex;
        end;
        DriverInput := 0;
    end;
    function DriverOutput( var DriverFile : TextRec ) : integer;
    var
        BufIndex : word;
```

Listing 17.10 continues

Listing 17.10 continued

```
begin
    with DriverFile do begin
        BufIndex := Ø;
        while BufIndex  < BufPos do begin
            DriverCharacterOutput( BufPtr^[ BufIndex ] );
            Inc( BufIndex );
        end;
        BufPos := Ø;
    end;
    DriverOutput := Ø;
end;
function DriverIgnore( var DriverFile : TextRec ) : integer;
begin
    DriverIgnore := Ø;
end;
function DriverClose( var DriverFile : TextRec ) : integer;
begin
    {*****************************
     *   Closing routines go here   *
     *****************************}
    DriverClose := Ø;
end;
function DriverOpen( var DriverFile : TextRec ) : integer;
begin
    with DriverFile do begin
        if Mode = fmInput then begin
            {***********************************
             *   Opening input routines go here   *
             ***********************************}
            InOutFunc := @DriverInput;
            FlushFunc := @DriverIgnore;
        end else begin
            if Mode = fmInOut then begin
                {***********************************
                 *   Opening Append routines go here   *
                 *   (If Append has special meaning)   *
                 ***********************************}
            end;
            {***********************************
             *   Opening output routines go here   *
             ***********************************}
            Mode        := fmOutput;
            InOutFunc := @DriverOutput;
            FlushFunc := @DriverOutput;
        end;
    end;
    DriverOpen := Ø;
end;
```

Listing 17.10 continues

Listing 17.10 *continued*

```
{$F-}
    procedure AssignDriver;   { var DriverFile : Text;
                                    FileName   : string }
    var
      DriverRecord : ^TextRec;
    begin
        {**************************************
         *  Special initiation code goes here  *
         **************************************}
        DriverRecord := @DriverFile;
        with DriverRecord^ do begin
          Handle    := $FFFF;
          Mode      := fmClosed;
          BufSize   := SizeOf( Buffer );
          BufPtr    := @Buffer;
          OpenFunc  := @DriverOpen;
          CloseFunc := @DriverClose;
          Name[ 0 ] := #0;
        end;
    end;
end.
```

Note that since DRIVER.PAS is a unit, you must compile it to disk to create a .TPU file.

The customized assign procedure is here named `AssignDriver`. Notice that it accepts two parameters: the text file identifier and the name of an actual disk file.

The customized `Open` and `Close` functions are here named `DriverOpen` and `DriverClose`, respectively. `DriverOpen` determines which `InOut` and `Flush` functions should be used, based on whether the file is opened for input or output.

The `DriverIgnore` function is used when you don't want a function to perform any activity. For example, the `FlushFunc` variable points to `Driver-Ignore` when the file is open for input.

Read-Only and Write-Only Files

As it's shown, the DRIVER unit is designed to be used for both input and output. Obviously, some text file devices (like the keyboard) are read only, whereas others (like the system printer) are write only. The drivers for those devices should be modified appropriately.

If the device is read only, make the following modifications:

1. Remove the DriverCharacterOutput procedure and the DriverOutput function.

2. In the section marked Opening output routines go here in the DriverOpen function, insert the statement RunError(1Ø5). This causes the program to terminate with run-time error 105 (File not open for output). Assign @DriverIgnore to both the InOutFunc and FlushFunc pointers.

If the device is write only, make the following modifications:

1. Remove both the DriverCharacterInput and DriverInput functions.

2. In the section marked Opening input routines go here in the DriverOpen function, insert the statement RunError(1Ø4). This causes the program to terminate with run-time error 104 (File not open for input). Assign @DriverIgnore to the InOutFunc pointer.

Not only do these changes help to ensure proper data transfer between your program and the device it accesses, but they also considerably reduce the size of the driver unit itself.

Using a Customized Device Driver

The Cypher unit in listing 17.11 is a device driver that supports text file encoding and decoding. The customized assignment procedure is called AssignCypher.

Listing 17.11

```
unit Cypher;
interface
    uses Dos;
    procedure AssignCypher( var DriverFile : Text;
                                FileName   : string );
implementation
{$R-,S-  Disable range and stack checking }
    var
        WorkFile   : file of char;
    function DriverCharacterInput : char;
    var
        ch : char;
    begin
        read( WorkFile, ch );
        if ch = #Ø then
            DriverCharacterInput := #255
        else
            DriverCharacterInput := Pred( ch );
    end;
```

Listing 17.11 continues

Listing 17.11 continued

```
       procedure DriverCharacterOutput( ch : char );
       var
          EncryptedCharacter : char;
       begin
          if ch = #255 then
            EncryptedCharacter := #Ø
          else
            EncryptedCharacter := Succ( ch );
          write( WorkFile, EncryptedCharacter );
       end;
{$F +}
       function DriverInput( var DriverFile : TextRec ) : integer;
       var
          BufIndex : word;
       begin
          with DriverFile do begin
            BufIndex := Ø;
            while not Eof( WorkFile ) and (BufIndex < BufSize) do begin
               BufPtr^[ BufIndex ] := DriverCharacterInput;
               Inc( BufIndex );
            end;
            BufPos := Ø;
            BufEnd := BufIndex;
          end;
          DriverInput := Ø;
       end;
       function DriverOutput( var DriverFile : TextRec ) : integer;
       var
          BufIndex : word;
       begin
          with DriverFile do begin
            BufIndex := Ø;
            while BufIndex < BufPos do begin
               DriverCharacterOutput( BufPtr^[ BufIndex ] );
               Inc( BufIndex );
            end;
            BufPos := Ø;
          end;
          DriverOutput := Ø;
       end;
       function DriverIgnore( var DriverFile : TextRec ) : integer;
       begin
          DriverIgnore := Ø;
       end;
       function DriverClose( var DriverFile : TextRec ) : integer;
       begin
          Close( WorkFile );
          DriverClose := Ø;
       end;
```

Listing 17.11 continues

Listing 17.11 continued

```
        function DriverOpen( var DriverFile : TextRec ) : integer;
        begin
            with DriverFile do begin
                if Mode = fmInput then begin
                    Reset( WorkFile );
                    InOutFunc := @DriverInput;
                    FlushFunc := @DriverIgnore;
                end else begin
                    Rewrite( WorkFile );
                    Mode      := fmOutput;
                    InOutFunc := @DriverOutput;
                    FlushFunc := @DriverOutput;
                end;
            end;
            DriverOpen := Ø;
        end;
{$F-}
        procedure AssignCypher;    { var DriverFile : Text;
                                     FileName   : string }
        var
            DriverRecord : ^TextRec;
        begin
            Assign( WorkFile, FileName );
            DriverRecord := @DriverFile;
            with DriverRecord^ do begin
                Handle    := $FFFF;
                Mode      := fmClosed;
                BufSize   := SizeOf( Buffer );
                BufPtr    := @Buffer;
                OpenFunc  := @DriverOpen;
                CloseFunc := @DriverClose;
                Name[ Ø ] := #Ø;
            end;
        end;
    end.
```

Note that since CYPHER.PAS is a unit, you must compile it to disk to create a .TPU file.

When the AssignCypher driver is used, text files opened for output "scramble" their data before writing to the disk. This data can only be correctly understood by another text file that uses the AssignCypher driver and is opened for input.

The ENCRYPT program in listing 17.12 uses the Cypher unit to scramble its output file. ENCRYPT accepts a "secret message" from the keyboard, encodes it by substituting the next higher ASCII value for each character, and writes the message to disk. The program terminates when a blank line is entered.

Listing 17.12

```
program Encrypt;
uses Crt, Cypher;
var
    CodeFile      : Text;
    SecretMessage : string;
begin
    AssignCypher( CodeFile, 'Secret.TXT' );
    Rewrite( CodeFile );
    ClrScr;
    writeln( 'Enter your message:' );
    repeat
       readln( SecretMessage );
       writeln( CodeFile' SecretMessage );
    until Length( SecretMessage ) = 0;
    Close( CodeFile );
end.
```

When ENCRYPT is executed, it displays Enter your message: and awaits data entry. A typical session is shown in figure 17.2.

Fig. 17.2. The original message you enter in the ENCRYPT program.

```
Enter your message:
Hello!  This message is being processed by a customized device driver that
converts keyboard input to an encrypted data file.  Each character will be
stored as the successor of the actual character.  That is, "a" becomes "b",
"b" becomes "c", and so on.
```

After the program terminates, you can examine the file it produced by entering the command

DUMP SECRET.TXT

The results of the file dump are visible in figure 17.3.

Remember that the DUMP program, which was discussed in Chapter 13, displays the hexadecimal value of each byte in the file in the six columns on the left. The corresponding character contents are displayed in the larger right column. The first five characters are *Ifmmp*. Subtracting one letter from each of these characters gives *Hello*, the first word in the encoded message!

The DECODER program in listing 17.13 can be used to read the contents of the file more directly. Again, the AssignCypher driver is used, but this time the file is opened for input. When DECODER executes, the original message (shown in fig. 17.2) is displayed on the screen.

Fig. 17.3. *The encoded file produced by the ENCRYPT program.*

```
secret.txt                      Page  1 of 1                    260 bytes

49666D6D 70222121 55696A74 216E6674 74626866 216A7421  Ifmmp"!!Uijt!nfttbhf!jt!
63666A6F 68217173 70646674 74666521 637A2162 21647674  cf.joh!qspdfttfe!cz!b!dvt
75706E6A 7B666521 6566776A 64662165 736A7766 73217569  upn.jᶜfe!efw.jdf!es.jwfs!ui
62750E0B 64706F77 66737574 216C667A 63706273 65216A6F  bu/ᴺᵝdpowfsut!Ifzcpbse!jo
71767521 75702162 6F21666F 64737A71 75666521 65627562  qvu!up!bo!fodszqufe!ebub
21676A6D 662F2121 46626469 21646962 73626475 66732178  !g.jmf/!!Fbdi!dibsbdufs!x
6A6D6D21 63660E0B 74757073 66652162 74217569 66217476  .jmm!cfᴺᵝtupsfe!bt!uif!tv
64646674 74707321 70672175 69662162 64757662 6D216469  ddfttps!pg!uif!bduubm!di
62736264 7566732F 21215569 6275216A 742D2123 62232163  bsbdufs/!!Uibu!jt-!#b#!c
6664706E 66742123 63232D0E 0B236323 21636664 706E6674  fdpnft!#c#-ᴺᵝ#c#!cfdpnft
21236123 2D21626F 65217470 21706F2F 0E0B0E0B           !#d#-!boe!tp!po/ᴺᵝᴺᵝ
```

Listing 17.13

```
program Decoder;
uses Crt, Cypher;
var
   CodeFile      : Text;
   SecretMessage : string;
begin
   ClrScr;
   AssignCypher( CodeFile, 'Secret.TXT' );
   Reset( CodeFile );
   while not Eof( CodeFile ) do begin
      readln( CodeFile, SecretMessage );
      writeln( SecretMessage );
   end;
   Close( CodeFile );
end.
```

Accessing Other Devices

Most of the time, the character input and output routines in a customized
text file device driver are considerably more complicated than those shown in
the Cypher example. Some devices (like a game adapter board) are accessed

using the Port or PortW arrays. Other devices (like a printer) are accessed with DOS or BIOS calls. Some amount of inline assembly language coding is usually required. The Turbo Pascal *Reference Guide* itself includes a relatively advanced example of a device driver for a modem.

Nevertheless, as the Cypher example clearly shows, customized text file device drivers offer an easy way to implement a variety of high-performance applications and at the same time eliminate the need for special code within the body of the main program itself.

Using the 8087 Coprocessor

The 8086-family processor is designed to handle all numeric data and operations within its 16-bit registers. Consequently, real numbers, which range in size from the 4-byte single type through the 10-byte extended type, must be processed "in pieces" in order to fit.

Although the accuracy of the final result isn't compromised, even a simple Turbo Pascal statement such as the addition of two real numbers can generate dozens of machine-language instructions, including:

❏ Translating each floating-point number to a fixed-point format

❏ Segregating each number into word-sized components

❏ Adding numbers at the word level, and so on

Needless to say, floating-point operations require considerably more time to execute than their integer counterparts.

On the other hand, the 8087-family coprocessor is specifically designed to accommodate floating-point numbers and instructions. Its register is 10 bytes long and consequently can manipulate even an extended real-number type in a single operation. In addition, the 8087 coprocessor can *directly* produce transcendental results, including all common trigonometric and logarithmic functions.

The 8087 is called a *coprocessor* with the 8086 because *both* chips monitor the instructions being sent to the CPU. The 8087 intercepts any instructions meant for it while allowing 8086 instructions to pass untouched. Similarly, the 8086 ignores instructions meant for the 8087, except for calculating any memory addresses the 8087 might need. The 8086 and 8087 operate simultaneously and consequently can together execute the awaiting instructions faster than the 8086 alone.

This section shows how to use Turbo Pascal to take advantage of the power of the 8087.

8087 Data Types

Quite simply, Turbo Pascal defines a *real number* as any number that contains a decimal point. There are five forms of real numbers, as listed in table 17.5.

Table 17.5. *Real-Type Numbers in Turbo Pascal*

Type	Size	Ranges of Allowed Values	Significant Digits
Real	6 bytes	2.9×10^{-39} to 1.7×10^{38}	11–12
Single	4 bytes	1.5×10^{-45} to 3.4×10^{38}	7–8
Double	8 bytes	5.0×10^{-324} to 1.7×10^{308}	15–16
Extended	10 bytes	1.9×10^{-4951} to 1.1×10^{4932}	19–20
Comp	8 bytes	$-2^{63} + 1$ to 2^{63-1}	19–20

Real numbers compress very large values into a very small number of bytes using a format similar to that of scientific notation. But while scientific notation uses base 10, floating-point types store the *binary* representations of a sign (+ or −), an exponent, and a base value:

$$(+/-) \text{ base } \times 2^{\text{exponent}}$$

The actual bit layout doesn't really matter. Notice, though, that both the base value and the exponent are stored as binary numbers; this is why the table of reals shows ranges that seem so unusual.

The {$N} Numeric Processing Directive

Even if an 8087 is installed in the system, a Turbo Pascal program doesn't automatically generate the code to use it. For a program to take advantage of a numeric coprocessor, the {$N +} compiler directive must be enabled at the beginning of the program.

If numeric processing is enabled, then the compiler tries to invoke the 8087 coprocessor whenever it encounters an instruction involving an operation on one or more real numbers. If the numeric processing option is disabled with {$N−}, the program executes just as if no 8087 is present.

The {$E} 8087 Emulation Directive

The {$E} 8087 emulation directive controls whether floating-point emulation software is to be included in the .EXE file of a compiled program.

Emulation software is code that acts just as if the 8087 is present. Whereas a real number operation might be handled by the coprocessor in a single step, the emulation software converts the operation to data and instructions that the 8086 can handle, then reassembles the answers when the operation is finished. Emulation software produces the same results as a coprocessor, although, of course, with far less speed. The standard Real number type is routinely processed with emulation software on the 8086.

In the default {$E +} state, the compiled program contains all the software necessary to emulate the operation of an 8087 coprocessor. All IEEE floating-point types are supported, including the single, double, extended, comp, and real data types. If 8087 emulation is disabled with {$E-}, the only software emulation that Turbo Pascal will include in the compiled program is code to support the 6-byte standard real.

Enabling the 8087

The {$N} numeric processing and {$E} 8087 emulation directives are most often used together to achieve the right combination of speed and program portability. Table 17.6 summarizes the four possible combined settings. Remember that the default state is {$E +,N- }.

Table 17.6. *Directive Combinations*

Options	Actions the Compiler Takes
{$E +,N +}	If an 8087 coprocessor is detected, it will be used for all floating-point operations; otherwise, software emulation will be used. Consequently, programs compiled in this state can run on any machine, regardless of whether an 8087 is available. All IEEE real number types are supported.
{$E +,N-}	Numeric processing is disabled. Even if an 8087 coprocessor has been installed, Turbo Pascal uses only software emulation. All IEEE real number types are supported.
{$E-,N +}	No software emulation is available for any real number other than the 6-byte real type. Therefore, if your program uses any other IEEE real numbers (single, double, extended, or comp), an 8087 coprocessor *must* be present. present.

Table 17.6 continues

{$E-,N-}	Only the standard 6-byte real type is allowed, and its implementation is accomplished with software emulation. Even if an 8087 coprocessor is installed, it will be ignored. The program *cannot* use any single, double, extended, or comp numbers, *even if an 8087 coprocessor is present*.

Summary

In this chapter, you have learned that the IBM open architecture design has fostered the introduction of a wide variety of add-in hardware. You have seen that there are three ways that this hardware can be accessed: through ports, device drivers, and—for the 8087 coprocessor—special software.

You have learned that a port is a channel between the CPU and its support circuitry. Almost all peripherals communicate with the CPU through one or more ports. The predefined arrays Port and PortW access the computer's input and output data ports. Programs that demonstrated the use of ports were presented.

You have learned that—to DOS—anything outside the main memory is considered a device and must be controlled by device driver software. Using this software, DOS controls each device with standardized commands. You have learned that Turbo Pascal programs communicate with DOS devices through text files. You have seen how the driver unit can be used as a model for creating your own device drivers, and you have seen an example of a practical device driver in the Cypher unit, which supports text file encoding and decoding.

You have learned that the 8087-family coprocessor is specifically designed to accommodate floating-point numbers and instructions. The 8087 handles five Turbo Pascal data types: Real, Single, Double, Extended, and Comp. The {$N} numeric processing directive determines whether the 8087 is used. The {$E} 8087 emulation directive controls whether floating-point emulation software is to be included in the .EXE file of a compiled program.

18

Interrupt Service
Routines

Probably for as long as you have known about computers, you have been hearing the phrase, "Computers can only do one thing at a time."

This isn't completely true. Even though the CPU focuses only on a single task, a great deal of activity might be taking place within the computer. Keys may be pressed, a printer may be producing a report, a disk may be spinning, a modem may be communicating with another computer over a phone line, and the screen may be filling with characters. If your machine has Turbo Lightning™ installed, you hear a "beep" whenever you misspell a word. Even more amazingly, as soon as you press a certain *hot key*, your favorite memory-resident program appears.

The CPU can't be in complete control of all this activity. However, your PC is designed in such a way that every legitimate claim for attention, such as a key being pressed, generates an *interrupt* signal that informs the CPU that it should temporarily suspend whatever it's doing (no matter what it is) and see what the fuss is about. The *interrupt* signal is well named; most of the time the CPU deals with the interruption quickly and then returns to its original pursuit.

Most interrupts automatically trigger the operation of a specific DOS or BIOS routine. (In fact, when you used the MsDos and Intr procedures in Chapter 16, you were requesting Turbo to execute interrupt routines.) When the routine terminates, the CPU returns to its original task.

Your PC can track up to 256 sources of interruption, so the CPU can stay aware (or more properly, can be *made* aware) of a great deal of activity and can react accordingly.

Interrupts are generated so frequently (every single key press generates an interrupt, for example) that programmers usually don't even want to know about them. But sometimes, as with the MsDos and Intr procedures, you may want to run one of the interrupt routines yourself. Other times, as discussed in this chapter, you may wish to create your own interrupt routines. Turbo Pascal provides a full set of procedures that enable you to accomplish all these tasks.

Types of Interrupts

Interrupts can be initiated either by hardware or software.

Hardware Interrupts

Hardware interrupts are generated by *physical* devices.

Interrupts 0 through 5 are called by the processor itself. For example, interrupts 1 and 3 are used for debugging. Interrupt 0 occurs when division by zero is detected. Interrupt 2 halts the system if a memory parity error is detected.

Interrupts 8 through $0F are generated by other hardware within the PC. For example, Interrupt 9 is triggered by each key press. On the AT, another eight hardware interrupts have been reserved in $70 through $7F.

Software Interrupts

Software interrupts really don't *interrupt* anything. They're called directly as part of the natural flow of a program. Your Turbo Pascal application may itself generate an interrupt. You can call any one of the BIOS services by using the Turbo Pascal Intr procedure. You can also access any one of DOS's services by using the MsDos procedure, which is nothing more than the execution of Interrupt $21.

The Interrupt Vector Table

Interrupts are always identified by number (from 0 through 255) instead of by name or address. Each subroutine is called an *interrupt handler* or an *interrupt service routine* (ISR).

By common agreement, all PCs use a standardized set of interrupt numbers for each specific task. Beginning at the bottom of memory (segment $0000 and offset $0000), DOS stores a table of pointers to every interrupt handler. Each pointer is four bytes (two words) long. The first word contains the offset and the second word contains the segment.

There are 256 possible entries, so this table, called the *interrupt vector table*, is 1K in size. When an interrupt is initiated, the CPU goes to the interrupt vector table, gets the appropriate address, and calls that routine.

(In engineering, a *vector* is something that defines both direction and magnitude. The term is frequently used by systems programmers to refer to addresses, because, after all, in order to move to a new address you need to know which direction to face and how far to go.)

Interrupts are listed in table 18.1.

Table 18.1. *The Interrupt Vector Table*

Interrupt	Cause
$00	Divide by zero
$01	Single-stepping (for use by debuggers)
$02	Non-maskable interrupt (NMI)
$03	Break point trap (for use by debuggers)
$04	Overflow
$05	Print screen
$06	Invalid opcode
$07	Processor extension not available
$08	System timekeeper
$09	Keyboard input interrupt
$0A	Reserved for MS-DOS
$0B	Asynchronous communications (COM2)
$0C	Asynchronous communications (COM1)
$0D	Fixed disk controller
$0E	Floppy disk controller
$0F	Printer controller
$10	Video display
$11	Equipment configuration check
$12	Memory size check
$13	Floppy disk, fixed disk driver (PC/XT)
$14	RS-232 communications port driver
$15	Cassette I/O, PC/AT auxiliary functions
$16	Keyboard driver

Table 18.1 continues

Table 18.1. *continued*

Interrupt	Cause
$17	Printer driver
$18	ROM BASIC entry code
$19	Bootstrap loader
$1A	Set/Read real-time clock
$1B	Ctrl-Break handler
$1C	Timer tick (18.2 times per second)
$1D	Pointer to video parameter table
$1E	Pointer to disk parameter table
$1F	Pointer to graphics character table for ASCII codes 128–255
$20	Program terminate (obsolete)
$21	MS-DOS function caller
$22	Terminate address for called programs
$23	Ctrl-C address
$24	Critical-error handler
$25	Absolute disk read
$26	Absolute disk write
$27	Terminate and stay resident (obsolete)
$28–$2E	Reserved for MS-DOS
$2F	Print spooler
$30–$3F	Reserved for MS-DOS
$40	Floppy disk driver (PC/XT)
$41	Fixed disk parameter table
$42–$43	Reserved for MS-DOS
$44	PCjr graphics character table (codes 0–FFh)
$45–$5F	Reserved for MS-DOS
$60–$67	User-definable
$68–$7F	Unused
$80–$85	Reserved for BASIC
$86–$F0	BASIC interpreter
$F1–$FF	Unused

If two interrupts are received at the same time, the one with the lower number is executed first.

Viewing the Interrupt Vector Table

An address in the interrupt vector table is the memory location of a sub-routine you want to execute. This is how the CPU knows what it is that you want it to do after you get its attention.

The Turbo Pascal procedure GetIntVec returns the address of a given interrupt. With this procedure (here, as part of the INTTAB1 program, listing 18.1), you can see the contents of the entire interrupt vector table.

Listing 18.1

```pascal
program IntTab1;
uses DOS;
type
   String2 = string[ 2 ];
   String4 = string[ 4 ];
var
   i,j,k,
   IntNumber : byte;
   VectorAddress : pointer;

function HexNybble( Number : byte ) : char;
begin
   if Number  < 10 then HexNybble := Chr( 48 +Number )
                    else HexNybble := Chr( 55 +Number );
end;
function HexBytes( Number : byte ) : String2;
begin
   HexBytes := HexNybble( Number div 16 ) + HexNybble( Number mod 16 );
end;
function HexWords( Number : word ) : String4;
begin
   HexWords := HexBytes( Hi(Number) ) + HexBytes( Lo(Number) );
end;
begin
   for i := 0 to 3 do begin
      for j := 0 to 15 do begin
         for k := 0 to 3 do begin
            IntNumber := i*64 + j + k*16;
            GetIntVec( IntNumber, VectorAddress );
            write( HexBytes( IntNumber ):7,
                   HexWords( Seg( VectorAddress^ ) ):5,
                   HexWords( Ofs( VectorAddress^ ) ):5 );
         end;
         writeln;
      end;
      readln;
   end;
end.
```

When INTTAB1 executes, it produces four "pages" of 64 interrupts. The first page is shown in figure 18.1.

Fig. 18.1. *The addresses of the first 64 interrupt service routines.*

```
00 204D 00CE    10 0DA1 003D    20 0E94 2814    30 F308 7EEA
01 0070 07D3    11 F000 F84D    21 0E94 26EB    31 0000 0000
02 F000 E2C3    12 F000 F841    22 05B4 028F    32 0000 0000
03 0070 07D3    13 C800 01CF    23 204D 00D5    33 0000 0000
04 0070 07D3    14 F000 E739    24 204D 009D    34 0000 0000
05 F000 FF54    15 F000 F859    25 00F3 0A78    35 0000 0000
06 F000 FF23    16 F000 E82E    26 00F3 0AC6    36 0000 0000
07 F000 FF23    17 0E94 2565    27 00F3 32AB    37 0000 0000
08 F000 FEA5    18 F000 E720    28 00F3 087D    38 0000 0000
09 0E94 56FB    19 C800 014E    29 050C 02D1    39 0000 0000
0A F000 FF23    1A F000 FE6E    2A 0000 0000    3A 0000 0000
0B F000 FF23    1B 27EB 012F    2B 0000 0000    3B 0000 0000
0C F000 FF23    1C F000 FF53    2C 0000 0000    3C 0000 0000
0D C800 01BE    1D F000 F0A4    2D 0000 0000    3D 0000 0000
0E F000 EF57    1E 0000 0522    2E 05B4 0343    3E 0000 0000
0F 0070 07D3    1F F000 0000    2F 0000 0000    3F 204D 00C6
```

If you run a program that attempts to divide by zero, the processor generates Interrupt 0. The CPU suspends execution and calls the subroutine that starts in segment $828F at offset $00CE. When that subroutine finishes, the CPU returns to its original activity.

A quick glance reveals that a large number of the entries in the interrupt vector table are empty. In fact, the rest of the table is almost completely unused.

Your PC might use different addresses. Some systems, for example, recognize that the interrupt vector table is intended to list subroutines that normally end with a "return" instruction. Instead of defining nil pointers as all zeros, these systems use the address of a subroutine containing nothing other than a "return" so that a call to an undefined interrupt won't hang up the machine.

Calling an Interrupt

Your Turbo Pascal program can execute any interrupt through the use of the Intr procedure. Its general form is as follows:

```
Intr( IntNumber, Regs );
```

IntNumber is the number of the interrupt selected from the interrupt vector table. Regs is a data structure of the following type:

```
Registers = record
            case Integer of
                  0: (AX,BX,CX,DX,BP,SI,DI,DS,ES,Flags: Word);
                  1: (AL,AH,BL,BH,CL,CH,DL,DH: Byte);
            end;
```

Many interrupts have subordinate functions or options; some interrupts return values upon completion. Although actual register use varies for each interrupt, the Regs record is always the mechanism used to pass arguments between your program and the called interrupt.

One of the most useful BIOS routines is Interrupt 5, the Print Screen function. Program INTSCR (listing 18.2) uses the for loop to fill the screen with numbers, then invokes Print Screen with the Intr procedure. Notice that for this call, no parameters are passed between the program and the BIOS code.

Listing 18.2

```
program IntScr;
uses Dos;
var
   i : word;

procedure PrintScreen;
var
   Regs : Registers;   { Dummy only }
begin
   Intr( 5, Regs );
end;

begin
   for i := 0 to 702 do write( i );
   PrintScreen;
end.
```

When the instruction is called, the processor looks up the address of the interrupt routine in the interrupt vector table. Because the table starts at the lowest point in memory (segment 0, offset 0) and consists of one segment and one offset word for each entry, you can determine the address of an interrupt routine by multiplying the number of the interrupt by four. The address of the Interrupt 5 ISR is stored at $0000:$0014 (decimal 20). The processor then jumps to this location and executes the code of the interrupt routine. When the routine finishes, control is returned to the next line in the program.

Replacing an Interrupt

When Intel originally announced its design for the 8086, the company reserved the first 32 interrupts for its own use. Not all were used in the final product, so IBM felt it could redefine the usage of interrupts $05 to $1F. Intel continued to treat those interrupts as reserved, so conflicts inevitably arose that resulted in compatibility problems, especially for the 80286 and 80386.

In order for software to remain *downward compatible* (that is, in order for a program designed for the 80386 to run successfully on the 8086 as well), the IBM interrupt usage must be followed even when it conflicts with the design of the chip. For example, Intel included a sophisticated new opcode in its design of the 80286 (now used in the AT) that generates an Interrupt 5 whenever an index is outside the limits of an array. However, IBM uses Interrupt 5 for the Print Screen function, so when the new function is actually used on the 80286 and the range error occurs, the screen is printed.

Programs that rely on the advanced features of the 80286 and 80386 must replace each unwanted interrupt handler with a customized version.

However, it isn't just the sophisticated applications that install customized interrupts. In a normal Turbo Pascal application, division by zero aborts the program with a run-time error. (According to Murphy's Law, a program will terminate only after a significant amount of time has been invested in processing data but prior to the time when the final results are either printed or saved to disk.)

Program ZERO1 (listing 18.3) demonstrates this phenomenon. It forces a division by zero prior to the completion of its processing.

Listing 18.3

```
program Zero1;
var
   Zero : byte;
begin
   Zero := Ø;
   writeln( 1Ø div 2 );
   writeln( 1 div Zero );
   writeln( 3Ø div 4 );
   writeln( 72 div 7 );
end.
```

When ZERO1 executes, it produces the following:

5

Runtime error 2ØØ at ØØØØ:ØØ45.

The third and fourth divisions are never performed. In ZERO1, the program abort isn't disastrous, but you can imagine how frustrating it would be if it occurred before you had time to print a report or save the file.

Division by zero is undefined, meaning that there's no right answer. Essentially, the CPU is notifying you in the only way it can that your program contains a serious error that demands your immediate attention.

But while division by zero is fatal, it's certainly not catastrophic. When the CPU encounters the situation, it generates Interrupt 0. By gaining control of that interrupt handler, you can arrange for a softer error message and still retain control of the program. You can do this by writing your own interrupt routine and substituting it for the ISR that would otherwise be used by default. Writing interrupt routines is usually a systems task, but Turbo Pascal makes it relatively easy.

An interrupt routine is written like an ordinary Turbo Pascal procedure, but with two main differences. First, the reserved word interrupt must be used immediately after the header declaration. Second, every interrupt procedure must be declared with register parameters. The format of a customized handler is as follows:

```
procedure CustomISR( Flags,CS,IP,AX,BX,CX,DX,SI,DI,DS,ES,BP : word );
interrupt;
begin
  :
  ...code...
  :
end;
```

Some or all of the parameters can be omitted, beginning with Flags and moving toward BP, depending on which registers are needed. For example, if you only needed the BX register, you might have defined the procedure declaration as follows:

```
procedure CustomISR( BX,CX,DX,SI,DI,DS,ES,BP : word );
```

If no registers are used to exchange data, then no registers need to be declared as parameters. The examples in this book include all registers just as a matter of form.

If your ISR is generated by a hardware interrupt, it can't include any Turbo Pascal input, output, or dynamic memory allocation procedures, nor can it include any BIOS or DOS calls.

You probably want to modify the interrupt handler only for the duration of your program, so you should save the original address before installing your routine. Then, when your program terminates, you can restore the original address.

The Turbo Pascal procedure GetIntVec is used to retrieve the current address of an interrupt handler. Similarly, the SetIntVec procedure can be used to modify the contents of the interrupt vector table.

Program ZERO2 (listing 18.4) demonstrates how to use the minimum amount of code to save the original Interrupt 0 address, replace it with the address of a customized handler, and restore the original address when the program terminates.

Listing 18.4

```
program Zero2;
uses Dos;
var
    Zero     : byte;
    SaveInt0 : pointer;

procedure ZeroDivide( Flags,CS,IP,AX,BX,CX,DX,SI,DI,DS,ES,BP : word );
interrupt;
begin
    writeln( 'You just divided by zero!' );
end;

begin
    GetIntVec( $00, SaveInt0 );
    SetIntVec( $00, @ZeroDivide );

    Zero := 0;

    writeln( 10 div 2 );
    writeln( 172 div zero );
    writeln( 30 div 4 );
    writeln( 72 div 7 );

    SetIntVec( $00, SaveInt0 );
end.
```

When ZERO2 executes, it produces the following:

```
5
You just divided by zero!
172
7
10
```

Notice that instead of aborting when the division by zero is encountered, the program simply displays a warning message. The division didn't occur, so the original value of 172 is returned.

Installing an Interrupt

As you will see in the following example, there's little difference between replacing an interrupt handler and installing one of your own.

One thing to do is identify a free address in the interrupt vector table. When you review the results of the INTTAB1 program from the beginning of the chapter, you will notice that almost every entry in the table is available. Arbitrarily, select interrupt $3A. (A more general approach would be to pick a starting point, then slide up the table until an open address was found.)

The SCRISR1 program (listing 18.5) demonstrates how parameters can be passed to an ISR. The ScreenISR procedure can be used either to save or to restore up to three screen images. If ScreenISR is called with a 1, 2, or 3 in the AX register, the current screen image is saved in buffer position 1, 2, or 3. Any position number can be used; no special sequence is implied. If ScreenISR is called with a 4, 5, or 6 in the AX register, the program restores screens 1, 2, or 3 respectively.

Listing 18.5

```
program ScrISR1;
uses Crt,Dos;
const
   VideoSeg = $B800;
var
   i           : word;
   Regs        : Registers;
   VectorSave  : pointer;
   VideoArray  : array [ 1..3 ] of array [ 0..1999 ] of word;

procedure ScreenISR( Flags,CS,IP,AX,BX,CX,DX,SI,DI,DS,ES,BP : word );
interrupt;
var
   i : word;
begin
   case AX of
      1..3 : for i := 0 to 1999 do
               VideoArray[ AX, i ] := MemW[ VideoSeg : i ];
      4..6 : for i := 0 to 1999 do
               MemW[ VideoSeg : i ] := VideoArray[ AX-3, i ];
   end;
end;


begin
   GetIntVec( $3A, VectorSave );
   SetIntVec( $3A, @ScreenISR );

   for i := 0 to 702 do write( i );

   Regs.AX := 1;
   Intr( $3A, Regs );

   GotoXY( 1, 10 );  write( '                                                   ' );
   GotoXY( 1, 11 );  write( ' Status message line 1 appearing here ' );
   GotoXY( 1, 12 );  write( ' Status message line 2 appearing here ' );
   GotoXY( 1, 13 );  write( '                                                   ' );
   Readln;
```

Listing 18.5 continues

Listing 18.5 *continued*

```
    Regs.AX := 4;
    Intr( $3A, Regs );
    Readln;

    SetIntVec( $3A, VectorSave );
end.
```

When SCRISR1 executes, it begins by filling the screen with digits. Then the current screen image is saved by a call to the ScreenISR procedure, after which the following message is displayed in figure 18.2.

Fig. 18.2. *Original display provided by the SCRISR1 program.*

```
012345678910111213141516171819202122232425262728293031323334353637383940414243 44
454647484950515253545556575859606162636465666768697071727374757677787980818283 84
858687888990919293949596979899100101102103104105106107108109110111112113114115 11
611711811912012112212312412512612712812913013113213313413513613713813914014141 421
431441451461471481491501511521531541551561571581591601611621631641651661671681 69
170171172173174175176177178179180181182183184185186187188189190191192193194195 19
619719819920020120220320420520620720820921021121221321421521621721821922022122 2222
232242252262272282292302312322332342352362372382392402412422432442452462472482 49
250251252253254255256257258259260261262263264265266267268269270271272273274275 27
                                89290291292293294295296297298299300301302 3023
Status message line 1 appearing here 316317318319320321322323324325326327328 329
Status message line 2 appearing here 234333443453463473483493503513523533543553 5
                                69370371372373374375376377378379380381 3823
833843853863873883893903913923933943953963973983994004014024034044054064074084 09
410411412413414415416417418419420421422423424425426427428429430431432433434435 43
643743843944044144244344444544644744844945045145245345445545645745845946046146 24
634644654664674684694704714724734744754764774784794804814824834844854864874884 89
490491492493494495496497498499500501502503504505506507508509510511512513514515 51
651751851952052152252352452552652752852953053153253353453553653753853954054154 25
435445455465475485495505515525535545555565575585595605615625635645655665675685 69
570571572573574575576577578579580581582583584585586587588589590591592593594595 59
659759859960060160260360460560660760860961061161261361461561661761861962062162 26
236246256266276286296306316326336346356366376386396406416426436446456466476486 49
650651652653654655656657658659660661662663664665666667668669670671672673674675 67
667767867968068168268368468568668768868969069169269369469569669769869970070170 2
```

After the Enter key is pressed, a second call to ScreenISR restores the original pattern of digits as in figure 18.3.

Disabling an Interrupt

When you boot your PC, the address for the overflow handler, Interrupt 4, is set to point to a procedure return instruction (technically, an IRET opcode). In other words, when an overflow interrupt is generated, the CPU

Fig. 18.3. *Restored image in the SCRISR1 program.*

```
0123456789101112131415161718192021222324252627282930313233343536373839404142434 4
45464748495051525354555657585960616263646566676869707172737475767778798081828384
85868788899091929394959697989910010110210310410510610710810911011111211311411511
61171181191201211221231241251261271281291301311321331341351361371381391401411421
43144145146147148149150151152153154155156157158159160161162163164165166167168169
170171172173174175176177178179180181182183184185186187188189190191192193194195 19
61971981992002012022032042052062072082092102112122132142152162172182192202212222
23224225226227228229230231232233234235236237238239240241242243244245246247248249
25025125225325425525625725825926026126226326426526626726826927027127227327427527
62772782792802812822832842852862872882892902912922932942952962972982993003013023
03304305306307308309310311312313314315316317318319320321322323324325326327328329
33033133233333433533633733833934034134234334434534634734834935035135235335435535
63573583593603613623633643653663673683693703713723733743753763773783793803813823
83384385386387388389390391392393394395396397398399400401402403404405406407408409
41041141241341441541641741841942042142242342442542642742842943043143243343443543
64374003944004144244344444544644744844945045145245345445545645745845946046146246 2
63464465466467468469470471472473474475476477478479480481482483404405406407408409
49049149249349449549649749849950050150250350450550650750850951051151251351451551
65175185195205215225235245255265275285295305315325335345355365375385395405415425
43544545465475485495505515525535545555565575585595605615625635645655665675685 695
70571572573574575576577578579580581582583584585586587588589590591592593594595 5 9
6597598599600601602603604605606607608609610611612613614615616617618619620621622 6
23624625626627628629630631632633634635636376386396406416426436446456466476486 49
65065165265365465565665765865966066166266366466566666766866967067167267367467567
667676867968068168268368468568668768868969069169269369469569669769869970070170 702
```

performs a procedure call that does nothing other than return control to the next line of code in the original program.

If, after careful thought, you wish to disable an interrupt completely, the safest way is to replace the address of the unwanted interrupt with the default address of the overflow ISR. To disable the interrupt resulting from division by zero, define a pointer variable (here, AddrWork) and use the commands:

```
GetIntVec( $04, AddrWork );
SetIntVec( $00, AddrWork );
```

After these lines are executed, a division by zero will produce an unpredictable algebraic result, but it won't cause your program to abort.

The DISABLE1 program (listing 18.6) uses this technique to disable the Print Screen function temporarily.

Listing 18.6

```
program Disable1;
uses Dos;
var
   i         : word;
   SaveInt5 : pointer;    { Global }

procedure DisablePrintScreen;
var
   AddrInt4 : pointer;
begin
   GetIntVec( $05, SaveInt5 );
   GetIntVec( $04, AddrInt4 );
   SetIntVec( $05, AddrInt4 );
end;

procedure EnablePrintScreen;
begin
   SetIntVec( $05, SaveInt5 );
end;

begin
   for i := 0 to 702 do write( i );    { Fills up screen }
   writeln;
   writeln( 'Print Screen is enabled' );
   readln;
   DisablePrintScreen;
   writeln( 'Print Screen is disabled' );
   readln;
   EnablePrintScreen;
   writeln( 'Print Screen is enabled' );
   readln;
end.
```

When DISABLE1 executes, it fills the screen with numbers, then displays the first of its status messages, Print Screen is enabled. At this point, you can still send the screen image to the printer. After the Enter key is pressed, Interrupt 5 is disabled by having its vector rerouted to an empty routine. Print Screen won't operate during this phase. When the Enter key is pressed again, Interrupt 5 is restored. The Enter key is pressed once more to end the program.

Concerns about Redefining Interrupt Routines

Before you consider redefining every troublesome interrupt, there are a few things to keep in mind.

Every interrupt gets the CPU's full attention. Therefore, every interrupt must be able to tell the CPU precisely what it should do, then enable it to return smoothly to its original activity. A poorly written program (or one that hasn't yet been completely debugged) is likely to cause the PC to "hang" and force you to reboot or actually turn off the machine.

If you execute the wrong interrupt, you may encounter more serious problems, such as accidental damage to disk files, if not the entire disk. Some problems are subtle; for example, you might unknowingly modify a portion of RAM memory that you won't use for another hour.

The bottom line is this: Take care when you work with interrupts. Think through the entire application. Test it incrementally. Don't include any potentially damaging line of code (a disk write, for example) until you have seen the results on the screen or printer. And most importantly, make backups frequently!

Summary

In this chapter, you have learned that an interrupt is a signal that causes the CPU to suspend whatever it's doing and execute the code in one of 256 predefined procedures. Each of these procedures is called an Interrupt Service Routine (ISR). The addresses of the ISRs are stored in the interrupt vector table, which begins at the bottom of the PC's memory.

You have learned that interrupts can be triggered either by hardware or software. Hardware interrupts are generated by physical devices, such as the keyboard. Software interrupts are called directly by Turbo Pascal programs through the use of the Intr and MsDos procedures.

Most ISRs consist of standard DOS or BIOS routines. You have learned, however, that Turbo Pascal provides several tools that you can use to create your own interrupt procedures. You have seen that the addresses in the interrupt vector table can be changed to reference specially modified procedures within your own program. You can now install your own custom ISRs, and you now know how to replace or disable existing ISRs.

CHAPTER 19

Memory-Resident Programs

When Borland first introduced SideKick® in 1984, it was a turning point for the software industry. From that moment on, the use of the previously little-known set of *Terminate-and-Stay-Resident (TSR)* DOS commands became the standard for programming convenience.

Although most commercial applications of TSRs incorporate extremely sophisticated memory management techniques that only people with systems-level programming skills can fully understand, the basic principles of TSRs are actually easy to follow.

This chapter discusses how you can use Turbo Pascal to write and install several simple but practical memory-resident programs.

Introduction to TSR Programs

DOS keeps a pointer to the memory address where it can load a program. When you run a series of programs, each one, in turn, begins at this same location.

In Chapter 12, you learned that the Program Segment Prefix (PSP) contains the address of the top of the program's memory.

Consider what would happen if, while a program was running, it copied its top-of-memory address into the special pointer that stores the location where DOS loads programs. Quite simply, DOS would be fooled into loading every subsequent program into the memory area *immediately above* the original program. Consequently, the original program would remain in memory while all subsequent programs are executed.

This is exactly what happens in a terminate-and-stay-resident program. TSRs replace the beginning program vector with the top-of-memory pointer. Every program executed after the TSR runs is loaded in the higher memory area and consequently doesn't overlay the memory used by the TSR program itself.

When you load several memory-resident programs (SideKick and Turbo Lightning, for example), each one uses this technique in turn, stacking up one program on top of the other.

Using a TSR Program

Now that you have tricked DOS into preserving the TSR's memory area, you are faced with the challenge of how to access it.

As in all Turbo Pascal programs, the basic useful unit is the procedure. When you first run the TSR program, you could use the @ operator to determine the address of the desired procedure, then write that address to a file. Any program you run later could read that file and execute the procedure with a far call. For each additional procedure and variable you want to access, you simply enlarge the data file by one record. In essence, the file is storing a table of pointers.

Now make one simplification. Instead of going to all the trouble to create and then read a pointer table, use one that's already available: the interrupt vector table. That way, if the procedure you want to make memory resident is written in the form of an interrupt service routine (ISR), any later program could access it with the Intr procedure.

An example should help. Chapter 18 showed the SCRISR1 program could be used to save screen images. With only a few changes, you can make the ScreenISR procedure memory resident.

Using the Keep Procedure

The Turbo Pascal Keep procedure terminates a program and allows it to stay resident in memory. Additionally, Keep takes a word-sized parameter and passes it along to DOS in the form of a program exit code.

When Keep is called, it copies the top-of-memory pointer from the PSP into the vector DOS uses to track the start of free memory. This effectively turns the top-of-memory location for the program that executed Keep into the bottom-of-memory for all subsequent programs.

By default, a Turbo Pascal program occupies all available free memory, so the top-of-memory pointer will be set to the highest memory location in the PC. Consequently, any program that calls the Keep procedure must use the {$M} compiler directive to minimize heap usage. If you forget this step, you will have to reboot the computer.

For the same reason, you can't run a would-be TSR program from within the integrated environment. *Your* program, not TURBO.EXE, must determine the contents of the PSP. Always compile a TSR program to disk, exit the TURBO.EXE compiler completely, and execute the TSR program directly from DOS. Do not run a TSR program within Turbo's OS Shell.

Through its action, Keep causes the entire program to remain resident. All global data, procedures, and program code are preserved. Therefore, the code required to actually insert the ISR into the interrupt vector table must be in a separate procedure (or in the main program body) from the ISR itself.

Keeping a Program

The SCRISR2 program (listing 19.1) contains the interrupt service routine and the code required to install it in memory. Arbitrarily, choose Interrupt $3A as the vector the ISR will use. Make sure that the vector you select on your machine is available; once installed, the ISR remains lodged in memory until you reboot. Unlike the self-contained SCRISR1 program in the preceding chapter, the $3A vector here isn't just being "borrowed" during the run of the program; it's being seized for the duration of your session on the PC.

Compile SCRISR2 to disk and execute the program from DOS. Do *not* execute the program through Turbo's OS Shell option.

Listing 19.1

```
program ScrISR2;
{$M 1024, 0, 0 }
uses Dos;
const
   VideoSeg = $B800;
var
   VideoArray : array [ 1..3 ] of array [ 0..1999 ] of word;

procedure ScreenISR( Flags,CS,IP,AX,BX,CX,DX,SI,DI,DS,ES,BP : word );
interrupt;
var
   i : word;
```

Listing 19.1 continues

Listing 19.1 *continued*

```
begin
   case AX of
      1..3 : for i := Ø to 1999 do
               VideoArray[ AX, i ] := MemW[ VideoSeg : i ];
      4..6 : for i := Ø to 1999 do
               MemW[ VideoSeg : i ] := VideoArray[ AX-3, i ];
   end;
end;

begin
   SetIntVec( $3A, @ScreenISR );
   Keep( Ø );
end.
```

SetIntVec places the starting address of the ScreenISR procedure into the interrupt vector table. Keep terminates the program with an error code of zero (normal termination).

Remember that although only the ScreenISR procedure responds to an interrupt, the entire program remains in memory. Consequently, the VideoArray screen array can be stored as a global variable outside the procedure itself.

The SCRISR3 program (listing 19.2) fills the screen with numbers, performs an Interrupt $3A to save the screen, displays messages, then performs a second Interrupt $3A to restore the screen. When it executes (assuming that the SCRISR2 program has already run), its output is identical to the SCRISR1 program in the preceding chapter.

Listing 19.2

```
program ScrISR3;
uses Crt,Dos;
var
   i    : word;
   Regs : Registers;

begin
   for i := Ø to 7Ø2 do write( i );

   Regs.AX := 1;
   Intr( $3A, Regs );

   GotoXY( 1, 1Ø );  write( '                                       ' );
   GotoXY( 1, 11 );  write( ' Status message line 1 appearing here ' );
```

Listing 19.2 continues

Listing 19.2 continued

```
    GotoXY( 1, 12 );  write( ' Status message line 2 appearing here ' );
    GotoXY( 1, 13 );  write( '                                       ' );
    Readln;

    Regs.AX := 4;
    Intr( $3A, Regs );
  end.
```

Categories of TSRs

A TSR is classified as being either *active* or *passive*, depending on how you activate it.

Passive TSRs execute as part of the normal flow of a program. The Screen-ISR procedure was passive; it ran only because it was explicitly called by another application.

The more interesting TSRs are active. Active TSRs are either constantly running or are invoked by a combination of keystrokes (commonly called *hot keys*) which have no meaning to the current program. An active TSR will usually—but not always—suspend the execution of the program running in the foreground.

Creating a Clock TSR Program

Your PC keeps time with a 1.19318 MHz clock. This frequency was chosen so that 64K (65,536) pulses or *ticks* occur each hour. Each tick generates an Interrupt 8.

In other words, your PC undergoes an Interrupt 8 approximately 18.2 times per second. Fortunately, the PC is so fast, you will never notice such a trivial inconvenience.

When each Interrupt 8 occurs, its ISR increments the four bytes beginning with memory location $0040:$006C. The word beginning at $0040:$006E contains the hour, and the word beginning at $0040:$006C contains the number of ticks in the current hour. The last action taken by the Interrupt 8 ISR is the generation of an Interrupt $1C, commonly called the *Timer Tick*.

When your PC first boots, Interrupt $1C doesn't have an ISR; the entry in the interrupt vector table points to a return instruction. By installing your own ISR in Interrupt $1C, you can gain control of your PC 18.2 times per second!

Using the Timer Interrupt

This process is best illustrated with an example. The CLOCK program (listing 19.3) displays a clock in the upper right corner of the screen in HH:MM:SS format. It first initializes the Hour, Minute, and Second variables, then installs the ShowTime ISR at Interrupt $1C. From then on, ShowTime is called 18.2 times per second and increments the TimerTick counter at the same rate. After every eighteenth tick, the Second counter is incremented. After the sixtieth increment of Second, the Minute counter is incremented. Finally, after the sixtieth increment of Minute, the Hour counter is incremented. The time is written directly to video memory once a second.

Compile CLOCK to disk, and execute it directly from DOS. Do *not* execute the program through Turbo's OS Shell option.

Listing 19.3

```
program Clock;
{$M 1024, 0, 1024 }
uses Dos;
const
    VideoSeg = $B800;
var
    Hour, Minute, Second, Sec100, TimerTick : word;
procedure ShowTime( Flags,CS,IP,AX,BX,CX,DX,SI,DI,DS,ES,BP : word );
interrupt;
begin
    Inc( TimerTick );
    if TimerTick = 18 then begin
      TimerTick := 0;
      Inc( Second );
      if Second = 60 then begin
         Second := 0;
         Inc( Minute );
         if Minute = 60 then begin
            Minute := 0;
            Inc( Hour );
            if Hour = 25 then Hour := 0;
         end;
      end;
    Mem[ VideoSeg : 144 ] := 48 + Hour div 10;
    Mem[ VideoSeg : 146 ] := 48 + Hour mod 10;
    Mem[ VideoSeg : 148 ] := ord(':');
    Mem[ VideoSeg : 150 ] := 48 + Minute div 10;
    Mem[ VideoSeg : 152 ] := 48 + Minute mod 10;
    Mem[ VideoSeg : 154 ] := ord(':');
```

Listing 19.3 continues

Listing 19.3 continued

```
        Mem[ VideoSeg : 156 ] := 48  + Second div 1Ø;
        Mem[ VideoSeg : 158 ] := 48  + Second mod 1Ø;
      end;
  end;
  begin
    TimerTick := Ø;
    GetTime( Hour, Minute, Second, Sec1ØØ );
    SetIntVec( $1C, @ShowTime );
    Keep( Ø );
  end.
```

Calling BIOS Routines

Writing directly to video memory is something of a pain. Why not just use ordinary Turbo Pascal routines like GotoXY and write?

The answer is that DOS routines are not reentrant. Instead of using the stack to save separate sets of data, each DOS routine stores data in the same set of global variables. If a routine is called and stores a return address, for example, and the ISR interrupts the CPU and calls the routine a second time, then the original return address is overwritten, the first routine transfers control of the program to the wrong location, and the system probably crashes.

When the CLOCK program is run, the ShowTime ISR executes 18.2 times per second or 65,536 times in an hour. If you called a routine like GotoXY or write that often, the odds are fairly high that sometime during the program's run, the GotoXY or write would try to use a DOS routine that's already in use.

In general, then, an active TSR must ensure that it doesn't call a BIOS function that is being executed by the program that was running when the TSR takes control. Although several rather technical means exist to accomplish this, you can avoid the problem entirely by writing directly to video memory.

Note that this problem arises only when the TSR—like the CLOCK program—is triggered by a hardware interrupt. Software interrupts called from and controlled by your program are different; every line of code prior to the Intr call must be complete before the Intr instruction is reached. Therefore, in a software interrupt, you can use any DOS, BIOS, or Turbo Pascal procedure you want because you can be confident that the routine you want isn't currently in use in another part of your machine. Just don't allow your ISR to call itself.

Accessing the Timer

Because CLOCK rounds off the 18.2-tick-per-second rate, you may object to the resulting 40-second-per-hour error. Unlike the BIOS limitation, this is a problem you can do something about. The revised program, CLOCK0 (listing 19.4), accesses the system clock by reading the four timer bytes beginning at $0040:$006C. (In principle, the "mod 24" and "mod 60" operations are superfluous, but they help you to avoid the inevitable one- or two-second-per-hour rounding error.)

Compile CLOCK0 to disk, and execute it directly from DOS. Do *not* execute it through Turbo's OS Shell option.

Listing 19.4

```
program ClockØ;
{$M 1Ø24, Ø, 1Ø24 }
uses Dos;
const
   VideoSeg = $B8ØØ;
var
   TimerTick : byte;
   Hour      : word;
   Minute,
   Second    : longint;
procedure ShowTime( Flags,CS,IP,AX,BX,CX,DX,SI,DI,DS,ES,BP : word );
interrupt;
begin
   Inc( TimerTick );
   if TimerTick = 18 then begin
      TimerTick := Ø;
      Hour   := MemW[ $4Ø:$6E ] mod 24;
      Minute := MemW[ $4Ø:$6C ];
      Minute := ((Minute * 5) div 5461) mod 6Ø;
      Second := MemW[ $4Ø:$6C ];
      Second := ((Second * 5) div 91) mod 6Ø;
      Mem[ VideoSeg : 144 ] := 48  + Hour div 1Ø;
      Mem[ VideoSeg : 146 ] := 48  + Hour mod 1Ø;
      Mem[ VideoSeg : 148 ] := ord(':');
      Mem[ VideoSeg : 15Ø ] := 48  + Minute div 1Ø;
      Mem[ VideoSeg : 152 ] := 48  + Minute mod 1Ø;
      Mem[ VideoSeg : 154 ] := ord(':');
      Mem[ VideoSeg : 156 ] := 48  + Second div 1Ø;
      Mem[ VideoSeg : 158 ] := 48  + Second mod 1Ø;
   end;
end;
begin
   TimerTick := Ø;
   SetIntVec( $1C, @ShowTime );
   Keep( Ø );
end.
```

Note that Minute is multiplied by 5, then divided by 5461. Similarly, Second is multiplied by 5, then divided by 91. This seemingly insane process is an integer approximation of the number of ticks in a minute and second, given that there are 65,536 ticks in an entire hour.

$$\frac{65,536}{60} \approx \frac{5,461}{5} \quad \text{and} \quad \frac{65,536}{60 \times 60} \approx \frac{91}{5}$$

In this technique, the errors aren't cumulative. You will use this idea again shortly.

Notice also that even though the ShowTime procedure is called 18.2 times per second, you change the clock display only once every 18 ticks.

Adding an Alarm

You can add a simple alarm feature to make the clock image flash at a predetermined time. The ALARM program (listing 19.5) gives a sample.

Compile ALARM to disk, and execute it directly from DOS. Do *not* execute it through Turbo's OS Shell option.

Listing 19.5

```
program Alarm;
{$M 1024, 0, 1024 }
uses Dos;
const
    VideoSeg = $B800;
var
    Index,
    HourW, MinuteW, SecondW, Sec100W,
    TimerTick, AlarmHour, AlarmMinute : word;
    Hour, Minute, Second             : longint;
procedure ShowTime( Flags,CS,IP,AX,BX,CX,DX,SI,DI,DS,ES,BP : word );
interrupt;
begin
    Inc( TimerTick );
    if TimerTick = 18 then begin
        TimerTick := 0;
        Hour   := MemW[ $40:$6E ] mod 24;
        Minute := MemW[ $40:$6C ];
        Minute := ((Minute * 5) div 5461) mod 60;
        Second := MemW[ $40:$6C ];
        Second := ((Second * 5) div 91) mod 60;
        Mem[ VideoSeg : 144 ] := 48 + Hour div 10;
        Mem[ VideoSeg : 146 ] := 48 + Hour mod 10;
        Mem[ VideoSeg : 148 ] := ord(':');
```

Listing 19.5 continues

Listing 19.5 continued

```
        Mem[ VideoSeg : 150 ] := 48 + Minute div 10;
        Mem[ VideoSeg : 152 ] := 48 + Minute mod 10;
        Mem[ VideoSeg : 154 ] := ord(':');
        Mem[ VideoSeg : 156 ] := 48 + Second div 10;
        Mem[ VideoSeg : 158 ] := 48 + Second mod 10;
        if (Hour    = AlarmHour  ) and
           (Minute = AlarmMinute) and
           (Second mod 2 = 0     ) then
             for Index := 72 to 79 do
                Mem[ VideoSeg : Index*2 ] := ord( '*' );
    end;
  end;
begin
    TimerTick := 0;
    GetTime( HourW, MinuteW, SecondW, Sec100W );
    writeln( 'The time is now ', HourW, ':', MinuteW );
    repeat
       write( 'Set the hour:   ' );
       readln( AlarmHour );
    until AlarmHour in [ 0..23 ];
    repeat
       write( 'Set the minute: ');
       readln( AlarmMinute );
    until AlarmMinute in [ 0..59 ];
    writeln( 'Alarm clock will ring at ', AlarmHour, ':', AlarmMinute );
    SetIntVec( $1C, @ShowTime );
    Keep( 0 );
end.
```

ALARM acts like the CLOCK0 program except that it prompts for the alarm
time in hours and minutes and blinks asterisks in the clock window when the
alarm goes off.

Calling an Active TSR

After a passive TSR is installed, it does nothing except wait for an interrupt.
An active TSR, on the other hand, either runs continuously or must forever be
testing for a triggering event.

So far you have seen how passive TSRs and continuously running TSRs work.
Now it's time to consider how a TSR can be triggered.

Using Predefined Interrupts

Through your keyboard, you have immediate access to three interrupts: Print Screen (Interrupt 5), Ctrl-Break (Interrupt $1B), and Ctrl-C (Interrupt $23). Each can be redefined for your own purposes.

Remember that Ctrl-C and Ctrl-Break are two different animals. The original purpose of Ctrl-C was to interrupt a process "softly," after the next write statement. Ctrl-Break was intended to be more brutal, with the interruption occurring immediately, without regard for what the main program was doing at the time of the call. The Ctrl-C and Ctrl-Break ISRs are too important to modify. The PrintScreen interrupt, however, can be redefined harmlessly.

If you are like most PC users, you may want to capture a screen image on disk instead of sending it to the printer. For example, you may want to include the screen image of a menu along with the program's documentation. You may also want to include the image of a spreadsheet as part of a memo. Such a feature is also useful if you write a book on Turbo Pascal and need a general tool to illustrate the output of your programming examples.

The SNAP program (listing 19.6) redefines the PrintScreen vector, Interrupt 5. After SNAP is installed, the PrintScreen command (Shift-PrtSC) copies the current screen image into VideoArray and increments the Image counter. SNAP is only designed to hold three screens, although your version could be modified to accommodate more.

Compile SNAP to disk, and execute it directly from DOS. Do *not* execute it through Turbo's OS Shell option.

Listing 19.6

```
program Snap;
{$M 1024, 0, 1024 }
uses Dos;
const
   VideoSeg = $B800;
var
   i,
   Image     : word;
   VideoArray : array [ 0..2 ] of array [ 0..1999 ] of byte;

procedure TakeThePicture( Flags,CS,IP,AX,BX,CX,DX,SI,DI,DS,ES,BP : word );
interrupt;
begin
```

Listing 19.6 continues

Listing 19.6 continued

```
    if Image < 3 then begin
        for i := Ø to 1999 do
            VideoArray[ Image, i ] := Mem[ VideoSeg : 2*i ];
        Inc( Image );
    end;
end;

begin
    Image := Ø;
    SetIntVec( $Ø5, @TakeThePicture );
    SetIntVec( $3A, @Image );
    SetIntVec( $3B, @VideoArray );
    writeln( 'Snap program now installed' );
    Keep( Ø );
end.
```

Notice that this program is redefining three vectors. Interrupt 5 contains the address of the TakeThePicture procedure; when PrintScreen is invoked, TakeThePicture is executed. The address of Image is stored in vector $3A and the address of VideoArray is stored in vector $3B. Once SNAP is installed, any program you run later can use the $3A and $3B vectors to determine how many screens you saved and what they contained when you saved them.

Accessing TSR Data

The SNAP program managed to save information within the memory area of the TSR program. The DEVELOP program (listing 19.7) retrieves the data. DEVELOP picks up the addresses from the $3A and $3B vectors, points to the Image variable, and checks to see if any screens were saved. If screens are available, the program appends them to the file called ScreenFile. (DEVELOP creates the file if it doesn't already exist.) Its final act is to reset the Image counter to zero so that even more screens can be captured.

Notice that a screen image is actually a continuous series of bytes. To make the screens more manageable, DEVELOP adds end-of-line markers to the file (via the writeln) every 80 characters.

Listing 19.7

```
program Develop;
uses Dos;
type
    ArrayType = array [ 1..3 ] of array [ Ø..1999 ] of byte;
var
    Image      : ^word;
    VideoArray : ^ArrayType;
    i,
    Screen     : word;
    Pntr       : pointer;
    ScreenFile : text;
    FileName   : string;
begin
    GetIntVec( $3A, Pntr );
    Image := Pntr;
    GetIntVec( $3B, Pntr );
    VideoArray := Pntr;
    case Image^ of
          Ø : writeln( 'No screens were found!' );
        1..3 : begin
                    FileName := 'Scrn.DAT';
                    Assign( ScreenFile, FileName );
                    {$I-} Append( ScreenFile ); {$I +}
                    if IOResult  <> Ø then
                        Rewrite( ScreenFile );
                    for Screen := 1 to Image^ do
                        for i := Ø to 1999 do begin
                            write( ScreenFile, chr( VideoArray^[ Screen, i ] ) );
                            if (i + 1) mod 8Ø = Ø then writeln( ScreenFile );
                        end;
                    writeln( Image^, ' screens were written to ', FileName );
                    Image^ := Ø;    { reset }
                    Close( ScreenFile );
                end;
        else    writeln( 'The SNAP program hasn''t been installed.' );
    end;
end.
```

Consider what you just did. The program used two open slots in the interrupt vector table to store the addresses of TSR variables, then used a second program to read and modify them. With this technique, you can devise applications that allow several independent memory-resident programs to communicate with one another.

Notice, though, that you didn't combine the functions of the two programs, immediately putting the screen image to disk. Here again, the program ran into a problem with hardware interrupts. You can't be sure what (if any) DOS or BIOS interrupt is running when PrintScreen is invoked. Consequently, you can't use Turbo Pascal routines, like write and writeln, that rely heavily on DOS and BIOS services. The TakeThePicture ISR in SNAP contains only non-recursive, nonreentrant code.

Defining Hot Keys

Redefining PrintScreen, Ctrl-Break, and Ctrl-C usually has limited appeal. For one thing, these three interrupts have other valid (and perhaps more useful) applications. It's quite conceivable (and, of course, inevitable) that you will want both an immediate printed copy and a disk version of the same screen image. The challenge is to find a way to use other keys as triggers.

Remember how the CLOCK program used the Timer Tick (Interrupt $1C) to tally up the passing seconds. You can take advantage of the frequency of the Timer Tick interrupt to scan for the presence of certain key combinations.

Chapter 9 showed how the Keyboard Status Byte at $0040:$0017 contains bits which indicate the state (pressed or not pressed) of the various toggle keys. If you test for certain bit combinations within an ISR that's executed as a result of the Timer Tick interrupt, you have a means of detecting when users press hot keys.

The SNAP1 program (listing 19.8) installs the TestHotKey procedure in vector $1C. As a result, TestHotKey tests, at the rate of 18.2 times per second, whether the Alt key and Right-Shift key have both been pressed. If these two keys are pressed simultaneously, the screen image is saved. (If this particular pair isn't convenient for you, feel free to use any other combination.)

When you activate the routine, you will undoubtedly hold the keys down longer than 1/18.2 seconds. Consequently, the keys should be ignored for a short period of time after the save is complete. By comparing the TimeNow and TimeHold variables, you ensure that the screen copying process is performed no faster than once every 91 ticks, which works out to around five seconds. (Of course, you should also test for when the hour changes, but as a practical matter, this can be ignored.)

Compile SNAP1 to disk, and execute it directly from DOS. Do *not* execute it through Turbo's OS Shell option.

Listing 19.8

```
program Snap1;
{$M 1024, 0, 1024 }
uses Dos;
const    VideoSeg = $B800;
var
    i,
    Image     : word;
    VideoArray : array [ 0..2 ] of array [ 0..1999 ] of byte;
```

Listing 19.8 continues

Listing 19.8 continued

```
    TimeHold    : integer;
    TimeNow     : integer absolute $0040:$006C;

procedure TestHotKey( Flags,CS,IP,AX,BX,CX,DX,SI,DI,DS,ES,BP : word );
interrupt;
begin
   if Image  < 3 then
      if abs(TimeNow-TimeHold) > 91 then { 18.2 * 5 }
         if Mem[ $0040 : $0017 ] and $09 = $09 then begin { Alt-R Shift }
            for i := 0 to 1999 do
               VideoArray[ Image, i ] := Mem[ VideoSeg : 2*i ];
            Inc( Image );
            TimeHold := TimeNow;
         end;
end;

begin
   Image := 0;
   TimeHold := TimeNow;
   SetIntVec( $1C, @TestHotKey );
   SetIntVec( $3A, @Image );
   SetIntVec( $3B, @VideoArray );
   writeln( 'Snap program now installed' );
   Keep( 0 );
end.
```

You can execute the DEVELOP program to copy any captured screens to disk.

Commercial TSR Programs

If you have a commercial memory-resident (TSR) program on your PC, you might have noticed that you were able to invoke it even while running the programs in this chapter. Clearly, TSR programs such as SideKick and Turbo Lightning use some triggering method other than overwriting the Interrupt $1C vector.

Most commercially available memory-resident programs intercept the keyboard BIOS at Interrupt 9. They do this by replacing the entry in the interrupt vector table with the address of one of their own procedures, which identifies the key(s) being pressed. At the end of the procedure, the TSRs chain to the original BIOS routine.

In a similar fashion, commercial TSR programs intercept other interrupts and test when nonreentrant BIOS routines are executing. The TSR then "pops up" only when all BIOS routines are in a safe state.

As you might imagine, this is a complicated process that isn't easily accomplished in Turbo Pascal without special BIOS calls or inline coding. Proper coverage of the topic is beyond the scope of this book.

Nevertheless, you can see from the examples presented in this chapter how—with few restrictions—Turbo Pascal can be used to implement extremely useful memory-resident programs.

Summary

In this chapter, you have learned how to develop Terminate-and-Stay-Resident (TSR) programs.

In Chapter 12, you learned that the Program Segment Prefix (PSP) contains a pointer to the address of the highest memory location used by the program. The Turbo Pascal Keep procedure copies the contents of this top-of-memory field into the special pointer that DOS uses to store the memory location where a program is loaded. As a result, every program that runs after the Keep procedure has executed will be loaded into the memory area immediately above the TSR program. Consequently, the TSR program remains in memory while all subsequent programs are executed.

Because the Keep procedure causes the entire TSR program to remain resident, all global data, procedures, and program code are preserved. You have seen that the addresses of these procedures and data can be stored in the interrupt vector table and accessed by any later program.

You have learned that a TSR is either passive or active depending on how it is activated. A passive TSR executes only when specifically called by another Turbo Pascal program. An active TSR is either constantly running or is invoked by pressing a special combination of keystrokes called "hot keys." You have learned how active TSRs test for hot keys. Several useful programs that demonstrate these features were presented.

Part IV

Reference

Procedures and Functions

Abs   System

Purpose: Returns the absolute value of a variable. The result returned by
            the function has the same type as the argument, which may be
            any integer or real value.

Syntax: Function Abs(X : AnyNumType) : AnyNumType;

Example: RootTerm := Abs(Sqr(B) - 4.0*A*C);

Addr   System

Purpose: Returns the address of the specified object. The argument may
            be any variable, procedure, or function identifier. The result of
            the function is in the form of a pointer to the object. Note that
            the @ operator produces the same result as the Addr function.

Syntax: Function Addr(X : AnyDataObject) : Pointer;

Example: PointerVar := Addr(WorkItem);

Append   System

Purpose: Opens an existing text file for appending. The `FileIdentifier`
variable must have previously been associated with an external
file using the `Assign` procedure.

Syntax: Procedure Append(var FileIdentifier : Text);

Example: Assign(DataStorage, 'DATA.TXT');
Append(DataStorage);

Arc   Graph

Purpose: Draws a circular arc of a specified `Radius` from starting angle
`StAngle` to ending angle `EndAngle`, using (`X`, `Y`) as the center
point. Angles are measured in degrees, running
counterclockwise, with 0 degrees in the three o'clock position.

Syntax: Procedure Arc(X, Y   : Integer;
                         StAngle, EndAngle,
                         Radius   : Word);

Example: Arc(100, 100, 0, 90, 50);

ArcTan   System

Purpose: Returns the angle, in radians, that has a tangent equal to the
value of the argument.

Syntax: Function ArcTan(X : Real) : Real;

Example: PIover4 := ArcTan(1.0);   { Returns one-fourth of pi }

Assign   System

Purpose: Assigns the name of an external file to a file variable. The `FileIdentifier` variable may be declared for any file type. `FileName` is a string containing the name of the external file.

Syntax: `Procedure Assign( var FileIdentifier;  FileName : String );`

Example: `Assign( DataStore, 'DATA.TXT' );`

AssignCrt   Crt

Purpose: Associates a text file with the CRT. The procedure is similar to the `Assign` standard procedure, except that instead of associating a `FileIdentifier` variable with an external file, `AssignCrt` associates the text file directly with the CRT.

Syntax: `Procedure AssignCrt( var FileIdentifier : Text );`

Example: `AssignCrt( UserMessageFile );`

Bar   Graph

Purpose: Draws a bar (that is, a filled-in rectangle) using the current fill style and color. The upper left corner of the bar is at (X1, Y1), and the lower right corner is at (X2, Y2).

Syntax: `Procedure Bar( X1, Y1, X2, Y2 : Integer );`

Example: `Bar( 10, 10, 40, 100 );`

Bar3D   Graph

Purpose: Draws a 3D bar (that is, a filled-in, three-dimensional rectangle) using the current fill style and color. The upper left corner of the bar is at (X1, Y1), and the lower right corner is at (X2, Y2). Depth is the number of pixels used to define the apparent thickness. If Top is True, a three-dimensional top appears on the bar. If Top is False, no top appears; Bar3D may be called again to stack another bar on top. Top can be set to one of the predefined constants: TopOn (True) or TopOff (False).

Syntax: Procedure Bar3D(X1, Y1, X2, Y2 : Integer;
                        Depth : Word;
                        Top   : Boolean);

Example: UpX := 30; UpY := 30; DownX := 50; DownY := 100;
           Bar3D(UpX, UpY, DownX, DownY, (DownX-UpX) div 4,
           TopOn);

BlockRead   System

Purpose: Reads one or more records from FileIdentifier into the Buffer. Count or fewer records are read. The optional parameter Result contains the actual number of records written to the buffer.

Syntax: Procedure BlockRead(var FileIdentifier : file; var Buffer;
                        Count : Word [; var Result : Word]);

Example: BlockRead(FromFile, Buf, SizeOf(Buf), NumberRead);

BlockWrite   System

Purpose: Writes one or more records from a Buffer into FileIdentifier. Count or fewer records are transferred from memory. The optional parameter Result contains the actual number of records written to the buffer.

Syntax: Procedure BlockWrite(var FileIdentifier : file; var Buffer; Count : Word [; var Result : Word]);

Example: BlockWrite(ToFile, Buf, NumberRead, NumberWritten);

ChDir   System

Purpose: Changes the current directory to the path specified in NewPath.

Syntax: Procedure ChDir(NewPath : String);

Example: ChDir('C:\TP\DATA');

Chr   System

Purpose: Returns the ASCII character for the specified ordinal number.

Syntax: Function Chr(X : Byte) : Char;

Example: write('This is line 1.', Chr(13), Chr(1Ø), 'This is line 2.');

Circle   Graph

Purpose: Draws a circle of a specified Radius using (X, Y) as the center
           point.

Syntax: Procedure Circle(X, Y : Integer; Radius : Word);

Example: Circle(100, 100, 50);

ClearDevice   Graph

Purpose: Clears the graphics screen using the current background color
           and moves the current pointer (CP) to (0, 0).

Syntax: Procedure ClearDevice;

Example: ClearDevice;

ClearViewPort   Graph

Purpose: Clears the current viewport. The fill color is set to the current
           background color, Bar is called using the dimensions of the
           viewport as its parameters, and the current pointer (CP) is
           moved to (0, 0).

Syntax: Procedure ClearViewPort;

Example: ClearViewPort;

Close   System

Purpose: Closes an open file of any type.

Syntax: `Procedure Close( var FileIdentifier : AnyFileType );`

Example: `Close( InputInfo );`

CloseGraph   Graph

Purpose: Shuts down the graphics system. `CloseGraph` restores the screen to the mode it was in before graphics was initialized and deallocates any heap memory used by the graphics scan buffer, drivers, and fonts.

Syntax: `Procedure CloseGraph;`

Example: `CloseGraph;`

ClrEol   Crt

Purpose: Clears all characters from the cursor position to the end of the line using the current setting of `TextBackground`. The cursor's position isn't changed.

Syntax: `Procedure ClrEol;`

Example: `ClrEol;`

ClrScr   Crt

Purpose: Clears the current screen (or the current window, if one is active) using the current setting of TextBackground. The cursor is moved to (0, 0).

Syntax: Procedure ClrScr;

Example: ClrScr;

Concat   System

Purpose: Concatenates a sequence of strings. The final string gets truncated if it exceeds 255 characters. Note that the + operator produces the same result as the Concat function.

Syntax: Function Concat(s1 [, s2, ..., sn] : String) : String;

Example: FileName := Concat('C:\', 'DataFile', '.TXT');

Copy   System

Purpose: Returns a substring of the Original string, beginning at Index, containing Count characters.

Syntax: Function Copy(Original   : String;
                             Index, Count : Integer) : String;

Example: Str := 'The quick brown fox';
               New := Copy(Str, 11, 5);   { "brown" }

Cos   System

Purpose: Returns the cosine of the argument. The input angle is
measured in radians.

Syntax: `Function Cos( X : Real ) : Real;`

Example: `C := Cos( AngleInRadians );`

CSeg   System

Purpose: Returns the current value of the CS register, which contains the
segment address of the current code segment.

Syntax: `Function CSeg : Word;`

Example: `StartingCodeParagraph := CSeg;`

Dec   System

Purpose: Decrements the value of any ordinal variable. If the optional
parameter n isn't specified, X is decremented by 1; otherwise, X
is decremented by the value of n.

Syntax: `Procedure Dec( var X : OrdType [; n : LongInt ] );`

Example:
```
Amount := 1Ø;
Dec( Amount );      { Amount now equals 9 }
Dec( Amount, 3 );   { Amount now equals 6 }
```

Delay   Crt

Purpose: Delays program execution for a specified number of
             milliseconds.

Syntax: Procedure Delay(MS : Word);

Example: Delay(500);   { Delays half a second }

Delete   System

Purpose: Deletes Count characters from the Original string, beginning at
             Index.

Syntax: Procedure Delete(var Original : String;
                                    Index,
                                    Count   : Integer);

Example: Str := 'Cat Dog Horse';
             Delete(Str, 5, 4);   { Returns "Cat Horse" }

DelLine   Crt

Purpose: Deletes the line containing the cursor. All lines below the
             cursor move up one row. A blank line appears at the bottom of
             the screen; the color of the blank line is defined by the current
             setting of TextBackground. The location of the cursor is
             unchanged.

Syntax: Procedure DelLine;

Example: DelLine;

DetectGraph   Graph

Purpose: Checks the hardware and determines which graphics driver and mode to use. GraphDriver and GraphMode contain values that can then be passed to the InitGraph procedure.

Syntax: `Procedure DetectGraph( var GraphDriver, GraphMode : Integer );`

Example: `DetectGraph( grDriver, grMode );`

DiskFree   Dos

Purpose: Returns the number of free bytes on a specified disk drive. A Drive of Ø indicates the current drive, 1 indicates drive A:, 2 indicates drive B:, and so on. If Drive contains an invalid number, DiskFree returns –1.

Syntax: `Function DiskFree( Drive : Byte ) : LongInt;`

Example: `RemainingOnFloppy := DiskFree( 1 );`

DiskSize   Dos

Purpose: Returns the total size in bytes on a specified disk drive. A Drive of Ø indicates the current drive, 1 indicates drive A:, 2 indicates drive B:, and so on. If Drive contains an invalid number, DiskSize returns –1.

Syntax: `Function DiskSize( Drive : Byte ) : LongInt;`

Example: `FloppySize := DiskSize( 1 );`

Dispose   System

Purpose: Disposes a dynamic variable previously allocated by the New procedure. The memory referenced by P is returned to the heap.

Syntax: `Procedure Dispose( var P : Pointer );`

Example: `Dispose( PtrVar );`

DosExitCode   Dos

Purpose: Returns the exit code of a subprocess. The low byte contains the code itself. The value of the high byte indicates the reason the subprocess terminated: 0 for normal termination, 1 for Ctrl-C, 2 for a device error, and 3 if the subprocess was terminated by the Keep procedure.

Syntax: `Function DosExitCode : Word;`

Example: `writeln( 'Exit code: ', Lo( DosExitCode ) );`

DosVersion   Dos

Purpose: Returns the DOS version number. The low byte contains the major version number, and the high byte contains the minor version number.

Syntax: `Function DosVersion : Word;`

Example: `writeln( 'Using DOS ', Lo( DosVersion ), '.', Hi( DosVersion ) );`

DrawPoly   Graph

Purpose: Draws the outline of a polygon containing NumPoints vertices, using the current line style and color. PolyPoints is an array of PointType, as shown here:

```
PointType = record
               X, Y : Integer;
            end;
```

Each PointType record contains the coordinates of a vertex of the polygon. For N vertices, PolyPoints must contain N + 1 PointType records; the first and last record must be identical.

Syntax: Procedure DrawPoly(NumPoints : Word; var PolyPoints);

Example: DrawPoly(SizeOf(Shape) div SizeOf(PointType), Shape);

DSeg   System

Purpose: Returns the current value of the DS register, which contains the segment address of the data segment.

Syntax: Function DSeg : Word;

Example: StartingDataParagraph := DSeg;

Ellipse   Graph

Purpose: Draws an elliptical arc from starting angle StAngle to ending angle EndAngle, using (X, Y) as the center point. XRadius and YRadius are the horizontal and vertical axes, respectively. Angles are measured in degrees, running counterclockwise, with 0 degrees at the three o'clock position.

Syntax:
```
Procedure Ellipse( X, Y              : Integer;
                   StAngle, EndAngle,
                   XRadius, YRadius   : Word );
```

Example: `Ellipse( 100, 100, 0, 90, 40, 20 );`

EnvCount   Dos

Purpose: Returns the number of strings contained in the DOS environment. Each environment string is in the form EnvStr = EnvValue.

Syntax: `Function EnvCount : Integer;`

Example: `writeln( 'Your system has ', EnvCount, ' environment strings.' );`

EnvStr   Dos

Purpose: Returns a specified environment string. The first string has an Index of 1. An empty string is returned if Index references a nonexistent environment string.

Syntax: `Function EnvStr( Index : Integer ) : String;`

Example: `EnvListItem := EnvStr( 1 );`

Eof   System

Purpose: Returns the end-of-file status of a file. Eof is True if the current file position is beyond the last character in the file, or if the file is empty; otherwise, Eof is False. If no FileIdentifier is provided, the standard Input file is assumed.

Syntax: Function Eof[(var FileIdentifier : AnyFileType)] : Boolean;

Example:
```
while not Eof( DataFile ) do begin
    readln( DataFile, InRec );
    writeln( InRec );
end;
```

Eoln   System

Purpose: Returns the end-of-line status of a text file. Eoln is True if the current file position is at an end-of-line marker or if Eof is True; otherwise, Eoln is False. If no Text file FileIdentifier is provided, the standard Input file is assumed.

Syntax: Function Eoln[(var FileIdentifier : Text)] : Boolean;

Example: if Eoln(DataText) then readln(DataText);

Erase   System

Purpose: Erases an unopened external file.

Syntax: Procedure Erase(var FileIdentifier : AnyFileType);

Example:
```
Assign( TempFile, 'Data.BAK' );
Erase( TempFile );
```

Exec   Dos

Purpose: Executes the program specified in the Path string with the
command line contained in ComLine. The PathStr and ComStr
types are defined as follows:

```
PathStr = String[79];    { Full file path string }
ComStr  = String[127];   { Command line string }
```

Syntax: Procedure Exec(Path : PathStr; ComLine : ComStr);

Example: Exec('\Command.COM', '/
               C DIR *.BAK');   { Lists all backups }

Exit   System

Purpose: Exits immediately from the current block. When used within a
subroutine, Exit causes the subroutine to end. When used
within the main body of a program, Exit causes the program to
terminate.

Syntax: Procedure Exit;

Example: Exit;

Exp   System

Purpose: Returns the exponential of the argument; that is, Exp returns
the base of the natural logarithms, e, raised to the power of X.

Syntax: Function Exp(X : Real) : Real;

Example: Power := Exp(Value);

FExpand   **Dos**

Purpose: Expands a file name into a fully qualified file name, consisting of the complete drive, path, and file name. The `PathStr` type is defined as follows:

```
PathStr = String[79];     { Full file path string }
```

Syntax: Function FExpand(Path : PathStr) : PathStr;

Example: BigName := FExpand('app.pas');   { 'C:\TP\PROGRAMS\APP.PAS' }

FilePos   **System**

Purpose: Returns the current record number of an opened file. The value can range from 0 through `FileSize( FileIdentifier )`. `FilePos` cannot be used on a text file.

Syntax: Function FilePos(var FileIdentifier) : LongInt;

Example: CurRecNum := FilePos(DataFile);

FileSize   **System**

Purpose: Returns the number of components in an opened file. If the file is empty, `FileSize` returns 0. `FileSize` cannot be used on a text file.

Syntax: Function FileSize(var FileIdentifier : AnyFileType) : LongInt;

Example: RecordCount := FileSize(DataFile);

FillChar   System

Purpose: Fills a variable X (declared to be of any type) with Count
characters of Ch, which may be any ordinal type. No range
checking is performed.

Syntax: Procedure FillChar(var X   : AnyType;
                              Count : Word;
                              Ch   : AnyOrdType);

Example: FillChar(NumVar, SizeOf(NumVar), Ø);

FillEllipse   Graph

Purpose: Draws a filled ellipse, centered at (X, Y), having horizontal and
vertical axes of XRadius and YRadius, respectively. The ellipse is
drawn with the current fill style and fill color and is bordered
with the current color.

Syntax: Procedure FillEllipse(X, Y   : Integer;
                                XRadius, YRadius : Word);

Example: FillEllipse(1ØØ, 1ØØ, 5Ø, 75);

FillPoly

Graph

Purpose: Draws and fills a polygon containing NumPoints vertices, using the current fill style and color. The border is drawn in the current line style and color. PolyPoints is an array of PointType, as shown in the following:

```
PointType = record
              X, Y : Integer;
           end;
```

Each PointType record contains the coordinates of a vertex of the polygon.

Syntax: Procedure FillPoly(NumPoints : Word; var PolyPoints);

Example: FillPoly(SizeOf(Shape) div SizeOf(PointType), Shape);

FindFirst   Dos

Purpose: Searches the Path directory mask for the first file having the attributes specified by Attr. The PathStr and SearchRec types are defined as follows:

```
PathStr = String[79];    { Full file path string }
SearchRec = record
                Fill : Array[1..21] of Byte;
                Attr : Byte;
                Time : LongInt;
                Size : LongInt;
                Name : String[12];
            end;
```

The SearchRec record F is used as input for the FindNext procedure.

Syntax: Procedure FindFirst(Path : PathStr;
                                    Attr : Word;
                               var F   : SearchRec);

Example: FindFirst('*.PAS', Archive, SRec);

FindNext   Dos

Purpose: Returns the next entry that matches the name and attributes specified in the SearchRec record F, obtained from a previous call to FindFirst. The SearchRec type is defined as follows:

```
SearchRec = record
                Fill : Array[1..21] of Byte;
                Attr : Byte;
                Time : LongInt;
                Size : LongInt;
                Name : String[12];
            end;
```

Syntax: Procedure FindNext(var F : SearchRec);

Example: FindNext(SRec);

FloodFill   Graph

Purpose: Fills a region containing the point (X, Y) and bounded by the Border color.

Syntax: Procedure FloodFill(X, Y : Integer; Border : Word);

Example: FloodFill(10, 25, Red);

Flush   System

Purpose: Flushes the buffer of a text file that is open for output.

Syntax: Procedure Flush(var FileIdentifier : Text);

Example: Flush(TextStuff);

Frac   System

Purpose: Returns the fractional part of the argument.

Syntax: Function Frac(X : Real) : Real;

Example: Decimals := Frac(3.14159); { Returns 0.14159 }

FreeMem   System

Purpose: Disposes (that is, deallocates) a dynamic variable P of a given
                Size that was previously created by a call to the GetMem
                procedure.

Syntax: Procedure FreeMem(var P : Pointer; Size : Word);

Example: FreeMem(ScreenBuffer, ScreenSize);

FSearch   Dos

Purpose: Searches for a file given by Path in a list of directories given by
                DirList. The PathStr type is defined as follows:

                    PathStr = String[79];   { Full file path string }

Syntax: Function FSearch(Path : PathStr; DirList : String) : PathStr;

Example: FSearch(RequestedFile, GetEnv('PATH'));

FSplit   **Dos**

Purpose: Splits the file name specified by Path into its three components;
the drive and directory are placed in Dir, the file name is
placed in Name, and the file extension is placed in Ext. If a
component is missing from Path, the corresponding output
string will be empty. The PathStr, DirStr, NameStr, and ExtStr
types are defined as follows:

```
PathStr = String[79];   { Full file path string }
DirStr  = String[C7];   { Drive and directory string }
NameStr = String[8];    { File name string }
ExtStr  = String[4];    { File extension string }
```

Syntax: Procedure FSplit(Path : PathStr;
                              var Dir : DirStr;
                              var Name : NameStr;
                              var Ext : ExtStr);

Example: FSplit(CompleteFileName, DirName, FileName, ExtName);

GetArcCoords   Graph

Purpose: Returns the coordinates of the last Arc or Ellipse command as a record of the type ArcCoordsType, defined as follows:

```
ArcCoordsType = record
                    X, Y            : Integer;
                    Xstart, Ystart  : Integer;
                    Xend, Yend      : Integer;
                end;
```

The center of the arc is at (X, Y). Its starting and ending coordinates are (Xstart, Ystart) and (Xend, Yend), respectively.

Syntax: Procedure GetArcCoords(var ArcCoords : ArcCoordsType);

Example: GetArcCoords(ArcData);

GetAspectRatio   Graph

Purpose: Gets the effective resolution of the graphics screen. The aspect ratio can be computed by dividing the Xasp parameter by the Yasp parameter.

Syntax: Procedure GetAspectRatio(var Xasp, Yasp : Word);

Example: GetAspectRatio(Xasp, Yasp);
               writeln('Aspect ratio is ', Xasp/Yasp);

GetBkColor   Graph

Purpose: Returns the index into the palette of the current background color.

Syntax: Function GetBkColor : Word;

Example: writeln('Background color index is ', GetBkColor);

GetCBreak   Dos

Purpose: Returns the state of Ctrl-Break checking in DOS. When checking is off (Break = False), DOS tests for Ctrl-Break only during I/O operations; when checking is on (Break = True), DOS tests for Ctrl-Break before every system call.

Syntax: Procedure GetCBreak(var Break : Boolean);

Example: GetCBreak(BreakTest);
writeln('Is Ctrl-Break checking on? ', BreakTest);

GetColor   Graph

Purpose: Returns the color value passed to the previous successful call to SetColor.

Syntax: Function GetColor : Word;

Example: writeln('Current color index is ', GetColor);

GetDate   Dos

Purpose: Returns the current date set in the operating system.

Syntax: Procedure GetDate(var Year, Month, Day, DayOfWeek : Word);

Example: GetDate(Year, Month, Day, DayOfWeek);
               writeln('Today is ',Month,'/',Day,'/',Year);

GetDefaultPalette   Graph

Purpose: Returns the palette definition record of the type PaletteType,
               defined as follows:

               PaletteType = record
                                   Size   : Byte;
                                   Colors : Array[Ø..MaxColors] of ShortInt;
                             end;

               The palette contains the original colors initialized by InitGraph.

Syntax: Procedure GetDefaultPalette(var Palette : PaletteType);

Example: GetDefaultPalette(PaletteRec);

GetDir   System

Purpose: Returns the current directory DirString of a specified
               DriveNumber. A DriveNumber of 0 indicates the current drive, 1
               indicates drive A:, 2 indicates drive B:, and so on.

Syntax: Procedure GetDir(DriveNumber : Byte; var DirString : String);

Example: GetDir(Ø, DirectoryName);
               CurrentDrive := DirectoryName[1];

GetDriverName   Graph

Purpose: Returns a string containing the name of the current driver.

Syntax: Function GetDriverName : String;

Example: OutText('Currently using driver ', GetDriverName);

GetEnv   Dos

Purpose: Returns the value of a specified environment variable.

Syntax: Function GetEnv(EnvVar : String) : String;

Example: writeln('Current path is ', GetEnv('path'));

GetFAttr **Dos**

Purpose: Returns the attributes of an unopened file. The file, F, can be tested for an individual attribute by logically ANDing the Attr parameter with one of the following predefined constants:

```
ReadOnly  = $Ø1;
Hidden    = $Ø2;
SysFile   = $Ø4;
VolumeID  = $Ø8;
Directory = $1Ø;
Archive   = $2Ø;
AnyFile   = $3F;
```

Syntax: Procedure GetFAttr(var F : AnyFileType; var Attr : Word);

Example:
```
Assign( StoredData, ExternalFileName );
GetFAttr( StoredData, FileAttribute );
if FileAttribute and ReadOnly  <>Ø then
    writeln( ExternalFileName, ' is write-protected' );
```

GetFillPattern **Graph**

Purpose: Returns an array containing the fill pattern set by the most recent call to SetFillPattern. The FillPatternType record type is defined as follows:

```
FillPatternType = Array[1..8] of Byte;  { User-defined fill style }
```

Syntax: Procedure GetFillPattern(var FillPattern : FillPatternType);

Example: GetFillPattern(PatternStyleArray);

GetFillSettings   Graph

Purpose: Returns the last fill pattern and color set by a previous call to
SetFillStyle. The FillSettingsType record type is defined as
follows:

```
FillSettingsType = record     { Predefined fill style }
                        Pattern : Word;
                        Color   : Word;
                   end;
```

Syntax: Procedure GetFillSettings(var FillInfo : FillSettingsType);

Example: GetFillSettings(PatternAndColor);

GetFTime   Dos

Purpose: Returns the date and time a file F was last written. Time may be
unpacked and read with the UnpackTime procedure.

Syntax: Procedure GetFTime(var F : AnyFileType; var Time : LongInt);

Example: GetFTime(StoredData, LastUpdate);

GetGraphMode   Graph

Purpose: Returns the current graphics mode.

Syntax: Function GetGraphMode : Integer;

Example: writeln('Current mode: ', GetModeName(GetGraphMode));

GetImage   Graph

Purpose: Saves a bit image of a portion of the screen into a buffer. The specified region is bounded by a rectangle with an upper left corner of (X1, Y1) and a lower right-hand corner of (X2, Y2). The buffer is defined by the variable BitMap.

Syntax: `Procedure GetImage( X1, Y1, X2, Y2 : Integer; var BitMap );`

Example:
```
Size := ImageSize( UpX, UpY, DownX, DownY );
GetMem( BufferArea, Size );
GetImage( UpX, UpY, DownX, DownY, BufferArea^ );
```

GetIntVec   Dos

Purpose: Returns the address stored in a specified interrupt vector.

Syntax: `Procedure GetIntVec( IntNo : Byte; var Vector : Pointer );`

Example: `GetIntVec( $Ø5, PrintScreenISR );`

GetLineSettings   Graph

Purpose: Returns a `LineInfo` record containing the current line style, pattern, and thickness as set by `SetLineStyle`. The `LineSettingsType` record type is defined as follows:

```
LineSettingsType = record
                       LineStyle : Word;
                       Pattern   : Word;
                       Thickness : Word;
                    end;
```

Syntax: Procedure GetLineSettings(var LineInfo : LineSettingsType);

Example: GetLineSettings(LineDataRec);

GetMaxColor   Graph

Purpose: Returns the highest color that can be passed to the `SetColor` procedure.

Syntax: Function GetMaxColor : Word;

Example: Color := GetMaxColor;

GetMaxMode   Graph

Purpose: Returns the maximum mode number for the currently loaded driver.

Syntax: Function GetMaxMode : Integer;

Example: ModeNumber := GetMaxMode;

GetMaxX   Graph

Purpose: Returns the rightmost column (X resolution) of the current graphics driver and mode.

Syntax: `Function GetMaxX : Integer;`

Example: `RightSide := GetMaxX;`

GetMaxY   Graph

Purpose: Returns the bottommost row (Y resolution) of the current graphics driver and mode.

Syntax: `Function GetMaxY : Integer;`

Example: `BottomLine := GetMaxY;`

GetMem   System

Purpose: Creates a new dynamic variable of the specified Size and places the address of the block in the pointer variable P.

Syntax: `Procedure GetMem( var P : Pointer; Size : Word );`

Example:
```
Size := ImageSize( UpX, UpY, DownX, DownY );
GetMem( BufferArea, Size );
GetImage( UpX, UpY, DownX, DownY, BufferArea^ );
```

GetModeName   Graph

Purpose: Returns a string containing the name of the specified graphics mode.

Syntax: `Function GetModeName( GraphMode : Integer ) : String;`

Example: `writeln( 'Current mode: ', GetModeName( GetGraphMode ) );`

GetModeRange   Graph

Purpose: Returns the lowest and highest valid graphics modes for a given driver.

Syntax:
```
Procedure GetModeRange(     GraphDriver   : Integer;
                        var LoMode, HiMode : Integer );
```

Example: `GetModeRange( CGA, Lowest, Highest );`

GetPalette   Graph

Purpose: Returns the current palette and its size in the `Palette` record. The `PaletteType` record is defined as follows:

```
PaletteType = record
                Size   : Byte;
                Colors : Array[Ø..MaxColors] of ShortInt;
              end;
```

Syntax: `Procedure GetPalette( var Palette : PaletteType );`

Example: `GetPalette( PaletteInfo );`

GetPaletteSize   Graph

Purpose: Returns the size of the palette color lookup table.

Syntax: Function GetPaletteSize : Integer;

Example: writeln('There are ', GetPaletteSize, ' colors available.');

GetPixel   Graph

Purpose: Gets the color of the pixel at (X, Y).

Syntax: Function GetPixel(X, Y : Integer) : Word;

Example: PixelColor := GetPixel(40, 25);

GetTextSettings   Graph

Purpose: Returns the current text font, direction, size, and justification as set by SetTextStyle and SetTextJustify. The TextSettingsType record is defined as follows:

```
TextSettingsType = record
                    Font      : Word;
                    Direction : Word;
                    CharSize  : Word;
                    Horiz     : Word;
                    Vert      : Word;
                  end;
```

Syntax: Procedure GetTextSettings(var TextInfo : TextSettingsType);

Example: GetTextSettings(TextOptions);

GetTime   Dos

Purpose: Returns the current time set in the operating system.

Syntax: `Procedure GetTime( var Hour, Minute, Second, Sec100 : Word );`

Example: `GetTime( Hour, Minute, Second, Sec100 );`
`writeln( 'It''s now ', Hour, ':', Minute, ':', Second );`

GetVerify   Dos

Purpose: Returns the state of the verify flag in DOS. When the flag is off (Verify = False), disk writes aren't verified. When the flag is on (Verify = True), all disk writes are verified.

Syntax: `Procedure GetVerify( var Verify : Boolean );`

Example: `GetVerify( Verify );`
`writeln( 'Are disk writes being verified? ', Verify );`

GetViewSettings   Graph

Purpose: Returns the current viewport and clipping settings, as set by
SetViewPort. The ViewPortType record is defined as follows:

```
ViewPortType = record
                    X1, Y1, X2, Y2 : Integer;
                    Clip           : Boolean;
               end;
```

The active viewport consists of the rectangle with upper left
coordinates (X1, Y1) and lower right coordinates (X2, Y2).
Clipping in the viewport is indicated by the state of the Clip
field.

Syntax: Procedure GetViewSettings(var ViewPort : ViewPortType);

Example: GetViewSettings(ViewPortData);

GetX   Graph

Purpose: Returns the X coordinate of the current position (CP).

Syntax: Function GetX : Integer;

Example: Xlocation := GetX;

GetY   Graph

Purpose: Returns the Y coordinate of the current position (CP).

Syntax: Function GetY : Integer;

Example: Ylocation := GetY;

GotoXY   Crt

Purpose: Positions the cursor at (X, Y).

Syntax: Procedure GotoXY(X, Y : Byte);

Example: GotoXY(4Ø, 12);   { Centers the cursor }

GraphDefaults   Graph

Purpose: Resets the graphics settings for the viewport; palette; draw and background colors; line style and pattern; fill style, color, and pattern; active font; text style; text justification; and user character size.

Syntax: Procedure GraphDefaults;

Example: GraphDefaults;

GraphErrorMsg   Graph

Purpose: Returns an error message string for the specified ErrorCode.

Syntax: Function GraphErrorMsg(ErrorCode : Integer) : String;

Example: ErrorCode := GraphResult;
writeln('Error: ', GraphErrorMsg(ErrorCode));

GraphResult   Graph

Purpose: Returns an error code for the last graphics operation, after
which the error code is reset to 0.

Syntax: `Function GraphResult : Integer;`

Example: `ErrorCode := GraphResult;`
`writeln( 'Error: ', GraphErrorMsg( ErrorCode ) );`

Halt   System

Purpose: Stops program execution and returns to the operating system.
The optional parameter `ExitCode` specifies the exit code of the
program. When `ExitCode` is omitted, `Halt(Ø)` is assumed.

Syntax: `Procedure Halt( [ ExitCode : Word ] );`

Example: `Halt( ExitNo );`

Hi   System

Purpose: Returns the high-order byte of the argument, which may be
either an `Integer` or a `Word`.

Syntax: `Function Hi( X : IntWord ) : Byte;`

Example: `writeln( 'Using DOS ', Lo( DosVersion ), '.', Hi( DosVersion ) );`

HighVideo   Crt

Purpose: Displays subsequent screen output in high-intensity characters.

Syntax: Procedure HighVideo;

Example: HighVideo;

ImageSize   Graph

Purpose: Returns the number of bytes required to store a portion of the screen. The selected region is in the form of a rectangle, with upper left coordinates of (X1, Y1) and lower right coordinates of (X2, Y2).

Syntax: Function ImageSize(X1, Y1, X2, Y2 : Integer) : Word;

Example: Size := ImageSize(UpX, UpY, DownX, DownY);
GetMem(BufferArea, Size);
GetImage(UpX, UpY, DownX, DownY, BufferArea^);

Inc   System

Purpose: Increments the value of any ordinal variable. If the optional parameter n isn't specified, X is incremented by 1; otherwise, X is incremented by the value of n.

Syntax: Procedure Inc(var X : OrdType [; n : LongInt]);

Example: Amount := 1Ø;
Inc(Amount);   { Amount now equals 11 }
Inc(Amount, 3);   { Amount now equals 14 }

InitGraph   Graph

Purpose: Initializes the graphics system and switches the hardware to graphics mode. If `InitGraph` is called when `GraphDriver` is equal to `Detect`—a predefined constant of 0—then the procedure automatically selects and initializes an appropriate graphics driver and mode. Otherwise, if `GraphDriver` is not equal to 0, `InitGraph` loads the graphics driver and mode corresponding to the values of `GraphDriver` and `GraphMode`. The `PathToDriver` string contains the name of the directory containing the graphics driver files. If `PathToDriver` is empty, the driver files must be in the current directory.

Syntax:
```
Procedure InitGraph( var GraphDriver: Integer;
                     var GraphMode   : Integer;
                         PathToDriver : String );
```

Example:
```
grDriver := Detect;
InitGraph( grDriver, grMode, 'C:\TP' );
```

Insert   System

Purpose: Inserts a `Source` string into a `Target` string, beginning at the `Index` position. If the resulting string would exceed 255 characters, it will be truncated after the 255th character.

Syntax:
```
Procedure Insert(     Source : String;
                  var Target : String;
                      Index  : Integer );
```

Example:
```
Target := 'abchijklmnopqrstuvwxyz';
Insert( 'DEFG', Target, 4 );   { "abcDEFGhijklmnopqrstuvwxyz" }
```

InsLine   Crt

Purpose: Inserts an empty line at the cursor position using the current
setting of TextBackGround. All lines below the cursor are moved
down one row. The contents of the bottom line are lost.

Syntax: Procedure InsLine;

Example: InsLine;

InstallUserDriver   Graph

Purpose: Installs a vendor-added device driver called DriverFileName to
the BGI device driver table. The pointer to an accompanying
autodetect function (if any) is given by AutoDetectPtr.

Syntax: Function InstallUserDriver(DriverFileName : String;
                               AutoDetectPtr : Pointer) : Integer;

Example: grDriver := InstallUserDriver('NewThing.BGI', Nil);
InitGraph(grDriver, grMode, 'C:\TP');

InstallUserFont   Graph

Purpose: Installs a new font called FontFileName that isn't built in to the
BGI system.

Syntax: Function InstallUserFont(FontFileName : String) : Integer;

Example: NewFont := InstallUserFont('OddShape.CHR');
grDriver := Detect;
InitGraph(grDriver, grMode, 'C:\TP');
SetTextStyle(NewFont, HorizDir, 1);

Int   System

Purpose: Returns the integer part of a real-type argument.

Syntax: Function Int(X : Real) : Real;

Example: WholeA := Int(3.14159);   { Returns 3.0 }
WholeB := Int(-3.14159);   { Returns -3.0 }

Intr   Dos

Purpose: Executes BIOS interrupt number IntNo. Any parameters are
passed with a record of the type Registers, defined as follows:

```
Registers = record
                case Integer of
                    0 : (AX,BX,CX,DX,BP,SI,DI,DS,ES,Flags : Word);
                    1 : (AL,AH,BL,BH,CL,CH,DL,DH          : Byte);
            end;
```

Syntax: Procedure Intr(IntNo : Byte; var Regs : Registers);

Example: Intr(5, Regs);   { Same as pressing Shift-PrtSc }

IOResult System

Purpose: If I/O checking is disabled with {$I-}, IOResult returns and resets the value of the internal error flag for the last I/O operation. A value of 0 indicates success; nonzero indicates that an error occurred. Whenever an error occurs while I/O checking is disabled, all subsequent I/O operations will be ignored until IOResult is called and the internal error flag is cleared.

Syntax: Function IOResult : Word;

Example:
```
Assign( InFile, FileNameString );
{$I-} Reset( InFile ) {$I +};
if IOResult <> Ø then
    writeln( FileNameString, ' wasn''t found!' );
```

Keep Dos

Purpose: Terminates the current program and makes it—in its entirety—stay resident in memory. ExitCode corresponds to the exit code parameter used in the Halt procedure.

Syntax: Procedure Keep(ExitCode : Word);

Example: Keep(Ø);

KeyPressed   Crt

Purpose: Returns True if a key has been pressed on the keyboard; otherwise, KeyPressed returns False. Special keys (such as Shift, Ctrl, and Alt) are ignored.

Syntax: Function KeyPressed : Boolean;

Example: if KeyPressed then
              ProcessTheKeystroke;

Length   System

Purpose: Returns the dynamic length of the Str string.

Syntax: Function Length(Str : String) : Integer;

Example: GotoXY((80 - Length(Message)) div 2, 10);
              write(Message);   { Centered in row 10 }

Line   Graph

Purpose: Draws a line from (X1, Y1) to (X2, Y2) using the line style and thickness set by SetLineStyle and the color set by SetColor.

Syntax: Procedure Line(X1, Y1, X2, Y2 : Integer);

Example: Line(0, 0, GetMaxX, GetMaxY);   { Draw a big X on }
              Line(0, GetMaxY, GetMaxX, 0);   {   the screen   }

LineRel   Graph

Purpose: Draws a line to a point located a relative distance from the current pointer (CP) using the line style and thickness set by SetLineStyle and the color set by SetColor. If (X, Y) is the position of the CP, then LineRel(Dx, Dy) is equivalent to Line(X,Y,(X + Dx),(Y + Dy)).

Syntax: Procedure LineRel(Dx, Dy : Integer);

Example:
```
LineRel( 20, 40 );      { ------------------------------- }
LineRel( 20, -40 );     { These three lines form a triangle }
LineRel( -40, 0 );      { ------------------------------- }
```

LineTo   Graph

Purpose: Draws a line from the current pointer (CP) to (X, Y) using the line style and thickness set by SetLineStyle and the color set by SetColor.

Syntax: Procedure LineTo(X, Y : Integer);

Example: LineTo(GetMaxX, 0);   { Draws line to upper right corner }

Ln   System

Purpose: Returns the natural logarithm of the argument, which must be positive.

Syntax: Function Ln(X : Real) : Real;

Example: LogValue := Ln(Num);

Lo   System

Purpose: Returns the low-order byte of the argument, which may be either an Integer or a Word.

Syntax: Function Lo(X : IntWord) : Byte;

Example: writeln('Using DOS ', Lo(DosVersion), '.', Hi(DosVersion));

LowVideo   Crt

Purpose: Causes all subsequent screen output to use low-intensity characters.

Syntax: Procedure LowVideo;

Example: LowVideo;

Mark   System

Purpose: Copies the current value of HeapPtr to the pointer variable P.

Syntax: Procedure Mark(var P : Pointer);

Example: Mark(HeapHold);

MaxAvail   System

Purpose: Returns the size, in bytes, of the largest contiguous free block in the heap, corresponding to the size of the largest dynamic variable that can be allocated at the time.

Syntax: `Function MaxAvail : LongInt;`

Example: `TopItemSize := MaxAvail;`

MemAvail   System

Purpose: Returns the sum, in bytes, of all free blocks in the heap.

Syntax: `Function MemAvail : LongInt;`

Example: `HeapSpaceFree := MemAvail;`

MkDir   System

Purpose: Creates a subdirectory specified by `SubName`.

Syntax: `Procedure MkDir( SubName : String );`

Example: `MkDir( 'C:\TP\WORKAREA\TEMP' );`

Move   System

Purpose: Copies Count contiguous bytes beginning with the first byte of Source to the first byte of Destination. The Source and Destination variables may be of any type. No range checking is performed.

Syntax: Procedure Move(var Source, Destination; Count : Word);r

Example: Move(X, Y, SizeOf(X));

MoveRel   Graph

Purpose: Moves the current pointer (CP) a relative distance from its starting location. If (X, Y) is the original position of the CP, then MoveRel(Dx, Dy) is equivalent to MoveTo(X + Dx, Y + Dy).

Syntax: Procedure MoveRel(Dx, Dy : Integer);

Example: MoveRel(50, 50);

MoveTo   Graph

Purpose: Moves the current pointer (CP) to (X, Y).

Syntax: Procedure MoveTo(X, Y : Integer);

Example: MoveTo(100, 200);

MsDos   Dos

Purpose: Executes a DOS function call from BIOS interrupt number $21.
Any parameters are passed with a record of type Registers,
declared as follows:

```
Registers = record
                case Integer of
                Ø : (AX,BX,CX,DX,BP,SI,DI,DS,ES,Flags : Word);
                1 : (AL,AH,BL,BH,CL,CH,DL,DH          : Byte);
            end;
```

Syntax: Procedure MsDos(var Regs : Registers);

Example: Regs.AH := $3Ø;
MsDos(Regs);
writeln('Running DOS ', Regs.AL, '.', Regs.AH);

New   System

Purpose: Allocates enough space in the heap for a dynamic variable of
the type pointed to by P. Next, the procedure sets P equal to
the location of the new variable, which can then be referenced
as P^.

Syntax: Procedure New(var P : Pointer);

Example: New(PtrVar);

NormVideo
Crt

Purpose: Selects the original text attribute read from the cursor location when the program began. Usually, all subsequent screen output appears in characters of normal intensity.

Syntax: Procedure NormVideo;

Example: NormVideo;

NoSound
Crt

Purpose: Turns off the internal speaker.

Syntax: Procedure NoSound;

Example: NoSound;

Odd
System

Purpose: Returns True if the argument is an odd number; otherwise, False is returned.

Syntax: Function Odd(X : LongInt) : Boolean;

Example: if Odd(Value Shl Bit) then
     writeln('Bit number ', Bit, ' is set.');

Ofs   System

Purpose: Returns the offset of the specified object.

Syntax: Function Ofs(X : AnyType) : Word;

Example: DataLocation := Ofs(Object);

Ord   System

Purpose: Returns the ordinal number of any ordinal-type value.

Syntax: Function Ord(X : OrdType) : LongInt;

Example: Ch := 'm';
writeln(Ch, ' is letter number ', Ord(UpCase(Ch)) - 64);

OutText   Graph

Purpose: Outputs TextString to the location of the current pointer (CP).

Syntax: Procedure OutText(TextString : String);

Example: OutText('Message string');

OutTextXY   Graph

Purpose: Outputs TextString to the location (X, Y).

Syntax: Procedure OutTextXY(X, Y : Integer; TextString : String);

Example: OutTextXY(100, 50, 'Message string');

OvrClearBuf   Overlay

Purpose: Clears the overlay buffer, forcing all subsequent calls to overlay routines to be reloaded from the overlay file or from expanded memory (EMS).

Syntax: Procedure OvrClearBuf;

Example: OvrClearBuf;

OvrGetBuf   Overlay

Purpose: Returns the current size of the overlay buffer.

Syntax: Function OvrGetBuf : LongInt;

Example: writeln('The overlay buffer was ', OvrGetBuf, ' bytes long.');
OvrSetBuf(OvrGetBuf + IncrementAmount);
writeln('It is now ', OvrGetBuf, ' bytes long.');

OvrInit   Overlay

Purpose: Initializes the overlay manager and opens the overlay file called FileName.

Syntax: Procedure OvrInit(FileName : String);

Example: OvrInit('SpredSht.OVR');

OvrInitEMS   Overlay

Purpose: If an expanded memory (EMS) driver and adequate EMS memory are detected, OvrInitEMS loads the overlay file into EMS and closes the overlay file on disk.

Syntax: Procedure OvrInitEMS;

Example: OvrInitEMS;

OvrSetBuf   Overlay

Purpose: Resets the size of the overlay buffer.

Syntax: Procedure OvrSetBuf(Size : LongInt);

Example: writeln('The overlay buffer was ', OvrGetBuf, ' bytes long.');
OvrSetBuf(OvrGetBuf + IncrementAmount);
writeln('It is now ', OvrGetBuf, ' bytes long.');

PackTime   Dos

Purpose: Converts a DateTime record into a four-byte, packed date-and-time LongInt used by SetFTime. No range checking is performed on the fields. The DateTime record is defined as follows:

```
DateTime = record
               Year, Month, Day, Hour, Min, Sec : Word;
           end;
```

Syntax: Procedure PackTime(var T : DateTime; var P : LongInt);

Example: PackTime(CurrentMoment, ClockField);

ParamCount   System

Purpose: Returns the number of parameters passed to the program on the command line.

Syntax: Function ParamCount : Word;

Example: if ParamCount > Ø then
                    for i := 1 to ParamCount do
                        writeln('Parameter', i:2, ' is ', ParamStr(i));

ParamStr   System

Purpose: Returns a specified command-line parameter. ParamStr will be empty if Index is zero or if it's greater than ParamCount.

Syntax: Function ParamStr(Index : Word) : String;

Example: if ParamCount > Ø then
    for i := 1 to ParamCount do
        writeln('Parameter', i:2, ' is ', ParamStr(i);

Pi   System

Purpose: Returns the value of pi (3.1415926535897932385).

Syntax: Function Pi : Real;

Example: Circumference := Diameter * Pi;

PieSlice   Graph

Purpose: Draws and fills a pie slice of a specified Radius, centered at (X, Y), from starting angle StAngle to ending angle EndAngle. Angles are measured in degrees, running counterclockwise, with 0 degrees in the three o'clock position. The outline of the pie slice is drawn with the current color. Its interior is drawn with the pattern and color defined by SetFillStyle or SetFillPattern.

Syntax: Procedure PieSlice(X, Y   : Integer;
                          StAngle, EndAngle,
                          Radius   : Word);

Example: PieSlice(1ØØ, 1ØØ, Ø, 9Ø, 5Ø);

Pos　　　　　　　System

Purpose: Searches for the substring SubStr in a string Str. If found, Pos returns the index of the first occurrence of SubStr within Str. If not found, Pos returns Ø.

Syntax: Function Pos(SubStr, Str : String) : Byte;

Example:
```
ActiveString := '   12.345';   { Replace blanks with zeros }
while Pos( ' ', ActiveString ) > Ø do
    ActiveString[ Pos( ' ', ActiveString ) ] := 'Ø';
```

Pred　　　　　　　System

Purpose: Returns the predecessor of the argument, which can be any ordinal type. The result is the same type as the argument.

Syntax: Function Pred(X : OrdType) : OrdType;

Example: XminusOne := Pred(X);

Ptr　　　　　　　System

Purpose: Converts a segment base and an offset address to a pointer compatible with all pointer types.

Syntax: Function Ptr(Seg, Ofs : Word) : Pointer;

Example:
```
MemPtr := Ptr( $4Ø, $13 );
writeln( 'There are ', MemPtr^, ' bytes of internal memory.' );
```

PutImage   Graph

Purpose: Copies the contents of `BitMap` into the rectangular region of the screen having an upper left corner of (X, Y). The `BitMap` buffer was originally created by `GetImage`; it contains the bit image to be displayed, in addition to the height and width of the region. The `DisplayOption` parameter determines how each bit is displayed; it can be set to one of the following predefined constants:

```
CopyPut = Ø;
XORPut  = 1;
OrPut   = 2;
AndPut  = 3;
NotPut  = 4;
```

Syntax:
```
Procedure PutImage(     X, Y          : Integer;
                    var BitMap;
                        DisplayOption : Word );
```

Example:
```
Size := ImageSize( Ø, Ø, GetMaxX, GetMaxY );
GetMem( BufferArea, Size );
GetImage( Ø, Ø, GetMaxX, GetMaxY, BufferArea^ );
PutImage( Ø, Ø, BufferArea^, NotPut );   { Inverts the screen }
```

PutPixel   Graph

Purpose: Sets the pixel at (X, Y) to the color of `PixelColor`.

Syntax: `Procedure PutPixel( X, Y : Integer; PixelColor : Word );`

Example: `PutPixel( 1ØØ, 1ØØ, Red );`

Random   System

Purpose: Returns a random number. If Range isn't specified, Random
returns a real-type random number that is within the range
$0 <= x < 1$. When Range is used, Random returns a word-type
random number within the range $0 <= x < $ Range. The
Randomize procedure should be called at the beginning of the
program to initialize the random number generator.

Syntax 1:   Function Random : Real;

Example: if Random < Ø.5 then writeln('Heads')
                          else writeln('Tails');

Syntax 2:   Function Random(Range : Word) : Word;

Example: writeln('The values of the dice are ',
                Random(6) +1, ' and ', Random(6) +1);

Randomize   System

Purpose: Initializes the predefined variable RandSeed—the seed of the
built-in random number generator—with a random value taken
from the system clock.

Syntax: Procedure Randomize;

Example: Randomize;

Read   System

Purpose: Reads one or more values from a file into one or more variables. FileID, if specified, may be either a text or typed file. If FileID is omitted, the standard text file Input is assumed. When your program reads from a text file, each individual variable must be a char, integer, real, or string type. When the program reads from a typed file, each individual variable must be of the same type as the file itself.

Syntax: Procedure Read[([var FileID : FileType;] v1 [,v2,...,vn])];

Example: Read(DataFile, Name, Address, City, State, Zip);

ReadKey   Crt

Purpose: Reads a character from the keyboard without echoing it to the screen. If a key has already been pressed, ReadKey immediately returns the character; otherwise, ReadKey waits for the next key to be pressed. Extended keys (such as F1, PgUp, and Alt-P) are returned as two characters: the first is null (#0), and the second is the extended key code. Hence, the value returned by ReadKey must be tested; if null, a second ReadKey routine must be executed.

Syntax: Function ReadKey : Char;

Example: Entry := ReadKey;
If Entry = #27 then   { Escape key }
    DoEscapeStuff;

Readln   System

Purpose: Executes the read procedure, then skips to the next line of the file. FileID, if specified, must be a text file; if omitted, the standard text file Input is assumed. Each individual variable must be a char, integer, real, or string type.

Syntax: Procedure Readln[([var FileID : Text;] v1 [,v2,...,vn])];

Example: Readln[(DataFile, Name, Address, City, State, Zip)];

Rectangle   Graph

Purpose: Draws a rectangle using the current line style and color. The upper left corner is at (X1, Y1) and the lower right-hand corner is at (X2, Y2).

Syntax: Procedure Rectangle(X1, Y1, X2, Y2 : Integer);

Example: Rectangle(Ø, Ø, GetMaxX, GetMaxY);   { Boxes the screen }

RegisterBGIdriver   Graph

Purpose: Registers a user-loaded or linked-in .BGI driver with the graphics system. If an error occurs while the system is loading the driver, the function returns a negative number; otherwise, the function returns the internal driver number.

Syntax: Function RegisterBGIdriver(Driver : Pointer) : Integer;

Example: Assign(CGADriver, 'CGA.BGI');
Reset(CGADriver, 1);
GetMem(CGAPointer, FileSize(CGADriver));
BlockRead(CGADriver, CGAPointer^, FileSize(CGADriver));
if RegisterBGIdriver(CGAPointer^) < Ø then
    writeln('Error in loading driver');

RegisterBGIfont   Graph

Purpose: Registers a user-loaded or linked-in .BGI font with the graphics system. If an error occurs while the system is loading the font, the function returns a negative number; otherwise, the function returns the internal font number.

Syntax: Function RegisterBGIfont(Font : Pointer) : Integer;

Example: Assign(TripFont, 'TRIP.CHR');
Reset(TripFont, 1);
GetMem(FontPointer, FileSize(TripFont));
BlockRead(TripFont, FontPointer^, FileSize(TripFont));
if RegisterBGIfont(FontPointer^) < Ø then
    writeln('Error in loading driver');

Release   System

Purpose: Returns the top of the heap to the location pointed to by P, which was assigned during the execution of the most recent Mark procedure.

Syntax: Procedure Release(var P : Pointer);

Example: Release(HeapTop);

Rename   System

Purpose: Renames an unopened external file to NewName.

Syntax: Procedure Rename(var F; NewName : String);

Example: Assign(SwitchFile, 'Orig.TXT');
              Rename(SwitchFile, 'New.TXT');

Reset   System

Purpose: Opens an existing file. If F is declared as a text file, Reset opens it for input only. If F is declared as a typed or untyped file, Reset opens it for both input and output. The optional RecSize parameter, which can be used only if F is declared as an untyped file, specifies the record size used for data transfers; if RecSize is omitted, Reset uses a default record size of 128 bytes.

Syntax: Procedure Reset(var F [: file; RecSize : Word]);

Example: Assign(InFile, 'Data.TXT');
              Reset(InFile);

RestoreCrtMode   Graph

Purpose: Restores the screen to its mode before InitGraph initialized
                graphics. RestoreCrtMode is used after SetGraphMode.

Syntax: Procedure RestoreCrtMode;

Example: RestoreCrtMode;

Rewrite   System

Purpose: Creates and opens a new file. If F is declared as a text file,
                Rewrite opens it for output only. If F is declared as a typed or
                untyped file, Rewrite opens it for both input and output. The
                optional RecSize parameter, which can be used only if F is
                declared as an untyped file, specifies the record size used for
                data transfers. If RecSize is omitted, Rewrite uses a default
                record size of 128 bytes.

Syntax: Procedure Rewrite(var F [: file; RecSize : Word]);

Example: Assign(OutFile, 'Data.TXT');
                Rewrite(OutFile);

RmDir   System

Purpose: Removes an empty subdirectory specified by EmptyDir.

Syntax: Procedure RmDir(EmptyDir : String);

Example: RmDir('C:\TURBO\DATA\TEMP');

Round   System

Purpose: Rounds a real-type value to an integer-type value.

Syntax: Function Round(X : Real) : LongInt;

Example: Three := Round(3.14159);

RunError   System

Purpose: Halts program execution and generates a run-time error. If the
optional parameter ErrorCode is omitted, the run-time error
number is assumed to be 0.

Syntax: Procedure RunError([ErrorCode : Word]);

Example: if Mode = fmInput then
        RunError(1Ø4);   { File not open for input }

Sector   Graph

Purpose: Draws and fills an elliptical sector from starting angle StAngle
to ending angle EndAngle, using (X, Y) as the center point.
XRadius and YRadius are the horizontal and vertical axes,
respectively. Angles are measured in degrees, running
counterclockwise, with 0 degrees at the three o'clock position.
The outline of the sector is drawn in the current color. The
interior of the sector is filled with the pattern and color
specified by SetFillStyle or SetFillPattern.

Syntax: Procedure Sector(X, Y   : Integer;
                    StAngle, EndAngle,
                    XRadius, YRadius   : Word);

Example: Sector(1ØØ, 1ØØ, Ø, 45, 3Ø, 5Ø);

Seek   System

Purpose: Moves the current position of an opened file F to the specified component CompNumber. The file variable F may reference a typed or untyped file, but not a text file. For a typed file, the component is the same data object as the type of the file. For an untyped file, the component is a record whose size defaults to 128 bytes, but which may be changed by the optional record-size parameter of the Reset or Rewrite procedure that opens it. The first component of the file is always number 0.

Syntax: Procedure Seek(var F; CompNumber : LongInt);

Example: Seek(RandomFile, RecordKey);

SeekEof   System

Purpose: Returns the end-of-file status of a text file. SeekEof behaves like Eof, except that it ignores all blanks, tabs, and end-of-line markers. If the optional file parameter F is omitted, SeekEof is assumed to reference the standard Input file.

Syntax: Function SeekEof[(var F : Text)] : Boolean;

Example:
```
while not SeekEof( DataFile ) do begin
    readln( DataFile, InLine );
    writeln( DataFile, InLine );
end;
```

SeekEoln   System

Purpose: Returns the end-of-line status of a text file. SeekEoln behaves
like Eoln, except that blanks and tabs are ignored. If the
optional file parameter F is omitted, SeekEoln is assumed to
reference the standard Input file.

Syntax: Function SeekEoln[(var F : Text)] : Boolean;

Example: while not SeekEoln(DataFile) do begin
    read(DataFile, CharItem);
    ProcessTheCharItem;
  end;

Seg   System

Purpose: Returns the segment of a specified object.

Syntax: Function Seg(X : AnyType) : Word;

Example: DataLocation := Seg(Object);

SetActivePage   Graph

Purpose: Selects Page as the active page for graphics output.

Syntax: Procedure SetActivePage(Page : Word);

Example: SetActivePage(1);

SetAllPalette   Graph

Purpose: Changes all palette colors as specified. Palette is an untyped parameter, but it usually conforms to the PaletteType record, defined as follows:

```
PaletteType = record
                Size   : Byte;
                Colors : Array[Ø..MaxColors] of ShortInt;
              end;
```

The Size byte is the length of the active part of the structure; that is, SetAllPalette only processes the first Size bytes of the Colors array. Each active byte may have a value from –1 through 15; if the byte is –1, the color is unchanged. Changes to the palette are seen immediately on the screen.

Syntax: Procedure SetAllPalette(var Palette);

Example: SetAllPalette(PaletteRecord);

SetAspectRatio   Graph

Purpose: Changes the default aspect ratio of the current graphics mode. The value must be specified as a fraction of whole numbers; the system computes the aspect ratio by dividing the Xasp parameter by the Yasp parameter. The GetAspectRatio procedure can be used to obtain the current aspect ratio.

Syntax: Procedure SetAspectRatio(Xasp, Yasp : Word);

Example: SetAspectRatio(Xaspect, Yaspect);

SetBkColor   Graph

Purpose: Sets the current background color to ColorNum—a value from 0
through 15. The actual color selected must be within the range
allowed by the current graphics driver and mode.
SetBkColor(∅) always sets the background color to black.

Syntax: Procedure SetBkColor(ColorNum : Word);

Example: if Color in [∅ .. Palette.Size] then
        SetBkColor(Color);

SetCBreak   Dos

Purpose: Sets the state of Ctrl-Break checking in DOS. If SetCBreak is
called when Break is False, DOS will only check for Ctrl-Break
during I/O operations. If SetCBreak is called when Break is
True, DOS will check for Ctrl-Break at every system call.

Syntax: Procedure SetCBreak(Break : Boolean);

Example: SetCBreak(True);

SetColor   Graph

Purpose: Sets the current drawing color to ColorNum—a value from 0
through 15. The actual color selected must be within the range
allowed by the current graphics driver and mode. Valid values
of ColorNum range from 0 through GetMaxColor.

Syntax: Procedure SetColor(ColorNum : Word);

Example: if Color in [∅ .. GetMaxColor] then
        SetColor(Color);

SetDate Dos

Purpose: Sets the current date in the operating system. Year must be within the range 1980 through 2099, Month within the range 1 through 12, and Day within the range 1 through 31. If an invalid date is specified, the request is ignored.

Syntax: `Procedure SetDate( Year, Month, Day : Word );`

Example: `SetDate( 1981, 5, 4 );   { May 4, 1981 }`

SetFAttr Dos

Purpose: Sets the attributes of the unopened file F. The desired attributes are chosen by using a value of Attr equal to the sum of an appropriate combination of the following predefined constants:

```
ReadOnly    = $Ø1;
Hidden      = $Ø2;
SysFile     = $Ø4;
VolumeID    = $Ø8;
Directory   = $1Ø;
Archive     = $2Ø;
AnyFile     = $3F;
```

Syntax: `Procedure SetFAttr( var F : AnyFileType; Attr : Word );`

Example: `Assign( WorkFile, ExternalFileName );`
`SetFAttr( WorkFile, ReadOnly );`

SetFillPattern   Graph

Purpose: Selects a user-defined fill Pattern and Color. The pattern is
formed as an 8 × 8 grid of pixels corresponding to the 64 bits
contained in the FillPatternType array, defined as follows:

        FillPatternType = Array[1..8] of Byte;

Syntax: Procedure SetFillPattern(Pattern : FillPatternType;
                                Color   : Word);

Example: SetFillPattern(CustomPattern, Red);

SetFillStyle   Graph

Purpose: Sets the fill pattern and color. The Pattern parameter may be
chosen from among the following predefined constants:

        EmptyFill   = Ø; { Uses the background color }
        SolidFill   = 1; { Uses a solid fill color }
        LineFill   = 2; { --- fill pattern }
        LtSlashFill   = 3; { /// fill pattern }
        SlashFill   = 4; { /// fill pattern with thick lines }
        BkSlashFill   = 5; { \\\ fill pattern with thick lines }
        LtBkSlashFill   = 6; { \\\ fill pattern }
        HatchFill   = 7; { Light hatch fill pattern }
        XHatchFill   = 8; { Heavy cross hatch fill pattern }
        InterleaveFill = 9; { Interleaving line fill pattern }
        WideDotFill   = 1Ø; { Widely spaced dot fill pattern }
        CloseDotFill   = 11; { Closely spaced dot fill pattern }
        UserFill   = 12; { User defined fill pattern }

ColorNum must be within the range allowed by the current
graphics driver and mode; valid values range from 0 through
GetMaxColor.

Syntax: Procedure SetFillStyle(Pattern, ColorNum : Word);

Example: SetFillStyle(HatchFill, Red);

SetFTime   Dos

Purpose: Sets the date and time an open file was last written. The Time parameter can be created by using the PackTime procedure.

Syntax: Procedure SetFTime(var F : AnyFileType; Time : LongInt);

Example: PackTime(CurrentMoment, ClockField);
SetFTime(ActiveFile; ClockField);

SetGraphBufSize   Graph

Purpose: Allocates BufSize bytes on the heap for the graphics buffer used for scan and flood fills. The default buffer size is 4K. The SetGraphBufSize procedure must be called before the call to InitGraph.

Syntax: Procedure SetGraphBufSize(BufSize : Word);

Example: SetGraphBufSize(8192);   { Doubles the buffer to 8K }

SetGraphMode   Graph

Purpose: Sets the system to the specified graphics Mode and clears the screen. All other graphics settings are reset to their defaults. SetGraphMode can be used to change the mode within the current graphics session or can be used after RestoreCrtMode to return to graphics in a new Mode.

Syntax: Procedure SetGraphMode(Mode : Integer);

Example: SetGraphMode(CGAHi);

SetIntVec   Dos

Purpose: Sets interrupt vector IntNo to point to the address specified by Vector.

Syntax: Procedure SetIntVec(IntNo : Byte; Vector : Pointer);

Example: SetIntVec(5, @NewPrtScProc);

SetLineStyle   Graph

Purpose: Sets the current LineStyle, Pattern, and Thickness. The LineStyle parameter controls the pattern of segments and spaces that actually form the line. Standard styles can be selected from among the following predefined constants:

        SolidLn   = Ø;
        DottedLn   = 1;
        CenterLn   = 2;
        DashedLn   = 3;
        UserBitLn = 4;

If UserBitLn is chosen, the line style takes the form of the sequence of bits within the Pattern byte; otherwise, the value of Pattern is ignored. The Thickness parameter chooses whether the line is normal or thick, depending upon the choice of the following predefined constants:

        NormWidth = 1;
        ThickWidth = 3;

Syntax: Procedure SetLineStyle(LineStyle, Pattern, Thickness : Word);

Example: SetLineStyle(DashedLn, Ø, ThickWidth);

SetPalette   Graph

Purpose: Changes the setting of the ColorNum entry in the palette to
NewColor. The choice of ColorNum must be within the range
allowed by the current graphics driver and mode; valid values
range from 0 through GetMaxColor.

Syntax: Procedure SetPalette(ColorNum : Word; NewColor : ShortInt);

Example: SetPalette(2, Red);

SetRGBPalette   Graph

Purpose: Modifies the palette entry ColorNum for the IBM-8514 and VGA
drivers. The choice of ColorNum must be within the range
allowed by the graphics driver: 0 through 255 for the
IBM-8514, and 0 through 15 for the VGA. RedValue,
GreenValue, and BlueValue enable the user to control the
intensities of the three CRT color guns.

Syntax: Procedure SetRGBPalette(ColorNum,
                              RedValue,
                              GreenValue,
                              BlueValue   : Integer);

Example: SetRGBPalette(Green, $FC, $14, $14); { Changes "Green" to Red }

SetTextBuf   System

Purpose: Assigns an I/O buffer of Buf to an unopened text file. The default buffer size is 128 bytes. If the optional Size parameter is specified, the buffer is set to the first Size bytes of Buf. If the Size parameter is omitted, the buffer size is assumed to be SizeOf(Buf) bytes.

Syntax: Procedure SetTextBuf(var F : Text; var Buf [; Size : Word]);

Example: Assign(BigText, ExternalFileName);
SetTextBuf(BigText, BufferPtr^);
Reset(BigText);

SetTextJustify   Graph

Purpose: Sets the text justification for strings output by OutText and OutTextXY. The Horizontal parameter selects left, center, or right justification based on the choice of one of the following predefined constants:

```
LeftText    = 0;
CenterText  = 1;
RightText   = 2;
```

The Vertical parameter selects bottom, center, or top justification based on the choice of one of the following predefined constants:

```
BottomText = 0;
CenterText = 1;
TopText    = 2;
```

Syntax: Procedure SetTextJustify(Horizontal, Vertical : Word);

Example: SetTextJustify(LeftText, CenterText);

SetTextStyle   Graph

Purpose: Sets the current text Font, Direction, and character Magnification factor. The Font is selected from one of the following predefined constants:

```
DefaultFont   = Ø;
TriplexFont   = 1;
SmallFont     = 2;
SansSerifFont = 3;
GothicFont    = 4;
```

The Direction of the output may be left-to-right or bottom-to-top, depending on the use of one of the following predefined constants:

```
HorizDir  = Ø;      { left to right }
VertDir   = 1;      { bottom to top }
```

The Magnification factor determines the size of the text.

Syntax: Procedure SetTextStyle(Font, Direction, Magnification : Word);

Example: SetTextStyle(GothicFont, HorizDir, 4);

SetTime   Dos

Purpose: Sets the current time in the operating system. Military time is used, with Hour ranging from 0 through 23, Minute and Second from 0 through 59, and Sec1ØØ from 0 through 99.

Syntax: Procedure SetTime(Hour, Minute, Second, Sec1ØØ : Word);

Example: SetTime(12, Ø, Ø, Ø);   { 12:ØØ noon }

SetUserCharSize   Graph

Purpose: Varies the character width and height for stroked fonts. Any factors may be used, but they must be expressed as fractions of whole numbers. The horizontal factor is given by MultX div DivX, and the vertical factor by MultY div DivY.

Syntax: Procedure SetUserCharSize(MultX, DivX, MultY, DivY : Word);

Example: SetUserCharSize(3, 2, 4, 1);   { 1.5x wide by 4.0x high }

SetVerify   Dos

Purpose: Sets the state of the verify flag in DOS. When the flag is off (Verify = False), disk writes aren't verified. When it is on (Verify = True), all disk writes are verified.

Syntax: Procedure SetVerify(Verify : Boolean);

Example: SetVerify(True);

SetViewPort

Graph

Purpose: Sets the size and location of the window to use for graphics output. The upper left corner of the window is positioned at (X1, Y1), and the lower right corner at (X2, Y2). Clipping is controlled by setting the Clip parameter, which can be either of the following predefined constants:

```
ClipOn  = true;
ClipOff = false;
```

Syntax:
```
Procedure SetViewPort( X1, Y1, X2, Y2 : Integer;
                       Clip           : Boolean );
```

Example: `SetViewPort( 25, 25, 100, 100, ClipOn );`

SetVisualPage

Graph

Purpose: Sets the visual graphics page number.

Syntax: `Procedure SetVisualPage( Page : Word );`

Example: `SetVisualPage( 1 );`

SetWriteMode   Graph

Purpose: Sets the writing mode for line drawing. The WriteMode
parameter determines the binary operation used to place the
line on the screen, as follows:

```
CopyPut        = Ø;      { MOV }
XORPut         = 1;      { XOR }
```

CopyPut uses an ordinary assembly language MOV instruction,
overwriting the contents of the screen. XORPut uses an XOR
instruction, which activates pixels when the screen is blank and
deactivates pixels when the screen is lit.

Syntax: Procedure SetWriteMode(WriteMode : Integer);

Example: SetWriteMode(XORPut);

Sin   System

Purpose: Returns the sine of the argument, which is expressed in radians.

Syntax: Function Sin(X : Real) : Real;

Example: SinValue := Sin(Pi/4);   { Sin(45 degrees) }

SizeOf   System

Purpose: Returns the number of bytes occupied by the argument, which
can be any variable reference or type identifier.

Syntax: Function SizeOf(X : AnyType) : Word;

Example: MemReqd := SizeOf(DataArray);

Sound   Crt

Purpose: Causes the internal speaker to generate a tone of Hz hertz
(cycles per second).

Syntax: `Procedure Sound( Hz : Word );`

Example: `Sound( 550 );`

SPtr   System

Purpose: Returns the current value of the SP register, which contains the
offset of the stack pointer within the stack segment.

Syntax: `Function SPtr : Word;`

Example: `StackPointerOffset := SPtr;`

Sqr   System

Purpose: Returns the square of the argument, which can be any integer-
type or real-type expression. The result returned by Sqr is the
same type as the argument.

Syntax: `Function Sqr( X : AnyType ) : AnyType;`

Example: `SideC := Sqrt( Sqr(SideA) + Sqr(SideB) );`

Sqrt System

Purpose: Returns the square root of the argument, which must be non-negative.

Syntax: Function Sqrt(X : Real) : Real;

Example: SideC := Sqrt(Sqr(SideA) + Sqr(SideB));

SSeg System

Purpose: Returns the current value of the SS register, which contains the segment address of the stack segment.

Syntax: Function SSeg : Word;

Example: StackSegmentAddress := SSeg;

Str System

Purpose: Converts a numeric value to a string Str. The number, X, may be any integer-type or real-type expression. The optional string Width and Decimals are integer-type expressions having the same formatting effect as a call to the write procedure.

Syntax: Procedure Str(X [: Width [: Decimals]]; var Str : String);

Example: Str(NumberValue, OutString);
OutText(OutString);

Succ $\qquad$ System

Purpose: Returns the successor of the ordinal-type argument.

Syntax: `Function Succ( X : OrdType ) : OrdType;`

Example: `Ch := Succ( 'B' );   { Returns "C" }`

Swap $\qquad$ System

Purpose: Swaps the high- and low-order bytes of the argument, which can be either an integer or a word. The value returned by Swap has the same type of the argument.

Syntax: `Function Swap( X : IntWord ) : IntWord;`

Example: `Flipped := Swap( $4567 );   { Returns $6745 }`

SwapVectors $\qquad$ Dos

Purpose: Swaps interrupt vectors prior to a call to the Exec procedure.

Syntax: `Procedure SwapVectors;`

Example:
```
SwapVectors;   { Saves interrupt vectors }
Exec( ProgName, ComLine );
SwapVectors;   { Restores interrupt vectors }
```

TextBackground   Crt

Purpose: Selects the background Color from one of the following
predefined constants:

Black	= 0;
Blue	= 1;
Green	= 2;
Cyan	= 3;
Red	= 4;
Magenta	= 5;
Brown	= 6;
LightGray	= 7;

Syntax: Procedure TextBackground(Color : Byte);

Example: TextBackground(Red);

TextColor   Crt

Purpose: Selects the foreground character Color from one of the following predefined constants:

```
Black         = 0;
Blue          = 1;
Green         = 2;
Cyan          = 3;
Red           = 4;
Magenta       = 5;
Brown         = 6;
LightGray     = 7;
DarkGray      = 8;
LightBlue     = 9;
LightGreen    = 10;
LightCyan     = 11;
LightRed      = 12;
LightMagenta  = 13;
Yellow        = 14;
White         = 15;
```

A blinking effect can be achieved by adding the constant:

```
Blink         = 128;
```

Syntax: Procedure TextColor(Color : Byte);

Example: TextColor(Green + Blink);

TextHeight   Graph

Purpose: Returns the height of a string in pixels. The value is calculated from the current font size and multiplication factor.

Syntax: Function TextHeight(TextString : String) : Word;

Example: Tall := TextHeight('Press Enter to terminate...');

TextMode   Crt

Purpose: Selects a specific text Mode from the following list of predefined constants:

```
BW4Ø        = Ø;      { 4Ø × 25 B/W on Color Adapter }
CO4Ø        = 1;      { 4Ø × 25 Color on Color Adapter }
BW8Ø        = 2;      { 8Ø × 25 B/W on Color Adapter }
CO8Ø        = 3;      { 8Ø × 25 Color on Color Adapter }
Mono        = 7;      { 8Ø × 25 on Monochrome Adapter }
Font8×8     = 256;    { Add-in for ROM font }
```

The Font8×8 value is added to one of the other options in order to use the additional lines available on VGA and EGA screens (43 and 50 lines, respectively). When TextMode is called, the screen is reset to its default values.

Syntax: Procedure TextMode(Mode : Integer);

Example: TextMode(CO8Ø);

TextWidth   Graph

Purpose: Returns the width of a string in pixels. The value is calculated from the length of the string, the current font size, and the current multiplication factor.

Syntax: Function TextWidth(TextString : String) : Word;

Example: Wide := TextWidth('Press Enter to terminate...');

Trunc   System

Purpose: Truncates a real-type value to an integer-type value.

Syntax: Function Trunc(X : Real) : LongInt;

Example: Num := Trunc(3.999);   { Returns "3" }

Truncate   System

Purpose: Truncates the file by deleting all records beyond the current file position.

Syntax: Procedure Truncate(var F : AnyFileType);

Example: Truncate(WorkFile);

UnpackTime   Dos

Purpose: Converts the four-byte, packed date-and-time LongInt Squish
returned by GetFTime, FindFirst, or FindNext into Legible, an
unpacked DateTime record, defined as follows:

```
DateTime = record
               Year, Month, Day, Hour, Min, Sec : Word;
           end;
```

The values of the individual fields are not range checked.

Syntax: `Procedure UnpackTime( Squish : LongInt; var Legible : DateTime );`

Example:
```
UnpackTime( SmallSize, ReadRec );
with ReadRec do
    writeln( Month, '/', Day, '/', Year-1900 );
```

UpCase   System

Purpose: Converts a character to uppercase.

Syntax: `Function UpCase( ch : Char ) : Char;`

Example:
```
Repeat
    write( 'Continue?  (Y/N) ' );
    readln( Ans )
until UpCase(Ans) in [ 'N', 'Y' ];
```

Val System

Purpose: Converts the original string value `Orig` to its numeric representation `Final`. If the string can't be converted, `Code` contains the index of the first troublesome character. No trailing spaces are allowed.

Syntax: `Procedure Val( Orig : String;  var Final;  var Code : Integer );`

Example: `Val( ParamStr(1), SelectedValue, TroubleItem );`

WhereX Crt

Purpose: Returns the X coordinate of the current cursor position, relative to the current window.

Syntax: `Function WhereX : Byte;`

Example: `Over := WhereX;`

WhereY Crt

Purpose: Returns the Y coordinate of the current cursor position, relative to the current window.

Syntax: `Function WhereY: Byte;`

Example: `Down := WhereY;`

Window   Crt

Purpose: Defines a text window on the screen. The window is in the
form of a rectangle, with upper left coordinates (X1, Y1) and
lower right coordinates (X2, Y2).

Syntax: `Procedure Window( X1, Y1, X2, Y2 : Byte );`

Example: `Window( 1, 1, 80, 25 );    { Resets screen to original size }`

Write   System

Purpose: Writes one or more values to a file. If the optional text file
identifier F is omitted, the standard Output file is assumed.

Syntax: `Procedure Write[( [var F : FileType;] v1 [ ,v2, ..., vn ] )];`

Example: `Write( DataFile, WorkLine );`

Writeln   System

Purpose: Executes the write procedure, then outputs an end-of-line
marker to the file. If the optional text file identifier F is
omitted, the standard Output file is assumed.

Syntax: `Procedure Writeln[( [var F : Text;] v1 [ ,v2, ..., vn ] )];`

Example: `Writeln( TextFileID, WorkLine );`

Compiler Directives

Although the Pascal language itself forces each line of your program to have one clear meaning, there are actually various ways the Turbo compiler can generate the machine-level output code. These different options are selected with compiler directives.

There are three categories of directives: switch, parameter, and conditional. *Switch* directives, as their name implies, act to switch particular code-generation options on or off. *Parameter* directives specify external file names and memory sizes. *Conditional* directives conditionally select which parts of a program to compile and which parts to ignore.

Compiler directives can be implemented within the integrated environment by selecting the desired directive with the Options/Compiler menu. Although many more directives exist than can be specified in this manner, this is the best way to establish your preferences for program defaults.

Alternatively, directives can be embedded within your source code or given in the command line of the command-line compiler. When given in the command line of the command-line compiler, the form must be /$<directive>. When included within your source code, the directive is written as part of a comment. In such a case the dollar sign is the first character following the opening comment delimiter, followed immediately by the particular symbol that designates the directive. If any blanks or other characters appear before the dollar sign, the compiler treats the entire line as an ordinary comment and ignores any directives it contains.

Although all these methods achieve the same result, you should remember that good programming entails good documentation; the preferred way to select a directive is to include it as part of the source code in your program. Further, you may want directives to be turned on or off within the same program as the situation requires; this is something that can be accomplished only with the embedded directive method.

Of course, many of your programs won't need to use any directives at all. However, when properly understood, directives are extremely useful for simplifying the pain of debugging troublesome programs and for considerably improving the speed and efficiency of your finished product.

Switch Directives

With switch directives, you can choose from among several code-generation options. Switch directives may be either *global*, meaning that the entire compilation is affected, or *local*, meaning that the effect exists only until the next use of the same directive. In other words, once a global directive is set, it cannot be changed, whereas local directives can be switched on or off as often as needed. Global directives must be declared immediately after the initial program or unit line. Local directives may appear anywhere in the program.

Several switch directives can be specified within the same comment line by separating them with commas, as follows:

```
{$A +,B-,C +,...  <any desired comment>}
```

A, B, and C may be any directive. The + indicates that the directive is enabled, whereas the – indicates that the directive is disabled. Any spaces appearing before a directive on a line cause the remainder of the line to be treated as a comment, and any additional directives are ignored.

A: Align Data

Syntax: {$A +} or {$A-}

Default: {$A +}

Type: Global

Menu: Options/Compiler/Align Data

With the Align Data directive you can choose between byte and word alignment when you store variables and typed constants. The directive has no effect on the functional operation of the program itself.

Alignment refers to the starting memory address. For example, when a segment must be *aligned* to a paragraph boundary, the memory address of the first byte in a segment must be evenly divisible by 16. Similarly, a *word-aligned* variable is one in which the memory address of the first byte in which the variable is stored is evenly divisible by 2.

In the default state {$A +}, every variable and typed constant requiring two or more bytes is stored in a memory location that begins on an even address. Because some memory locations may be skipped over, the resulting .EXE file may be a *few* bytes larger than it would be if the option weren't used. The Align Data directive affects only *individual* variables; it has no impact on *compound* variables such as the fields in a record or the elements of an array.

When word alignment is disabled with {$A–}, all data items are stored continuously in memory, without any consideration for their individual sizes or beginning addresses.

Some processors, such as the 8088, only have an 8-bit data bus and, consequently, always fetch data a single byte at a time. Word alignment offers no efficiency improvements for those machines.

However, other processors, such as the 8086 and the 80286, have a 16-bit data bus and can fetch a word in a single operation. Therefore, word alignment can considerably enhance the performance of most PCs.

B: Boolean Evaluation

Syntax: {$B +} or {$B–}

Default: {$B–}

Type: Local

Menu: Options/Compiler/Boolean Evaluation

The Boolean Evaluation directive allows the option of evaluating a Boolean expression only as far as necessary to determine the result of the entire expression.

In the following code:

```
W := 3;
X := 4;
CondA := False;
if ( W  < X ) or ( Y > Z ) then begin
   Proc1;
   Proc2;
end;
if CondA and CondB then
   Proc3;
```

the Proc1 and Proc2 procedures are always executed because 3 is less than 4; the values of the Y and Z variables are irrelevant. Similarly, because CondA is False, Proc3 cannot be executed no matter what the state of CondB.

In the default {$B–} state, the compiler generates code containing exits that allow the program to end the Boolean evaluation after the result of the entire expression becomes evident. Although in this example the {$B–} directive still creates code to compare Y and Z and to evaluate CondB, during program execution those code segments will simply be bypassed because they wouldn't have any effect on the condition of the entire sentence. This feature is commonly known as *short circuit Boolean evaluation*.

If the {$B +} directive had been enabled in the example, the entire Boolean expression would have evaluated, even though in each case the final result could have been determined within the first clause.

Using the {$B +} directive results in slightly smaller output files because programs compiled in the default {$B-} state contain extra conditional jump instructions. However, the adverse effects of the larger program size and the additional condition tests are usually trivial. Depending on the structure of a Boolean expression, the default {$B-} directive may significantly improve the speed with which the program executes. For example, if the following statement is executed repeatedly:

if (A > B) or ((((C + D) > E) and (F < G)) or ((not H) and (I > J))) then

considerable execution time will be saved if the default {$B-} directive is used and A is almost always greater than B. In general, whenever you use the {$B-} directive, you should remember to arrange the clauses of a Boolean expression to optimize program efficiency.

One negative consequence of the {$B-} directive is that using functions as Boolean operands can produce strange results. For example, consider the SWITCHB program (listing 1).

Listing 1

```
program SwitchB;
var
   GlobalX : integer;
function BumpUp : integer;
begin
   inc( GlobalX );
   BumpUp := GlobalX;
end;
begin
   GlobalX := 37;
   writeln( '1: GlobalX = ', GlobalX );
   if ( 4 > 2 ) or ( BumpUp > 67 ) then          { Test 1 }
      writeln( '2: GlobalX = ', GlobalX );
{$B +}
   if ( 4 > 2 ) or ( BumpUp > 67 ) then          { Test 2 }
      writeln( '3: GlobalX = ', GlobalX );
{$B-}
   if ( 4 > 2 ) or ( BumpUp > 67 ) then          { Test 3 }
      writeln( '4: GlobalX = ', GlobalX );
end.
```

When executed, the program results in the following:

```
1: GlobalX = 37
2: GlobalX = 37
3: GlobalX = 38
4: GlobalX = 38
```

Because 4 is always greater than 2, the if statements of Tests 1 and 3 were completely determined by the first clause. In Test 2, however, the {$B +} directive forced the if statement to evaluate the second clause unnecessarily. As a consequence, the BumpUp function was invoked and the global variable GlobalX was changed.

D: Debug Information

Syntax: {$D +} or {$D-}

Default   {$D +}

Type: Global

Menu: Options/Compiler/Debug Information

When the Debug directive is enabled with {$D +}, the Turbo Pascal debugger can relate a program's source code to the machine code produced by the compiler. The Debug directive is what allows the TURBO.EXE integrated development environment to respond to a run-time error by automatically returning to the editor and highlighting the offending source code.

In addition, the Debug directive provides the information needed for Turbo's built-in debugger to allow a program to run freely, to be "single-stepped," or to run until a user-defined breakpoint is reached—all while displaying the effect of the program's statements.

The Debug directive is usually enabled in conjunction with the Local Symbol directive {$L +}. The Local Symbol directive allows the debugger to track individual local symbols, whereas the Debug directive can relate those symbols to specific lines of program code.

Use of the Debug directive increases the size of an output file, but the resulting information is contained separate from the normal machine code. Consequently, it has no effect on execution speed.

E: Emulation

Syntax: {$E +} or {$E-}

Default: {$E +}

Type: Global

Menu: Options/Compiler/Emulation

The Emulation directive controls whether floating-point emulation software is included with a compiled program.

In the default {$E +} state, the compiled program contains all the software necessary to emulate the operation of an 8087 coprocessor. The program may use any floating-point data types, including single, double, extended, and comp.

If 8087 emulation is disabled with {$E-}, the only software emulation that Turbo Pascal includes in the compiled program is code to support the 6-byte real data type. The program may still use the single, double, extended, and comp data types, but if it does, it can only run on a PC in which a math coprocessor has been installed.

The .EXE file for a program is considerably smaller when a program is compiled with the Emulation directive disabled. Furthermore, the program runs faster because it doesn't include additional software to dynamically decide which machine code will handle which operation. Nevertheless, such a program isn't portable. The directive should only be disabled when you are certain that the program will always run on a PC in which a coprocessor has been installed.

F: Force Far Calls

Syntax: {$F +} or {$F-}

Default: {$F-}

Type: Local

Menu: Options/Compiler/Force Far Calls

The Force Far Calls directive determines whether the code generated for making procedure and function calls uses the near or far call model.

Far calls allow the program to reference a subroutine anywhere in memory. Both the segment and offset values must be specified; four bytes are required to contain the address. Near calls can only reference a subroutine within the current segment; only the two-byte offset is specified.

All of the code within a single unit resides in the same segment. Different units place their code in different segments. In the default state (when the directive is disabled), the compiler automatically determines whether a procedure or function call is referencing a routine outside of the current segment (which then results in a far call) or if the routine is within the current segment (which results in a near call).

When the directive is enabled with {$F +}, *all* calls use the far model.

By themselves, the extra two bytes used by the segment address may seem negligible; however, during execution, code must be generated to save, replace, and restore the segment registers. Further, the compiler believes that the routine is in another segment, so any variable parameter used by the routine is referenced by both its segment and offset addresses.

Because of these inefficiencies, the Force Far Calls directive should be used sparingly.

I: Input/Output Checking

Syntax: {$I +} or {$I-}

Default: {$I +}

Type: Local

Menu: Options/Compiler/I/O Checking

The I/O Checking directive controls whether code is generated to test for input and output errors.

When the directive is enabled with {$I +}, the compiler automatically tests every I/O procedure and function. If any problem is detected, the program immediately terminates with a run-time error.

When the directive is disabled with {$I-}, a single I/O error suspends all further input and output activity but won't cause program termination. In this case, I/O errors can be detected—and I/O processing restored—by calling the IOResult function. If IOResult returns zero, the operation was successful; a nonzero value corresponds to an error code that the program can use to determine an appropriate response. Note that when I/O Checking is disabled, the IOResult function *must* be called after every individual input and output statement.

Consider the simple integer squaring program SWITCHI1 (listing 2).

Listing 2

```
program SwitchI1;
var
   Selection : integer;
begin
   write( 'Please enter an integer value: ' );
   readln( Selection );
   writeln;
   writeln( 'The square of ', Selection, ' is ', Sqr( Selection ) );
end.
```

If an integer value is entered for the Selection variable, the program responds with its square. If a letter, real number, or some other noninteger value is entered, the program terminates with the message: Error 1Ø6: Invalid numeric format.

This inconvenience can be avoided by disabling the I/O Checking directive with {$I-}. The IOResult function can then be used to determine if an error has occurred, as shown in SWITCHI2 (listing 3).

Listing 3

```
program SwitchI2;
var
   Selection : integer;
   IOAction  : integer;
begin
   repeat
      write( 'Please enter an integer value: ' );
{$I-}
      readln( Selection );
{$I +}
      IOAction := IOResult;
      if IOAction <> Ø then
         writeln( 'Please try again.' );
   until IOAction = Ø;
   writeln;
   writeln( 'The square of ', Selection, ' is ', Sqr( Selection ) );
end.
```

In this program, if a noninteger value is entered, the IOAction variable will contain a nonzero error code (actually, it will be 106, just as before).

By developing your own error-processing routines, you can make your programs virtually "crash proof" from inadvertent (or deliberate) I/O errors.

L: Local Symbol Information

Syntax: {$L +} or {$L-}

Default: {$L +}

Type: Global

Menu: Output/Compiler/Local Symbols

The Local Symbol directive determines whether local symbol information is included as part of the program's output.

For a debugger to examine and modify local variables, information about them (specifically, their names, types, and locations within the program) must be summarized in the same output file that contains the program's machine code.

When the Local Symbol directive is enabled with {$L +}, the Turbo Pascal integrated debugger can access a program's local variables. In addition, you can use the Debug/Call Stack menu option to analyze the parameters passed in procedure and function calls.

The Local Symbol directive is usually enabled in conjunction with the Debug directive {$D +}. The Local Symbol directive allows the debugger to track individual local symbols, whereas the Debug directive can relate those symbols to specific lines of program code.

Use of the Local Symbol directive increases the size of an output file, but the resulting information is contained separate from the normal machine code. Consequently, it has no effect on execution speed.

N: Numeric Processing

Syntax: {$N +} or {$N-}

Default: {$N-}

Type: Global

Menu: Options/Compiler/Numeric Processing

The Numeric Processing directive determines whether an installed 8087 coprocessor will be used to handle floating-point operations.

By default, the Numeric Processing directive is disabled. The program executes just as if no 8087 coprocessor is present—regardless of the actual configuration of the PC.

In the {$N +} state, the compiler tries to use the coprocessor whenever it encounters an instruction involving an operation on one or more real numbers. If no coprocessor is present, emulation software may be invoked, depending upon the setting of the {$E} Emulation directive.

O: Overlay Code Generation

Syntax: {$O +} or {$O-}

Default: {$O-}

Type: Global

Menu: Options/Compiler/Overlays Allowed

The Overlay Code Generation directive enables or disables the generation of the special code that allows a unit to be used as an overlay. This code consists of slightly different parameter-passing routines, which—while not as efficient as the default routines—nevertheless have the same functionality. Therefore, the use of the {$O +} directive doesn't *force* the unit to be used as an overlay; it simply tells the compiler that the unit *can* be used as an overlay.

R: Range Checking

Syntax: {$R +} or {$R-}

Default: {$R-}

Type: Local

Menu: Options/Compiler/Range Checking

The Range Checking directive enables or disables the generation of code designed to perform range checking in an executing program.

When you enable the Range Checking directive with {$R +}, Turbo Pascal generates code to ensure that each reference to the subscript of an array or string is within the defined bounds of the variable. In addition, the compiler ensures that each assignment to a scalar or subrange variable is within the appropriate range. If the range-checking code detects any out-of-bounds condition, the program will terminate with a run-time error.

Because code is generated for every occurrence of a limit condition, compiling with the Range Checking directive enabled results in a larger and slower program. However, programs compiled without range checking may exhibit unpredictable effects. Consider the SWITCHR program (listing 4) that follows.

Listing 4

```
program SwitchR;
var
    i : byte;
    X : array [ 1..3 ] of integer;
    Y : integer;
    Z : integer;
begin
    Y := 14;
    Z := 35;
    for i := 1 to 5 do X[ i ] := Ø;
    writeln( 'Y = ', Y, ' and Z = ', Z );
end.
```

When executed, SWITCHR produces the following result:

Y = Ø and Z = Ø

The for loop placed zeros in the first five elements of the X array. However, because X was defined as having only three elements, the fourth and fifth entry overflowed the array and affected the values in the Y and Z variables. If the Range Checking directive had been enabled with {$R +}, the program would have terminated with the run-time error's message: Error 2Ø1 : Range check error.

Note that the Range Checking directive is a run-time test only. If the SWITCHR program had contained a statement such as

writeln(X[5]);

the compilation would have terminated with the compile-time error's message: Error 76: Constant out of range, no matter how the Range Checking directive had been set.

Range-checking errors generally produce far more subtle problems than those demonstrated here. Consequently, it's a good idea to turn on the Range Checking directive until a program is completely debugged.

S: Stack Overflow Checking

Syntax: {$S +} or {$S-}

Default: {$S +}

Type: Local

Menu: Options/Compiler/Stack Checking

The Stack Checking directive enables or disables the generation of code to check whether a stack-overflow condition is encountered. In the default state {$S +}, the compiler generates code to calculate—*prior* to a function or procedure call—whether there is sufficient stack space remaining to contain both the passed parameters and any local variables. In the SWITCHS program (listing 5), the stack size is set deliberately low by means of the {$M} option and recursive calls are made to the Shrinker procedure.

Listing 5

```
program SwitchS;
{$S + Keep the default;  that is, check stack size }
{$M 1024, 0, 1024   The stack and heap are relatively small. }
var
   BigInt : longint;
procedure Shrinker( StartNumber : longint );
begin
   if StartNumber > 0 then begin
      StartNumber := StartNumber - 1;
      Shrinker( StartNumber );
      writeln( StartNumber );
   end;
end;
begin
   readln( BigInt );
   Shrinker( BigInt );
end.
```

If you enter a number less than or equal to 62, the program displays all integers from zero through 1 that are less than the selected number. If you enter a number greater than or equal to 63 (that is, if 64 or more procedure calls are made), the program terminates with the message: Error 202: Stack overflow error.

If the Stack Checking directive had been disabled with {$S-}, the exact results would have been unpredictable, but a system crash would have been likely.

Note that the Stack Checking directive has no effect on the *contents* of the stack. The same amount of stack space is available regardless of whether the directive is enabled. Programs that rely heavily on recursion should be developed with the Stack Checking directive enabled. The directive should then be disabled only after the program has been thoroughly debugged. Alternatively, because the directive is local, it could be enabled only for a few functions or procedures.

V: Var-String Checking

Syntax: {$V +} or {$V-}

Default: {$V +}

Type: Local

Menu: Options/Compiler/Var-String Checking

The Var-String Checking directive determines whether strict type checking is performed on strings passed as variable parameters to functions and procedures.

In the default {$V +} state, formal and actual string parameters must be the same type. When the directive is disabled, a subroutine accepts strings of any size.

Although strong-typing helps to ensure that variables are properly used, disabling Var-String Checking enables you to develop generic string routines. Consider the SWITCHV program (listing 6).

Listing 6

```
program SwitchV;
type
   String10 = string[ 10 ];
   String100 = string[ 100 ];
var
   Var1 : String10;
   Var2 : String100;
procedure StringUp( var TestString : String10 );
var
   i : byte;
begin
   writeln;
   writeln( 'Processing ''', TestString, '''' );
   writeln( 'It has a size of ', SizeOf( TestString ), ' characters' );
   writeln( 'It is ', Length( TestString ), ' characters long' );
   for i := 1 to Length( TestString ) do
      TestString[ i ] := UpCase( TestString[ i ] );
   writeln;
end;
```

Listing 6 continues

Listing 6 continued

```
begin
        Var1 := 'xyz';
        Var2 := 'abcdefghijklmnopqrstuvwxyz';
        StringUp( Var1 );
        writeln( Var1 );
{$V-}   StringUp( Var2 );
        writeln( Var2 );
end.
```

When executed, SWITCHV generates the following output:

```
Processing 'xyz'
It has a size of 11 characters
It is 3 characters long
XYZ
Processing 'abcdefghijklmnopqrstuvwxyz'
It has a size of 11 characters
It is 26 characters long
ABCDEFGHIJKLMNOPQRSTUVWXYZ
```

In the SWITCHV program, the `StringUp` procedure is designed to work on 10-byte strings. However, by disabling the Var-String Checking directive, a 100-byte string was successfully processed.

Parameter Directives

Whereas a procedure or function parameter serves to pass information to a subroutine, a program parameter passes information to the operating system. Program parameters are principally concerned with file names and DOS memory allocation requirements.

I: Include File

Syntax: {$I filename}

Default: None

Type: Local

Menu: Options/Directories/Include Directories

The Include File directive instructs the compiler to insert the contents of the named file immediately after the occurrence of the directive. The directive may appear anywhere in your program, except that it cannot be located within a begin...end statement block.

The default file name extension for include files is .PAS. A directory may be specified. If the file isn't found, the compiler searches the directories named in the Options/Directories/Include Directories menu (or those specified with the /I option of the TPC command-line compiler).

Include files may be nested up to eight levels deep.

L: Link Object File

Syntax: {$L filename}

Default: None

Type: Local

Menu: Options/Directories/Object Directories

The Link Object File directive identifies a file to be linked with the program or unit currently being compiled. Files to be linked must be in proper Intel relocatable object file (.OBJ) format.

The default file name extension for link files is .OBJ. A directory may be specified. If the file isn't found, the compiler will search the directories named in the Options/Directories/Object Directories menu (or those specified with the /O directive of the TPC command-line compiler).

M: Memory Allocation Sizes

Syntax: {$M stacksize, heapmin, heapmax}

Default: {$M 16384, Ø, 655360}

Type: Global

Menu: Options/Compiler/Memory Sizes

The Memory Allocation directive specifies the amount of memory to be allocated for the program's stack and heap.

Default, minimum, and maximum sizes are shown in table 1. Only integer values are accepted.

Table 1. *Sizes of Memory Allocations*

	Default	*Minimum*	*Maximum*
stacksize	16,384	1,024	65,520
heapmin	0	0	655,360
heapmax	655,360	heapmin	655,360

The Memory Allocation directive is global. It can appear only within the main module; the directive is ignored if you include it in a unit.

O: Overlay Unit Name

Syntax: {$O unitname}

Default: None

Type: Local

Menu: No equivalent

The Overlay Unit Name directive tells the compiler which units are to be processed as overlays.

The directive must appear after the unitname is referenced by the uses clause. If the directive appears within a unit, or if it references the System unit, it is ignored.

Conditional Compilation Directives

Conditional compilation allows separate sections of a single program to be compiled, based entirely on user-defined conditions. This feature is particularly useful for debugging large programs and for tailoring a general program to fit a variety of specific applications or installations.

The conditionally compiled portions of code are placed within logical block structures that are entirely independent of any program logic. The basic format of a conditional compilation block is:

{$IFxxx }	The $IFxxx statement tests a condition.
. . . .	
. . . .	
. . . .	These statements are compiled only if the
. . . .	condition in the $IFxxx statement is True.
. . . .	
. . . .	
{$ELSE}	The optional Else designates alternate code.
. . . .	
. . . .	
. . . .	These statements are compiled only if the
. . . .	condition in the $IFxxx statement is False.
. . . .	
. . . .	
{$ENDIF}	One Endif is required for each If block.

Any legal Pascal statement may appear within a conditional compilation block, including directives, data, and program code. The {$IFxxx} statements may be nested up to 16 levels deep, but each must be terminated with an {$ENDIF} statement. Whenever an {$ELSE} appears, it always refers to the most recently defined {$IFxxx}. If conditional compilation statements are used within an include file, you must ensure that each file has balanced pairs of {$IFxxx} and {$ENDIF} statements.

The {$IFDEF} and {$IFNDEF} statements evaluate symbols defined by other conditional compilation statements or predefined within Turbo Pascal. Symbols are defined and undefined (that is, set to True and False) with the directives:

```
{$DEFINE SymbolName}
{$UNDEF SymbolName}
```

The {$UNDEF} directive cancels a previous definition; if SymbolName had not been previously defined, it would have automatically evaluated to False.

Conditional symbols can also be defined with the command-line compiler through the use of the /D directive. Within the interactive development environment, conditional symbols can be defined with the Options/Compiler/Conditional Defines menu.

The predefined conditional symbols are listed in table 2.

***Table 2.** Predefined Conditional Symbols*

Symbols	Defined (True) When
VER40	Current compiler version is 4.0
VER50	Current compiler version is 5.0
MSDOS	Current operating system is MS-DOS or PC DOS
CPU86	CPU is an Intel 80 ×86 processor
CPU87	80 ×87 coprocessor is present during compilation

As an example, the Numeric Processing directive could be controlled with the following:

```
{$IFDEF CPU87}
{$N +}
{$ELSE}
{$N-}
{$ENDIF}
```

The {$IFOPT} statement evaluates as True or False, depending on whether the directive is enabled or disabled, as indicated. For example, if a program contained the directives just listed for enabling numeric processing, it could additionally allow 8087 emulation to be disabled as follows:

```
{$IFOPT N +}
{$E-}
{$ENDIF}
```

DEFINE

Syntax: {$DEFINE name}

The DEFINE directive both defines a conditional symbol for use by other directives and sets the symbol to Boolean True. If name has already been defined, the directive is ignored.

UNDEF

Syntax: {$UNDEF name}

The UNDEF directive removes the definition of a conditional symbol. In effect, the symbol is set to Boolean False. If name has already been undefined, the directive is ignored.

IFDEF

Syntax: {$IFDEF name}

The IFDEF directive compiles the following section of code if the conditional symbol name has been defined using a DEFINE directive.

IFNDEF

Syntax: {$IFNDEF name}

The IFNDEF directive compiles the following section of code if the conditional symbol name has not been defined with a DEFINE directive or if name has been undefined with an UNDEF directive.

IFOPT

Syntax: {$IFOPT switch}

The IFOPT directive compiles the following section of code if the switch directive is enabled or disabled, as indicated.

ELSE

Syntax: {$ELSE}

The ELSE directive compiles the following section of code if the most recent IFxxx is not True.

ENDIF

Syntax: {$ENDIF}

The ENDIF directive marks the end of the most recent IFxxx or ELSE section.

Index

E

P

More Computer Knowledge from Que

LOTUS SOFTWARE TITLES

1-2-3 QueCards................................. 21.95
1-2-3 QuickStart 21.95
1-2-3 Quick Reference......................... 6.95
1-2-3 for Business, 2nd Edition 22.95
1-2-3 Business Formula Handbook............... 19.95
1-2-3 Command Language 21.95
1-2-3 Macro Library, 2nd Edition............. 21.95
1-2-3 Tips, Tricks, and Traps, 2nd Edition ... 21.95
Using 1-2-3, Special Edition 24.95
Using 1-2-3 Workbook and Disk,
    2nd Edition............................... 29.95
Using Lotus HAL............................... 19.95
Using Symphony, 2nd Edition 26.95

DATABASE TITLES

dBASE III Plus Handbook, 2nd Edition 22.95
dBASE IV Handbook, 3rd Edition 23.95
dBASE IV Tips, Tricks, and Traps, 2nd Edition 21.95
dBASE IV QueCards 21.95
dBASE IV Quick Reference..................... 6.95
dBASE IV QuickStart 21.95
dBXL and Quicksilver Programming:
    Beyond dBASE 24.95
R:BASE Solutions: Applications
    and Resources 19.95
R:BASE System V Techniques
    and Applications.......................... 21.95
R:BASE User's Guide, 3rd Edition............. 19.95
Using Clipper................................ 24.95
Using Reflex................................. 19.95
Using Paradox, 2nd Edition................... 22.95
Using Q & A, 2nd Edition..................... 21.95

MACINTOSH AND
APPLE II TITLES

HyperCard QuickStart: A Graphics Approach 21.95
Using AppleWorks, 2nd Edition 21.95
Using dBASE Mac 19.95
Using Dollars and Sense 19.95
Using Excel.................................. 21.95
Using HyperCard: From Home to HyperTalk.. 24.95
Using Microsoft Word: Macintosh Version 21.95
Using Microsoft Works 19.95
Using WordPerfect: Macintosh Version 19.95

APPLICATIONS
SOFTWARE TITLES

CAD and Desktop Publishing Guide 24.95
Smart Tips, Tricks, and Traps................ 23.95
Using AutoCAD................................ 20.95
Using DacEasy 21.95
Using Dollars and Sense: IBM Version,
    2nd Edition 19.95
Using Enable/OA.............................. 23.95
Using Excel: IBM Version..................... 24.95
Using Managing Your Money 19.95
Using Quattro 21.95
Using Smart 22.95
Using SuperCalc4............................. 21.95

WORD-PROCESSING AND
DESKTOP PUBLISHING TITLES

Microsoft Word Techniques and Applications 19.95
Microsoft Word Tips, Tricks, and Traps 19.95
Using DisplayWrite 4......................... 19.95
Using Microsoft Word, 2nd Edition........... 21.95
Using MultiMate Advantage, 2nd Edition 19.95
Using PageMaker on the IBM................. 24.95
Using PFS: First Publisher................... 22.95
Using Sprint................................. 21.95
Using Ventura Publisher...................... 24.95
Using WordPerfect, 3rd Edition 21.95
Using WordPerfect 5 .... 24.95
Using WordPerfect Workbook and Disk 29.95
Using WordStar, 2nd Edition................. 21.95
WordPerfect Advanced Techniques 19.95
WordPerfect Macro Library 21.95
WordPerfect QueCards........................ 21.95
WordPerfect Quick Reference................. 6.95
WordPerfect QuickStart 21.95
WordPerfect Tips, Tricks, and Traps,
    2nd Edition 21.95
WordPerfect 5 Workbook and Disk........... 29.95

HARDWARE AND
SYSTEMS TITLES

DOS Programmer's Reference 24.95
DOS QueCards 21.95
DOS Tips, Tricks, and Traps................. 22.95
DOS Workbook and Disk..................... 29.95
IBM PS/2 Handbook 21.95
Managing Your Hard Disk, 2nd Edition 22.95
MS-DOS Quick Reference.................... 6.95
MS-DOS QuickStart.......................... 21.95
MS-DOS User's Guide, 3rd Edition........... 22.95
Networking IBM PCs, 2nd Edition........... 19.95
Programming with Windows 22.95
Understanding UNIX: A Conceptual Guide,
    2nd Edition 21.95
Upgrading and Repairing PCs 24.95
Using Microsoft Windows 19.95
Using OS/2 .... 22.95
Using PC DOS, 2nd Edition 22.95

PROGRAMMING AND
TECHNICAL TITLES

Advanced C: Techniques and Applications ... 21.95
Assembly Language Quick Reference 6.95
C Programmer's Library 21.95
C Programming Guide, 3rd Edition........... 24.95
C Quick Reference........................... 6.95
C Standard Library.......................... 21.95
Debugging C 19.95
DOS and BIOS Functions Quick Reference... 6.95
QuickBASIC Quick Reference 6.95
Turbo Pascal for BASIC Programmers 18.95
Turbo Pascal Program Library 19.95
Turbo Pascal Quick Reference 6.95
Turbo Pascal Tips, Tricks, and Traps........ 19.95
Using Assembly Language 24.95
Using QuickBASIC 4......................... 19.95
Using Turbo Pascal 21.95
Using Turbo Prolog......................... 19.95

SELECT QUE BOOKS TO INCREASE
YOUR PERSONAL COMPUTER PRODUCTIVITY

Turbo Pascal Quick Reference

Developed by Que Corporation

Programmers can speed up their Turbo Pascal programming with the quality information in this compact reference. Now it's easy to find information on Turbo Pascal 5.0 guidelines, syntax, and conventions —without wading through pages and pages of inapplicable information! Help your customers put Turbo Pascal protocol at their fingertips with Que's *Turbo Pascal Quick Reference*!

DOS Programmer's Reference

by Terry Dettmann

Intermediate and advanced programmers will find a wealth of information in Que's *DOS Programmer's Reference*. Designed for serious applications programmers, this "nuts and bolts" guide contains sections on DOS functions and their use; IBM-specific programs; expanded and extended memory; and the use of DOS with various languages, such as C, BASIC, and assembly language. A combination of tutorial and reference, this text helps you gain a greater understanding of what your operating system has to offer. Choose *DOS Programmer's Reference*, the definitive guide to DOS applications programming.

Using Assembly Language

by Allen Wyatt

Using Assembly Language shows you how to make the most of your programs with assembly language subroutines. This book helps you understand assembly language instructions, commands, and functions —how they are used and what effects they produce. You will learn to develop and manage libraries of subroutines, successfully debug subroutines, access BIOS and DOS services, and interface assembly language with Pascal, C, and BASIC. Now you can harness assembly language's speed, versatility, flexibility, and code compaction—with Que's *Using Assembly Language*!

C Programming Guide, 3rd Edition

by Jack Purdum, Ph.D.

A completely new edition of a Que classic. Rewritten to reflect C's ongoing development—including the new ANSI standard—this text contains many programming tips that let readers benefit from the author's practical programming experience. Also included are a complete keyword reference guide, a host of program examples, and a tear-out quick reference card. This is the perfect guide for beginning programmers in the C language.

ORDER FROM QUE TODAY

Item	Title	Price	Quantity	Extension
935	Turbo Pascal Quick Reference	$ 6.95		
107	Using Assembly Language	24.95		
76	DOS Programmer's Reference	24.95		
850	C Programming Guide, 3rd Edition	24.95		

Book Subtotal _____

Shipping & Handling ($2.50 per item) _____

Indiana Residents Add 5% Sales Tax _____

GRAND TOTAL _____

Method of Payment

☐ Check   ☐ VISA   ☐ MasterCard   ☐ American Express

Card Number _____ Exp. Date _____

Cardholder's Name _____

Ship to _____

Address _____

City _____ State _____ ZIP _____

If you can't wait, call **1-800-428-5331** and order TODAY.

All prices subject to change without notice.

FOLD HERE
- -

_____

_____

_____

_____

Que Corporation
P.O. Box 90
Carmel, IN 46032

REGISTRATION CARD

Register your copy of *Using Turbo Pascal*, and receive information about Que's newest products. Complete this registration card and return it to Que Corporation, P.O. Box 90, Carmel, IN 46032.

Name _____ Phone _____

Company _____ Title _____

Address _____

City _____ State _____ ZIP _____

Please check the appropriate answers:

Where did you buy *Using Turbo Pascal*?
- ☐ Bookstore (name: _____)
- ☐ Computer store (name: _____)
- ☐ Catalog (name: ____ _____)
- ☐ Direct from Que _____
- ☐ Other: _____

How many computer books do you buy a year?
- ☐ 1 or less
- ☐ 2–5
- ☐ 6–10
- ☐ More than 10

How many Que books do you own?
- ☐ 1
- ☐ 2–5
- ☐ 6–10
- ☐ More than 10

How long have you been programming in Pascal?
- ☐ Less than 6 months
- ☐ 6 months to 1 year
- ☐ 1–3 years
- ☐ More than 3 years

What influenced your purchase of *Using Turbo Pascal*?
- ☐ Personal recommendation
- ☐ Advertisement
- ☐ In-store display
- ☐ Price
- ☐ Other: _____
- ☐ Que catalog
- ☐ Que mailing
- ☐ Que's reputation

How would you rate the overall content of *Using Turbo Pascal*?
- ☐ Very good
- ☐ Good
- ☐ Satisfactory
- ☐ Poor

How would you rate *Part I: Learning Turbo Pascal*?
- ☐ Very good
- ☐ Good
- ☐ Satisfactory
- ☐ Poor

How would you rate *Part II: Advanced Programming*?
- ☐ Very good
- ☐ Good
- ☐ Satisfactory
- ☐ Poor

How would you rate *Part IV: Reference*?
- ☐ Very good
- ☐ Good
- ☐ Satisfactory
- ☐ Poor

What do you like *best* about *Using Turbo Pascal*?

What do you like *least* about *Using Turbo Pascal*?

How do you use *Using Turbo Pascal*?

What other Que products do you own?

For what other subjects would a Que book be helpful?

Please feel free to list any other comments you may have about *Using Turbo Pascal*.

_____

_____

_____

_____

_____

_____

_____

FOLD HERE

_____

_____

_____

_____

Que Corporation
P.O. Box 90
Carmel, IN 46032